ADAPTING GREEK TRAGEDY

Adaptations of Greek traged[illegible] attention as a dynamic way of engaging with a dramatic genre that flourished in Greece some 25 centuries ago but remains as vital as ever. In this volume, fifteen leading scholars and practitioners of the theatre systematically discuss contemporary adaptations of Greek tragedy and explore the challenges and rewards involved therein. Adopting a variety of methodologies, viewpoints and approaches, the volume offers surveys of recent developments in the field, engages with challenging theoretical issues, and shows how adapting Greek tragedy can throw new light on a range of contemporary issues – from our relation to the classical past and our shifting perceptions of ethnic and cultural identities to the place, function and market value of Greek drama in today's cultural industries. The volume will be welcomed by students and scholars in Classics, Theatre, Drama and Performance Studies, as well as by theatre practitioners.

VAYOS LIAPIS is Professor of Ancient Theatre and Its Reception at the Open University of Cyprus. He is the author of *A Commentary on the Rhesus Attributed to Euripides* (2012) and co-editor of *Greek Tragedy after the Fifth Century* (Cambridge, 2018). He is the recipient of the 2018 National Prize for the Translation of Ancient Greek Literature into Modern Greek (Hellenic Ministry of Culture and Sports).

AVRA SIDIROPOULOU is Associate Professor of Contemporary Theatre Theory and Practice at the Open University of Cyprus, and Artistic Director of Persona Theatre Company. She is the author of *Directions for Directing: Theatre and Method* (2018) and *Authoring Performance: The Director in Contemporary Theatre* (2011). She was nominated for the 2020 Gilder/Coigney International Award by the League of Professional Theatre Women in New York.

ADAPTING GREEK TRAGEDY

Contemporary Contexts for Ancient Texts

EDITED BY

VAYOS LIAPIS

Open University of Cyprus

AVRA SIDIROPOULOU

Open University of Cyprus

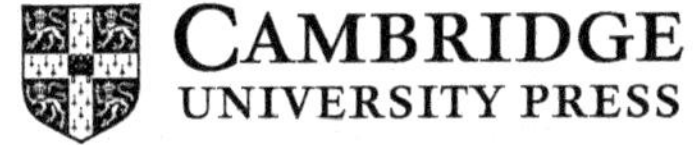

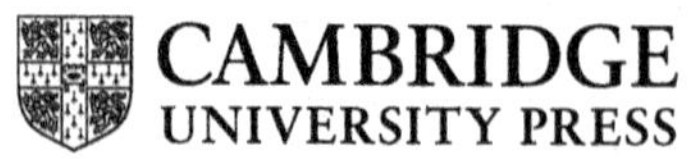

Shaftesbury Road, Cambridge CB2 8EA, United Kingdom

One Liberty Plaza, 20th Floor, New York, NY 10006, USA

477 Williamstown Road, Port Melbourne, VIC 3207, Australia

314–321, 3rd Floor, Plot 3, Splendor Forum, Jasola District Centre, New Delhi – 110025, India

103 Penang Road, #05–06/07, Visioncrest Commercial, Singapore 238467

Cambridge University Press is part of Cambridge University Press & Assessment, a department of the University of Cambridge.

We share the University's mission to contribute to society through the pursuit of education, learning and research at the highest international levels of excellence.

www.cambridge.org
Information on this title: www.cambridge.org/9781316609408

DOI: 10.1017/9781316659168

First published 2021
First paperback edition 2023

A catalogue record for this publication is available from the British Library

Library of Congress Cataloging-in-Publication data
NAMES: Liapēs, Vaios, editor. | Sidiropoulou, Avra, 1972– editor.
TITLE: Adapting Greek tragedy : contemporary contexts for ancient texts / s edited by Vayos Liapis, Avra Sidiropoulou.
DESCRIPTION: Cambridge, United Kingdom : Cambridge University Press, 2021. | Includes bibliographical references and index.
IDENTIFIERS: LCCN 2020052322 (print) | LCCN 2020052323 (ebook) | ISBN 9781107155701 (hardback) | ISBN 9781316609408 (paperback) | ISBN 9781316659168 (epub)
SUBJECTS: LCSH: Greek drama–Modern presentation. | Greek drama (Tragedy)–Adaptations.
CLASSIFICATION: LCC PA3238 .A33 2021 (print) | LCC PA3238 (ebook) | DDC 882/.0109–dc23
LC record available at https://lccn.loc.gov/2020052322
LC ebook record available at https://lccn.loc.gov/2020052323

ISBN 978-1-107-15570-1 Hardback
ISBN 978-1-316-60940-8 Paperback

Contents

Figures

Contributors

Anastasia Bakogianni is Senior Lecturer in Classical Studies at Massey University, New Zealand.

Peter A. Campbell is Associate Professor of Theatre History and Criticism and Dean, School of Contemporary Arts at Ramapo College of New Jersey.

Erika Fischer-Lichte is a professor at the Institut für Theaterwissenschaft at the Freie Universität Berlin.

Lorna Hardwick is Professor Emerita in Classical Studies at the Open University.

Katja Krebs is Senior Lecturer in Performance and Theatre Studies at the University of Bristol.

Adam Lecznar is Lecturer in Classical Languages and Literature at the University of Leeds.

Vayos Liapis is Professor of Ancient Theatre and Its Reception at the Open University of Cyprus.

Peter Meineck is Professor of Classics in the Modern World at New York University.

Jane Montgomery Griffiths is former Professor of Theatre Practice and Head of the Centre for Theatre and Performance at Monash University.

Simon Perris is Associate Professor of Classics at Victoria University of Wellington.

Avra Sidiropoulou is Associate Professor of Theatre Studies at the Open University of Cyprus.

Elke Steinmeyer is Senior Lecturer in the Classics Programme at the University of KwaZulu-Natal.

Preface

This volume grew out of the editors' shared interest in the long and variegated reception of Greek tragedy as material for adaptation. The project was conceived in late 2012, at a time when the growing body of contemporary adaptations of Greek tragedy, despite having already attracted a significant amount of scholarly attention, had not yet found the comprehensive treatment it seemed to require. During the extraordinarily long period in which this volume was in preparation, new monographs and edited volumes appeared, which tackled various aspects of adaptation studies, especially with regard to modern and contemporary adaptations of Greek tragedy (see Introduction). Still, even after this spate of relevant publications, we trust that the present volume remains the first thorough and wide-ranging exploration of contemporary adaptations of Greek tragedy from a variety of perspectives. We hope that it will be of interest to students, researchers and scholars in classics, theatre, drama, and performance studies, as well as to theatre practitioners.

We are grateful to all the contributors to this volume for their good humour and exemplary patience, as well as for the excellent quality of their chapters. We are also grateful to the three eminent theatre practitioners, Charles L. Mee, Suzuki Tadashi and Ivo van Hove, for the interviews they graciously accorded to co-editor Avra Sidiropoulou. Last but not least, we extend our warmest thanks to Dr Michael Sharp for his interest in this project and for his guidance, to the Syndics of Cambridge University Press for accepting this book for publication, to the Press's anonymous readers for careful and astute remarks which improved the overall quality of the volume, and to our copy-editor, Damian Love, for his eagle-eyed attention to the manuscript and for countless editorial improvements.

Chapter 5 uses photographic portraits of (alphabetically) Charles L. Mee, Suzuki Tadashi, and Ivo Van Hove. We thank the above for their permission to reproduce their respective portraits.

Chapter 12 uses images from the National Theatre of Greece's productions of Euripides' *The Trojan Women* (dir. Sotiris Hatzakis, 2015) and Sophocles' *Antigone* (dir. Stathis Livathinos, 2016). We thank the National Theatre of Greece for their permission to reproduce the above images.

Chapter 13 uses text excerpts from *Antigonick* by Anne Carson (pp. 11–12, 14–15, 15–16, 17–18, 20, 22 24, and 28–36), copyright ©2012 by Anne Carson. We thank New Directions Publishing Corp. for their permission to reproduce the above excerpts.

Chapter 13 also uses illustrations by Bianca Stone from *Antigonick*, copyright ©2012 by Anne Carson (pp. 5, 7, 8, 10), copyright © 2012 by Bianca Stone. We thank New Directions Publishing Corp. for their permission to reproduce the above illustrations.

Vayos Liapis
Avra Sidiropoulou

Introduction

Vayos Liapis and Avra Sidiropoulou

Contemporary Perspectives on Adaptation: Definitions and Theoretical Issues

In the last decades of the twentieth century, and at the beginning of the twenty-first, adaptation has come to the forefront of theoretical debates about the limits (or lack thereof) of our engagement with the classical past. At the same time, the adaptive process takes on an increasingly performative character, moving away from the text-centred approaches that had dominated earlier eras and towards new idioms that privilege visuality at least as much as textuality, or enhance the text through its scenic realisations and refractions. Theorists are now careful not to 'treat performance as merely a derivative citation of the text';[1] text and performance are viewed as being in a state of constant interaction, complementarity, and mutual redefinition, in which performance may actuate in numerous ways the performative potential of the dramatic text, while the text may be conceptualised afresh as a result of being performed. In particular, to study the adaptation of Greek tragedy in both textual and performance media is not only to explore intertextual or 'intervisual' relations but also to map out the various avenues through which plays once considered sacrosanct, qua indisputedly part of the Western cultural paradigm, are increasingly being appropriated into different performance and cultural contexts, value systems, and conceptual frames, and are as a result often challenged, questioned, contested.

Definitions: Adaptation, Translation, and Related Modalities

Typically, 'adaptation' comprises a large gamut of activities that may range from the rather modest exercise of abridging the source text to make it

[1] Quotation from Mee and Foley (2011), 11.

suitable for audiences or performance conditions different from the original ones to more ambitious projects, such as expanding, enriching or otherwise crucially altering the source text. Frequently, adaptation involves the transcoding of the source text into a different medium (e.g. drama into film) or genre (e.g. fiction into drama), although adaptation within the same generic boundaries is also possible. Rather inevitably, a degree of re-contextualisation is inherent in adaptation. Such is the case of, e.g., 'updated' versions of classical dramas transferred into modern settings, or of classical plays relocated into different cultural contexts (see further Sanders 2016, 3). By committedly engaging with the source text, adaptation is more thorough and systematic than allusion or quotation, and may come across (though not necessarily) as more conspicuous in its respect for the source text than parody:[2] these are merely a few of many boundaries that can be posited between adaptation and related modalities.

The question of definitions is treated in detail by Katja Krebs in Chapter 1 of this volume ('Definitions: Adaptation and Related Modalities'), which explores the notion of adaptation both in terms of recent theoretical positions claimed within adaptation studies and in relation to the theatre-making process. More precisely, Krebs attempts to establish what we mean by 'adaptation' when discussing classic Greek tragedy in performance and to what extent such terms as 'translation', 'version', '(re)writing', or '(re)imagining' can or indeed should be distinguished from one another. In addressing some of these questions, Krebs investigates whether notions of performance of the classics and notions of adaptation are in a constructive relationship with each other. In order to do so, she adopts a case-study approach: looking at (inter alia) recent theatre adaptations of *Medea*, *Iphigenia at Aulis*, and *The Persians*, Krebs explores the relationship between performance of the classics and notions of adaptation.

It is also imperative to think about translation as adaptation. Even when 'faithful' to the source text, translations involve a degree of re-encoding not only into a different language but also into a different cultural framework, involving 'a whole set of extra-linguistic criteria'.[3] Etymologically, *translatio* is a transfer, a process of transplanting both a text as a verbal event and its underlying cultural assumptions into different contexts. Qua re-contextualisation, a translation can and (at its best) does become a creative work in its own right. As Lorna Hardwick shows in Chapter 3 ('Translation and/as Adaptation'), translations of Greek tragedy in particular, by reconfiguring and resignifying the originals for modern audiences, can address and

[2] Cf. Sanders (2016), 6–7. [3] Quotation from Bassnett (2002), 22.

even shape modern sensibilities. In transferring dramatic texts from an ancient culture that is both fundamentally alien and (by virtue of its classic status) partially similar to that of the modern West, translations of Greek tragedy can both affirm and challenge feelings of cultural rootedness or superiority. Contrariwise, by foregrounding cultural disparities or by drawing on non-mainstream linguistic communities (such as sociolects), translation can revitalise texts whose classical-ness may be taken to imply immobility and fixedness. In the context of this dual opposition, Hardwick explores the relationship between vernacular and source language, both in terms of the details of the formal and lexical aspects of rewriting and in terms of the sociocultural contexts and the epistemological and affective impact on the new texts. Hardwick situates the translation/adaptation of drama in a broader context, to include an investigation of the ways in which it bears on the dialogical relationship between ancient and modern, especially since it invites an acute awareness of the palimpsestic effect of the mediating traditions, texts, and performances. In this connection, Hardwick provides a critical commentary on changes in assumptions about what the term 'translation' covers in its literary forms and in its mediation of ancient texts to the modern stage.[4]

The methodological issues raised by Hardwick's chapter may be complemented by Adam Lecznar's 'The View from the Archive: Performances of Ancient Tragedy at the National Theatre, 1963–1973' (Chapter 6), which shows how archival material can augment our understanding of modern adaptations of ancient Greek tragedy, while simultaneously opening up new avenues of creative interpretation. Lecznar focuses on the National Theatre of Britain and its production history of adaptations of Greek tragedy over the first ten years of its existence (from 1963 to 1973), by discussing three case studies: William Gaskill and Keith Johnstone's version of Sophocles' *Philoctetes* (1964); Peter Brook's production of Ted Hughes' translation of Seneca's *Oedipus* (1968); and Wole Soyinka's *The Bacchae of Euripides: A Communion Rite* (1973). Thanks to insights drawn from these case studies, Lecznar broadens his chapter's focus to explore more general issues attendant on viewing modern performances from the vantage point of the archive. On the one hand, he argues, such a perspective can historicise the adaptations in question and locate them more securely in their immediate sociocultural context; on the other, it can disrupt received scholarly ideas about the significance of these adaptations

[4] See also Hardwick (2007b).

by drawing attention to the different, and sometimes hidden, investments of the various parties involved.

Adaptation as a Problematisation of the Canon

In most cases, adaptation involves, at least to a degree, a reconfiguration of the source text's semantic properties, which it reframes by interposing perceptual filters between classical texts and modern consumers, and by forcing the latter to re-evaluate both their perception of the source text (especially when it has the status of a 'classic') and their own cultural assumptions. This rearrangement of the constituents of the source text is presupposed even in relatively uncomplicated adaptations, such as those based on abridgement or expansion, let alone in more wide-ranging reworkings. Thus, adaptation openly breaks the illusion of textual autonomy by establishing itself as an intertextual act and by advertising its 'derivativeness' as one of many possible ways of actualising meaning at the point of reception.[5] Precisely by virtue of its 'derivativeness', adaptation constitutes a particularly appropriate lens through which to view tensions, ambivalences, and inconsistencies.

Indeed, adaptation often contests the notion of the classic as an inviolable, authoritative model, one relying on (or imposing) specific cultural, semantic, or interpretive assumptions. Adaptation of Greek tragedy, in particular, engages in a variety of ways with an inalienable part of Western cultural capital, which is historically invested with significations that are perceived as familiar qua constituents of a specific (Western) identity. But precisely because it has played a central role in shaping our perceptions of the classical world as a defining paragon, Greek tragedy is especially suitable for often dissonant rewritings (both textual and performative). On the one hand, adaptations of Greek tragedy play on the audience's presumed familiarity with foundational texts of the Western canon, thereby seeming to perpetuate its existence; on the other, they may proceed to perform 'a dissonant and dissident rupturing' of the value systems and hierarchies associated with canonical writing.[6] In the latter case, they may set themselves up as rival readings of the source text and its

[5] Especially in recent years, when the proliferation of media (film, television, radio, musicals, electronic media, graphic novels, video games, etc.) has dramatically increased the number and quality of suitable outlets for adaptation, routine dismissals of adaptation as a derivative activity have increasingly given way to serious critical attention and to attempts to reconsider its cultural valuation. See Hutcheon (2006), xi–xii.

[6] See Sanders (2016), 12, whence the quotation.

associated values; or as rereadings that configure afresh the source text's established meaning(s); or as new points of departure that privilege ambiguity, problematise the source text's current valuations, and question the dominant discourse about what constitutes 'the classic' in literary, performative, or cultural terms. In other words, modern reworkings of classical myth presuppose and build on the notion of authoritativeness in order to negotiate or even negate the very idea of a monumentalised manifestation of the classic and the concomitant notions of semantic fixity and originary meaning. As pointed out by Lianeri and Zajko, the very notion of what constitutes a classical text is far from stable; on the contrary, it 'continues to be mediated and configured by changing historical circumstances, which present the construction of the classic as a historical relationship between past and present'. By negotiating 'the contradiction between the two mutually oppositional sides of the classic, the timeless and the contingent',[7] adaptation at once asserts the death of the classic and promotes its transhistorical, perpetually redefinable identity.

Almost by definition, adaptation raises important questions of canonicity and dissidence, authority and provocation, deference and confrontation. These are some of the issues discussed by Peter Meineck in chapter 2 ('Forsaking the Fidelity Discourse: The Application of Adaptation'), which seeks to identify the cultural and even political stakes involved in the act of adaptation. Meineck interrogates the fidelity discourse as applied to Greek drama and explores the ways it has sometimes led to adaptation being treated dismissively. Meineck challenges the oft-unquestioned premise that we have access to the original versions of the Greek plays and suggests ways in which we can approach adaptation as a positive act of creativity, which has enabled the work to survive. Further, Meineck illustrates how the fidelity discourse continues to exert a negative influence on the adaptation of Greek drama, by using examples from his own work on adaptations with the Aquila Theatre, whose target audience is the veteran community in the United States. By describing these performance projects, Meineck demonstrates how an informed approach to adaptation can produce new ways in which to increase engagement with, and knowledge of, ancient dramatic works.

One of the most exciting vehicles of the aforementioned renegotiation of the canon is the association between Greek and non-Western performance traditions. Such associations, which frequently focus on the non-verbal elements of performance, often aim to re-establish a sense of

[7] Both quotations from Lianeri and Zajko (2008), 4.

'otherness' by alienating modern audiences and their Stanislavskian sensibilities. In his epoch-making *Trojan Women* (1974) and *Clytemnestra* (1986), director Suzuki Tadashi challenged Western theatre traditions by creating his own Eastern ritual from elements of traditional Japanese theatre, such as Noh drama, as well as from his own intensely contemporary sensibilities.[8] In Ninagawa Yukio's *Medea* (1978), the merging of Eastern and Western traditions was effected by the use of an all-male cast and of (sometimes subverted) dramatic techniques borrowed from Kabuki, thereby reinforcing a sense of traditional ritual.[9] More recently, there have been attempts to tap into other Asian traditions, for example by Yanna Zarifi, who utilised modern Tajikistan dirges in staging the chorus' lamentation in Aeschylus' *Persians*; by Sadanam Balakrishnan, who adapted *Alcestis* and *Helen* into the Kathakali idiom; and by China's Hebei Bangzi theatre, which adapted Medea as a *hebei bangzi* opera in 1989.[10] Western-derived versions of Greek tragedy have also been in dialogue with non-Western cultures. A famous case in point was the gospel version of Sophocles' *Oedipus at Colonus* by Lee Breuer and Bob Telson (*The Gospel at Colonus*, 1983), which brought Sophocles' *Oedipus at Colonus* alive as a sermon performed by African American singers and actors before an African American gospel chorus.[11] One of the most prominent points of contact between Western and Oriental theatre traditions is provided by Ariane Mnouchkine's work (notably *Les Atrides*), whose narratives are mostly derived from the Western literary canon and history but systematically absorb from, and interact with, Oriental presentational and distancing elements in movement, costume, mask, and make-up to add a more global sensibility to her stage, as well as foregrounding (in league with Artaud) non-Western modes of representation as an alternative to word-dominated forms.[12] Finally, an important example of adaptation of Greek tragedy from a distinctly non-Western point of view was the Alaskan *Yup'ik Antigone* (1985), which included a shaman Tiresias and tribal masks and music that enhanced the heroine's stirring defence of traditional Inuit mores.[13]

Issues of identity and alterity are treated in detail by Erika Fischer-Lichte in Chapter 10 and by Elke Steinmeyer in Chapter 11 of this

[8] See further Goto (1989), 108–19; Foley (1999), 8; Carruthers and Takahashi (2004), 124–79.

[9] See further Smethurst (2002).

[10] See Tian (2008), 193 and cf. Fischer-Lichte, this volume.

[11] Further on *The Gospel at Colonus* see Goff and Simpson (2007), 178–218.

[12] On Mnouchkine see J. G. Miller (2007); particularly on her *Les Atrides* see Goetsch (1994) and Glynn (2015).

[13] See Foley (1999), 2.

volume. In her 'Adaptations of Greek Tragedies in Non-Western Performance Cultures', Fischer-Lichte explores and analyses the increasing interest (by scholars and theatre practitioners alike) in associations between Greek and non-Western traditions of performance. Such associations create unexpected fusions between vastly different theatrical aesthetics, which may invest the source text with fresh political potential – witness, for example, Amitava Dasgupta's 'Brechtian' versions of Greek tragedies in Delhi and elsewhere. Alternatively, cross-cultural adaptations may aim to reimagine the Dionysiac feel of an Athenian performance event, or simply to explore the intrinsic allure of such cross-cultural experimentation. In West Africa, in particular, such adaptations (among which Wole Soyinka's version of *Bacchae* takes pride of place) functioned not only as responses to the centrality of Greek drama in British colonial ideology but also as a means of exploring affinities between the Greek and West African cultures. Fischer-Lichte's scope here is quite expansive: it encompasses, for instance, such notable Japanese productions as Suzuki Tadashi's and Ninagawa Yukio's adaptations of Greek tragedies, as well as tracing the history of adaptations of Greek drama in India and China.

In particular, modern adaptations of Greek plays, as Mee and Foley aptly remark, 'are important for the ways in which they use the Western canon to challenge Western value systems and assumptions about culture, and for the ways in which they decentre Western culture . . . adaptation can be more of a challenge to the "original" than a derivative to it'.[14] From this perspective, it is particularly instructive to look at the topic of Elke Steinmeyer's chapter in this volume ('Cultural Identities: Appropriations of Greek Tragedy in Post-Colonial Discourse'). Steinmeyer looks at how Greek tragedy has been employed by African, Afro-Caribbean, and African American playwrights as a means of offering alternative mythopoeic models of approaching and debating crucial political and social issues.[15] She discusses how the classical tradition, a long-time staple of colonial education, has often been challenged and ironised as an imperial relic, but it has also given rise, in the cultural context of alternative African traditions (both within and outside Africa), to the creation of a distinct corpus of adaptations that both foster and deconstruct encounters between ancient Greece and contemporary African cultures. In particular, Steinmeyer discusses post-apartheid playwrights and stage directors, e.g. Mark

[14] Mee and Foley (2011), 4.

[15] This is a topic on which much of value has been written: see, e.g., Hardwick and Gillespie (2007); Goff and Simpson (2007); Greenwood (2010).

Fleishman and Mervyn McMurtry, who tend to refocus Greek tragic themes on instances in which victims and oppressors face each other, as well as their traumatic past, in the spirit promoted by the Truth and Reconciliation Commission.[16] In a similar vein, an exciting recent trend in European theatre has been the expansion of theatre culture to the under-privileged outskirts of modern urban sites. The *banlieues*, inhabited mostly by 'new Europeans', immigrants from former European colonies, now often provide venues for the performance of classical plays, which not only cater to the cultural needs of those communities but also encourage questioning and dissent.[17] Among other things, such projects bring out and problematise the narrowness of certain concepts of European (or national) identity.

Adaptation and the malleability of myth

One of the crucial factors that permit the kind of (re)negotiations described in the previous section is the malleability of classical myth.[18] As a traditional, originally oral tale, myth is not only authoritative but also, crucially, susceptible of being constantly remodelled and reformulated through successive retellings and through subsequent readings and interpretations. As Moddelmog (1993) observes, the essential quality of myth is that it initiates interpretive acts by its recipients, involving them in a quest for an essential meaning that is absent (i.e. unrealised) until the interpreting subject recognises it as an object of enquiry. There is thus an 'ontological gap' between the mythic tale and the meaning(s) assigned to it by its recipients – a gap that can never be closed, insofar as 'myth is discourse that generates discourse and thereby brings with it an elaborate literary and interpretive history'.[19] Thus, myth perpetually generates acts of 'interpretation, including the interpretation of retelling and translation', in a constant flux of semiotic mobility, whereby the semantic constituents of myth are selectively privileged, questioned, challenged and/or renegotiated, in a continuous interplay of different versions and reinterpretations.[20]

To the extent that they retain recognisable mythic components, adaptations of Greek tragedy may establish a dynamic relationship with tragic

[16] On this topic see also, e.g., Mezzabotta (2000); McDonald (1999); Steinmeyer (2009); van Zyl Smit (2010).

[17] See esp. Treu (2009).

[18] This section is largely based on Liapis (2014b) 92–3.

[19] Moddelmog (1993), 3–4 (quotations from 4), building on important insights from Gould (1981), esp. 6, 183, 186–7.

[20] Cf. Moddelmog (1993), 4–5 (quotation from p. 4).

myth, whereby the reader or viewer is invited to pursue the interpretive potentialities of the dialogue between the modern text and its mythic antecedent.[21] This involves a partial 'updating' of tragic myth, a re-contextualisation of the ancient tale for modern concerns and sensibilities, whereby readers/viewers are encouraged partly to detach myth from its perceived 'original' context (in this case, Greek tragedy) and to invest it with qualities associated with subsequent temporal and cultural contexts. At the same time, by grafting its product on the template of ancient (tragic) myth, adaptation invites its consumers to disassociate it from its contemporary time-frame and to imbue it with a temporal depth it might otherwise have lacked. This process initiates an interpretive interplay between modern text or performance and mythic subtext, whereby the modern work is illuminated by ancient myth but also causes us to reinterpret the myth it appropriates.[22]

Questions arising from the contemporisation of ancient tragic myth inform Simon Perris in Chapter 9 ('Violence in Adaptations of Greek Tragedy'), which deals with depictions of verbal and physical violence in modern retellings of Greek tragedies. Perris shows how contemporary adaptations, operating without the constraints of Greek stage conventions, do sometimes embrace physical violence as a nod to its predominance in contemporary visual (especially cinematic) culture. Through a series of case studies – including *Greek* by Steven Berkoff (1980), *Phaedra's Love* by Sarah Kane (1996), and *By the Bog of Cats...* (1998) and *Ariel* (2002) by Marina Carr – Perris explores the ways in which instances of violence in Greek tragedy, although ostensibly familial (and thus predominantly personal), are overtly politicised in modern adaptations. Thus, Berkoff's play transfers the Oedipus myth to a run-down London suburb in the days of Margaret Thatcher's premiership; Kane's work represents physical brutality in grotesquely extreme forms; and Carr's two plays feature re-enactments of shocking violence that engage with Euripides' *Medea* and Aeschylus' *Oresteia*. In these and other cases discussed by Perris, violence and aggression are used as a vehicle for bringing out debates associated with ethnic conflict, social marginalisation, political dissent, gender antagonism, and other issues of contemporary (but also timeless) concern.

Issues of contemporisation are also addressed in Chapter 12 by Anastasia Bakogianni ('Trapped between Fidelity and Adaptation? On

[21] Further on this type of dialogue, see Moddelmog (1993), 16–17.

[22] Cf. Moddelmog (1993), 8: 'if it is true that the myth tells us something about the modern story, it is equally true that the narrative's appropriation of the myth causes us to reinterpret the myth'.

the Reception of Ancient Greek Tragedy in Modern Greece'), which revisits the perennial tension between the 'authenticity' imperative and the quest for updating and relevance in the context of the reception of ancient Greek drama in modern Greece. As Bakogianni shows, modern Greek reception of ancient Greek drama has often been encumbered by a proprietary mentality and a (usually conflicted) sense of epigonalism. As a central part of modern Greece's perceived cultural heritage, Greek tragedy has been a crucial factor in the formation of a poetics and a politics of modern Greek national and cultural identity. Both a privilege and a burden, modern Greece's special relationship with its classical past has generated, in some quarters, an essentialist quest for an ever-elusive 'genuine' meaning to be puzzled out by modern theatrical engagements with Greek drama. By contrast, in other, more recent and non-traditionalist quarters, this relationship has led to approaches which, rather than privileging Greek drama as a locus of crystallised collective remembrance, initiate a dynamic process of cultural and ideological interaction, in which modern concerns are fed into the ancient texts and vice versa, thereby establishing a circuit of reflective debate and self-questioning. Bakogianni's analysis focuses on four representative modern Greek productions of ancient drama from the first two decades of the twenty-first century, namely Sophocles' *Oedipus Tyrannus* directed by Vasilis Papavassiliou (2000), Euripides' *Trojan Women* by Sotiris Hatzakis (2015), Sophocles' *Antigone* by Stathis Livathinos (2016), and, at the more experimental end of the spectrum, Nikos Perelis' *Traps and Killings: The Machines of Dolos and Terror* (2000), a collaborative pastiche from five dramas by Euripides. These productions range from the predictably canonical to the provocatively adventurous, and it is the latter (especially Perelis' production) that Bakogianni singles out as paradigms of a creative reappropriation of Greek drama, which can resonate with modern audiences' sensitivities.

Adaptation and/in Performance

When actuated through performance, the various modes of reconfiguration operative during the adapting process become even more complex. In the case of staged adaptations of classical texts, 'the essentially new work that the ... adaptor has brought into being', a work that is already a 'strongly inflected ideological and cultural product', is further filtered through the multiple layers superimposed by the numerous interpretive agents involved in performance (director, actors, stage-set designer, choreographer, lighting designer, etc.).[23] In this case, performance of an adapted drama, as well as renegotiating the source text, measures itself against a long series of earlier performances and/or adaptations of that text, thereby engaging in a process of palimpsestic 'intervisuality' as well as intertextuality.[24] Setting aside such regulatory notions as faithfulness to the 'original', as well as critically naive concepts of textual autonomy, contemporary adaptations of Greek tragedy focus on the intertextual/intervisual act itself, on the enterprise of appropriation undertaken thereby, on the processes of acculturation or foreignisation involved therein, and on the sets of assumptions and values that are negotiated, promoted, questioned, or reconfigured by the adaptation.[25] A considerable number of contemporary dramatic and directorial revisions of the Greek classics have been ambivalent in their intended reception of the theatre event, thus reflecting a broader disquiet regarding the treatment of the 'great narratives', and prioritising ambiguity, fragmentation, and insecurity over fixity of meaning and contentedness in cultural supremacy.

In this connection, an issue of primary importance – explored in detail by Sidiropoulou and by Montgomery Griffiths in this volume (Chapters 4 and 7 respectively) – is the ethics of stage adaptation. As argued by Avra Sidiropoulou ('Adaptation as a Love Affair: The Ethics of Directing the Greeks'), stage adaptation is a form by definition open, volatile, and thus susceptible to both the marvels and the injuries of interpretation; as such, it is forever attached to the unresolved debate pertaining to directors' so-called 'respect' and 'loyalty' towards the 'original'. Whether adaptation is seen as an invitation to deepen and expand the source material or (at the opposite extreme) as a gratuitous statement of ultimately uninspired defiance, one needs to address and perhaps attempt to settle the issue of directorial freedom and/or mediation in a process that is inevitably indebted to an inceptive core. Deciding on the boundaries of directorial intervention is often another way of asking ourselves where interpretation ceases and rewriting begins, and when it really becomes necessary to speak of a new work, which will abolish even the comforting anchor of such theatrical euphemisms as 'inspired by', 'based on', and 'adapted from'. Focusing on auteur directors' adaptations of Greek tragedy, Sidiropoulou interrogates such controversial notions as authority and/or deference to the received primary agent of creativity, namely, the author of the original text – a text which, qua material for adaptation, bears the brunt of change,

[23] See E. Hall (2004b), 61 = (2010b), 15, whence the quotations.

[24] Hall (2004b) 66–7 = (2010b), 18.

[25] Cf. Hardwick (2003), 9–10.

be that appropriation, growth, abuse, or subversion. The problem of directorial freedom is especially pronounced in the case of 'canonical' texts, which are customarily regarded as agents of authority and may generate a gamut of audience expectations and directorial responses that range from absolute reverence to the text's accepted meaning to a radical reinterpretation of the source text.

In the context of her own approach to similar questions, Jane Montgomery Griffiths ('Compromise, Contingency, and Gendered Adaptation: The Case of the Malthouse's *Antigone*') uses Australian productions of Greek drama in order to explore broader issues regarding feminist and gendered retellings of Greek tragedies. In view of the remarkable resurgence of Greek drama in Australian theatre over the last years, Montgomery Griffiths investigates this trend by providing a thorough analysis of a recent adaptation of Sophocles' *Antigone*, which she authored and in which she performed a version of Creon, for Melbourne's Malthouse Theatre. Montgomery Griffiths argues that the adaptive mentality can be mapped onto the way we perceive and comprehend difference, and that our processing, understanding, and reception of adaptation are deeply ingrained in an often subliminal system of preconceptions and epistemologies that has the potential to sustain both a reactionary and an emancipatory hermeneutic. Looking at the numerous and unpredictable contingencies inherent in the theatrical process, at the mediation that necessarily contextualises translation, and at the situated nature of 'readings' done both by artists engaged in adapting the source text and by critics engaged in analysing the target text, Montgomery Griffiths argues that the adaptive mentality, when seen through the lens of gender, can be a liberating force to unleash new interpretations and subvert the normative expectations of canonical force.

Another aspect of adaptation that becomes particularly prominent in performance is its celebration 'of the cooperative and collaborative model of creativity' (Sanders 2016, 6). Performance conspicuously involves non-textual elements (such as music, dancing, costuming, actors' bodies), and contemporary performances in particular attempt, ever more frequently and aggressively, to challenge the logocentric model by experimenting with a variety of alternative forms. These forms may foreground non-representational elements such as abstract sets or stylised choreography; they may defy notions of textual cohesion, semantic fixity, or aesthetic unity by adopting bricolage techniques (e.g. found texts) or pastiche methods; and they are likely to engage with a variety of cultural and performance traditions (especially non-Western ones) and of different media (especially multimedia technologies) in an effort to question representational conventions by fragmenting the performance's cultural, visual, and temporal landscape. In all such cases, adaptation not only involves an interaction between the source and the adapted text but also embraces the collaborative model in seeking to enrich the end-product by opening itself up to disparate and even conflicting materials, artistic media, aesthetic attitudes, ideological assumptions, and creative processes.

An idiosyncratic case of symbiosis between the textual and the visual is investigated by Vayos Liapis in his chapter on 'Adaptation and the Transtextual Palimpsest: Anne Carson's *Antigonick* as a Textual/Visual Hybrid' (Chapter 13), which explores hybridity between text, intertext, and image. Canadian poet and classicist Anne Carson's *Antigonick* (2012) makes ample use of techniques associated with postmodernism, such as pastiche, bricolage, and fragmentation. Ostensibly a translation/adaptation of Sophocles' *Antigone*, Carson's *Antigonick* visibly holds itself out as a handcrafted cross-media collage: pages of text, in Carson's own handwriting, alternate with images by illustrator Bianca Stone, which are printed on translucent paper and can thus be superimposed on the text. The resulting effect is one of multiple layers of meaning, in which the textual and the visual become inextricably intertwined. This enforced symbiosis of text and image creates a collage effect, which is supplemented by a different type of hybridity, one created by frequent and violent intrusions of intertextual references (e.g. Hegel, Beckett, Brecht) into Carson's translation of Sophocles' text, as well as by equally frequent and equally violent shifts of stylistic register (e.g. solemn tragic diction giving way, all of a sudden, to colloquialism or even vulgarity).

Postmodern Aesthetics: Amalgams, Hybrids, and New Technologies

As part of the gradual loss of the playwright's authority in the latter part of the twentieth and in the beginning of the twenty-first century, adapters and/or (auteur) directors have been experimenting with alternative textual forms, or with forged amalgams or hybrids. Such unapologetic adaptations of Greek tragedy devise what is essentially a new text by altering, interpolating, extracting, or contextualising the source text into radical rereadings and/or restagings, often by acknowledging postmodern and post-dramatic sensibilities. In these experiments, the 'bricolage' metaphor – understood as the creative and resourceful use of whatever materials or fragments are available from an earlier product – seems particularly apt. For instance, in *Fragments of a Greek Trilogy* (*Medea*, *Electra*, *The Trojan Woman*, 1972–4), director Andrei Şerban distilled Euripides' *Trojan Women* and *Medea* as well as Sophocles' *Electra* into intensely physical, electrifying scenes performed in Greek, Latin, and African and Amerindian tribal languages. Sound provided the predominant axis of the devising process and, as a result, the impact of the orgiastic energy of Şerban's masterpiece was visceral rather than intellectual.[26] Sound and music were also the fundamental components in the experimental Dutch theatre collective Dood Paard's *MedEia* (1998), a choral text version of Medea devised primarily out of the 'found text' of English-language pop songs. The play was derived from different versions of Medea's story (source material included the various 'lives' of Medea told through the ages by writers as diverse as Euripides, Seneca, Pasolini, and Müller), and was narrated from the perspective of the Chorus.[27] Ten years later, Warlikowski's *(A)pollonia*, a four-hour-long collage of Euripides (*Alcestis*) and Aeschylus (*Oresteia*) with Jonathan Littell (*Les Bienveillantes*), Hanna Krall (*Apollonia*) and J. M. Coetzee (*Elizabeth Costello*), was celebrated as one of the most thrilling productions ever inspired by Greek tragedy.[28]

Also of relevance here are the strategies used by auteur directors to contemporise classical Greek tragedy by moving away from the predominance of logos towards more sense-informed (visual or aural) intimations of mood, together with a creative amalgamation of disparate styles. Such strategies have included, among other things, stylised choreography, non-realistic pacing, abstracted sets, filmic devices, and suggestive soundscapes. Introducing a predominantly painterly perspective to the appreciation of performance, Robert Wilson's version of *Alcestis* (1986) offered a spectacular, rather than meditative, reading of Euripides' play of self-sacrifice. Featuring a prologue by Heiner Müller (significantly entitled 'Description of a Picture') and a Kyogen play as an epilogue foregrounding the exaggerated burlesque of Japanese comic theatre, Wilson's performance offered ample opportunity for visual contemplation and relish.[29] In the same vein, Robert Woodruff's versions of *Medea* (1998) and *Oedipus* (2004) together with his *Iphigenia at Aulis* (2008–9) are iconoclastic renderings of

[26] One discerns here the legacy of Artaud's 'Theatre of Cruelty', with its emphasis on a universal (physical) language and a bringing-together of the stage and the auditorium. Further on Şerban's trilogy, see Green (1994), 42–68; Hartigan (1995), 45–6; Foley (1999), 6–7.

[27] See further Gallagher-Ross (2009); Monaghan (2009).

[28] For a video of Warlikowski's *(A)pollonia* with English subtitles, see https://ninateka.pl/film/apollonia-krzysztof-warlikowski-english-subtitles (accessed 9 March 2020). Cf. also Sidiropoulou, Chapter 4, this volume.

[29] On Wilson's *Alcestis*, see further Hartigan (1995), 121–3; Foley (2012), 116–20.

Euripides' and Sophocles' tragedies, with formal considerations of staging going hand-in-hand with a profound analysis of the ancient texts, through which the hypotext is thoroughly illuminated and, as a result, the poetry of the plays is made fresh and relevant. Postmodern pastiche aesthetics were evident both in Wilson's *Alcestis* mentioned above and in Tina Landau's production of Charles Mee's *Iphigenia 2.0* (2007), which interweaved traditional songs and dances with stylised speech, musical comedy, and girl talk, while managing, all the same, to keep the political undertones of the play intact.

The interchange between live stage action and technologically mediated audio or visual elements increasingly inhabits postmodern and post-dramatic refashionings of the classics as a means of questioning the representation of reality and identity. Deconstructed versions of Greek tragedy often engage in a forceful application of technology, combining live and mediated presences, recorded voice, and rigorous segmentation of theatrical time, no less in order to comply with than to compete against the aesthetics of the digital era. At the antipodes of Artaud's adulation of a metaphysical theatre based on the immediacy of the actor's body, the integration of multimedia forms has been a powerful engine in radical performance ever since the 1980s. When engaging with ancient classical texts, technology registers a sense of resistance to psychologically validated interpretation, by collapsing common representational conventions and addressing such questions as what realism and reality ultimately do mean in (virtual) postmodern culture. The inevitable sense of distance and defamiliarisation generated thereby forces us to look beyond our established horizon of expectations for meaningful connections between text and hypotext, while at the same time entertaining the possibility of an end-product that undermines or incapacitates logocentrism. In effect, 'the oedipal *logos* is now understood as pre-existent discourse that needs to be re-marked and contextualised so that an understanding of its affiliations to culture and to various acculturating agencies can be exposed'.[30] At the same time, technology contemporises performance and facilitates shared cultural understanding, functioning as an interlocutor between the contingencies of live action and our technologised intuitions.

Multimedia stagings of tragedy have proliferated in recent years. A prominent example is Katie Mitchell's *The Oresteia* (1999), which featured constant use of the video camera, while at the same time Clytemnestra's and Agamemnon's speeches were recorded by the Chorus

[30] Quotation from Vanden Heuvel (1994a), 63.

to be played back later on, and Orestes' name was repeated on tape loop to indicate how memory and history continue to haunt us ad infinitum. In a more recent example, Jan Fabre's *Prometheus – Landscape II* (2011) presented the titular hero pitted against a huge globe of fire, which was projected on a screen, thus becoming the focal point of the stage composition and engulfing spectators with its simulation of a dangerous, yet thrilling locus of power and potency.[31] In Krzysztof Warlikowski's *(A) pollonia* (2009), mentioned above, the action was filmed on stage, with the video being projected on the back wall. The convergence of theatre and film created simultaneity and tension between the Greek narrative and the intended modernisation of the performance's reception, while at the same time the video projection generated a destabilising, yet ultimately stimulating and challenging multifocal perception. More generally, the inclusion of filmic devices in stage performance forces viewers to reconsider familiar assumptions about temporality and spatiality and urges them to activate a multiple consciousness to match the multiplicity of stimuli propelled on them.

Technology-mediated productions and adaptations of Greek tragedy are the topic of Chapter 8 ('Technology, Media, and Intermediality in Contemporary Adaptations of Greek Tragedy') by Peter A. Campbell, who argues that, by using as their primary source material artefacts from what is considered as the cradle of Western civilisation and drama, such productions attempt to engage spectators in examinations of human culture and behaviour that are not only timely, but have deeper historical and emotional resonances, even when the productions themselves destabilise and sometimes undermine the cultural position of their ancient Greek referents. Furthermore, Campbell explores several significant examples of technological media in contemporary productions of Greek tragedy and seeks to show how they use materials from Greek tragedy to express and reflect the changing demands of a media-saturated world, even though individual approaches may differ – e.g. from the use of video as scenography to audience immersion into theatrical landscapes fragmented through media. Reference is made to a large gamut of such performances, from, e.g., the En Garde Arts production of Charles Mee Jr's *Orestes 2.0* (1993) and John Jesurun's adaptation of *Philoktetes* at the Soho Repertory Theatre in 2007 to Katie Mitchell's 1999 production of Ted Hughes' translation of *The Oresteia* at the Royal National Theatre, Jay Scheib's *Medea* (self-styled

[31] On Fabre's *Prometheus*, see Velle (2011); Constantinidis (2016), 272–3; also Campbell, Chapter 8, this volume.

as a 'play with mixed music and mixed media, after Euripides, Seneca, Mueller, Cherubini'), and Jan Fabre's *Prometheus – Landscape II*.

Political and Commercial Issues in Adaptation

We saw above how adaptation can acquire political implications in the context of transforming and manipulating textual sources generally held to be sacrosanct qua classic. Adaptation is essentially an act of self-assertion on the adapter's part, one that challenges regulatory notions of authority or authorship, and forces its recipients to renegotiate their values, assumptions, and even cultural identities. To adapt is by definition to deny the source text's fixedness as the product of a single author and to affirm its mutability in the hands of potentially endless adapters. In other words, it is the very idea of a centre, of a point of origin guaranteeing meaning and coherence, that is at stake in all adaptations. On the other hand, adaptation cannot ignore canonicity, which it implicitly presupposes: whether it subverts or it celebrates the canon, adaptation must define itself in relation to it. This contradiction is at the core of the politics of adaptation and invites reflection on such issues as canonicity and dissidence, authority and provocation, deference and confrontation.

Relatively recently, Wiles (2011) discussed how theatre shapes spectators into communities of active citizens by functioning as a social and political focus of collective ethics and emotions. Theatre, as the 'shared physical presence in a public space' of humans interacting with each other in complex ways, constitutes a nodal point connecting art with the public realm.[32] One of the aims of this volume is to explore how the community-building power of the theatre is channelled specifically through stage adaptations of Greek tragedy, a communal genre par excellence, which performed and projected collectivity through its inalienable component of a citizen chorus. Modern adaptations of 2,500-year-old dramas negotiate questions related to nationhood, political identities, or cultural communities in our world by engaging with issues urged on us by globalisation, the affirmation or problematisation of diversity and assimilation, and ideologies pertaining to the collective *imaginaire* in its numerous constructions and manifestations. A central question here is whether there is an antinomy between the privileging of individual autonomy in the West and the predominance of collectivity (together with the concomitant performance of the downfall of powerful individuals) in Greek

[32] See Wiles (2011), 5, whence the quotation.

tragedy. And if there is, how does this antinomy play out in modern adaptations of Greek tragedy? Chapters in this volume – especially those by Fischer-Lichte, Meineck, Montgomery Griffiths, and Steinmeyer – explore this question and describe various modes of engagement with different audiences.

An often neglected parameter that needs to be taken into account is that of commercial considerations. Modern adaptations of Greek tragedy would seem to capitalise on a body of ancient dramatic texts considered marketable; as a result, such adaptations help maintain and even increase the market value (as well as the cultural valuation) of ancient tragedy in the modern world. On the other hand, Greek tragedy commonly lends itself to experimental adaptations that may seem, at least ostensibly, to target select or elite audiences and thus to pursue ambitions that claim to rise above the merely commercial. As a result, Greek tragedy in modern performance, including its textual and stage adaptations, would seem to stand both within and without the framework of market values that otherwise drive much of the production and consumption of culture in the modern world.

On Adapting Greek Tragedy Today: State of the Art

Adaptation, as is obvious from the above, can be a significantly more layered and complex process than may appear at first sight. Above all, it can be a paradoxical pursuit, at once asserting (qua relying on) and challenging prevailing canons and dominant paradigms. Chronological subsequence cannot and should not be reduced to mere dependence or (worse) inferiority: adaptation ought rather to be seen as a challenge to prevailing notions of authenticity, authority, and even authorship. By renegotiating and transforming the source text, especially when it is considered a classic, adaptation questions the classic's status as an authoritative statement: it revisits its intellectual make-up, it reassesses its political foundations and cultural assumptions, it reshapes its formal design, and it alters its outlook. In this process of potentially endless renegotiation (since adaptations may give rise to further adaptations), the very notion of authorship can become secondary or even irrelevant. Once the source text comes to be treated as material for adaptation rather than prioritised as a 'source', implying dependence, or an 'original', implying the obligation of faithfulness,[33] then questions of authorship no longer seem to matter.

[33] Cf. Hutcheon (2006), xiii; Mee and Foley (2011), 8; Meineck, Chapter 2, this volume. On the problematisation of authenticity, see further Gamel (2010).

From fixed products of a single intellect, texts become parts of a nexus of complex mutual relations, in which they are constantly reshaped and reorganised. Always in a flux of intertextual mobility and mutability, they become instances of signification that influence and define each other in a potentially never-ending process.

In recent years, adaptation has been increasingly attracting the attention of scholars working in the fields of literature as well as drama and theatre performance. To begin with, adaptation has been the focus of two fundamental monographs, namely Hutcheon (2006) and Sanders (2006, 2nd edn 2016), both of which deal extensively with manifestations of adaptation (and appropriation) in literature, and with the theoretical issues involved therein. At about the same time, the studies included in Hardwick and Gillespie (2007) drew attention to adaptations of Greek tragedies by African playwrights, poets, and novelists, and discussed appropriations of Greek tragedy in the context of post-colonial politics and debates. Working again with post-colonial theory, Goff and Simpson (2007) explored adaptations of Sophocles' Theban plays as a means of articulating 'postcolonial moments in Ghana, Nigeria, South Africa, the Caribbean, and the United States'.[34] A few years earlier, Wetmore (2003) had discussed, among other things, adaptations of Greek tragedies (especially *Medea*) that 'transcultured' the ancient plays into African American contexts. The emphasis of these discussions on African, African American, and/or Afro-Caribbean adaptations and on post-colonial discourse is reflected and enhanced in Elke Steinmeyer's chapter in this volume.

More recently, Mee and Foley (2011) have addressed an array of modern responses, often in non-Western contexts, to Sophocles' *Antigone*, offering in-depth studies on an impressive range of individual theatre productions. Their volume addresses mainly the political ramifications of adaptation but also its power to cut across cultures and performance media, thereby establishing a dialectics between textuality and visuality, as well as between cultural products that come from different temporal and spatial frames to inhabit and affect our own. In a similar vein, Foley (2012) shows how Greek tragedy produced on the American stage has found resonances with contemporary debates, throwing them into an unexpected and often disorienting light.

The last few years have seen a remarkable surge in academic publications on adaptation in general, and on the adaptation of Greek drama in particular. The major *Oxford Handbook of Greek Drama in the Americas*[35] offers a

[34] Goff and Simpson (2007), 1. [35] Bosher, Macintosh, McConnell, and Rankine (2015).

thorough interdisciplinary exploration of the reception (including adaptations) of Greek drama in the Americas from the nineteenth century onwards. It provides an in-depth analysis of regional (North and South American) instances of Greek drama reception, taking account of those regions' colonial histories and emphasising both the individualities of the performance reception of Greek drama in the Americas and its cross-boundary continuities.

In the same year, Komporaly (2015) offered an analysis of 'radical' adaptations (by Ostermeier, Purcărete, Tocilescu, and the Rimini Protokoll) of key texts, ranging from *Hamlet*, *Julius Caesar*, and *Faust* to 'unadaptable' texts such as *Das Kapital* and *Mein Kampf*. Komporaly's interest is in contemporary adaptations that engage with the precursor text in ways that challenge authority, involve a high degree of risk, pursue avant-garde experimentation and provocative recreation (often including cross-genre and cross-media explorations), and invite a renegotiation of accepted truths and/or lazy assumptions. As well as assessing the potential of such works to open new pathways in performance practice, Komporaly's book also discusses the limits of adaptability in theatre.

The related theme of the ethics of adaptation – a topic treated by Sidiropoulou and Montgomery Griffiths in their respective chapters in this volume – is the central concern of O'Toole, Pelegri Kristić, and Young (2017), an edited volume whose contributors explore a range of ethical issues involved in the practice of adaptation, translation, and dramaturgy, which they treat as part of a continuum of ethical and political questions. A particular attraction of this volume is its wide coverage of theatrical forms and traditions, from Shakespeare and Ibsen to contemporary forms of theatre (verbatim, immersive, interactive, devised, post-dramatic, etc.), as well as its exploration of the ever-present problems of untranslatability and of the ethical challenges involved in intercultural adaptations.

The year 2017 was an *annus mirabilis* for adaptation studies, especially with regard to modern and contemporary adaptations of Greek tragedy. The volume edited by Rodosthenous (2017) focuses on contemporary auteur theatre directors' visions regarding the adaptation of Greek tragedy for the stage. The volume offers a rich overview and in-depth analysis of international productions by a broad array of acclaimed contemporary directors, from Mitchell and Sellars through Terzopoulos and Fabre to Suzuki, Ninagawa, Şerban, and Schechner. Contributing authors explore how these and many other directors respond to and refashion the source texts for different contexts, and discuss (among other things) the tensions between the authority of the 'classic', directorial authority, and audience reception.

In the same year, Fischer-Lichte (2017) offered an innovative narrative, which sought to explore how performances of Greek tragedies in Germany since 1800 may be used to gauge developments in the cultural identity of the educated German middle class (the so-called *Bildungsbürgertum*) during that period. Among other things, Fischer-Lichte explored performances of Greek tragedy from Goethe's Weimar *Ion* (1802) down to the new genre of choric theatre, and showed how Greek tragedy and its adaptations served to consolidate German cultural (but also national and nationalist) identities, especially in reaction to the earlier French influences that had dominated German high culture.

Yet another publication of that year, Ioannidou (2017), discusses adaptations of Greek tragedy from 1970 to the mid-2000s, in an attempt to unearth and reconstruct latent but significant dialogues with postmodernism. The prevailing notion Ioannidou seeks to challenge is the idea that tragedy, as an aesthetic form and as a *Weltanschauung* privileging coherence, stability, and meaning, is incompatible with postmodernism, which favours ambivalence, dissolution, and fragmentation. With insights from Nietzsche, Benjamin, Brecht, Steiner, and Marxist (or Marxist-inflected) criticism, Ioannidou examines a number of contemporary adaptations – or rewritings, as she calls them – of Greek tragedy (by Berkoff, Cixous, Crimp, Friel, Hugh, Kennely, Soyinka, as well as Greek authors like Matessis and Staïkos) to explore such issues as the manipulation of the politics of viewing, the interrogation and renegotiation of the authority of classical texts and textuality, and the questioning of power structures implicit in fixed definitions and interpretations of tragedy.

A fifth volume on adaptation to appear in that year was Brodie and Cole (2017), an edited volume which focuses on the challenges of translating for the stage and staging works in translation, but also (inevitably) discusses adaptations of classical drama, especially at the turn of the twenty-first century. Using a large number of case studies, contributors to that volume explore the multiple intersections between translation and adaptation – a topic discussed in detail by Hardwick in the present volume – and contest the deep-seated but ultimately counter-productive dichotomy between literality and performability.

A more recent major publication, *The Routledge Companion to Adaptation*,[36] explores a broad spectrum of issues regarding the theory and practice of adaptation, with a strong interdisciplinary focus. One of that volume's many strong points is its emphasis on cross-media

[36] Cutchins, Krebs, and Voigts (2018).

adaptations (e.g. novel-to-stage, stage-to-film, dance, radio, television, new media) and its broad-ranging coverage of the interactions between adaptation and historiography, identity formation, audience reception, and technology. Among other things, contributors to that volume examine the tensions between adaptation and source-text, the role of adaptation and perceptions of history and historical narratives, confrontations with the concept of the canon (including fidelity and originality), the role of adaptation in the development of regional identities, as well as issues of contemporary relevance, such as queer studies, new media, or videogame adaptations.[37]

A Brief Overview of the Present Volume

The present volume seeks to develop and enhance many of the adaptation-related topics and questions raised in the works discussed in the previous section. As its subtitle indicates, this volume focuses on *contemporary* adaptations of Greek tragedy – i.e. on the dramatic and theatrical production of the last few decades. In the wake of the publications mentioned above, we are concerned not only with 'close adaptations', i.e. modern scripts that maintain a perceptibly close relationship with the Greek original, but also with 'new versions' or 're-makings', i.e. dramatic works which, although essentially new, presuppose a familiarity with the source text.[38] Thus, our volume's scope includes both textual adaptations/new versions – works that endeavour, to a greater or lesser degree, to remake the source text – and performances that offer revisionist takes on Greek tragedy, whether by keeping the source text essentially intact while attempting a re-contextualisation of the text's received meaning through an innovative mise-en-scène, or by developing a more or less radically adapted or remade script.

The volume is structured in two parts. After a 'Prelude' by Vayos Liapis surveying adaptations of Greek tragedy from a historical perspective, the first part, entitled 'Adapting Greek Tragedy: Definitions, Conceptual Foundations, Ethics', deals with the foundations of adaptation as an act which both asserts the validity of an established dramatic text and promises an often radical reinvestigation of its premises. This part serves as an overarching theoretical framework and sets out the methodological parameters for the subsequent chapters. The second, and larger, part

[37] This overview does not take account of publications that came to our attention after October 2018.
[38] For the distinction, cf. Mee and Foley (2011), 8–9.

('Adaptation on the Page and on the Stage: Re-inscribing the Greek Classics') examines textual and especially performative adaptations of Greek tragedy in the context of contemporary intellectual and political debates, which may problematise or endorse the classical tradition as a bulwark of Western culture, as well as a variety of ways in which contemporary directing practices approach Greek tragedy in seeking to adapt it for a contemporary performance medium.

A novelty of this volume is Chapter 5 ('Speaking Up: Theatre Practitioners on Adapting the Classics'), which serves as an 'Interlude' between Parts I and II. Here, leading contemporary theatre directors are interviewed by Avra Sidiropoulou, in an attempt to bring together and juxtapose playwrights' and directors' voices on the subject of the adaptation of Greek tragedy. Specifically, three of the theatrical avant-garde's most acclaimed auteurs – Mee, van Hove, and Suzuki – discuss questions relentlessly encountered in contemporary directing practice, such as the boundaries of directorial freedom and the redefinition of directorial interpretation in the process of adapting from, revising, and/or deconstructing Greek tragedy, together with the broader notions of authority, trust, loyalty, and subordination. This chapter not only reveals the richness of opinions over the practice of adaptation, but also brings to the fore the ways in which the artist's point of view is not limited to an understanding of the text's dramaturgical particularities and potentialities, but can serve to reshape and contextualise the source material through a series of metaphors, which will ultimately render it meaningful for contemporary audiences.

Prelude

Adapting Greek Tragedy: A Historical Perspective

Vayos Liapis

This Prelude, which may be read as a supplement to the Introduction, aims at situating adaptations of Greek tragedy in their historical context. This volume's contributions programmatically focus on late twentieth- and early twenty-first-century adaptations of Greek tragedy, but this must not be taken to imply that adapting Greek tragedy for the page or for the stage is a recent development. It is to be hoped that the following historical overview will help avoid or dispel presentist fallacies by demonstrating both that Greek tragedy was an act of adaptation since its inception and that the reception of Greek tragedy has proceeded, to a considerable extent, in concert with its adaptation in theatre and dramatic literature.

Antiquity to the Eighteenth Century

Greek Tragedy in the Fifth and Fourth Centuries BCE

From very early on, dramatic literature and theatrical performance in the West have been anchored in practices that we may reasonably classify as forms of adaptation. The earliest extant works of Western dramatic literature, the plays of the Greek tragic authors, are largely products of an ongoing dialogue with pre-existing mythic nuclei, which had previously been actuated in epic or choral narrative as well as in the oral tradition. The staple stories of Greek tragic drama – e.g. Oedipus and his family, the internecine Atreid house, the Trojan War with its preliminaries and aftermath – are theatrical instantiations of an infinitely malleable material, which had been subjected for centuries to innumerable forms of telling and retelling in a variety of media. Early Greek drama draws its themes mainly from the epic cycle, i.e. from epic poetry *outside* Homer, which may seem surprising given the undisputed primacy of Homer as cultural capital.[1] However, Homer becomes increasingly a prime source for tragic adaptations in the fourth century, when a number of tragedies entitled *Achilles* or *Hector* (by Astydamas, Chaeremon, and others) draw inspiration from the *Iliad*; moreover, the pseudo-Euripidean *Rhesus*, probably a fourth-century work by an unknown playwright, is largely though not exclusively an adaptation of *Iliad* 10.[2] In this context, Greek theatre soon became a major, and indeed privileged, cultural depository and capacitor, in which collective cultural memory was concentrated, renewed, and disseminated, in a constant flux of reworkings.[3]

None of those reworkings seems initially to have been intended or perceived as authoritative, although of course eventually the three great fifth-century tragic authors did achieve canonical status as paragons of dramatic art.[4] As a result, tragic production in the fourth century BCE appears, to a considerable extent, to gravitate towards the same mythic cycles as fifth-century tragedy. Not only do titles like *Ajax*, *Alcmeon*, *Antigone*, and *Athamas* (to stay only within the letter A) recur time and again in our sources, but also tragic playwrights now explicitly engage, whether in a centripetal or a centrifugal manner, with the 'classic' versions formulated by their fifth-century forerunners.[5] But even the canonical texts themselves, which after 386 BCE were reperformed regularly as part of the programme of the annual Great Dionysia festival in Athens, were evidently tampered with by actors, who would interpolate parts of their

[1] As far as we can tell, of the considerable fifth-century dramatic output only one Aeschylean tragic trilogy (*Myrmidons*, *Nereids*, *Phrygians*) and one Euripidean satyr drama (*Cyclops*) engage with specifically Homeric material.

[2] On fourth-century tragedies titled *Achilles* (at least five of them) and on Astydamas' *Hector*, see Duncan and Liapis (2018), 184; Liapis (2016). On *Rhesus* see Liapis (2012); Fries (2014).

[3] Greek tragedies on historical rather than mythic subjects, such as Phrynichus' *Phoenician Women* (mid-470s BCE) and Aeschylus' *Persians* (472 BC), may have arisen in a spirit of experimentation with the generic features of tragedy, perhaps as a contribution to the Panhellenic 'celebration culture' following the Greek victory at the Persian Wars (so Taplin 2006). Soon, however, such plays became outliers, as tragedy came to focus on the mythic past – although there was a brief revival of the 'historical tragedy' subgenre in the Hellenistic era (see Hornblower 2018, 99–101, 102–3). Equally exceptional were tragedies like Agathon's late fifth-century *Antheus* (Aristotle, *Poetics*, 1451b19–23), in which both plot and characters were entirely made up rather than based on pre-existing myths.

[4] On the canonisation of the three great tragic poets in the fourth century, see Hanink (2014); cf. Duncan and Liapis (2018), 180–90.

[5] For examples of 'centripetal', deferent engagement with the fifth-century canon cf., e.g., the charmingly naive scene of an illiterate rustic describing, in verbal images, the letters spelling out Theseus' name in an inscription – a scene first found in Euripides' *Theseus*, then in Agathon's *Telephus*, then in a fourth-century play by Theodectas. As examples of a 'centrifugal', non-conformist engagement, suffice it to mention Astydamas' *Antigone*, in which Antigone and Haemon survive to have a child together, and Carcinus' *Medea*, in which the eponymous character does *not* kill her children. For all of the above, see Liapis and Stephanopoulos (2018).

own making, perhaps as a means of showcasing their skills – so much so that the Athenian statesman Lycurgus found it necessary to decree that performances of classic dramas should henceforth be based on official copies of the plays.[6] In more than one way, the evolution of Greek tragedy into precious cultural capital went hand in hand with various, and often non-formal or even underhanded, processes of adaptation.

Roman Republican Tragedy; Seneca

Greek tragedy enters the cultural sphere of Rome in a self-aware, programmatic act of 'cultural transfer', whereby Roman plays are produced, on the basis of models from the Greek language and culture, for consumption by Roman audiences.[7] The Romans never attempted to conceal the Greek origins of their dramatic literature; on the contrary, they advertised it through the titles and themes of their plays, and even through such genre-specific terms as *tragoedia* (a Latinised form of the Greek *tragōidia*) and *fabula crepidata* (an allusion to the genre's Greek origins, since *krēpides* = the Greek tragic actor's boots). It is important to realise, however, that this cultural transfer was not an act of literal translation but sought freely to recreate one of the defining manifestations of Greek culture as a vehicle for Roman values and identities.[8]

From the point of view of the Western theatre tradition, the most prominent early adapter of Greek tragedy is Seneca. His surviving tragedies (barring the apocryphal *Octavia*) are creative reworkings of plays by the three great Greek tragedians. Thus, for instance, *Hercules Furens* is a recreation of Euripides' *Herakles*; *Troades* remoulds material from Euripides' *Trojan Women* and *Hecuba*; and *Phaedra* engages in a complex intertextual dialogue with Euripides' surviving *Hippolytus*, with the same author's now-lost *Hippolytus Covering Himself*, possibly with Sophocles' lost *Phaedra*, and with Ovid's *Heroides* 4 (a fictional letter from Phaedra to Hippolytus).[9] The case of *Phaedra* in particular reveals the complexity of Senecan adaptation as the point of confluence of various literary strands

[6] See esp. Hanink (2014), 60–89; Hanink (2018), 327–9.

[7] Cf. Manuwald (2011), 21, from whom I borrow the term 'cultural transfer'.

[8] See further Manuwald (2011), 20–1, 133–9 (on cultural transfer and the Romanisation of Greek models), 190–225 (on Roman Republican tragedy authors), 282–92 (on the varieties of the Roman adaptation of Greek models).

[9] On Seneca's tragedies, see Conte (1994), 416–20; Boyle (1997), esp. 32–137. On the *Octavia*, see Ferri (2003). On Seneca's engagement with Sophoclean tragedy in particular, see Holford-Strevens (1999).

ranging from Greek drama to Hellenistic and Augustan poetry. This intertextual palimpsest is supplemented and enhanced by the play's multilayered ideological make-up, which incorporates characteristically Roman concerns, from the triumph of *pietas* over the lust for power to the quest for Stoic ideals such as *otium*.[10] Thanks to its far-reaching polyvalence, and despite a predilection for the grotesque which today comes across as overblown, Senecan drama takes pride of place among our earliest evidence for the literary and ideological potential of adaptation as an act of cultural appropriation.

The Eastern Roman Empire

In the Eastern Roman Empire (more commonly, but inaccurately, known as 'Byzantium'), the only surviving trace of an interest in the canonical Greek tragic theatre is, intriguingly, an idiosyncratic text that was programmatically conceived and realised as an act of adaptation. This is the anonymous text known as *Christus Patiens* (Χριστὸς Πάσχων), or *The Passion of the Christ*, a lengthy (2,632 lines) *cento*, in which lines from Euripidean tragedies are taken out of their original context and recombined, often with modifications, to produce a dramatised narrative of the passion, death, and resurrection of Jesus. One of the underlying ideas behind this *cento* may be that inklings of Christian truth lurk even in pagan texts and can be brought to light by shrewd cherry-picking and rearrangement – that is, by a procedure of wide-ranging adaptation. In general, *Christus Patiens* may be seen as an act of Christian cultural hegemonism seeking to appropriate some of the outstanding canonical texts of the pagan tradition and to put them into the service of Christian ideology. As one among many examples, the anonymous author repeatedly excerpts lines from Euripides' *Bacchae* in particular, an act which bespeaks a desire to recast the myth of Dionysus – a god who, like Jesus, reveals himself in human form, is resisted, suffers, and eventually triumphs – in the context of Christian doctrine.[11]

[10] On the palimpsestic aspects of Senecan tragedy, see Boyle (1997), 85–111; on Stoicism and Senecan drama, see Rosenmeyer (1989).

[11] Further on the *Christus Patiens*, see the sensitive and intelligent analysis of Pollmann (2017), 140–57, to which the above remarks are indebted. For a synoptic presentation, see also Puchner and White (2017), 77–80.

Renaissance Tragedy

The rediscovery of classical drama as stage material in the Renaissance is, again, inextricably associated with adaptation. Modern French drama was born out of a landmark performance, at Lyons in 1548, of Bernardo Dovizi da Bibbiena's *La Calandria*, an adaptation of Plautus' *Menaechmi*. The same Plautine comedy, in a modernised adaptation by Juan de Timoneda (1559), is among the earliest specimens of classical drama in Spain, together with Fernán Pérez de Oliva's *La venganza de Agamenón* (1528), an adaptation of Sophocles' *Electra*, and the same author's *Hécuba triste* (*ca.* 1530?), an adaptation of Euripides' *Hecuba*.[12] In Italy, Lodovico Dolce produced his notable versions, or rather creative rewritings, of Euripidean tragedies, in which his own share is at least as substantial as Euripides'. Dolce's fame reached well beyond Italy, and his *Giocasta* (an adaptation of Euripides' *Phoenician Women*) served as the model for one of the earliest English performances of Greek tragedy, namely George Gascoigne and Francis Kinwelmershe's *Jocasta* (1566).[13]

As often in that era, Dolce's dramatic writing went hand in hand with a critical interest in the theory of drama, especially as laid out in Aristotle's *Poetics*. That interest was shared also by one of the great Italian dramatists of the time, Giambattista Giraldi (Cinzio), who explored the Aristotelian principles of dramatic composition in his tract *Discorso delle commedie e delle tragedie* (1543), as well as producing the first modern classicising tragedy, *Orbecche* (1541), a 'Senecan' drama of revenge, horror, and extreme violence, which was tremendously successful in its time.[14] An awareness of theoretical issues, and a critical engagement with Greek forerunners, seem to accompany the modern era of adaptations of Greek tragedy almost since its inception.

12 Highet (1949), 120–1, 133–4. As is well known, Plautus' *Menaechmi* later provided the material for a much more famous adaptation, Shakespeare's *The Comedy of Errors*.

13 See Dolce 1560; Terpening (1997), 92–4. On Gascoigne's and Kinwelmershe's *Jocasta*, see Ward (2013), 62–71.

14 Dolce's and Giraldi's engagement with Aristotelian principles of dramatic composition led to their respective *Didone* plays, in which they attempted to dramatise an episode from Virgil's *Aeneid*, in accordance with Aristotle's (*Poetics*, 1456a10–18) recommendation that tragedy should avoid taking on subjects of epic scope (i.e. should refrain from containing a multiplicity of poorly connected plots); see Terpening (1997), 105–27.

Neoclassical Tragedy: Baroque Retellings

An engagement with the theory of drama, especially in its post-Renaissance manifestations that claimed to derive from Aristotle, is also characteristic of neoclassical tragedy, as represented by the plays of Corneille, Racine, and Dryden, as well as by Milton's solitary and experimental outlier *Samson Agonistes*. Milton's *Samson* (1671), a distant and perhaps unwitting descendant of Ezekiel's biblical tragedy *Exagōgē* (composed sometime between the mid third and the mid first century BCE), combines a biblical theme, from the Book of Judges, with the diction and themes of Greek tragedy, as well as with a serious interest in the theoretical underpinnings of dramatic writing. In his preface to the published text of his tragedy, Milton foregrounds Aristotelian catharsis as a homeopathic cure 'purging' violent emotions like pity and terror by exciting them in the controlled environment of 'reading or seeing those passions well imitated'.[15] What sets *Samson Agonistes* apart from the other dramas of that era is that it constitutes 'a pure re-creation of Greek tragedy', which assimilates themes, style, and dramatic techniques from all three Greek tragedians.[16] With its unpredictable variety of metres and its lack of such structural divisions as acts and scenes, Milton's 'Greek' tragedy cares little for the rigid rules of dramatic composition we usually associate with neoclassical drama.

By contrast, Pierre Corneille's two 'Greek' tragedies, *Medée* (1635) and *Œdipe* (1659), strictly adhere to the rules of neoclassical tragedy (unities of time, place, and action, verisimilitude, and *bienséance*, or decorum). They are largely based on Seneca's and Sophocles' plays of the same titles, albeit with a distinct (and typically neoclassical) tendency to downplay the characters' moral failings and to privilege psychological interest mainly in the form of amorous liaisons or love triangles.[17] Cultural context is of the essence here: neoclassical adaptations, under the influence of the highly centralised politics of the French Academy, tend to comply with strict rules

[15] Quotation from Milton's prologue ('Of that sort of Dramatic Poem which is call'd Tragedy') to *Samson Agonistes*: Milton (1671), 3. See further Mueller (1980), 193–212; Wood (1992). On Ezekiel's *Exagōgē*, see Lanfranchi (2018) with earlier bibliography; on its date see Lanfranchi (2006), 10.

[16] Quotation from Highet (1949), 294, who also points out that Milton was the only poet of the period who 'knew and assimilated all three Greek tragedians'.

[17] On *Médée* see, e.g., Tobari (1985). On *Œdipe* see, e.g., Mueller (1980), 131–6; Zanin (2008), 74–7. By contrast, Corneille's wildly successful *Le Cid* (1637) showed little concern for the neoclassical constraints imposed by the French Academy; as a result, it provoked a public debate and a condemnation, on behalf of the Academy, by Jean Chapelain in his tract *Les Sentiments de l'Académie sur la tragi-comédie du Cid* (*The Sentiments of the Academy on the Tragicomedy of Cid*, 1637).

in regard both to structure and to content, and thus to validate and enhance the canonical nature of the classical models, even when attempting to better them, as Corneille and others sometimes purported to do. Corneille's three theoretical essays, or *discours*, on drama deal with some of the central themes of Aristotle's *Poetics* (the 'utility' and structure of the dramatic work, the construction of the dramatic plot according to probability and necessity, etc.). Corneille often puts his theoretical insights to dramatic use by, e.g., offering, in his *Œdipe*, a central character who is always in control and is thus deemed superior to his Sophoclean and Senecan predecessors, or by introducing an element of dynastic intrigue intertwined with an amorous interest in the invented person of Dirce, daughter of Laius and Jocasta, who considers herself the legitimate heir to the throne of Thebes and intends to marry Theseus, himself covetous of the Theban kingship. A less successful romantic subplot is introduced in Voltaire's *Œdipe* (1718) in the invented story of Jocasta's earlier chaste love for Philoctetes, whom the Queen had to reject in order to marry Oedipus out of patriotic duty.

Of all neoclassical tragic playwrights, Jean Racine is the one whose engagement with Greek tragedy is the most sustained, explicit, and self-aware. Some of his greatest tragedies are programmatically and self-avowedly modelled on the classics of Greek dramaturgy, so much so that he deliberately seeks to downplay collateral influences from his contemporary theatre. Thus, in the preface to his early *La Thébaïde ou Les Frères ennemis* (1664), Racine declares that he 'designed the plot more or less following Euripides' *Phoenician Women*',[18] when it is evident that his sources also included Statius' *Thebaid* and Jean Rotrou's *Antigone*.[19] In the earlier of his two prefaces to his *Andromaque*, Racine invokes Aristotle's *Poetics* in defence of his portrayal of Pyrrhus; and in the later preface to the same play, while admitting that he has considerably distanced himself from Euripides' *Andromache*, he invokes another Euripidean play (*Helen*) as a precedent for a dramatist's licence to diverge from the accepted version of a myth.[20] Here, once again, he suppresses his debts to contemporary authors, from Corneille (*Pertharite*, *Sophonisbe*) to Rotrou (*Hercule mourant*).[21] In his late masterpieces, *Iphigénie* (1674) and *Phèdre* (1677), Racine

[18] 'Je dressay à peu prés mon plan sur les Phenicienes d'Euripide': Racine (1951) i. 161.

[19] See P. Mélèse in Racine (1951), I.155–9.

[20] Racine's *Andromaque* was produced in 1667; the earlier preface appeared in the 1668 and 1673 editions; in the 1676 edition it was replaced by the later preface. See Racine (1951), II.23–5, 115–16.

[21] See P. Mélèse in Racine (1951), II.15–16.

shows himself, if anything, even more anxious to establish the (neo) classicist credentials of his plays. In the preface to *Iphigénie* he offers a near-exhaustive list of the myth's classical sources, evidently as a means of demonstrating that the remarkable novelties of his treatment – Iphigenia is spared both an undeserved death and an implausibly miraculous salvation; Achilles and Iphigenia are romantically involved – are an improvement upon the traditional material rather than the symptom of an unscholarly author.[22] Racine's background research was remarkably extensive in the case of his *Phèdre*. His principal model was, of course, Euripides' *Hippolytus*, although the shift of dramatic focus from Hippolytus to Phaedra (hence the French piece's title, which replaced an earlier *Phèdre et Hippolyte*) is due to Seneca's *Phaedra*. Once again, as is his wont, Racine says nothing in his preface about his debts to near-contemporary sources, such as Gilbert's *Hippolyte ou le garçon insensible* (*Hippolytus or the Unfeeling Lad*, 1647) and Bidar's *Hippolyte* (1674).[23] Whatever his literary debts, Racine, the former pupil of Port-Royal Jansenists, must of course be credited with the fundamental conception of a Phaedra who, deprived of divine grace, is carried away by vice, despite herself.

Perhaps no other Greek-themed play of that era is more explicitly conscious of its epigonal status than *Oedipus* by John Dryden and Nathaniel Lee (licensed in 1678 and published in 1679). In their prologue, after paying the obligatory homage to Sophocles' *Oedipus Tyrannus* as the best tragedy classical antiquity has produced, the authors confront more recent treatments, which they dismiss rather summarily. Seneca, they claim, 'is always running after pompous expression, pointed sentences, and Philosophical notions, more proper for the Study than the Stage'.[24] Nonetheless, they own to having lifted from Seneca the conjuring of Laius' ghost, which in their play not only reveals Oedipus' crimes but also lays claim on Jocasta's love.[25] As for Corneille, they say, 'a judicious Reader will easily observe, how much the Copy is inferiour to the Original' – although they do borrow from Corneille the motif of the chaste amorous liaison (between Adrastus and Eurydice), which they admit to having introduced as a concession to 'an unsatiable Audience';[26] a similar concession to popular tastes, we may add, is their decision to kill off spectacularly all major characters by the end of the

[22] Racine (1951), IV.21–7. [23] See P. Mélèse in Racine (1951), IV.129–31.

[24] Quotation from Dryden and Lee (1679), A3.

[25] In Seneca, however, Laius' ghost does not appear onstage: its revelations about Oedipus' guilt are communicated in hair-raising detail by a reluctant Creon (*Oedipus*, 530–658), which gives Oedipus cause to suspect a plot against him, as in Sophocles' play (*Oedipus Tyrannus*, 380–403, 531ff.).

[26] Quotations from Dryden and Lee (1679), A2.

play. What is remarkable in all this is, above all, the uncommon candour with which Dryden and Lee confront the complexities of their role in the revival and recreation of Greek tragedy. On the one hand, they situate themselves in a long line of – usually inadequate, as they claim – heirs to one of the greatest artistic achievements of Greek antiquity. On the other, they are anxious to establish their artistic ascendancy in an environment in which earlier engagements (e.g. by Seneca and Corneille) with the classical canon had added layers of intertextual accretions, which inevitably determine the framework that later adaptations must acknowledge, contend with, or break out of.[27]

Overall, neoclassical tragedy, especially in its French instantiations, while claiming to follow in the steps of its classical models, imposes on itself restrictions – such as the 'three unities', the rigid metrical structure, the squeamishly aristocratic decorousness – that are to be found nowhere in Greek or Roman tragedy. Also, it presupposes, in order to be fully appreciated, a familiarity with the classical models that goes beyond anything the majority of its contemporary audiences will have been conversant with. In other words, it is a genre to be enjoyed by a happy few rather than by the large popular audiences of Greek, Roman or, for that matter, Elizabethan drama.[28] Nonetheless, neoclassical tragedy is an important landmark in the history of the adaptation of Greek tragic drama, as it programmatically goes beyond the mere emulation of the tragic canon to construct a precise and systematic (if too rigid) framework for the reception and dynamic recreation of the classical heritage.

Romanticism and the Spirit of Revolution

What the eighteenth century revolted against was (despite the worn-out cliché) not classical antiquity per se but its hijacking by the political, social, religious, and ideological establishment and its straitjacketing into perverse, artificial, and (often) absurd rules that had nothing to do with the classical authors themselves. In fact, 'in the general movement of revolt, the examples of Greece and republican Rome were among the most urgent forces . . . The revolutionaries believed themselves to be *more* classical than their opponents.'[29] From constituents of a tyrannical canon, Greece and Rome are now transformed into agents of political, spiritual, social, moral, religious, and even sexual liberation.

[27] Further on the three aforementioned Oedipus plays (by Corneille, Dryden/Lee, and Voltaire), see Burian (1997), 240–7.

[28] See further Highet (1949), 295–302.

[29] Quotation from Highet (1949), 356.

Among the most prominent cases in point is Vittorio Alfieri, a fervent opponent of tyranny in all its forms, who loathed despotism and the French Revolution in equal measure. Alfieri wrote numerous tragedies inspired by Greek and Roman antiquity, four among which are reworkings of myths known from Greek tragedy: *Polinice* (1781), *Agamennone* (1783/8), *Antigone* (1783/9), and *Oreste* (1776/83). Typically for Alfieri's tragic production, these plays are characterised by a pared-down, almost unhewn style, a single-minded focus on a central heroic character and on a theme divested of subplots, and above all a celebration of anti-tyrannical sentiment and popular revolt. The odious figure of the tyrant is materialised in, for instance, *Polinice*'s Eteocles, who attempts to poison his brother Polynices, and in *Oreste*'s Aegisthus, who apprehends Orestes and Pylades only to provoke a popular revolt and end up being slain by Orestes (who also kills Clytemnestra accidentally).[30]

The revolutionary spirit is equally, if more subtly, detectable in the dramatic work of Percy Shelley, a towering figure of the Romantic movement, and a radical to boot, both in his politics and in his religious views.[31] It is in the context of Shelley's radical politics that we should read his two major attempts to recreate Greek tragedy, namely *Prometheus Unbound* (1820) and *Hellas* (composed in 1821 and published in 1822). As Shelley himself pointed out, his fervently Philhellenic *Hellas* was inspired by Aeschylus' *Persians*. The correspondences are quite transparent. For instance, Shelley's tragedy takes place at Sultan Mahmud's seraglio in Constantinople, as Aeschylus' play takes place at the Persian king's palace at Susa. Also, Mahmud, troubled by uneasy dreams, conjures the ghost of an ancestor, just as the Persian Queen and the chorus in Aeschylus conjure Darius' ghost as a response to the Queen's ominous dream. Most important, perhaps, Shelley presents Turkish defeat from a Turkish perspective, just as Aeschylus had presented the Greek victory at Salamis from a Persian perspective – although Aeschylus' Persian chorus is now replaced by a chorus of Greek captive women, who provide a contrapuntal Greek perspective on the nation's hope for liberation.[32]

30 On Alfieri's politics as manifested in his tragedies, see Merola (1981).

31 Shelley's 1811 anonymous pamphlet *The Necessity of Atheism* led to his being expelled from Oxford. His 1811 anonymous poem *Political Essay on the Existing State of Things*, long-lost and rediscovered in 2006, is a virulent attack on government, religion, war, imperialism, and the monarchy. And his 1812 *Address to the Irish People* advocated nothing less than a repeal of the Acts of Union (1800/1801), which Shelley viewed as an instrument of English oppression over Ireland.

32 See further Løkse (1994), 1–15, with remarks on Shelley's sources, which also include Milton and Calderón; Mulhallen (2010), 177–207.

With *Prometheus Unbound*, Shelley took greater freedoms with the traditional material. Indeed, in the preface to that work, he shows himself perfectly aware that the Greek tragic dramas themselves were adaptations of stories already current – adaptations which asserted their agents' authorial physiognomy: 'The Greek tragic writers ... by no means conceived themselves bound to adhere to the common interpretation or to imitate in story as in title their rivals and predecessors.' Shelley retains the kernel of the Aeschylean version (Prometheus is riveted on a rock in the remotest regions of the earth as a punishment for his disobedience), and even replicates some of the more emotional points of the Aeschylean *Prometheus Bound* (e.g. Prometheus' poignant address to the elements, or his violently proud reaction to Mercury's mission as a messenger of Jupiter). However, he purposely deviates from the Aeschylean *Prometheus Unbound* (Προμηθεὺς Λυόμενος), a drama which now survives only in a handful of fragments and mentions by later authors, in that he precludes any possibility of reconciling Prometheus with Jupiter, 'the Champion with the Oppressor of Mankind'. Such an outcome, says Shelley, would annihilate 'the moral interest of the fable', for then Prometheus would be 'unsaying his high language and quailing before his successful and perfidious adversary'[33] – an idea found already in Goethe's earlier version of *Prometheus* (1774, publ. 1789), a two-act dramatic fragment in which Prometheus repeatedly resists the bribes offered him in return for his submission to Zeus' rule.[34] Shelley's Jupiter falls as a result of his confrontation with Demogorgon, and humankind is released from the tyranny of the supreme god: 'the man remains | Sceptreless, free, uncircumscribed, but man | Equal, unclassed, tribeless, and nationless, | Exempt from awe, worship, degree, the king | Over himself'.[35]

Shelley's anti-monarchical sentiments were vented also in his *Oedipus Tyrannus, or Swellfoot the Tyrant* (1820), a satirical rip-off of Sophocles' play adapted to suit the contemporary Queen Caroline affair.[36] There is more Aristophanes (and Commedia dell'arte and pantomime theatre) than Sophocles to Shelley's comedy, and the piece is generally not on a par with the rest of Shelley's work.[37]

[33] All quotations are from Shelley (1820), vii–viii.

[34] See further McDonald (2003), 40–1.

[35] Shelley (1820), 120. Further on *Prometheus Unbound*, see Mulhallen (2010), 47–75.

[36] Upon his ascension to the English throne, King George IV attempted to bar his adulterous and estranged wife, Caroline of Brunswick, from claiming royal privileges, but the latter managed to garner Whig and popular support.

[37] On *Swellfoot the Tyrant*, see further Erkelenz 1996; Mulhallen (2010), 209–34.

A more important, and artistically accomplished, adaptation of *Oedipus Tyrannus* is Heinrich von Kleist's comedy *The Broken Jug* (*Der zerbrochne Krug*, 1806–11), a work which Goethe himself, despite some reservations, staged at the Weimar Court Theatre for a single performance (2 March 1808) – the play was hissed off the stage, although it has since gained considerably in popularity. The dissolute judge Adam, a latter-day Oedipus whose very name identifies him as archetypally sinful, presides over a trial in which the point at issue is a broken jug. After much contestation, and despite Adam's delaying tactics, it transpires that the jug was broken by Adam himself, who was in the house of the jug owner, one Frau Martha Rull, on the previous night, trying to seduce her daughter, the appropriately named Eve. His guilt discovered, Adam hobbles away to impunity, while Frau Martha's case remains undecided. The play rehearses the fundamental Oedipal motif of the judge who is himself the guilty party, except that Adam, in contrast to Oedipus, is perfectly aware of his guilt, does everything in his power to avoid detection, and in the end escapes punishment. As a satire of the greed and corruption of state officials, *The Broken Jug* employs adaptation of Greek drama as an ideological tool for the castigation of social ills.

As well as being instrumental in *The Broken Jug*'s ill-fated first stage production, Goethe himself authored two major adaptations of Greek tragic drama. His *Iphigenie auf Tauris* (1779–86)[38] largely rehearses the plot of Euripides' play and follows the conventional five-act structure of neoclassical tragedy. Goethe's major contribution is his emphasis on purity, salvation, and moral ennoblement as objectives to be attained by the individual rather than conferred by divinity. Thus, Orestes has a vision of Hades in which his sinful forefathers (Atreus, Thyestes) live together in peace; and Iphigenia, foregoing her Euripidean predecessor's deceitfulness, succeeds in persuading King Thoas to yield to his better nature by allowing her and her brother to depart. Goethe's play exemplifies an instance not only of tragedy averted (thanks to the happy ending it shares with its Euripidean forerunner) but also of 'partial or arrested tragedy',[39] in that it opens up the perspective of forgiveness and reconciliation early enough for any possibility of tragic fall or disaster to be precluded: it is an almost Christian tragedy by a non-Christian author.[40]

[38] The play's first (1779) and second (1781) versions were in prose; its third (1786) and definitive version is in verse.

[39] For the term, see Steiner (1961), 185.

[40] On Goethe's *Iphigenie* and its dialogue with Greek antiquity, the standard treatment is still Maass (1912), 330–54.

Late in his life (1827), Goethe published his 'classic-romantic phantasmagoria' *Helena*, which was later integrated into his *Second Faust* (Act III). This tripartite drama, which partly evokes the meeting of Menelaus and Helen in Euripides' *Trojan Women*, breaks free from almost all neoclassical rules, as it moves casually between different epochs and places, while its plot is loosely structured around the figure of Helen. From Menelaus' palace in Sparta the drama moves to Faust's castle in (apparently) medieval Peloponnese, and from there to an idealised Arcadia, where Faust and Helena have a child, the short-lived Euphorion, whom Goethe explicitly saw as an incarnation of the spirit of Romantic poetry and, more specifically, of Lord Byron, whose untimely death in Greece in 1824 was still fresh in European memory.[41] However, it is hard not to see behind 'Euphorion' also an allusion to the name shared by Aeschylus' father and son, and thus perhaps to the generative force animating Greek tragedy. The manner of Euphorion's death, designed to evoke that of the mythic Icarus, is a manifestation of Romanticism's cult of fiery vitality and vigour leading to an untimely death,[42] but also perhaps a comment on the impossibility of bringing about a long-lasting revival of the spirit of Greek tragedy, at least in the hands of northern Europeans like the Gothic Faust.

The Nineteenth Century

Robert Browning Rewrites Euripides

Perhaps no other nineteenth-century adaptation of Greek tragedy has caused more critical perplexity than Robert Browning's *Balaustion's Adventure* (1871; henceforth *BA*), a lengthy (2,705 lines) narrative of how Balaustion, a young woman from Rhodes, arrived in Sicily soon after the disastrous defeat of the Athenian expedition in the late fifth century and saved herself by recreating, in narrative form, in the theatre of Syracuse, a performance of Euripides' *Alcestis* which she had herself attended.[43] Remarkably, Browning's narrative problematises his contemporary fidelity discourse by having a 'critic and whippersnapper', who castigates Balaustion for arbitrarily reading the dramatic characters'

[41] See Gumpert (2001), 198. [42] Cf. Highet (1949), 389.

[43] Browning's implicit hypotext here is Plutarch's famous story (*Life of Nicias*, 29.2–5) of how a number of Athenian prisoners in Syracuse gained their freedom as a reward for reciting or singing portions from Euripides' plays – such was the local population's fondness for the poet.

emotions behind their masks, receive the reply that poetry is 'a power that makes' and energises all human senses even though it speaks only to one of them (*BA* 318–35).[44] It is ironical that, for some twenty-five years after its publication, Browning's version remained the object of hostile criticisms precisely for its perceived 'unfaithfulness' to the Euripidean original.[45] It is true that Browning condenses or even suppresses some of the Euripidean chorus' expressions of sympathy for Admetus, thus casting him as weaker and more selfish, whereas he divests Heracles of whatever burlesque elements he has in Euripides to present him as an incarnation of heroic magnanimity, an almost Christ-like figure of selfless sacrifice.[46] And not only this: Browning's Balaustion takes even further creative liberties with the original, as she adds a *second* retelling of the Alcestis story, one in which she assigns the figure of Admetus more charitable attributes, thus going Euripides one better by improving the moral content of the tale. According to Balaustion's second retelling, the music Apollo played as he tended Admetus' flocks inspired in the latter's heart the wish 'to rule henceforth | In Pherai solely for his people sake, | Subduing to such end each lust and greed | That dominates the natural charity' (*BA* 2449–52). When, however, the fated moment of Admetus' premature death arrives, his wife Alcestis informs him that she has already arranged to die in his stead so that he may accomplish his life project of becoming a just king. At the moment of their last embrace, the power of Alcestis' soul enters her husband and redoubles his strength; as a result, Persephone feels herself cheated because 'The life, that's left behind and past my power, | Is formidably doubled' (*BA* 2634–5). Thus, before her shadow can enter Hades, Alcestis is released from the grasp of death. Rather than having a heroic redeemer like Heracles rescue her from Hades, Alcestis saves herself through the power of her conjugal love and works with her husband for the benefit of the kingdom. Thus, the possibility is opened up for personal salvation through the individual's re-enactment of the Christian story.[47]

44 See further Ryals (1973), 1043, 1045.

45 For a survey of such criticisms, see Tisdel (1917), 519–24.

46 Cf. Tisdel (1917), 525–8, 539–41; on Heracles' Christ-like traits, see Ryals (1973), 1044; Prins (2015), 522–3.

47 See Ryals (1973), 1046–7, on whose phrasing I have occasionally drawn in this section. Considerations of space prevent any detailed discussion of Browning's translation, or 'transcript', of Euripides' *Heracles*, incorporated into his *Aristophanes' Apology: Including a Transcript from Euripides, Being the Last Adventure of Balaustion* (1875), or of his translation of Aeschylus' *Agamemnon* (1877). On these translations, see Prins (2015), 516–18, 524–35.

André Gide: Between Paratragedy and Moral Treatise

Shortly before the end of the nineteenth century, the world saw the first fully and consciously 'anachronistic' adaptation of Greek tragic drama. This was André Gide's *Le Prométhée mal enchaîné* (1899), or *Prometheus Ill-bound*,[48] in which the time and place of action are Gide's contemporary Paris, and the plot departs quite radically from that of *Prometheus Bound*. Gide's *Prométhée* is structured as a series of brief prose narratives, which feature a disparate assortment of characters, from the corpulent 'Zeus the banker' to the waiter and patrons of a Parisian café to Prometheus himself, who breaks free from his shackles on Caucasus to take a stroll in the Parisian boulevards. In conversation with two café patrons, Prometheus identifies himself as a manufacturer of matches (a transparent parody of his mythic role as the bringer of fire to humans) and summons his pet eagle, which comes to feed on his liver. The police intervene, Prometheus and his eagle are imprisoned, and the vulture continues to feed on its owner's liver until the latter becomes so light that the eagle is able to carry him out of prison. This account of Gide's narrative, selective and incomplete as it is, gives an idea of the typically Gidean mélange of superficial frivolity and underlying seriousness that pervades *Prométhée*. In particular, the episodes involving Prometheus' eagle, for all their grotesque comedy, point to the fundamentally tragic theme of suffering as both a consequence and a precondition of the human struggle for freedom.[49] It is worth pointing out that Gide's half-comic capitalist Zeus acquires much more sinister and violent undertones many years later, in Tom Paulin's *Seize the Fire* (1989), a rewriting of *Prometheus Bound* in the context of the question of Northern Ireland's independence.[50]

At about the same time, Gide also wrote *Philoctète* (1898), a 'play' emphatically not written for the stage,[51] in which he generally follows the plot of Sophocles' homonymous drama, except that his Philoctetes outwits Odysseus, who has been trying to trick him out of his bow, by knowingly and willingly drinking the drug offered him by Neoptolemus, so that his weapons may be stolen from him during his sleep. Thus, he accepts to be left alone, but happy, on his desert island – indeed, 'Je suis heureux' ('I am happy') are the last words of the play, after which the stage

[48] See Gide 1925 and, for an English translation, Gide 2007.

[49] See further Sheridan (1999), 158–60.

[50] See further McDonald (2003), 43–4.

[51] In his prefatory note to the printed edition, Gide (1948), 102, specifies that *Philoctète* is a 'moral treatise' rather than a play, and adds (no doubt tongue-in-cheek) that he has included it in a volume of treatises the better to demonstrate that it has no claim to the stage.

directions indicate that he enters a state of beatific transcendence.[52] The play's eventual title, *Philoctète ou Le Traité des trois morales*, brings out its character as a 'moral treatise' (see fn. 51 above), in which each of the dramatis personae embodies a different kind of morality, namely patriotism and duty to the motherland (Ulysse); charity and empathy for one's fellow humans (Néoptolème); and a more complex morality, patiently cultivated by the individual in extreme solitude, and transcending, in Nietzschean fashion, the duality of good and evil in order to arrive at a mystic contemplation of God and truth (Philoctète).[53]

The Twentieth and Twenty-first Centuries

A common theme linking the three nineteenth-century adaptations surveyed above is the valorisation of the individual, an act variously manifested as a quasi-Nietzschean process of self-creation in Gide's *Philoctète*, or as a quest for freedom through self-sacrifice in *Le Prométhée mal enchaîné*, or as a struggle for individual salvation through the creative reappropriation of the classical past in Browning's *Balaustion's Adventure*. These three seminal nineteenth-century texts articulate the transition of the adaptation discourse into the twentieth century not only qua celebrations of individualism but also through their self-reflexive character, especially prominent in *Balaustion*'s second-degree adaptation of its source text and in *Prométhée*'s ironic retelling of the Aeschylean myth.

A similar interpretive self-awareness is also characteristic of many twentieth-century adaptations of Greek tragedy. The fidelity imperative that had animated neoclassical adaptations, with their strict adherence to purportedly classical rules, is now superseded by a more fluid approach, which both acknowledges the canonicity of the classical source texts and challenges it by endorsing different and even conflicting discourses. Progressively, twentieth-century adaptations – a trend that continues into the twenty-first century – contest the very idea of an authoritative centre regulating the creation of meaning: they celebrate polyvalence, diversity and eclecticism, and they even advance anti-classical and anti-canonical agendas. There is a growing tendency of radical revisionism, which both recognises the centrality of 'the old' and urges the breathing of new life

[52] Gide (1948), 145: 'Sa voix est devenue extraordinairement belle et douce; des fleurs autour de lui percent la neige, et les oiseaux du ciel descendent le nourrir' ('His voice has become extraordinarily beautiful and gentle; flowers all around him burst through the snow, and birds fly down from the heavens to feed him').

[53] See further Conacher (1955), 125–7; Sheridan (1999), 162–4.

into it, by infusing it with a new vitality derived from the most disparate periods, stylistic registers, and genres.

Dominant Myths I: Electra and Orestes

Few myths have attracted as strong an interest in twentieth-century adaptations of Greek tragedy as those of Oedipus and Electra. Doubtless, this is due as much to those myths' dramatic potential (seeing how they combine themes ranging from incest and intrafamilial violence to dynastic struggles) as to their central place in psychoanalytical theory. As is well known, the Oedipus myth, and Sophocles' *Oedipus Tyrannus* in particular, play a cardinal role in Chapter 5 of Freud's *Interpretation of Dreams* (1899), in which Oedipus' patricide and incest are seen as representative of an important stage in the psychosexual development of the human male.[54] As for the Electra myth, it is fundamental to Carl Jung's 'Electra complex', first introduced in his Fordham lectures of 1912 as the female equivalent of the Oedipus complex, in which the girl develops feelings of sexual antagonism against her mother as she desires the attentions of the father, but also remains in a state of unsatisfied longing for a father who is perpetually absent.[55] It is no doubt symptomatic of this renewed interest in the Electra and Oedipus myths that Max Reinhardt's efforts to revive interest in the Greek theatre included monumental performances of plays drawing precisely on those myths: Aeschylus' *Oresteia* (1911, 1919), Sophocles' *Oedipus Tyrannus* (1910), and Hugo von Hofmannsthal's *Elektra* (1903).[56]

Almost a decade before Jung's Fordham lectures, inklings of what was to become the 'Electra complex' are evinced in Hofmannsthal's *Elektra*. In it, the visceral, almost physical quality of Electra's incessant mourning[57] is combined with her equally physical abhorrence at the carnality of her mother's adulterous liaison with Aegisthus, an abhorrence which bespeaks a smouldering sexual jealousy, evinced by Electra's disgusted references to 'laboring breath' when the couple 'are alone together'.[58] When Electra asks her sister Chrysothemis to help her slay Aegisthus,[59] she does so in

[54] See e.g. Freud (1999), 201–3. [55] See Jung (1961), 154–5, 168, 245.

[56] See McDonald (2003), 23–4.

[57] Electra compares herself to a vulture devouring her own body, and the women of Argos to 'muck-flies' trying to 'feed upon the sweetness of [her] torment' (Hofmannsthal 1908, 7, 9). The image of the women of Argos as 'muck-flies' resurfaces in Giraudoux's and especially Sartre's image of the Erinyes as flies (in *Électre* and *Les Mouches* respectively).

[58] Hofmannsthal (1908), 17–18. [59] Hofmannsthal (1908), 52–9.

language that intermingles the lethal with the sexual: the sisters are to wait for Aegisthus as if for a bridegroom; Aegisthus at the moment of his death will 'look up at [Chrysothemis'] slender body'; and Chrysothemis herself will be rewarded for her courage 'with shudderings of rapture, night for night'.[60] Finally, at the recognition scene (which is largely modelled on Sophocles' *Electra*), Electra confesses to Orestes, in erotically charged language, that the spectral presence of their dead father has prevented her from achieving sexual fulfilment: 'For jealous are the dead, | And [Agamemnon] has sent me hatred for a bridegroom, | Hollow-eyed hatred. And that horrible thing, | Breathing a viperous breath, had I to take | Into my sleepless bed, that it might teach me | All that is done between a man and wife.'[61] In 1909, Hofmannsthal rewrote *Electra* as a libretto for Richard Strauss' opera of the same title, which foregrounded even more blatantly Electra's sexual obsession with her father.[62]

The 'Electra complex' is made glaring use of in O'Neill's *Mourning Becomes Electra* (1931), in which Lavinia (the titular 'Electra') is disconcerted to find herself attracted by her mother's lover, who bears an unsettling resemblance to her father.[63] The play refracts Aeschylus' *Oresteia* through the prism of the American Civil War (1861–5), a cardinally important event which consolidated American national and political identities, just as Aeschylus' trilogy had retrospectively granted mythic legitimacy to Ephialtes' recent radical political reforms.[64] *Mourning*'s (rather loose) parallelisms with the *Oresteia* include the murder of the victorious general Ezra Mannon ('Agamemnon') by his adulterous wife Christine ('Clytemnestra'); Christine's sexual affair with Ezra's cousin Adam Brant ('Aegisthus'); her son Orin's murder of Adam (whereas Christine, in a departure from the relevant Greek myth, commits suicide, thereby mitigating the horror of the matricidal act that provides the climax of the Greek Electra plays); and Orin's imaginary pursuit by the ghosts of his dead forebears, which evokes his literary ancestor Orestes' pursuit by

60 Hofmannsthal (1908), 56, 58, 59.

61 Hofmannsthal (1908), 69–70. On 24 May 1905, Freud's 'Wednesday Society', of which Jung was a member, held a discussion of Hofmannsthal's *Electra*, which some critics had seen as a dramatisation of Freud's and his mentor Breuer's studies on female 'hysteria' – an idea they found confirmation for in Electra's 'maenadic' dance at the end of the play. See Lensing (2006); Martens (1987); Scott (2005), 57–80.

62 Further on Hofmannsthal's *Electra*, see Mueller (1986) (dramatic models including Sophocles' *Electra*, Goethe's *Iphigenie* and even Wilde's *Salome*); Ewans (1984) (with emphasis on Strauss' opera).

63 On Jung's influence on O'Neill, which the playwright explicitly admitted (Nethercot 1960, 247–8), see Törnqvist (1998), 22–3.

64 On the political substratum of the *Oresteia*, see further Goldhill (2004), 8, 10–11, 83–4.

the Furies. However, O'Neill also introduces a complementary 'Oedipal' element by having Orin nourish quasi-incestuous feelings towards his mother and, later, towards his sister. By choosing as the trilogy's setting the aftermath of the American Civil War, an age of nascent identities and political integration, O'Neill invests *Mourning* with a primeval quality comparable to that of Greek plays about the Trojan War, that defining moment of Greek historical and national self-awareness, which established the paradigmatic antithesis between Greece and Asia, thus helping forge Greek national identity.[65]

Yet another family drama with oblique political implications is Jean Giraudoux's *Électre* (1937).[66] The play ironically undermines the elevated style and exalted ethos of Greek tragedy by introducing incongruously mundane plot elements. For instance, it foregrounds trite disputes (over, e.g., who is responsible for baby Orestes' fall from his mother's arms more than twenty years in the past), thereby offering an ironical counterpoint to the titanic conflicts of Greek tragedy; also, it introduces comical characters like the bourgeois Théocathoclès couple,[67] whose behaviour (Agathe Théocathoclès systematically cheats on her husband) bathetically mirrors the relationship between the adulterous royal couple of Agamemnon and Clytemnestra.[68]

Psychoanalytical echoes, albeit distilled through a Christian ideology of personal salvation, are also to be found in T. S. Eliot's *The Family Reunion* (1939),[69] which engages in an intertextual dialogue with Aeschylus' *Oresteia* (esp. *Libation Bearers* and *Eumenides*). When Harry, Lord Monchensey, returns to his family estate to take possession of his patrimony, it becomes immediately apparent that he suffers – rather like his dramatic predecessor, the Euripidean Orestes of *Iphigenia in Tauris* and *Orestes* – from delusions in which he is persecuted by Furies as a punishment for his self-avowed murder of his wife (a crime for which his guilt is

[65] See further E. Hall (1989), 101, 110 (with nn. 29–31), 164–5, 193–4, 196–7.

[66] The play was written in an era when Nazism in Germany and Fascism in Italy and Spain were on the rise, and some of its themes – such as Aegisthus' transformation from petty tyrant to enlightened monarch, or the impending threat of the besieging Corinthian army – are perhaps covert comments on contemporary political events.

[67] In this mockery of a Greek name, the first (*théo-*) and last (*-clès*) components allude to the Greek words for 'god' (cf. *Theo*-doros) and 'glory' (cf. Peri-*cles*) respectively, but these grand connotations are undermined by the middle component (*-catho-*), which evokes *katō*, the Greek word for 'downwards' or 'below'.

[68] Further on Giraudoux's *Électre*, see, e.g, Laizé (1997); Boulogne (2007). On its political aspects, see Albert (1970).

[69] On psychoanalytical influences on Eliot's work, including *The Family Reunion* in particular, see Smidt (1961), 132–3, 230.

never actually established). In the play's conclusion, Eliot's Erinyes are transformed from demonic agents of vengeance to 'bright angels' (Eliot 1964, 111) of grace and expiation, complete with evocations of the triumphal torch-lit procession at the end of the *Eumenides*. Thus, 'the *Oresteia*'s theme of communal absolution is transformed into a tale of personal salvation',[70] in the context of 'a modern Freudian and Christian myth, mingled with an ancient tragedy'.[71] However, as Eliot himself later admitted, his Erinyes 'never succeed in being either Greek goddesses or modern spooks'.[72]

If Eliot adapted the Electra story into a tale of personal salvation, Jean-Paul Sartre gave it an existentialist twist, a few years later, in his *The Flies* (*Les Mouches*, 1943), a composite adaptation drawing on a number of Greek Electra plays.[73] Like his Sophoclean counterpart in *Electra*, Sartre's Orestes arrives at Argos after a period of exile, except that this is an Argos whose citizens wallow in a perverse cult of self-incrimination for imaginary sins against the departed. Orestes is soon seized by a painful awareness of his rootlessness and realises that the murder of Aegisthus and Clytemnestra would at least enable him to appropriate a personhood by adopting a deeply personal life-project. The murderous act over, Orestes finally proclaims himself free – from guilt, biology, social norms, and the ethics of repentance. Like his Greek predecessor, he is pursued by the Erinyes: this is the price he has to pay for accomplishing his life-project and for constructing a freely chosen identity even by means of a criminal act.[74] The cultic and primitivist undertones of many of Sartre's scenes may have inspired Jean-Louis Barrault's staging of the *Oresteia* in 1955, which introduced re-enactments of voodoo rites in an attempt to highlight the 'primitive rawness' which he saw as a feature of Greek tragedy.[75]

As well as focusing on the individual's painful existence within the meshes of the family, Marguerite Yourcenar's *Électre ou La Chute des*

70 Quotation from Burian (1997), 258. 71 Quotation from McDonald (2003), 27.

72 Eliot (1951), 30. *The Family Reunion* is unique among Eliot's 'Greek' plays in making its source text recognisable enough. By contrast, his *The Cocktail Party* (derived from Euripides' *Alcestis*), *The Elder Statesman* (from Sophocles' Oedipus plays), and *The Confidential Clerk* (from Euripides' *Ion*) are extremely cryptic reworkings of Greek plays – something that Eliot himself admitted (1951, 31) à propos of *The Cocktail Party*. On Eliot's 'Greek' plays see, e.g., Heilman (1953); A. C. H. Smith (1963), 147–240; Tanner (1970); McDonald (2003), 182–3, 188; Pattie (2012), 98–118.

73 Cf. Burian (1997), 258; Liapis (2014a), 126.

74 Further on Sartre's *The Flies*, see Blasi (1974); McCall (1969), 9–24; Leonard (2005), 217–23.

75 See McDonald (2003), 28, whence the quotation. The power of ritual music and dance is brought out much more forcefully in Wole Soyinka's *The Bacchae of Euripides: A Communion Rite* (1973), on which see McDonald (2003), 189–92, Ioannidou (2017), 121–8, as well as the chapters by Fischer-Lichte (10), Lecznar (6), and Steinmeyer (11), this volume.

masques (*Electra or The Fall of the Masks*, 1944)[76] is also remarkable in that it explicitly offers a fusion of the Orestes story with that of Hamlet (in both stories, the avenging son punishes the adulterous couple who have usurped his father's throne), albeit with a surprising twist: Orestes realises that he is, in fact, the natural son of the adulterous usurpers. Married (as in Euripides) to a commoner, Electra plans, with help by Orestes and Pylades, the murder of her mother, whom she lures to her death by pretending that she is pregnant (yet another nod to Euripides' *Electra*). As for Orestes' murder of Aegisthus, it is constructed as a patricidal act that frees him from the tyranny of both his putative and his actual father.

Yourcenar revisited the Atreid myth in her monologue 'Clytemnestra or The Crime' ('Clytemnestre ou le crime'),[77] in which the eponymous character offers an *apologia pro vita sua* (which is far from being an apology) and reveals that she is condemned to replay the family drama (especially her toxic relationship with Agamemnon) ad infinitum. The idea is also present in Jean Anouilh's play *Tu étais si gentil quand tu étais petit* (*You Were So Kind when You Were Little*, 1972), in which Aegisthus and Clytemnestra are likewise sentenced to an endless series of reperformances of their drama, though Aegisthus comes across as a more sympathetic figure than his Greek counterpart, and is filled with understanding for Orestes, who eventually grows disgusted with Electra's self-perpetuating hate.[78]

Dominant Myths II: Oedipus and Antigone

Moving now to the story of Oedipus, the second of the two myths dominating twentieth-century adaptations of Greek tragedy, we begin with André Gide's *Œdipe* (1931), a play in which the titular character emerges emphatically as an individualistic self-made man. When Œdipe finds out that he is an adopted child, he is filled with a sense of self-discovery, as he feels free to create his selfhood away from the stifling influence of his father.[79] Œdipe's celebration of selfhood, however, soon turns to smug self-assurance, which is eventually shattered by his discovery of his true identity. Blaming the gods for deceitfully fostering his delusion, Œdipe blinds and exiles himself as a final act of self-fulfilment.[80]

[76] See Yourcenar (1971), 9–79.
[77] See Yourcenar (1974), 119–30.
[78] See further McDonald (2003), 28–9. Further on the reception of the Electra myth (esp. in opera, in Victorian art, and in Cacoyannis' film), see Bakogianni (2011).
[79] Gide (1942), 271–2.
[80] Cf. Conacher (1955), 131–2. See further Burian (1997), 248–51; McDonald (2003), 69–70.

A few years later, Jean Cocteau's *La Machine infernale* (*The Infernal Machine*, 1934) offered a kaleidoscopic phantasmagoria of alternately pathetic and parodic scenes, often reminiscent of Cocteau's cinematography. The variegated quality of the play is evident already at the outset, where we are presented with a comic, almost burlesque dialogue between two anonymous soldiers, who discuss the recent appearances of Laius' ghost on the ramparts of Thebes. This is a transparent parody of the opening scenes of *Hamlet* (Act 1, sc. i, iv, v) but also of the earlier use of Laius' ghost in Seneca and in Dryden and Lee (see earlier in this chapter). The Sphinx, who has lost the will to live and desperately hopes for someone to solve her riddle so that she may kill herself, reveals to Oedipus the answer – although the hero, rather obtusely, is convinced that he has hit upon the solution unaided. The incestuous marriage of Oedipus and Jocasta is accomplished in spite of repeated warnings by Tiresias; and although Oedipus, while looking into the old seer's blind eyes, visualises a happy future of conjugal bliss, the illusory vision is eventually shattered, when the truth comes to light in a manner similar to Sophocles' *Oedipus Tyrannus*.[81]

One of Jean Anouilh's last works, *Œdipe ou Le Roi boiteux* (*Oedipus or the Lame King*, 1978), focuses, predictably, on the myth's psychoanalytical elements, while emphasising the story of Oedipus as emblematic of the human condition in general. Oedipus and Jocasta blissfully narrate their first sexual union in language celebrating the Freudian aspects of their incestuous bond, which is for them a source of profound pleasure. Anouilh's choral odes dwell on Oedipus' lameness as a metaphor for human life (humanity proceeds with one foot in the clear path of light and the other in mud and darkness), and the epilogue likewise proclaims Oedipus' story to be emblematic of the human condition: 'Misfortune, such as that of Oedipus' story which you've just witnessed, is not always the exception. . .'[82]

Anouilh's exploration of 'Oedipal' sexuality is far from being a unique example: it is preceded, as we saw, by Cocteau's *La Machine infernale* and followed by Steven Berkoff's *Greek* (1980), a play which updates and relocates the Oedipus myth in a London East End skid row in the heyday of Thatcherism. In his new context, 'Oedipus', now renamed Eddy, is violent, amoral, and interested only in brutishness and sex. He couples

[81] On Cocteau's play, see further McDonald (2003), 68–9; Renger (2013), 75–89.

[82] Anouilh (1986), 93–4: 'Le malheur, comme dans l'histoire d'Œdipe que vous venez d'entendre, n'est pas toujours exceptionnel. . .' See also McDonald (2003), 73–5.

with his own mother (a role played by the actress who also plays the Sphinx), without any remorse when the truth comes to light, and kills (unawares) his own father in a local pub over the tritest of reasons. Intriguingly, the murder is committed with words: Eddy 'verbals' his father to death, just as the old Oedipus of Sophocles' *Oedipus at Colonus* (1373–4, 1387–8) had effected his sons' death with the words of his curse.[83] Contrary to his Greek predecessor, Eddy, when confronted with the truth, triumphantly admits and celebrates his personal responsibility for the patricide and incest he has committed.[84]

More recently, Rita Dove's *The Darker Face of the Earth* (1994, revised 1996) relocates the Oedipus myth in the antebellum American South. A white slave-owner, Amelia, conceives a child with one of her black slaves; the child, Augustus, is taken away from her, but returns as an adult, has a liaison with his own mother and kills his own father. Augustus also kills Amelia's husband, and his mother commits suicide (like Jocasta), but Augustus, true to his name, becomes the leader of a group of black slaves fighting for freedom.[85]

Rita Dove's overtly political reading of the Oedipus myth has at least two major precedents, namely Jean Anouilh's *Antigone* (1944) and Bertolt Brecht's *Antigone* (1948). Directed by André Barsacq, Anouilh's play ran for a stupendous 500 performances at the Théâtre de l'Atelier, its popularity partly explained by its anti-Nazi and anti-Vichy nuances, however subdued these were. Contrary to what happens in Sophocles' *Antigone*, Anouilh has his own heroine perform Polynices' symbolic burial even before the play begins, thereby setting the action on its inexorable course to disaster. This is in line with the play's general atmosphere, which is pervaded by a sense of grim inevitability: tragedy, as the chorus says, is a set of predetermined events ready to unwind, like a coiled spring (a metaphor reminiscent of Cocteau's 'infernal machine'); tragedy is 'clean' and 'restful' because 'you know there's no lousy hope left'.[86] In an embodiment of *Realpolitik* tactics, Creon at first attempts to hush up Antigone's act in

83 See further Perris, Chapter 9, this volume.

84 On Berkoff's play, see most recently Ioannidou (2017), 45–52. For a post-colonial take on the Oedipus myth, namely Ola Rotimi's *The Gods are Not to Blame* (1968), see Goff and Simpson (2007), 78–134, and the chapters by Steinmeyer (11) and Fischer-Lichte (10) in this volume. For a summary and brief discussion of the play, see also McDonald (2003), 70–3.

85 On Dove's play, see further Goff and Simpson (2007), 135–77; also, Steinmeyer, Chapter 11, this volume.

86 Quotation from Barbara Bray's translation (Anouilh 2005, 26); cf. Anouilh (1946), 54: 'C'est propre, la tragédie ... Et puis, surtout, c'est reposant, la tragédie, parce qu'on sait qu'il n'y a plus d'espoir, le sale espoir'.

order to prevent a popular uprising, and in his effort to persuade Antigone to acquiesce in the cover-up, he goes as far as to let her in on a shocking secret: both her brothers were thuggish traitors intent on killing their father; it is not even certain that the body lying unburied is Polynices', since one brother's mangled and unrecognisable corpse was left unburied and the other given funeral honours merely for reasons of political expediency. Antigone is shaken, but regains her earlier feistiness when Creon makes the mistake of advocating happiness as the ultimate life goal: she refuses to abase herself in exchange for 'snatch[ing] her own little scrap of happiness'.[87] The last scenes of the play follow, more or less, the Sophoclean source text (Antigone, Haemon, and Eurydice commit suicide), except that after the tragic dénouement Creon continues his government business as usual – although we are uneasily aware, as he must be, that there is an angry crowd outside the palace threatening to burst in.[88]

More evident are the political inflections of Brecht's *Antigone*, especially in the form in which it premiered in Chur, Switzerland, in February 1948. The *Vorspiel*, or 'Prelude', which Brecht added for that performance was set in Berlin at the end of World War II and featured, apart from the two sisters, an SS officer and a Polynices who came back from the war as a deserter only to be hung from a meat hook as a punishment. Brecht's play was a substantial revision and adaptation of Friedrich Hölderlin's idiosyncratic 1804 translation, which had itself come under attack from philological circles for a number of perceived errors. In other words, Brecht's version was twice removed from the Sophoclean source text: it was 'a transformation of Hölderlin and a further departure from Sophocles'.[89] The staging, which used masks and four totem poles with horses' skulls at the top, underlined the presumed 'barbarism' of Greek tragedy and reinforced the distancing effect Brecht is famous for.[90] The politicisation of the Antigone myth is evident throughout: Antigone and Ismene are factory workers; Polynices is killed not by Eteocles but by Creon himself for desertion; and Tiresias exposes Creon's victory propaganda by revealing that the war is actually not going well at all for Thebes. Creon is thus an unqualified tyrant, who loses the war, is faced with a popular uprising (a detail given greater emphasis in Brecht than in Anouilh), and witnesses

[87] Quotation from Anouilh (2005), 46 in Barbara Bray's translation; cf. Anouilh (1946), 92: 'Quelles pauvretés faudra-t-il qu'elle fasse elle aussi, jour par jour, pour arracher avec ses dents son petit lambeau de bonheur?'

[88] Anouilh (1946), 102, 106; cf. Anouilh (2005), 50, 52. Further on Anouilh's *Antigone*, see Sachs (1962); Krüger (1967); Hunwick (1996).

[89] Quotation from Cairns (2017), 187.

[90] See Cairns (2017), 187–8.

the collapse of his household (his sons Haemon and Megareus die, although there is no mention of Eurydice). Although ostensibly an allegory of the last days of the Third Reich, Brecht's version is more than that: 'it has important things to say to us about the disconnect between rulers and ruled, about the multitude of sins that may be concealed behind appeals to state security, and about the ways in which the symbiosis between government and the military-industrial complex drives both external aggression and internal repression'.[91]

Against the Tyranny that is Greece: Politics, Aesthetics, Sexuality

Mindless violence and deviant (even grotesque) sexuality are also central themes of Sarah Kane's *Phaedra's Love* (1996),[92] a fin-de-siècle adaptation of the Phaedra and Hippolytus myth. Kane's Hippolytus, who has degenerated into an obese and apathetic youth, attracts Phaedra's hopeless love nonetheless; the latter even pleasures him onstage, eliciting from him nothing but cynical apathy. As in the traditional versions of the myth, Phaedra commits suicide, leaving behind a note accusing Hippolytus of rape, and Hippolytus – more as a way of relieving his own boredom than out of genuine emotion for Phaedra's death – pleads guilty to the police. In the end, after his sister Stophe has been publicly raped by her own father Theseus, and Theseus himself has committed suicide, Hippolytus is dismembered by a frenzied crowd in a cannibalistic orgy, his last words being 'If there could have been more moments like this'.[93] With her 'in-yer-face' use of profanity and onstage pornography, Kane attempts to reinvigorate the ancient myth's shocking potential, but the result is often grotesquely cartoonish rather than genuinely upsetting – it is a 'dramatizatio[n] of cruelty for its own sake', and a far cry from the Greek theatre's studious avoidance of onstage violence.[94] Like Berkoff's *Greek*, Kane's play flies in the face of the conventions of Greek tragedy, which avoids both stage violence and the enactment of (or even explicit reference to) sexuality. But

[91] Quotation from Cairns (2017), 198. On Brecht's *Antigone*, see further F. Jones (1957); Weisstein (1973); Philipsen (1998); Taxidou (2008). More recent landmarks in the reception of the Antigone story include Kamau Brathwaite's *Odale's Choice* and Femi Òsòfisan's *Tègònni: An African Antigone*, on which see Goff and Simpson (2007), 219–38, 322–64, and the chapters by Steinmeyer (11) and Fischer-Lichte (10) in this volume.

[92] Kane (2001), 63–103. [93] Kane (2001), 103.

[94] McDonald (2003), 40; cf. also p. 171: 'The Phaedra-Hippolytus theme has evolved from individual suffering to political farce and simply rehashing news from a scandal sheet; much is lost at this end of this spectrum.' On violence in modern adaptations of Greek tragedy (including Kane's own), see Perris, Chapter 9, this volume.

Kane's play lacks the political awareness of Berkoff's *Greek*, in which sex and violence are overtly politicised in the context of social marginalisation and ethnic conflict in Thatcherite Britain, thus injecting into the ancient myth a sense of social urgency not normally found in Greek tragedy.

Several decades before Kane, the contestation of the classical paradigm and the problematisation of the concomitant authority discourse had given rise to a highly idiosyncratic mélange of sensuality and lyricism, namely *Hippolytus Temporizes* (1927) by Hilda Doolittle (henceforth H.D.).[95] Ostensibly an adaptation of Euripides' *Hippolytus*, H.D.'s play is in fact an original composition, which remythologises the Hippolytus story in a sensualist, even erotic spirit. Albeit fanatically chaste, H.D.'s Hippolytus is, almost unconsciously, in love with an unwilling Artemis – a projection of his attachment to his dead mother, herself a devotee of carnal chastity, who had been raped by Theseus. At the opposite end, the sensual Phaedra lures Hippolytus to her seaside tent by suggesting to him the idea that Artemis dwells there. As well as bearing the traits of H.D.'s lifelong interest in psychoanalysis, *Hippolytus Temporizes* also evidences its author's struggle – in which she joined her contemporary modernist pioneers Gertrude Stein, Marianne Moore, and Virginia Woolf – to forge a new language that would break free from the fetters of patriarchal writing.[96] At the same time, by conspicuously departing from its source text, *Hippolytus Temporizes* also problematises the oppressive authority of the classical paradigm – 'this tyranny of spirit | that is Greece'.[97]

A version of the Phaedra and Hippolytus myth set in rural New England, Eugene O'Neill's *Desire Under the Elms* (1924) features a widowed landowner, Ephraim Cabot ('Theseus'), whose recent marriage to a young woman, Abbie Putnam ('Phaedra'), upsets his three sons, who fear that the family property will go to her. One of the sons, Eben ('Hippolytus'), intent on acquiring the farm as a way of honouring his dead mother's memory (since the latter had been the farm's original proprietor), is sexually accosted by Abbie but rebuffs her. Abbie accuses him to Ephraim of attempted seduction but also persuades him to keep his son in the farm. Eventually, stepmother and stepson become lovers, and Abbie becomes pregnant by Eben, but pretends to her husband that the child is his, since he had promised her to make her sole heir to the property if she could beget a son. Realising that he has been used, and that he is now

[95] Doolittle (2003), 1–138. [96] Cf. Camper in Doolittle (2003), ix–x.

[97] Quotation from *Hippolytus Temporizes*: Doolittle (2003), 49.

cut out of the family property, Eben confronts Abbie, who decides to kill the child in order to convince him that she became involved with him out of true love, with no ulterior motives. In the end, Eben claims joint responsibility for the infanticide. In this play, O'Neill 'reinforce[s] the basic sexual tension of the Greek original with the American obsession for owning property',[98] and (as in *Mourning Becomes Electra*) exploits Freudianism and Jungian depth psychology to portray Eben's frustrated attempts to fill the gap left by his mother's death by seeking love first in the arms of the local prostitute Minnie, then in the surrogate mother figure of Abbie.[99] The mother's spectral presence is embodied in the farm's surrounding elms, which are invested with 'a sinister maternity . . . a crushing, jealous absorption';[100] one is reminded of Hippolytus' being haunted by his dead mother in Hilda Doolittle's play (see above).

An almost unique case of radical remaking of Greek tragic myth, Heiner Müller's Greek-themed plays resist categorisation and, often, interpretation, as they programmatically reject – in keeping with the aesthetics of post-dramatic theatre – the unified, well-wrought coherence of conventional drama (including Greek tragedy) to espouse fragmentation, lack of cohesion, and disconnectedness, and to explore incertitude, non-clarity, ambiguity, and paradox.[101] Denying conventional theatre's valorisation of the spoken word over visuality, Müller's plays allow the visual to break free from the fetters of logocentrism, so that the distribution of stage signs becomes a fundamental component of drama, and the physical aspect of performance is no longer merely a vehicle for the dramatic text.[102] Post-dramatic theatre aesthetics are exemplified in Müller's *Medeaspiel* (1974), a set of stage-directed images for a pantomime performance, in which the Euripidean version of the myth is revisited from a feminist point of view, by nakedly foregrounding Jason's male sexual aggression and Medea's slaughter of her children.[103] In *Medeamaterial* (1982),[104] the Müllerian

[98] Quotation from McDonald (2003), 161.

[99] On *Desire Under the Elms*, see further Ranald (1998) 65–6; Wainscott (1998), 104–5; Lauriola (2015b), 464–5.

[100] Quotation from O'Neill (1988), 318; cf. McDonald (2003) 162.

[101] On Müller as an emblematic author of post-dramatic theatre, see Lehmann (2006), 26–7, 32, 113–14, 123, 147; cf. also Kalb (2001). On the renunciation of representationism and on the aesthetics of fragmentation in post-dramatic theatre, see Lehmann (2006), 22, 37, 82–3, 85–7, 127; Sugiera (2004), 21, 24. Especially on Müller's experimental construction of scenic space as against traditional stagecraft. see Fuchs (1996), 98, 105–6, 136–8. Further on post-dramatic aesthetics in adaptations of Greek tragedy, see Campbell (2012).

[102] See Lehmann (2006), 89–94 (esp. 93–4), 95–7.

[103] See McDonald (1992), 149.

[104] See McDonald (1992), 147–69 (also with the text of a lecture by Theodoros Terzopoulos on his staging of *Medeamaterial*); Ioannidou (2017), 156–63. Müller's *Medeamaterial* was published as

Medea embodies the empowered female/worker/work of art breaking free from the confines of capitalist commoditisation and violently turning against the male/capitalist oppressors. In his *Philoktet 1950*, Müller ostensibly rehearses, more or less, the plot of Sophocles' *Philoctetes*, albeit with subtle but significant deviations. Rather than being bitten by a snake, Müller's Philoctetes suffers from leprosy (thus becoming emblematically a social outcast), although, contrary to his Sophoclean precursor (cf. *Philoctetes* 260–316, 676–717), he seems to have carved out a reasonably comfortable livelihood on his desert island. His only moral victory – if such it is – is the unwillingness with which he lets the Greeks drag him to Troy. In his readings of the Heracles myth (*Heracles 2, or the Hydra*, 1972; *Heracles 13, after Euripides*, 1991; and *Heracles 5*, 1996), composed over a period of years, Müller uses the themes of madness and destruction with varying foci both as a depiction of an archetypical state of human obsession and as a political allegory of Germany.[105] Finally, Müller's poetic monologue 'Aias zum Beispiel' ('Ajax for Example', 1994) plays with the traditional image of Ajax as the eternal loser, in consequence of his adherence to noble but obsolete patterns of life. Conspicuously autobiographical, the monologue casts Ajax as Müller's alter ego, who finds himself, in the post-cataclysmic context of a reunified Germany, unable to share the paroxysmal consumerism of a post-communist world.

Müller's use of Greek myth as a political commentary on post-communist Germany is far from unique. Another German author, Christa Wolf, in her aggressively political novel *Medea* (1996), offers a radically revisionist adaptation of the Medea myth. Through a series of narratives by six different voices, Wolf's text articulates a novel version of the story, in which Medea neither kills her brother (who is instead sacrificed by his own father, King Aeëtes, in exchange for seven more years of monarchic rule) nor slays her children – on the contrary, she discovers that Creon, the King of Corinth, has sacrificed his own daughter for fear that she might oust him. False accusations force Medea to flee Corinth, while the Corinthians stone her children to death, after putting about a story that their mother has murdered the king's daughter, Glauke. The Corinthians' suspicious hostility towards Medea and the group of Colchian refugees accompanying her brings out perennial questions of otherness and integration, which are particularly relevant to the

part of a volume entitled *Verkommenes Ufer; Medeamaterial; Landschaft mit Argonauten* (*Despoiled Shore; Medea-material; Landscape with Argonauts*): Müller (1984).

105 See further McDonald (2003), 172.

divisiveness and distrust faced by Wolf's (formerly) East German compatriots ('Ossis') after the reunification of Germany in 1990. At the same time, Medea, the swarthy foreign female in possession of supposedly arcane arts, is a victim of the myth of matriarchy, constructed for the perpetuation of patriarchal order.[106] Wolf's version develops themes already found in Franz Grillparzer's 1882 dramatic trilogy *The Golden Fleece* (*Das goldene Vlies*), in the third part of which Medea's feelings of exclusion and betrayal lead to the infanticide, although there both Creon and his daughter come across as more sympathetic.[107]

The Medea myth also provides the material for an allusively political reading in Jean Anouilh's *Médée* (1946), a play which is a transparent fusion of Euripides and Brecht. While retaining elements of the Euripidean version (e.g. the opening dialogue between Medea and her Nurse, cf. *Medea* 96ff.), Anouilh's play is set on a stage dominated by a wagon in which Medea lives – a striking visual symbol of her nomadic existence, which inevitably evokes Mother Courage's itinerant wagon in *Mutter Courage und ihre Kinder* by Bertolt Brecht and Margarete Steffin (written in 1938–9 and performed in 1941). A shocking example of unmotherly unconcern, Mother Courage is indifferent to her own children's lives when her own is at stake, pretending not to recognise her own dead son's body, and paying some peasants to bury her daughter's corpse while she makes off to continue her war-profiteering. In a less cynical vein, Anouilh's play foregrounds Medea's nature as an agent of uncontrollable subversion and chthonic disorder, in contrast to Jason, who seeks to disentangle himself from Medea's demonic charms and pursue a life of calm obscurity.[108]

More obviously political is Cuban playwright José Triana's *Medea en el espejo* (*Medea in the Mirror*, 1960), in which the mixed-race Maria ('Medea') is abandoned by her lover Julio ('Jason'), who prefers to marry the daughter of a rich white man. Maria poisons the white boss and his daughter, and kills Julio and their children through voodoo-doll magic. Maria's marginalisation in her own culture is a central theme here, and the extremity of her actions is the price she has to pay for her empowerment and the assertion of her selfhood against white oppression. At the end of the play, Maria is protected by her people against Julio's murderous intentions: 'she is hoisted high by the chorus and she declares herself

[106] Further on Wolf's *Medea*, see Arnds (2001) (*Medea* as an act of cultural translation); Lü (2004) (relevance to post-reunification Germany); Weingartz (2010) (feminist reading).

[107] On Grillparzer's trilogy, see McDonald (2003), 146.

[108] On Anouilh's *Médée*, see Pronko (1961), 30, 65, 88–90; Kaliss (1971); McDonald (2003), 146–7.

God',[109] in an obvious nod to her Euripidean counterpart's escape on a winged chariot provided by the Sun-god.

A play constructed as a direct response to then-recent events, Hélène Cixous' *La Ville parjure, ou Le Réveil des Érinyes* (*The Perjured City, or The Erinyes Awaken*, 1993) was conceived in the aftermath of the French blood-transfusion scandal of the mid-1980s, when it transpired that a number of hemophiliac patients had received HIV-contaminated blood. Blood is as central an idea to Cixous' play as it is in Aeschylus' *Oresteia* – an idea condensed in the Erinyes' memorable dictum (*Eumenides*, 261–3) that 'it is very hard to draw a mother's blood back from the ground where it is spilled; the liquid is drained through the soil and gone'.[110] *The Perjured City*, which takes place in a cemetery, features the mother of two dead hemophiliac boys and, among other characters, Aeschylus as the caretaker and a chorus of outlaws living in the cemetery. The Erinyes come back from their chthonic residence, where they had confined themselves 'for the past 5000 years',[111] in order to avenge the grieving mother but also because in their absence the world of humans has degenerated into festering rottenness. Confronted with an array of lawyers and doctors, who refuse to assume responsibility for their murderous malpractice and ask for forgiveness, the mother and the chorus turn to the newly elected president, who is, however, willing to offer the mother only compensation, not real justice, and even orders the cemetery to be flooded and its outcast residents to be drowned. The play ends with a call for action addressed to the audience: 'It is your turn to insist that what is just | Comes to pass justly.'[112]

Greek tragedy is also used as a vehicle for exposing the discontents of America by playwright Charles Mee. Matching a collage structure with the freshness and precariousness of everyday conversation, Mee's adaptations are playful, but often vicious, commentaries on the ailments of contemporary society, in which language expresses cultural disenchantment. His *Orestes 2.0* (1992), inspired by Euripides' tragedy, as well as by a large variety of intertextual sources (sometimes as disparate as *Vogue*, *Soap Opera*

109 Quotation from McDonald (2003), 148. On Triana's *Medea*, see also Lauriola (2015a), 396; Nikoloutsos (2012).

110 Cixous (2004), 89, after citing the *Eumenides* passage in the prologue to her *Perjured City*, comments that '"Blood" once spilled can never be spilled again. Irreversible is the loss of blood shed by murder. It is this irreversibility that Aeschylus sang and decried.'

111 Cixous (2004), 110.

112 Cixous (2004), 182–3. On Cixous' play, see further Walker (2001); Ayres (2005); Weltman-Aron (2012); Ioannidou (2017), 52–62.

Digest, William Burroughs, and Apollinaire), is part of what Mee calls 'the (re)making project'.[113] Non-linear narratives shift between dialogue and monologue forms, interspersed with media imagery and excerpts from the political and historical discourse. Commenting on the absence of meaning in the power dynamics between the matricidal Orestes, his accomplice Electra, and the state of Argos, the play is filled with obsessive language, as societal disruptions and trauma are verbally carried through. Fragmentation and pastiche suggest a state of moral chaos, while the interplay between the archaic chorus convention and the displaced experience of today's politics creates a parodic effect. His *Agamemnon 2.0* (1994) is set out as a debate between Herodotus, Thucydides, Homer and Hesiod – all physically impaired – with notable philosophical flair. The play is a critique of American politics, interspersed with images of violence, such as rape and bodily mutilation. *Big Love* (2001), Mee's reading of Aeschylus' *Suppliant Women*, concludes with a modern-day ceremony, complete with bouquet-throwing and fireworks, but the overriding darkness undermines the forced atmosphere of mirth. Mee's 'remaking project' depicts 'the horror of the human condition, without the grandeur that we f[i]nd in Greek tragedy'.[114]

The preceding overview, partial and selective as it is,[115] may help us situate adaptation in a historically aware cultural perspective, within which we may identify some of the parameters determining, over the ages, the dialogue between source texts and the adaptations that engage with them. One conclusion that seems to emerge from this survey is that the fidelity imperative, so much prized among certain circles now and in the past, was almost never a determining factor in the adaptation of Greek drama. Even neoclassical dramatists, working within strict rules purporting to encapsulate the principles of classical dramaturgy, took liberties with regard to the classical source texts and even presumed to better them by aligning them to what they perceived as Aristotelian precepts, even as they ostensibly validated and enhanced the canonical nature of their models. Contestation of classical models begins, somewhat timidly, with Browning's *Balaustion* and its second, morally improved retelling of the Alcestis story and,

[113] www.charlesmee.org/orestes.shtml. See Campbell (2011).

[114] Quotation from McDonald (2003), 40. I am grateful to my co-editor for contributing the above section on Charles Mee.

[115] I have purposely left out opera adaptations of Greek tragedy, for which see Brown and Ograjenšek (2010). I have also refrained from discussing modern Greek adaptations of Greek tragedy, since the topic is treated in the contributions to Liapis, Pavlou, and Petrides (2017) and in Chapter 12 by Bakogianni in this volume.

more aggressively, with Gide's *Prométhée*, which as we saw chooses a genre-bending, seriocomic medium to explore human suffering as part of the struggle for freedom. Contemporary contextualisations (psychoanalytical, existentialist, Christian, etc.) of Greek tragic myths are variously offered by O'Neill, Sartre, Eliot, Cocteau, and others, while more recent adaptations (by, e.g., Berkoff, Kane, and Müller) explicitly contest the very idea of an authoritative centre, programmatically celebrate fluidity and eclecticism, and endorse different and even conflicting cultural discourses.

PART I

Adapting Greek Tragedy

Definitions, Conceptual Foundations, Ethics

CHAPTER I

Definitions
Adaptation and Related Modalities

Katja Krebs

This chapter aims to explore what we mean by 'adaptation' both in terms of recent positions claimed within adaptation studies as well as in relation to the theatre-making process. More precisely, it attempts to establish what we mean by 'adaptation' when discussing classic Greek tragedy in performance and to what extent terms such as translation, version, (re)writing, (re)imagining, etc. can or indeed should be distinguished from one another. Arguably, the juxtaposition of the canonical classical play with its contemporary theatrical (re)imaginings[1] can simultaneously contribute to, as well as complicate, notions of the so-called original and its adaptation(s). Here are some questions I shall be raising in this chapter: are performance and adaptation related modalities? Is the relationship between text and performance analogous to that of source text and target text?[2] Or are other considerations necessary when discussing contemporary theatrical revisions of Greek plays? Can a relationship which involves a considerable degree of transcoding, updating, and/or recontextualisation be legitimately described as adaptation? Or do we need to employ an alternative conceptualisation of the relationship between the classic text and the contemporary performance, and thus invoke a more specific nomenclature? In addressing some of these questions, this chapter will investigate whether notions of performance of the classics and notions of adaptation are in a constructive relationship with each other. In order to do so, the chapter will adopt a case-study approach: looking at recent theatre adaptations of

[1] I make a distinction between theatrical and dramatic (re)imaginings in that 'theatrical' refers to the practice of theatre-making, and 'dramatic' to the practice of playwriting. Thus, drama is to be understood as the play in its written, textual format, while theatre is the ephemeral performance of such a text. The focus of this chapter lies with theatrical (re)imaginings in the form of performance rather than dramatic ones.

[2] 'Source text' and 'target text' are terms widely used within translation studies in order to distinguish between a translation and its so-called original while avoiding the ideological bias inherent in the notion of 'original' and 'originality', in which the 'original' is assumed to have greater value than its translation or adaptation, which is deemed 'secondary'.

Medea, *Iphigenia at Aulis*, and *Hippolytus*, it will explore the relationship between performance of the classics and notions of adaptation.[3]

Text and Performance: Drama or Theatre

To consider the staging of a classical Greek play as an example of adaptation is to make some very clear assumptions about the relationship between written text and embodied text – namely, that the two modes are in a temporal if not a hierarchical relationship to one another. Written drama and performance are not seen as being integral to each other: one is not necessarily regarded as a trace of the other. As Michael Walton argues,

> A legitimate engagement with the text as handed down, at least insofar as such engagement is possible: that is surely a responsibility of the translator. The re-creation, rooted in this original, but not wholly dependent on it, of something for a contemporary audience which takes account of the past but thrusts it firmly into the present: that is the responsibility of the director. (Walton 2006, 194–5)

Such a distinction between translation as 'legitimate engagement with text' and performance as 're-creation' is a very specific position to take, but it is also tendentious. Importantly, such a position vis-à-vis the creative theatrical process assumes that the roles inherent in theatre-making, such as translation and directing amongst others, are easily separable: the translator as independent and clearly distinguishable from the director. It is questionable, however, to what extent such a clean and structured division of labour is possible or even desirable in the, arguably, messy and quite often unpredictable collaborative process that is theatre (see also Montgomery Griffiths, Chapter 7, this volume). The position which clearly distinguishes textual production and theatrical production, as implied by Walton, limits itself to a consideration of a very specific kind of theatre steeped in an understanding of a creative process which is based upon a (hierarchically) structured relationship; at the helm of this relationship stands either the figure of the director or the figure of the playwright, depending on the historical context,[4] but never both.

[3] All examples in this chapter of recent theatre productions of Greek plays are British ones. This is by no means a value judgement in terms of importance or quality but merely a reflection of my own personal geographical context.

[4] Historical context may, for example, be that of twentieth-century British theatre, which very much favoured the playwright over the director, while twentieth-century German theatre was far more director-focused.

This position is very closely wedded to a historically as well as culturally specific understanding of theatre, which excludes, for example, non-Western, pre-nineteenth-century, or post-dramatic practices.

In contemporary theatre practice, there are numerous instances in which the translator/adaptor and director work very closely together. As a result, the textual production by a translator/adaptor and the theatrical (re)imagining by a director are intertwined to such an extent that it is no longer possible or even necessary to distinguish the two processes. This intertwining is, of course, further complicated as it includes the other agents who are responsible for theatrical adaptation (actors, theatre managers, set designers, etc.). This was arguably the case with the Kneehigh theatre company's *Bacchae* (2004).[5] While the text was published in 2005, and Carl Grose and Annamaria Murphy were acknowledged as writers, the anthology of which *Bacchae* was a part, and which also includes *Tristan and Yseult*, *The Wooden Frog*, and *The Red Shoes*, is presented as being authored by Kneehigh itself. And Emma Rice, Kneehigh's artistic director, reminds us in her foreword that 'these texts are just one layer of the worlds Kneehigh creates',[6] thus acknowledging the complexity of the relationship between text and performance.

Similarly, the Gate Theatre's[7] recent reworking of the Iphigenia at Aulis myth resulted in a publication of the plays *Agamemnon*, *Clytemnestra*, *Iphigenia*, and *Chorus* to accompany the production of the quartet in 2016. Yet, the writing process of all four plays was a collaborative one: all four writers took part in joint workshops as part of their creative writing process, which was considered very much part of the theatrical process and guided by the Gate's artistic director, Christopher Haydon. Furthermore, from the moment they bought their ticket and registered an e-mail address, the audience were allowed to witness some of this process, which was documented by blogs, recordings of rehearsals, discussions, etc.

Leaving such important considerations as the relationship between text and performance to one side for a moment, the investigation of Greek tragedy necessitates a decision as to which performances and/or plays should be considered adaptations, which translations, appropriations, or (sub)versions. Are all performances of classic Greek plays adaptations, or

[5] Kneehigh is a theatre company based in Cornwall, UK, and adaptation is central to their artistic vision. See www.kneehigh.co.uk for further details.

[6] Kneehigh (2005), n.p.

[7] The Gate Theatre is a small theatre above a pub in Notting Hill, London. It has a maximum capacity of 75 seats and has a reputation for being a so-called teaching theatre, which supports new and up-coming theatre-makers. See www.gatetheatre.co.uk/about-us for further details.

only those which make considerable changes to a so-called original?[8] And who decides what the nature of such a considerable change might be? Would textual changes stay within the domain of translation, while (re) localisation or (re)contextualising, for example, make it an adaptation? Does that mean that plays inspired by specific classic tragedies, such as Sarah Kane's *Phaedra's Love* (1996), are seen as adaptations even though their source may be manifold (Euripides' *Hippolytus*, Seneca's *Phaedra*, and Racine's *Phèdre*)? Is Kane's *Phaedra's Love* an original play, Power's *Medea* (2014), produced at the National Theatre of London, an adaptation, and Kaite O'Reilly's *The Persians* (2010), commissioned by the National Theatre of Wales, a translation, because they are presented as such in the accompanying programme notes, reviews, etc.? Or is the fact that Kane, Power, and O'Reilly had no knowledge of ancient Greek, and thus no access to the original text of Euripides' and Aeschylus' plays, the decisive factor in such a classification? Do we follow Gideon Toury's seminal definition of translation as 'any target-language utterance which is presented or regarded as such within the target culture'[9] and apply this to adaptation? Or does the classification of a text or rather performance as adaptation, translation, or original depend on our knowledge of the writers' linguistic abilities? One might, of course, call O'Reilly's *Persians* a so-called 'free translation' based on existing translations rather than on the ancient Greek source, but it is questionable to what extent this is at all helpful or even meaningful in relation to the theatrical event that was the performance of O'Reilly's *Persians*.[10]

As we can see here and as argued elsewhere,[11] the distinction between adaptation, translation, appropriation, version, and even original, is a complicated one. And while Walton offers a tentative series of seven different categories ranging from literal to faithful and actable, and from adapted to original play,[12] such categorisation is very often, if not always, an enunciation made through various kinds of reception following the process of (re)writing rather than preceding it, and one in which the position and expertise of the audience are key. In other words, the nomenclature depends not so much on the specific act of (re)writing but

[8] While there may be very few performances of classic Greek plays in their original language, it is the possibility of it that needs to be acknowledged as part of an unpicking of the relationship between translation and adaptation, and text and performance.

[9] Toury (1985), 20.

[10] See Krebs (2012) for a more detailed discussion of O'Reilly's *The Persians* in a production directed by Mike Pearson for the National Theatre of Wales.

[11] Krebs (2014, 2012).

[12] Walton (2006), 182–3.

on the specific position of (re)reading. As Hardwick argues, 'Different constituencies of readers and spectators stand in different relationships to what has gone before, textually, theatrically, culturally and in terms of the unexpected that strikes as they watch, listen and read.'[13] Hardwick's position responds to Toury's: it is the position the text has been assigned by its own receiving culture that is the decisive factor in the nomenclature of a text as either translation, adaptation, appropriation, version, or original. Such classifications are not an inherent characteristic of a text, inscribed into it during its specific kind of creation; rather, they are attached to a text and/or performance once it has been received. And some of the various positions of (re)reading, which Hardwick alludes to, are made visible by theatre reviews.

This is not merely to transfer the problem of classification from the level of authorial intention to that of audience reception. As we shall see in detail below, reception (and the concomitant classification of a performance as 'version', 'translation', 'adaptation', etc.) is more amenable to analysis than authorial intention insofar as one can identify some of the parameters that influence and shape it.

Medea: (Re)Writing as Translation

Ben Power's *Medea* was produced at the National Theatre, London, in 2014, starring Helen McCrory as Medea and Danny Sapani as Jason. Art-pop duo Will Gregory and Alison Goldfrapp wrote the music, and the production was directed by Carrie Cracknell, who had previously won critical acclaim for her 2013 Young Vic production of Ibsen's *A Doll's House*. The production, and Helen McCrory's performance in particular, were reviewed mostly positively by all major theatre reviewers in the UK, both in print and online, and the production was also screened as part of the NT Live programme in cinemas across the UK and forty or so other countries.[14]

In theatre reviews, Power's *Medea* is variously classified as a translation, a version, or (re)writing, and value judgements are made in relation to the terms employed. Charles Spencer, theatre critic of the conservative broadsheet the *Telegraph*, celebrates this particular *Medea* as a translation and offers a theatrical frame of reference by locating it alongside Cracknell's

[13] Hardwick (2013a), 338.
[14] See http://ntlive.nationaltheatre.org.uk/venues for a list of all countries and venues which screened *Medea*.

previous production of Ibsen's *A Doll's House* and implicitly comparing Medea to Nora: 'The director, Carrie Cracknell, is clearly fascinated by women at the end of their rope. Few who saw it will forget her stunning production of Ibsen's *A Doll's House*, in which the heroine, Nora, walks out on her patronising husband and children in order to discover her own identity.'[15] Spencer's frame of reference is, in this case, not *Medea*'s own production history or indeed textual history; instead, it is the director's earlier production of an Ibsen play, itself with its own production history. And while the performance context of *Medea* is given priority over a discussion of the relationship between dramatic source and theatrical practice, Spencer clearly identifies the play as a translation rather than as an adaptation, version, or even appropriation: 'Ben Power's translation has a stark eloquence without an ounce of fat on it.'[16] Spencer's formulation may suggest that Power's translation works well as a piece of translated literature in its own right: he implies that it is svelte, eloquent, and free of the usual redundancy and stiltedness that characterise many translations. But his phrasing may also be taken, at least by some readers, to imply that, normally, translation 'adds fat' to its source, or rather layers of surplus flab that result in corpulent, unwieldy (re)writings, to stay with Spencer's metaphor. Potential members of theatre audiences who form this newspaper's readership are on the whole, arguably, concerned with conservative cultural values and notions of authenticity, as well as the safeguarding of an accepted Western dramatic canon to which classic Greek drama belongs. Thus, they may be more comfortable celebrating a faithful translation – the review of the production is on the whole very positive – of a Euripidean tragedy than what could be described as a free adaptation or indeed version. The translation label brings with it a certification of authenticity in terms of the production and a certification of cultural expertise in relation to its spectators.

That is not to say that the decision to label a text a translation, or for that matter an adaptation or version, is one that is universally applied. With regard to Greek drama, Tony Harrison may be one example: his translation of Aeschylus' trilogy *The Oresteia* (1981) is presented as a *version* rather than a translation in its published format. Used for the National Theatre's production of *The Oresteia* (1981), which was directed by Peter Hall and screened two years later on the then relatively young Channel 4, Harrison's *The Oresteia* has also been regarded a translation, as

[15] Spencer (2014). [16] Spencer (2014).

well as an adaptation.[17] In this instance then, the same text has been assigned three different classifications – version, translation, adaptation – depending on its context of reception, i.e. reader, theatre audience, and film audience. Such a change in nomenclature could point to a downgrading process from the more faithful relationship with the text, as exemplified by a translation, to a perceived betrayal represented by a version or adaptation. Yet, it might also indicate an acknowledgement of creative agency: Tony Harrison, the well-known poet, is no longer 'merely' a translator of the text but instead an authorial figure, and the published text of *The Oresteia* is inextricably linked to its production by the National Theatre. Labelling it a 'version' may also be another iteration of Emma Rice's position: that the text is just one layer of many and cannot necessarily be seen as independent from its theatre production (see Kneehigh 2005).

Medea: (Re)Writing as Version

A similar shift in emphasis, from translation to adaptation or even version, is apparent in reviews of Power's *Medea*. While the *Telegraph* identifies *Medea* as a translation, Catherine Love, writing for the review section of the website *What's on Stage*, settles for 'version'. At the same time, she credits Power with the creative agency reserved for a playwright rather than adaptor or indeed translator.

> In his version of Euripides' tragedy, which he [Power] describes as 'the ultimate divorce play', Power hopes to explore 'how this story . . . can actually be a story about families and marriages'. Blending the classic and contemporary, he is also interested in how the play can 'explode out of something quite located and recognisable into something timeless and epic.' (Love 2014)

Describing *Medea* as 'the ultimate divorce play', the reviewer's frame of reference, similarly to Spencer's review above, is one of psychological realism as well as popular culture with its allusion to soap-opera story lines and one-dimensional dramatic narratives. Both are presented here as perfectly appropriate means to blend, if not replace, the classic with the contemporary. There seems to be an underlying suggestion that without adaptation, the classic play is stuck in its remote temporal location, unrecognisable and out of touch, its very canonicity doubtful. The attitude displayed in this particular context is far removed from what Christopher Balme terms the 'idealizations of Greek theatre as an ideal-typical public

[17] Translation: Cavendish (2013); adaptation: www.imdb.com/title/tt5524714/?ref_=nv_sr_2.

sphere';[18] instead, we witness a celebration of a theatre which is concerned with an un-politicised private sphere. As Balme observes, 'The darkened auditorium has become to all intents and purposes a private space.'[19] The journalistic context of Love's review is one that celebrates the individual. An online magazine focused on UK theatre in general and London theatre in particular, *What's on Stage* contains a 'News and Reviews' section in which reviews are presented alongside a collection of 'This Week's Top Stories' revolving around well-known individuals within the London theatre scene.[20] The important thing here is not canonicity so much as creative agency and individual talent as agents of cultural worth; what matters most in assessing an adaptation is not so much its relation to its Greek source as its display of personal truths in a postmodern sense.[21] In other words, it is not necessarily the plays that are of primary interest here, but the individuals involved in the productions. Celebrated as 'making London's National more exciting',[22] Ben Power's reading of *Medea* is, arguably, of more interest to the readers of *What's on Stage* than of Euripides, and the classification of *Medea* as a version, written by Power, needs to be seen in this context of reception rather than as an assessment of this version's relationship to its ancient Greek source.

Medea: (Re)Writing as Mistranslation

The most detailed discussion as to whether we are to view the Ben Power production as a performance of a translation, an adaptation, or a variation on a theme can be found in the *Times Literary Supplement*. While *What's on Stage* may focus on notions of celebrity, the *TLS* defines itself, according to its tag line, as the 'leading international weekly for literary culture'. Its emphasis on literary culture is apparent in its theatre reviews, and of the various particular constituencies of readers and spectators, to employ Hardwick's terminology,[23] the *TLS* is most likely to address the position of the literary expert and, in this context, that of the classicist. Here is an excerpt from Mary Beard's *TLS* review of Power's production.

> Impressive, certainly – but is it Euripides? With all due honesty, Ben Power's script is billed as a 'new version' of the play, not as a 'translation'.

[18] Balme (2014), 29. [19] Balme (2014), 3.

[20] Alongside reviews of current productions, the reader is presented with an array of links to items and stories related mainly to individual performers and artistic directors.

[21] For further considerations on how individual talent ultimately determines the ethics of adaptation/directing, see Sidiropoulou, Chapter 4, this volume.

[22] Costa (2013). [23] Hardwick (2013a), 338.

> Though parts of it are recognizably based on Euripides' words, much of it is hard to match with anything in the original Greek. There is, of course, a long and honourable history – going back to antiquity itself – of such 'variations on the theme' of an ancient text. But the questions always are: what violence has been done to the original, was it worth it, and what has been lost? In this case, there are awkward tensions between Euripides and Power; occasionally the original text seems more of a victim of his rewriting than a willing collaborator in it. (Beard 2014)

Written by a professor of Classics at the University of Cambridge, this review emphasises the relationship between 'original text' and Power's (re) writing, and while issues of staging and performance are mentioned, they are seen as witnesses to the relationship between two literary texts – Euripides' and Power's *Medeas* respectively – rather than in terms of theatrical performance. The National Theatre's production of *Medea* is discussed not so much in terms of its theatrical context as in terms of aligning staging and performance with textual knowledge and comparison to the source:

> By far the most radical change that Powers has introduced is in the very last scene of the play. In this production Medea walks off dragging the bodies of her children. It makes for a haunting and terrifying few minutes, with McCrory at her finest. But it bears no resemblance whatsoever to the climax of Euripides' original . . . (Beard 2014)

While, of course, Carrie Cracknell, the director, is complicit in the creation of this specific ending, it is discussed here as an authorial rather than collaborative choice, a textual rather than theatrical one, and creative agency is ascribed to Power, the writer, rather than Cracknell, the director, or indeed to the creative team as a whole. In this case then, it is not the director, nor the performers, nor the hosting venue that is of primary importance but the text itself. While Spencer praises Power's eloquent translation, and Love celebrates the individual artist, Beard labels the production as a 'very constructive re-working of the text (or, less charitably . . . wilful mistranslation)'.

***Phaedra*: (Re)Writing as Radical Updating**

What these examples demonstrate is that the classification of a play as adaptation, translation, version, or any other related modality is first and foremost a culturally specific act of reception. While the act of (re)writing asserts the validity of an established dramatic text and promises a sometimes radical reinvestigation of its premises, as is certainly the case with

Kane's *Phaedra's Love* and to a lesser extent with Power's *Medea*, it is the act of reception and the relationship the audience has 'to what has gone before, textually, theatrically, culturally'[24] that is the deciding factor in terms of the classification of (re)writing as adaptation, translation, or so-called original. The act of reception is, of course, not confined to the general public as theatre audiences but it includes theatre-makers, reviewers, publishers, and the like, all of whom play their part in the nomenclature of (re)writing. And while it may be the relationship to what has gone before that is crucial, it is also the framework within which these classifications are made that is of importance: a publisher of the dramatic text will assign a classification for reasons to do with marketing and the business of selling books; a reviewer of a production will assign a classification in terms of their own ideological positioning and in relation to their assumed readership; a writer and theatre-maker will assign a classification in relation to their artistic and dramaturgical position; an expert may assign a classification in terms of their own understanding of the source; and so on. While we may want to be able to define adaptation and related modalities in an absolute manner, these categories will always be relative to their context of reception.

In Sarah Kane's case 'what has gone before', to use again Hardwick's formulation, includes not only Racine, Seneca, and Euripides, but also her other authored plays as well as her own figure as a tragic *enfant terrible* of 1990s British theatre. The contemporary spectator first and foremost sees *Phaedra's Love* in the context of *Blasted*, *Cleansed*, *4.48 Psychosis*, and possibly Kane's rise to Royal Court fame, and related tabloid outrage.

> '"I [Sarah Kane] think a lot of people won't see beyond the fact that there was a lot of nasty stuff in *Blasted* and there's even more in this." I [David Benedict] point out that this time, the suicide, lust, hatred and murder are in the original. "Yeah," she agrees grinning, "it's not a tea party. Blame it on the Greeks."' (Benedict 1996)

As her 'Blame it on the Greeks' demonstrates, Kane clearly sees her play as an adaptation. Yet, in terms of Walton's classification, Kane's play is an original work inspired by specific classical tragedies – in this case, by Racine's *Phèdre*, which was inspired by Seneca's *Phaedra*, which in turn was a (re)writing of Euripides' *Hippolytus*.[25] To a large extent, Kane's *Phaedra* is a 'mythical appropriation' as a 'means for contemporary authors

[24] Hardwick (2013a), 338.

[25] The chain of (re)writings doesn't end there, as Euripides' *Hippolytus* itself is a (re)writing of his earlier, now lost, *Hippolytos Kalyptomenos* as well as of the Hippolytus myth.

to carry out self-conscious investigations into the artistic process'.[26] The reception of the play tends to relate it first and foremost to Kane's *oeuvre* rather than assess it in terms of its palimpsestic relationship with the Greek, Roman, and/or French versions of the same myth. When the Greek, Roman, and/or French versions are mentioned, it is in order to celebrate Kane's apparent superiority to classic playwrights. Lyn Gardner, for example, writing for the *Guardian*, claims that the 'Greeks offer nothing quite so mercilessly tragic, quite so mercilessly honest'[27] as Kane does, while Aleks Sierz, known for coining the phrase 'In-Yer-Face Theatre' during the early 1990s, states:

> the play is a radical updating of Seneca's *Phaedra* play. Kane's version is not a translation, but a completely new version . . . Now, of course, what strikes me more is the pared-down crispness of much of her writing, and the subversiveness of her attitude to ancient Greek tragedy: instead of keeping the wildness off stage, she brings it on stage right in front of our eyes. (Sierz 2011)

Such celebration of (re)writing, (re)imagining, updating, or whatever terminology is employed in order to foreground artistic agency, is not necessarily a modern phenomenon, as similar creative strategies were also employed by the Greek playwrights. As Hardwick argues, Greek playwrights themselves were 'playing with and adapting stories', and their adaptive dramaturgical choices brought together 'the mythical and the contemporary'. The specifics of such bringing together, according to Hardwick, trigger 'the ways in which the spectators related the theatrical occasion to their own sense of . . . identity'.[28] Sourvinou-Inwood discusses this coming together of the mythical and the contemporary as being achieved by the employment of zooming and distancing devices found in Greek tragedy. She argues that

> the double perspective in the relationship between the world of the audience and the world of the play . . . was clearly fundamental in allowing tragedy both to explore problems and issues at a distance, and to relate them directly to the audiences' experiences, with the distances manipulated through distancing and zooming devices. (Sourvinou-Inwood 2003, 23)

And just as Sophocles melds together the mythical and the contemporary, or, in Sourvinou-Inwood's words, employs distancing and zooming devices, arguably so do Kane and Power respectively, whether *Medea* is turned into a divorce play or *Phaedra's Love* becomes a critique of the royal

[26] Sanders (2006), 65. [27] Gardner (2005). [28] Hardwick (2013a), 327.

family: 'With hindsight – and the death of [Princess] Diana – it [i.e. *Phaedra's Love*] seems starkly satirical and strangely prescient about our own dysfunctional royal family.'[29]

Iphigenia: Collaborative (Re)Writing

Another example which elucidates the difficulty of establishing boundaries between original writing and adaptation is the Gate Theatre's *Iphigenia Quartet* (2016). As discussed above, the genesis of the *Iphigenia Quartet* problematises notions of singular authorship and illustrates the collaborative nature of contemporary theatre-writing as well as theatre-making. Furthermore, its presentation and reception make a classification of the text as either original writing, adaptation, or any other related modality very difficult indeed. The production of the *Quartet* was accompanied by a print version of all four plays: *Agamemnon*, *Iphigenia*, *Clytemnestra*, and *Chorus*. A single author was also attributed to each play: Caroline Bird is credited for *Agamemnon*, Suhayla El-Bushra for *Iphigenia*, Lulu Raczka for *Clytemnestra*, and Chris Thorpe for *Chorus*. As became clear during a podium discussion[30] which accompanied the production of the *Quartet* in 2016, the playwrights themselves did not necessarily pay much attention to the difference between authorship, adaptation, or indeed translation during their creative processes. Yet the reviews of the productions emphasise the adaptive nature of all four plays and by extension of the *Iphigenia Quartet* as a whole. Tim Bano, writing for *The Stage*, identifies all four plays as 'adaptations' in his review of the productions at the Gate Theatre, and Claire Allfree of the *Telegraph* labels the *Quartet* a 're-telling' and 're-imagination' of Euripides' *Iphigenia at Aulis*.[31] The *Guardian* settles for 'response' and 'retelling', while the *Times* prefers 'reinvention'.[32] The theatre itself may have decided upon a nomenclature which protects Bird's, El-Bushra's, Raczka's, and Thorpe's position vis-à-vis copyright, artistic agency, and ownership by identifying all four as authors in the published text, yet the reviews decided to view all four as (re)writers, if not adaptors, rather than as authors.

The act of (re)writing asserts the validity of an established dramatic text; it confirms that a text belongs to the category of classic drama. At the same time, it promises an often radical (re)investigation of its premises. In a

[29] Gardner (2005). [30] See Brodie and Cole (2018).
[31] See, respectively, Bano (2016); Allfree (2016).
[32] See, respectively, Gardner (2016); Maxwell (2016).

number of these cases we witness a rather radical shift from Greek theatre to our contemporary preoccupation with psychology and naturalism, or what Laera identifies as 'the bizarre but very popular adaptation strategy that attempts to humanize what is ultimately a set of mythological (not psychological) characters'.[33] The zooming devices identified by Sourvinou-Inwood as being (together with distancing ones) central to Greek tragedies become the overriding technique in contemporary (re)writes, versions, or indeed adaptations. This is echoed by Caroline Bird's description of her process of (re)writing as 'zooming in on mainly what I thought about Agamemnon and his experience'.[34] Relating an adaptation to the present and to contemporary audiences' concerns through a focus on characters as individual human beings becomes the dominant mode of contemporary adaptations of Greek drama.[35] '[T]he double perspective in the relationship between the world of the audience and the world of the play', which Sourvinou-Inwood argues 'was very important in Greek tragedy',[36] takes a back seat in favour of the single perspective of the psychological character. This shift, then, provides us with an insight into contemporary concerns rather than into the Greek sources. It is not an indication of misunderstanding or disrespecting the source, but instead it is symptomatic of a current malaise of, and preoccupation with, the individual self. Adaptation and related modalities, then, become an important witness to cultural shifts and allow us to identify contemporaneous affairs and anxieties, rather than necessarily elucidate their source.

Thus, the distinction between so-called original, adaptation, and related activities or modalities such as translation, appropriation, and so forth, is not down to an a priori difference between these modes of (re)writing; the positing of such boundaries is necessarily embodied, in different ways, by the text and/or the performance itself. Importantly, they are enacted also by the expert witness, the creative agents of the process, and crucially by spectators. Of course, this does not mean we must give up trying to classify (re)writings we encounter or indeed give up trying to define the boundaries between adaptation, appropriation, version, etc. But we need to recognise that such attempts to position boundaries may say more about our own context of reception than about the examples of (re)writing under discussion. In other words, we as spectators in the shape of reviewers,

[33] Laera (2015). [34] Plastow (2018).
[35] This can often lead to overly psychologising mythical (i.e. bigger than ourselves) figures. For more on this, see Sidiropoulou, Chapter 4, this volume.
[36] Sourvinou-Inwood (2003), 23–4.

theatre practitioners, expert witnesses, and so forth, enact the boundaries between these categories. And such an enactment of boundaries depends very much on the specific access a spectator has to the 'dialectical relation'[37] between source and adaptation: a spectator with knowledge of the source will enter the dialectical relationship at a different point from a spectator who has no knowledge of the source. The expert witness may very well have a different perspective and entry point from other members of the audience as well as the creative agents. As such, local concepts of adaptation may vary according to the ideological and cultural positioning of the numerous cultural agents involved. While this is not meant to lead to a devaluing of the position of the expert, it may help to explain the popularity of adaptation: adaptation exists in the eye of all spectators, creative agents, and expert witnesses, and is thus a democratic process of shared ownership.

This applies to all adaptations and is not specific to the canon of classic Greek drama. Also, there are numerous kinds of access to the dialectical relation between source and adaptation which Bruhn, as we saw, talks about. Julie Sanders argues that if 'assessing the similarities and differences between texts, . . . which we have elsewhere argued is fundamental to the . . . experience of adaptation, is to be possible it requires prior knowledge of the text(s) being assimilated . . . by the adaptive process'.[38] Yet, the knowledge of the text(s) can be multifarious and, especially in the case of canonical works such as those under discussion in this volume, can relate entirely to 'a generally circulated cultural memory',[39] to other (re)writings of the same source text, and only sometimes, because of the specialist knowledge necessary, to what we regard as the source. In my case, my knowledge of the source texts is limited to their contemporary theatrical (re)presentations; I have no access to the original texts but relate to the various examples as part of a specific theatrical memory as well as 'a generally circulated cultural memory'.[40] As Linda Hutcheon observes, 'If the adapted work is a canonical one, we may not actually have direct

[37] Bruhn (2013), 86.

[38] Sanders (2006), 65; cf. Sanders (2016), 152: 'The pleasure of assessing the similarities and differences between texts, and of judging the levels of conformity and dissent in their approaches, requires prior knowledge of the work(s) being assimilated, absorbed, reworked and refashioned.'

[39] Ellis (1982), 3, as cited in Hutcheon (2006), 122.

[40] This lack of access to the original is very much specific to my own position as a theatre historian and adaptation scholar without a classicist background. It echoes my reluctance to discuss dramatic adaptations alongside theatrical ones as, arguably, the comparative element necessary for such textual analysis demands a textual expertise with regard to the source which I don't have.

experience of it . . . we tend to experience the adaptation through the lenses of the adapted work, as a kind of palimpsest'.[41]

The Persians: Faithful (Re)Writing

In some cases, it is not only the spectator who experiences the adapted work as a kind of palimpsest. In the programme notes accompanying the National Theatre of Wales' production of *The Persians*, directed in 2010 by Mike Pearson, Kaite O'Reilly, credited with (re)writing this version of Aeschylus' play, is at pains to establish her trustworthiness as translator despite not having knowledge of ancient Greek: 'Although I'm not a linguist and therefore unable to read the text in Ancient Greek, through my close reading of 23 translations, made across three centuries, I like to think I have caught a sense of the bass line.'[42]

In this case, then, O'Reilly's version of *The Persians* is in itself an act and product of reception, where the experience of multilayered palimpsests is at the heart of the creative process that is the (re)writing of a canonical text. She distances herself from the process of adaptation and instead authenticates her creative process by employing terminology which implies that her translation in general, and her (re)writing in particular, are trustworthy: 'I chose not to reinvent. I chose to be as faithful, as far as I could perceive it, to that "initial" voice and trust that the extraordinary location in which the performance takes place would create a context with more resonance than anything I could ever fabricate.'[43]

O'Reilly's description of her process demonstrates the agency of the translator/adaptor: faithfulness becomes a choice rather than a compulsion, impulse, or even necessity. It also demonstrates the intricate relationship between (re)writing and the performance itself. Text and performance are not autonomous elements of production, and they are not in a hierarchical or temporal relationship to each other: rather, they are symbiotic. Just as source and adaptation are in a symbiotic relationship, as each of them exists in terms of the other, so are text and performance. And while an emphasis on text rather than performance, as apparent, for example, in the *Times Literary Supplement* review of *Medea*, may be able to prioritise text over elements of the production, such elements of production are of the

[41] Hutcheon (2006), 122. [42] O'Reilly (2010), n. p.

[43] O'Reilly (2010), n. p. The 'extraordinary location' O'Reilly refers to here is the site in the Welsh Brecon Beacons in which the performance took place. Normally not accessible to the public, the site consists of a mock German village which was constructed at the height of the Cold War and is still used as a training site for battlefield scenarios by the British Military.

utmost consequence in the context of *The Persians*. Performed as a National Theatre of Wales production on a military training site in the Brecon Beacons, a mountain range and National Park in South Wales, O'Reilly's *The Persians* is not discussed or reviewed as a text separate from the performance, or from its location for that matter, but always as part of it; so much so that the (re)writing itself – be it translation or adaptation – is considered as intrinsically and unequivocally linked to the performance. And while Power is very much assigned an authorial position in most reviews of *Medea*, and the text exists independently from the production, O'Reilly's *The Persians* is discussed and acknowledged by herself as a playtext independent from the performance only when discussing her own process of (re)writing in the programme notes accompanying the production.

Just like *Medea* and *Phaedra's Love*, this production of *The Persians* is witness to the complexities of the relationship between adaptation, related modalities, and performance. Yet where does that leave our understanding of adaptation in terms of contemporary revisions of the classic Greek play? Is any given adaptation of Greek drama simply a variation on a theme, an inevitable violence done against its source text, whereby the source becomes the victim of the adapted text, which is perceived as a flabby layer around a lean core, or a radical, timeless (re)imagining, essential to the canonicity of the Greek play, as some of the reviews cited above indicate? What happens to our understanding of classic Greek tragedy if we embrace the notion of the fluid text, the reciprocal relationship between source and adaptation, text and performance? Regina Schober alerts us to the 'multiple contextual entanglements of adaptations',[44] and adaptations of classic Greek plays in performance seem to proliferate such entanglements exponentially. As we have seen above, each review and assessment of the adaptations under discussion here are governed by these contextual entanglements, whether these are the contextual engagement with Sarah Kane's other plays, or the context of the populist assessment of West End stars in *What's on Stage*'s review of Ben Power's *Medea*. Such contextual entanglements do not stop here, of course, but go further and include the performance as well as translation and adaptation histories, the context of venue, spectators, as well as the theatre-makers and (re)writers themselves, and so forth. The current volume may indeed unravel some of these contexts but also, in its own way, contribute to the entanglement.

[44] Schober (2013), 110.

Conclusion: (Re)Connecting Adaptation and Its Related Modalities

As we have seen in this chapter, we talk about adaptation as translation, version, and mistranslation, and can consider the adaptive process as one of radical updating, collaborative (re)writing, or faithful adaptation. And while this is not an exclusive list of the modalities of adaptation, what becomes clear is that there is no presumptive and inferred notion of adaptation common to all. Instead, what all these (re)writings have in common is the fluidity and variability of notions of adaptation, translation, version, etc. A similar variability and fluidity also governs the reception process. The examples discussed above bear witness to adaptation 'as a process of forming connections'[45], which may be seen as acts of violence, or of radical updating, or anything in-between or beyond.[46] Importantly, however, all such forming of connections needs to be understood as enacted by the spectator, at the point of reception, as much as (if not more so than) by the adaptor/translator/(re)writer. Thus, the connections are anything but stable entities fixed in time and place. As a result, *Medea*, *Iphigenia*, or *The Persians* can no longer be understood as singular literary entities but, instead, they become ever-shifting, unstable, dialogic events. Just as Power's Medea drags the bodies of her children in full view of an audience, and is thus physically and metaphorically forever linked to the event of their deaths as well as to the existence of their bodies, adaptations, translations, versions, and all modes of (re)writing are forever linked to their sources; they are witnesses to, as much as modifiers of, their sources and in turn responsible for their death as well as their eternal existence.

Arguably, such a reciprocal relationship as the one that Schober identifies is already inherent in all text-based theatre, where the production history of a play is in a dynamic relationship with a contemporary production as well as with our current understanding of the play as written text. Adaptation, then, is a necessarily dramaturgical act, which is not better for not having an 'ounce of fat on it', *pace* Spencer (2014). On the contrary, adaptation is itself flabby as well as adding flab to its source. It stands in a messy, multifarious, collaborative and, importantly, reciprocal relationship with the source play. In other words, the source does not imply one single performance or reading; the source exists and is envisaged as a constellation of infinite adaptations, or rather (re)writings, which cross-pollinate each other like the palimpsest Hutcheon evokes (2006).[47]

[45] Schober (2013), 91. [46] Violence: Beard (2014); updating: Sierz (2011).
[47] See also Sidiropoulou, this volume.

Arguably, the agenda of adaptation and related modalities is 'to reposition the originating text in a new cultural context'.[48] Yet, the originating text is not necessarily a singular, textual entity, but in itself a plurality of texts and, in the case of Greek tragedy, a plurality of performances. And if this does not lead us to a straightforward and self-sufficient analysis of the process, product, and reception that is adaptation, or indeed to an a priori categorisation of the difference between adaptation, version, and (re)writing, blame it on the Greeks, as they started it by 'playing with and adapting stories'.[49]

[48] Bryant (2013), 54. [49] Hardwick (2013a), 327.

CHAPTER 2

Forsaking the Fidelity Discourse
The Application of Adaptation

Peter Meineck

> There *isn't* one true version. There isn't. There isn't one story – a line of truth that stretches start to end. That doesn't happen anymore, maybe it never happened, but even as I say this now, as I say *this* now, in each of your minds you create your own versions, different lenses pointing at the same thing at the same time and *seeing that thing differently*.
>
> (Icke 2015, 108)

This passage is taken from the end of Robert Icke's *Oresteia*, staged at the Almeida Theatre in London in 2015. In many ways, it encapsulates an important issue in the development and reception of classical works for the stage. This is the continuing prevalence of what has been termed 'fidelity discourse' and has tended to dominate the perception of new adaptations of ancient Greek plays.[1] Fidelity discourse, a term that became prevalent in film studies, is described by Bortolotti and Hutcheon as 'a common determination to judge an adaptation's "success" only in relation to its faithfulness or closeness to the "original" or "source" text.'[2] This reinforces the idea that an adaptation of a canonical work tends to have less cultural capital even though it is 'in fact, a common and persistent way in which humans have always told and retold stories'.[3] The critical response to Icke's *Oresteia* stands as a recent example of how the misguided application of the fidelity discourse impacts the ways adaptations of Greek drama are critiqued and valued. Many London critics measured Icke's *Oresteia* based on its relationship to what they perceived as the original work, presumably some faithful exemplar of Aeschylus' *Oresteia* produced in 458 BCE.

1 Andrew (1980).

2 Bortolotti and Hutcheon (2007), 444. They cite Stam's list of 'moralistic' terms used to describe adaptations such as *infidelity*, *betrayal*, *deformation*, *violation*, *vulgarisation*, and *desecration*, 'each accusation carrying its specific charge of outraged negativity' (Stam 2000, 54).
Bortolotti and Hutcheon (2007), 444.

3 For a defence of fidelity in appraising adaptations, albeit in cultural context, see Hermansson (2015).

The problem is that nothing of the sort exists. Yet, the production was variously described as a 'very free adaptation', a 'new version', a 'completely new play', and one critic even remarked that 'Icke can't resist having his mischievous intellectual way with Western culture's cornerstone drama.'[4]

In this chapter, I examine the fidelity discourse as applied to Greek drama and the ways in which it has affected assessments of adaptations of ancient plays. I challenge its fundamental applicability to this genre by pointing out that we have no access to the original versions of these plays at all. Instead, influenced by an evolutionary model, I propose ways in which adaptation can be perceived as a positive act of creativity, which has enabled the work to survive, rather than as a kind of debasement from a presumed canon. I hope to demonstrate my thesis in action by using examples drawn from my work with Aquila Theatre's public programming aimed at the veteran community in the United States. By briefly describing these performance projects, I also hope to show how an informed approach to adaptation can produce new ways in which to increase engagement with, and knowledge of, ancient dramatic works.

One noted critic's response to Icke's 2015 *Oresteia* can help to illustrate the limitations of the fidelity discourse and the ways in which it can misguide both critical and audience response to Greek drama. The production was generally very well received by audiences, and had a sold-out run, but it seems to have been held to a far different standard by critics than if the Almeida Theatre had mounted a production of say, Shakespeare, Shaw, or Chekhov. Shakespeare stands as a good example of how productions are now hardly ever judged against a preconceived set of ideas about 'faithfulness' or 'fidelity' to the original work. Of course, we know far more about the staging of Elizabethan drama than we do about the Athenian theatre in the fifth century BCE, and yet with Shakespearean productions, most people now accept directorial conceptualisations, actor interpretations, and even textual reordering, and have developed sophisticated ways in which to judge their effectiveness. This may be because there is an unbroken theatrical tradition of producing Shakespeare spanning 400 years, and the scholarly community widely accepts that the earliest texts of his plays are themselves adaptations by touring companies or copies of actors' prompt books, not original authorial texts. Furthermore, Shakespeare has always existed in the theatrical tradition as well as in

[4] Cavendish (2015).

scholarly circles, whereas Greek drama is a reconstructed genre understood primarily through scholarship, philology, and literary criticism.

Icke's *Oresteia* and other productions of Greek plays are often held to a far different standard than other period plays by critics who are largely uninformed about the advances in scholarly interpretations of Greek drama during the past thirty years or so. Partly this is the fault of an ever-increasing specialisation in academia, even though several noted classical scholars have advised and informed some high-profile professional productions of Greek drama. For Aeschylus alone, these include Oliver Taplin on Peter Hall's *Oresteia* in 1977, Helene Foley on Aquila's *Agamemnon* with Olympia Dukakis in 2004, and Simon Goldhill on Icke's *Oresteia*. In his introduction to Icke's adaptation, Goldhill is emphatically against the perpetuation of any kind of fidelity discourse when he states: 'The fact that Aeschylus himself was redrafting the old and privileged stories to talk directly to new and insistent politics demands that each new version of his masterpiece speaks to its modern condition.'[5] He also makes the important point that while *The Oresteia* is one of the greatest works of world theatrical culture, 'it needs continual and active re-engagement with its immense potential to make it speak with its true insistence and power'.[6]

Despite Goldhill's appeal that Icke's *Oresteia* be placed in a tradition of adaptation that threads back to Aeschylus, Michael Billington, the respected theatre critic for the *Guardian*, commented: 'Icke sometimes substitutes neurotic intensity for what a Greek professor once called "the formal calm that pervades Aeschylus and Greek tragedy."'[7] Billington does not reveal his source for this quote but this misconceived notion of 'tragic calm' has a long history within the academy. In a survey of twentieth-century classical scholarship, William Tarvin identified several similar concepts applied to Aeschylus: these include 'serenity and harmony', 'release and repose', 'repose and serenity', 'pleasurable calm', 'calmness and readiness', and several others.[8] Can such lofty notions really be applied to a work involving intra-familial murder, the enactment of hideous and dangerous underworld demons, personal terror, and the threat of pestilence and plague? Even in antiquity, we hear the famous apocryphal anecdote that women miscarried and men fainted at the sight of Aeschylus' Furies,[9] and in *Frogs* (963) Aristophanes describes Aeschylus' stagecraft with the made-up adjective *kōdōnophalaropōlous* ('full of the

[5] Goldhill (2015), 4. [6] Goldhill (2015), 7. [7] Billington (2015). [8] Tarvin (1990), 5.
[9] *Life of Aeschylus* §6.

clattering of the battle armour of horses'). There are certainly no ancient Greek references to Aeschylus' works being particularly calm. What then would we make of Aristotle's famous statement that tragedy elicited *katharsis* by means of pity and fear and other emotions,[10] or the fact that Isocrates, Aristotle, Polybius, and others wrote that tragedy had the power to 'stir the soul'?[11] Tarvin rightly concluded that this concept of tragic calm was an arbitrarily imposed notion and deprived many tragedies 'of their essential ambivalence, paradox, and tension'.[12] Yet, even though most scholars would now agree about the emotional power of ancient tragedy in performance, this outdated and wrongheaded notion of a stately, rarefied Greek theatre prevails and is once again used here as a critical yardstick by a highly respected commentator on the contemporary British theatre.

With prolific scholars such as Simon Goldhill advocating the necessity of translation and adaptation, why then does fidelity discourse stick so stubbornly to Greek drama? Perhaps one reason is that, since antiquity, Greek drama as performance first came to the notice of most people in the late nineteenth and early twentieth century from productions mounted at elite universities, often performed in ancient Greek, beginning with Oxford University's *Agamemnon* in 1880. Even though there had been some professional productions of adaptations of Greek plays in Europe and the Americas before that, these academic productions exerted a great deal of cultural impact. For example, the Harvard *Oedipus Tyrannus* was transferred to Broadway in 1882, and the University of Pennsylvania brought Aristophanes' *Acharnians* to Broadway in 1886.[13] The influence of the academy was so strong that when the famous performer Margaret Anglin decided to star in her production of *Antigone* at Berkeley in 1910, she hired the classics professor George Riddle to direct. This was also true in Canada, where the University of Toronto mounted an *Antigone* in 1882 directed by the classicist Maurice Hutton. The Canadian Little Theatre Movement, a progenitor of the professional stage in that country, was active at the university and continued to mount several Greek plays, helping to foster a new performance tradition of Greek drama. In the early twentieth century, artists such as Jean Cocteau, Bertolt Brecht, Isadora Duncan, Gordon Craig, and W. B. Yeats became interested in Greek drama as a means of exploring a kind of European 'primitivism' inspired

[10] Aristotle, *Poetics*, 1449b26–7.

[11] Isocrates, *Evagoras*, 2.10 and 2.49; Aristotle, *Poetics*, 1450b16–21; Polybius, *Histories*, 2.56.11. Cf. also Gorgias, *Helen*, 10, and the pseudo-Platonic *Minos*, 321a.

[12] Tarvin (1990), 24.

[13] For academic Greek theatre in America, see Meineck (2016).

by Jane Harrison and the Cambridge Ritualists.[14] Bold new productions started to spread from the avant-garde theatre to the professional stages of Europe and the Americas.

One of the best-known productions of Greek tragedy in the twentieth century was first staged in Canada, at the new Stratford Festival in 1954. This was Tyrone Guthrie's *Oedipus Rex* with James Mason in the title role. The new stage at Stratford, which was built for the festival and later made permanent, consisted of a large thrust stage protruding into the auditorium. This design was based on contemporary ideas about the form of ancient Greek theatres and their circular orchestras. Guthrie also hired Tanya Moiseiwitsch, who designed huge stylised masks and elaborate costumes and was also heavily influenced by Harrison and the Cambridge Ritualists.[15] This production, now with Douglas Campbell in the title role, was filmed in 1956, and since then has had an enormous influence on generations of students who experienced it in educational settings or saw the photographs reprinted in many theatre history textbooks. Even today, in a recent Google image search of 'Oedipus Rex', eight of the first eighteen images displayed were of the Guthrie production, now more than sixty-five years old.[16] What was at its time a fairly radical staging has itself come to reinforce preconceived notions about 'stately' and 'noble' Greek drama, with its fixed masks, limited movement, and intoning actors.

One would have thought that perhaps by the early twenty-first century, and given the plethora of adaptations of Greek plays that have exploded around the world, the theatre's dependence on academia for validation of what is or what is not a 'faithful' production might have subsided. Yet, the roots of the European and American tradition of performing Greek drama are still firmly entrenched in outdated academic notions that most scholars working in the field today would not now advocate. The important point here is that most aesthetic conditions attached to the fidelity discourse have far more to do with the social, cultural, and artistic conventions of elite American and European universities in the late nineteenth century than anything that Aeschylus did with his *Oresteia* in 458 BCE. His masked, music- and movement-based open-air production conditions had more in common with Balinese Topeng drama or Japanese Noh theatre than with the Victorian stage. This was impressively demonstrated in the early 1990s by Le Théâtre du Soleil's *Les Atrides*, directed by Ariane Mnouchkine, which combined performance styles from several different cultural

[14] Taxidou (2017). [15] Foley (2012), 164. [16] Google image search, 4 August 2017.

traditions, including Indian Kathakali and Japanese Kabuki. Also, Yukio Ninagawa's *Medea* was a large-scale production that originated in the late 1970s and toured extensively for the next 20 years, which fused traditional Japanese with European theatrical traditions and cinematic visuals. Despite these kinds of productions, when actors, teachers, and directors often talk in hallowed tones of 'going back to the Greeks', they are probably not aware that the actual performance tradition of these works is no more than 150 years old, not the 2,500 years that have elapsed since the first known Athenian productions.

Adapt to Survive

There tend to be several questions that are frequently asked whenever a new production of a classical Greek play is staged, and these have been influenced by the fidelity discourse.

- How close is the new work to the original?
- Has the director/translator/designer taken 'liberties' with the classic work?
- Is the production a revival, a faithful version of the original, or an adaptation?
- What is the difference between an adaptation and a faithful version?
- Just what is the faithful version being faithful to, exactly?
- What are the formal dictates of classical tragedy or comedy and how has the new production departed from them?
- Why has the director/writer/translator/designer 'changed' the original play and for what purpose?

These questions are all predicated on the idea that the adaptation can be compared to an original work, although we possess no authorial text from fifth-century Athens, and have a very limited idea about how the plays were staged, what was actually on view to the audience, what the music sounded like, how the lines were delivered, what dance steps and movements were performed, and even what the form of the theatre space itself was at the time.[17] Such questions also imply a marked distinction between what is considered an adaptation and what is viewed as a revival of the original play. For example, in the introduction to his book on the survival of Greek tragedy, Garland stated: 'Adaptations, though these have played a major role in keeping the "spirit" of Greek tragedy alive, are largely

[17] Meineck (2012).

ignored, even though it must be conceded that the defining line between translation and adaptation is extremely tenuous.'[18] In this single sentence, Garland noted the significant contribution of adaptations but also suggested that they are different from a translation, which he presumably regarded as an accurate rendering of the play in English. However, Lorna Hardwick, who has explored this question from the perspective of performance, writes:

> Theatre translation is a connector between ancient and modern audiences, but its operation is not confined by linear temporalities of transmission nor constrained by a settled relationship between ancient and modern or, indeed, between text and performance. It shifts perceptions of both ancient and modern, and this makes it important for the understanding of cultural change.[19]

Julie Sanders has provided a useful theoretical framework to help articulate this discrepancy.[20] For Sanders, an adaptation deliberately signals a relationship with an informing source, whereas what she calls an appropriation offers a more decisive journey away from its informing source into 'a wholly new cultural product and domain'.[21] Sanders' description would imply that there is an original version that the adaptation is relating to, and the appropriation is moving away from. But for Greek drama we are on slippery ground: can we really talk about an original play? And what is the source that is being adapted/appropriated exactly? Though we have limited knowledge of the staging conditions, we do possess texts, many that can be securely traced back to the tenth century CE. But for the 1,500 years before that our knowledge is highly fragmentary; we only catch glimpses of the plays in the quotations of other authors, or on scraps of papyrus from the dry sands near the ancient Greek towns of Egypt. That any Greek dramas survive at all is nothing short of a cultural miracle, and even if we could be entirely sure that these texts were a record of the original production, despite hundreds of years of interpolation, copying, correcting, emendation, and interpretation, we still would only possess the words, and theatre is performance, not literature. Furthermore, even if we knew much more than we do about the original productions, we should still perceive them as adaptations of earlier material. It was, after all, a conscious act of adaptation on the part of the ancient playwright that brought the work to life in the first place. Therefore, instead of constantly seeking to define an adaptation based on fidelity to an unknowable

[18] Garland (2004), xvi. [19] Hardwick (2007b), 361. [20] Sanders (2006).
[21] Sanders (2006), 26.

original, we need a new method of appraising and appreciating adaptations of Greek drama.

Julie Sanders writes that adaptation is

> a transpositional practice, casting a specific genre into another generic mode, an act of re-vision in itself. It can parallel editorial practice in some respects, indulging in the exercise of trimming and pruning: yet it can also be an amplificatory procedure engaged in addition, expansion, accretion, and interpolation.[22]

If we apply this theoretical framework to what we know of the Athenian theatre, the notion that all Greek drama should be viewed as adaptation becomes clearer. For example, we can say that the creation of the first production of the play was transpositional, in that the ancient dramatists took existing material from other performance genres, such as choral lyric and epic, and wove it into a new dramatic form. We can also deduce a kind of parallel editorial process where the adaptation was trimmed and pruned as playwrights mostly adapted commonly known myths and organised the events to suit their dramatic purposes. For example, they exploited narrative reorderings for dramatic effects, such as the entrance of Aegisthus at the end of *Agamemnon*, which placed the killing of Agamemnon solely in the hands of Clytemnestra, in contrast to the Homeric account (*Odyssey* 1.28–31, 3.234–75). This kind of adaptation was an important feature of the composition of Greek drama, a point made by Aristotle who argued in *Poetics* (1450b35–1451a6) that a tragic plot (*muthos*), as well as being well ordered, should also arouse wonderment (*thaumasios*) by devices such as reversals (*peripeteia*) and unexpected recognitions (*anagnorisis*). Athenian audiences came to expect their theatre to adapt known mythic material, and tragedy, satyr drama, and comedy became vehicles for adaptive inter-genre innovation. In *Laws* (700a–e) Plato has his conservative Athenian complain that the tendency of performing artists to mix genres and adapt new styles has led to a 'theatrocracy' (*theatrokratia*) – the rule of the theatre audience, who feel empowered to express political opinions because they have been allowed to judge the value of these works as new adaptations.

We must also assume that, as the ancient productions were revived and reperformed, further cuts and edits must have been made to suit budgets, local conditions, the theatrical aesthetics of the day, and casting needs, among much else. Editing was, of course, an essential part of the

[22] Sanders (2006), 22–3.

subsequent manuscript tradition, beginning with the emendations and *scholia* made by the Alexandrian scholars, to the corrections and interpretations by generations of copyists, Byzantine scholars, philologists, and literary critics. Furthermore, amplificatory procedures have been central to the process of textual transmission with the addition of actors' interpolations and glosses. However, a good deal of the work of scholars over the past several hundred years has focused on attempting to purge the manuscripts of what they saw as amplificatory intrusions to the 'original' text from later reperformances, rather than viewing them as part of an ongoing adaptive process. Yet, as Finglass has recently pointed out, 'investigating the mutual relationship of re-performance and the transmission of texts should not force us to choose between either attempting to get as close as possible to the author's text or appreciating the social and cultural circumstances which led to the adaptation of these texts in the decades that followed'.[23]

Sanders also explains that adaptations can offer commentary on a source text, and this is a distinguishing factor in identifying an adaptation. By this measure, we can take the Electra plays of both Sophocles and Euripides and label them as adaptations of Aeschylus' *Libation Bearers*, or perhaps of each other, based on their respective recognition scenes. Euripides' adaptation not only offers what Sanders describes as 'a revised point of view from the original' but sometimes actively alludes to it. The classical playwrights also used staging devices to refer to existing cult practices, political activities, and contemporary social norms, such as hymns, paeans, processions, wedding ceremonies, and often included references to existing sanctuaries, cult sites, and political venues. For example, *The Oresteia* culminates at the Areopagus, the seat of the old Athenian aristocratic council, whose powers had been severely curtailed just one or two years before the performance. Orestes is told to fall at the feet of Athena's statue in Athens, a city that had only just erected a colossal new bronze statue to the goddess on the Acropolis, and whose small statue of Athena Polias had been evacuated during the Persian occupation just twenty-two years earlier.[24] Finally, the Furies are given a new cult in the city which is affirmed by their joining a procession as if they were participating in the Dionysia or Panathenaea.

Another important marker of an adaptation for Sanders is the attempt to make a work relevant or more comprehensible to new audiences 'via a process of proximation and updating'.[25] While this is easy to discern in

[23] Finglass (2015), 274–5. [24] Meineck (2013). [25] Sanders (2006), 19.

many modern translations and productions, can we say the same about the ancient works? I think this is appropriate for Greek tragedy: the political allusions inherent in the plays and the works' close relationship to contemporary cult practices would seem to bear this out. Additionally, according to Aristotle, playwrights clustered their narratives around a few well-known mythic households to offer a comprehensible structure replete with the kind of surprising plot devices needed to grab attention and evoke an emotional response (*Poetics* 1453a17–23). This is in itself a description of the adaptation of existing well-known narratives.

What we can clearly discern is that Athenian drama stands in a rich tradition of mythic and performative adaptation. Instead of debating a misguided fidelity discourse, we should be seeing the production of Greek drama for what it has always been – a dynamic process of theatrical adaptation. Once we take this step, we can begin to appreciate that in the theatre, just as in nature, it has been the process of adaptation that has allowed Greek drama to survive and thrive.

Such an evolutionary model has been proposed by Bortolotti and Hutcheon (2007), who have compared the biological processes of replication, mutation, and selection to how adaptations are culturally transmitted. They too have pointed out that 'the critical tendency has been to denigrate [adaptations] as secondary and derivative in relation to what is usually (and tellingly) referred to as the "original"'. Bortolotti, an evolutionary biologist, and Hutcheon, a literary scholar, propose the following:

> Our hope is that biological thinking may help move us beyond the theoretical impasse in narrative adaptation studies represented by the continuing dominance of what is usually referred to as 'fidelity discourse.' This common determination to judge an adaptation's 'success' only in relation to its faithfulness or closeness to the 'original' or 'source' text threatens to reinforce the current low estimation (in terms of cultural capital) of what is, in fact, a common and persistent way humans have always told and retold stories.[26]

This model views adaptations as successful cultural products and descendants of an earlier source that have mutated to survive and thrive in new and different environments. The same kind of idea about the positive biological traits of adaptation was proposed by Barthes in 1978:

> As for the Text, it reads without the inscription of the Father [author]. Here again, the metaphor of the Text separates from that of the work: the latter

[26] Bortolotti and Hutcheon (2007), 444.

> refers to the image of an organism which grows by vital expansion, by 'development' (a word which is significantly ambiguous, at once biological and rhetorical); the metaphor of the Text is that of the network; if the Text extends itself, it is as a result of a combinatory systematic (an image, moreover, close to current biological conceptions of the living being).[27]

Another Aeschylean work can help to demonstrate this point. *Seven Against Thebes* is based on the legends of Thebes that existed in the older Greek oral epic tradition with links to Mesopotamian mythology. Aeschylus adapted these legends, probably influenced by the lyric poet Stesichorus, for the new medium of the theatre. Subsequently, many tragedians adapted this material, including Achaeus, Sophocles, Euripides, Agathon, and Timotheus.[28] It was again adapted by Astydamas, Theodectes, and Antimachus of Colophon in the fourth century, and then notably by Statius and Ovid in Rome, among others. These and other literary and artistic adaptations allowed different parts of the narrative to survive. The story was adapted in the twelfth century in France as *Le Roman de Thèbes*, by Boccaccio in Italy in his *Teseida*, and by Chaucer in England in 'The Knight's Tale', which in turn inspired Shakespeare's *Two Noble Kinsmen* and provided the background to *A Midsummer Night's Dream*. The evolution of *Seven Against Thebes* is no more linear than the kind of genetic variabilities that exist in biological organisms, which help maximise survival. Thus, as the text *of Seven Against Thebes* and its variant forms were obtained, copied, edited, published, and then translated, the errors and emendations that occurred during this process of textual transmission may be compared to evolutionary mutation pressure – the accumulation of errors in DNA replication over time. Likewise, the adaptive journey of *Seven Against Thebes* is a process of mutation from an unknown original progenitor, and this ancient story of the seven avenging warriors and the after-effects of their war on Thebes has continued to inspire adaptations in other media. Examples in film include Kurosawa's *The Seven Samurai*, Sturges' *The Magnificent Seven*, and G. P. Sippey's *Sholay*, which have in turn acted as influences in their own right on Will Powers' hip-hop musical adaptation of the Aeschylean play from the first decade of the twenty-first century, which he named *The Seven.*[29] There are many more versions and adaptations we could add, of course, but the point is to demonstrate that the process of adaptation does not follow a linear diachronic pattern, but acts more like a network of cultural

[27] Barthes (1978), 161. [28] Wright (2016), 85–6.
[29] Grene and Lattimore (2013), 1.69; McClain (2009), 359; Hunt and Wing-Fai (2010).

influences transmitting different facets of the adapted material at various times. Bortolotti and Hutcheon would see these adaptations as part of the normal human process of how we receive, adapt, and pass on narratives, and propose that we examine the process of adaptation with these different cultural contexts in mind. Their point is that whereas the basic question posed in biology has been 'Why does life exist in such a dazzling array of forms?', the cultural equivalent might be 'Why do the same stories exist in such a startling array of forms?'[30]

One way of examining this question would be to seek an explanation as to why Will Power used *Seven Against Thebes* as his theatrical vehicle, and not judge its merits based on how close his version is to some misguided idea of an original. This can both provide insights into the reception of the ancient work in a particular cultural context but also, in some cases, even shed more light on the themes, theatrical dynamics, and cultural functionality of the ancient piece by approaching it from a new perspective. In interviews, Will Power has stated that he wanted to use the play to articulate a social tension in his own culture, that is, the absence of fathers in many African American families due to structural racism, poverty, incarceration, and other social factors.[31] He took the hip-hop technique of 'flipping' source material to make something new and applied it to Greek drama. Whereas, in music, hip-hop artists flipped records and rapped over them (one of the first break-out hip-hop tracks *Rapper's Delight* by the Sugar Hill Gang did this by setting new lyrics over a famous guitar riff from *Good Times* by Chic), Power 'flipped' Aeschylus, via the 1961 Philip Vellacott Penguin translation. The form of Power's *The Seven* was one of active adaptation, and therefore he was free to import influences from any genre that suited his artistic purposes. One of the more notable was to import the character of Oedipus into the *Seven Against Thebes* to bring the main point of his adaptation into sharp view. This was Oedipus as a 1970s 'pimped-out Mac Daddy' messing with the minds of his sons and thereby tearing them apart, just as he had been torn from his own family and killed his father. In making this decision, Power tapped into the mythic material that had influenced the Aeschylean version and unknowingly reconnected the ancient material to part of its wider story (Power did not originally know that *Seven Against Thebes* was part of a trilogy which included the story of Oedipus). There is a good deal we can learn from the adaptive process of hip-hop when it comes to better understanding how

[30] Bortolotti and Hutcheon (2007), 446. [31] Meineck (2006).

stories mutate, develop, and change.[32] Power's total acceptance of the primacy of the adaptive process via hip-hop's practice of flipping completely freed him from the artificial constraints of the fidelity discourse to produce a vital new work.

Will Power's adaptive process is not unlike Aristotle's views on plot construction found in *Poetics*: 'the function of a poet [is] to relate not things that have happened, but things that may happen, i.e. that are possible in accordance with probability (*to eikos*) or necessity' (1451a36–b1). *Eikos* refers to the concept of probabilistic thinking and is also used by Aristotle to describe *peripeteia* in *Poetics* (1452a24); it was fundamental to methods of political deliberation, judgement making, and the narratives of Greek drama. *Eikos* involved the fluid consideration of differing perspectives and active adaptation of perception to form a collective judgement rather than the promulgation, and then entrenched defence, of a fixed idea.[33] This is analogous to contemporary cognitive theories about how humans perceive the world around them, make subsequent decisions, and then act on them. Predictive processing asserts that the human mind deals with the enormous amount of sensory information in the world by quickly comparing what is sensed with what is known, and it is only the perceived 'errors' or variances to this constant bottom-up/top-down flow that warrant our cognitive and bodily attention.[34] These are the places where we utilise 'action inferences' – we look, touch, smell, or move to find out more, to analyse and to receive more sensory information and update and adapt our perception. According to this cognitive model, prediction is the cornerstone of human perception. When we predict the world around us, we actively adapt the percepts stored in the mind, and our subsequent responses also adapt as a result. Thus, by extending the Bortolotti and Hutcheon notion of biological adaptation into a model of distributed cognition, the idea that the mind is not 'brain-bound' and that thought is extended out through the body, the environment, and back again, we can surmise that adaptation is not only an evolutionary process but an essential part of what makes us able to perceive and interact with the world we live in. The whole idea of a fidelity discourse would have been

[32] For example, see Williams (2014) and George (2004). I thank my reader for these sources and for pointing out that Dub, which originated in the Caribbean, is also an important influence on hip-hop (Hebdige 2003). On the connections between Homer, West African orature, and hip-hop, see Banks (2010).

[33] Kirby (2012), 422.

[34] For an excellent discussion of predictive processing, see A. Clark (2015). For its application to Greek drama, see Meineck (2017).

anathema to Aristotle's theories on drama, since it was he who suggested that playwrights should adapt traditional stories in skilful new ways (1453b23–6). It was the possibilities of these new adaptations and the way they were received by the audience at the time that in large part made Greek tragedy such an absorbing and enthralling experience. To quote Victoria Wohl, Greek tragedy was 'the genre par excellence of *eikos*'.[35]

If human cognition is a process of actively adapting the ways in which we sense the world around us to better understand that world, then the process of adaptation in drama should certainly not be regarded as debasement, degradation, or corruption. Rather, adaptation is an essential part of what makes us all human. If we conceive a play as a kind of mimetic mind for the audience it plays to, in that it must be reflective of their cognitive processes to be understood, then we can start to examine its forms of adaptation as a means of specific cultural production. Some of the questions we might want to be asking could look as follows:

- What are the existing perceptions of the canonical work within the culture for which the play is being performed?
- What are the new ways in which the play has been adapted and what is the artist trying to communicate by these acts of adaptation?
- Is the adaptation aware of its source material in an intertextual or interperformance sense, or is the source not so apparent?
- How has the adaptation utilised current theatrical and cultural practices, and do they work with the existing source material?
- Is the adapter fully aware of an existing source, or are they responding to a common cultural trope that may have at one time been influenced by the source which is now not so apparent?
- Is the adaptation attempting to elucidate the source, challenge it, or use its themes as inspiration for something else entirely?
- Does the new adaptation provide new insights on the source(s)?

Aquila's Adaptations with the American Veteran Community

Having set out some of the main points that surround the issue of fidelity discourse, the remainder of this chapter will focus on the application of adaptation in the public sphere and the work of Aquila Theatre with the American veteran community from 2007 to 2017.

[35] Wohl (2014), 5. On *eikos* and tragedy, see also Meineck (2017), 30–47.

Aquila Theatre was founded in 1991 with the express idea of creating innovative productions of classical drama and bringing that work to underserved communities. The company sought to challenge ideas about classical drama, make it accessible to new audiences, and expand what most people considered the classical theatrical canon. Aquila has mounted productions of ancient works including Homer, Aeschylus, Sophocles, Euripides, and Aristophanes as well as modern classical authors such as Shakespeare, Rostand, and Ibsen. Additionally, they have explored Heller (*Catch 22*), Bradbury (*Fahrenheit 451*), Brontë (*Wuthering Heights*), Shelley (*Frankenstein*), and Orwell (*1984*), and mounted collaborative projects with modern dance groups and artists from other disciplines. The company is known for its highly physical style with small multi-talented casts, innovative design elements, and a certain irreverent iconoclasm, which emanates from a developed understanding of the plays and the conditions in which they were first presented. The overall mission of Aquila is to free the essential spirit of the original work through research, experiment, and innovation, and to defy pedantic and conservative ideas about classical drama. With this in mind, all of Aquila's theatrical works have been, in differing shapes and forms, acts of theatrical adaptation.

In the early 2000s, the company became interested in expanding their public engagement work, beyond pre- and post-show talks, participatory workshops, and additional special educational performances, into the area of public discourse. They posed the question of how ancient works could offer modern Americans material for understanding more about their society and its actions. This was particularly relevant after September 11, 2001, when the United States soon found itself fighting two very long wars. One of the main inspirations for this programming was Aquila's involvement in the National Endowment for the Arts' *Shakespeare in American Communities* project in 2004, which placed a professional Shakespeare production and accompanying public programme in all fifty states, including many US military bases. A special performance of Aquila's *Much Ado About Nothing* was staged in the East Room of the White House for then-President George W. Bush, the first artistic event his administration had held since taking office four years earlier. This performance had already been adapted for eight actors doubling and tripling in roles and had an irreverent, 1960s 'Go-Go' feel. At the White House, it was restaged again and shortened to fit the president's schedule. In discussions, before and after the play, with George and Laura Bush, it was clear that classical drama could raise important issues about education, arts in society, public funding, and contemporary culture across the political spectrum.

That night, a distracted president heading an administration not particularly friendly to the arts was momentarily enthralled by a small group of highly committed actors performing a classical work in a new way and then inspired to recommit federal funds for the arts in America.[36]

Aquila's new model was not only to produce and tour full productions of classical drama, but to further adapt its work so that it might inspire people from different backgrounds to come together in person, in non-traditional spaces, in order to discuss issues that mattered to them in the here and now. In the mid-2000s, America was increasingly becoming politically polarised, a trend that has continued to the present. Part of the reason for this growing divide was the increasing lack of public discourse and the diminishing ability for people on the right or left to find any common ground for their social and cultural viewpoints. The rapid development of the internet and cable TV was completely changing the social fabric of American cultural life with the result that attendance at live artistic events was dropping rapidly. Increasingly, people were experiencing discourse in the technological echo chamber of social media and self-affirming news feeds, and one of the most important places Americans had frequented to find out information was in peril: this was the American public library.

Homer's *Iliad*: *Page and Stage*

Aquila was approached by the National Endowment for the Humanities to develop a public programme that might create a new model for library public programming, one that combined reading groups, public talks, performance, and discussion, and would place adaptations of ancient Greek drama at its core. The first of these innovative public programmes, called *Page and Stage*, visited sixteen libraries in twelve US states in 2007 with a programme based around Homer's *Iliad*. It was during the presentation of this new programme that Aquila began its engagement with the American veteran community. In many ways, by developing ancient works and adapting them for an entirely new purpose, the company learned far more about those works than when they were developed solely for the professional stage. But the implementation of these

[36] This kind of political outreach was impossible during the Trump administration, which proposed the eradication of both the Arts and Humanities endowments. Additionally, no Aquila artist would have agreed to perform at the Trump White House, an indication of how much more polarised American politics has become since 2016.

programmes and the future adaptations they inspired also ran headlong into the critical maelstrom of the classical fidelity discourse, which will be detailed below.

Page and Stage involved the formation of reading groups led by specially recruited and trained local scholars, who also presented public talks, convened and contextualised film screenings, and moderated discussions after performances of *The Iliad: Book One* by the Aquila actors. These performances were staged wherever space could be found, including library meeting rooms, in the lobby, or by temporarily pushing back the book stacks to create space.[37] This adaptation of Homer was based on Aquila's 1999 production, which was first staged at Lincoln Center's Clark Studio in New York.[38] The work was a physical theatre piece that involved a cast of seven, using just four large black boxes, the equipment they carried, a very simple, stark lighting design, and an original musical score. In development and rehearsals, the company had devised the work with the intention not of mounting a literal staging of the *Iliad*, but instead of asking what would happen if a group of modern soldiers and civilians, thrust together in a highly stressful situation, started to perform the *Iliad* themselves. In this way, the production was an enacted embodiment of the act of appropriating, adapting, and reperforming a classical work, and of showing how the *Iliad*'s characters and situations reflected the conflicts and concerns of the modern people who appeared in the play. To create some temporal distance, the decision was made to set the adaptation during World War II, although this was never expressly stated, and only represented by costume. The cast played three American GIs, a German soldier, a civilian priest, a teenage girl, and a civilian woman, and the premise of the production, which was also not stated, only enacted, was that they were thrust together in the basement of a ruined house on the coast of France on D-Day 1944 at the time of the Allied invasion. The inspiration for this idea came from the cover art for Stanley Lombardo's 1997 translation published by Hackett, a black and white coastguard photo of American GIs storming a beach from a landing craft called 'Into the Jaws of Death'.[39]

Lombardo rendered *The Iliad* in the spare vernacular of the American GI, which created a tense emotional atmosphere of potent immediacy. The critic Daniel Mendelsohn writing in the *New York Times* commented: 'in taking the existing text of Homer as a starting point for a brand-new performance of his own, Stanley Lombardo is following in the footsteps of

[37] Tessman (2010). [38] Bruckner (1999). [39] Lombardo and Murnaghan (1997).

the company of 'Homers' who assembled that text, to begin with – not breaking with tradition but joining its powerful current'.[40] By contemporising Homer's language, one might even say by adapting it, as all translators must do, Lombardo had created a new text with the kind of immediacy and visceral power that helped propel a taut and dynamic production.

Lombardo's translation and book cover helped inform the central conceit of the production: not to attempt to stage Homer but instead to explore what it means to tell a classic story again, and perhaps even why it needs to be told. Once this idea was established in rehearsal, then a whole physical language of deliberate anachronism could be developed. Arrows of sickness sent by Apollo could be presented as a gas attack, the debate over human chattel became a means to diffuse a tense hostage situation, and the presence of the gods as the distant rumbling of aircraft overhead stopped the action and reminded us of the modern war going on outside. Yet, for all the wilful anachronism, something interesting developed: as the company explored enacting Homer with only what they carried on to the stage, so objects with iconic relevance for one historical setting could be transformed by the repurposing of their usage to become equally significant as ancient, mythic props. An example of this was the iconic GI helmet: when worn, it created the archetypal silhouette of the American soldier of the mid twentieth century, but when repurposed as a ceremonial basin and used in a coordinated movement sequence of purification, the object became a material anchor for the projection of audience imagination. It had been adapted.

The way in which an object can come to act as a kind of cognitive scaffolding for the contemplation of the immaterial and the spiritual has been termed 'material fetishism' by Appadurai.[41] Thus, a recognisable object that at first seems firmly tied to a time, place, and use can be physically transformed by the way it is repurposed and reused on stage. Yet, this transference of time, space, and function is far from stable, as the object in this adaptive context does not become 'translated', in that it has not wholly transformed from one thing to another. It is not simply a sign system with a fixed representational meaning, like a writing system: it is, as Lambros Malafouris has put it, an 'enactive sign'.[42] This means that the object treated in this way is not a mere signifier of one commonly understood meaning, but something that can bring forth a multiplicity of connotations at the same time. Hence, the GI helmet is at once a functional piece of head protection, a visual marker of an American soldier,

[40] Mendelsohn (1997). [41] Appadurai (1988). [42] Malafouris (2013).

an evocation of war in the mid twentieth century, a soldier's grave marker when placed on a vertical rifle, and (when used in a cleansing ceremony) a basin to contain water, a means of making an offering to the gods, and a sacred object. The instability of an object used in this way on stage lies at the heart of the theatrical adaptive process and drama's ability to provoke imagination and create entire fictive worlds from the merest of physical elements. Perhaps then, this is why we struggle to perceive a text similarly. The written word is a signifier which acts as part of a representational sign system to fix meaning. Even though many words can still have multiple meanings, and many writers exploit this fact, most readers and writers seek a singularity of meaning and communication when they read.

The foundation of the fidelity discourse in classics rests firmly on texts, but like the repurposed prop, the uttered word in performance is also an enactive element, especially when partnered with movement, music, actor reactions, vocal inflection, intention, and action. Thus, a word heard provides a different cognitive experience from a word that is read. When an ancient dramatic text is analysed as momentary utterances nested within the broader context of all the corresponding elements of the performance, we can sometimes catch glimpses of how the ancient dramatists exploited this kind of verbal instability. One example is the use of the term *baphê* in Aeschylus' *Oresteia.* The word may refer to the dying of an object and to the dyed object itself. The English word *baptise* is derived from it and it resonates as an onomatopoeic sequence of plosive sounds like either a sheet of fabric or hot metal being plunged into water (*baphê* can also refer to the tempering of metal). Aeschylus uses a feminine form of the term (*baphas*) to describe the saffron veil of Iphigenia as it slips off her head at the moment of her slaughter (*Agamemnon* 239). This provokes the conflation of two powerful images: a ceremonial bridal unveiling, and blood pouring from her severed neck. *Baphas* is also used to describe the crimson tapestries Agamemnon treads to enter his house to his death (*Agamemnon* 960), the bloodstains on the tangling robe that ensnared him in the bath (*Libation Bearers* 114), and the dyed crimson cloaks worn by the Furies as they are inducted into the cults of Athens at the end of the trilogy (*Eumenides* 1028).

Aeschylus projects the multiplicity of meanings of this highly charged word in the *Oresteia* and makes an aural connection between the past, present, and future when Clytemnestra uses the term to describe her loyalty to her husband in the message she wants the Herald to relay back to her husband (*Agamemnon* 612). A lexical textual translation of her οὐδ' οἶδα τέρψιν οὐδ' ἐπίψογον φάτιν | ἄλλου πρὸς ἀνδρὸς μᾶλλον ἢ χαλκοῦ βαφάς might be: 'I know as much about the pleasures of another man as I do of steeping bronze.' However, in performance, the audience heard this speech end with the phrase *khalkou baphas*, which must have surely reminded them of *krokou baphas* which was uttered by the chorus describing the veil/blood of Iphigenia (*Agamemnon* 239). Additionally, Aeschylus names Khalkis first when referring to the region where Iphigenia was killed when describing how the fleet 'on the other side of Khalkis' was trapped by the swelling tides off Aulis (190–1). Khalkis is just 4.5 miles to the north of Aulis across the straits of Euripus on the coast of Euboea and was the main city of that region in antiquity. Its name means something like 'Copper' or 'Bronze Town' and both copper and iron were mined and exported in Khalkis in the archaic and classical periods.[43]

With this in mind, we may infer from Clytemnestra's statement at least two further meanings in addition to the utterance made to be understood in the present: 'I measure my loyalty based on what happened at Khalkis' (past action) and 'I am going to plunge metal into him' (future action). By its very nature, translation seeks to find a close linguistic equivalent in the target language, and this can obfuscate how words uttered in performance can provoke a multiplicity of immediate meanings and operate at a subliminal and multitemporal level. In translating Clytemnestra's pledge as text, we seek to fix meaning, and while recognising possible multiple interpretations, linguistic puns, and ironies, this representational clarity does not work in the same way in which we process the associative sounds of a live utterance. The kind of ambiguities and multiple meanings that are sometimes inherent in speech can often be eradicated by the fixedness of text. If the practice of translation is, according to Hardwick, not constrained by a settled relationship between ancient and modern, then the relationship between word and utterance of both the ancient and the modern theatre audience is even more unsettled.[44]

Ancient Greeks and Modern Warriors

A fundamental element of Aquila's public programming was the way in which passages from ancient dramatic works operated in performance as verbal anchors for association and projection, in that they could elicit multiple meanings and elide temporal distinctions. Additionally, the

[43] Healy (1978), 57–8. It is also notable that the chorus members of Euripides' *Iphigenia at Aulis* who watch the events surrounding the sacrifice of Iphigenia are from Khalkis.

[44] Hardwick (2007b), 361.

canonical status of ancient Greek plays as 'classics' has helped foster productive discourse on sometimes highly charged themes. This is appropriate for the performance of this kind of mythic material, as the ancient audience also experienced their dramatist's adaptations of existing well-known stories and projected on them their contemporary political and social concerns. The inherent ability of Greek dramas to act as projective devices has often confounded critics informed by the fidelity discourse, who have tended to misunderstand mythic material as offering distant 'universality' rather than perceiving how relevant it can be in the here and now. By enacting the myth again, a stage adaptation offers a certain aesthetic fixedness, such as the World War II costumes of Aquila's *Iliad.* However, just as classical vase painters rendered their Homeric heroes in the battle dress of their day, modernising a myth or moving it into another historical period in no way diminishes its potential to operate effectively, and can often increase its contemporary relevance. However, proponents of fidelity discourse might not share this view; this is something I will return to address at the end of this chapter by using a recent example.

After the initial public programme was concluded, Aquila expanded it into a three-year project, called *Ancient Greeks/Modern Lives* (*AGML*), visiting 100 locations across the United States. Here, material culled from earlier Aquila stage adaptations was adapted into a staged reading format comprising five different seven-to ten-minute scenes of Greek literature interspersed with brief introductions by a trained programme scholar and followed by a moderated audience discussion. This adaptation of the ancient material allowed the programme to focus on certain themes, which could then be used to anchor discussion. This moved the conversation away from aesthetics (costume design, staging choices, etc.) and back to programme themes, which included returning from war, the impact of war on civilians, democracy and war, the clash of ethics, and women at war. The programme's simplicity of staging allowed it to be presented in many more non-traditional spaces. *AGML* aimed to get Americans reading and thinking about ancient literature and the ways in which it related to their lives today. Libraries were given book donations of new translations of ancient works, and the overall mission was the promotion of the study of classics as something meaningful in contemporary culture. As new veterans from the wars in Iraq and Afghanistan started to return home, and *Page and Stage* had seen engagement from veterans of earlier conflicts, a section of *AGML* was devoted to the veteran community. As the programme ran through 2010–13, it became clear that there was an urgent need to place veterans in dialogue with the public about their experiences and attitudes to war and homecoming – or as Vietnam veteran and actor Brian Delate described it, to help Americans become more literate about war, something essential in a viable democracy.

This adaptation of ancient material to provoke discourse was in practice quite remarkable. In effect, a theatre programme became a venue for public political dialogue on the role of warfare in American society, the commercial and governmental connections to war, public engagement with the wars, or lack thereof, the effect of warfare on civilians, leadership, the ethics of war, warrior homecoming, moral injury, post-traumatic stress, and the inequalities of military service.[45] The status of the ancient work as a classic seemed to help validate the experiences of many people, who found distinct parallels between the mythic characters and their own lives. Sophocles' *Ajax* launched many intense discussions on military suicide; *Philoctetes* on moral injury and the treatment of disabled veterans; Euripides' *Herakles* on reintegration, the family, and PTSD; Aeschylus' *Agamemnon* on the struggle between duty and family, state and home; and Homer's *Odyssey* on the trials of homecoming and questions of leadership. One of the hallmarks of *AGML* was placing veterans on an equal footing with the scholars, in that their experiences of war made them uniquely qualified to offer insights into ancient works that have been described by Jonathan Shay as 'theatre by combat veterans, for an audience of combat veterans, performed by combat veterans'.[46] In this way, without reflecting any one ideological alignment, plays created for the ancient polis became, once again, political.

Using Greek drama to draw attention to issues surrounding war in America became an urgent endeavour. Simons and Lucaites have pointed out that the United States has been at war for 93 per cent of its history, and those born since September 11, 2001 have never known a time when America was not at war.[47] They write that 'one might imagine that given such circumstances, the US population would be in a continual state of mobilization . . . or at least there would be a pronounced and significant anti-war movement . . . But neither has been the case.'[48] They describe the recent US conflicts as 'invisible wars' fought by a volunteer army and professional contractors with very little impact on most of the American population. In real terms, in 2017 there were approximately 1.4 million

[45] For analyses of Aquila's veterans programming, see Lodewyck and Monoson (2015); Hankir et al. (2017), 198–9; Adamitis and Gamel (2013), 296–7.

[46] Shay (2002), 152–3.

[47] Simons and Lucaites (2017), 1.

[48] Simons and Lucaites (2017), 1.

Americans in the military. This corresponds to 0.4 per cent of the total population. Simons and Lucaites perceive a paradox in American culture: that war is simultaneously seen and unseen, visible and invisible; war is, in effect, displaced. Civilians are made very aware of the threat of terror and participate in the security measures connected with it, while simultaneously being unaware of the wars being fought by their troops overseas. The authors cite the prevalence of what they describe as the Military-Industrial-Media-Entertainment network (MIME) as providing the mimetic means to normalise war via films, television shows, and video games. One can go further and see how these highly popular representations can create a false paragon for how and why wars are fought and how Americans should behave while fighting them. The reality on the ground, of course, is far more complicated. In general, the MIME network and its associated news media outlets do not tend to offer complexity or ambiguity when addressing issues of foreign policy and war.

Ambiguity lies at the heart of what makes mythic material so effective in being able to seem to speak to immediate concerns, both to ancient and modern audiences. It is also attractive to many veterans who have experienced first-hand the inherent ambiguities of warfare and the ways in which mythologies of patriotism, nationalism, or the idea of democracy have been deployed to validate military campaigns. Yet perceptions about what is considered a classic work and why, and just who maintains and polices the classical canon, are bound up with complex issues of race, ethnicity, colonialism, class, and privilege. Therefore, when veterans use this material, it can frequently reveal tensions about who has the right to adapt it, particularly if that adaptation is intended for an overtly political purpose. One commonly found tenet of the fidelity discourse as applied to Greek drama is that it should not too closely reflect current political or social tensions, as to do so would debase its 'universality'. Of course, Greek drama was always inherently political, and yet moving it from the realm of pure aesthetics into the political is now frequently viewed as not only controversial but somehow destructive.

Adapting the Chorus of *Herakles*

At the end of *Ancient Greeks/Modern Lives*, it was decided to mount a production of Euripides' *Herakles* in New York and adapt the play to reflect some of the remarkable associations made by veterans during the programme. The *Herakles* production developed an idea of using different art forms to create a dialogue between the fictive world of the ancient play and the ways in which Greek plays were being interpreted by modern combat veterans. To achieve this, the chorus parts of the play were analysed and developed into a series of questions based on the content of the text, such as 'Who were your mythical heroes and what were their memorable deeds?', 'Who was your bitterest enemy?', 'What do you remember about coming home after a deployment?', or 'What is your reaction to a hero destroying his own family?' Then a small team travelled around the country interviewing veterans from different ethnic groups, genders, age groups, and regions, both enlisted and officers who had served in World War II, Korea, the Vietnam War, the Cold War, Iraq, and Afghanistan, and posed these questions after describing the play and each choral ode. Their responses were recorded by a filmmaker, who then worked with the company to edit them into short 'chorus films'. These were then played on a large screen in place of the choral odes, in between the action of the play performed by live actors.

The discontinuity between the two-dimensional films and the three dimensions of the live action caused something of an aesthetic schism between chorus and scenes, but it also acted to highlight the testimonies of the veterans in a way that transcended the documentary level. The stories of the veterans were both viscerally real and at times quite mythic, painful, heartfelt, and disturbing, but also funny, poignant, and sensitive.[49] When the messenger told of how Herakles went insane and killed his children, the veterans each told their own harrowing story of witnessing children being killed in war. While Euripides' chorus sang of the deeds of Herakles, the veterans spoke of their heroes, such as a one-eyed Buddhist warrior in Vietnam who rescued a young American officer and believed he was invulnerable except for his one good eye. In this way, *Herakles* became for these veterans a work that encapsulated the difficulties of the returning warrior, the ravages of combat, and the tension between family and duty. These are certainly not the only themes one can find in the play, but in its way, this adaptation brought home some truths about combat and its effects to an audience who for the most part had never experienced the wars fought in their name.

One criticism of Aquila's *Herakles* was that the adaptation of the veterans' own stories into the fabric of the play, spoken by the veterans themselves, was so moving that the actors performing the mimetic story where overwhelmed. Another criticism was that the veterans' stories eroded the distance between Euripides and us, that *Herakles* is not a play

[49] For a review in the *New York Times*, see Zinoman (2013).

about war or a veteran returning home, but a story of an unattainable mythic character beset by ineffable gods. But surely the success of any adaptation is that it can be both.

The perpetuation of fidelity discourse and its desire to erode the inherent ambiguity of mythic material can prove problematic when adapting ancient drama to highlight contemporary issues. In the case of veterans, it can run the risk of overly simplifying the veteran experience, and even cause reputational damage to the veteran community. For example, one high-profile for-profit programme called *Theater of War* advertises its work thus: 'Rooted in discussions about the invisible and visible wounds of war, the company's hallmark project [*Ajax* and *Philoctetes*] is designed to increase awareness of psychological health issues, disseminate information on available resources, and foster greater community cohesion.'[50] This is an attractive mission, and I have written about the effectiveness of *Theatre of War* in promulgating this message.[51] But there is a concern in the veteran community that the advancement of such a seemingly compelling idea, namely that Greek drama can help destigmatise psychological injury and create understanding between military and civilian populations, is a gross oversimplification of the individual and variated experiences of veterans. Furthermore, it runs the risk of harming the community it is seeking to help by further marginalising them as modern-day Ajaxes – and in effect by advancing the misguided trope of the broken warrior. While post-traumatic stress is a real issue for many veterans and their families, it is also a complicated one and cannot be applied to all those who served. If the public perceives veterans as people liable to 'snap' like Ajax and commit sudden acts of violence, how does this help veteran reintegration, employment opportunities, or community understanding? Thus, a valid criticism of *Theater of War* is that it perhaps perpetuates a negative and simplistic stereotype of the veteran.[52]

To a certain extent, the continued presence of the fidelity discourse is due to the fact that it also adapts to reflect current conservative and elitist attitudes. *Theatre of War*, though well-meaning in its aims, has also succumbed to a one-dimensional view of ancient drama and the veterans it purports to be helping. Presenting returning veterans to the civilian population as psychologically damaged from their experiences of war might be seen to fit a narrative that casts these wars as politically toxic. Here the veterans play the role of the one-time believer, i.e. the volunteers

[50] From the Theater of War website (https://theaterofwar.com/projects), accessed 14 January 2020.
[51] Meineck (2009). [52] Adamitis and Gamel (2013); Powers (2018), 172–209; Doerries (2015).

who signed up to fight for their country, and now publicly represent the failure of those wars and the damage they caused, both to the countries they fought in and to themselves. In conforming to a certain political and cultural viewpoint, both the ancient work and the veterans run the risk of becoming oversimplified and perhaps even unwittingly exploited. Funding bodies and foundations prefer simple mission statements, and the idea that the cultural riches of ancient Greece can offer solace to veterans is a highly attractive one. Yet, Greek dramas tend to be morally ambiguous and ethically confusing; they question social norms and frequently expose tensions, both in the society they were created for and also today. While they can certainly allow people to draw all kinds of parallels and can be used to highlight particular issues, plays like *Ajax* and *Philoctetes* are in themselves far from single-issue works; on the contrary, they offer the kind of narrative complexity that is the essence of Greek drama's continuing ability to enthrall and engage different types of readers and audiences. One reason that *Theater of War* has been successful is its brilliantly simple and unambiguous messaging (Greek drama cures veterans!); it seems a validation of the humanities at a time when they are so under threat. However, the program's attractive claims of 'timelessness' and 'universality' are really just well-worn tropes of the classical fidelity discourse. Instead, it is Greek drama's inherent ambiguities and complexities that make the plays still so compelling today, and importantly, so eminently *adaptable.*

Philoctetes and Refugees: *The Warrior Chorus*

In working closely with members of the veteran community, Aquila next developed a programme with them to seek to counter the marginalisation and oversimplification of the veteran experience. *The Warrior Chorus* was created with the express purpose of training veterans to devise and present their own programming. From 2013 to 2016, the project placed the adaptation of Greek plays at the centre of its programming, using them to explore a variety of themes that the veteran participants wanted to communicate. Three shows were produced: *A Female Philoctetes*, focused on women at war, produced at the Brooklyn Academy of Music in New York and then in Athens at the Cacoyannis Foundation; *Philoctetes*, with an all-veteran cast at GK Arts in Brooklyn; and *Our Trojan War*, a new work incorporating veterans' writing, also presented at the Brooklyn Academy of Music.[53]

[53] Powers (2018), 177–209.

A Female Philoctetes took Sophocles' all-male play and recast the title role as a woman, using this adaptation to act as a provocateur for questions surrounding the issue of women in combat. While women have always been both involved in and affected by war, it was the campaigns in Iraq and Afghanistan that forced the US armed forces to recognise that women were actively participating in combat roles in both theatres of operations, even though under the provisions of the 1948 Combat Exclusion Policy women were expressly barred from carrying out combat roles. It was not until 2013 that this ban was lifted, and only in 2016 were women actually incorporated into some combat units. This meant that many women veterans who were serving in combat zones in Afghanistan, Iraq, and earlier conflicts were not recognised as combat veterans, nor had they access to the resources and benefits available only to male combat veterans.

The cast was made up of both Aquila actors and veterans who had participated in an acting training and rehearsal programme with the company. The chorus was comprised of combat veterans, with the director, Desiree Sanchez, incorporating both tactical and drill movements into their choreography. This full production was then adapted again into four scenes, which were incorporated into a discussion programme staged at several institutions, including the Metropolitan Museum of Art in New York and the Cleveland Humanities Festival. While performing the production in Athens, this group partnered with a refugee theatre programme and the cast of a new adaptation influenced by Aeschylus' *Persians* entitled *We Are the Persians*, directed by Yolanda Markopoulou. This adaptation was described as a piece of documentary theatre in dialogue with Aeschylus' play, which used the ancient text, translated into modern Greek, to help teach the migrants the language and to inspire the telling of their own stories. The production brought together members of the refugee community in Athens – people from Syria, Iraq, Pakistan, and Afghanistan – to perform their stories of displacement.

The cast of *A Female Philoctetes* was in Athens in July of 2015, just as the Greek government ordered the banks shuttered and restrictions placed on cash withdrawals. Apart from the demonstrations and counter-demonstrations, Athens was uncharacteristically quiet, with many shops, bars, and cafes shuttered. Despite these difficult conditions, the performances of *A Female Philoctetes* went ahead, albeit to smaller audiences than normal. However, it was the wordless improvisational workshops, based on themes found in *Persians* and *Philoctetes*, between the cast members of the show and *We Are the Persians*, that opened a new chapter in the adaptation of Greek drama as an applied theatre project. These brought together people from different communities experiencing ongoing conflicts, working together on ancient material in the very place where that material was created. Veterans who had served in the wars in Iraq and Afghanistan were now working creatively alongside people who at one point may have been regarded as their enemy, or at least potentially hostile inhabitants of a country under foreign military occupation. Likewise, many of the refugee participants were performing with members of what had been an occupying force in the countries they had left, or representatives of American military power, with all the connotations associated with it. One workshop was particularly striking: a large former US Marine Corps officer who had served in Iraq and Afghanistan was partnered with a considerably smaller Pashtun man from Afghanistan and an Aquila actor. As the workshop, which was based on the theme of isolation, got underway, the Marine and the Afghan started to size each other up. Then the Afghan tried to push the Marine from his spot, and soon the two men were grappling until the Marine eventually pinned the Afghan man across his legs in a kneeling position. Yet the Afghan would not stop struggling to escape this wrestling grip, and the struggle continued, controlled and yet right on the edge of being more than a workshop and turning into a real conflict. Then it broke; the Marine cried out and ran into the theatre wings, and the Afghan ran the other way, the onlookers watching an empty stage infused with a kind of futile rage. Then both men, visibly emotional, walked towards each other slowly, and embraced.

What transpired in that workshop was something quite profound, inspired by a Greek text as an act of physical adaptation. The contextual frame of the classic work allowed these two men, perhaps former enemies, to express something communal about their relationship to the wars they had endured. While is it not possible to comment on whether this was therapeutic in any way, the format provided by this kind of applied adaptation allowed for something to transpire that seemed very empathetic. That night, these two men, accompanied by a large group of veterans, refugees, and artists, sat down to a meal together, talked, joked, laughed, and enjoyed each other's company, all based on a play that was first performed in that same city some 2,500 years earlier.

In the spring of 2017, a new veteran-performed work inspired by ancient texts, entitled *Our Trojan War*, was produced in New York and toured to five US states. This was produced by Aquila's *Warrior Chorus* project, which established three groups, in New York, Austin, and Los Angeles. Each group comprised around twelve veterans and was led by a veteran coordinator and a classics scholar. The groups met weekly to read and discuss classical texts and to develop their public programmes within their respective geographic locations. The Los Angeles group decided to focus on filmmaking and developed several short films adapted from Greek tragedy, which were screened at five public events followed by an audience discussion. The Austin group chose to develop readings based on political discourse and took their presentations to community centres and cultural organisations in and around Austin. In New York, the group wrote their own pieces based on reading Homer and Greek drama, and it was decided to develop a full production that interwove these pieces with selections of ancient texts including the *Iliad*, the *Odyssey*, *Oedipus Tyrannus*, *Antigone*, Aristophanes, Plato, and the *Aeneid*.

The aim of this approach was to create an adaptation that would include both ancient works and the new writings by veterans inspired by them. After the tumultuous US presidential election of 2016, the group felt that the mood in the country was not one of reflection about the recent wars; instead, there was a palpable sense of urgency about perceived abuses of democratic institutions and inflammatory rhetoric about immigrants, refugees, women, and minorities. Furthermore, the Trump campaign had quite callously used veteran causes to attempt to garner public support. While the Aquila programme veteran participants were well aware of the cynicism of this empty rhetoric, they also knew that they occupied something of a unique position in this cultural moment in having the ear of both sides of the ever-increasing political divide in the United States. It should be noted that the members of the programme in each of the three locations were a diverse group of people, who held a wide range of political, social, and religious views. Yet it was found that the ancient material acted as a contextual anchor for the kind of deep discourse on certain inflammatory issues that had become very polarised in social, print, and televised media.

For *Our Trojan War*, a theatrical frame was developed to create a world in which several ancient pieces could be staged. This was imagined as a raid on a house in a Middle Eastern country where a teacher and his daughter had been teaching in secret and hiding books, among them Greek classical texts. From the discovery of these books came the performance of both the ancient scenes and the modern works by the veterans. The main thrust of the piece was an exploration of the meaning of democracy, by addressing questions of hospitality, relationships with people from different cultures, the use of military power, and the deployment of classical works by American leaders from George Washington to Robert Fitzgerald Kennedy. After the performances, there were veteran-led audience discussions with several invited participants organised by the New York Veterans' Alliance and faculty from the Military College at West Point.

The Fidelity Discourse Applied

The final production was something of an experiment in adaptation and drew favourable reviews and audience responses. One piece, published online by the *New Yorker*, by Bard College ancient historian James Romm, used the production to explore some of the issues that surround adapting this kind of ancient material.[54] This article was not a review but a culture piece, the only critical remark being that the production was 'powerful'. Romm's commentary took a position that seemingly negated the validity of veterans appropriating ancient material to advance what he perceived as a political cause. The concept of modern veterans taking ancient material and using it to reflect their own experiences of war in Iraq and Afghanistan was questioned, and rather than regarding this as an example of the continuing relevance of ancient works for yet another audience, it was argued that this kind of interpretation inhibited the 'universality of the mythic material'.

The bulk of the article was a refutation of the work of psychiatrist Jonathan Shay and other scholars who have sought to show how reflections of combat trauma can be found in ancient literature, and it stated that 'For classical scholars, putting an emphasis on the material and physical aspects of war, taking the battles so literally, risks diminishing the mythic legacy of the Greeks.' But why would a focus on an important aspect of a poem like the *Iliad*, its frequent vivid descriptions of warfare and the effects it has on people, somehow diminish the ancient Greek text? And what is this 'mythic legacy of the Greeks', and just whom was this legacy bequeathed to? Can veterans not participate in that legacy too and find meaningful parallels between the ancient poetry and their own experiences? From the Persian Wars on, Athens in the fifth century was in a state of almost constant warfare, every adult male citizen had to serve in the military, and

[54] www.newyorker.com/culture/cultural-comment/a-misguided-impulse-to-update-the-greek-classics, accessed 15 June 2017. The original article included a paragraph on ways in which the experiences of ancient Greek warriors were not at all analogous to modern American service personnel, and stated that 'he [the ancient Greek warrior] was rarely forced to deal with foes of a different race, language, or religion, nor was he ever, at least in classical times, stranded in alien jungle or desert landscapes'. Many drew the editor's attention to Xenophon's *Anabasis*, an account of a classical Greek army stranded in Persia and fighting a foreign enemy. The article was subsequently corrected with a note. This is an example of how the fidelity discourse dictating and even ignoring the ancient evidence can be highly problematic.

the evacuation of Athens, long sieges, and the plague would have seriously affected the entire population. Throughout this time, Homer was taught and performed and continued to influence Greek drama. Furthermore, the continual reality of war must have been a major factor in the production and performance of classical Athenian drama, and we can see its reflections in every Greek play we have. No wonder people who have experienced war first-hand find powerful resonances in these works.

Romm's piece then focused on whether ancient Greek soldiers suffered any kind of combat trauma, a pertinent question to be sure and one that has been recently examined in detail.[55] Yet *Our Trojan War* contained no references or representations of combat trauma, unless one views the fact of being in a war zone as traumatic for soldiers and civilians alike. Here, the fidelity discourse reveals itself by inhibiting the understanding of different meanings in adapted ancient material. For some, like Romm, Greek epic poetry and drama are perceived as communicating a sense of universal suffering; therefore, to use it to highlight the suffering of veterans is culturally acceptable (this is analogous to *Theater of War*), whereas using these plays to explore the current state of American democracy, through the lens of a group who have traditionally not been afforded a voice in this kind of discourse, is not. To be sure, there is suffering aplenty in Greek drama, but this is not the only thing these plays are about. Furthermore, in accepting a psychological, therapy-based notion of tragedy, this article was engaging in the kind of cultural equivalency it condemned. Just like the works it wants to preserve and protect, the fidelity discourse is also subject to its own kind of adaptation in that it tends to reflect the current acceptable premises of the particular elite group engaged in its enforcement.

Perhaps the best articulation of the frustration at the attitudes found in Romm's article that was felt by many veterans who experienced the programme was expressed by Kristen Rouse, who served as a captain in the US Army and is now the Executive Director of the New York Veterans Alliance. As the main objective of *Our Trojan War* was to let the veteran's voice be heard, it seems only appropriate to reproduce a portion of her unpublished letter to the *New Yorker* here.

> As a veteran who served three combat tours in Afghanistan – a war that has raged on seeming autopilot for more than sixteen years now – I've grown accustomed to the American public's prevailing and persistent disinterest in

[55] Meineck and Konstan (2014).

our nation's longest and most expensive war. But now we have a classics scholar telling us that ancient masterpieces centered on ancient warfare, the rage of military leaders against each other, and warriors' long and arduous return home shouldn't be the domain of current-day combat veterans who are inviting a bored and disconnected American public to connect with our current conflict that has no end in sight – and to hear and understand anew these ancient lessons that apply equally today.

For those of us whose lives and families have been deeply impacted by America's wars and political leadership, this new production isn't about 'therapy.' We're not simply repackaging great literature in our tired military uniforms to feel better about ourselves. We are a new generation of veterans who are emerging as leaders, as writers, and as artists who have made it our lives' work to let our fellow Americans know the complexity and impacts of our current wars that Americans keep failing to connect with, and that none of this is new – these lessons applied as much to the ancient hoplite as to today's infantryman patrolling the mountains of Khost Province, Afghanistan. Our nation and our world have too much at stake right now for us to be silent, or to let classical literature remain as dusty books on the shelf for only academics to access and interpret for us.[56]

Epilogue

The original premise of this chapter was to describe and discuss the political aspects of adapting Greek drama. As a translator and director, I have been doing just that for many years alongside my career as a classics scholar. The two most pressing 'political' questions that persist are the application of the fidelity discourse as an instrument of class and elitism, and the issues that are raised whenever an adaptation moves into an overtly political area. In this chapter, I have tried to briefly unpack some of the main misconceptions surrounding the fidelity discourse and to illustrate a political/social applied approach to adaptation in Aquila's veteran public programming. New adaptations, novel ways to adapt ancient material, and fresh voices threaten the viability of the fidelity discourse. These same approaches can bring a type of misguided condemnation and criticism from some quarters of the academy that can, in turn, do great harm to the public's perception of these fledgling works. What we need instead is a more sophisticated methodology to better understand and appreciate the

[56] The focus of the *Warrior Chorus* is on providing a place of community for veterans, fostering a veteran/civilian dialogue, training and paying veterans to develop and lead their own programming, letting the veteran voice be heard directly, and trying to show the complexity of both the veteran experience and the effects of war on society.

process of adaptation and the reasons why Greek plays continue to attract artists, activists, and authors. To adapt a Greek play, which was itself already an adaptation, is an act of cultural adoption that can bring new perspectives and new audiences to the material. In the evolution of the reception and application of Greek drama in the modern world, to adapt *is* to survive. As Icke's Orestes says at the end of his adaptation of Aeschylus' *Oresteia,* what we need instead are 'different lenses pointing at the same thing at the same time and *seeing that thing differently.*'

CHAPTER 3

Translation and/as Adaptation

Lorna Hardwick

i: testimony

KLYTEMNESTRA: A great ox –
As they say –
Stands on my tongue.

As she begins to speak – the CHORUS all turn their heads to the right, to listen to her.

TRANSLATOR: Ndise ndayinkukhw' isikw' umlomo.
[A GREAT OX. . .
AS THEY SAY. . ..
STANDS ON MY TONGUE.] (Farber 2008, 22)[1]

Developments in translation theory and practice have made translation a more flexible and often heuristic tool for engaging with literature and with performance (Bassnett 2014). Recognition that translations are works in their own right as well as transmissions of ante-texts has been accompanied by greater understanding of the interrelationships between creativity and scholarship in the making and evaluation of translations. Moreover, the 'cultural turn' in translation studies has been characterised by attention to the way in which translation of works from other times, places, and languages is itself a form of reception and of cultural commentary.[2] Such commentary embraces the source text, the mediating texts, and the new work, bringing all of them into conversation in diverse cultural contexts that can sometimes be mutually hospitable, sometimes adversarial, and often embrace elements of both. The 'cultural turn' has been mirrored by a

[1] The lines are from the Watchman's opening speech in Aeschylus' *Agamemnon*, 1–39. The English words used by Farber are taken from Louis MacNeice's 1936 translation. Klytemnestra's further words in this opening sequence are taken from the English translation by Robert Fagles (1977).

[2] Bassnett (2014), 30–2.

'translation turn' in literary and cultural studies.[3] Both these 'turns' have also influenced the study of dramatic texts and performance. That field has experienced its own paradigm shifts, and the prominence accorded in recent scholarship to staging of plays has been described as a 'performative turn'.[4] This 'turn' highlights the distinctiveness of drama in relation to the broad field of translation norms. Expectations that translations of Greek tragedy should (or could) be evaluated according to the faithfulness of their relationship to a linguistically, culturally, and sometimes ideologically authoritative source text immediately raises problems for performance translation. These problems are not only in terms of theory (because belief in the immutable stability of text and interpretation has been eroded), but also in terms of practice, because fidelity to the ancient conditions of production would never be possible.[5] Performance is by definition ephemeral. As the playwright and theatre poet Blake Morrison put it: 'Writing for the stage is different from writing for the page: the effect has to be immediate, in the moment, and can't be dwelt on or revisited'.[6] The expectation is that drama translations have a limited life, needing renewal and rewriting for each new theatre generation.[7]

Furthermore, where performance is concerned, translation can never be solely a matter of the words in the acting script. Visual and physical aspects of expression and communication shape, and are shaped by, the interaction with words that is permitted and framed by theatre. Performance analysis has to include nonverbal sound (music, storms, lamentations, screams, groans, laughs) and must be sensitive to the impact on mood and direction of the gaze (for actors and spectators) that is contributed by lighting design, silhouettes, costume, and stage properties.[8]

[3] The work of Lawrence Venuti pioneered recognition of the historical and ideological invisibility of the translator in literary and cultural agency and the need for discussion of the agency of the translator (Venuti 1995, 1998, 2013). In developing that argument, Venuti also advocated an ethical obligation on the translator to signal difference, i.e. the linguistic and cultural distance between the ante-text and the receiving context.

[4] For discussion and further bibliography, see Hardwick 2005, 207–11.

[5] Even a scholar as sensitive to theatre issues as Michael Walton has had to frame his typology in philological rather than performance terms (Walton 2006, 181–4).

[6] Morrison (2010), 254. Commissioning a new translation can also offer the opportunity for director, translator, designer, and other practitioners to work together in creating the new performance. Such is the basis of adaptation.

[7] To say nothing of needing to be attuned to developments in scholarship. See further Hardwick (2010), 195–8, which discusses how a translation prepared by a scholar can act as a mediating text between an ancient play and a modern acting script.

[8] In Greek drama, stage properties notably include puppets (for instance to represent the dead children in *Medea*, or in the *Agamemnon* to convey visually and aurally how Cassandra's body and identity were manipulated; Hardwick (2007c), 313–14 with n. 14. For a discussion of costume in performance reception, see Wyles (2010).

The performing body, individual and group movement, dance, and gesture are all crucial to the energising effects of the bodily co-presence of players and spectators.[9] Video and multimedia of various kinds can often form part of the mise-en-scène for Greek drama (see further Campbell, Chapter 8, this volume), whether it is staged in the original Greek or in translation, and may function as a commentary on the words and action on the stage and/or as a further translational technique in alerting the spectators to resonances between the Greek context and that of subsequent events.[10] It is at the interfaces and interactions between translation and adaptation that modern productions of tragedy are remaking their connections between ancient and modern, and between performers and audiences.

Probing the nature and effects of those interrelationships in translations made for the stage, which are themselves adapted in the process of creating the performance, underlies the approach taken in this essay.[11] Writerly translation and practitioners' creativity work together. Innovative combination and recombination introduce as part of the creative process features such as imitation, allusion, quotation, excerpting, parody, pastiche, all of which signal cultural encounters of different kinds.[12] Particular translation excerpts can constitute raw material from which a playtext is fashioned (as is the case with the epigraph to this essay). Translation has increasingly taken a prominent place in the models of reception and performance analysis now used by scholars, alongside the categories of body, mimesis, memory, psyche, contingency, temporal orientation, and political potency.[13] To these may be added spatiality, an analytic tool that includes use of space and communication of location on and around the stage, situation of the playing space in the wider environment, and the 'outreach' of the performance culturally and globally.[14]

The verbal and visual aspects of translation to the stage are central to communication and interpretation of those resonances. David Johnston has summed up the situation of the theatre translator, who not only has to be a reader and a (re)writer but also an engaged spectator, creating a text

[9] Fischer-Lichte (2010); Montgomery Griffiths (2016).

[10] For example, in Katie Mitchell's 1999 production of Ted Hughes' version of *Agamemnon*, *The Home Guard*; see Hardwick (2005), 218–19. In Jane Montgomery Griffiths' production of Sophocles' *Electra* in the original Greek as the Cambridge Greek play, 2001, video clips showing Orestes and Electra as children appeared at key points (for performance documentation and reviews, see database ID no. 2639, www.open.ac.uk/arts/research/greekplays, accessed 2 February 2017).

[11] Cf. Hardwick (2013a). [12] Hardwick (2010), 194. [13] E. Hall (2010b).

[14] See the essays in Monaghan and Montgomery Griffiths (2016).

that 'will simultaneously move between and across different histories and geographies, locating and uprooting the historical and cultural imagination of the spectator in ways that seek to overcome the twin separations implied by aloofness and subjection'.[15] In discussing this insight, Susan Bassnett adds the gloss that '[the translation] is a point through which different dimensions of the text, both written and performative, can flow'.[16] As a result, Bassnett rightly sees translation for the theatre as a collaborative undertaking. In the examples that are discussed in this essay, I develop this point by showing how the concept of agency in performance creation has also to include all the key practitioners. Just as there is a tension between holistic analysis of the performance itself and the contribution of the translator/writer, so the designer, choreographer, composer, and musicians also shape the experience of the spectators and link outwards to the creative traditions of their own crafts.

Adaptation adds a further theoretical and practical layer to this mix. As with translation, recent scholarship and practice has pushed the limits of the concept, with the result that there is no longer a simple dichotomy between translation, which used to be thought of as an activity that *transmits* a text by transposing it from one language to another with the aim of preserving and communicating its essence, and adaptation, which was categorised as an activity that separated out and *altered* component parts of a text, even adding further material to produce a work that might still be a 'distant relative' of the source text but which differed from it in ways that were determined by its receiving context and media and were reflected in changes in the form, narrative, and idiom that was (dis) inherited from the ante-text. Like translation, adaptation brings with it its own forms of paramaterial (notes, commentaries, interviews) and raises issues about the agency of practitioners in shaping and realising the relationship between a particular adaptation and its forerunners and successors.

Adaptation theory in general has tended to put the emphasis on what is changed, what is marginalised or excised, and on the media, forms, and poetics through which the new version is created, and for whom it is created.[17] However, classical texts, and especially drama in performance, have not hitherto been embedded in the development of adaptation analysis to anything like the same extent as has classical material in the

[15] Johnston (2011), 19. [16] Bassnett (2013), 155.

[17] Hutcheon (2006). Hutcheon's has been the most influential study of adaptation but does not specifically engage with Greek tragedy.

recent developments in translation studies. In particular, there have not as yet been paradigm shifts in adaptation theory that correspond to the watersheds signalled by the 'cultural turn' in translation studies, the 'translation turn' in literary and performance studies, and the 'performative turn' in classical drama studies.[18]

Where classicists have considered adaptation and translation together, adaptation has sometimes been seen as a kind of 'second phase' that *follows* translation; as Constantinidis observes, drawing on Foley,

> 'Translations are routinely adapted by dramaturgs (including directors and commissioned authors). Some of these rewrites acculturate [a play] to such a degree that it loses its Greek manners of speech, gesture and thought. The Americanization of a Greek tragedy, for instance, usually serves its director's vision about which scenes and lines might be performable and appealing to audiences in the USA. And the entire process of adapting a Greek tragedy through rewrites, workshops or rehearsals repeatedly confirms the belief that no translation is necessarily performable just because it is faithful and readable.'[19]

Even this type of sequential model for the relationship between translation and adaptation adds two elements to the imperatives associated with staging: performability and appeal to the target audience.[20] It is a main aim of this essay to bring these together in order to explore what happens when translation and adaptation are seen as interdependent rather than consecutive phases of bringing Greek plays to the modern stage. To that end, I have chosen case studies that open up some of the most interesting interactions between translation and adaptation. Those interactions involve recontextualising and reconfiguring the ante-text and refining and extending the perceptual filters brought by staging.

[18] A partial exception might be the analyses that have probed the analogies between the adaptation of Greek drama in post-colonial contexts and diaspora theory (see Hardwick 2004 and essays in Hardwick and Gillespie 2007) but these affect notions of a Euro-centric 'classical tradition' rather than reshaping adaptation theory as such.

[19] Constantinidis (2016), 18; cf. Foley (2012), 6. Some critics and scholars take this disjunction further and challenge attempts to privilege the ancient text or to categorise adaptations as derivative. For example, Charles L. Mee asserts that 'there is no such thing as an original play' and uses the term 'remaking' to indicate how he combines aspects of an ancient tragedy with modern plays in order to speak to a new audience (www.charlesmee.org, quoted and discussed in Mee and Foley 2011, 9); see also Charles Mee's interview in this volume, Chapter 5. Fischer-Lichte (2014b) addresses related issues through the concept of *sparagmos*, or tearing apart (sc. of the ante-text).

[20] There are many examples of cases in which a performance concept imposed by a director on a pre-existing text has resulted in a disjunction between the translation/version and the staged adaptation. For example, Seamus Heaney's *Burial at Thebes*, a poetic rewriting of Sophocles' *Antigone*, was not well served by the director's approach when it premiered at the Abbey Theatre Dublin in 2004; see further Wilmer (2007); Hardwick (2007c).

Like translations, adaptations speak to one another as well as to the Greek works. In his thoughtful Introduction to a collection of essays on the reception of Aeschylus, Stratos Constantinidis discusses how translation reconstitutes and rearticulates meaning rather than transferring it intact from one language and its culture into another.[21] This activity is analogous to that of adaptation, which involves 'fitting of meaning' to a new setting or environment, particularly when a tragedy moves from the page to the stage or to another performance genre (such as opera) or to another mode or register (such as melodrama or parody or burlesque).[22] 'Remakes' can be seen as revisions of meaning, brought about when a play is re-envisioned to please and communicate with a different type or generation of spectators. Constantinidis gives as his example Terence's *Adelphoe*, which in the second century BCE was a remake of Menander's *Adelphoi* and/or Diphilus' *Adelphoi* from the late fourth century BCE.[23] That example serves as a very useful reminder that the tragedians of fifth-century Athens were themselves adapting and remaking myth.[24] Like the Greek plays, adaptations energise theatre to build and transform public imagination and community understanding of itself and others. An emerging – and in some respects surprising – feature of the adaptation/translation nexus is that adaptation can serve to preserve some features of the ante-text precisely because it confirms its viability in new contexts (both aesthetic and material). That is an aspect to which I will return at the end of this essay.

Nevertheless, the raw material provided by Greek tragedy in the translation/adaptation nexus brings its own complications. Some of these derive from the fifth-century BCE context; some have been added by subsequent cultural history and by scholarship. Privileging words-as-text can lead us to

[21] Constantinidis (2016), 5.

[22] Constantinidis (2016), 6, n. 13 helpfully distinguishes his approach from that in Hutcheon (2006), explaining how he has drawn on the insights of Sanders (2006), who emphasises ways in which adaptation can be a transpositional practice. It should also be noted that sometimes a particular translated text can so dominate that it comes almost to replace the source text as the touchstone of a particular work. For example, millions of readers have encountered Homer only in the translations of the *Iliad* and the *Odyssey* made by E. V. Rieu and published in the popular Penguin editions (1950, 1951). This phenomenon is less true of Greek tragedy because of the distinctiveness of performance and the mix of translation, adaptation, and remake. In terms of tragedy, 'iconic' is just as likely to be a term applied to a performance as a whole than to its constituent parts (script/star role/music). This will emerge from the examples discussed in the rest of the essay.

[23] Constantinidis (2016), 6, n. 14.

[24] Equally, the Homeric resonances and verbal allusions in tragedy were remade and transposed in the internal contexts of the plays (Goldhill 1997, 129–30). Athenaeus (*Deipnosophistae* VIII, 347e) refers to Aeschylus' remark that his plays were 'slices from Homer's great banquets'. The multifaceted dynamic of Homer reception in antiquity is discussed in Barchiesi (2015).

overlook the fact that the Greek tragedians were adapting and transposing myth, not translating it. Similar processes apply to reading and spectating. As Charles Martindale has put it, 'a "text" is never "just" itself . . . rather it is something that a reader reads, differently'.[25] Over the centuries the associations between tragedy and canonicity have intensified, with the result that adaptation can be seen as a divergent activity, presenting a challenge to norms of authenticity, authority, and authorship. The cultural freight attached to tragedy has brought with it a paradigm shift from its status as a popular and community art form in the ancient world to 'high' culture in the modern. Such constraining stereotypes have been challenged by recent research into the performance histories of plays, their pliability of form across genres, and their place in the social histories of culture.[26] As a result, scholars working in the field have to grapple with a cluster of partly overlapping explanatory frames which have constantly to be tested against the evidence provided by examples.[27]

In the next part of this essay, I look at three very different case studies, each of which informs and tests a particular aspect of my overall argument. I use the first case study, a short film of the opening sequence of Aeschylus' *Agamemnon*, to identify some of the issues involved in re-envisioning the relationship between text, translation, medium, and adaptation aesthetic. That discussion in turn raises questions about the creative agencies involved in negotiating the translation/adaptation nexus, and I pursue this by using paramaterial as a source for the insights of director and designer. The longer case study that follows, an analysis of Yaël Farber's *Molora*, aims to bring together those threads in a more holistic way by investigating the relationship between translation, adaptation, formal elements, and wider performance context. Finally, I look briefly at some trends in performance and scholarship that bring adaptation into a 'ring-composition' relationship with the ancient texts and performances.

Destabilising Expectations: Language, Translation, Medium, and Audience

Study of the relationship between translation and adaptation in performance practice reveals overlapping, intersections, and tangential encounters between the categories. Those encounters can provide a potentially abrasive mix or produce a rewarding synergy. Furthermore, the contexts in

[25] Martindale (2006), 2–3. [26] Hall, Macintosh, and Wrigley (2004); Hall and Macintosh (2005).
[27] See Hardwick (2018), 24 and (2019), 13–15.

which these encounters take place are constantly developing. This brings me to the first of my case studies, one which challenges some of the expectations associated with a Greek text and its translation and adaptation. A short film was released online in 2017, presenting a seven-minute performance of the Watchman's scene that opens Aeschylus' *Agamemnon* (lines 1–39).[28] The film was the first in a series developed by a new company called Barefaced Greek.[29] The aim of the company's project is to create enhanced digital resources for access to and study of classical plays, especially by the 'YouTube generation'.[30] The scene was set at night on the flat roof of a high-rise building in a large city from which the Watchman looked down on a main thoroughfare and other buildings, some of which were lit and shown silhouetted on the skyline. He was bearded and wore a dark trench coat, woolly hat, and fingerless mittens, had a sleeping blanket and played with dice. He poured liquid from a thermos flask. He had a hand lantern and warmed his hands at a brazier. His appearance was that of a well-equipped rough-sleeper in twenty-first-century London. The film was shot in high definition colour. During the edit process a sepia filter was added to the colour grading.[31] Changes in the perspectives brought to the sequence were enhanced by the flickering lights in the cityscape.

The actor (Leon Scott) spoke the lines in Greek and there were subtitles in English on the screen. The actor involved the viewer by sometimes speaking directly to camera, with close-ups of his facial expression (for instance, when saying that he was 'crouched like some watch-dog'). This is a form of direct address to the off-stage spectators that was unusual in tragedy. When addressing the gods he lay down and looked either contemplatively at the sky or at the ground, in a posture that recalled prostration. When he at last spotted the beacon fire that signified that Troy had fallen, his dance movements resonated not just with musical

[28] *The Watchman*, the first in a series of short films devised and produced by the Barefaced Greek company, featuring Leon Scott as the Watchman, produced by Mairin O'Hagin, directed by Helen Eastman, music composed by Ben Pearson. See www.youtube.com/watch?v=Vh6gN8nQWSk (accessed 29 January 2017).

[29] www.barefacedgreek.co.uk (accessed 19 March 2017). The website will be developed to provide information and links to future films in the project.

[30] I thank the director Helen Eastman for providing background information on the aims and funding of the project (personal communication, 28 February 2017). Initial financial support came from organisations dedicated to promoting and disseminating classics (the Gilbert Murray Trust, the Hellenic Society, the Oxford University Classics Faculty) and from a research institute (the Archive of Performances of Greek and Roman Drama, University of Oxford), but it is planned that further phases of the project will also involve crowdfunding.

[31] Depending on the specification and situation of the receiving technology, the colour mix varies.

theatre but with a celebration by a football fan. The performance concept of this gripping film defied fixed categories. It exploited translation, transposition, and adaptation to communicate directly to viewers. It used Aeschylus' Greek text and yet also aimed to be accessible to viewers who had never heard of Aeschylus or of the *Oresteia*. The use of subtitles is not only a method of reaching viewers who do not know Greek, it also exploits the dominance of hand-held devices, whose users are habituated to seeing captions. Moreover, the captions can be added in multiple languages, so the short film exploits the international reach of modern technology to promote awareness and understanding of the ancient Greek text to a new demographic. An additional aspect of this particular example was that its screening via YouTube enabled viewers to encounter other examples of Greek drama, with which the film was clustered by YouTube. Most notably these included clips from Tony Harrison's version of the *Oresteia* (see the case study below, pp. 120–3), which is not easily available on DVD or video in the UK.

The ways in which the short film *The Watchman* pushes against some of the norms of translation and adaptation thus act as a prompt for revisiting how the aims, methods, and interpretative insights of creative practitioners might inform and revise the models used in scholarship. In terms of scholarship, the energising of contemporary theatre aesthetics through the performances of tragedy has been the concern both of classical reception studies and theatre studies.[32] In terms of practice, Greek plays and their close adaptations have almost become a *rite de passage* in the careers of young directors as well as highpoints in the careers of established practitioners. Much of the most interesting recent scholarship brings together performance and literary studies.[33] The move has been away from a binary distinction between text and performance and towards recognition of the ways in which theatrical performances 'shape perceptions of textuality'.[34] These perceptions recognise the embodiment in the performance text of material and physical experiences outside and beyond the written and spoken word.[35] The balance struck between these elements by contempo-

[32] Ioannidou (2017), 5, n. 7, with bibliography.

[33] For a critical assessment that questions the extent of this 'turn', see Perris (2010).

[34] Ioannidou (2017), 6.

[35] Perceptions of performance textuality are reflected both in the scholarship associated with visual and musical analysis (Heck 1999; Ferrario 2016) and in performance scholarship (Fischer-Lichte 2010; Ioannidou 2017).

rary productions is partly shaped by commissioning and commercial pressures but is usually dominated by the director's concept.[36]

Practitioners' Voices 1: The Director's Perspective

From these practitioner-led and scholarly trends[37] it follows that the perceptions of theatre practitioners provide important evidence for scholars.[38] The director Helen Eastman set out and addressed some of the main issues in an extended interview published in a collection of essays that probed the dialogical relationships between past and present.[39] Three main points relate closely to the key issues of adaptation summarised in the Introduction to this volume. Firstly, Eastman commented on the distinctions between new texts that are created by dramatists and those created by poets. She notably reversed the conventional sequence of 'page to stage' by pointing out that in practice 'stage to page' is equally likely:

> A dramatist is often trying to solve the play for a modern audience dramatically, and is trying to reconstruct it. [...] poetic translations very rarely restructure [...] Quite a lot of the texts you read, you have to remember, are constructed on the page after they've been developed in rehearsal [...] there are very few dramatists who don't attempt solutions to what they think the problems are with Greek tragedy for contemporary audiences. As a result they make other plays. (Eastman [2013] 32)

On audience engagement, Eastman commented on how changes of title can attract new audiences, and also pointed to the indirect and open-ended ways in which theatre can be transformative:

36 See Hardwick (2015) for discussion of tensions between these aspects.

37 The open-access e-journal *Practitioners' Voices in Classical Reception Research* was established to promote understanding of artistic, literary, and theatre creativity in the reception of Greek and Roman texts and material culture (www.open.ac.uk/arts/researchpvrcs, accessed 20 March 2017).

38 For a critical evaluation of the value of interviews with practitioners as part of classical reception research, see Burke and Innes (2004, rev. 2007). To interviews as a source of evidence should be added other paramaterial, such as prefaces. The cognate research discipline of book history also has an important role in identifying the texts, translations, and versions available to playwrights and practitioners at particular times. Studies of intertextuality need to take account of mediating texts as well as of direct dialogue between ancient and modern. Analysis of intertextuality has its performance counterpart in theatre history and semiotic comparative analysis.

39 Eastman (2013). The interview on which the published version was based was recorded in 2009. Eastman studied classics and English at Oxford and while still an undergraduate took a production of Seamus Heaney's *The Cure at Troy*, a version of Sophocles' *Philoctetes*, to the Edinburgh Festival Fringe (her production was revived many times from 1999 to 2005). She subsequently trained as a theatre director at LAMDA and later founded her own company. She also researched a doctoral thesis (King's College, London) focused on the Northern Broadsides theatre company.

> it's interesting whether a production's aiming at a very specific political message or whether it's aiming at an emotional transformation. In some ways it's not transformative for us to empathize in the theatre with certain characters, it doesn't necessarily make us go out and live our life in a different way or change things but it does keep us emotionally alive and responding communally to fundamental human stories. (Eastman 2013, 34)

Discussing her experiences of working in different environments and theatre spaces, Eastman contrasted ancient and modern experience and suggested that the textuality of performance is shaped by configuration of the playing space,[40] by landscape and setting, and by light and dark:

> The open air thing is really interesting because although, yes, you're further away from the performers and they're wearing masks, importantly you can all see each other as an audience . . . The moment somebody puts you in the dark, it invites you to be individualistic . . . It invites you to be passive . . . So yes, you're further away in a Greek theatre . . . but you are very visually part of a group in a way that most modern theatres manage to prevent. (Eastman 2013, 36)

Practitioners' Voices 2: Writer and Designer Collaboration in Text and Performance: The Mask

My next example probes different aspects of how the forms and mythical narratives of Greek tragedy interact through translation and adaptation for modern performance contexts. The focus is on how a central feature of ancient performance, the mask, interacts with the modern creativity of the designer in bringing a translated and adapted text to the stage. This example shows how the words that are the stuff of translation were brought into a relationship with the visual and physical properties of performance in a production that has often been cited as iconic in modern performance reception. On 28 November 1981, Tony Harrison's translation of the *Oresteia* was performed in the Olivier Theatre at the National Theatre in London, directed by Peter Hall, with music composed by Harrison Birtwistle.[41] The same company performed the play in July 1982 in the

[40] For instance, in modern terms, proscenium arch, thrust stage, theatre in the round, and promenade theatre have different implications for directing the spectator's gaze, for how the performers relate to one another, and for how the spectators relate both to the performers and to each other.

[41] The production has been documented in detail by the Archive of Performances of Greek and Roman Drama (www.apgrd.ox.ac.uk) and the Open University's Classical Reception Project Greek drama database (www.open.ac.uk/arts/research/greekplays, database ID number 207, last accessed 4 February 2017), which includes information on critical reviews.

Greek theatre at Epidauros.[42] Harrison added a note to the published text: '*This text is written to be performed, a rhythmic libretto for masks, music, and an all-male company.*'[43] My concern here is with the distinctive contribution of the designer, Jocelyn Herbert, and with how this collaboration was viewed by the translator, Harrison.[44] To explore the collaborative aspects of the creation of performance I draw extensively on paramaterial as well as text and design.[45]

Jocelyn Herbert (1917–2003) was associated with productions of a considerable number of Harrison's plays, translations, adaptations, and creative versions, including *The Trackers of Oxyrhynchus* (1988) and *Square Rounds* (1992), as well as the *Oresteia*.[46] After the publication of her *Theatre Workbook* (Herbert 1993), she also worked on other classically orientated material, with Harrison's *The Kaisers of Carnuntum* (1995, performed in a Roman amphitheatre near Vienna), *The Labourers of Herakles* (1995, Delphi), and the film-poem *Prometheus* (Channel 4 TV, 1997). In the Preface to Herbert's *Workbook*, her editor Cathy Courtney commented on the comparative lack of attention previously given to theatre design, especially in its creative relationship with others in the creative process:

> There are countless books on actors and directors but virtually none on the contribution of the designer, whose role is little understood and almost never discussed by audiences and critics ... This *Workbook* tries to recreate a little of the chemistry that at its best flows between director, designer and writer through the process of bringing a play to the stage, and to show how deeply the design may influence the production values as a whole.[47]

[42] The cast list of Chorus members featured many actors who have been extensively associated with productions of Greek tragedy and comedy, including Greg Hicks, Tony Robinson, and Barrie Rutter.

[43] Harrison (1985), 187 (italics in original). The writing of the translation was a ten-year enterprise. In a letter to Peter Hall dated 22 December 1975, Harrison observed that, although he had worked through the Greek text, commentaries, and other translations, he could not progress in isolation from the direction and the performance concept; see Harrison (1991), discussed in Bassnett (2014), 155.

[44] Herbert studied painting in Paris and then theatre design at the Slade School of Fine Art. She then joined the London Theatre Studio in 1936 but her work was interrupted by the Second World War and by bringing up her four young children. In 1956 she joined the English Stage Company at the Royal Court Theatre and continued her work as a designer to an advanced age.

[45] For the importance of collaboration in the creative process, see n. 6 above. For the range and importance of paramaterial, see n. 38 above.

[46] See, respectively, Herbert (1993), 129–33, 135–7 and 118–27. The archive of Herbert's work is housed at Wimbledon College of Art, University of the Arts, London. See www.jocelynherbert.org (accessed 1 February 2017).

[47] The director Peter Hall also gave an account of his work with Harrison and Birtwistle, and of the Chorus and mask rehearsals; see P. Hall (1983).

Tony Harrison has acknowledged the distinctive contribution of Herbert's approach to design and its considerable influence on him. He pointed out how her commitment to words helped her to understand that Greek theatre created its strongest effects by *not* illustrating the text. This ensured that design was not subservient to the text but developed its own aesthetic in conversation with the text. He went on to explain how Herbert's insights and the resulting symbiosis between words and visuals was crucial to the use of masks in the play and to understanding the relationship of this to form:

> The discovery we made about what is called *stichomythia* in Greek tragedy, formally matched pairs of question and answer which are at the heart of the plays and have a great bearing on the use of masks and also the style of the language ... Actors tend to look on these exchanges as a bit of 'real' dialogue and their instinct is to play them naturalistically. It doesn't work like that ... What we discovered was that the *stichomythia* represented a kind of formal 'gear change' in which the mask could have its emotion turned from one colour to another.[48]

Herbert's reflections on the processes of creating the *Oresteia* production add practical elements to Harrison's analysis, but from her different starting point she also focuses on the formal conventions of the plays: 'In all the Greek tragedies, none of the violence or bloodletting is ever shown on the stage; it all happens offstage and the audience is told about it. A mask allows the text to emerge more fully and gets rid of the very human face contortions which, quite naturally, happen when an actor describes scenes of horror.'[49] She also comments on the importance of the physical and material space for the staging: 'The *Agamemnon* needs a palace behind the walls of which all the terrible things happen.'[50] The nature of the theatre space also shaped her design. She notes that for the indoor set at the Olivier she worked with the shape of the auditorium, while for the staging in the ancient outdoor theatre at Epidauros she 'made a huge doorway and façade of what looked like the stones of Epidauros with a curtain at the back and a platform in front with steps leading down to the ground. It was

[48] Herbert (1993), 230. The example given by Harrison was the Herald's speech and exchanges with the Chorus in the *Agamemnon* (503–680) in which he moves from conveying elation at the victory to the bad news of the wrecked ships and losses on the homeward voyage.

[49] Herbert (1993), 120. [50] Herbert (1993), 119.

about twenty five feet high and the scale was marvellous . . . Harry Birtwistle's music sounded quite beautiful in that space.'[51] It is as if Herbert's collaboration with Harrison and Hall involved a triple-framed translation – not just from language to language but also back to the performance conventions of the Greek and outwards to the physical environments of the performances.[52]

The texture of the Harrison/Hall/Herbert *Oresteia* raises intriguing questions about the trajectory away from and towards Aeschylus. It is still common to find open or covert assumptions that in modern performance translation is likely to be (or should be) grounded in the ancient text, while staging allows for a freer and perhaps more ideologically oriented adaptation, in tune with modern audiences and theatre spaces.[53] However, in the case of this *Oresteia*, the acting script, although written by a poet well-schooled in Greek, moved its rhythms and idiom away from the ancient, whereas the design, and especially the masks, grounded the performance in the forms and conventions of ancient tragedy. It was the interaction between the two that used ancient theatre conventions to avoid the naturalism that a modern translation might have prompted. Thus, design was as influential as verbal idiom in setting the tone and register of the performance.

Translation and Adaptation in Symbiosis

In discussing the potential of theatre to bring both political and emotional transformation, Helen Eastman cited Yaël Farber's *Molora*, a version of the *Oresteia*, which communicates a self-conscious recognition that translation is embedded in adaptation.[54] The cultural theorist and novelist Ngũgĩ wa Thiong'o has pointed out how translation is 'the language of languages. It opens the gates of national and linguistic prisons. It is thus one of the most important allies of world literature and global consciousness.' Ngũgĩ calls

[51] Herbert (1993), 126. A TV film 'The Oresteia at Epidauros' was shown on Channel Four in the UK on 5 October 1983. The filming followed the company from its arrival in Greece to the final performance. See www.youtube.com/watch?v=qSRB_b2YcN4 (accessed 22 March 2017).

[52] Interestingly, it was the relationship between performance and design that attracted most critical acclaim. The words of Harrison's translation came in for some criticism, as did the tones of the delivery: the theatre critic Martin Esslin commented in *Plays and Players*, January 1982: 'Tony Harrison is a brilliant translator and a fine poet. But the idiom he has couched the Aeschylean text in is very peculiar . . . somebody, translator or director, has made the decision to let the play be spoken in a kind of stage North of England hybrid Lancashire-Yorkshire accent with a hint of the Beatles.'

[53] Jenkins (2015), 25.

[54] Published text 2008, preceded by an extensive performance history.

for an understanding of 'interactive connections and their mutual impact in the local and global space', which he thinks may also mean 'the act of reading becoming a process of self-examination'.[55] Those insights provide an unwitting comment on Farber's play and its international performance and reception.[56] *Molora* was based on Aeschylus' *Oresteia* and is described in the published text as 'created and adapted' by Yaël Farber. The paramaterial at the front of the text includes a list of the translations of *Agamemnon*, *Libation Bearers*, *Electra* (Sophocles) and *Electra* (Euripides). Quotations and excerpts from all of these were used in the play.[57] Many of these are also flagged up in footnotes. Material from Euripides' *Iphigenia in Aulis* and Jean-Paul Sartre's *Les Mouches* (*The Flies*) has also been identified, along with Shakespeare's *Merchant of Venice* and the biblical books Genesis and Exodus.[58]

The list of acknowledgements in the published text of *Molora* also includes the translations into Xhosa (by Bongeka MPongwana) and vernacular translations contributed by cast members.[59] The Foreword (by Farber) and the short introduction 'The Power of Speech' (by Sophie Nield) amplify this. Farber comments that

> The ancient *Oresteia* trilogy tells the story of the rightful heirs to the House of Atreus, dispossessed of their inheritance ... The premise of this ancient story was striking to me as a powerful canvas on which to explore the history of dispossession, violence and human-rights violations in the country I grew up in [sc. South Africa]. I had long been interested in ... the choices facing those shattered by the past. *Molora* is an examination of the spirals of violence begat by vengeance, and the breaking of such cycles by the ordinary man ... *Molora* (the Sesotho word for 'ash') is the truth we must all return to, regardless of what faith, race or clan we hail from. (Farber 2008, 7–8)

The Foreword is followed by Nield's observations. These make specific connections between the events enacted in the play and the recent political

[55] Ngũgĩ (2012), 61.

[56] The performance history of *Molora* dates from its premiere at the Grahamstown Festival, Eastern Cape, South Africa in 2003. The performance in Oxford, UK, of 14 June 2007 is extensively documented and analysed at www.open.ac.uk/arts/research/greekplays (database ID number 2797, last accessed 2 February 2017). On *Molora*, see also Steinmeyer, Chapter 11, this volume.

[57] Farber (2008), 16.

[58] Van Zyl Smit (2010), 130. Van Zyl Smit suggests that Farber's emphasis on the role of the people in achieving resolution is adopted from Sartre.

[59] The role of the interpreter in *Molora* reflects the practice of the South African Truth and Reconciliation Committee hearings, in which people testified in the language of their choice, so every participant was by turns 'insider' and 'outsider'. Cf. the approach used by Dorinda Hulton in her 2004 production of the *Agamemnon* in Wolverhampton, UK (discussed in Hardwick 2007c).

conditions in South Africa. She starts by describing how in the play a human being is subjected to torture by the 'wet bag' technique, in which the person is handcuffed and a wet bag applied to their face so that they begin to suffocate. This also prevents speech, and the victim is denied the right to be heard. Nield quotes the Chair of the South African Truth and Reconciliation Commission (TRC), Archbishop Desmond Tutu, on the commitment enshrined in the TRC to *ubantu*, a Bantu word denoting the philosophy of being human, being open and affirmative of others, knowing that humans belong in a greater whole and are diminished when others are humiliated, tortured, or oppressed.[60] Nield uses this concept and the belief that a person is 'a person through other persons' to make the claim that 'the theatre represents the world to us . . . the characters stand in for and speak to us all . . . We can find reconciliation in the theatre.'

These are large claims. Betine Van Zyl Smit (2010) has made a detailed study of how *Molora* was part of an extensive South African theatrical engagement with the myth cycle of the house of Atreus. She identified differences between the handling and reading of the myth pre- and post-apartheid, demonstrating how the final settlement depicted in the *Oresteia* resonated with the aims of the Truth and Reconciliation Commission and contributed to a political theatre that, by recognising suffering and its place in the cultural memory, also sought to reconcile past enemies.

That context is, however, only part of Farber's dramatic strategy in *Molora*. Translation provides a bridge both between ancient and modern, via quotation and adaptation from the Greek, and between different modern ethnic and cultural traditions. Adaptation involved some selection and reworking of the myth, including interweaving of different ancient sources. The result was a performance in which virtually no one, on stage or in the audience, would understand everything that was being said or enacted because they were unlikely to be familiar with all the languages used.[61] This combination of unknowing and knowing audiences, within the play and in the off-stage spectators, created an environment in which everyone was open to transformation of their knowledge and understanding but was not tempted into thinking they had understood everything. Translation and adaptation worked together in the way in which Greek theatrical forms – prologue, *agon*, messenger speech, and Chorus – were used in the play to create an aesthetic in which an encounter could take place.

60 Farber (2008), 10.

61 There are eleven official languages in post-apartheid South Africa.

The Chorus was particularly important, both because of the associations of its members and in how it related to the action of the play. At the very beginning, a Xhosa woman moved from the audience into the performance space. Her dress was that of an elderly woman from the rural Transkei. She had a blanket round her shoulders and clay on her face. She dragged away a plastic covering to reveal a red earthen floor, in the centre of which was a grave. She then picked up a traditional calabash bow and sang in Xhosa: *Ho laphal'igazi* ('Blood has been spilt here').[62] She was then joined by the other Chorus members who moved from among the audience on to the playing space. The seven members of the Chorus were actors and musicians from the Ngqoko Cultural Group, six of whom were female, and one male. Their instruments provided the live music for the performance.[63] They were witnesses to the action, sang and chanted in the vernacular, and participated in some of the action (for example, as midwives assisting Klytemnestra when in her dream she gave birth to a snake). Like the Elders of Argos in Aeschylus, they were custodians of cultural memory.

Translation and adaptation were thus enmeshed, combining to create a rich and thickly layered performance. Performance analysis similarly requires 'thick' models that take account of the layers of cultural, literary, and theatre contexts that underlie both theatre practice and scholars' search for interpretation and meaning.[64] The aesthetic of the play and its context in relationship to the Truth and Reconciliation Commission combined to create an art work that displayed heightened receptivity and required matching sensibilities from its audiences.

Future Trends: The Postdramatic and Beyond

The determination to avoid naturalism discussed by Herbert (see above) opens up a perhaps unexpected route for comparison with the theories of performance that have been developed in respect of postdramatic theatre

[62] Quoted from the stage directions in Farber (2008), 20.

[63] Instruments included the *uHadi* (percussion bow) and the *inking* (friction bow).

[64] 'Thick' is a term borrowed by classicists and performance scholars from anthropology, especially the 'thick description' conceptualised by Clifford Geertz (Geertz 1993). 'Thick' images a combination of sectional and layered analyses and recognition of their interactions. Geertz argued that cultural phenomena are embedded in complex communication systems and that individual examples have to be deciphered in terms of their relationships to these wider systems. This in turn raises issues about the assumptions made within cultural systems and brought by those who seek to analyse them. My discussion aims to build on the notion of 'thickness' by relating thick description to 'thick' analysis of adaptations in performance. For discussion of 'thick' in relation to translation studies, see Appiah (1993).

and its enactment of tragic experience. In his study of tragedy and dramatic theatre, Hans-Thies Lehmann has discussed production concepts that marginalise or exclude character and naturalism while privileging image, sound, and affect, as they explore the pliability of myth in the late twentieth- and early twenty-first centuries.[65] Suggestions that this trend marks (yet another) demise for Greek tragedy have been challenged by practitioners and scholars who argue that the worldview generated by postdramatic theatre and the concerns of Greek tragedy in many respects converge. For example, Paul Monaghan has cited the Dood Paard company's observations on their website that their productions embody the actors' attempt to relate to the world of the present and that every production asks the questions 'what do we know? what is our situation and what do we think?'; Monaghan also argues that this is the reason why Dood Paard, and others, turn again to the Greek plays which address analogous questions.[66] 'Thick' analysis of the mutually enhancing relationship between translation and adaptation informs analysis of postdramatic tragedy, especially when it illuminates the palimpsestic aesthetic created in performing plays that draw not only on the Greek texts but also on intervening mediations. Examples include Sarah Kane's *Phaedra's Love* and the Wooster Group's *To You, the Birdie!* The latter takes Racine's *Phèdre* as its initial springboard but non-teleologically exploits Euripides' *Hippolytus* to challenge the French neoclassical aesthetic.[67]

The relationship between translation, translation for the stage, and adaptation, in addition to the relationships that each has with the Greek texts and performance contexts as well as with each other, is also at the hub of larger theoretical issues. Two of these seem to me to be especially important and to warrant further research and debate. The first is the contribution of translations and adaptations of tragedy to an understanding of temporal-spatial relationships, for example as conceptualised in Bakhtin's notion of the

[65] Lehmann (2006).

[66] Monaghan (2016), 216. Monaghan's hypothesis that, despite differences between ancient and postdramatic dramaturgies, some aspects of the contemporary aesthetic can resonate with some aspects of tragedy is based on his analysis of Aeschylus (Monaghan 2016, 251). Further work is needed to assess this and to test its viability in terms of the other tragedians. Emma Cole's recent monograph in the Oxford University Press Classical Presences series takes the investigation further (E. Cole 2019). I am grateful to Dr Cole for information and discussion about her research in advance of publication.

[67] For documentation of performances, see www.open.ac.uk/arts/research/greekplays, database ID 2640 (*To You, the Birdie!* accessed 20 March 2017) and 869, 2633, 2757 (*Phaedra's Love*, accessed 20 March 2017). For detailed analysis of these and other postdramatic approaches to Greek tragedy, see Cole (2019).

chronotope.[68] David Wiles has discussed how Bakhtin's insistence that space and time are not just Kantian modes of cognition but have a more concrete, historical existence opens the way to understanding how Greek tragedy and its reception performs relationships in spaces that have their own history.[69] Wiles also suggests that the intersections between mythological and historical time and place encountered in tragedy and its reception provide a way of engaging with post-Enlightenment paradigms without denying the historical force of the ideas of the Enlightenment.[70] Thus, recreations of Greek plays help participants, spectators, and critics both to be a part of their own world and to see it from outside. Examples of the relationship between translation and adaptation at key moments of heightened receptivity, such as those discussed in this essay, and perhaps especially the role of formal elements in holding in tension the ancient and modern imperatives, provide some raw material for remodelling the temporal-spatial aspects of performance reception (and by extension of classical receptions more broadly).

The second issue that has been lurking at several points beneath the surface of my discussion is that of repression. There are many positive ways in which translation and adaptation transpose the forms, content, and narratives of tragedy, and create links between Athenian and subsequent patterns of thought (including disjunctions in understanding and the paradigm shifts that may result from these). Much reception scholarship is focused on those continuities and discontinuities and the ways in which they are mediated into subsequent work. However, reception can also involve erosion. Although texts and performance can be 'sticky' in that they retain and transmit mediations and accretions, they are also overtly and covertly selective. Chiara Thumiger has characterised this as 'an experience of loss and oblivion'.[71]

Classicists have discussed extensively how the reworking of myth in the Athenian tragedies of the fifth century BCE involves displacement of issues to another time and another place, allowing transformation of understanding through critical distance.[72] Simon Goldhill has pointed to ways in which both Athenian tragedy and its subsequent stagings and receptions

[68] See Monaghan (2016), 13–14 for discussion of how the concept relates to Kant's and Einstein's ways of looking at the world and at how experience and cognition are framed and communicated.

[69] Wiles (2016), 96.

[70] Wiles (2016), 103–4.

[71] Thumiger (2013), 39. I discuss this issue in Hardwick (2019).

[72] Easterling (1997b), 171–2.

operate through what he calls 'the dynamics of distance': '[tragedy] is set in other places at other times and involves other people', but nevertheless making a detour via tragedy's otherness enables the discovery that a Greek play 'turns out to be about ourselves'.[73] This adds a classicist's focus on temporality to the emphasis on spatiality in the theatre translation scholar David Johnston's view that theatre translation is a 'mobile practice, in which nothing can be fixed, because not only are languages and cultures different but so also are theatre systems, including conventions of performance and audience expectations'.[74]

The multiple and dense shadings of translation and adaptation in subsequent times can work together to *reconnect* the present and the past, overcoming the erosion of links that is a feature of the intervening cultural displacements. Reconnection of past and present paradoxically allows the reinstallation of critical distance and hence the transformation of sensibilities and understanding. In its wider context, the dynamics of translation and adaptation of Greek tragedy also highlights watersheds in perceptions of the relationship between the traditional classical canon and new creative work, and indicates how the paradigms, vocabulary, and grammar of critical and affective reception are changing, both among scholars and critics and among the wider public. The heightened receptivity displayed in iconic theatre performances, in the associated creative processes, and through the scholarly analyses they provoke is enhanced by sensitivity to the interplay between translation and adaptation.[75]

Translation and adaptation operate symbiotically at moments of heightened receptivity, both within a play and in its immediate context of production, as well as in subsequent contexts of performance and reception. Heightened receptivities are transformative both within the performance and in the subsequent effects on the spectators and the public imagination. Performance creation processes as diverse as those of the *Oresteia* of Harrison, Hall, and Herbert, the *Molora* of Yaël Farber and the Ngqoko Cultural Group, and the postdramatic rewritings of tragedy can all contribute to revised models of receptivity of the tragic experience.

[73] Goldhill's observations (Goldhill 2007, 125–7, 151) are also discussed in Monaghan (2016), 279, in relation to postdramatic theatre.

[74] Johnston (2011), discussed in Bassnett (2014), 154–5. For discussion of audience expectations, see Hardwick (2013b). For case studies of the geographical and cultural scope of modern performances of translations and adaptation of Greek tragedy, see Mee and Foley (2011).

[75] The relationship between specific appropriations and times of heightened receptivity is not confined to Greek tragedy. See further Haubold (2013), 21–3, with bibliography.

Such models will also carry implications for studies of the construction of cultural memory (including disjunctions and inventions) and the associated shifts in epistemologies, emotional sensibilities, and intelligence. Those studies will in their turn inform current and shape future conceptions of what it is to be human.

CHAPTER 4

Adaptation as a Love Affair
The Ethics of Directing the Greeks

Avra Sidiropoulou

> The integral authority of the classic is such that it can absorb without loss of identity the millennial incursions upon it, the accretions to it, of commentary, of translations, of enacted variations.
>
> (Steiner 1984, 296–7)

> A classic is a work which relegates the noise of the present to a background hum, which at the same time the classics cannot exist without.
>
> (Calvino 2000, 8)

> I'm faithful to the texts; I invent nothing. Our duty as directors is to be good readers.
>
> (Mnouchkine 1992)

First Impressions

Adaptation, argued Wooster Group's iconoclastic director Liz LeCompte in an interview, is 'when you take something familiar, something you know, or think you know, subject it to every conceivable transgression of interpretation and form, and return it to you illuminated and deepened'.[1] In LeCompte's nonchalant definition, the words 'transgression' and 'illuminated' co-exist unapologetically, as if to soothe any feeling of anxiety or guilt that the very term 'adaptation' has come to generate.

This chapter makes the case that adaptation is a vital and loving companion to any dramatic work. New versions of the canon serve to perpetuate its established value. In the case of Greek tragedy, they can guarantee its longevity, providing a continuous acknowledgement of its merit and relevance. At their best, they elucidate the ancient texts anew, offering fresh insights and stimulating new reactions in spectators. But even at their weakest, revisionist readings contribute additional

[1] Quoted in Kramer (2007), 49.

perspectives to the ongoing discussion on fidelity, betrayal, and the ethics of directing. Part of this discussion is parochially attached to a kind of marital discourse when, ideally, the encounter of text and performance should be fuelled by excitement, passion, and surprise. In my essay, I will address some recurrent issues in adaptation studies from the point of view of staging. With references to some emblematic productions of Greek tragedy,[2] I will try to illustrate that adaptation is no hostile activity (at least not intentionally so), no attack on a vulnerable source that must remain foolproof against directorial invasion. Rather than an inimical scheme against the author, the adaptatory siege of the literary text[3] could be viewed in terms of a growing love affair: that of a perennially attractive text often 'playing coy', yet deep down longing to surrender to the persistent, sometimes aggressive, but altogether amorous attentions of yet another suitor.[4]

Invariably, the conversation on the ethics of directing, which has become an indispensable component of the fidelity discourse on adaptation, references the so-called 'spirit' of the original work. The term awkwardly strives to capture the literary author's assumed intentions, which will, for the most part, especially in the analysis of Greek tragedy, remain unrecoverable. The implied supremacy of the 'classical, canonical, literary author' over the 'second-in-order' author (the director) may now feel obsolete; still, many critics and spectators continue to assume that fiddling with the classics, far from being a valid artistic venture, undermines established authority. In effect, the fidelity discourse that has pervaded adaptation scholarship implies that any product of recreation involves the practice of trespassing. 'Blasphemous' directors and theatre companies choosing to revise works of the canon in a radical manner are often blamed for tampering with someone else's property, instead of *protecting* it, as they were supposed to do. Shrouded in an aura of scandalous transgression, the act of adaptation winks back at the audiences

[2] Obviously, this study is neither historical nor exhaustive; the discussion of adaptation can always be replenished with endless case studies and production material.

[3] For the siege metaphor in relation to the translation of the classics, see Pope (1812), 206 à propos of his progress on the translation of Homer's *Iliad.*

[4] The governing metaphor of adaptation as love affair, initially featured in Sidiropoulou (2015a), has parallels in critical theory and, in particular, in translation. Indeed, translation as romance and passion is a well-established trope. On the 'erotics of translation' see Reynolds (2011), esp. Part III, which explores romantic and erotic metaphors for translation in English poetry and contains six chapters under the umbrella title 'Translation as "Friendship," as "Desire," and as "Passion"'. See also Jacques Poulin's novel *La Traduction est une histoire d'amour* (Poulin 2006), which has been translated into English by Sheila Fischman as *Translation Is a Love Affair* (Poulin 2009).

with a self-indulgent, conspiratorial smirk. And while the anticipation of being thrown off-balance is a deep-seated aspect of the theatre-going experience, it is especially pronounced in productions that advertise their 'deviant' approach'.[5] The mystery goes further: the spectators' voyeuristic impulses are in battle with their guilt-ridden duty to see the text handled with care through to its conclusion.

The question of whether Greek tragedy needs protection appears to lie in the heart of the present debate. Is it not precisely the classic's openness to the turbulence of change that has rendered it universal and timeless in the first place? A multitude of similar questions duly arises. Does ownership of an adaptation imply authorship of a new, autonomous artistic product? Is adaptation an objectionable behaviour, bordering on the distasteful and the sacrilegious? How can artists and critics deal with the insidious agenda of artistic decorum when discussing adaptation? Could directorial intervention function as a legitimate attempt to 'improve' a weak play, or at the very least decode its greyer areas as best as possible? How is artistic agency established? Should a director pay the necessary dues to the play's canonical status and if so, what exactly is it that constitutes 'canonicity'? Who controls the material? Who owns the text? What, in the end, qualifies as theatre *text*? These are only a few of the issues – some admittedly old, some less so – springing right from the unsettled and unsettling relationship between directing, adaptation, and authorship.

An unwritten, nebulous, and silently shared consensus postulates that as long as the playwright's words remain untouched, the production script still carries the stamp of the writer's authorship.[6] This assumption, however, leads to a circuitous examination of inadequate definitions. If the original words are all still there, what should we label as 'adaptation'? What are we to make of performances, in which the setting has been well overwritten, the dramatis personae utterly reconceived, and the cultural circumstances tailored to the present? Because the mise-en-scène is 'not an execution of the text, but its discovery',[7] the tensions that permeate the source–adaptation relationship may alert us to the cautiousness surrounding the hierarchies of meaning inherent in any act of rewriting. Any

[5] Stam (2000), 54 hits the nail on the head in castigating the condemning terminology of the fidelity discourse: 'Infidelity resonates with overtones of Victorian prudishness; betrayal evokes ethical perfidy; deformation implies aesthetic disgust; violation calls to mind sexual violence; vulgarization conjures up class degradation; and desecration intimates a kind of religious sacrilege toward the "sacred word".'

[6] Sidiropoulou (2011), 98. [7] Pavis (2008), 118.

situation where cohabitation is established presents a variety of challenges for both partners, where one must be careful not to infringe on the life of the other.

Courtship and Foreplay

Today, hundreds of contested theatre versions and extended scholarly debates later, we are still caught up in a dialectic that one would think to be by now obsolete. A profound mistrust separates text from performance, classics from adaptation, readers from spectators, obliging artists from naughty offenders, and so forth. However, engaging with the classics helps both artists and spectators re-understand fundamentals and reconsider absolutes from a (safe) distance, even when confronted with painful, violent, or atrocious emotions. Moreover, with all its tantalising imagery and heretical characterisation, adaptation can legitimise directorial choices that are still unacceptable in mainstream theatre. At one point of their career or another, renowned directors – such as Peter Hall, Peter Stein, Suzuki Tadashi, Peter Sellars, Robert Wilson, and more recently, Katie Mitchell, Ivo van Hove, Romeo Castellucci, Anne Bogart, Olivier Py, Jan Fabre, and several younger-generation artists whose names would expand this list beyond salvation – have tackled the innate challenges of the genre. Some have accepted tragedy's linguistic, structural, and contextual limitations as a sacrosanct given, and have accordingly employed more conventional modes of staging. Others have continued to tamper with the form with a critical eye and a desire for subversion or provocation, consciously or unconsciously divulging a sense of entitlement over the interpretation of tradition.[8]

Simply retelling the stories that Euripides or Sophocles have already given us, with no consideration of the factors that can still render them relevant, is no longer a viable artistic endeavour. In some straightforward versions claiming affinity to the ancient conventions of performance, the vital text falls into a deep slumber and eventually fades out into oblivion; indeed, it appears about to collapse under the weight of the centuries that it has carried on its shoulders. Modern theatre fails to arouse genuine reactions in its largely disillusioned audiences partly because of a fallacy: that of being able to recreate or slavishly ape the imagined conditions of an era no longer applicable or interesting to us. What Patrice Pavis terms *archaeological reconstruction* has long ceased to be the 'representational ideal

[8] Sidiropoulou (2015a), 32.

of a classical work',[9] ignoring, as it does, the unique circumstances of the audience at the point of reception and thus resulting in an *echo* – rather than a *distillation* –of the original story.[10] On the other hand, the term 'contemporary' has also been abused by otherwise well-meaning experimentalists. Its alluring connotations are frequently subjected to various degrees of misunderstanding, which are sadly bound to the clichés of deconstruction. In identifying as *historicisation* the process of interpreting plays 'from the point of view that is ours at the present time', with situations, characters, and conflicts shown in their historical relativity, Pavis has produced a useful typology, which draws attention to the dangers involved in the artists' tendency 'to explain the present too much, by forcing the plays to say what suited us at the time'.[11] Being much more than a mere alternative to the 'everyday', the realistic, and the vernacular, the application of a 'contemporary' reading could function as a barometer of pertinence, as a powerful indicator of the original material's level of relevance to what is familiar and important today.

In theatre criticism, radical performances of tragedy remain the locus of contention regarding the need for as well as the future viability of 'straight' readings. Consistently, theatre-makers have manifested an ambivalent attitude towards the Greeks. Faltering, irresolute ways of reframing the source text resound a broader disquiet vis-à-vis the treatment of the 'great narratives', and harbour some of the insecurities that Roland Barthes had already voiced in his 1972 analysis of Greek drama. Barthes' succinctly theorised dialectic is still apposite today, as it keeps open the polarised discussion on the ethics of directing:

> we never manage to free ourselves from a dilemma: are the Greek plays to be performed as of their own time or as of ours? Should we reconstruct or transpose? Emphasise resemblances or differences? We always vacillate without ever deciding, well-intentioned and blundering, now eager to reinvigorate the spectacle by an inopportune fidelity to some 'archaeological' requirement, now to sublimate it by modern esthetic effects appropriate, we assume, to the "eternal" quality of this theatre.[12] (Barthes 1972b, 59)

The heated debate raised annually at major international theatre festivals on whether 'solid' – if tame and tepid – versions of the Greek plays are

[9] Pavis (2013), 207. [10] Sidiropoulou (2015a), 45. [11] Pavis (2013), 208.

[12] Interestingly, Barthes is also one of the most prominent modern theorists of the erotics of literature and language, from which this essay draws its prevailing metaphor: see Barthes (1973) and (1977), respectively (and characteristically) entitled *Le Plaisir du texte* (*The Pleasure of the Text*) and *Fragments d'un discours amoureux* (*Fragments of an Amorous/Amatory Discourse*).

preferable to more adventurous adaptations is a reflection of this ambivalence. It may be true that subversive productions have as a matter of course enraged smaller or bigger parts of the audience with their nonconformist aesthetics. Yet, it is also the case that those directors who proudly fly the flag of experimentalism have helped gather a new kind of sophisticated spectatorship around them, contributing to an increase in attendance and tickets sales. If anything, adaptation is more of an act of defiance against time and decay than an interruption of historical continuity.

In determining whether innovation or temperance is a better approach to the act of adaptation, it is tempting to take sides according to one's own theatre-going experience. Criticism of adventurous practice features variations on the 'victimisation' theme, which castigate the violation of the text by an iconoclastic mise-en-scène. In principle, the tension that surrounds adaptations has to do with audiences' opposing sets of expectations of fidelity. On the one hand, the conservative attitude privileges 'faithfulness' to the original work. On the other, there is always a furtive, unacknowledged desire to be surprised by the product. But fidelity is 'no more than an illusion'. Directors have come to accept their work as an 'inevitable and productive betrayal regarding a so-called truth of the text which, according to them, never existed and had neither meaning nor appeal'.[13]

As a cultural product both foreign and familiar, the old and yet timeless text foregrounds its complex duality through mediating influences, traditions, and production histories. Trusting in the existence of *one* correct reading or interpretation is no less utopic than identifying the so-called 'author's intentions'. Conceivably, it would be much more constructive if scholars, critics, artists, and audiences looked for common recurrent patterns in different adaptations, identifying elements that appear to have influenced, over the years, one's way of experiencing the *old* as *new*. This way, they might eventually rid themselves of the 'moralistic language'[14] of adaptation criticism, and build new sets of criteria that could render the dialogue between ancient texts and modern performances less fragile.[15] If and when that happens, theatre practice may gradually discard the discourse of guilt that has come to attach itself to any act of adapting, revising, reimagining, and rewriting. Recycling is, for that matter, anything but a demeaning activity. As Linda Hutcheon explains, 'Stories do get retold in different ways in new material and cultural environments; like genes, they adapt to those new environments by virtue of mutation – in their "offspring" or their adaptations. And the fittest do

[13] Both quotations from Pavis (2008), 119. [14] Stam (2005), 3. [15] Sidiropoulou (2015a), 32.

more than survive; they flourish.'[16] Classical works have repeatedly astonished us with their resilience, bouncing back each time a director launches a ferocious attack.

Fertile Encounters

What exactly qualifies as adaptation? Thomas Leitch raises a valid point when examining whether all productions should be considered 'adaptations', especially in light of the fact that 'every text is an intertext whose stability and integrity are social and political rather than ontological'.[17] The question where 'adaptation proper crosses the boundary and becomes adaptation improper'[18] is anything but rhetorical and puts into perspective the debate about directorial authorship and auteurism. Similarly, Julie Sanders' distinction between adaptation and appropriation can prove helpful in one's venture to demarcate the boundaries of directorial freedom. According to Sanders, 'an adaptation signals a relationship with an informing sourcetext original'. Appropriation, on the other hand,

> frequently effects a more decisive journey away from the informing text into a wholly new cultural product and domain. This may or may not involve a generic shift, and it may still require the intellectual juxtaposition of (at least) one text against another . . . But the appropriated text or texts are not always as clearly signalled or acknowledged as in the adaptive process. (Sanders 2006: 26)

Most directorial reformulations are adaptations in a double sense: on the one hand, they rewrite pre-existing texts, in various degrees of radicalism. On the other, they also reflect previous stagings of the same source,[19] being 'palimpsests, tracing within themselves a history of other productions, other theatrical moments'.[20]

Is, then, adaptation a 'recoding of reproduction into production'?[21] Since adaptation claims legitimacy as a *separate product* – and not as a *reproduction* of artwork – directors' centrifugal attitudes towards the original text can no longer be considered heretical. In so far as any interpretive act can be considered an original agent of meaning and not an illustration, directing should no longer be conceived as an art of recreating, but of

[16] Hutcheon (2006), 32. [17] Leitch (2012), 88. [18] Leitch (2012), 88.

[19] Suzuki Tadashi uses the term 'requotation' to suggest that the original story has been 'rearranged and transformed' (Neely 1987, 515).

[20] Abrams and Parker-Starbuck (2007), 99–100. For more on the palimpsestic function of adaptation, see Liapis, Chapter 13, this volume.

[21] Cobb (2012), 110.

creating, composing, producing, giving birth. Inevitably, the passage from page to stage, from literature to performance, is full of turbulence. However, there is also an element of textual completion and maturity that characterises the encounter of writer and adapter (director). In discussing (film) adaptations, Cobb identifies a 'transfer of ownership', which, 'gained by the recoding of adaptation into a productive activity, becomes a signifier of authority and originality – two signs central to the image of the auteur'.[22]

The blessings and handicaps of a revisionist mise-en-scène are a constitutive part of any discussion on adaptation. Increasingly, audiences have grown weary of self-proclaimed 'avant-garde' approaches, which, as a matter of course, lazily resort to heavy-handed, provocative, and ultimately reductionist metaphors.[23] We shall discuss the matter further in the following section. The above observations notwithstanding, we should also admit, in (partial) defence of experimentalism, that without strong, potentially insolent metaphors, theatre readings of the classics risk being reduced to cultural curiosities. Directors can no longer play it safe. The attempt to achieve historical verisimilitude by recapitulating the original performance will eventually bounce back since any presumed knowledge is for the most part hypothetical. Erika Fischer-Lichte draws attention to the distance of the ancient texts, which any staging should bring to the light. She insists that revivals are unable to access the past because it is 'lost and gone forever. What remains are only fragments – play texts torn out of their original contexts – which cannot convey their original meaning.'[24] Her compendious remark hits the nail on the head: 'whatever we think we know about the past is a kind of reinvention – a construction, a fantasy'.[25]

Thanks to its *adaptability*, the dramatic canon has been revisited across different mediums and practices, becoming universally popular. It is worth examining what makes Greek tragedy, *in particular*, flexible and accommodating of bold experimentation with content and form. Fundamental and primordial, myths – reworked through the mediating hand of the tragic poets – reach out to us indiscriminately, impervious to cultural conditioning. Within the dramatic form, myth is expanded and ripens as it spreads.[26] Because of its universal themes, it helps contextualise the

[22] Cobb (2012), 108.

[23] Such is, for example, the metaphor of King Pentheus donning 'a slinky green cocktail dress' (Billington 2007) upon Dionysus' invitation for him to 'come out' in a deconstructed version of Euripides' *Bacchae* in the 2007 National Theatre of Scotland's production of David Greig's new version, directed by John Tiffany. According to critic Michael Billington, the tragedy's sexual politics were treated as a homosexual coming out.

[24] Fischer-Lichte (2005), 234. [25] Fischer-Lichte (2004), 352. [26] Barthes (1972a), 149.

human condition, which in turn leads to a mature attitude towards history. In daring to put out in the open essential if unresolved issues, it also provides a forum for helping us deal with mental and psychological unrest. Tragedy's expansive inner space – mythical as well as historical – can liberate performance, freely housing the perennial extremities of humanity. Often, tragedy reflects current sociopolitical anxieties, and for this reason, directors turn to it for guidance and wisdom. The old plays are 'not simply a thing of the past, an archaeological relic [but] totally projected into the future... [something] inevitable'.[27]

Ordinarily, spectators enjoy hearing the words of texts to which they have been variously exposed either through formal education, theatre-going, or personal study of original versions and derivative adaptations in different media and forms. Even so, despite feeling at home with familiar myths and quotable quotes, they also appreciate being surprised, exposed to alternatives that encourage them to perceive myths in a new light. Fully aware of this paradox, artists must confront the ancient, fixed, irretrievable reality of antiquity, also bearing the awareness and experience of the *plastic* (to quote Barthes again) fragmentary present, which imposes different hermeneutic criteria. American director Anne Bogart, whose work on tragedy has typically received critical acclaim, thinks of plays as 'little pockets of memory'. Her fascination with revisiting old works is part of a need to reclaim something that has been lost: 'the sense that theatre has this function of bringing these universal questions through time'.[28] Similarly, American playwright Charles Mee – whose inspired adaptations of the Greeks include *The Trojan Women: A Love Story*, *Orestes 2.0*, and *Big Love* (a surrealist take on *The Suppliant Women*) – suggests that because these 'old narrative structures are in some fundamental way authoritarian ... part of the struggle in the arts is to figure out a way for a person sitting alone in a room to come up with a structure that allows other people to take part in the making of the experience'.[29]

The interpretation of tragedy carries within itself the conflicting desire to remember and to change, to revive and to bury.[30] In any adaptation, it is the interaction of past and present that builds interpretation. One cannot really ignore the current reality, any more than altogether dismissing the play's reception at the time in which it was originally produced. In either case – denial or oblivion – this would lead to an inchoate rendition

[27] Castellucci in Laera (2013), 185. [28] Bogart in Shewey (1984). [29] Mee (1999), 189.

[30] Hutcheon (2006), 9 is right to observe that 'With adaptations, we seem to desire the repetition as much as the change.'

lacking a viable inner pulse. At the same time, one of the harshest criticisms that adaptation has incurred decries choices of extreme recontextualisation. The critique may not always be warranted, given that adaptations also serve an educational function: they make old texts freshly popular through proximation and updating, bringing them 'closer to the audience's frame of reference in temporal, geographic, or social terms'.[31] Suzuki Tadashi's work, for example, uses this strategy to great effect. By instilling ritual and vestment elements of his native Noh tradition into the equally formalised genre of Greek tragedy,[32] the director processes the social and political transformations of Japanese history, traditions, and identity.[33] The acclaim that Suzuki's approach has generally met with helps explain why to do justice to any director and any production, one must take into account the special conditions of reception. Interpretations that seem trivial or blasphemous to one audience can be highly appropriate to another, especially when they illuminate specific cultural circumstances. The question of ethics should then also be addressed in terms of context, which ultimately 'conditions meaning'.[34]

Being the 'closest "other" there can possibly be',[35] placed as it is in a kind of public domain, tragedy has become an ideal place for directors to channel their existential, social, political, and ideological discontent. How does one infuse the elastic and vital subject matter with pertinence and connection, while simultaneously respecting, and even highlighting the essential remoteness of the tragic form?[36] Could such a felicitous compromise offer a way out of tragedy's inherent paradox and regulate the uneasy balance that exists between its ecumenical and culture-specific, foreign properties? Staging the Greeks' constitutional strangeness is no easy matter. Many a director has lost sleep over solving the 'chorus problem', the actual or implied presence of the gods,[37] and tragedy's elevated language. Similarly, many adapters have struggled to conceive of metaphors that could substitute for indices of alterity, heroics, and grand stature on today's

[31] Sanders (2006), 21.

[32] See Suzuki's *Clytemnestra* (1983), based on the tragedies that focus on the myth of the House of Atreus. Soon after the son (Orestes) murders the mother, she comes back as an avenging white-faced Noh ghost who kills him while he is committing incest with his sister, Electra.

[33] Allain (2002), 20. [34] Hutcheon (2006), 145. [35] Revermann (2008), 110.

[36] Many directors keep reminding us of this distance, which they tend to pronounce through recourse to emblematic set, movement, and costume features of ancient ritualistic drama. See, notably, Peter Hall's *The Oresteia* (1981) at the Royal National Theatre and Ariane Mnouchkine's *Les Atrides* (1990–2).

[37] For an in-depth analysis of the problem of the gods in contemporary theatre, see Goldhill (2007), 189–224.

stage; in other words, to make mise-en-scène serve equally the distance and the *presentness* of the ancient text within the context of contemporary reflections, life, and culture. In Pavis' words,

> A further reason for the success of classical texts: historical, geographical, or social distance; production of ambiguity and enigmas which change a work hitherto monosemic into one that is complex and undecidable. If the mise-en-scène can, in a new concretization of the text, suggest new zones of indeterminacy, organize possible trajectories of meaning between them, the classical dramatic text may recapture the glow tarnished by the passage of time and by banal interpretations. This phenomenon of recycling grants the classical text a perennial life by founding this life, not on permanent and unchanging significance, but on change and adaptation.[38]

Consummation and Betrayal

With all that in mind, it is worth pondering whether a director's ethical outlook on revisiting tragedy must be concerned with credibility rather than originality and creativity. If the key to a meaningful adaptation is the ability to make the text personal and thus autonomous, what is the ethics of directing when an artist confronts a canonical work?

The privileging of literature over the arts of the spectacle has steadily spread its surreptitious bias in adaptation criticism.[39] The metaphor of the text's identity as a sacrificial victim within the ritual of performance, amply theorised by Fischer-Lichte,[40] is quite fitting. As early as the 1960s, directors turned 'against the text', disparaging those celebrated, 'sacred' words, downplaying – if not wholly dismissing – drama's discursive character, and challenging the thus far prevailing verbo-centricity of theatre. Analysing Klaus Michael Grüber's production of *Bacchae*, a part of the Antiquity Project at the Berlin Schaubühne (1974), Fischer-Lichte has examined the revised hierarchical structure between text and performance in 'directors' theatre' (*Regietheater*). She evokes Nietzche's understanding of 'dismemberment', a process of tearing apart the original text, for the performance to take shape. In her view, every classical text is subjected to a *sparagmos*, a dismemberment analogous to that suffered by Dionysus' victims or Dionysus himself in the myth.[41] In the same vein, Italian

38 Pavis (1986), 7.

39 Stam (2000), 58 locates the hierarchical superiority of literature precisely in the love for words ('logophilia') and the fear of images ('iconophobia'). The combination of the two conditions has rendered literature by definition 'superior' to any other artistic medium.

40 See below.

41 Fischer-Lichte (2005), 233–4.

theatre artist Romeo Castellucci rejects literature in favour of literality and argues that there can be no text if there's theatre. In his words, 'what happens if you pursue a text, the text-testicle, is that you end up in the [*sic*] sort of funerary cult by celebrating the dead'.[42] While for Castellucci text is primarily associated with knowledge, confirming culture, it is significantly the 'derangement of structure' that 'penetrates into the body of the spectator'.[43] Other revisionist directors, however, claim to be 'servants' to the text, adapting the visual mise-en-scène through modernising, while leaving most or the entire of the original lines intact. Ivo van Hove's attitude to adaptation translates into a process of understanding and highlighting what lies underneath the words. He insists that 'as a director you have to understand what the author wanted', and that the text is the only thing he has. However, he clarifies the function of text as *material*, 'like when you have a car. You need to put in petrol, and only then you can start. Without petrol, nothing happens. A text in itself is not alive. I have to make it alive.'[44] Van Hove is adamant that he does not 'do adaptation',[45] but that his work is to interpret. Contrary to Castellucci, who understands text as primarily (static and irrevocably dead) verbal material for use, van Hove treats it as a dynamic entity, which carries the potential for resurrection and transformation.

As a rule, the degradation of textual primacy is counterbalanced by lavish imagery. Often, visual dramaturgy helps unearth, resolve, or enrich aspects of the original text that are obscure to modern audiences. However, the avidity for iconographic ammunition and recyclable cultural material can oversaturate interpretation. Back in 1986, Robert Wilson directed a visually ravishing version of *Alcestis*, for which he assumed full authorship: 'I was working with a complete translation of Euripides' text then, but I felt I had to make it more my own. So that's what I did. Rewrote it myself.'[46] The production was nevertheless criticised for its emphasis on spectacular, extravagant effects over content. See, for example, *New York Times* critic Mel Gussow's caustic account:

> When the play reaches a point of sacrifice, it seems to swerve into another landscape. A goat-like figure is eviscerated and its 'blood' is used to paint the characters; a laser beam shoots from the back of the theatre and carves a hole in the mountain. At this moment, one unavoidably thinks not of

[42] Castellucci quoted in Laera (2014), 96–7.
[43] Castellucci quoted in Laera (2014), 99.
[44] Van Hove quoted in Laera (2014), 55.
[45] For more on van Hove's attitude on adaptation, see the section 'Speaking Up: Theatre Practitioners on Adapting the Classics', Chapter 5 in this volume.
[46] Quoted in Fuchs (1986), 86–7.

> Mr Wilson but of Steven Spielberg, wondering if the Temple of Apollo had not been somehow confused with the Temple of Doom. (Gussow 1986)

'Mix-and-match' strategies are constant echoes of deconstruction's firm hold on the practice of adaptation, with postmodernist aesthetics being held responsible for several adaptations' permissive attitude to textuality. In his review of Peter Sellars' 1985 production of Chekhov's *Seagull*, Gussow takes the director to task for his 'aberrant approach – tricks, quirks and sight gags', and renounces directors' 'tearing apart a text, shuffling its parts and leaving the skeleton exposed'.[47] The critic takes an unequivocal stand in the debate on the ethics of auteurism. He contemptuously dismisses Sellars' 'search of directorial signatures' as something that prohibits him from keeping his mind on the play's values.[48] Stylish and comfortably heretical, the theatre of American director Joanne Akalaitis has been subjected to similarly caustic criticism. Her 2009 interpretation of Euripides' *The Bacchae* was castigated for its apparent frivolity and for downplaying the elemental savagery of the text. Some of the reviews reveal that the emotional impact of the performance was extremely lukewarm. Ben Brantley of the *New York Times* dismissed the production as a 'light operetta', and sarcastically described the energetic soundscape as a constant accompaniment to a 'hip' chorus, embodied by 'a dozen actresses clad in outfits that suggest Abba gone Indonesian'. He also attacked the production's 'toothless' outlook during the play's most climactic point: 'As Pentheus' tragically deluded mother, [the actress] Joan MacIntosh speaks of blood-letting revels with the prosaic satisfaction of someone fresh from a cutthroat sale at Bergdorf's.'[49]

Central in directors' over-reliance on form is the desire to construct modern equivalents that can correspond to the elevated style of the classical work. Reversing expectations of standard forms of storytelling is a way of training audiences to enjoy less conventional modes of staging. We are stunned by Castellucci's transcendental scenography, Wilson's ever-expanding colour palette, Mnouchkine's exotic figures, and Mitchell's mediascapes. We are grateful for the beauty and the visual insights they bring to the plays. This is when form deepens, magnifies, and amplifies the source, building worlds that transform the writer's imagination into a moving sensory experience. Such encounters are fuelled by a burning desire to understand, to express, to connect. When such a

[47] Both quotations from Gussow (1985). [48] Gussow (1985).
[49] Both quotations from Brantley (2009).

desire is absent, however, extreme stylisation can yield cold results. Productions that rely on the eclectic marrying of different performance traditions without a solid underlying rationale to give them coherence and substance seem fated to reproduce demystified, emotionally dehydrated art forms. The aspects of myth that can move or invite critical understanding are flattened out by reductive 'directorialism'. As a result, far from embarking on an experiential journey, spectators are coerced to accept a watered-down, if splendid-looking spectacle as the *only* viable alternative to a period reconstruction. An overly aestheticised style can feel ossified; many shows are castigated as 'icily formalized', 'austere', and 'diamonded', on the grounds that they 'too angularly refract, too tightly contain the fiery Dionysian god at their core'.[50]

Formalism is generally the product of a rather cerebral – as opposed to instinct-driven – operation, and formalist performance is often perceived as academic and speculative; if anything, we can detect the kind of mental investment that has gone into it. Herbert Golder's critique of revisionist 'stylized, cerebralized, intellectualized, conventionalized, orientalized, multiculturalized' productions of Greek drama is quite fierce. He protests that the term 'contemporary' is in itself constrained by 'its own, already modishly outmoded conventions', and aptly notes that 'just because an image or idea is new, does not necessarily mean it is fresh'.[51]

One may argue that striking ideas and visual imagination can absorb tragedy's political and philosophical scope and produce meaning only when the artistic vision is strong; in other words, when they reveal how a contemporary artist speaks to and about the world. It is a connection that holds the material together and keeps it alive against all the odds. The inability of form to echo content underlies the fundamental criticism against New Formalism as an 'increasingly self-absorbed focus upon form and structure in its own right'.[52] An airtight concept vehemently protected against the cracks of textual interpretation will inevitably deflate or diffuse the audience's experience of the tragic. In addition, when their emotional range is framed rigidly, actors seem doomed to perform 'choreographically', unable to fully develop their creative impulses.

At the same time, an exaggerated investment in the aesthetic value of the work can empty it of its social and historical perspective. Although directors' experiments with form and image have boosted theatregoers' faith in and enthusiasm for *auteur theatre*, visual éclat appears to offset their deeper lack of commitment: to text, to context, to interpretation.

[50] Golder (1996), 185. [51] Golder (1996), 185. [52] Kaye (1994), 46.

What happens, for example, when flamboyance and portentousness are dressed up as taste, metaphor, and relevance? Problematising further the relationship between our assumed knowledge of the original and its flesh-and-blood incarnation on stage, the intention to generate subversive readings can lead to a rushed, naive 'mumbo jumbo' of stage signs. Such confused extravagance will gradually strip any sense of urgency or vitality off the play. Because the social, civil, and religious import of tragedy is part and parcel of its cultural specificity, depoliticising it by employing aesthetic filters divests it of a perspective at once historical and timeless. In this sense, while formal innovation is a desideratum of directing practice, one must gauge carefully the degree to which the emphatic use of postdramatic signifiers will bring life and meaning to the ancient works. Obliterating dramaturgical specificity can compromise tragedy's metaphysical viewpoint.

The list of mishaps and betrayals is long. For example, the experience of witnessing a diminished version of tragedy's epic stature is most destabilising, even though 'proximation'[53] can be an effective method of bringing the text closer to today. Occasionally flirting with parody, such operations can also conjure up a non-heroic, post-tragic present, in the context of which valiant kings and demigods show up on stage as failed rock-stars, feeble politicians, or incapacitated laymen. The attempt to modernise ancient characters can feel patronising, and extreme domesticisation may hit against the very structure of tragedy, a genre where psychocentric analyses sit uncomfortably. Expedient metaphors, after all, lead to another kind of mannerism. By way of example: British director Deborah Warner's stunning interpretation of *Medea* (2002) nevertheless conveys the sort of unease that many directors face when confronted with the fundamental unnaturalness of having lofty and often supernatural heroes embody human sentiments. This is why the production's focus was on causing spectators to 'identify with weakness',[54] as Fiona Shaw, who performed the Medea role as a 'very normal' modern housewife, argued.[55] In Warner's production, the depiction of Medea as 'the happy housewife of Corinth' defied Euripides' portrayal of the character as a 'female reincarnation of one of the most anguished, outsized, titanic dramatic heroes in the ancient canon'.[56] The show's intended psychologisation

[53] See Sanders (2006), 3, 19; cf. Sanders (2016), 5.

[54] Cf. Shaw and Warner (2001): 'Audiences can identify with weakness. I think the Greek playwrights knew that. That they could entice the audience into an emotional debate about failure and dealing with being a failed person'.

[55] Shaw and Warner (2001).

[56] Mendelsohn (2003).

stripped the audience of the chance to experience the extraordinary sense of alterity – Medea being both a 'barbarian' and a sorceress – that is so central to the play. Instead, one rather felt compassion for the plight of the 'woman-next-door'. In general, because the force and energy that epitomise the classical frame hold a different type of affect, the desire to bend structure and stature to create believable characters is worth noting. More than anything, one ought to consider whether a form as open as that of tragedy could ever be made to fit the dictates of more private affairs.

The occasional hollowness we experience after many a night out in the theatre can be attributed to directors' 'refusal to interpret'[57] – an attitude of treating the text as a soluble material whose meanings never add up to anything more than fleeting impressions. Such refusal also draws from Barthes' famous postulation of the text being not 'a line of words releasing a single "theological" meaning (the "message" of the Author-God), but rather, a multi-dimensional space in which a variety of writings, none of them original, blend and clash', a 'tissue of quotations drawn from the innumerable centres of culture'.[58] Barthes' thesis has forced us to acknowledge the existence of multiple author-gods involved in both reading and writing, which can be assumed to happen concurrently. The realisation that the less fortunate side of multiplicity is neutrality (an approach that favours a generous 'anything goes' attitude) helps explain why directors, performers, and spectators resort to the convenience of narrative dispersal and fragmentation.[59] It also raises another question: is the text merely some 'signifying matter awaiting meaning',[60] and if yes, should this grant directors the right and the luxury of postponing interpretation for as long as possible? Revisionist practices, with all their complacent detachment, create an uncomfortable space for spectators; the audience must now dive into the deep and murky waters of antiquity without the anchor of the director's vision, evidently a firm departure point for any act of interpretation. The reliance on *material* rather than on *text* is equally treacherous. When dramaturgical complexity and logic are randomly relinquished to serve an *au courant* visual statement, the classical play becomes depoliticised, denarrativised, removed from its cultural context. Tragedy's discursive and metaphysical perspective is tossed aside amid all kinds of extraneous linguistic, sonic, and visual debris. A 'hermeneutic nostalgia'

[57] Pavis (1986), 10. [58] Barthes (2000 [1988]), 148.

[59] This way, the textual or theatrical heritage is treated as 'no more than *memory* in the technical sense of that word, as an immediately available and reusable memory bank' (Pavis 1986, 1).

[60] Pavis (1986), 11–12.

will then set in, 'a melancholic and thus unresolved grieving, an unfulfilled longing for the familiar, or ... for canonical, reified readings of [Greek tragedy]'.[61]

Here, a brief run-down of what are often considered unwarranted directorial 'transgressions' is perhaps in order. As already argued, setting the play in a modern context is one of the most popular mechanisms – and the most adventurous one at that – of staging the Greeks. In this area, the Greek 'war plays' have been particularly blessed. In 1986, the pioneering director-adapter Peter Sellars made Sophocles' *Ajax*[62] into a story about an imagined American war in Latin America. American General Ajax was played by a deaf-mute actor (Howie Seago), whose lines were spoken by a five-person chorus usurping the hero's voice against a photo projection of the Pentagon. In 2007, Calixto Bieito's version of Aeschylus' *The Persians* (subtitled *Requiem for a Soldier*) offered an extreme reformulation of the politics of the play as a musical interpretation of the US war in Afghanistan in 2003. The stage represented a desert with car wrecks all over, but the attitude towards the winners and losers of the war focused on the Spanish army rather than on the Asian 'other'. This choice suggested that Western troops were the real 'barbarians' of the twenty-first century.[63] Notably, at the beginning of the performance, a chorus of soldiers in military uniforms sang a patriotic anthem celebrating Spain, accompanied by a live band. In another updated mise-en-scène, that of Katie Mitchell's 2007 production of Euripides' *Women of Troy*, the image of the ransacked city was transported to an industrial cityscape, near a modern-day port site. The sight of suffering was highly symbolic. Lamenting their plight, the immaculately dressed females of the chorus were locked in a nightmarish iron prison, where they danced to familiar tunes and smoked cigarettes: a ritual of mourning for their dead husbands.

At times, the revised context of the myth is not limited to one single sociohistoric dimension. Anne Bogart's 2011 modern-dress *Trojan Women (After Euripides)* at the Brooklyn Academy of Music, reworked by dramaturg Jocelyn Clarke, was interspersed with 'flashes of the Russian Revolution, the Holocaust [and] the Balkan wars',[64] so that the audience could 'summon any Armageddon at any locale domestic or international'.[65] Bogart insisted that the play was 'as far from a historical artefact

[61] Forsyth (2009), 27.

[62] The production script had been adapted from the original by Robert Auletta, who also worked on Sellars' version of *The Persians*.

[63] Laera (2014), 246. [64] Zenowich (2011). [65] Henerson (2011).

as anything that I can imagine ... Hecuba, when she looks out upon her wrecked city, is talking about the devastation after Hurricane Katrina or Hurricane Sandy, or a recently bombed Palestinian village.'[66] As its subtitle indicated, Bogart's and Clarke's production pointed to a robust intervention on the source text.

In 2015, British director Robert Icke based his celebrated free adaption of the *Oresteia* trilogy at London Almeida Theatre in a contemporary abstract space, which merged the stark reality of the present with the nightmarish but all-too-real memories of past crimes. The action was framed as part of an investigation. An interrogator looking for evidence questioned Orestes. A large bathtub at the back of the stage highlighted Agamemnon's crime scene. Opaque screens, sliding open and closed, concealed what was behind them, 'allowing people to glide like ghosts'.[67] The adaptation began with a family dinner, around a long table downstage, where everyone (including Iphigenia) was present. Icke depicted the story of Iphigenia's killing by her father not as a sacrifice but as a clinical operation, brought to the foreground against the ancient Greek convention of never representing crime on stage. In its domesticity, while the audience watched adults put to death a child during several minutes, the sacrifice scene felt excruciatingly violent, particularly as the young tiny girl's 'little legs innocently kick, while she drinks her fatal dose'.[68] In the words of a critic, 'this is not destruction but revelation. You can almost see the dust flying off the old master.'[69] Icke's revisionist approach was also applied in his 2019 adaptation of *Oedipus Rex*, produced by the International Theater Amsterdam. The director set the action on the eve of a state election, where popular politician Oedipus pledged an inquiry into the death of Laius, while awaiting the election results. This all took place in a modern-day conference room, with TV monitors, campaign posters directly referencing the Obama campaign, and, notably, a stopclock ticking down the time to the results. The real-time quality of the story-telling heightened the masterful plot's suspense, fully serving the argument that adaptations can reveal and accentuate latent or prevailing dynamics in the source play. Icke's adaptation, as one critic put it, 'stays true to the governing forces of the Sophocles original while touching a 21st-century nerve in its discussion of honesty, truth and cover-ups in public life'.[70]

[66] McKee (2013). [67] Clapp (2015a). [68] Clapp (2015a). [69] Clapp (2015a).
[70] Fisher (2019).

Additional distancing techniques involve casting against type and cross-gender and cross-racial casting. Similarly, in many productions the visual layering bears little relation to the language of the text. The tension that results from dialogue, action, and setting standing in opposition to each other can be truly compelling. For the most part, such patterns of defamiliarisation force us to look beyond the predictable elements for a stronger correspondence between text and subtext. In Polish director Krzysztof Warlikowski's five-hour-long epic collage *(A)pollonia* (2009),[71] texts by Euripides and Aeschylus, J. M. Coetzee, Hanna Krall, and Jonathan Littell provided the narrative structure for an exploration of the theme of sacrifice. On stage were Agamemnon and Clytemnestra, Iphigenia and Alcestis, Admetus and Heracles, Orestes, and the perpetrators of the Holocaust and its victims – most notably a Polish woman named Apolonia Machczyńska, who lost her life in her attempt to save twenty-five Polish Jews during World War II. They gathered together to perform a series of brutal rituals of purgation, telling each other ancient and modern-day tales in a conspicuously post-mythical space. In one of the most memorable scenes, a family dinner between a despondent Admetus, his pregnant wife Alcestis, his elderly parents, and a doctor and master of ceremonies from the office of Thanatos (Death) disintegrated into a harrowing affair: Alcestis was seen rushing on and off the stage in choreographed repetition, each time trying on a different dress for her husband. Eventually, she slashed her wrists, drawing with her blood a little picture of a small house, such as a child might sketch, on the transparent walls of her room. This emotionally fraught image heightened the structural pattern of pointless resistance and ultimate surrender to death.[72]

Wishing to undermine the heroic ideals of tragedy, theatre artists will sometimes express defeat or decay in savage forms. For Romeo Castellucci, the performer's body serves as a mirror of physical impotence, which extends to social, cultural, and existential malaise. His 1995 *Orestea* had the god Apollo performed by an actor missing his arms. Castellucci commented visually on the inability of the homicide's instigator to provide 'a helping hand' to Orestes. The latter's weakness was also captured viscerally. The emasculated Orestes was incapable of carrying out his

[71] The production premiered in Warsaw's Teatr Nowy in May 2009.

[72] Warlikowski's production did not remain unscathed by criticism. One reviewer for the *Guardian* (Nestruck 2009) commented on the director's 'inventive if sometimes baffling staging', which 'includes a Skype call between Orestes and Apollo and a drunken, cowboy-hat-wearing Heracles in a one-man foam party'. She also observed that some of 'his contrasts are more head-scratching than thought-provoking'.

mission, and was therefore assisted by a mechanical contracting arm, which helped him commit the act of matricide. In marked, ironic contrast to Orestes' anorectic presence, the obese bodies of both Electra and Clytemnestra stood for their ample determination and hunger for power, respectively.[73] Such controversial representation functions as a metaphor for an ailing society – in effect, for a 'post-sense world'.[74] Attaching itself to Artaud's Theatre of Cruelty, where the actor is sanctified in his or her pure, anti-mimetic presence, Castellucci's company, Socìetas Raffaello Sanzio, employs the performative strategy of the 'Dis-Human' and the 'Dis-Real': an 'erasure of traditional construction of humanness and identification on stage'.[75] For artists like Castellucci, the Greek plays and myths validate the extremity of human emotions and actions, since, as already pointed out, the tragic mode offers a generous space wherein to address discomfort and unease. Articulating violence in a variety of formal ways may very well challenge our limits of tolerance and aesthetic perception, revealing tragedy's vital significance, its mental and psychological power.

This discussion of directorial ethics can only conclude with the most challenging of all formal elements of tragedy, namely, the chorus. A representative of the moral sentiment of the public, it has been one of directors' most exciting problems, and, equally, the most vulnerable of all sacrificial victims in the name of experimentation and updating. The chorus presence can be humorous, as in Mitchell's 2001 version of Euripides' *Iphigenia in Aulis*, where five women in scarves, hourglass dresses, and handbags, 'cluck onstage, representing the populace as a flock of fickle, gaggling, fashionable geese', while Clytemnestra paraded on stage with baby Orestes in a pram.[76] The effect can also be shocking, as in Lithuanian auteur Oskaras Korsunovas' 2002 heretical staging of Sophocles' *Oedipus Rex*, where the chorus, led by Coryphaeus disguised as a huge bear, featured a number of uncanny creatures, some masked as big-headed babies and others in black Mickey-Mouse guise. An 'uninvited guest'[77] in contemporary performance, the chorus has stretched the limits of directorial interpretation to phenomenal extremes. Repeatedly, directors have been forced to reimagine and defend its awkward status as a defunct convention that must nonetheless be maintained. Sometimes, its central position reveals a politically and socially driven perspective. Reinforcing the complex identity of the Greek plays, a revamped chorus also suggests the tension inherent in a 'collective body' that is simultaneously foreign

[73] Sidiropoulou (2015b), 34. [74] Kuppers (2005), 79. [75] Causey (2001), 202.
[76] Moroney (2001). [77] Laera (2013), 132.

(qua archaic convention) and public (qua representing the humanistic and democratic ideals of community). To that effect, German collective Rimini Protokoll's 2010 *Prometheus in Athens* transformed Aeschylus' *Prometheus Bound* into an extended choral part embodying the current cultural make-up of the Greek capital, with 103 Athenians representing the city, drawing from official demographical statistics. Athenian citizens from all over the city, of different age groups, professions, and ethnicities – including undocumented immigrants – re-enacted the Prometheus myth, each identifying with a character from the tragedy, which they introduced to the audience. The chorus members voiced their responses to the tragic themes, especially to the conflict between freedom and acquiescence to autocratic rule. Parts of the original text were adapted and adjusted to the contemporary reality of Athens, rendering the performance a compelling manifesto of communal values in a time of crisis. Thanks to the open dialogue between the stage and the auditorium, the spectators were no simple voyeurs: they became public voice.

Maturing into Love

Concerning his production of the *Oresteia*, director Robert Icke explained that an adapter has to be '100 percent faithful not to the letter of the original but the impulse that motors the whole thing forward', adding characteristically: 'adaptation is like using a foreign plug. You have to find the adaptor which will let the electricity of now flow'.[78] It is no surprise that the lofty, enduring status of tragedy, with its larger-than-life characters and the representation of forces beyond human comprehension, has in one way or another become a compelling medium for artists to comment on the absence of grandeur and heroics today and to seek solace in the idea that our lives are ultimately determined by a variety of agencies that exist outside of ourselves. Far from sabotaging or annihilating the tragic spirit, revised forms can act as a kind of umbilical cord that keeps the original text alive. No longer dictating our response to the old plays – which are always appreciated and enjoyed beyond form and style – adaptation can nourish the relationship between past and present. As directorial indulgence threatens to conceal or smother the pulse of texts and performances, it would not be out of line to suggest that the so-called ethics of directing may well have to do with a revolt against the closure of form. Having settled on a fixed, seemingly secure relationship between the updated mise-

[78] Cited in Clapp (2015b).

en-scène and the original text, often directors, actors, and designers become victims to the form they have invented, unwilling to transgress its boundaries, to explore and exploit its potential. Resisting retraction to easy pattern – one of the most common dangers associated with the decay of avant-garde art – is ultimately part of the ethics of any creative act.

The discussion on adaptation remains just as open and accommodating as the classical work. One can never hope to have reached definitive answers or discovered a fool-proof recipe for a 'strong reading', such as the one Harold Bloom believed to be 'the only text, the only lie against time that endures'.[79] While in any directorial project it is still useful to 'distinguish between deconstruction and provocation,'[80] the question in the end becomes how intelligent an adaptation is: how setting, time, language, character portrayal, and action can be reframed and retuned to our society's rhythms. In the process of generating new artistic and perceptual criteria, inspired adapters will extend the frontiers of interpretation neither out of a sudden whim to provoke or shock, nor through a flaccid attitude to analysis and interpretation. The desire to revisit, revise, render novel and meaningful can also indicate a genuine need to preserve and enrich tradition by means of creative ownership.

Although any attempt to gauge an adaptation's success must take into account the source's popularity, a flood of additional questions and concerns will continue to issue forth, possibly ad infinitum. Is the 'untouchable', 'pure' classic more valuable than the one that has received various reproductions and revisions? Is fidelity to one's auteur status in itself a guarantee of solid investment in the work? What are the boundaries of directorial intervention? Where does or can interpretation cease and rewriting begin? Can we really talk about an ethics of stage direction and if yes, who is to set the limits of directors' freedom to interpret?'[81] There are no easy answers to any of the above questions.

It could be that directors' unfaithful moments 'make possible the auteur's ability to be faithful to himself in the process of adaptation'.[82] Hence, one might want to consider whether the ethics of directing is a matter of remaining faithful to the playwright or one's directorial identity. On a more technical, legalistic note, there are, in theory, fewer complications in those productions that acknowledge their status as 'rewritings' (as opposed to 'plain' stage interpretations), establishing their adaptation

[79] Bloom (1979), 7. [80] Pavis (2013), 233. [81] Sidiropoulou (2011), 156.
[82] Cobb (2012), 112.

status in their very title.[83] In modifying the source title with appropriate prefixes or suffixes, such projects vindicate their authorial function, even when lines are cut, new material and text interpolated, characters added or eliminated, the timeframe switched and the action altogether relocalised. Extracting whatever feels essential and urgent in the original, directors can rewrite tragedy using new dramaturgical and stage-informed co-ordinates, without being blamed for cheating. This approach to adaptation is both honest and mature. The production recognises the existence of an original author but clarifies from the outset its intention to diverge from the source. This way, adapters can prepare the audience for what is bound to be a different version of a familiar story and, in turn, spectators may anticipate a visionary, unorthodox experience, one that they can enjoy without fear or guilt. Irrespective of style, form, or context, the source of inspiration remains the one 'original' work. On that account, 'irreverent' adaptations can be viewed as intuitive operations intended to expand the original, engaging a variety of mediums and approaches. In their most fortunate manifestations, they have been known to add unexpected layers of meaning, which revamp the source text.

Adaptatory processes always activate intricate networks of intentions, ambitions, and balances. Because adaptation originates in a desire to remain true to one's authorial voice, it is often assumed that to claim one's autonomy as an artist, one must somehow 'betray' the original author. Such betrayal, however, as many adaptations testify, can be fraught with passion and excitement for both creators and receivers. Revisionism notwithstanding, any mise-en-scène is potentially a new adaptation insofar as it engages with the world of the play and with the world outside. While 'ethical' adaptations seem anchored on the idea of commitment, *avoidance* – a resistance to interpretation – is where one should locate the slackening of directing ethics. For a director, such avoidance may be the result of insecurity or indifference or both. For a spectator, it can be driven by the need for comfort, a lack of investment, or quite simply, boredom. In either case, there is an unwillingness to immerse, not so much in a text as such but rather in a world of ideas, of emotions, of rigorous mental and psychological (self-)interrogation. Whether iconoclastic and irreverent, deconstructive or formalist, a strong mise-en-scène is ultimately a mise-en-scène that remains in love with its stable, unfaltering companion, even as it betrays it.

[83] As was the case with Anne Bogart's production of *Trojan Women (After Euripides)*.

PART II

Adaptation on the Page and on the Stage
Re-inscribing the Greek Classics

CHAPTER 5

Interlude

Speaking Up: Theatre Practitioners on Adapting the Classics

Avra Sidiropoulou

Given the multi-perspectival context of our volume, we thought it necessary to bring three renowned theatre artists into the room and invite them to share with our readers their insights on adaptation as a practice of high interpretative value. To this purpose, I conducted a series of interviews with two theatre directors and one playwright, all of whom internationally acclaimed. The discussion that some of the questions generated addressed the challenges – dramaturgical, stylistic, and ethical – that are part and parcel of the philosophy and the special dynamics of adaptation; in other words, of the conceptual base from which directors and writers embark and of the creative choices they make in their attempt to bring Greek tragedy closer to the emotional, aesthetic, and intellectual needs of the present-day spectator.

The interview with Flemish director Ivo Van Hove took place in New York City on 21 October 2014. At that time, Mr van Hove was rehearsing for his production of *Antigone*, starring Juliette Binoche.

The interview with Japanese director Suzuki Tadashi took place at the village of Toga, in Toyama Prefecture, Japan, on 24 March 2016. Professor Uchino Tadashi acted as interpreter from Japanese into English. I am also grateful for the help provided by Mr Kameron Steele, Suzuki Tadashi's official translator.

Finally, the interview with American playwright Charles (Chuck) Mee took place in New York City on 7 October 2016.

All three interviews were conducted in person by Avra Sidiropoulou.

Charles L. Mee

—*When was your last project working on the Greeks? When was the very last time New York audiences got the chance to see something?*

—Well, the last production in New York was when *Big Love* came back about a year ago at the Signature Theatre, directed by Tina Landau, but that had first been done in 2001, I think.

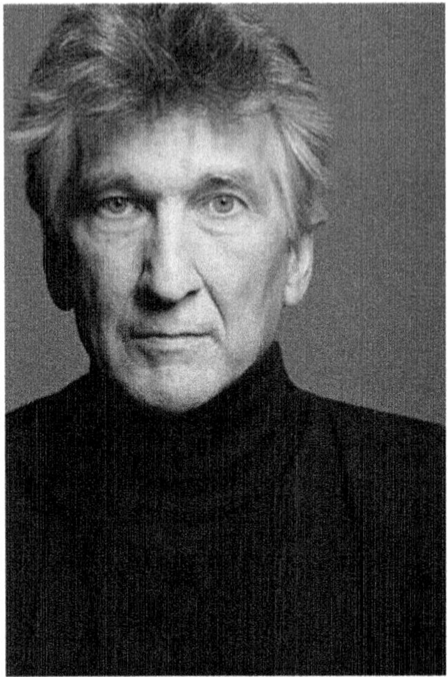

Figure 5.1 Charles Mee.

—*What was the reception?*

—I think it was very enthusiastic. I think the younger people really loved it. The older audience maybe didn't love it quite so much. And that's been, I think, consistent. It's been produced at almost every College and University in United States. I think younger people are crazy about it.

—*Do you think there is an audience for a Greek tragedy per se in the United States? Besides adaptations or new works inspired by Greek plays?*

—I don't think anybody does faithful productions. So I don't know if there's an audience or not.

—*What is a faithful production and what's an unfaithful production?*

—Well, I guess a faithful production would be an attempt to reproduce exactly what happened over 2,000 years ago. And that would be faithful. But, of course, nobody really knows exactly what that is. And so, I think they'd give up before they start. And, anyway, I don't even try, I'm not interested in doing a faithful version of anything myself. I just feel, growing up in the United States we were always told that the greatest playwrights were the Greeks and Shakespeare. And none of them ever wrote an original play. They all stole their plays from somebody else and then did their version. And I don't think any of them tried to be faithful necessarily. I mean, if you take just, for instance, Hippolytus or a story of Phaedra, there are different versions of Phaedra.

—*Seneca, Racine . . .*

—So you could take the story of Phaedra and then at the end Theseus could murder Phaedra or Theseus could murder Hippolytus or Hippolytus could murder Theseus or Phaedra could murder both Hippolytus and Theseus if you wanted to. I mean, anything could happen. What's the faithful version of that story? There are so many possibilities. In my own version, Theseus shoots Phaedra and then himself.

—*It makes a lot of sense actually.*

—But then in fact my version didn't kill either one of them, so they end up with Phaedra and Hippolytus living in an apartment next door to the apartment that Theseus lived in.

—*It would make sense to a contemporary audience. Do you call your work adaptation?*

—I guess, I call it unfaithful adaptation.

—*Do you think that's the only way for you to perpetuate whatever was there to begin with, the original myth? The only way to keep it alive?*

—It seems to be.

—*So, in a sense, adaptation is necessary but it's not that new of a practice.*

—Yeah. It's several thousand years old. We're adapting existing adaptations of myths pretty much, whatever was there before the Greek playwrights.

—*I'm interested in what your American-ness brings to these plays. Do you think the American perspective is stronger than, say, a universal twenty-first-century perspective, or do they always come together to inform the new writing?*

—Well, I hope they come together. But I don't think I'm doing just an American version. Years ago, I did a version of Orestes. At the time, we were at war in Iraq, and those were the earliest days of the Internet. So, I was on the Internet and I found blogs written by soldiers in Iraq about being on the battlefield, being at war. Then I took those blogs and I put them into the middle of the play. There is a soldier speaking from the front line, and I put other things into it that came from now, today. It's just a mix of how war has been for the past several thousand years.

—*What's your next Greek play?*

—I think I've done eleven or twelve of them by now. And the next one that I'm going to be working on today and tomorrow and next week and next month, is not, like, really a Greek play. It's a play that you might call *Love* and so it takes material from Greek plays, about things about love. But it would be done with Anne Bogart and with Elizabeth Streb, who has a company of acrobats. So, the acrobats will be swinging on ladders and fall into the ground.

—*While speaking your text.*

—Climbing up on top of things and falling off. So, it will be beautiful and fascinating and lovely and frightening and horrible, scary.

—*Like the Greek plays themselves.*

—Like the Greek plays, and like love.

—*It doesn't seem to be about ownership or appropriation, it's more like sharing, which is a very generous attitude to the classical works. Many think it's a no-no, and it's very much an irreverent thing to do. But I think, ultimately, it is very generous to keep the works alive and to add to them.*

—Did I tell you I got very involved in anti-Vietnam war politics and wrote a number of books about American foreign policy? And it turns out that when you quote Winston Churchill, you can't make up what he says. You have to quote exactly what he said. And that's evidence of what he thought. And so, when I write plays, I appropriate material from the world I live in and I don't rewrite it because that's evidence of who and how we are today. So, I don't get to change it. I have to deal with it somehow.

—It's more of an editing process, it seems.

—It is. But also, I take the Greek plays because that's the culture we come from. I take bits and pieces of that and I take bits and pieces of our cultural and political history and pieces of the world today and put them together. And it's all appropriated, I don't get to change it. Then, of course, I do write some of my stuff. But having done that, having stolen all of that material, I don't feel like I've been copyrighted in the old-fashioned sense of the word, and so I can't claim that I own it. So that's why I've put it back in the world and say, 'Hey, you take it, do whatever you want.' It's not so generous on my part, it just feels kind of honest that I stole it, so now they steal it from me. That's what we do in our civilisation. We steal stuff from the past, I actually steal stuff from now, we put it together, living our lives, that's how it is.

—There seem to be layers and layers of adaptations in your work. I like the idea of literature and art flowing through space and never becoming stationary. It can go on forever. Do you get bits and pieces from the actual text or the circumstances, situation, characters?

—All of it.

—Do you keep any of the original text?

—Sometimes, yeah.

—So why the Greeks?

—Well it started with Robert Woodruff. It started with a guy named Gordon Davidson, who ran the Mark Taper Forum Theatre in Los Angeles, and Gordon telephoned Woodruff one day and said: 'I was having some people do a workshop here in my theatre and now they can't do it, so we have a space and a budget for a workshop for a new play. Why don't you come and do it?' And Woodruff called me saying they were going to do a workshop and that would be a great chance for us to work together. At first, I told him I didn't have anything and couldn't write that fast, but then I said: 'Well, here we're into this war in Iraq, why don't we take a Greek play about war? Like, you and I we both know the play *Orestes*. You go out to LA – I can't go now, I have to stay in New York – but you go and work with the actors, and then I will fax you some material while you're there, and you can stick it into the play.' And he said, okay. So, he went to Los Angeles, I faxed him all this material. It is like if you read *Orestes*, it would make you think of things, and you would write that in the margin. So, I faxed him all of the marginal notes and texts that it'd made me think of. And so, after the workshop was over, he came back with this big pile of junk and said: 'So, here's the stuff that we've put together.'

I said: 'Oh great, now how would you make a play out of this? Oh, I see, you just throw away the original and what's left we'll call it a modern version of it.' So, that was it. That was the first Greek play.

—*And what kind of things did they come up with?*

—Oh, all kinds of stuff. I mean, there was the interview of the guy in jail who had murdered his whole family. All kinds of things. And when Woodruff brought this material back to me and I put it together, and then made this play *Orestes*. That's when I fell in love with Greek theatre and I thought 'Well, this is the great theatre where they take no small problem that can be solved by the time of the commercial break at the top of the hour on television. Boys murdered their fathers, people murdered their mothers, and they murdered their husbands and wives and children. They take big problems and then they try to say: 'How is this done? Could we do better than that?' And when you go to Delphi and you go to the top of the mountain, and there are the ruins of the old houses and the ruins of the government buildings and the ruins of the religious institutions, the ruins of the oracle, and at the top of all the ruins the theatre, and you think: 'Oh right, so people would go from their houses to the theatre, look at a play, and behind the play are the houses and the city they live in and the fields they work in. So, it happens in their world and they must be sitting there thinking "That's what Oedipus did, could we be better than that?"' I mean, you know, in running our city, in taking care of our neighbours, in being leaders. And so, I fell in love with just the huge stakes that were involved. The structure of a Greek play is that the principal characters advance the plot and then the chorus riffs. I thought, 'Oh, so Shakespeare woke up one morning and thought the chorus riffs', but that's not ten people saying the same thing at the same time, that's ten individuals. It's like you would walk down the street with a microphone and say to somebody 'What do you think of the war in Iraq?' And repeat the same question to someone else, and again, to someone else. These are all individuals, but all together they are the voice of a community. So, Shakespeare thought: 'Huh, I'll call them subplots.' So those are his [subplots], the gatekeeper and the people who are the 'other people' in most of Shakespeare's plays. Then, by the time you get to the nineteenth century, to Ibsen and Chekhov, you have the principals advance the plot, there was no chorus. By the time you get to Pina Bausch, the chorus riffs.

—*There are no principals.*

—And I thought, 'Oh now I get it.' So, in other words, you can make a theatre piece and you can have as [many] of the principals as you want and as much of the chorus as you want, and the chorus doesn't just talk, they sing and they dance and they do other stuff. So, now you can make a play with music and movement and physical theatre and text and put it together however you want. So, that's what I got from Greek plays. And that's why I've written another ten or eleven of the same style.

—*I've always wondered what happened in-between the Greeks and Shakespeare when it comes to the chorus. How did the chorus get eliminated? You seem to suggest that it didn't, really, it just became more individualised.*

—Right, yes.

—*And part of the problem of doing tragedy today is how to address the 'chorus problem', cliché though it sounds.*

—But the chorus problem . . . If you think of the chorus as the voice of the community, and you think Ibsen eliminated the voice of the community, so all you have is the well-to-do middle-class family in their living room saying how they think and feel about things. That's a little bit self-absorbed and a little bit not paying attention to the world they live in. And sometimes . . . I mean obviously, with Ibsen and Chekhov, they try and also say 'choral' things. But now I think it's interesting that in the beginning all art was about the gods, and then you can trace the history of democracy by seeing, then it became about the Emperor and the Emperor's family, then the King and the King's family, then the aristocrats, and by the time you get to the nineteenth century, it's about the middle class. And that's exciting and revolutionary at the end of the nineteenth century, but by now it's a little bit boring. We've been doing this, and it finally gets down to home hysteria. But now, mostly in American theatre, what you have is all well-to-do middle-class white people in the Connecticut suburbs in their living room. And they are the ruling class, they think they rule the world, they think they are the Emperors.

—*Do you feel that we miss the individual voices of the people in the writing?*

—Yes. We're missing the world. But not in European theatre, where with Pina Bausch it's chorus, chorus, chorus. And Pina Bausch would take her company to a town in Sicily, and they would all go out into the town and meet people and hear their stories and come back and put it all together, so that it was Sicily as a choral event.

—*But it's interesting to think about the difference between having a chorus speak in a unified way and express a common view as it was in the Greek plays, where they all pretty much agree on the things they say, and have the 'chorus' of individual people who speak their mind as they wish. So, there is a little bit of a difference here, isn't there?*

—Well, I'm not sure. You know, in an unfaithful production of a Greek play, you could take that choral text and give it to ten different actors and have one of them speak very nicely and one of them speak a little bit unhappily or angrily. And it could be the voice of the community having different opinions and feelings about things.

—*I haven't seen that done.*

—No, but you can do it.

—*So the chorus doesn't have to be a problem. Isn't there something missing when a director determines that the chorus is the first thing to go? You can still keep the chorus, as you're suggesting, but make it part of a different structure.*

—And why doesn't it [the chorus] sing and dance?

—*Which it did in the past.*

—Yeah. And why are there not individual dancers and individual singers? And then a group of three or four singers, as one individual dances and then somebody speaks?

—*You have worked with the same directors time and again, like Tina Landau and Anne Bogart and Robert Woodruff. What about the relationship that develops between the adapter, you, and the director? How much of your adaptation gets adapted by these directors? Are they 'free' to add even more stuff in terms of the dramaturgy of it?*

—Yes. Years ago, I was spending a lot of time in Europe, seeing productions of things. I thought, 'Oh, the playwrights who get the best production are the dead playwrights.' And maybe that's because they don't go to rehearsals. So, I stopped going to rehearsals. I never, ever go to rehearsals. So, the director and the actors are free to do whatever they want. And some of them do very unfaithful versions of my plays, and some of them can be very faithful versions of my plays — I think Tina Landau would do a faithful production in my spirit. But it will mean she would do a lot of stuff that's faithful to the guy she knows that I am.

—*Can you give an example?*

—In the direction she did in *Big Love*, there were 438 things that were not in the script that she did but I thought were perfectly faithful to everything I felt and thought.

—*Does 'faithful to the spirit' mean that you and the director think along the same lines, and then the director can complete and fulfil your vision, by taking it further?*

—Yeah, and has her own ideas, and because we're such good friends we both love those ideas.

—*But why do you feel that you don't want to be in rehearsals? I'm sure this kind of dialogue can really help the actors feel totally emancipated.*

—But playwrights will go to rehearsals; what happens is, they say 'Oh that's interesting but that's not really quite what I had in mind; what I was really thinking was this and that.' That ends their exploring that thing that they were doing, which might have been wonderful, or it might have been wrong, but by exploring it and continuing to explore it, the actors would have gotten somewhere else. Nobody knows if they're ever going to get there, but they do, and it's fantastic. So, you stop the process of exploration. And then the actor will say to the playwright, 'Oh Chuck, you know, I'm not sure I quite understand my motivation here, could you write a few lines that really say, you know, what I . . .' So, then, if you're being a nice person, you write a few lines that make it obvious and that make it, you know, not as challenging. One thing Robert Woodruff said to me years ago was that he'd love to direct a play designed by George Tsypin, because George Tsypin designs the set that you *cannot* stage a play on. So, in overcoming that obstacle, you're forced to be more resourceful and creative. And I thought, 'Okay, I'm a playwright, I'm going to do that; I'm going to put obstacles into my plays that cannot be acted and cannot be directed and cannot be put on stage.' But I'm not in rehearsal to fix it, so they have to figure out how to do that, and then they're forced to do something that nobody has ever thought of.

—*The actors will have to create their own form, they'll find a way to deal with the limitations.*

—Right. Instead of my fixing it and making it easy for them so they don't have to deal with any limitations.

—*It sounds as if the presence of the playwright in the room can occasionally stall interpretation.*

—Yes.

—*Even if it's somebody as open as you are, obviously?*

—No, because then I force them to explore. But if I were in the room, because I think I'm a nice guy, I would make it easy for them, I would rewrite that part and make it easy.

—*Have you ever worked with a dramaturg?*

—Never.

—*And just to get back to what you were saying about working with all those wonderful directors, have there been cases where you felt unpleasantly surprised?*

—Oh sure. People who do things that I think are awful. But it's also true that I'll go to a production that I haven't seen any rehearsals of, and I'll think 'Oh my God, that's fantastic. Wow, look what they did.' And I'm amazed because they've found things that I didn't even know they were there, right?

—*It's like a gift.*

—Yeah. And also thinking about dramaturgs and working with a dramaturg: dramaturgs will have their own ideas of what's right and what's wrong. And I don't want to do what they think is right. I want to do what *I* think is right. I want to do just what I love. And since I'm the world's leading expert on what I love, I can't be wrong. So, even if nine out of ten people think, 'Oh, that's stupid and awful and wrong', I want to do it.

—*What's your opinion about the tendency in contemporary performance to make those Greek characters more human, common and understandable? And sometimes perhaps overly psychologised?*

—I'm against it. I don't think that Greek playwrights left the psychological understanding out of their plays because they were too stupid to know what that would be. They left it out on purpose, because they were doing something else. And, so, whatever else they were doing, I think it was quite amazing.

—*What were they doing?*

—I don't know. You and I might not have the same reaction but I think they were talking about how we live on earth and how our civilisations have been made, how we make it, and are we doing this as well as we could, could we do better? Do we have to do what others did? Or could we do something different, as we watch the play, sitting in the theatre of Delphi? Or is there another version of evidence to be written? No, we knew that was his mother and his father and that's how badly we wanted to be kings.

—*There is always a moral imperative that is extremely political at the same time.*

—Yes. We are the creators of our civilisation. So, how do we want to make it? What do we need to do to make it how we want it to be?

—*And this is exactly what I think is missing from many plays today, this big moral imperative and the idea that drama should ultimately be about our place in the world.*

—Yeah. Right.

—*I think what you're bringing to the table is that connection with the outside.*

—Yeah. The connection not just to a child and your psychological life and your intimate family relationships, but about how you're making the civilisation of the world you are living in. Are you doing a good job? Thank you, Donald Trump.

—*I was coming to that as a final question. At this moment in time in history in America [October 2016], what would you think would be the ideal Greek play to borrow from, to steal from, to describe what's happening now, all the anxiety we're faced with?*

—I'm not sure there is an evil character in any Greek play that's evil enough for a drama just now. So, that's a hard question.

—*Past anything even the Greeks could imagine.*

—Exactly.

—*Thanks so much, Chuck, this was great. Looking forward to your next Greek play!*

—Many thanks, Avra. And do *Big Love* in Europe! It's not weird to do it now since it's about people fleeing, trying to get into another country. Which is what's happening everywhere now.

Suzuki Tadashi

English translation by Uchino Tadashi

—*I'm going to start with a very general and perhaps slightly naive question. Ultimately, are you an optimist or a pessimist?*

—Well, it's hard to be candid about something like this when speaking of myself. But, fundamentally, I'm pessimistic about our collective global future. There are too many persistent conflicts. On the other hand, no matter how pessimistic our worldview may be, the fact that we're still able to create theatre is cause for optimism. In my case, the issue isn't about being pessimistic or optimistic. The function of art is to provide new, critical perspectives on the events that transpire in our world. It's for this reason that I choose narratives where human beings are placed in situations of extremely high risk.

—*The extremes that you were describing in* Culture is the Body.

—Those are the only kinds of situations that attract my interest. I'm simply not drawn towards the quotidian. Greek tragedy fascinates me because essentially every protagonist is a murderer of some sort.

—*Like any of us watching could potentially be a murderer.*

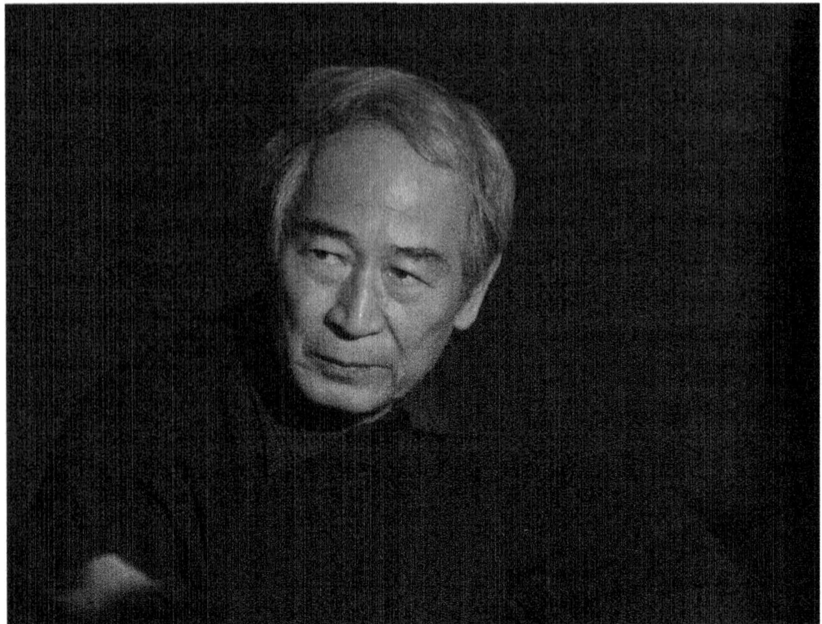

Figure 5.2 Suzuki Tadashi

—So when we think about why Greek tragedy put the homicidal act at the centre of so many of its narratives, we realise that this act poses the largest threat to the continuity of any given group's social order. Whether for political or religious reasons, whether in warfare, in acts of terror, or amongst members of a family, the act of murder, and how we collectively view it, is a central human concern, especially in our age of globalisation. In short, we must analyse how context influences the way we interpret and communicate the homicidal act in contemporary society.

—*And understand the motivation that is behind evil or in our nature?*

—The numbers of people being killed every day in our world is catastrophic. In Russia, in America, if you look at the numbers, they are really shocking. Of course, many people were killed in the two World Wars, but if you look at the daily numbers of dead in these countries in peacetime, there are probably more. Each group responsible for the killing tries to rationalise their actions, and so it's extremely difficult to objectively ascertain what is right and wrong. For example, today [24 March 2016] Trump threatened to drop an atomic bomb on ISIS. It's hard to believe that things have come to this pass.

—*Are there any answers that Greek tragedy gives us? Does it show us a pattern? Does it try to rationalise the irrational?*

—Greek tragedy is not concerned with giving us solutions. Rather, it presents the issues to us. Greek tragedies are asking us questions, and we must imagine the solutions. And I think that is perhaps Greek tragedy's most potent aspect: its questions are universal, timeless, and so can resonate with us in the contemporary world.

—*The questions are there, so the very fact that we dare face those questions is important.*

—Yes, the problem is that most are avoiding these questions. The Tokyo theatre in particular avoids them. I believe that art shouldn't concern itself with problems that can be resolved within the context of our quotidian lives. The great artists, including novelists, treat issues that can't be solved in daily life.

—*What is the role of the artist today as a product of his or her country and as an international entity?*

—Well, like I've been saying here, we have to consider why such violence is occurring between different groups, like ISIS and the EU, for example. Both groups have their own rationale which in their minds justifies the act of killing. You can find this same rhetoric in how the USA defended dropping the atom bomb on Nagasaki and Hiroshima, or how the Japanese justify the Nanking massacre. So, beyond arguing about who was right or wrong in each of these cases, the real issue we need to interrogate is why human beings have continued to slaughter each other throughout history. As artists we must ask: why can't we, as a species, coexist in peace? The 'why' here is very important. Why has there been so much killing throughout history? Greek tragedy and Shakespeare in particular explore this question, which is one of the main reasons I'm attracted to their texts. There are few questions as important as this. We could say another [question] is: 'Why does poverty exist?' Why such an economic gap between people? The why of poverty and killing are the two major questions facing the world now.

—*There seems to be a tendency in contemporary theatre to treat all these matters either very lightly, from a distance, and somewhat formalistically, without really thinking about them, and, reversely, through propaganda theatre. So, the violence never becomes convincing, you don't feel the violence in your gut.*

—I agree. The reason why I'm drawn to Greek tragedy is because these plays clearly show how human beings haven't changed over history. Of course, we think we have progressed. But if we consider ISIS and EU's reaction to it, these actions seem to reflect a return to the brutal times of the ancient Greeks. We can see the actions described in today's news reflected in a play like *The Trojan Women*. George W. Bush described the terrorists as an 'axis of evil' to justify his attempts to erase them, just as the Greeks erased the Trojans. The rhetoric of ISIS has the same slant. We live in a time when traditional warfare centred on national borders no longer exists. Instead we are experiencing a borderless World War III in action. We can no longer consider the violent events in Belgium and France as terrorism. This is the way a weaker opponent responds to aggression. This is referred to as 'terrorism', but ultimately, it's a state of war.

—*In the sense that terrorism is a perspective, a one-sided perspective.*

—In Japan, it has taken the form of nationalism. If it's in the nation's interest, we don't call it terrorism. But when you colonise people, you are essentially terrorising them.

—*You said in Culture is the Body that ultimately Greek tragedies are a kind of social theatre that evaluates our shared values. I think this is a wonderful way to capture the spirit of a tragedy. Do you think there is any chance that in the future other forms of writing can equal the force of social engagement that Greek tragedy inspired in its audience?*

—I doubt it. During the eras when Greek tragedy and Shakespeare's plays were written, and even probably even at the time of Chekhov, theatres were influential, they had social power, and their effectiveness was much stronger, their status was much higher. Up until that time communication was based on animal energy, which was a vital part of society. Nowadays, everyone communicates via smartphones. The emergence of a great playwright who can inspire a dynamic use of animal energy via their text and thus make a strong social impact seems almost impossible today. Today, filmmakers and screenwriters have more impact. The cinema has taken away that power of the theatre. Because more people watch cinema, more money can be invested in it, and ultimately it is more socially effective. So, naturally, less and less people are eager to participate in theatre-making. This is the source of my pessimism about the future. In the age of Greek tragedy, TV and cinema didn't exist. Theatre was one of the only viable means of public communication.

—*And it was promoted by society itself, it was part of the festivals that were being supported by the state.*

—And it was free of charge.

—*I also wanted to ask you about animal energy. In contemporary theatre in Japan, certain theatre-makers have been replacing actors with androids and robots. Do you fear that in the future we may be talking about a theatre with no living actors?*

—I don't agree with you, actually. I believe the more technology comes to dominate the theatre, the stronger the likelihood that we will see a countermovement of people who say we need to go back to the theatre's live roots. If technology starts to dominate the human in the theatre, sooner or later we will realise that this technology is no longer useful.

—*That was the question: is it a passing trend?*

—Yes, sooner or later we will reach a tipping point, where the dominance of technology will have driven us into a state of desperation. The problem now is we haven't quite reached that point yet. People are not desperate enough, not disappointed enough to return to their roots in the theatre. But it is becoming clearer that technological advances such as nuclear power plants, the personal computer and the Internet are actually making the world a more miserable place. It is technology that makes it easier for us to kill each other.

—*It's interesting that you say that, because I've noticed that, for example, in today's crisis-ridden Greece, theatre has had a resurgence. There are a lot more artists now, the audiences have increased, and even though the money is much less, theatre is flourishing.*

—That is probably happening, but we still need a leader, not a great leader, but a talented leader who has a superior perspective about the world. A leader in the theatre world, not a political one. There used to be such people, like Peter Brook, for example. But there are no more leaders in the theatre world who can cross the borders and still have some say and influence on people.

—*What does it take to be a leader in the theatre?*

—The leader has to speak up, he or she has to get the message through. It can't be just a playwright. But when this happens, it is usually the combination of a good director and a good playwright. Chekhov and Stanislavski, for example.

—*In collaboration.*

—Such a combination of great playwrights and directors today you may perhaps find in Germany, which has a lot of good directors. Yes, Germany is in a very good position, because it also has a lot of material, a rich history. But still we have to cross the national borders and work together.

—*Do you think international collaboration can be a partial solution to this, or in the very least, provide some kind of opening?*

—In that case, the message must be that there is an ongoing crisis. Right now, collaboration is just a commercial enterprise.

—*Festivals.*

—Festivals, yes. So, there has to be the bonding of those who can send out the message that there is this particular crisis here. Back when we created the Theatre Olympics [established in Delphi in 1993], it was like that, that was the idea behind it. Everybody's now very old or dead, the next generation has to do it.

—*But to me, watching how things go, it feels like we are running a little behind. We have a generation of people like you and Ariane Mnouchkine, and then Heiner Müller is gone, and even Robert Wilson's form is getting old, and there haven't been many artists who were able to go beyond that, they have been moving alongside, rather.*

—So that's why I am trying to help out, inviting Chinese directors and younger artists to create theatre here.

—*You said that Greek tragedy is 'a drama precipitated by excess', which is a great thought. There are contemporary directors who tend to psychoanalyse these monumental characters and turn tragedy into drawing-room drama. What happens to the excess and to the spirituality of tragedy, then?*

—One of the reasons why that happens is because the status of the theatre people in the world is now very low. Unlike politicians and those in the financial sector, theatre people have great difficulty learning about the broader spectrum of the world. So, when people speak with someone from politics or finance, they usually feel defeated, as if they're being persuaded against, because those people have better understanding when analysing the world. And certain theatre people are just talking about their very personal hobbies. The younger generations of Japanese theatre artists cannot actually analyse what is happening now. However, I believe theatre people in other parts of the world have a say, they can analyse what the problem of the world is. The solutions may be different among politicians, finance people, and artists. They understand what the problems are, they can share those ideas. And of course, it ends up with all the artists saying they don't have enough money. They are only complaining, without doing much. But here there's nobody that will even ask what the future of this world is, this country, this nation, nobody will discuss these big issues.

—*Would that require some special training and education, or is it just a matter of being engaged with society and with what goes on in the world?*

—If you don't have an education, it is very difficult to properly engage with society. Education is necessary.

—*And as a result, 'big' plays such as Greek tragedy and Shakespeare get shrunken into this tiny network of relationships.*

—Yes, that's true. So, when [directors] say they have contemporised Greek tragedy, it means it has become something very small. And, in my opinion, it's not really contemporary, anyway.

—*And what about the chorus? That's always a big challenge for directors. Is it the mouthpiece for the author, a representative of the audience, the voice of the gods, a collective democratic body making suggestions and decisions?*

—Greek tragedy is basically signed by one author, which means that the chorus is essentially the voice of the author. Contemporary playwrights tend to write their text with one opinion in mind, their own opinion. But in Greek tragedy the characters have different opinions. Overall, completely different perspectives are presented by the chorus, and that is how Greek tragedies operate, namely, in a dialogic relationship, in controversy. That's why Greek tragedians are great.

—*Argument, argument, argument. All thought process.*

—But towards the modern and contemporary audience the message has to be singular, and that is by the author himself. It is a kind of purification of the message. There is no argument here. Ibsen has one idea, and that's why he's writing his texts. Arthur Miller too. Greek tragedies are not like that. That is why it's so interesting that the text says there are different opinions. There is no conclusion. No resolution. Formally speaking, the *deus ex machina* is actually the formal resolution, but no real resolution. By contrast, Ibsen says 'I have an opinion and I need this text to express my opinions.' And that's why I think those texts are not interesting. If there is only one opinion, that is just one partial point of view. In fact, the chorus is always telling the audience that this is only a subjective point of view, there are lots of different things underneath, so your subjective opinion may be wrong. That is an excellent thing about Greek tragedy. The chorus questions the protagonists' subjectivity. It communicates to the audience the notion that humans are imperfect, and also that there might be something beyond the mere existence of a human individual, something transcendental, something more than what our existence is about. In *Oedipus Rex*, for example, it's clearly stated that the individual point of view, the individual judgement, does not solve any problems. Oedipus is continuously questioning himself, like a prosecutor. But if you keep interrogating and questioning yourself, this can only result in unhappiness. So, in other words, in Greek tragedy, they interrogate in order not to be happy.

And as a result, they become unhappy, which is why it's very interesting. In order to be unhappy, they want to know the truth. Think of Pentheus too, in the *Bacchae*. He wants to know the truth.

—*It's also some kind of acceptance that our life is full of conflict and there will be no resolution.*

—That is the greatness of Greek tragedy. Nobody ever became happier in Greek tragedy. Everyone's intentionally becoming unhappy.

—*Intentionally! That's the important word here.*

—And that, in my point of view, is what is happening now. Americans try to become richer and happier, and as a result everybody's becoming unhappy. ISIS, as well. They also want to be happy, but they may unconsciously become unhappy. Their intention is to be happy, but actually they're trying to become more unhappy.

—*Do you think there is something in Western thought in general about aggressively pursuing things and not going with whatever the flow is?*

—The *logos* cannot explain everything, the *logos* cannot explain human beings, as the chorus says. Not everything is a matter of logic.

—*Perhaps this is one of the messages: we, the audience, must accept that.*

—That is the best, the strongest message.

—*The "why" doesn't always lead to a "because" . . .*

—Yes, exactly. That is the greatness of the Greek tragedy.

—*Just to wrap up a little bit and talk about adaptation, since our book is about adapting Greek tragedy. I personally tend to think of adaptation as a love affair, where artists remain in love with the object of their affection, the text, even as they 'betray' it.*
I wonder what your take is on the fidelity question. How necessary or useful is it to think about how faithful a director is to the ancient text? What does 'faithful' mean, even?

—So, we should discuss what the assumption behind this question is, namely, who is the audience, who are we creating this piece for? Everything depends on that.
I don't really rewrite the text, but I adapt and reinterpret it, because I have the image of the audience in my mind, and so this has to change, to become this way for this particular audience, that's why I do that. That is my reason for adapting. I'm not creating theatre for an audience in general. I'm only making theatre for those who have the basic knowledge of the European literary history and about the relationship between Japan and Europe. Also, for those who think and sometimes wonder about what we should do about this relationship and all these different intellectual histories. I'm only creating my pieces for those people. I do say that to the public, in general: 'You don't understand, and it's okay that you don't, because I love creating this for you.' Some university professors in Tokyo say, 'Maybe you are wrong.' And I'm also saying to the Japanese politicians and intellectuals that they misunderstand Europe, and that as a Japanese, you should learn things from the European texts. So, I'm considering those who are already intellectuals or opinion leaders and those who will be future opinion leaders, and I'm also considering those people who will never be.

—*Really interesting take on adaptation. What about re-quotation? It's a term you yourself devised.*

—That's because I have a particular type of audience in my mind. Therefore, it's not simply a quotation but a re-quotation. As a director I'm not only looking at a text and thinking 'This has to be changed like that.' I'm looking at the audience and going back to the text and thinking about how to change the text. I'm not trying to appeal to the audience, intellectuals or would-be intellectuals, but I'm trying to change their minds, change their ways of thinking. I'm not really trying to appeal to the audience's intellect, but I'm trying to change their mind, to change their way of thinking. I'm not answering to the needs of the audience but trying to create new kinds of audiences and cause them to change.

—*And showing them what they really need, perhaps?*

—Or that human beings are like that. You have to look at human beings this way. The reason why I write a lot about society is because I want to tell politicians to change themselves. So those words are coming out on the basis of an understanding of what is happening in the world right now.

—*Do you feel that Japanese society is still isolated from the rest of the world? In terms of an awareness of what's happening in the rest of the world?*

—I don't think I'm representing Japan. I'm friends with directors from other countries, and in that sense I'm not isolated. However, I'm perfectly isolated in my country. I am very difficult to understand within Japan. I think it's always like that with the best artists all over the world, like in China or Russia or Germany: it's difficult to be understood. Ibsen couldn't go anywhere, he was cast away. The best artists are always fighting against the majority of a particular nation. And that can create a bond with the other artists who are also having their own struggle to fight within their own national boundaries. When we say we understand Arthur Miller, we are not saying that we understand America through Arthur Miller, but that we understand Arthur Miller, who was fighting against America. That's why we can bond. Lubimov, Brecht, too. And that kind of understanding can become a bond.

—*The better side of globalisation, in some ways.*

—The 'back alley'. Art is by definition that. That one culture is different from ours, that's the basic understanding. Culture is for managing the homogeneous community. The nation or community, that's what culture is there for, and that's why conflict is inevitable. The traditional community within one culture tends to conflict more with other communities. But the artist is somewhat out of that. The artist does not accept one culture all the way. He's interested in other cultures as well. Politicians tend to think that they can unify people within one culture, like in China. The artists are those people who can discover they can be critical or find different kinds ways of thinking.

—*You're saying you're isolated in Japan. In Europe, where I come from, you are considered one of the inspirational voices in Japanese theatre, which is so interesting because your theatre is very global, always mixing traditions and different forms. So, if there were one thing to say about the Japanese theatre to the rest of us, what would it be?*

—I don't like to be called 'Japanese theatre'.

—*What I meant is that you're one of the very few Japanese artists that we know, whose work we've seen, although you are obviously beyond national borders. But let's say an outsider comes, like me, and asks 'what is the state of Japanese theatre today?' And I'm not talking about Suzuki's theatre.*

—Because there is no formal training in the educational system of this country, everything becomes very small, like a hobby. It's a kind of liberation for the artists from their frustration with social tensions. Because the liberation from the frustration is a reality for those who are actually doing it. But I don't think that this kind of liberating from the frustration can be meaningful when artists are thinking about the global issues that we are actually very severely facing today. So, during the time of the communist regime, I feel that theatre was liberating audiences from oppression. So, liberation in the theatre has a meaning within the social context of a communist regime. In China, as well. In the case of a communist regime, artists analyse the frustration, they understand it is coming from communism itself. But for contemporary Japanese so-called 'artists' and for people in general, when one tries to resolve frustration, one resorts to a very small resolution, small reasons, everything small. So, people from other nations cannot share it because it's so private. Ibsen, Chekhov, Heiner Müller, or Arthur Miller, they all deal with this notion of frustration, but their way of treating this liberation from frustration can be shared by other people from other cultures and other nations. Of course, Arthur Miller is American, he is not writing for Japan or Germany, but we can understand how frustration operates in America.

—*He starts from the national and makes it global.*

—Yes. My understanding is that maybe some younger artists are doing a little bit more, in Korea, for example, or in Europe, but that's a very generational thing. Heiner Müller's West can be shared beyond generations. It's not a generation issue.

—*Maybe we just need to wait and see how to look back on these younger generations after years. Only time will tell.*

—I expect there is somebody who can create that kind of art, but what I see is that most artists are just moving in very small ways. That's how I feel.

—*That's pessimistic.*

—Trust me . . .

—*One last thing, because we talked about optimism, pessimism, and finally I'm getting the feeling that you're not an optimist at all — and how can any thinking person be? Are there any gods left for us today? Who are they? How do we find them?*

—I think we need them. There is a tradition in Japan that everything that has a beginning, nature itself, is God. Everything besides me, myself, the subject, is God. So, in the Japanese psyche there is this kind of priority or selection, something transcendental, the things that inspire us and make us happy. For me, nature in Toga Village probably is God because it inspires me, it gives me energy. So, God is something that will give you energy, like for some people, God is money or women.

—*I was talking about a spiritual connection . . . But I can fully understand why you moved to Toga.*

—I can create theatre here, I can work surrounded by this nature, it is a gift from God. Usually you can't do theatre in this kind of environment, you can't create or build an audience in these surroundings, it's very ambitious. This is my heart's homeland.

—*Thank you so much for this. And for your wonderful hospitality.*

—Thank you.

Ivo Van Hove

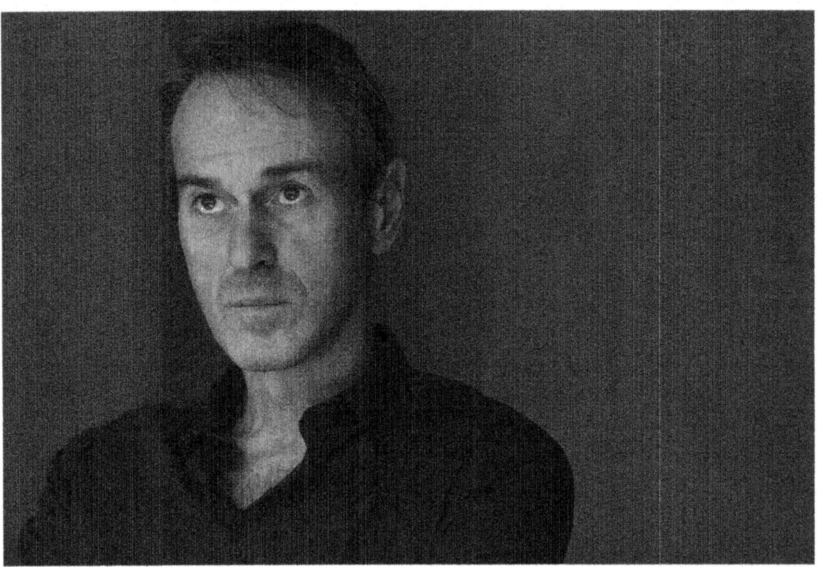

Figure 5.3 Ivo van Hove © Jan Versweyveld, reproduced with permission of Ivo van Hove

—*Thank you very much for all your wonderful work and for taking part in this. Would you talk a bit about your earlier work on the Greek plays, besides the* Antigone *production?*

—I did *Bacchae* twice. Different versions. Then I did *Ajax/Antigone* in one night.

—*Was that the whole play?*

—No, I cut things, I cut it down, it's a long time ago, 1991. *The Bacchae* was in 1986, and then I did *The Bacchae* again in Germany but in a totally different version. It was in 1992 or 1993, I believe, and *Ajax/Antigone* I did in '91.

—*Why start with these plays?*

—If you want to become a theatre director, there's a few things you cannot avoid to do, that's Greek tragedy, that's Shakespeare, and that's Chekhov. If you don't try to do that, why be a director?

—*Is it the challenging form, the content, or the global scope of the plays that drew you to them?*

—Everything. Everything is a challenge in a Greek tragedy, for me anyway. But you have to think, because they are very short most of the time, and Shakespeare is long. Greek tragedy takes about an hour and 40 minutes. It's like a nuclear bomb. It's not easy. Because you have few words, you don't have a lot of words to do that.

—*What really amazes me about your work is the way you always find the right metaphor. How do you work with metaphors? When you read the text, do you immediately identify what it is that will make it relevant?*

—Sometimes yes, sometimes not at all, sometimes it's a search. I'm going to do *Antigone*[1] again now, as you know, with Juliette Binoche. We are starting and we will tour for ten months in New York, London, Paris, everywhere. So, I'm preparing it now. Totally new, in a new translation specifically made for us. So, I'm thinking about that a lot now, and again I have the same problems as I had before. Namely, there are only a few scenes, where I have to bring out a very complex layer of content, complex people, complex themes, and only a short amount of time to do that.

—*Do you start from the themes and the people and not so much from the context? And by 'context' I mean the politics in the play. Sometimes directors go for an easy metaphor, which makes the production of the play very simple and very sort of literal, in a way.*

—That's the difficulty in tragedy: it can easily become not a Greek tragedy, which is of course about deep things. I have not seen a lot of productions of Greek tragedies that are gripping, that really touched me, that really irritated me or moved me. No, I haven't seen a lot of them. I only need one hand to count them.

—*Why do you think that is?*

—Because it's difficult. Greek tragedy is minimalist, it is about minimalism. Within minimalism there have to be maximum results, maximum effects. It's very hard, and it can easily become a vehicle for star actors. Everybody wants to play Oedipus, everybody wants to play Medea. So, it can easily become this comforting bourgeois evening. And I think, when you really look at Greek tragedy, it's very disturbing material, it's deeply political, but not political in the sense that it's about right and wrong. Also, in *Antigone*, who is right and who is wrong is not so easy to answer. You become totally confused by this text, and this confusion, this ambivalence is what I want to bring on stage when I do a Greek tragedy. That's what I try to do, anyway.

—*Do you stress the essential otherness of the tragedy? Several times we witness directors tending to psychologise the Greeks by, for example, making Medea the housewife*

[1] *Antigone*, produced by Toneel Groep Amsterdam, premiered at the Barbican Centre in London, in March 2015, and thereafter toured internationally.

next door. How do you feel about that?

—Sometimes it works, but of course Medea is not a housewife next door. She is a princess from another culture, being an outcast in that society that she enters, where she is accepted until Jason doesn't need her anymore, and then she is expelled to the other side. So, of course it's domestic, it's partly a domestic tragedy, but it becomes much more than that, and it's the same with Antigone when she wants to bury her brother. Yes, but she is also the descendant of Oedipus, and she has lost her father a few weeks before the play starts. She has lost her two brothers the night before, and she has already lost her mother long before that. There's only loss in her life. She is, as I call it, in a deep mourning process. And so Greek tragedy is always recognisable, but at the same time it's larger than life. You have to fight hard to find this delicate balance.

—*There's always an outside force that cannot be ignored.*

—Yes. In *Antigone*, for instance, it's nature. The Guard says it from the start, there has been a storm, and suddenly the body was buried, it's two burials: it's nature that does it, and there is Antigone who does it, with her libations. So, it's like the force of nature, something that we still have here, in New York. In New York it was devastating with [hurricane] Sandy two years ago. Devastation all over. The city was empty, a whole section of the city was cut off for weeks, no electricity, nothing. Nature can be a destructive force. There was no weapon against it, and that's this deep force, something that drives, something that's there in the cosmos. That's all in Greek tragedy, it's all there. And that you have to bring on stage. I try not to reduce it into a domestic drama, something which is happening a lot these days.

—*You are also very strong working with subtext. Is there subtext in Greek tragedy?*

—Of course. There's not so much speech, there's little speech.

—*Isn't everything said and spelled out?*

—I don't think so. I think there are layers there. Greek tragedy is not Brechtian for me. In a Brechtian drama everything is said and exemplified. But in a Greek tragedy there's a huge mystery, there's a huge hidden force. We talk about hidden forces now in *Antigone*, that's a play that has been very much in my mind. But in the *Bacchae*, for instance, the character of Dionysus is a liberator, and he is a dark character at the same time, because he's also a destroyer. That's very dark, very ambivalent. I think Greek tragedies are full of ambivalence. It's never as clear as good and evil. That's what's so great about it, that's what attracts us still in Greek tragedy. It's still this mystery of our life. That Sophocles, Aeschylus, Euripides try to explain something, but it's like an open-heart surgery.

—*How so?*

—That's what a Greek tragedy is for me. You see everything in its raw brutality. The heart beating, the veins, and then the people. I think Greek tragedies are brutal dramas, they are about brutality. Greek tragedy is not civilised at all, it's very rough. But that's what I try to do anyway.

—*Yes, we get a sense looking at the page that it is very structured speech but then there are different poetries, elemental poetries.*

—Yeah.

—*Would you describe your directing process on the classics as adaptation?*

—No, I don't like that. For instance, now I specifically asked for a translation of *Antigone* made by Anne Carson. She is proficient in Greek, she works from the Greek language. So, she made it and she called it all by herself not an adaptation but a translation. She calls it a new translation. That's what it is. So, of course, it's in the language of today. That's what I want. I don't want adaptations done in a free way, that's not what I'm interested in.

—*Where would you draw the line between a new translation, an inspired translation and a creative translation or adaptation?*

—Adaptation means that you can, for instance, change Medea into a housewife. Of course, I can do it also in my production, but an adaptation changes texts. A translation tries to translate into modern, into our language, what we believe the Greek intended. That's what the translation tries to do.

—*But in a director's work, adaptation can also involve messing around with the text, restructuring scenes, adding text, etc.*

—Yeah, but that's what I never do. People think I do that, but I never do that.

—*In this sense, how do you feel about those uneasy terms, 'loyalty' and 'respect' to the text and the playwright?*

—I think I'm totally loyal to the text. I had a professor when I went to school to learn how to direct, and I never forgot him. He used to be an actor himself and he said there is no objectivity in any text in the world. Nobody knows what the intentions of the author are, even the author himself might not know. A text is there in order to be interpreted. And I make an interpretation of the text based on my own experiences in life, what I've read, what I've seen, what I've encountered, my experiences. Somebody else will read something else in the same line. When I teach or give a speech, I always use a very simple line, the phrase 'I love you.' And then I ask five people to say it and immediately I have five different ways of saying 'I love you.' I can say 'I love you' in the way that I'd say 'I hate you.' And I can say 'I love you' in a very tender way. I can say 'I love you, but you don't love me.' I can say 'I love *you*, not somebody else.' Even in these three words there are thousands of possible interpretations. So, the idea that there is objectivity in a text is stupid. A text is a sponge and it absorbs time, otherwise we wouldn't play Greek tragedies anymore. It absorbs the times we're living in, and Antigone is still around. For me, for instance, living in Holland, this Malaysian Airlines plane that was shot down, we still don't know by whom, it was a very intense thing. Then all these people were lying dead for a week in the open-air, under the sun. It makes you think of Polynices lying there. It was so barbaric, like a Greek tragedy. And then the Dutch brought the dead back. There could have been seventy funeral cars, and they went to a whole country. For me it was like going back to the civilised world. Showing respect for people who have died. And that's what Antigone does. But people misunderstand Antigone a lot, thinking that she's ideologically driven. She's not ideologically driven, she's driven by pure emotion, she does a human gesture. I discovered that in *Oedipus at Colonus* she speaks to Polynices, and she says 'don't fight your brother, don't do it, it's wrong', so she's very negative about him. And then suddenly in *Antigone* she wants to die for him. I understand that, it's like being a mother. A mother whose son has killed somebody and is in prison will go to prison to visit him.

—*You just opened up the play for me. It's not about ideology, it's more about emotion. How do you get your audiences to feel things?*

—I don't know. The audience I don't care about. At this very moment I have a show here in New York that's playing. At the same time, I have a show at BAM Brooklyn, and I have a show in Holland. I don't know what my audiences are. I can only do what I think I can do, and I hope that they will be moved but not moved just emotionally, they can also be moved rationally. But I cannot know when I play for a house of 900 people, it's 900 individuals, and I don't know them. I don't care about them.

—*The question of the chorus is another issue. It's the one element that feels completely foreign to us and from which we've been quite alienated.*

—No, it's not foreign to us. Chorus is people. Community. That's not foreign to us. There are a lot of communities, but it's different communities from those in the past. We have communities, for example, there's Facebook. I'm not in it, but Facebook is a whole community of so-called friends. There are a lot of communities. For instance, here in New York there are communities in the big buildings, people I lived with in a big building here, downtown, it was 500 apartments and it felt like a community, like a little village. We met each other only in the elevator, and then you said 'Oh, how are you? Are you back from Europe? Yes, how are you doing?' You cannot claim that this is a good community and that the other one is a bad community. There are communities, and when you have to deal with Greek tragedy you have to think about what community means today.

—*Exactly. In Greek tragedy the community feels very connected. The chorus represents common sense, the common voice of the city people. I wonder if we have that here in New York or in Athens. I guess we do, although it's very hard to find what is common in the people.*

—But the chorus in *Antigone* has a different opinion in every scene of the play. It totally develops, it's not a static thing. I think that the chorus in *Antigone* is one of the best in Greek tragedy, anyway. But in other cases, like in the *Bacchae*, the chorus is a totally different thing from the chorus in *Antigone*. I think every play, every text in Greek tragedy, has a different kind of chorus. In *Medea* they are with Medea, in the *Bacchae* they are with choice, not with Dionysus.

—*Right.*

—But you have to think about what it represents in our time, and it's one of the things that a lot of directors evade because it's so challenging. The meaning, what it means today.

—*And the community of it. You mentioned different communities, but honestly, when you read and watch Greek tragedy you feel that these people are very connected, they practically breathe together, and I don't get the sense that this is what we have in our contemporary community space. But you're not afraid of the chorus.*

—I'm afraid of it, but I have to deal with it. I will do the whole text and we'll see what happens, and I think in the case of *Antigone* it's a very dramatic chorus because they really listen, they really try to. The chorus is a real character in *Antigone*. It's not just like a little feedback or something like that, it's much more. They think and they consider and reconsider, and you suddenly see the historical context of everything.

—*I like the idea of the chorus not being just feedback. That's a great way to put it.*

—Yeah.

—*Will Creon ever become the protagonist of the play?*

—That's my challenge. Because the play's called *Antigone*, not *Creon*.

—*Do you always pay a lot of attention to the title?*

—That's what I do all the time. For instance, with *Othello*. In a lot of productions that I'd seen, Othello was not the main character, Iago was. When I did *Othello*, I told my actors the play's called *Othello*. It's his drama, it's his tragedy. The play is called *Romeo and Juliet*, not only *Romeo*, not only *Juliet*. *Macbeth* is called *Macbeth*, not *Lady Macbeth*. She is very important, but still the play is called *Macbeth*. So, when Shakespeare wanted a play to be about two characters, he would call it *Antony and Cleopatra*, which is two characters. I think you should take the title seriously. That's what I do. *Antigone* is called *Antigone* because of her presence, what she's about, what she provokes, what she destroys, and also because she is not only a positive character, she is also a destructive and a self-destructive character. All these things I want to do.

—*Also the idea of going against the title is going against the dramaturgy, which is just there for you as a director, and ultimately if you try to fool around with it, it may just collapse.*

—I agree.

—*This may sound somewhat naive, but do you find Greek tragedy culturally bound or global in scope or both?*

—Culturally bound? Of course. But from a long time ago. Because also the Greek society now is a different society from what it used to be at that time. So, yes, it's culturally bound, like Shakespeare was culturally bound, but it has supported the power of the universal language, universal themes that still haunt us, that are still not solved, that we still fight with, that we still have nightmares and dreams about.

—*What about the language itself, the text, the way the language is formed and structured, even in translation? I know you disagree, but aren't those long speeches real arguments?*

—Have you ever read a play by Eugene O'Neill?

—*Yes.*

—Talking about long monologues. At this moment I'm directing *Mary Stuart* by Schiller. That's like a rhetorical text, and very hard to deal with. But you have to deal with it in order to do the play. But that's also what's so great about our job, since we are married to just plain realistic language. And now *Mary Stuart* uses a lot of metaphors in the text, and you have to deal with that. That's great, that's a challenge. It's the same in paintings. We still like to see a Turner painting, but we also like to see a Rothko painting. Or we like to see a David

Hockney painting or whatever. We don't listen to the same music every day, so for me the language of the Greek tragedies is of course a different kind of music, a different kind of colouring from what we hear or see in a French classic or a Shakespeare or a Chekhov. Chekhov is not from our time, it's also an older language from over a century ago.

—*Again, it's how you take that text and make it speakable, hearable, contemporary. This is why the work on the subtext is so important.*

—Yeah, right. I think that's something that the twentieth century has brought. Subtext didn't exist before. But I think that's what we can bring to it, now.

—*Could you describe the beginning of your rehearsal process for a Greek tragedy?*

—The first rehearsal of a Greek play I did was of thirty years ago, so that's a long time ago. But it will be the same as always. I do a reading, I talk a little bit about it, that's the first day. Just a plain routine, and a little bit of explaining the ideas of the world [of the play]. What I have to do as a director is to get to my set desires, to create the world where it's playing. I try to explain a little bit about the house that we have built for them, where will you live for the next ten months. And then the next day we start with Scene One. But I work in the same way with Shakespeare as with Arthur Miller. I always do the same thing.

—*What about the space? Considering that the Greek plays were intended for an open-air theatre, where you have the whole world coming in and the sun in the sky right above your head, how easy is it to just stage tragedy in a room basically, no matter how large? Do you miss the cosmos coming in?*

—No, ultimately I will bring the cosmos in, you will see.

—*I can't wait.*

—You will see. No, I think it's a very important issue. I have a set designer, Jan Versweyveld, who loves Greek tragedy and has a deep connection to it. He is very much aware that it's always about cities. A city wall that's protecting the city against outside influences or enemies, or whatever. So, the city wall was for this play very important. Of course, what I said in the beginning about the force of nature is also very important. And we will bring that into the production, too. For me it's very clear from the beginning that this is part of the production. It's this outside world that's also an inside world, because when you're inside a city wall, you're a part of the community, and when you're outside of it, you're outside of the community. So, that idea is very important.

—*In tragedy you have the entrances and it's the entrances from the left coming from the countryside and the right coming from the port. Do you follow those rules?*

—That's what we don't do. I don't use this type of conventions. That's what they call traditional things, and they don't resonate to anyone, anymore. You have to know in order to understand it. Otherwise it makes no sense. Left or right.

—*How does the outside communicate with the city?*

—Well, it's very easy, we have a wall and we have a door here.

—*And people come in.*

—You come in and then you're inside. I've used video here, and also when people go outside, we have images from outside.

—*Which it's a little bit what you did with* The Misanthrope, *with the outside of the theatre coming in.*

—Well, that's different. I like to expand always, I use the theatre, even when it's a conventional theatre, as a site-specific venue. That's how we use it.

—*So, we don't see the borders of the stage.*

—No. And that's where video helps us. Because it can go out.

—*Finally, why* Antigone *of all plays?*

—I've already said lots of things about it. Juliette [Binoche] wanted to do a project with me. I met her and we immediately started talking about Greek tragedy. We never talked about anything else and immediately we went there, I don't know why. It's an impulse. And we talked about different things, and after a year and a few conversations, we ended up with *Antigone*. Juliette loves the character, I think because it's very mysterious. I repeat myself here, but Antigone is a character with a lot of layers. She is vengeful, she is in mourning, she is sometimes stubborn, she is suicidal, she doesn't want to suffer anymore because she's suffered too much already, I can go on forever. It's an endless range of what's within us. And you see all that in one person, one character, only for just an hour and a half, all this. I think that's very intense.

—*Like a palimpsest.*

—Yes. And, of course, again, as I said earlier, we tend to like her but also to dislike her. And I have a lot of questions about her: do I like her, don't I like her? I like the idea that I don't know.

—*The ambivalence you were talking about.*

—And that's why this play is the climax of ambivalence. Also, it's the same way with Creon. In the beginning, he is a very positive character, a new leader. He really thinks about this curse of Oedipus and his family taking over the power. He thinks he has to stop them, because the curse brings all the violence, all the destruction. And he wants to be a modern leader. But, of course, he doesn't know how to handle them because he is also in stress about the civil war that just only ended yesterday evening. He's not relaxed. He is full of stress.

—*Usually we start with disliking him.*

—I will make you like him in the beginning.

—*And then what?*

—Also at the end, of course, when he's a broken man. Even though everything he did was wrong, you have to feel for him. You want to show the suicide of Antigone so that you can really see how far she goes. That is something that we talked about. So, I will do something that's forbidden in Greek tragedy, I will show things on stage. Also, the burial, I want to show it on stage.

—*Totally breaking the rules.*

—Yes, but hopefully I will bring out what is really there. The ugliness, the rotting body, what it means when a body that's lying there and that someone cares about it.

—*The rawness of pain.*

—Yes, I think that's what the play is about.

—*Thank you so much for sharing your thoughts. I look forward to the production.*

—Thank you.

CHAPTER 6

The View from the Archive

Performances of Ancient Tragedy at the National Theatre, 1963–1973

Adam Lecznar

Archives of grief I see falling upon this house
Death on birth birth on death there is no end to it
Some god is piling them on
One last root was reaching up for the light in
The house of Oidipous
But the bloody dust of death
Hacks her down mows her down
All the tall mad mountains of her mind.
(Carson 2012, n.p.)

Anne Carson, in her 2012 adaptation of Sophocles' *Antigone* entitled *Antigonick*, translates Sophocles' phrase 'ἀρχαῖα ... πήματα' at lines 594–5 as 'archives of grief'. In this volume, Vayos Liapis points out the aptness of Carson's response to this Sophoclean line. Liapis demonstrates that at the same time as 'archives of grief' draws on the homophony of the English word 'archive' and the Greek word *arkhaios*, meaning 'ancient', it also appeals to the etymological origin of the word 'archive' in the Greek word *arkheia*, meaning 'public records'.[1] On this reading, the tragic archive of ancestral curses invoked by Sophocles and Carson becomes an index both of depth of time and extent of renown. They are the famous but repressed stories from the dark vaults of Greek mythology that are not told explicitly in this moment but which silently surround and animate the story we are watching. The translation further gestures towards the reams of lost plays that would have been an integral part of the ancient corpus of tragedy alongside the thirty-three plays that survive today. These 'archives of grief' represent the mythologies that tragic literature does not preserve but that structure the unfolding events as absent presences, haunting the action across the millennia of tragic performances but never seen on stage.[2]

[1] See Liapis, Chapter 13, this volume.
[2] On Carson's *Antigonick*, see further Liapis, Chapter 13, this volume.

Following Carson's lead, I want to use this chapter to explore different ways of understanding the relationship between tragedy and the archive, and to examine how the resources of the archive can offer exciting possibilities for the reconstruction and interpretation of modern adaptations of ancient Greek tragedy.[3] As we will see, the view from the archive can help us understand the ambivalence that fuels modern adaptations of ancient tragedy, torn between an impulse to forget and a demand to bear witness. Irving Velody declared in a 1998 article that, 'As the backdrop to all scholarly research stands the archive. Appeals to ultimate truth, adequacy and plausibility in the work of the humanities and social sciences rest on archival presuppositions.'[4] Here, Velody suggests that what one critic has termed the 'allure' of the archive, and what another critic has described as its 'seduction', is the promise that it can provide unmediated truth about the past.[5] But the idea that the authority of the archive lies in its ability to adjudicate on the veracity of historical claims has provoked a rich tradition of dissent. One of the main propagators of this dissent was Michel Foucault, who argued that the archive was as much an engine of repression as it was of truth, and that its main role was in deciding what should be remembered rather than allowing its users to find out the details of historical truth for themselves.[6] Another was Paul Ricoeur, who has discussed the role of the archive in mediating between the personal act of memory and the institutional practice of history, suggesting that it creates the parameters for traditions of cultural remembrance through the particular 'traces' of events and actions that it chooses to preserve.[7]

Jacques Derrida launched a particularly reverberative critique of the archive in his 1996 book *Archive Fever: A Freudian Impression* (first delivered as a lecture at London's Freud Museum in 1994). Derrida, like Carson after him, exploits the richness of the ancient Greek language to explore a different resonance of the archive, examining its relation to the word *arkhē*. Derrida teases out the conflicting implications of this Greek root, differentiating between the word's meanings of 'beginning' and 'power', as 'the *commencement* and the *commandment*':

> This name apparently coordinates two principles in one: the principle according to nature or history, *there* where things *commence* – physical,

[3] For a good introduction to archive theory and for further bibliography, see McGillivray (2011). Further useful sources are Macintosh (1997); Steedman (2001); Hamilton et al. (2002); Freshwater (2003); Burton (2005); Craven (2008); Michelakis (2010a).

[4] Velody (1998), 1. [5] See Freshwater (2003) and Michelakis (2010a), esp. 105.

[6] Foucault (1972), esp. 128–31. [7] Ricoeur (2004), esp. 166–76.

> historical, or ontological principle – but also the principle according to the law, *there* where men and gods command, *there* where authority, social order are exercised, *in this place* from which *order* is given – nomological principle.[8]

Derrida's ontological and nomological principles might also be parsed as the competing logics of memory and forgetting; drawing on Freud, he argues that the physical space of the archive, along with the actions of its human guardians, strictly controls access to its material as a means of limiting the easy exchange between the public and private spheres of understanding. Derrida makes clear, in line with Foucault, that the archive is as much interested in creating a particular version of the future as it is in preserving the past: 'The archive has always been a *pledge*, and like every pledge, a token of the future.'[9]

I will return to Derrida in the conclusion; but for now it is enough to note the divide between understandings of the archive as a space for reconstructing a truer version of the past, and as a space for finding out why a particular version of the past has come to be remembered. This tension is crucial in debates about performance archives. While the performance archive can serve as a way of understanding a performance *as it really was* by means of video or audio recordings, and thus of gaining access to the elusive performative moment, it simultaneously offers a unique opportunity for understanding how a performance might have been otherwise.[10] This is something that Jane Montgomery Griffiths discusses in Chapter 7, which describes the various situations, contingencies, and mediations that gave rise to a controversial production of *Antigone* in Melbourne, Australia, in which she was involved as translator and actor. From this privileged perspective, Montgomery Griffiths skilfully reconstructs a subjective account of how, as she puts it, 'the reified theatrical entity that is subject to analysis has often only ended up in that form because of a series of unplanned disappointments, practical compromises, and pragmatic solutions'. This is the same position that I wish to explore in this chapter; but as we will see, the view from the archive is more *objective* than the view of the participant in that it relies on the material remains of performance. Through its preservation of discussions and conversations between the people who were involved in its creation, be that through letters, memoranda, telegrams, or other types of record, the archive can shed an oblique light on the contingency of the performative moment and

[8] Derrida (1996), 1. Original emphasis throughout. [9] Derrida (1996), 18.

[10] See Phelan (1993) for seminal discussion of the performative moment.

the very human desires and commitments that led to its final form. As Glen McGillivray points out, 'Writing performance history is writing about hidden things deduced from the physical traces and remnants, or detritus of performances which . . . have become enigmatic metonyms for that which has now vanished.'[11] In what follows I try to balance these two archival imperatives. First, I show how its resources can take us closer to understanding what happened on stage by filling in the silences of the published texts of the plays in question; second, I show how a performance can also be understood as a patchwork of the myriad human encounters that facilitated its birth on the part of (amongst others) actors, directors, producers, spectators, reviewers, translators, and poets.

To this end, this chapter will focus on three performances of ancient drama by the Royal National Theatre of Great Britain (henceforth 'NT') in the first ten years of its existence, from 1963 to 1973.[12] Prior to this, some seminal productions of Greek tragedy, like the Prussian version of Sophocles' *Antigone* that was performed in 1845 at London's Covent Garden and featured a score composed by Felix Mendelssohn-Bartholdy, had emphasised the archaeological accuracy of the stage set in an attempt to recover the historical resonances of the plays in question. Others, like the performances of Gilbert Murray's translations of Euripides at London's Court Theatre in the first decade of the twentieth century, had made the plays speak to the contemporary theatrical fashion for the drama of Henrik Ibsen and George Bernard Shaw.[13] As we will see, the NT proved themselves from their very inception to be committed to performing innovative versions of ancient plays, something that was in tune with the spirit of the 1960s, when, as Edith Hall puts it, 'Greek tragedy began to be performed on a quantitatively far greater scale, from more radical political perspectives, and in more adventurous performance styles than it had been before.'[14]

The first play that I examine is Sophocles' *Philoctetes*, which was also the first ancient Greek play to be performed at the newly founded NT in April 1964. Here, I explore how the NT tried to frame the performance as offering an innovative angle on Greek tragedy by means of its programme

[11] McGillivray (2011), 17.

[12] Some of the material on these plays and on the NT more generally has been reworked from the first two chapters of Lecznar (2014).

[13] See Macintosh (1997, 2015) for good introductions to this history. See also E. Hall and Macintosh (2005), 488–520 and Macintosh (2007) on the performance of Gilbert Murray's translations.

[14] E. Hall (2004a), 1.

material. Second, I discuss the performance of Ted Hughes' translation of Seneca's *Oedipus* from March to August 1968. As we will see, the people involved in the play explicitly understood it as an alternative version of Sophocles' Oedipus tragedy Here, I use audience responses to show how the archive can shed light on performative moments that might otherwise have been lost. Finally, I discuss the performance of Wole Soyinka's *The Bacchae of Euripides: A Communion Rite* between July and October 1973 in order to bring to light the long history of the NT's desire to put on Euripides' tragedy that involved two unsuccessful attempts to stage the play before they were finally successful with Soyinka. This chapter argues that the details of these two hypothetical productions can help us understand what the NT expected when they finally came to perform Soyinka's play, and demonstrates that documents and records preserved in various archives can help us construct a narrative of what the NT wanted to achieve in these early productions.[15]

Sophocles' *Philoctetes* (1964)

Though the NT did not become a fully functioning theatre company until November 1963, it had been in the pipeline since the late nineteenth century, when critics and drama professionals including Matthew Arnold, Harley Granville-Barker, and William Archer had campaigned for Britain to have a national theatre company similar to France's Comédie Française.[16] These desires gained a concrete form in 1949 when the National Theatre Act was passed by the British Parliament; fourteen years later the NT took up residency at London's Old Vic theatre under the leadership of its first Artistic Director, Sir Laurence Olivier. Its first production was Shakespeare's *Hamlet*, directed by Olivier. This choice of first play testified to a particular understanding of the role of a national theatre in two ways. First, the decision to begin with Shakespeare appeared to suggest that the NT was primarily a theatre for the performance of canonical British (or perhaps more accurately, English) plays; second,

[15] I have used three physical archives in the writing of this piece: the National Theatre Archive on The Cut near the present home of the National Theatre at London's South Bank (NT Archive); the Theatre and Performance Archives of London's Victoria and Albert Museum in Blythe House in Earl's Court (V&A Theatre Archive); and the University of Bristol Theatre Collection (Bristol Theatre Collection). Another electronic archival resource that has greatly facilitated archival research on the performance of ancient drama is the Archive of Performances of Greek and Roman Drama (APGRD) at the University of Oxford. See www.apgrd.ox.ac.uk for further details.

[16] See Elsom (1976), 161–81; Findlater (1997); Shepherd (2009), 1–17.

Olivier's vision for *Hamlet* took clear visual cues from the 1948 Academy Award-winning film that he had directed and in which he had starred in the eponymous role.[17] Both of these positions attested to a conservative commitment to tradition that was at odds with the ideas of the theatre's first Literary Manager, the former theatre critic Kenneth Tynan. Tynan was keen that the theatre should understand its national role differently, suggesting in a speech he gave to the Royal Society of Arts in 1964 that the aim of the NT should be to 'offer the public the widest possible selection of good plays from all periods and places'.[18] Tynan's position speaks to a desire to be more cosmopolitan and inclusive, with less emphasis on the canon and more on seeking out new plays from across history and around the world. This double imperative of conservatism and innovation made the position of ancient Greek tragedy particularly fraught at the founding of the NT. While it might serve as the starting point of the European theatrical tradition of which *Hamlet* was a part, it could just as easily be a casualty of Tynan's desire to expose the British public to a wider range of theatre from around the globe.

The choice of Sophocles' *Philoctetes* as the NT's first version of an ancient drama, produced in April 1964 as part of a double bill with Samuel Beckett's *Play* (1963), tried to balance respect for tradition with drive for innovation. The NT was keen on doing an ancient Greek tragedy at this early stage, and chose to do *Philoctetes* after they were unable to put on a planned version of Euripides' *Bacchae* (more on which below). William Gaskill directed this version of Sophocles' play in an adaptation by Keith Johnstone: both Gaskill and Johnstone were recent recruits from London's Royal Court Theatre, which had become synonymous with experimental productions in the mid-twentieth century.[19] Other details of the production suggest that *Philoctetes* was selected with innovation in mind, including the decision to stage it alongside Beckett's *Play* even though Beckett's piece was twenty minutes long and Sophocles' tragedy lasted just over an hour.[20] As we will now see, the programme that accompanied this performance and the frame that it tried to furnish for the action on stage in the mind of the spectator demonstrate the NT were

[17] F. Beckett (2005), 111–29. [18] Tynan (2007), 243 (see 235–44 for the whole speech).

[19] This Royal Court connection extended to the production of Beckett's *Play*, where the director was George Devine: Gaskill, Johnstone, and Devine had collaborated intensively at London's Royal Court Theatre during the fifties when Devine had been in charge (Gaskill would return to the Royal Court two years later in 1966 on Devine's death). See Rebellato (1999).

[20] These numbers come from the stage manager's reports for the performances, which list the exact length of every performance of the different plays. Accessed in NT Archive.

attempting to marry together antiquity and modernity in their first foray into ancient Greek drama.

The programme begins with material on *Play*, including a full-page photo of Samuel Beckett, a biography of his life up until April 1964, and a two-page essay on how best to understand Beckett's theatrical style by the play's director George Devine.[21] After this, the reader encounters a photo of a statue of Sophocles followed by a four-page excerpt from the influential essay 'The Wound and the Bow' by the American critic Edmund Wilson.[22] After three pages of sketches by Sam Kirkpatrick, the production's costume designer, of the appearance of the character Philoctetes and of the stage itself, comes a three-paragraph essay by the play's director William Gaskill:

> The interpretation of myths is as risky as the interpretation of dreams. While we sleep it is the dream itself, its succession of images, which holds us. In the morning we may analyze it; but not while we are dreaming. This is not to say that dreams, myths and plays from myths cannot be interpreted: the point is that in the moment of experiencing them we cannot submit them to rational analysis. Having seen 'Philoctetes', we may decide that its 'theme' is integrity under pressure (represented in different ways by Philoctetes and Neoptolemus); but this decision is a logical afterthought, it is not part of the theatrical experience.
>
> The myth of Philoctetes rests on one irreducible fact. It shows a man in extremity. So do the plays of Samuel Beckett. Beckett, too, places his characters in total extremity – buried up to their necks in the earth, confined in dustbins or jars – but he gives them nothing with which they can combat their misfortunes. They are powerless. But Philoctetes not only has a terrible wound; he also has an invincible bow.
>
> This is a myth about human beings in a realistic situation. It is less concerned with divine justice than most of the better-known Greek plays; the problem it poses is a human problem, calling for a human solution. Hercules, who appears at the end, is a highly personalised god; he was once

21 The fact that Beckett's play comes first in the programme attests to the fact that for the first twelve performances the running order was first Beckett, then Sophocles; however, as a slip included in the programme on Saturday 16 May declares: 'It has been decided that the balance of this programme is improved by reversing the order of the two plays. "Philoctetes" will be given first and "Play" second.' This is borne out in stage manager's reports for the thirteenth performance of the drama on 16 May, where a note confirms 'Order of programme reversed.' Documents accessed in NT Archive.

22 Programme accessed in NT Archive. See Wilson (1961), 244–64 for the essay. Wilson argues that the play is 'a parable of human character' (263) and emphasises the psychological elements of Sophocles' drama; he also suggests that the story of Philoctetes was popular among rebellious artists like André Gide in the twentieth century because it provided a mythical metaphor for 'the idea that genius and disease . . . may be inextricably bound up together' (259).

> a man, and in addition he was Philoctetes' master. In most Greek drama, the gods dictate the course of the action from the very beginning. Here, almost deliberately, Sophocles seems to soft-pedal the divine element in order to emphasise the human one. 'Philoctetes' is not a play about man against the gods, but a play about man against man.[23]

In this lapidary piece, Gaskill consistently subverts scholarly understandings of *Philoctetes.* By stressing the links between Sophocles and Beckett he places both dramas on a human plane, and thus downplays the manifest mythological and divine elements of the Greek play, such as in the significance of an oracle and in the appearance of the spirit of Heracles as *deus ex machina* at the play's conclusion.[24] On this reading, *Philoctetes* is removed from its ancient Greek context and cast as a drama with universal human resonance that might prove an appropriate match with Beckett's sparse, psychologically introspective drama. Gaskill's fundamental aim is to emphasise the antique innovation that he associates with Sophocles' play, and it is as a way of showing this that he contrasts *Philoctetes* successively with 'better-known Greek plays' and 'most Greek drama' as a means of emphasising the freshness of the NT's choice.

The remaining content of the programme continues to explain the NT's innovation: after excerpts about Sophocles' play from Gotthold Ephraim Lessing's 1766 aesthetic treatise *Laocoön* and William Wordsworth's 1827 poem 'When Philoctetes in the Lemnian Isle', comes a final piece, of uncertain authorship, entitled 'Philoctetes Philanthropist':

> As far as we can ascertain, the National Theatre production of 'Philoctetes' represents the first occasion on which the play has been publicly performed by professional actors in this country. It has, however, been staged several times by amateurs. The following account of one such production appeared in 'The Times' on April 21, 1933, under the heading 'BELFAST UNEMPLOYED IN A GREEK PLAY':
>
> 'A Greek play, the "Philoctetes" of Sophocles, was performed by 21 unemployed Belfast workers in the large hall of the Queen's University here this evening. This was an experiment introduced by Professor Meredith, President of the Queen's University Dramatic Society, who produced the play to provide instruction and recreation for unemployed workers. Over 1,400 of the Belfast unemployed are receiving instruction in a variety of subjects ranging from English and Latin to shorthand ...
>
> 'The proceeds of the Greek play will be devoted to a fund to provide textbooks for these unemployed students. It is the first time that

[23] Accessed in NT Archive. [24] See Roisman (2005) for a good introduction to *Philoctetes.*

> 'Philoctetes' has been staged in Belfast, and the unemployed performers and their friends took a great interest in the production and provided their own scenery and stage effects ... A large audience really enjoyed the performance tonight, and a good sum has been realised for the unemployed students' textbook fund.[25]

The NT organised their programme in order to introduce their *Philoctetes* as a theatrical departure for the theatre: after Gaskill has read the tragedy as a play concerned with transhistorical, human ideas, as opposed to the divine, culturally specific concerns of other extant Greek texts, the references to Lessing and Wordsworth emphasise the play's appeal to writers and artists throughout history. Finally, the excerpt from a 1933 newspaper article stresses both the NT's innovation in the professional sphere, and hints at their desire to balance an emphasis on the intellectual prestige of Greek tragedy with the suggestion that this play might have appeal to audience members who do not have prior knowledge of classical literature.[26] With their production of *Philoctetes*, the NT declared an intention to balance the approaches of Olivier and Tynan by subverting the canon and choosing a lesser-known tragedy; but this was an uncontroversial beginning to what would become a much more provocative tradition.

Seneca's *Oedipus* (1968)

The second play to be performed at the NT with a close (if indirect) relationship to ancient Greek tragedy was Seneca's *Oedipus* in 1968. The impetus behind this play was complex. Tynan seems to have been alerted to the play's potential when he received an unsolicited translation from a BBC radio producer called David Turner in early 1967. As Tynan later declared in a letter, 'I've always been fascinated by Seneca and [Turner's translation] seemed a pretty good attempt to render a strange and unique flavor. Olivier thought the play was streets ahead of Sophocles.'[27] With Olivier convinced, the theatre company issued a contract to Turner for his translation. At first Olivier was also going to direct; but he shortly grew ill and abandoned the project, and in the summer of 1967 the NT contacted the then head of the Royal Shakespeare Company, Peter Hall, to ask if he would permit Peter Brook to take over the production. Brook had gained international acclaim for his productions of *Titus Andronicus* and *Marat/*

[25] Accessed in NT Archive.
[26] See Hardwick and Harrison (2013) and Stead and Hall (2015) for explorations of similar issues.
[27] See letter dated 10 November 1967 from Kenneth Tynan to Ted Hughes. Accessed in NT Archive.

Sade at the RSC in the earlier sixties and was a bright directing talent. On reading Turner's text, Brook decided that he wanted a poet to go over the translation; the NT Archive preserves an urgent telegram that Tynan sent to the poet Ted Hughes at his home in Devon on 8 November 1967:

> HAVE YOU READ THE OEDIPUS OF SENECA STOP WE ARE PRESENTING PLAY AT NATIONAL THEATRE IN MARCH DIRECTED BY PETER BROOK WHO WOULD LIKE YOU TO REVISE OUR TRANSLATION STOP IF INTERESTED PLEASE WIRE ME OR TELEPHONE WAT 2033 REGARDS KEN TYNAN THENAT LONDON SE1.[28]

Hughes responded positively and a collaboration began between himself, Brook, and the NT.[29] Eventually Hughes seems to have completely rewritten the text he inherited, which left the NT in a difficult position since they had already issued a contract to Turner. After extensive wrangling over the terms of the royalties, they eventually resolved the issue by declaring on all material related to the production that Ted Hughes had adapted the play 'from a translation by David Anthony Turner'.[30] As we will see in the discussion of the *Bacchae* below, the NT was prone to lengthy negotiations over translations of ancient Greek tragedies; in this section I want to examine how the archive can give us access to elements of performance that are invisible in published versions of texts.

In a short essay that accompanied the publication of his translation in a special edition of the classics journal *Arion* in late 1968, Ted Hughes was quick to emphasise the significance of extratextual, performative concerns to the NT's decision to stage Seneca's *Oedipus*:

> Our guiding idea from the start was to make a text that would release whatever inner force this situation still has, with the minimum of interference from surface detail in word, plot, or movement. Sophocles' version would not have served the special purposes of this production nearly so well as Seneca's, which is less a play than a series of epic descriptions connected by artificial and at times rudimentary dialogue. It is easier to see the form of the Seneca as that of the ritualised account of a sacred event. Out of the possibilities of this, Peter Brook drew the whole style of his production, the

[28] Accessed in NT Archive.

[29] See Fleming (2013) on Hughes' translation. The collaboration between Hughes and Brook would also result in the 1971 performance of *Orghast* at the Shiraz Arts Festival in Iran. As well as interweaving parts of Aeschylus' *Prometheus Bound* and *Persians*, Hughes also invented a language (called Orghast) for the production. See A. C. H. Smith (1972) and Sagar (2009), 6–13.

[30] Programme accessed in NT Archive. See Stead (2013) for further archival research on the relationship between Hughes and Turner.

> limited movement of the actors, the heightened style of delivery, and the over-all headlong musical impetus.[31]

Hughes explains that Seneca has been chosen over Sophocles because it has an internal dynamism lacking in the Attic tragedy. Crucially, this manifests itself in the production through a variety of performative, and thus non-textual techniques, including the movement of the actors, their rhetorical style, and the production's use of music. In a longer essay that appeared alongside the published text of his translation in 1969, Hughes described this untapped power with a rather different emphasis:

> The Greek world saturates Sophocles too thoroughly: the evolution of his play seems complete, fully explored and in spite of its blood-roots, fully civilized. The figures in Seneca's *Oedipus* are Greek only by convention: by nature they are more primitive than aboriginals.[32]

This focus on the 'primitive' had not been part of the NT's approach to Greek tragedy four years earlier with *Philoctetes*: then, the play had been located mostly within a European intellectual tradition populated by Beckett, Lessing, and Wordsworth. The turn from Sophocles to Seneca thus hinges on the belief that the Roman playwright had captured the primal heart of the Oedipus myth in a way that would allow it to become a modern ritual and an attempt to resacralise the theatrical space. Again, we will see these themes were picked up in the later production of Soyinka's *Bacchae*; but for now I want to use the archive to see how they played out in the performance on stage.

This is most evident in the finale to the production, which Ted Hughes' translation represents with the following enigmatic stage-direction:

> (*The* CHORUS *celebrate the departure of* OEDIPUS *with a dance*)[33]

What this entailed is preserved in a review of the performance by Ian Scott Kilvert, which was published in the same 1968 edition of *Arion* as Hughes' translation:

> The epilogue was evidently devised to illustrate Peter Brook's theory that applause has become an automatic and possibly quite irrelevant tribute to a performance and that a more appropriate reaction might be silence. The stage is cleared and a litter is brought on supporting a tall object draped in red silk and covered with ivy leaves, which when the veil is twitched away is revealed to be an enormous golden phallus. The chorus enter and stream through the auditorium, led by a brass band playing 'Yes, we have no

[31] Hughes (1968), 325. [32] Hughes (1969), 8. [33] Hughes (1968), 371; (1969), 55.

bananas' in the style of a New Orleans jazz group returning from a funeral service: the chorus follow it, executing a bacchanalian jive . . .[34]

By discussing applause, Kilvert picks up on Peter Brook's essay in the programme of the production that included the comment 'we clap our hands mechanically because we do not know what else to do, and we are unaware that silence is also permitted, that silence also is good.'[35] Brook objected to the way that applause allowed the audience a sense of celebratory closure at the end of a play, preventing silent deliberation over what had taken place on stage. To stop this, he did not conclude the production with the sombre departure of Oedipus from Thebes, but rather had all the members of the chorus, as well as the actor who played Creon, change costume from all-brown into gold so that they could participate in a 'carnival', dancing around a golden phallus.[36] The intrusion of jazz music, particularly in the style of a 'Second Line' procession from New Orleans, points again to the NT's new attempt to disassociate Greek tragedy from its exclusive connections with a white European tradition.

While this finale is not preserved in the published text, it has nevertheless become part of the production's lore.[37] But the archive can give us some sense of the hitherto-lost ramifications this directorial decision had for the audience, and what they meant for specific performances of the play. On 29 April 1968, a member of the public wrote to the secretary of the NT board, Kenneth Rae, to express her horror at the conclusion:

Dear Mr Rae

I am writing in protest about the final scene in the current production of 'Oedipus' at the Old Vic.

I have seen most of the plays that the National Theatre has staged recently, and have been generally impressed; but I have never before, either at the Old Vic or any other theatre experienced the shock of gratuitous obscenity that I received at the appearance on the stage, at the focal point of an irrelevant finale, of a large gilt penis.

This I consider inexcusable, because it had no dramatic point and no connection with the play itself. It compared shabbily with the scene of

[34] Kilvert (1968), 507.

[35] Accessed in NT Archive. This comment came from Brook's then-yet-to-be-published theatrical manifesto *The Empty Space*: for its published context, see Brook (1968), 47.

[36] This is clear from the costume files of the production: next to every member of the cast except Sir John Gielgud, who played Oedipus, and Irene Worth, who played Jocasta, there is listed '1 Gold Costume' alongside their outfit of 'Brown wool sweater/Brown Jersey trousers/1 pair black socks/1 pair brown suede shoes'. Accessed in NT Archive.

[37] E.g. J. Clark (1991), 83–4. Clark's information was also gleaned from reviews of the original production – see Clark (1991), 183, n. 4.

> Jocasta's suicide, which was also shocking, but, because it had a dramatic point, acceptable. As played in Peter Brook's production, the last scene was superfluous, disgusting and an insult to the audience, and in my view it should be omitted from subsequent presentations. The play would not be harmed.
>
> In addition, in fairness to any teacher who might consider taking his pupils, it should be made clear on the handout that the play in its present form is not suitable for this. Indeed, I was perturbed to see that a matinee was presented on 21st March for the I.L.E.A.
>
> I should be grateful if you would draw this letter, of which I am sending a copy to Mr. Brook, to the attention of your Board.
>
> Yours sincerely,
>
> Susan Maunsell[38]

Unlike most of the disapproval and criticism to be found in the letters of complaints preserved in Olivier's papers (there are none in the NT's official archives), Susan Maunsell's dissatisfaction was not rooted solely in personal dislike of the production, but had also grown out of a belief that its finale precluded its being performed to school audiences, as had happened on 21 March in the matinee for the Inner London Education Authority that she mentions. Two days later, Kenneth Rae wrote a letter in response that tried to assuage her concerns:

> With regard to the ILEA matinee, which you mention, I think I should tell you that the performance was stopped before the messenger's speech. Mr Brook then explained to the audience how the play ended, giving them full details. Educational officials were present and, after a request had been made that anyone under 16 should leave the theatre, the performance proceeded at the request of the audience.[39]

Rae's story of a performance that had taken place over a month earlier is confirmed by the stage manager's report for 21 March: while the production of *Oedipus* generally lasted an hour and forty-five minutes, this performance (the third of the run) lasted two hours and nineteen minutes. The report includes a handwritten note:

> There was a 30 min break at the end of Act 4 when Mr. Brook and Mr. [Geoffrey] Reeves talked to the audience. It was decided to continue the play to the end inc. the carnival.[40]

[38] Letter dated 29 April 1968 from Susan Maunsell to Kenneth Rae, BL Manuscript Add. 80412.

[39] Letter dated 1 May 1968 from Kenneth Rae to Susan Maunsell, BL Manuscript Add. 80412.

[40] Stage manager's report dated 21 March 1968, accessed in NT Archive.

What emerges from these documents is an extraordinary event in theatrical history. One of the twentieth century's most avant-garde directors interrupted a performance to come on stage before the end of the play and check that a young audience understood the significance of one of his theatrical choices. The exact explanation that Brook offered is not preserved; but what does survive is his angry response to a request from the NT the night before this performance that he might consider changing the ending for this particular school audience:

> I make no bones about being deeply mistrustful at the moment so I would like to put everything on record. I received a request from George Rowbottom to consider eliminating the phallus from Oedipus for the schools matinee. The following points were the essence of my reply:
>
> 1. To ask if it could be explained to me very simply on what grounds we might fear having a phallus seen by children between the age of 12 and 16. Was our concern that it might provoke certain questions? If so, would such questions be in any way contrary to the general practice of sex education in schools today?
> 2. As a help to accepting the genuineness of such anxiety could I be assured that certain lines of Shakespeare had been omitted in the past from school performances?
> 3. I naturally applaud and admire the theatre's sense of responsibility towards its young audience. Consequently, I can safely assume that before rushing into accepting bookings from school parties, the question of the possibly disturbing effects on young adolescents of the themes of this play have been thoroughly discussed and weighed. I admit that, learning for the first time about school parties, I am very concerned to know whether the horrors described by the Messenger and the profoundly horrible event of a woman sticking a sword up her vagina might not be genuinely traumatic.
>
> I hope this question is being given attention.[41]

The rest of the negotiations must have taken place via face-to-face meetings or on the phone, as no record survives of how they decided on the final form of the performance. Brook's response provides a startling insight into the immediate, vigorous response of a theatrical revolutionary when faced with an anxious theatre company, worrying about a perceived disjuncture between its role as a public institution and its duty towards theatrical innovation. First, Brook suggests that if the young audience is shocked by the sight of a phallus, then this suggests their sex education

[41] Internal memorandum from Peter Brook to Frank Dunlop, dated 20 March 1968. Accessed in NT Archive.

classes are not preparing them well enough for the world; second, he invokes the counter-example of Shakespeare's obscenity as a reason not to cut the final scene; finally, he argues that the NT is being at best myopic and at worst hypocritical in their desire to get rid of his final phallic carnival but to keep unquestioned the shocking visual representation of Jocasta's suicide, as the actor Irene Worth 'slowly and grotesquely impailed [*sic*] herself through the womb by lowering herself onto one of several long thin obelisks that earlier in the play had seemed mere stage decoration'.[42]

Again, the NT used an adaptation of an ancient Greek tragedy to exploit the tension between tradition and innovation in their dramatic project. Olivier had starred in a seminal version of Sophocles' *Oedipus* in 1945 at the Old Vic, which had received great critical acclaim; and since that performance, the APGRD performance database suggests that there were at least twenty-five stage productions of Sophocles' play around the United Kingdom between 1945 and 1968, with two taking place in 1968. The fact that the NT's performance was the only one in England of Seneca's *Oedipus* during the same period suggests that it was an appropriate play for a theatre company invested in doing unusual and rarely performed ancient dramas, as they had already demonstrated in their choice of *Philoctetes*.[43] Similarly, Hughes' belief that Seneca's play was 'primitive' informed the decision to include a final ritual, scored with jazz music, that would upset the preconceptions of a European audience about how the average theatrical experience should conclude. As we will see, when the NT turned to ancient Greek tragedy for the third and final time in the first decade of its existence, this desire to disrupt the expected conventions of ancient Greek tragedy continued to prove controversial.

Wole Soyinka's *The Bacchae of Euripides: A Communion Rite* (1973)

Wole Soyinka's *The Bacchae of Euripides: A Communion Rite* (1973) was performed twenty times under the direction of Roland Joffé at the Old Vic between 31 July and 18 October 1973.[44] This production was one of the last productions of the NT under the leadership of Olivier and Tynan, and by this juncture the theatre had reached a time of great upheaval. After a

[42] Helfer and Loney (1998), 146.

[43] Statistics taken from a search on APGRD online productions database (including two productions of Jean Cocteau's adaptation of Sophocles' play, *La Machine infernale*). The index cards for professional plays of this production held at the V&A Theatre Archive list thirteen productions in total during this period, and three in 1968.

[44] See Goff (2005) for this production.

protracted handover, Peter Hall was on the verge of taking over from Laurence Olivier as the theatre's Artistic Director; Kenneth Tynan, due to long-standing disagreements with Hall, was also planning to leave the company. Nobody was keen to take responsibility for this production, and it was only performed at this point because Soyinka threatened to give his script to a different theatre company.[45] Furthermore, the performance was not a success, and Hall eventually stepped in to cancel the production before the end of its run, citing negative critical reviews and poor ticket sales.[46] But despite this apparent failure, the details of the performance that survive give us access to the long history of the NT's wish to perform the *Bacchae,* and provide a backdrop for the debates that accompanied their performance.

The first time that the NT tried to do the *Bacchae* was in 1963, the first year of the theatre's existence, when they almost offered a contract to Neil Curry for the use of his translation of the play.[47] However, they had to back out at the last minute because two other London theatres, the Mermaid Theatre and The New LAMDA Experimental Theatre Club (based in the London Academy of Music and Dramatic Art), had announced their plans to do versions of the same tragedy, staged in October 1963 and February 1964 respectively.[48] Although this plan was eventually shelved, there is intriguing evidence of what this particular performance might have looked like at the NT. In April 1963, seven months before the foundation of the NT, and while William Gaskill was still at the Royal Court, Laurence Olivier wrote to him with the following elliptical question:

> Do you wish me to go into a thing with Edith about Agave, or would you settle for Margaret Leighton, who is, I hear on all sides, very anxious to join us; or would you prefer Pamela Brown?[49]

[45] See memorandum from Tynan to the Planning Committee dated 5 January 1973, BL Manuscript Add. 87887.

[46] See letter from Hall to Soyinka dated 20 August 1973, BL Manuscript Add. 80404.

[47] It seems possible that the NT hierarchy had got to hear of Curry's translation through its performance in February 1960 by the Tavistock Repertory Company at London's Tower Theatre, in a double bill with *Something Unspoken* by Tennessee Williams. See details in V&A Theatre Archive.

[48] Contract details from NT Archive.

[49] The results of a Google search (performed 5 January 2020) for 'Margaret Leighton Pamela Brown Edith' suggests that the 'Edith' referenced here may have been the British actor Edith Evans (1888–1976), though at the age of 75 she may have been considered too old for the role of Agave. Letter BL Manuscript Add. 80404, dated 30 April 1963.

In an undated response, Gaskill stated that he preferred the idea of Margaret Leighton.[50] On its own, this document takes us only so far: we have a version of the *Bacchae* directed by William Gaskill and using a translation by Neil Curry that would possibly have been the first Greek tragedy at the theatre (it was this slot that Sophocles' *Philoctetes* came to fill in April 1964). But preserved in Laurence Olivier's personal papers is a handwritten letter dated 30 October 1972 from a disgruntled black British actor called Clifton Jones that sheds a rather different light on Gaskill's investment in the *Bacchae*. It was written, as we will see, after Jones had discovered that the NT were going to perform Soyinka's translation of the *Bacchae*:

> Dear Sir Laurence,
>
> The announcement that a black playwrite [*sic*] has been commissioned to do a version of 'The Bacchae' for the National Theatre. I realize that it is part of the archaic conceit of the Englishman that only he can appreciate important talented black men and that only he can perform drama. Black men therefore have no place in the important parts of the theatre here. I write this because I have a secret suspicion that this is the version of 'The Bacchae' that Bill Gaskill wanted to do some time ago with an all black cast.
>
> If this is so I think it a pity that it should be performed by the mummies at the National Theatre rather than the fresh exciting young actors available, living and performing in this country. As it is possible that I might be known in your theatre to be an actor, I would like to state that I am neither seeking a place in the production nor at the National as nothing on earth could persuade me to work there.
>
> I am, Yours disrespectfully,
>
> Clifton Jones
>
> p.s. I only hope that Mr Soyinka does not get another awful production here for his reputation's sake. C. J.[51]

Unlike with Susan Maunsell's letter, and unlike most letters of complaint or approbation in Olivier's papers, no reply from Olivier or anyone

[50] Undated letter from Gaskill to Olivier, BL Manuscript Add. 80404.

[51] BL Manuscript Add. 80404, letter dated 30 October 1972. During the sixties, Soyinka's plays had received three prominent performances in British theatres: *The Road* at the Theatre Royal, Stratford East, *The Trials of Brother Jero* at the Hampstead Theatre Club, and *The Lion and the Jewel* at the Royal Court, both in 1966. Despite Jones' claims, these often received positive reviews: see e.g. Gilliatt (1980). Furthermore, the performance of *The Trial of Brother Jero* shared the 1967 John Whiting Award for young playwrights with Tom Stoppard's *Rosencrantz and Guildenstern are Dead.* See Goodwin (1988), 36.

else at the theatre accompanies Jones' letter.[52] Nevertheless, it was kept; and it suggests that a further element of Gaskill's potential production was that it would use a cast entirely made up of black actors. Events between the original idea in 1963 and Jones' 1972 letter suggest that this was a plausible desire on Gaskill's part. In 1966, the director had put on a version of Wole Soyinka's play *The Lion and the Jewel* at the Royal Court Theatre that had used the Ijinle Theatre Group, a London-based acting troupe made up solely of West African actors.[53] Indeed, Clifton Jones seems well disposed towards Gaskill's idea, and objects only to it being done at the NT. As we saw, Gaskill would go on to direct Sophocles' *Philoctetes* while trying to emphasise its transhistorical similarities to Samuel Beckett; but it is interesting to consider what the history of twentieth-century productions of ancient Greek tragedy would have looked like if the NT's first performance had been a *Bacchae* that featured only black actors.

The second attempt by the NT to put on the *Bacchae* took place between February 1966 and December 1971, when they made an extensive effort over almost six years to convince Jerome Robbins, the American choreographer and director, to travel to London and direct a production. Robbins was very enthusiastic about the project in its early stages, though he eventually had to decline due to other commitments in New York. In March 1967 he sent a short sketch of his ideas about the *Bacchae* to Olivier that offers a tantalising insight into his intentions for the production:

> Fall '68 is okay as a flexible plan. Would Gielgud be interested in BACCHAE? It might be masked – thus he (or you) could play *any* role or even triple parts as they were originally done. My ideas are not just formalistic but go toward a raw, religious ritual filled with hallucinations, ecstasies and poetry. Images: the great African tribal masks, Noh masks, and some awesome Fate and God masks. The piece achieves its stature not through a large and heavy production but through the intense and intimate focus of three actors playing out the roles in a fierce and meaningful ritual.
>
> All the above are just the instinctive rumbles of my searchings. The *how* I haven't made concrete.

Robbins' comments demonstrate that not only was this play planned for the autumn of 1968, at around the time when Seneca's *Oedipus* was

[52] A Wikipedia search for 'Clifton Jones' (performed 5 January 2020) shows that he was a prominent British television actor in the seventies and eighties who was born in Jamaica in 1942. He would therefore have been thirty years old when he sent the letter.

[53] See esp. a letter from William Gaskill to Dennis Duerden, dated 12 September 1966. Accessed, along with other material about the production, in V&A Theatre Archive.

eventually performed, but it was also intended to feature that play's leading actor, Sir John Gielgud. Similarly, Robbins' ideas straddle antiquity and modernity in their attempt to stay faithful to the ancient Greek practice of having three actors play multiple roles in the theatre, as well as in the intended use of masks, and also to give a sense of the global resonances of tragic ritual in non-European cultures by bringing in 'African tribal masks' and 'Noh masks'. The reference to 'hallucinations, ecstasies and poetry' also reflects his discussions with Robert Graves over the significance of the ancient Greek myth and its relationship to the sixties Zeitgeist of a Dionysus who represented the possibility of countercultural revolution, as best represented in Richard Schechner's *Dionysus in 69*.[54]

While the planned Robbins adaptation did not explicitly call for a black cast, it again assembled its ideas about the *Bacchae* around a core concern with racial and geographical difference. Though no evidence survives for exactly why the NT finally decided to approach Wole Soyinka, it is plausible that their commissioning a young Nigerian playwright had something to do with a desire to have their *Bacchae* tackle ideas of racial exclusion in the European theatrical tradition.[55] Soyinka places heterogeneous geographical, cultural, and religious traditions side by side in his adaptation of Euripides' *Bacchae*. At different points his Dionysus is an ancient Greek god, an avatar of the Yoruba god Ogun, and a proto-Christ, and the syncretic result highlights what Soyinka viewed to be the fundamental ritual and spiritual similarities between these different manifestations of the religious impulse (whence his closing scene, and subtitle, 'A Communion Rite'). Soyinka also incorporates a chorus of slaves into the play as a means of elaborating his theory of the symbolic and historical significance of liberation to the worship of Dionysus, blending ancient and modern contexts of slavery as a comment on Greek tragedy's modern relevance to a black author. But the eventual production of Soyinka's play at the Old Vic was very different from the one that is contained in its published text.[56] First, its title was changed in the production material to

[54] See Vaill (2007), 380–6. This countercultural perspective was trialled in the NT's 1969 production of Maureen Duffy's *Rites*, a feminist play that took some inspiration from Euripides' *Bacchae*. For more on *Rites*, see Perris, Chapter 9, this volume. Little evidence survives of this production, though there is some material in the NT Archive, the V&A Theatre Archive, and the Bristol Theatre Collection (from the latter, see the cast list at OVP/79/36). For *Dionysus in 69*, see Zeitlin (2004) and Fischer-Lichte (2014b), 27–47.

[55] The first mention of Soyinka in the NT Archive dates to January 1972, with an internal memorandum acknowledging the receipt of a signed contract from the playwright. See BL Manuscript Add. 80404, memorandum dated 24 January 1972.

[56] See particularly Lecznar (2014) and (2020), 161–92.

downplay Soyinka's input: rather than 'The Bacchae of Euripides: A Communion Rite by Wole Soyinka', the programme and cast list declared 'The Bacchae of Euripides. Adapted by Wole Soyinka'. Secondly, the production's prompt-book, the script that included the cues for the lighting and sound in the performance to make sure that they match up with the words spoken on stage, demonstrates that many changes were made to Soyinka's published text: indeed, the text was altered so much that in one letter Soyinka quipped: 'My first instinct on reading the "scissors-and-paste" job done on *The Bacchae* was to ask you to transfer the full authorship back to Euripides and treat with me as "dramatic consultant" or something along those lines.'[57]

Another point of contention was the racial diversity of the cast. In a production note, Soyinka comments:

> The Slaves and the Bacchantes should be as mixed a cast as is possible, testifying to their varied origins. Solely because of the 'hollering' style suggested for the Slave Leader's solo in the play it is recommended that this character be fully negroid.[58]

Soyinka points up his main alteration to Euripides' text here, the inclusion of a slave chorus to accompany the chorus of Asian bacchantes that appear in the ancient Greek original: but more than this, he emphasises that he wants the actors of the chorus to be of 'varied origins' with only one actor, the Slave Leader, to be 'fully negroid'. This would immediately seem to preclude a production that followed in the spirit of Gaskill's hypothetical all-black *Bacchae* from 1963: but an exchange in January 1973 between Olivier, Tynan, and the director of this production, Roland Joffé, demonstrates otherwise.[59] This exchange began on 10 January 1973 in Tynan's record of a conversation with Joffé that stressed 'RJ *does want* coloured actors.'[60] This was followed by a brief note from Olivier to Joffé on 22 January:

> One thing I did want to ask you and that is this. Would you please re-consider using Negro actors. Ken Tynan tells us that Wole Soyinka does not insist on this, and I'm sure you will appreciate that it will make it a very

[57] Accessed in MS Thr 427 (2395) in Houghton Library, Harvard University, letter dated 28 May 1973.

[58] Soyinka (1973), 234.

[59] It is not clear why Joffé was eventually made director, but it seems that he may have been chosen because he had previously directed a successful version of Sophocles' *Oedipus* at London's Young Vic in September 1970, a theatre with which the NT had a close relationship at the time. Details of this production accessed in the V&A Theatre Archive.

[60] Record of a conversation with Roland Joffé dated 10 January 1973. Found in NT Archive.

> expensive operation for us as it is unlikely that we shall be able to use them all in other productions. If you feel you must have them in THE BACCHAE, do you think you could limit it to just one of each sex?[61]

Olivier excuses his desire to have fewer black actors on budgetary grounds: it would be impossible to find enough roles for so many non-white actors in the plays that the theatre wished to perform. But his comments also hint at the particular racial bind that confronted a European national theatre in the aftermath of colonialism and empire. Though these theatres primarily performed plays by white European playwrights that dealt with white European concerns, this was not a self-evidently appealing corpus for a growing proportion of the nation's audience, not to mention its actors. Clifton Jones' letter emphasises this: in a country where a black playwright like Soyinka was becoming increasingly successful, these issues of racial difference could not be ignored for much longer. Indeed, it is striking in the context of this comment that a 2009 production at the NT of Wole Soyinka's *Death and the King's Horseman* featured an all-black cast that 'whited up' by painting their faces with white paint to play the roles of white European characters.

Joffé's production eventually followed Olivier's advice and included only three black actors: Leslie Rainey and Ram John Holder split the role of the Slave Leader, while Isabelle Lucas played the leader of the bacchantes. This final decision angered Soyinka, who commented in his later account of his experiences:

> all the principal actors among the slaves and the followers of Dionysos were black – which, observe, is something of a feat in British theatre: the leading Bacchante was black, and the two who shared the principal role of Slave Leader were black, a reduction along racial lines which neither Euripides nor I his adapter ever indicated.[62]

It is debatable whether Soyinka is being entirely ingenuous in these comments: his production note (quoted above, p. 201) does offer some precedent for their decision, and the NT were perhaps right in thinking this would be a suitable approximation of the 'mixed cast' of 'varied origins' that he described there.[63] But whatever the case, understanding this performative conflict from the perspective of the archive allows us to see that what seems like a local disagreement between playwright and

[61] Letter from Olivier to Joffé dated 22 January 1973, BL Manuscript Add. 80404.
[62] Soyinka (1993), 54.
[63] See above, n. 58. The production's Dionysus, played by Martin Shaw, was styled as a South Asian Tantric guru. See Soyinka (1993), 50.

theatre company over the role of race in one particular performance of ancient Greek tragedy had a much longer history. This history also includes two embryonic productions of the *Bacchae* that never took place, as well as the NT's two previous performances of ancient drama: in *Philoctetes* and *Oedipus* we can perceive a repeated desire to offer a fresh reading of ancient Greek tragedy that would depart from the (then) common associations of the genre. This final production of ancient Greek tragedy during the first decade of the NT makes it clear that the archive can be important in allowing us to understand what *did* happen in a performance against the backdrop of what did not.

Conclusion

In this chapter, I have explored three different case studies that demonstrate the sorts of material that the archive holds, and the different modes of enquiry, and critical questions, that it can encourage us to pursue in relation to adaptations of ancient Greek tragedy. I hope to have shown not only that can we discover new information about the productions in question by using the resources of the archive, but that we can also piece together narratives about the significance of ancient Greek tragedy in the modern world that might be otherwise lost if the productions are discussed separately and without reference to their documentary remains. I want to conclude by returning to Derrida in order to think further about the connections between tragedy and the archive.

One of the most important avenues of contemporary scholarly inquiry concerning this connection has focused on how the archive can help modern communities work through their tragic histories of violence, hatred, and destruction.[64] Derrida's second prominent engagement with the archive was related to this, since it took place in connection to the real-life tragedy of apartheid in South Africa. In 1998, Derrida spoke about the country's Truth and Reconciliation Commission at a conference at South Africa's University of the Witwatersrand. Here, he commented that the significance of the archive to the lived tragedy of South African history might, ideally, be one of forgetting.

[64] See Trouillot (1995) on the difficulty of remembering the Haitian revolution of the late eighteenth century; Hamilton et al. (2002) on post-apartheid South Africa; Bastian (2003) on the ravaged history of the US Virgin Islands; Caswell (2014) on the legacy of the Khmer Rouge in Cambodia. In a similar vein, Ricoeur (2004) is centrally concerned with the ethics of memory in relation to the Shoah. Cf. Steinmeyer, Chapter 11, in this volume, on adaptations of Greek tragedy in post-colonial contexts.

> So, suppose that one day South Africa would have accomplished a perfect, full archive of its whole history – not simply apartheid, but what came before apartheid, and before before, and so on and so forth, and a full history – suppose that such a thing might be possible – of course it is impossible – let us suppose it's possible – everyone in this country, who is interested in this country, would be eager to put this in such a safe that everyone could just forget it, okay? And perhaps, perhaps, this is the unconfessed desire of the Truth and Reconciliation Commission. That as soon as possible the future generation may have simply forgotten it, okay? Having kept everything in the archive, meaning the libraries, in the hands of remarkable archivists, okay, just let us forget it to go on, to survive. That's what we are doing – just archive against memory.[65]

For Derrida, tragedy creates an impulse to forget: the Truth and Reconciliation Commission, he speculates, is an archive of tragic events within human history that aims at the obliteration of those events, and that hopes to allow future generations to live without the experience of their violent weight. But Derrida is sure to flag up the impossibility of this eventuality, since no archive could ever be large enough to contain the uncountable human experiences that make up any given historical event. Indeed, running counter to his argument is the idea that what the archive often ensures is precisely the *unforgettability* of a performative moment that might otherwise have disappeared in the grand narratives of history. The story of distraught mothers disrupting TRC hearings by throwing a shoe at the police officers accused of murdering their sons captures a subjective response to this trauma that ought not be forgotten, since it is itself a spur towards remembering the human cost of past violence and the necessity of its future avoidance.[66] In a similar way, every adaptation of ancient Greek tragedy, including the three that I have examined in this paper, bears witness to a foundational ambivalence in their treatment of modernity's tragic archive, as the desire to revisit and reperform ancient artworks manifests itself in an attempt to make them speak for the present and the future.

In this way, there is something elegiac and spectral about the archive; despite the long passage of time and the necessary inevitability of eventual forgetting, it preserves the urgent ideas and impassioned hopes of people who are collaborating over and watching performances that flared so briefly and brightly in the world. One outcome of pursuing the archival remains of the adaptations that we want to discuss is that we can bear

[65] Derrida (2002), 54.

[66] See C. M. Cole (2010), 18–25. With thanks to the anonymous CUP reader for this suggestion.

witness to the ideas of William Gaskill, the anxieties of Susan Maunsell, the anger of Clifton Jones; and by finding a space to remember these things we can grasp some small part of the significance that ancient Greek tragedy had in their lives, and become better aware of what tragedy continues to mean today. This is something captured in the 2015 production of Sophocles' *Antigone*, using Anne Carson's translation, at London's Barbican Theatre under the direction of Ivo van Hove and featuring the French film-actor Juliette Binoche. At the point when the chorus spoke Carson's lines about the 'archives of grief', they all stood with their backs to the audience, joining in with the view from the auditorium and watching fuzzy projections of family gatherings in old home movies that were playing along the back wall of the stage. Here, a view of the archives united the production's chorus with the audience as both pored over poignant recordings of happier pasts, and tried to work out the chain of events that had led to the all-too-tragic present unfolding before their eyes.

CHAPTER 7

Compromise, Contingency, and Gendered Reception
The Case of the Malthouse's Antigone

Jane Montgomery Griffiths

For several months in 2013, adaptation was the theatrical hot topic in Australia's arts communities.[1] Following a spate of radical revisionist productions of the classical repertoire on the main stages of Australia's state theatre companies, adaptation had become a theatrical cause célèbre. From Brisbane to Perth, Adelaide to Sydney (not to forget that hub of theatrical cognoscenti, Melbourne), theatre critics, arts journalists, playwrights, directors, and academics weighed in on the relative merits of staging adapted classics.[2] The argument inflamed passions, 'angry and perplexed on one hand, blithe and overruling on the other'.[3] It solicited personal testimony, provoked ad hominem attacks, caused a re-evaluation of theatrical funding and programming, and ultimately prompted soul-searching on the state of the artistic nation. And all this, from something as seemingly simple as whether adaptation can be seen as new work, or whether it is merely 'standing on the shoulders of giants'.[4]

This debate was in many ways indicative of what is known in Australia as 'the cultural cringe': the embarrassed feeling that we slavishly follow 'the mother country', Britain, or unthinkingly assimilate the best, and often worst, of the US; the insecurity that we have yet to attach the prefix 'post-' to the 'colonial' of our heritage; the schizophrenia that we simultaneously resent and aspire to the history of others while ignoring our own country's ghosts. As director and academic Julian Meyrick pointed out, the debate was an illustration of Australian theatre's 'adaptive mentality'.[5]

1 This debate was precipitated by Rosemary Neill in *The Australian.* Meyrick (2014) gives a comprehensive list of the main players in the argument, as well as the context for the contention.
2 For the purposes of this debate, 'the classics' were considered to be the theatrical canon of great Western plays, which included, but was not exclusive to, those of ancient Greece and Rome.
3 Meyrick (2014), 15.
4 This is a centuries-old concept, expressed by Newton (1676): 'If I have seen further, it is by standing on the shoulders of giants.'
5 Meyrick (2014), 15.

Meyrick's assessment of the debate is fascinating: in itself, it is as contentious as the subject matter and not without its own resultant criticism. Several years down the track, as one who became embroiled in the adaptation debate, I want to take the idea of 'the adaptive mentality', but to shift it from Meyrick's critique of national identity to one of gendered identity. In this chapter, I want to argue that the 'adaptive mentality' can be mapped onto the way we perceive and comprehend 'difference' in translation; that our processing, understanding, and reception of adaptation are deeply implicated in an often subliminal system of preconceptions and epistemologies that have, simultaneously, the potential to be both a reactionary and an emancipatory hermeneutic. I will do this through an analysis of a recent adaptation of Sophocles' *Antigone* which I wrote, and in which I played a version of Creon, for Melbourne's Malthouse Theatre. My aim in doing so is not to rehash well-worn arguments about authority and reception (although I shall touch on them), but rather to examine how the process of translation and adaptation of such a canonical work can demonstrate what Martindale calls the 'situated, contingent, mediated' place of reception,[6] and how, from that, 'the adaptive mentality' can become a force that challenges both artists and audiences through appropriation and subversion. Looking at the contingency inherent in the theatrical process, at the mediation that necessarily contextualises translation, and at the situated nature of 'readings' done both by artists engaged in adapting the source text and by critics engaged in analysing the target text, I shall argue that 'the adaptive mentality', when seen through the lens of gender, can be a liberating force with a capacity to unleash new interpretations and subvert the normative expectations of canonical force.

The Adaptive Mentality: The Situated Reader

In *The Feminist Spectator as Critic*, Jill Dolan writes:

> Culture is not an innocent preoccupation ... representational, expressive media both shape and reflect who we are to ourselves and to one another. We learn from seeing in performance how gender and race relations are embodied and enacted. (Dolan 2012, 1)

To any scholar of performance studies, this assertion by Dolan would seem both self-evident and incontestable. The performativity of gender, the

[6] Martindale (2006), 3.

implicated 'readership' of practitioner and audience, the tyranny of gender, sex, and sexuality, are well-worn tropes in academic discourse in my discipline. Yet in the practice of theatrical adaptation, in the very *un*theoretical world of actually putting on a play, of audience responses, and of critical reception, Dolan's seemingly obvious words are both contentious and revolutionary – perhaps not in an obvious way. Perhaps most theatremakers and critical audiences would like to think themselves sufficiently aware to realise the full ideological potential of their engagement with the power of performance. Yet in the day-to-day practicalities of the theatre, the full implications of a potential *complicity* – of willing or unwilling, or witting or unwitting entanglement with the political power[7] of performance – are provocations generally too problematic to resolve. We theatremakers become immersed in the endless compromises required to get the play on stage. We critics become trapped in the greater priority of making deadlines and creating entertaining copy. We academics become enmeshed in the productivity imperatives underlying our research. In other words, all too often the practical reality of the theatre prevents us from exploring the revolutionary in its potential.

Adaptation, however, is, in its essence, a revolutionary form. This is not simply because the process necessitates a re-evaluation of the source-to-target relationship. It is not simply because in the reshaping of a pre-existing form to a new medium, a new genre, a new audience, adaptation tests the parameters of both the 'original' and the new work. It is because the very process creates the potential for a radical reconfiguring that, in its innovation, can shake up preconceived ideas, 'shape and reflect'[8] a source in a way that makes us reconsider the state of the target, and ultimately engage in a dialogue between past and present, source and target, so as to question the implicit and the complicit in our reading of the new. In this way, to paraphrase Pearce, 'reading' the new text of an adaptation is no longer something we 'do' to texts;[9] it is something texts 'do' to us, 'whenever we [take] the leap into their uncharted territories'. Theatrical adaptation, because of its ontological oscillation between the idea of a non-material originary source text and the embodiment of a very material 'secondary' theatrical 'text', sails deep into these 'uncharted territories'. There is something strangely anarchic about the (seemingly oxymoronic) circumscribed openness of theatrical adaptation that can be truly

[7] I mean political in the broadest context here: something that connects with the broader community (the 'polis'), as well as something that touches on government's political policy decisions.

[8] Dolan (2012), 1.

[9] Pearce (1997), 2.

revolutionary. And in this way, the 'adaptive mentality' that Meyrick criticises can also be a springboard to a radical re-evaluation of our relationship with our cultural, canonical paradigms.

For Hardwick, adaptation belongs to a contested cultural space.[10] It carries with it the ideological baggage that is unavoidably attendant on the very idea of the canon, its transmission, and its currency. It is prone to arguments of authority, authenticity, fidelity, and originality. Like its twin, translation, it is subject to a 'hierarchy of correctness', as Bassnett notes, which validates an essentialist belief in 'authorial intent', 'original genius', and the desirability of finding the core meaning that resides in a stable originary text.[11] These theoretical arguments about translation and adaptation have gone backwards and forwards over the decades with often depressing predictability:[12] they have leapt between post-structuralism and editorial theory, deconstructionism and textual criticism, translation studies and adaptation studies, performance studies and reception studies. In essence, the argument is always the same: for those who believe in a stable originary text, translation and adaptation are at best a form of faithful rebirth, at worst a type of parasitic abortion; for those who believe in the inherent polyvalence of all texts, translation and adaptation are mechanisms for new creation which will itself branch off into infinite possibilities of hermeneutic openness.

In the theatre, the theoretical, not to say occasionally metaphysical, nature of this '*traduttore, traditore*' ('translator, traitor') debate is counterbalanced by practical necessity. When an artistic director chooses to programme a canonical classic, particularly a Greek tragedy, the question of the production's intended level of fidelity is dependent on so many factors external to the translator/adaptor – factors which I shall shortly articulate – that the primacy which theorists would attribute to this search for equivalence becomes, in practice, all but non-existent. There are, nonetheless, pervasive echoes of the argument's key themes even within the practicalities of production. In a theatrical incarnation, fidelity to a source text or to original production practices might not focus as strongly as they do in areas of academic discourse. When it comes to artistic integrity and control, however, issues of authenticity, hierarchy, authorship, and the ideological space of hermeneutics and reception are just as

[10] Hardwick (2006), 204. [11] Bassnett (2014), 90.

[12] For an overview of the ongoing debates on adaptation, see Sanders (2016) and Hutcheon (2012). Worthern's (1997) analysis of arguments for and against the originary text is still one of the most compelling.

present.[13] From the very moment of programming, this is evident. As a theatre company announces its forthcoming season, multiple hierarchical layers are at play. The Season Launch might seem innocuous: amongst the glitter, cheap bubbly, and canapés, a theatre company is merely publicising its choice of plays for the forthcoming year. Yet underlying that announcement are elements of everything that comprises the adaptation debate. The choice of play is predicated upon a cultural context that validates one play over another, that conforms to and perpetuates its own sense of hierarchies by a simple act of one inclusion and multiple exclusions. The choice of whether a Greek tragedy is to be staged, and if so, which, and if so, how, consequently has substantial significance in the cultural context of the receiving environment. Unlike in the UK in the last few years, Greek tragedy comes around very infrequently in Australia.[14] Professional productions are few and far between, and so the programming of one will necessarily carry with it expectations: expectations from those audience members who long to see the canon resurrected; expectations from those with a cynical attitude to the validation of Dead White Males; expectations from those whose lack of awareness of the genre makes their 'horizon of expectations' potentially infinite.

With the choice of play, comes the nomenclature, the crediting by-line. In recent years in Australia, the European influence of the postdramatic has led to an interesting shift in authorial control. The deferential, sometimes obsequious, occasionally invisible, role of the translator has been replaced by the rise of the director-'auteur', who happily rewrites the source text with none of the concerns of fidelity that plague his literary counterpart. Part of the furore in the Australian adaptation debate has been caused by this increasing attribution of authorial credit to this type of director:

> there is a catch-all category of cultural transposition, where something 'other' is recoded into a more familiar register . . . This elasticity is reflected in the nomenclature accompanying a diversity of production approach: 'based on', 'a version of', 'after' etc. . . . That many of these are associated with their director's [*sic*] hints at the power relations underlying apparently

[13] See Sidiropoulou, Chapter 4, this volume, for a fascinating complementary discussion on the ethics of directorial adaptation/appropriation and the interesting provocation that directorial adaptation can actually be the manifestation of a love affair, rather than a power-play.

[14] For instance, in one week in October 2015, I was able to see a new *Hecuba* at the RSC, a *Medea* at the Almeida, and two *Oresteias* at the Globe and the Trafalgar Studios. This is, I grant, not usual practice for UK theatres, but it contrasts notably with Melbourne, where there have been only two fully professional productions of Greek tragedy (*Women of Troy*, 2008, and *Antigone*, 2015, both Malthouse Theatre) in the past decade.

> literary choices. If, as some argue, the playwright is downgraded in the process of adaptation, it is clear enough who has benefitted. While it can be handled collaboratively, adaptation is often channelled through a narrow set of roles chief of which is that of the director.[15] (Meyrick 2014, 23)

In contemporary Australian adaptation, the author may be dead, but the auteur is very much alive. Before a word has been written, or an actor has walked into a rehearsal room, a new form of hierarchy has been established, and established pragmatically, not to say cynically, in a board room or a marketing department, as a way of tapping into the currency of 'youthful genius', which celebrates the myth of the exceptional young maverick over the reality of collaborative interpretation. Theatre is, intrinsically and inescapably, a collective endeavour. The practical reality of the process of theatrical creation means that the very idea of the 'auteur' is as logically fragmented as the idea of original authorial intention or of a stable originary text. Yet the myth of the 'auteur', that single, always male, theatrical wunderkind, persists.[16] And in its persistence, the myth parallels literary and academic arguments for and against authorising power, hermeneutic essentialism, and textual monovalence. The numerous instances of authorial attribution given primarily to the director set up false assumptions of singular creativity that is belied by the very means by which the end product will be embodied. Ironically, in this paradigm, this directorial 'adaptive mentality', which promotes itself as innovative and iconoclastic, is ultimately as conservative as the canonical text whose image it tries to break: it is merely substituting one authorial hierarchy for another.

Meyrick sees the rise of this directorial adaptation as potentially negative: something that undermines the emerging creative voices of new playwrights; something that traps us in an aping of an ancient and alien culture's values and stories. Yet 'the adaptive mentality' that both validates the director as adaptor and the adapted canonical text as 'new' is not necessarily detrimental to the receiving culture when viewed from the lens of reception studies. That is because reception studies, at their core,

15 There is a whole other article to be written on the distinction between the director who stages an adaptation which has been created by a playwright, and a director who creates, through bricolage and devising, her/his own one. Meyrick's argument points to the fact that, with the rise of the auteur director, the distinction is beginning to blur.

16 The gendered nature of this is perhaps singular to Australian culture at the moment and is certainly not reflected in Europe, despite the serious, ongoing gender imbalance in theatre directing. The critical reception of young male directors, such as Benedict Andrews and Simon Stone, is very different from that received by female directors such as Adena Jacobs and Emma Valente, although they are all radically revisionist directors of canonical texts. I would argue that in Australian theatrical culture, 'auteur', just as 'wunderkind', is exclusively applied to young men.

acknowledge the multiplicity of creation and comprehension. While adaptation can potentially create new hierarchies which invalidate collaborative creativity, it is also possible that, when exercised from a marginal position, 'the adaptive mentality' can confound hierarchical authority. What happens if the model of the auteur is shaken up through an overtly collective process? What if 'the adaptive mentality', far from accepting single authorship uncritically, takes the licence of adaptation to explode persistent linear structures of authorship? What if, also, the process of adaptation becomes subject to so many variables that its very existence belies arguments of textual stability or originary authority? I would argue that 'the adaptive mentality' can be a revolutionary form, just as much as it can be a reactionary one, through acknowledgement of the 'situated, contingent, and mediated' imperatives of the process.[17] As I have discovered in the process of adapting *Antigone*, what might initially have had no revolutionary motivation can end up being radically political and profoundly subversive, through the happenstance of reception.

Nowhere is the force of the 'situated, contingent, and mediated' more present than in theatrical adaptation of the classics. Indeed, the very process, from commission to first critical reviews, can be seen as the very reification of the theory of reception. It is as ontologically complicated, it is as hermeneutically fraught, and it is as ideologically driven. The test case of Malthouse Theatre's *Antigone* will demonstrate just this. As the creative process for the production shows, there are significant parallels between the illogicality of claims for a stable originary text and that of claims for a single theatrical auteur. Similarly, the acts of interpretation and reception which accompanied the production will demonstrate the gendered and ideologically situated act of reading by the creatives (that is to say, the director, designer, writer, and composer), audience, and critics alike. The series of compromises and alterations that occurred in the process of the production will exemplify the importance of contingency in interpretation and reception. Finally, the production's eventual manifestation and critical reception will exemplify the potential of adaptation as reception to explore

> the imperfect of our past and the future perfect of our present (our desire) . . . the point of reception: where words, not my words, not your words, intersected with the past (memory, tradition, even individual history, and, of course, the unconscious) and the future (desire, chance, and ideology) are repeated in the future perfect of the present. (Batstone 2006, 18–19)

[17] Martindale (2006), 3.

The Background

Antigone was staged by Malthouse Theatre, Melbourne's premier company for theatrically innovative work, in August 2015. A year earlier, Marion Potts, the then artistic director of the company, had commissioned me to write a new adaptation of Sophocles' play, working towards an open brief, but with the caveat that there could only be a cast of five. Over the next few months, the design team of The Sister Hayes was brought on board, together with lighting designer Paul Jackson, and sound designer Jethro Woodward. From August 2014 to January 2015, intermittent development meetings were held with this team to discuss concepts for the production, and I began work, first on a literal translation of Sophocles' Greek, then a gradually culled-down and adapted version. The production process shifted significantly in February 2015, when Marion Potts was appointed Theatre Director of the Australia Council, and so resigned from the project. Director Adena Jacobs, who already had a substantial reputation for the visceral sensibility of her work at Sydney's Belvoir Theatre,[18] was brought in as replacement, and the development process began from scratch, with the same creative team, but with a notably different aesthetic. By May 2015, all parts in the play had been cast, with the exception of Creon. Nine months of trying to cast the role had failed (I will come to the reasons for that later), and the impossibility of finding the right actor for the role led to a major rethinking of the project, resulting in the part being rewritten as a female head of state. After several attempts to cast this part with an 'A-list' actor, I was finally cast in the part about three weeks before rehearsals commenced. The final production broke Malthouse box office records, yet was their most critically contentious show of 2015, with critics sharply divided along gendered lines in their appraisal of the play. This in turn led to heated online debate about gender bias in reviewers, which prolonged the production's life long after the show had closed.

This is a very quotidian summary. The dullness of it belies the year-long creative process that inspired, incensed, perplexed, and fulfilled in equal measure. But the bare facts are worth noting, because they speak to the

[18] Belvoir is one of Australia's premier nationally funded and state-funded theatre companies. For many decades, it had been the home of new Australian writing and relatively 'straight' productions of the theatrical canon. Under the artistic directorship of Ralph Myers (2010–15), the company developed a more radical approach, with the conscious employment of more female directors and more openness to devised and avant-garde theatre. Adena Jacobs, as Associate Director of the company, worked primarily on radical reworkings of classics, such as a male *Hedda Gabler*, a nightmarish feminist evaluation of *The Wizard of Oz*, and a two-person, almost silent meditation on *Oedipus at Colonus*.

issues of contingency and mediation that this chapter addresses: circumstances mediate intention. The artistic drive, what we might call the intentionality that also underpins the idea of 'the originary', is in reality endlessly mitigated by contingency, and in *Antigone*, this is nowhere more apparent than in the enactment and the reception of the political context of the play.[19]

Contingency and Mediation

It seems so obvious to say *Antigone* is political.[20] Of course it is. It questions the authority of the state. It questions the autonomy of the individual. It questions the demarcation of gender roles. It is, in other words, eternally current and eternally provocative, since what it questions is our subjectivity in our 'past ... future ... [and] future perfect of the present'.[21] Yet even with the weighty knowledge of the play's place in political theory and political theatre, the nature of *Antigone*'s political force has come as a shock to me. And part of that shock has been the way in which the definitions of what is 'the political' shape-shift in the context of reception. It has been political not in the way I imagined, but in a way that has been entirely framed by the mediation of audience expectations of what can be, and should be, addressed in an adaptation of a canonical classical text.

The choice of *Antigone* as the first Greek tragedy to be staged by Malthouse Theatre in seven years carried political weight. Malthouse positions itself in Australian theatre as 'a creative site, an *engine for change*'. It is 'dedicated to extending the boundaries of the performing arts'. It aims to make work that is 'inventive, provocative and entertaining; ignites political, social and civic conversation; [is] capable of influencing and generating change' and is 'Australian and Global'.[22] It is seemingly the perfect venue for, and producer of, theatre that is both provocative and

[19] For discussion of the tangle of compromises that beleaguer theatrical programming, casting, and the staging of adaptations of Greek tragedy, see Lecznar's Chapter 6 in this volume. Lecznar goes further than most theatre historians in not just describing past productions but also demonstrating how archival research can elucidate the journey from intention to execution in professional theatre.

[20] It would take volumes to document the political significance of *Antigone*, the influence of which has been pervasive from classicist discussions of the political in Greek tragedy to political philosophy and psychoanalysis. The best current overviews and analyses of its currency are Honig (2013) and Leonard (2015). See also now Cairns (2016). Among earlier contributions, I would single out Ahrensdorf (2009).

[21] Batstone (2006), 19.

[22] These quotations are taken from Malthouse Theatre's mission statement for 2015.

political. A production at Malthouse carries with it expectations of a progressive political stance, expectations that it will challenge the status quo (in terms of both performance tradition and contemporary Australian politics). The genesis of the Malthouse's *Antigone* had, however, no such overtly political intentions; it was, rather, more an act of compromise.

In 2014, Marion Potts, the then Artistic Director, and I had been working on ideas for an epic adaptation of Milton's *Paradise Lost*. The project was ambitious – too ambitious for the limited resources of this middle-scale-funded theatre – and was ultimately shelved. In its place, Marion suggested we work on an adaptation of *Antigone*. I demurred, partly because the change from the mooted twelve hours of durational Miltonian epic to the suggested ninety minutes of chiselled Sophoclean perfection seemed like a big leap; partly because, as a classicist who had variously spent three decades studying Sophocles, I baulked at the thought of appropriating the playwright who had been the most seminal writer in my life, and I was thoroughly aware of the irony of adapting this genius playwright who had examined so deeply the dynamics of hubris. 'Why?' I asked. Not, 'Why produce the play? Why here? Why now?' Those questions are compelling and necessary, but there is a ready answer. The reception and production history of this play teaches you that. The play is horrifyingly current. It speaks endlessly, timelessly, in multiple incarnations through multiple voices, at every time. Its power is not in some faux universality, but in its mutating specificity: something that generations of theatre-makers around the globe have found can speak to the world they need to interrogate. Sophocles' play has a profound political power and terrifying urgency. So, my question was not, 'why stage it?' but 'why *adapt* it?' Why rewrite something almost perfect in its current structure, tagged with the Hegelian accolade of being 'one of the most sublime and in every respect most excellent works of art of all time',[23] written by a writer so great he shaped the course of literature and theatre (not to mention psychoanalysis) – a play so potent that it really needs no translation. The answer to my question was pragmatic. The theatre could only afford a cast of five actors. If the cast were not to double (which neither of us wanted), adaptation rather than a 'faithful' translation was a financial necessity.

Here is the stark economic imperative that belies theoretical ideas of the transfer of authorial control implicit in adaptation. In this case, there is no sense of the auteur's voice: Potts had no great vision for the play, no

[23] Hegel (1998), 464.

burning political motive to stage it, and, other than the haunting images of strewn body parts from the MH17 plane crash, which had little to do with the ethical and political imperatives of *Antigone*, no specific visual provocations to inspire a production. There was no artistic reason to rewrite the text; no theatrical vision to justify an appropriation. It was pragmatic programming: the passion project of *Paradise Lost* was unfeasible, so a financially viable alternative, which could be a school set text and would draw in an audience because of its classical cultural kudos, was an acceptable compromise.

These practical realities are often ignored in the reception theorist's analysis of classical adaptation. Academic deconstruction of a production rightly explores cultural context and performative decoding. Mee and Foley's collection on *Antigone* in performance (2011) is an exemplary case in point, where the interaction between source and target, and between theatre-makers and audience, is scrutinised in impressive detail for the political force of reception. What is neglected, however, is an understanding that the reified theatrical entity that is subject to analysis has often only ended up in that form because of a series of unplanned disappointments, practical compromises, and pragmatic solutions.

If we begin to acknowledge that, we can start to discard the 'intentional fallacy' that the adaptor and director *necessarily* have a grand vision behind adaptation; and if we do that, we start to see something profound about the very nature of the adaptive process. We see something that begins to undermine hierarchies of authorship and tyrannies of authority, opening the door to the anarchy of chance that can liberate both creativity and reception. If the choice to adapt is not ideological, or artistic, but pragmatic, if it is not desire, but necessity that prompts the process, if the end-result is not the realisation of intention, but a dance with circumstance, the relationship of fidelity between source and target becomes very different. There is not an intentional wish to rewrite; there is a practical requirement to do so. The constraints of theatrical pragmatism confound the theoretical division between fidelity and betrayal that has, at its root, essentialism and intentionality. In so doing, the process necessarily embraces the contingency and mediation that reception studies posit. The relationship between source and target becomes more open because it is no longer burdened by an authorial hierarchy. It might be burdened by happenstance, but the aleatory consequences of unforeseeable accident offer a different type of circumscription: something that is potentially more creative in terms of responsivity and collaborative problem-solving; something that perforce assimilates the variables and polyvalence of reading and interpretation. The search for source/target equivalence ceases to be a linear hermeneutic pathway and becomes instead rhizomatic.[24]

This model of rhizomatic equivalence is probably a more useful, and certainly a more honest way of viewing theatrical adaptation than the idea of direct authorial control. The multiple offshoots of the rhizomatic model certainly form a more accurate analogy for the tangled pathways of adaptation. When we come to stage canonical plays, we are always undertaking multiple simultaneous acts of interpretation, adaptation, and translation, which become both the means and the ends of the reception process. We are always dealing with the contingency of practical interpretive decisions, with the situated understanding of the source and target text, and with the mediation of the theatrical signs which we employ to convey meaning to be decoded by the audience. Each of these elements creates a root that can bend or snap, that can grow crooked or straight, and that can wither or flourish. Each root is integral to the whole, will remain largely unseen, but will feed the final production. This root system will grow to be so complex that it will become almost impossible to see a straight, homogeneous, interpretative line. The multiple contingencies of theatre make the search for a single creative through-line as doomed as trying to unravel a pot-bound geranium. To demonstrate, I wish to draw on just two key elements of the process: that of casting and that of directorial vision. As the case of *Antigone* demonstrates, both are key contingencies in the mediated process of theatrical adaptation.

Within the tangle that is the adaptive process, theatrical translation, through adaptation, becomes much more than the search for linguistic equivalence. Theatre is a medium that engages all the senses, and the body – that of the performer and of the audience – is at its centre. As Perris states, 'aesthetic experience of the performing human body differs fundamentally from aesthetic experience of the book'.[25] Similarly, the aesthetic experience of witnessing *as a body* differs fundamentally from the sensation of reading *as a body*. Theatre conveys meaning through multiple correlations and affective synergies, so that translation for the stage is not bound by the logocentricity of the imprinted word, but by the somatocentricity of the body in performance. As such, the stage translator must, as Woodruff says, find 'the terminology to capture the essence of adaptation' *and* 'the

[24] For 'rhizomatic' as opposed to 'arborescent' hierarchies of understanding, see Deleuze and Guattari (1999).
[25] Perris (2010), 187.

essence of what is being adapted' through the interplay of bodies and language.[26]

This is the ventriloquism, the mimetic embodiment at the core of performance studies. The terminology of what is being adapted is created not through words on a page, but through the assimilation of those words into the physical being of the actor and through the affect of that sensory relationship with the mechanisms of theatre; if you like, the *opsis* of Aristotle's *Poetics*. Consequently, a significant element in articulating the 'essence' of adaptation must come in the act of matching of bodies – real human bodies – to the play's characters of our imagination. Bert O. States describes the actor as 'the entire perceptual ground' of the character:[27] it is through her or his physical presence – through her mannerisms, voice, physiognomy, energy – that the audience's understanding of the play will be constructed. However adept a translator might be, her work will be meaningless on stage without the voice in the body that will inhabit those words.

Casting, however, is no easy business, and is dependent on so many practical and economic factors, that artistry becomes one of the least important issues in its process. There is a lot at stake in this one decision: the play's success will ultimately hinge on the embodiment of character. The casting of Antigone and Creon is, therefore, a crucial element not just to the aesthetic success of a production, but also to the creation of the political frame of reception. In initial discussion on casting, Potts and I had substantial disagreement on whom to cast. Potts wanted a young actress known for playing ferocious and commanding roles; I suggested an actress who had a certain strangeness to her, a type of uncanny quality on stage, who was particularly good at dealing with text. We both had very different ideas on the character, on what the actor needed to play her, on presence, age, experience. We had both received the character – in Potts's case, through the translations she had read of the play, and in my case, through the study I had done of the text in the Greek – in entirely different ways. It was a multiply layered mediation of the character, through the conduit of language transmission, to be transferred to the conduit of physical flesh and blood. Ultimately, Potts and I reached agreement, but it was not what either of us initially wanted: Potts would cast a young, relatively inexperienced actor who was very unlike our individual initial ideas of the role. In one phone call and one conversation, our entire situated reading of our eponymous hero had radically changed, and as a consequence the entire

[26] Wetmore (2014), 631. [27] States (1992), 373.

tenor of the political and gendered discourse of the play also changed through the casting of this young woman who would create the audience's perceptual framework.

The adaptor's job, then, is already shaped by a crucial contingency: that of casting and actor availability. Casting meant I would be writing for a very different Antigone from the one I had initially imagined. Availability meant that I would end up not only having to change the gender and rewrite Creon but would also ultimately embody the character myself. After a ten-month fruitless search to cast a 'big name' as Creon, and with only two months before rehearsals began, the decision was made to make the part female. This pragmatic compromise – one that seemingly went against all the gender politics which I, as a classicist, knew were so crucial to the play, and one at which I initially baulked – was entirely prompted by practical circumstance: the failure to find an eminent middle-aged actor willing to play the role.

It is no exaggeration to say that in all theatrical adaptation, this casting imperative – something often beyond the director's, and certainly beyond the writer's, control – has the power ultimately to shape the entire production and its reception in a way hardly imagined by critics and scholars. This imperative is, I would argue, the key element in the contingency that shapes creative reception and transmission. In many ways, the mapping of a character that initially only lives on the page and in the imagination onto the flesh and blood of a human body is itself an adaptive act: one that has the potential to be revolutionary. The restrictions imposed by it are constraining, but they are also liberating. It is in this contingent happenstance that the emancipatory potential of theatrical adaptation can, paradoxically, be seen. Restriction leads perforce to new forms of creativity. The restriction of only five actors forces the relationship of characters and the dramaturgy of the narrative to change.[28] The strictures become an energetic propulsion: while compromise is inevitable, the adaptor must use interpretative creativity as a way to circumvent the limitation. In Malthouse's *Antigone*, therefore, the restriction of a cast of five had major creative ramifications for the role of the chorus. This would have to be radically re-envisioned. The absence of physical bodies to comprise the chorus in this production meant that the choral function would need to be reconfigured to become something other: rather than the

[28] One could see parallels with the constraints imposed by the use of three actors in Attic tragedy, which led to creative doubling of roles, although the decision neither to double nor use masks in the Malthouse production changed the parameters of the constraints.

interplay of the communal and the individual voice trying to comment on society, it would have to become a silence to demonstrate the redundancy of comment. In the world gradually materialising in the stark, utilitarian design of The Sisters Hayes,[29] this emptiness became fitting: it is a society which has consciously tried to put state-controlled ritual above individualised ritual, which pits political rhetoric against the words and deeds of family ties, which has no organic communal identity to enable the choral voice. The chorus would therefore become an intended absence – a gap on stage that demonstrates an impossibility. Individuals might incorporate lines from the chorus, but there would be, could be no communal voice. And I would need to find some other way to convey the subliminal effect of the chorus's metre and rhythmic drive, something which would be done now only through collaboration with Paul Jackson's lighting design and Jethro Woodward's soundscape. Translation, therefore, moves from single authorship to multiple responsibility through the various means of theatrical effect.

The constraints of cast size ultimately necessitated other substantial changes. The guard and messenger were combined to form a new character, The Bureaucrat, who was also given the chorus' *Polla ta deina* ode. Eurydike would have to be cut. Haemon and Ismene would remain, but were given new lines, which assimilated thoughts, images, and arguments from the chorus. Most radical of all was the cutting of Tiresias and the allocation of his lines to Antigone as she was awaiting execution. On her way to death, Antigone would become her father and Tiresias in one: her ambivalent love affair with the dead, her incestuous longing to join her *philoi* in the underworld, her erotic desire to be subsumed into their blood, would morph her into the ghost of her dead father. She would share both the blindness and insight of Oedipus and Tiresias. And on the limen between life and death, between the abject and the sublime, between ignorance and omniscience, elevated through suffering, androgynous and asexual, she would, in her impotence, have the strange and infecting force of Tiresias as he warns Creon.

This decision to meld Antigone and Tiresias was, of course, partly practical, but it was also the result of the collaborative engagement. In this, we see the contingency that is implicit in the theatrical process: one that is entirely shaped by the collaborative synergies between the creative team. By the time I was writing the script's second draft, Marion Potts had

[29] The Sisters Hayes are a highly successfully Australian sibling trio of graphic artists and theatrical designers who consciously meld a variety of cultural aesthetics in their work.

resigned from the project, and Adena Jacobs had taken over as director. The change of director from Potts to Jacobs initiated a radical re-envisioning of the work, and with that, the potential to explore an entirely different aesthetic frame. Jacobs has a growing reputation in Australia as an innovative, radical theatrical voice, interested in exploring the aesthetics of gender, sexuality, and viscerality. Her work is informed by a deep knowledge of Irigaray, Kristeva, and Cixous, and her productions to date have been marked by what we might call a theatrical *écriture feminine.* For Jacobs, the materiality of the body on stage supersedes overt political contextualisation. Bodies are, in themselves, political, burdened as they are with the performativity of gender, ethnicity, and sexuality. Approaching *Antigone*, Jacobs wanted to highlight the affective and semiotic power of the body on stage.

When Marion Potts commissioned the piece, she programmed it under a season's subheading, 'Ritual'. For *Antigone*, this is an ironic provocation. The play is less about ritual than about the denial of it: the refusal of a state to show compassion; the inability of a society to show emotion (unless covertly); the limiting of grief to politically motivated, state-sanctioned memorial services; the classification and demonisation of the enemy as 'the other'. In this world, the rites of mourning and the messy business of life and death are untidy inconveniences that should be vacuum-packed in clingfilm to stop possible contagion. As Jacobs took over the production, the place of ritual – or of its lack – came together with her interest in the body: Antigone's body became the site of ritual. Drawing from Kristeva and Mary Douglas,[30] Jacobs would focus on the abjection of the corpse, the infection of the plague, the liminality of Antigone's living death. Drawing on the desensitising emptiness of the postdramatic, she would look for an aesthetic context for the production that maintained the ritualised formality of Greek drama but subverted it with deferral and the uncanniness of Antigone's androgynous nakedness.

Antigone's and Creon's fates would be reinvented in this ritual-less world. Antigone's body would become the abject site of the materiality of flesh, where insides seep outside, just as Polyneices' corpse infects as its fluids pool. Creon would suffer a fate, the tragedy of which is not the loss of family, but the inability to step outside the constraints of a de-ritualised society to acknowledge the loss. As in Sophocles, neither character learns; in this version, however, they would wear their continuing ignorance differently.

[30] In particular, Jacobs was inspired by Kristeva's *Powers of Horror* and Douglas' *Purity and Danger.*

I, in turn, looked for a theatrical language to match the directorial vision. All translators for the stage must walk a perilous line between fidelity to, and betrayal of, the source text, because, unlike the philologist, the theatrical translator does not see language as the be-all and end-all, but rather as just one medium of translation. The play's language needed to match the aesthetic that was developing: a style of language that, while retaining a formal, although sometimes shifting, verse style, would have a visceral muscularity undercut with desensitised banality. The result closely followed Sophocles, but acknowledged the intertextual heritage of transmission, with the occasional subliminal nod to the viscerality of Seneca and Artaud, and the equivocation of Anouilh:

BUREAUCRAT: You've sacrificed your freedom,
And for what?
To save a rotting body from the sun?
It's already back there, oozing in the heat.
Your actions did no good. They made no change.

The people aren't rebelling,
All's the same.
Nothing is happening –
Except in the corpse –
That is oozing and swelling
That is sighing and breathing
That slowly seeps
While the skin pulsates
With a thousand flies
And the maggots dance
In the humming flesh
And the body starts to swell and plump
And insides become outsides
And the solid liquefies

And the dead are livid.

As I say,
Your actions made no change.
Achieved a mild hiatus in decay.
That's all.

The theatrical adaptor's job is, I believe, not to start an ill-fated quest to create syntactical and rhythmic equivalence, but to look for *affective* correlation: in other words, to find some linguistic means of conveying meaning from one medium to another, from one culture to another, within the parameters of the collaborative creative process to which they are contributing. There can be no preciousness in this process. This is theatre, where the writer serves the production, not the other way around, and where the developing text is subservient to the collaborative creative process. It is consequently quite possible that the adaptor's role is to cut text, as meaning can be conveyed in other conative ways. Theatrical equivalence is more than just language, and meaning can be conveyed, theatrically, in ways more interesting and effective than a doomed attempt at linguistic fidelity. Consequently, the adaptation gradually became a work of finding a context for the language that would provoke with the political force of the play, and of creating affective equivalence that would give some sense of contemporary tragic catharsis in a desensitised world.

It is in this theatrical language, at once semiotic and affective, that the utter distinction between the philological and the performative is most apparent. It is also the most controversial area for the purist who looks for fidelity to an originary. The example of these first few lines of the Malthouse *Antigone* is a vivid illustration of this. In Adena Jacobs' production, designed by The Sisters Hayes, the setting is empty, soulless, mechanised, dehumanised. The vast dark stage of the Merlyn Theatre is stripped back to its theatrical nakedness. In the centre of the stage is a rigid rectangular playing area of grey linoleum, with a raised prefab office sitting in utilitarian ugliness at the back. A single heavy chain hangs downstage right from the flies. The production begins in silence, with a clothed man carrying a naked body down the office stairs and laying it on the downstage floor beneath the chain. At this stage, it is impossible to tell whether the body is male or female. Gradually the other cast members descend from the office, variously disrobe to show their underwear, and assume positions of physical shame. From the tableau, the naked corpse begins to sing lines in Greek until, on the final lines, a sound cue swells, so loud that the entire world of the play seems to buzz like a corpse infested by flies. As the sound fades, the Leader, a middle-aged woman dressed in the female politician's uniform of tailored black suit, blond short hair, and heels, pronounces the state's edict on Polyneices. She exits to the office with the rest of the cast, leaving the prostrate naked body on stage. It becomes clear that this figure is Antigone as she now runs up the staircase to ask Ismene to help her with the burial. Steiner (1984, 208) says of the first lines of *Antigone*:

> The opening line consists of five words of which two, 'O' and 'Ismene' are straightforward. The other three have been the object of voluminous exegesis. The semi-darkness in which they are spoken seems to cling to them.

The framing of the image, two sisters, one fully clothed with long hair, one naked and androgynous, standing dangerously, erotically close to each other as their scene is urgently whispered, did more to convey the oddness of Sophocles' opening two lines than any English translation could. Exposed in the brutal light, 'the semi-darkness' still clung to them. Bodies on stage, not semantic equivalence, translated language through connotation, affect, and presence. Those bodies in turn – through their very performativity – would profoundly affect the audience reception of the play.

Situation

I have argued that the practical happenstance of contingency and its subsequent effect on the mediation implicit in translation and adaptation weigh far more heavily in the theatrical process than intentional ideas of fidelity. To return to Martindale's triad, this leaves us with 'situated' – our situated reading of the text, our situated mediation of it, and our situated reception of the production. This for me is where *Antigone* became so political, in a way I had not predicted, and where the adaptive mentality became emancipatory.

As I have said, the production was Malthouse's most critically contentious of 2015. The criticism lined up on gendered battle lines, with all (bar one) male critics hating the show, and all (bar one) female critics loving it. I was accused of not understanding Greek tragedy, of 'tinkering' with greatness, of creating a play that was cold, boring, banal, arrogant, pretentious, an ego-trip, that was too political, that was too contemporary, that was too obvious, and that had the temerity to make Creon into a woman. My acting was similarly attacked – somewhat bizarrely – for being too good: I was 'too strong', I was 'absurdly good' and 'so good' I 'breed a special kind of resentment'. I have written elsewhere about this critical controversy and so shall not restate arguments here.[31] What does strike me now, however, is the sheer power that adaptation as a theatrical medium must have to elicit such vitriolic responses. The critics who loathed the production did so because their situated readership had been challenged. The security of their canonical knowledge was not so safe anymore: it had been unsettled by two women, Adena and me, in the creative process, and by two women, Antigone and the Leader, on stage. While most of the negative critics mentioned my academic credentials, none would allow

[31] For negative criticism of the production, see Woodhead (2015), Bache (2015), Fuhrmann (2015). For the most considered positive analysis, see Croggon (2015). For my response and the subsequent heated online debates, see Montgomery Griffiths (2015b).

even the possibility that that might just mean my adaptation was informed by knowledge of Greek tragedy. Rather, our creative decisions were dismissed as being based on ignorance, arrogance, or hubris.

The vehemence of these attacks, especially when contrasted with the critical praise of the female critics, says something very interesting about how adaptation can be, whether wittingly or not, a political form. Most classicists would respond as I initially did to the idea of making Creon a woman. It is a terrible idea. It goes against the grain of every Hegelian understanding of the play, of every Segalian structuralist analysis of its gender binaries.[32] And yet, and yet ... If we allow adaptation to be an emancipatory force, to have the power to shake up preconceptions and entrenched presumptions, the idea of making Creon into a woman is actually not so bad. Contextually, gender politics have changed from ancient Athens. 'Translating' Creon's sexism over two and a half thousand years and several thousand miles is as doomed as finding a satisfying English translation for Sophocles' *ta deina*. The embodied reification offered by theatrical adaptation provides us with the opportunity to reassess what the political is, and what the gendered politics of the play could be. Now, as we are still smarting from the excruciating misogyny that precipitated the political demise of Gillard in Australia and Hillary Clinton in the 2016 US presidential elections, the politics of gender – and the politics of how we receive that gender – warrant re-evaluation and provide a more provocative theatrical test case than the overt misogyny of a misguided patriarchal tyrant. In the case of the Leader, that re-evaluation came in her denial of gender as an issue. As the female world leaders before her, she made the tough decisions to put state above emotion. She transgressed the role of carer and nurturer laid down for her; she put *Realpolitik* above her ovaries; and for that crime, the critics would have a field day. In the criticism of the Leader's callous heartlessness, the reviewers betrayed more about their situated reading of powerful women than about their understanding of Greek tragedy. In this *Antigone*, gender became more, not less, politically potent because of the absence of the patriarch. It left the audience without the easy option of safe identification, and without the security of comfortable reception. Adaptation became a liberation from and provocation to preconceived ideas.

[32] See Segal (1999) for an example of his masterful application of structuralist anthropological analysis to Sophocles.

'Nobody loves an adaptation', says Boyum,[33] and adaptation, more than most theatrical genres, can provoke the most entrenched resentment. In its worst reception, it is the medium of the plagiarist, the receptacle of the derivative: no adaptation can live up to the expectations of those who value originality, nor escape the opprobrium of those who believe in the originary. Yet as Mee and Foley point out, 'Antigone has always been already adapted',[34] and that process of adaptation is what makes *Antigone* endlessly, timelessly political. As just the past few years in Australian theatre have demonstrated, adaptation is an ideological battleground, where issues of cultural appropriation, national identity, gender performativity, and creative practicalities contest the field. But the soil of that battleground is remarkably fertile, and the roots and shoots of multiple variants and multiple creative synergies are ready to burst through from just below the surface. It is liberating when they do.

[33] Boyum (1985), 15. [34] Mee and Foley (2011), 6.

CHAPTER 8

Technology, Media, and Intermediality in Contemporary Adaptations of Greek Tragedy

Peter A. Campbell

> The theatrical is … what we have while we wait to find out … whether theater is a phase the culture will pass through en route to new forms, or whether… theater has become an enabling form – not only a way to the new, but the scene itself.
>
> (Fuchs 1996, 157)

Every art form expresses itself through media. From the cave paintings of ancient peoples to the tragedies of fifth-century Athens and the digital video of the twenty-first century, art needs a medium through which to be expressed. For theatre and performance, even in the face-to-face mode of storytelling between performers and spectators, there is still the literal air that sound and vision traverse, and all of the physical, physiological, and psychological intermediaries involved in those complex processes. The contemporary context, in which technological media have become the dominant representational mode, also demands that we consider not only the intended use of the media, but the role of media in our processes of creation and understanding. As Arnold Aronson says in 'Theater Technology and the Changing Aesthetic',

> The relationship of technology to the theater is neither direct nor obvious. The mere addition of video monitors or remote tilt-and-pan spotlights – the typical sort of nods toward modern technology in the theater – does not, in and of itself, create new forms of theater. Technology, rather, alters our perceptual mechanisms; it changes the way we see and, more importantly, the way we think.[1]

In fact, the hegemony of the mediated image through television, film, and the Internet has changed the ways that audiences view live theatre, so that it is no longer obvious that there can be a critical distance between the spectator and the medium. Since we already live in a mediated world, our

[1] Aronson (2005), 46.

'perceptual mechanisms' have already changed, thus making our observations and attempted analysis of the mediated world always already mediated.

Theatre, Media, and Perception

Theatre, as Elinor Fuchs explains in the epigraph above, has become a potent place for exploring this postmodern mediatised world because of its liminal place in the relationship among words/images and representation/reception. In attempting to find the language to describe the movement from a culture of logos, or the relative certainty of language and words, to one in which the 'logos loses its stability and begins to dance with undecidability',[2] Jacques Derrida illustrates the transition to undecidability with the language of the theatrical. Fuchs, in her reading of Derrida, observes that in their historical moment, specifically the late twentieth century in which Derrida and Fuchs were writing, 'the Platonic tradition of writing-as-truth is interrupted by a new type of writing in the form of a stage performance'.[3] Stage performance subverts Platonic and logocentric ideas of truth, instead offering what Fuchs calls 'reality-effects', which create a 'de-ontologized world'.[4] In other words, theatre is the perfect place to express the uncertainty of the logos and of ideas of truth, because it is in itself a medium that depends upon the ontological untruths of acting and representation.

Athenian tragedy likewise upended the traditional logos of the early fifth century BCE by using imitation and stage performances that inevitably introduced elements of uncertainty, aesthetics, and 'reality-effects' that were clearly representational and not reality. The Athenians, of course, were well aware of these complications and often played with the reinterpretation of their own myths and traditions, and even their metaphysical beliefs, through the tragedies and their performances. In this way, even then, well before those tragedies were interpreted using electronic media, ancient Athenian tragedy, like theatre today, was, as Fuchs suggests, 'not merely the *model* of that world, or the exemplary transition into that world ... It is, with its perpetual mysterious *mise-en-scène* of emerging inscription, *in itself* that world.'[5] Theatre has been and remains problematic because it is only 'written' as it exists in its stage performance. Every other attempt at forcing it into a form of logos creates a new logos that

[2] Fuchs (1996), 149. [3] Fuchs (1996), 149. [4] Fuchs (1996), 149.
[5] Fuchs (1996), 149 (emphasis in the original).

exists beyond the stage performance itself, and thus reveals the relativity of truth as a consequence of 'reality-effects'.

Video and audio media in performance have significantly changed the way artists and spectators approach Greek tragedy. In this chapter, I will address the use of media in contemporary productions and adaptations of Greek tragedies that have used the form, narratives, and cultural cachet of Greek tragedy for explorations of the contemporary world. By using artefacts of what is considered the cradle of Western civilisation and drama as their primary source material, these productions are attempting to create work that engages spectators in examinations of human culture and behavior that are not only timely, but have deeper historical and emotional resonance, even when the productions themselves are destabilising and sometimes undermining the cultural position of their ancient Greek referents. While the approaches differ, from the use of video as scenography to the immersion of the audience into theatrical landscapes fragmented through media, this chapter will explore several significant examples of technological media in contemporary productions of Greek tragedy, and examine the ways in which they use materials from Greek tragedy to express and reflect the changing representative demands of a media-saturated world.

The presence of technological media in theatre, especially since the development of digital and audio technology that is readily available and easy to use, brings up deeper questions about representation. This technology extends the possibilities of what can be represented in live theatrical performance and consequently collapses many traditional dramatic and theatrical expectations. Philip Auslander's idea of televisual intimacy, for example, posits that a contemporary audience whose existence is dominated by moving video images sees in those images a more convincing representation of the real than a live theatrical performance.[6] As live theatre by definition is happening in the shared space and air of performers and spectators, it would seem to have the representative advantage of presence. The use of media technology such as microphones and video in live performance accentuates the undermining of the logocentric from a Derridean point of view while at the same time complicating Fuchs' idea that theatre can be '*in itself* that world'. Live theatre represents the hegemony of presence, whereas video and audio technology imposes an element of absence – a sort of Derridean 'trace', whereby the signifier is neither wholly present nor wholly absent. The 'trace' provided by

[6] Auslander (1999), 12–16.

mediation through digital technologies might create the kind of representative separation, or absence, that spectators require in a mediated world. The intimacy and shared space and time of live theatrical performance, ironically, become less 'real' because they are less familiar than the hegemonic media to which many of us are now accustomed. The mediated world, in this construction, makes us desire absence in order to feel intimacy.

The bounds of reality and the real, then, are changed by mediation. Johannes Birringer describes television as 'our continuous, uninterrupted history; an endless flow of images, sounds, stories, and news events in living color', which, through its dominant cultural presence, sustains the myth that 'electronic communication simultaneously channels knowledge, information, and expression ... ignoring national borders or differences of time and space'.[7] In this way, the proliferation of media has not only changed our ideas of representation, but also the way in which we see and understand the world and our human history and culture. The traditional binaries between 'live' and 'mediated' have become, in a sense, outdated, victims of the ubiquity of mediation. As Herbert Blau argues: 'There is nothing more illusory in performance than the illusion of the unmediated.'[8] While this does not mean that there are no longer meaningful comparisons to be made between the live and the mediated, those debates are always informed by mediation. Indeed, mediation and media seem to be so integrated into performance in some form or other – be it video screens, microphones, or lighting – that they are often paradoxically 'invisible'. Even the least technology-infused theatre, the live performance in an outdoor venue, say, without artificial lighting or electronic amplification, still exists in a word in which most spectators will be comparing it to some sort of mediatised representation.

The Wooster Group, *Phèdre*, and the Postmodern

As in every discussion of media in theatre, reference must be made to the Wooster Group. And with good reason, because, since it first used video in *Route 1 & 9 (The Last Act)* in 1981, the Wooster Group has been an innovator in using audio and video technology in theatre to do more than create scenography. The Group's work regularly engages the central issues of media in contemporary culture and representation. According to Michael Rush, in their work the stage is composed of 'video monitors,

[7] Birringer (1998), 5. [8] Blau (1987), 164.

movable scenery, microphones', and 'live performers compete for viewers' attention with videotaped versions of themselves'.[9] All of these elements are not just to grab attention or distract the spectators, but are ways that the text or texts with which they are working is/are fragmented. The incorporation of video and audio in these ways creates opportunities both to use well-known texts in new ways but also, as a reflection of postmodern culture, to demonstrate the artistic potential of these media.

In *To You, the Birdie!*, the Wooster Group's adaptation of Racine's *Phèdre*, video and audio are used to show the fragmentation of bodies, which clearly expresses the general postmodern fragmentation of the world. There are three mobile video screens that show body parts of the actors, with the actors sometimes partially obscured by the screens and thus made 'whole' by the video version of the rest of their bodies. For example, the performance begins with performers Scott Shepherd and Ari Fliakos, portraying Theramenes and Hippolytus respectively, sitting behind the screens so we see their upper bodies live but their lower bodies enlarged slightly on the screens in front of them. This makes for what one might call a literal intermedial body – half live and half 'mediated'. *To You, the Birdie!* also separates the live voice from the actor, as Shepherd speaks most of Phaedra's lines through an amplified microphone. Greg Giesekam observes that this further supports the themes of the play as the 'disjunctive voicing of her [viz., Phaedra's] lines and the video dislocations of her body also operate as figures of her being torn apart, disintegrated, by her passion for Hippolytus'.[10] However, since each of the characters is subject to the video dislocation, the theme of fragmentation is clearly one that affects the entire theatrical world, and speaks clearly to the spectators not only about the characters of the play and the themes of the story of Phaedra, but of their own fragmented world. This perception of emotional detachment is a common response to the postmodern, and is not surprising, since an important premise of the postmodern is the alienation of human beings from each other and their history. Phaedra's text is voiced by another actor, and thus disembodied from the body of the character, creating a clear example of the fragmentation of character. The emotional and physical detachment of voices and bodies exemplifies Fredric Jameson's postmodern idea of 'speech in a dead language', a 'blank parody' of the original text without humorous or malicious intention, but with the recognition of the lack of any 'healthy linguistic normality'.[11] In this world, characters do not speak for themselves or move for themselves, and thus they do not speak

[9] Rush (1999), 65–9. [10] Giesekam (2007), 109. [11] Jameson (1993), 74.

and act like normal human beings. Or rather, from a postmodern perspective, they speak and act exactly like human beings – in a dead language and detached from psychological intention or consciousness. Even though the text itself adheres rather closely to Racine's text, the use of media is intentional in creating a visually contemporary and complex version of the classical characters that denies them the potential of a unified psychology and therefore works against the kinds of empathetic responses that Racine's neoclassical adaptation of the Greek myth usually elicits. Instead, the use of media expresses the kind of 'waning of affect' and consequent subjugation of interpretable expressive emotion that is a part of the uncertainty of the postmodern.[12]

This postmodern uncertainty through mediated detachment is also evident in the En Garde Arts production of Charles Mee Jr's *Orestes 2.0*, directed by Tina Landau in 1993. In what Mee deems the 'crazy trial' scene of the play, Landau's production used microphone technology to emphasise the private conversations of the nurse and hospital patient characters over the public trial of the public actions of Orestes, Electra, and Pylades.[13] The foreground text was spoken by the nurses, who were sitting at a table speaking over microphones, and was amplified at an exaggerated volume, making the background text not only quieter but actually quite difficult to hear at all. The movement of the 'public' legal trial to the background and the foregrounding of Mee's 'private' choral elements through mediation is not only emblematic of the corrupt and distracted system of jurisprudence in Orestes' situation (and the analogous contemporary one), but also discourages emotional identification with the Greek tragic characters. By mediating only the 'intimate' text, Mee and Landau subvert the importance of the 'public' narrative, which is of course the central concern of the Greek tragic plot and characterisation. The spectators might struggle to hear the text of the legal trial but are prevented from focusing on it entirely by the louder personal material. Mee uses media to play upon the idea that our interest tends towards the prurient because our 'private' interests tend towards it; in this context, the discourse of the Greek characters is simply not that compelling, and the judgements that come from it are equally unimportant or even irrelevant.

Video has also been used to express postmodern uncertainty and detachment in recent adaptations of Greek tragedy. Theatre artist John Jesurun began using projected images and film techniques in his live theatrical productions in the early 1980s. When he staged the United

[12] Jameson (1993), 69–70. [13] Mee (1998), 127.

States premiere production of his adaptation of *Philoktetes*, at the Soho Repertory Theater in 2007, the set consisted only of two rectangular projection screens, one covering the floor of the small stage and another raised above the back edge of the stage space. The projections on these screens began with repeated images of waves and changed to other resonant images over the course of the piece: billowing smoke, strong winds, what looked like a nuclear explosion devastating some trees, the moon, and a stand of green trees, before the waves again covered the screens at the end of the play. None of these images were attempts to physically create a specific setting or time period, although projected images of bombing patterns from the 2003 invasion of Iraq, while not obvious to all spectators, did certainly contain resonances of contemporary war. During most of the scenes, the images were in constant, repetitive motion, while the actors remained, for the most part, quite still. There was some use of a camera to project the faces of Neoptolemus and Philoktetes in large close-up, a sequence of debate between Odysseus and Philoktetes with a brief moment of physical combat, and a climactic kiss between Neoptolemus and Philoktetes near the end.

Jesurun 'wants us to look at how our minds have been conditioned' by language and the media through which we perceive and communicate.[14] His theatre has been called 'cinematic' and 'cinematographic' primarily because of its self-consciously film-influenced scenography.[15] His use of film techniques was an effort to 'do away with transition and exposition' by exploiting film conventions; however, it was not because he thought either film or theatre a more valid or truthful medium: 'Making films always seemed so fake to me . . . and then I started doing live things, and that also seemed contrived. So I thought I'd push the contrivance farther by applying film ideas to live performance.'[16] Jesurun's acknowledgement of the contrivance of both media is clear in his production of *Philoktetes*, which makes no attempts to create naturalistic stage environments, physical actions, or dialogue.

These productions are attempting to speak in a new language that involves media as a part of the visual, thematic, and aural landscape. *To You, the Birdie!*, for example, subsumes the traditional dramatic interest in

[14] C. Carr (2008), 217.

[15] Fried (1985), 57 calls it 'Cinematic Theater'. Lehmann (2006), 114 calls it 'cinematographic'. Fried's term emphasises both the spoken language and scenography of the cinema and theatre, while Lehmann's term emphasises the visual, even though his analysis also emphasises both spoken and visual elements.

[16] Jesurun quoted in Fried (1985), 57.

psychology and emotion into a viewing experience in which character and narrative are not necessarily the central issues at hand in the theatrical event. Instead, by juxtaposing mediated images, both live and recorded, with live action, the Wooster Group's work complicates the 'reality' of the performance event for the spectators in order to make them consider their own spectatorship, as viewers of an event and members of a society and civilisation that consumes such representations. This 'intermediality' uses media in a live performance setting to encourage 'the multiple semantic potential offered' in such a setting

> by communicating gaps, splits, and fissures, and broadcasting detours, inconsistencies, and contradictions. Therefore, intermedial effects ultimately inflect the attention from the real worlds of the message created by the performance, towards the very reality of mediation, and the performance itself ... Thus, intermediality manages to stimulate exceptional, disturbing, and potentially radical observations, rather than merely communicating or transporting them as messages, as media would traditionally do.[17]

By highlighting the functioning of media, intermedial work is not simply expressing the common theme of alienation in an over-mediated society. Instead, the intermedial addresses the fact that our own forms of representation, in live theatre and elsewhere, have taken on more and more of the elements of those media and are thus affecting spectator responses to those representations. Intermediality in theatre attempts to create work in which 'the usually transparent viewing conventions of observing media are made palpable, and the workings of mediation exposed'.[18] This echoes the transitional phase that Derrida describes in his work, as a culture moves from the certainty of the logos to a new world of uncertainty and simulacra. The intermedial, though, does not necessarily involve a movement towards the cinematic or away from the theatrical. It is more in line with Fuchs' thinking: a representation of the transitional world and an example of that world itself.

Katie Mitchell's *Oresteia*: Media as Amplification

According to the British director Katie Mitchell, who used video and audio technology in her 1999 production of Ted Hughes' translation of the *Oresteia* at the Royal National Theatre, there are two basic functions for

[17] Boenisch (2006), 115. [18] Boenisch (2006), 115.

video in theatre. The first is 'To support the set design in communicating the world and ideas of the play. For example, using recorded footage of clouds in the sky moving across a white cyclorama.'[19] This use, as a type of scenography, is quite common in contemporary theatre, and is not significantly different from more traditional set design techniques that use painting and textured materials. As in Jesurun's *Philoktetes*, they might not be realistic depictions, but they nonetheless serve a primarily scenographic and atmospheric role. While projected (or otherwise) visible video has the potential, as in Mitchell's example, of providing movement, light, and color in ways that a more static design does not, the function is still to establish place, atmosphere, setting, mood, and the potential changes in those elements throughout a production.

Mitchell's second function for video, however, is where the use of media can complicate the theatrical setting. She proposes that video can function

> To act as a live participant in the performance, with almost equal status to the actor. For example, video footage of a person – recorded or live – may literally replace one of the actors. Alternatively, an actor might 'perform' the upper body of a character, whilst pre-recorded footage relayed on a screen shows what the lower body is doing, as in the Wooster Group's recent production of *Phaedra*.[20]

Mitchell's idea of the media as a performer leads to the concept that a piece of technology becomes central to the action of the work, or at least central to its consideration. While this clearly has some intermedial effects, as the Wooster Group's work demonstrates, Mitchell's use of technology is intended to help in her goal of 'representing behavior and emotion'.[21] In showing multiple projected images, both live and recorded, of the performers and other elements of the production, Mitchell is attempting to create a contemporary theatre that is active, engaged, phenomenological, and visceral. Her use of media is not meant to create the kind of alienation or distance for a commentary about the mediated, fragmented world.

For Greek tragedy, which already struggles with reaching contemporary audiences because of the translation problems of historical and performance traditions, media are most often used, as Mitchell suggests, to create a contemporary sensibility for the piece, to overcome the boundaries of history and culture and create a new sense that the dramatised world of the Greek tragedy is alive and current. In practice, this is often done in the way that Erwin Piscator and others used projected newsreels to highlight

[19] Mitchell (2009), 90. [20] Mitchell (2009), 90. [21] Shevtsova (2009), 200.

contemporary political events of film in live German epic theatre in the 1920s, in order to ground the spectators in the contemporary reality of the time.[22] However, as will become clear in the following examples, the media are usually doing several things at once; and despite their ubiquity in contemporary culture, they are still almost always recognised as mediation within a live theatrical context.

The most common use of video technology is what Mitchell describes in her first point: the extension of the scenographic to include video, in support 'of the set design in communicating the world and ideas of the play'.[23] In her 1999 production of the *Oresteia* at the Royal National Theatre in London, Mitchell used the central back door of the Cottesloe Theatre stage as both the door to the palace in Argos and a projection surface for several different kinds of images. The first of these were prerecorded images that helped the audience gain information about the play. For example, between 'the prologue and the parodos, images of celebration (dancing feet and sparklers) were projected on to the palace door', a visual representation of the celebratory mood of Argos on Agamemnon's return.[24] Later in the same scene, however, when the chorus mentioned Calchas' fears about the safety of Agamemnon and Argos, a ghostly image of Iphigenia was then projected on to the giant sliding door of the palace. The image of her face was cast at exactly the point when Calchas' fears implied Clytemnestra's revenge, visually underscoring the direct translation of Hughes:

> Filling the furious womb of the woman [*image projected*]
> Who waits in this palace . . .[25]

The projected image of the dead Iphigenia, who is also represented by a live actor on the stage in this production, informs (or reminds) the audience that Agamemnon sacrificed his daughter at Aulis, and that her death is what Clytemnestra uses as justification for her killing of Agamemnon. The video serves here to illustrate the spoken text, a strategy that Mitchell uses in several other parts of the performance, and which is evidence that her primary purpose in using video is to provide information and familiarity for her contemporary audience, help them understand the text, and amplify thematic concerns. It also reminds the spectators that there is an absent body that is being communicated to them only through the mediated image at that point. The example above demonstrates how

[22] Giesekam (2007), 40. [23] Mitchell (2009), 90. [24] Burke (2005), 275.
[25] Burke (2005), 292.

Mitchell rejects a purely literary theatre that depends upon the spectator's understanding of often dense and unfamiliar spoken text, and instead hopes to use media to create an engaged audience through a more visual and visceral representation of stage action. In other words, she amplifies the emotional and psychological world of the play and the characters through the use of mediated images, making it easier for spectators to connect to material with which they might not be familiar.

Most of the video in Mitchell's production, however, was not of pre-recorded images. Instead, she used live camera operators to find focal images and project them. As Alison C. Burke describes it:

> the door to the palace (and later the cave of the Eumenides) also served as a screen on to which live black and white video images were projected, which thereby provided another acting zone that existed simultaneously with the live physical performance in the rectangular stage.[26]

In some cases, the information provided by these projections was logistical, as when during Clytemnestra's speech describing the lighting of the beacons an actor playing one her attendants 'filmed the map and projected the image on to the back wall/palace door. As Clytemnestra named the stages on the beacon's journey, a laser highlighter illuminated the respective spot on the map.'[27] In other cases, the projected images provided information that had emotional or thematic resonance. For example, later in the same scene Clytemnestra 'burned the map in the bath. The image of the burning flames was then projected on to the palace door. The sight of the map burning, coupled with the giant image of the flames, provided a physical symbol for the imagery in Hughes' text' of the burning of Troy and the beacon flames.[28] Again, Mitchell uses these images to amplify the text for the spectators to clearly understand the mythological events and their significance within the production.

Mitchell also used video and audio in ways that were less informative of content or theme but instead had the technology 'act as a live participant in the performance'.[29] The clearest example of this was in the second play, titled *Daughter of Darkness*, in an extended scene from Aeschylus' *Libation Bearers* in which Orestes and Electra are discussing their father, Agamemnon, who is in his tomb. In an interview after the production, Struan Leslie, the movement director for Mitchell's *Oresteia*, explained the rationale for the camera placement in relation to the demands of the play

[26] Burke (2005), 274. [27] Burke (2005), 300–1. [28] Burke (2005), 301–2.
[29] Mitchell (2009), 90.

for a contemporary audience. Since the hole where Agamemnon is buried became the focus in the second play, Mitchell had 'The idea of the camera being down the hole … The camera is there because of the downward focus. They are talking about the earth for an hour. You just can't do that.'[30] This allowed them to look down into the camera, and at the ground, while the spectators saw the front of their faces directly through the projections. In its original Athenian context, the actors were clearly not expected to look down on Agamemnon in the ground while speaking about him. They would have been speaking out towards the spectators in order to be heard (and so that their masked faces could be seen). However, in the kind of stage naturalism that Mitchell is attempting to achieve, the gesture of looking down at the tomb while speaking to it was deemed a necessary representation of the psychological and emotional states of the characters and their respective actions. As Leslie noted, 'The camera being down there really feels very natural.'[31] So the camera works to fulfil a contemporary stage naturalism, while also breaking it up with a projected image. Michael Billington's review of the production validates Mitchell's choice by referring to the kind of resonance it created, of the inevitability of death and the human condition: 'As the onstage screen gives us a worms-eye-view of Electra with her feet straddling his resting place, we are inescapably reminded of Beckett's "They give birth astride of a grave."'[32] The projections of the actors' faces, magnified to larger-than-life size, provide the audience with familiar images from film and television. At least in this example, the video is also a rejection of a more traditional theatrical relationship, which would accept the convention of speaking out towards the audience and not demand the cinematic or televisual reality of the camera's close-up and frontal perspective. In this way, the video projections domesticise the space of tragedy, rendering it more intimate, in the sense that Auslander suggests.[33]

The camera also focused sometimes on the spectators themselves.[34] This mirroring of the spectators through the use of projected video is the most obvious example of the spectators being made aware of the technology and their own place within the mediated world. This awareness of self through media, as a part of the event and an observer of the event, might have reminded the spectators of their common spectatorship, something that would certainly have been significant for the spectators in the Theatre of Dionysus watching the original productions. In the very least, it makes

[30] Leslie, quoted in Burke (2005), 363. [31] Leslie, quoted in Burke (2005), 363.
[32] Billington (1999). [33] See n. 6 above. [34] Llewellyn-Jones (2002), 10.

them aware of their own presence. In this way, the use of media becomes the subject of these moments as much as the spectators' recognition of their own shared spectatorship.

The video projections in Mitchell's *Oresteia* were black and white, and many commentators note that they felt as if they were from an earlier time, as 'the images that were projected were in black and white and had the grainy quality of a World War II film … implicitly inviting a modern comparison to the way war is filmed as a spectacle and documentation'.[35] This sense of time period for Mitchell is not necessarily used to make a specific historical analogy, but instead to resonate ideas of memory and war. As Leslie observed, 'The video has a number of resonances in terms of war – the whole Gulf War thing about watching war on video, watching bombing raids. So we have an association with it.'[36] Mitchell's anachronistic and eclectic use of costumes and props from several time periods that sometimes refer to different wars (in the former Yugoslavia and Northern Ireland, for example)[37] also works against a specific analogy. Instead, Mitchell seems to use the historical-feeling video to resonate with the idea of memory, and perhaps even achieve a strong sense of memory. Robert E. Jones thought that the primary use of film in the theatre would be to depict dreams and memories, and Mitchell seems to be using this mode in her images of Iphigenia especially, which are in soft focus and filtered to seem dream-like.[38]

Mitchell's production also uses mediated audio to affect the audience, especially in terms of their sense of history and memory. In the first play, *Home Guard*, the chorus did not vocalise the quotations from Calchas and Agamemnon. Instead, a chorus member played a tape recording of their voices, which 'were reminiscent of a World War II wireless broadcast: the crackled quality of the broadcast and the Received Pronunciation voices echoed the broadcasts of Neville Chamberlain or Winston Churchill.'[39] The elements that Burke identifies might have the specific resonances she describes with older audiences especially, who are more familiar with the historical referents. But even for those who do not make those identifications, the sense of the historical past is clearly communicated through these tapes. Their significance is also intermedial of course, as they interrupt the live choral voices and are presented as archives of history, of the real, even

[35] Burke (2005), 275–6. [36] Leslie quoted in Burke (2005), 363. [37] Burke (2005), 259.

[38] As R. E. Jones (1965 [1941], 18) wrote, 'Some new playwright will presently set a motion-picture screen on the stage above and behind his actors and will reveal simultaneously the two worlds of the conscious and the unconscious …'

[39] Burke (2005), 290.

though they only exist in the theatrical event at this point as recorded sound. Their power is further demonstrated by the actor portraying the ghost of Iphigenia, who moved towards the tape recorder each time her father's voice was played on it.

Peter Sellars also used microphones to 'project, distort, and cover the human voice' like a 'Greek mask'[40] in his 1993 production of Robert Auletta's Gulf War-inspired adaptation of *The Persians* at the Salzburg Festival. Because Sellars, a pioneer of the use of technology in productions of Greek tragedy, thinks that the mediated voice also reminds the spectators of broadcast journalism, it also gives it the authority, or at least the perception, of 'truth', and a relationship to history. At the same time, Sellars uses it to offer, along the lines of Auslander's analysis about intimacy, 'the intensity of a secret interior monologue'.[41] He is not interested so much in the fragmentation strategy of the Wooster Group or Jesurun as in the complications of the human voice as a mode for storytelling that is clearer and more intimate by using mediation. Like Mitchell, Sellars thinks that the audio mediation can complicate the subject for the spectators, while also giving them a familiar context to help them listen to and understand the text.

Mitchell's production demonstrates some relatively straightforward uses of media that help the spectators to process the information from the Greek narrative and contextualise it in terms of more contemporary content and form. The video especially is used to provide emotional and psychological support to the storytelling, as in the case of the images of the ghost of Iphigenia and the projected text, and to help the audience feel less distance from the plot and characters by using familiar televisual and cinematic strategies, as in the projections of Electra and Orestes looking down at Agamemnon's tomb. Furthermore, the cameras are used to create a sense of communal experience through mediation, especially by showing spectators on the projections. Finally, Mitchell uses both video and audio to create a sense of other or parallel worlds that reference history and memory: the ghost of Iphigenia, the black-and-white projections, and the recorded voices made to sound like old radio footage.

With Mitchell, then, we are still dealing primarily in the realm of psychological realism, with some mediation to help reinforce emotional, logistical, or brief intermedial elements. Mitchell's work in the *Oresteia*, which was innovative in 1999 and still remains significant because of its liberal use of mediated technologies, uses media to illuminate and express

[40] Auletta (2006), xiii. [41] Auletta (2006), xiii.

the characters and actions of a traditional dramatic plot in a mediated theatrical environment that is still recognisable as such by most contemporary theatre spectators. In fact, one of Mitchell's more recent productions, *Fräulein Julie* (2013) at the Schaubühne in Berlin, transformed the stage into a set for the express purpose of making a film of Strindberg's play. The spectators watched the filming simultaneously while watching the film, which is edited and produced live, on a large projection screen in the centre foreground of the stage.

Jay Scheib's Intermedial *Medea*

A project similar in some ways to Mitchell's *Fräulein Julie*, Jay Scheib's *Platonov, or The Disinherited*, was staged at the Kitchen in January 2014 while a live film of the production was shown at a nearby cinema. Scheib calls this attempt part of a 'continued effort to be more live than live' and, like Mitchell, is actually 'privileging film over theater' in order to achieve this.[42] Scheib reverses the usual expectations of the live/mediated binary, finding the 'present' not in the live event but in its televised manifestation. In his construction, the elements usually accorded to the 'live', like breath, are instead accorded to the televisually intimate mediated sports event.[43] This idea speaks clearly to Auslander's propositions about liveness, and Scheib, for one, embraces the challenges that the dominance of mediation sets forward for live theatre.

Scheib nearly always uses media in his pieces in order 'to amplify the real, the live, the source'.[44] His production of *The Medea* (2005) used the basic framework of Heiner Müller's *Despoiled Shore*, *Medeamaterial*, and *Landscape with Argonauts* along with fragments of the texts of Euripides, Seneca, and Franz Grillparzer. The production also referenced films of the story of Medea made by Pier Paolo Pasolini and Lars von Trier. Scheib used a live camera feed of onstage action with large projections of the camera feed above the stage. In the opening scene, Jason is onstage as the spectators enter the Club at La Mama E.T.C. in New York City. He is underneath a large wooden board, a representation of his death underneath the rotten mast of his ship, the Argo, and is facing upstage so that his face remains invisible to the audience. When he starts to speak, the projection shows his face in extreme close-up. At this point, the spectators immediately look to find the location of the camera to determine the relationship

[42] Quoted in Soloski (2014). [43] Soloski (2014). [44] Soloski (2014).

of the staging to the projection. Thus, the audience is focused on the act of mediation, in this case the camera angle.

Part of the performance space is inside a room built on stage, with four walls so that it can only be seen when the door is open or on the screens that capture the action through multiple cameras inside the room. As Scheib describes:

> Michael Byrne's design re-envisions a classical Greek Skene in the shape of an oversize fitting-room-living-room. For the Greeks it was behind the closed doors of the Skene that unspeakable violence took place. For Seneca, the violence was central and ostensibly on-stage. We split the distance and try to make it feel like America – partially seen, partially screened.[45]

This enclosed room functions as an onstage sound stage and is always visible but only through two changing camera perspectives projected on two large screens above the stage. By obscuring both live and mediated images, the production presents disconnected and fragmented images of the action of the actors, expressing and representing a fragmented and disconnected world. Scheib and video designer Leah Gelpe call this style 'DEVOLUTION/NOT EVOLUTION',[46] as instead of seeing a progression of elements coming together to create a unified dramatic world, Scheib and Gelpe intentionally set out to show its fragmentation by actively taking it apart. The phrase explains to some extent how both artists use media to subvert, complicate, and obfuscate the dramatic and theatrical elements of the Greek story and its adaptations.

Scheib uses multiple actions in distinct spaces, simultaneous live and projected images, live and recorded music seemingly unrelated to the story, and a casual, conversational acting style, as he thinks this is what best represents contemporary reality.

This style uses classical texts like Euripides' *Medea* but juxtaposes them with stylistic influences such as reality television and other popular media like American soap operas. It creates moments of recognition for the spectators through the emotional vulnerability and expressiveness of the actors. It has much in common with Hans-Thies Lehmann's idea of 'hypernaturalism', which is derived from Baudrillard's hyperrealism: 'a non-referential, media-produced, heightened resemblance of things to themselves, not the adequacy of images to the real'.[47] The reality television comparison is particularly relevant here, since the 'reality' of those shows is

[45] Scheib (2005). [46] Scheib (2005). [47] Lehmann (2006), 117.

not much more 'real' than the perceived artifice of Euripides or Strindberg to a contemporary audience. However, the resemblance of this style to contemporary life, and the ubiquity of its modes of representation through television and the Internet, make it seem more real to a contemporary audience accustomed to those conventions.

The most intimate scene in Scheib's *The Medea* is not mediated. In the forestage in front of the enclosed onstage room, less than two metres from the closest spectators, Jason and Medea have their extended reconciliation scene, in which the two actors have a brutal and loud seven-minute sex scene. While there was little nudity involved, and it was clear that the actors were not actually having sex, the scene was sexy and frightening in its violence and intimacy – a gesture towards the Artaudian principles of presence and live bodies as the central purpose of theatre. Scheib's projected images are filled with the energy and vibrancy of the performances, even when they are mediated. While this is somewhat related to the themes of the works themselves, the embrace of the intermedial, with the complexities of the live and filmed existing at the same time in the same space, also creates a tension in the performance itself. By privileging the film so much, Mitchell makes it detrimental to the theatre experience because it deprives 'the live theater of some of its particular strengths of physical, emotional, kinetic energies and resonances'.[48] The vitality of Scheib's intermediality survives through the media because of its engagement not just with the emotional or psychological, but with the physical and the visceral. In his attempts to create a new kind of performed reality, Scheib embraces the physicality of bodies and their presence while insisting that their existence through media is essential to our engagement with and understanding of them.

Jan Fabre's Promethean Viscerality

Along similar lines, Troublyn's production of Aeschylus' *Prometheus Bound*, retitled by its auteur director Jan Fabre as *Prometheus-Landscape II,* uses media to create a landscape that also informs the environment and themes of the production, in ways reminiscent of Mitchell's uses of media in her *Oresteia*. But while media is ever-present and dominant in the visual sphere of *Prometheus-Landscape II*, Fabre's engagement with the physical body is central. In the world premiere performance, in Montclair, New Jersey in January of 2011, the primary mode of mediation was an

[48] Lehmann (2006), 225.

enormous projection that filled nearly the entire backdrop with a ball of fire, a representation of the sun which had a diameter three times the size of the actor playing Prometheus, who was bound and suspended in the air for the entirety of the performance. The prologue to the piece, with the curtain down, consists of a large, nearly naked actor standing centre-stage wrapped in ropes, while another actor speaks a text that climaxes with a series of curses on modern psychologists like Freud and Jung, and, finally, a desperate call for heroes. The ball of fire, which shone more brightly at times and dimmed to a moon-like sphere at others, was front-projected, so that Prometheus' dark shadow was constantly visible on it. The story of Prometheus, the Titan who brought fire to humankind, is in Fabre's production turned into a fable about courage, vision, and their lack in humankind despite the sacrifices of those who, like Prometheus, have struggled and are eternally tortured in their attempts to illuminate humanity. While Prometheus watches, a series of characters tell their stories, which consist primarily of screaming rants and orgiastic dances.

Fabre puts fire everywhere in the production. There are many devices that shoot fire and smoke, and there are also strategically placed and utilised red buckets of sand and industrial-size fire extinguishers that extinguish the real fire that is brought on stage, but also, especially in the case of the fire extinguishers, move bodies with the pure force of the carbon dioxide jets that are released from them. The performers also light matches against sandpaper placed over their genitalia and swallow the tiny bits of fire repeatedly. There is even a moment when performer Gilles Polet attempts to use his own penis to ignite a fire, unsuccessfully rubbing it between his hands like one would a stick into another stick. For Fabre, fire is sex, power, and knowledge, and an artist is meant to play with fire and pass it along to audiences. Fabre sees Athenian tragedy

> at the core of how I perceive this medium [i.e. theatre]. All ancient gods and heroes are very important to me. Prometheus was the man who brought fire to humanity. Sometimes I feel that as an artist, I have this fire, and I pass it on to other people, other artists. We form a team, which I really like. Of course, there's the question of who contemporary society's heroes are. We live in a world that bars us from using fire. Fire is banned from every fucking museum or theater. In this sense, we are also barred from being creative. We think about the contemporary world, about Prometheus, we keep talking about fire, but we can't start one![49]

[49] Semenowicz (2011).

For Fabre, there is great irony in the representation of fire through media, and even though the piece is dominated by actual fire, this is always controlled, as fire needs to be for the safety of the performers and spectators on the stage. But Fabre's desire for the viscerality, presence, and danger of fire also evokes the question of media in the theatre. Fabre would rather 'look people in the eye ... smell their scent' than be 'kissed by a computer'.[50] He emphasises the material body and the shared presence of live theatre, and even though he uses video, its function in *Prometheus-Landscape II* suggests what he thinks about its role in theatre and in culture: while it is a huge part of the landscape, dominating it to a large degree and causing great suffering through its power, it is not the most interesting or vital element of theatre or life. Despite the dominance of media, we remain human beings, whose psychologies, behaviours, and bodies are still the reasons why, in the end, artists and spectators participate in theatre.

While Fabre's marked focus on the body is not representative of every contemporary production of Greek tragedy, the most meaningful ones tend to challenge the styles of naturalism and realism. Even Mitchell's *Oresteia*, which tended towards a modern psychological interpretation of character, included a ghost and used media to upset the illusion of a unified narrative world. Media are often the vehicle by which contemporary practitioners avoid the demands of stage realism to make the Greek stories more contemporary and, perhaps ironically, more visceral. The use of intermedial practices often helps in this engagement, as it forces the spectators not only to pay attention to the psychology of the characters or the progress of the action, but also to actively relate to the elements of the theatrical world. In a sense, productions such as Jesurun's *Philoktetes*, Mitchell's *Oresteia*, and Scheib's *The Medea* allow spectators to imagine possibilities for the stories and characters through their negotiation of the live and the mediated:

> By rejecting the totalizing mediation as well as the lures of immediacy and particularism, intermediality aims to provide an alternative both to the unification promised in different ways by dialectical systems (the legacy of Hegelianism and orthodox Marxism) or the grand narratives of modernity ... and to the dispersal bemoaned or celebrated as the hallmark of the postmodern condition.[51]

[50] Semenowicz (2011). [51] Oosterling and Plonowska Ziarek (2011), 1.

These adaptations of Greek tragedies take the foundational texts of Western drama and create contemporary theatrical experiences that both embrace and reject traditional dramatic principles. By focusing on the relationship of media to contemporary culture and representation and using the well-established tragic texts of fifth-century Athens for these productions, they manage to encapsulate the rapidly changing world and, at the same time, show theatre as, to use Fuchs' term, an 'enabling form' for representation. The mediated adaptation of Greek tragedy, then, is not just a representation of how media affect traditional drama, representation, and the contemporary world; it is 'the scene itself'.

CHAPTER 9

Violence in Adaptations of Greek Tragedy[*]

Simon Perris

Then Peneleus stabbed Ilioneus, right under the eyebrow and into the root, and the eyeball popped out; the spear went through the socket and out the nape of his neck. Ilioneus sat down, both hands outstretched, but Peneleus drew a sharp sword, hacked square at his neck and chopped off his head, helmet and all. The long spear was still sticking out of the eye-socket. Peneleus picked up the head – like a poppy-head – showed it to the Trojans and shouted a boast . . .

(*Iliad*, 14.493–500)[1]

MENELAUS: You will never take this woman from my hands.
 You can be sure of it.
PELEUS: Yes I will, once I've smashed your head bloody with
 this sceptre . . .
MENELAUS: Come over here, just try laying a finger on
 me – then you'll see!

(Euripides, *Andromache*, 588–9)

Why, I oughta – !

(Moe Howard, The Three Stooges)

I

I begin by reproducing – and not for the first time – a well-worn cliché: Greek tragedy is violent.[2] But not in the usual way of film, television, or videogames. On the one hand, violence (Greek: *bia*, *aikia*, *hybris*;

* I thank the editors for inviting me to contribute to this volume and for their comments and suggestions. The audience who heard an earlier version in Wellington gave much helpful feedback. Special thanks to Charlotte Simmonds for reading and commenting on a full draft. This essay was substantively complete by late 2015; I have not systematically updated it to take into account scholarship published since then.

1 Unless otherwise specified, all translations are mine. I restrict discussion to English-language adaptations.

2 Perris (2011a), 37. See Goldhill (1991); Sommerstein (2010).

Latin: *vis*) can be understood as a kind of forceful physical contact. And Greek tragedy did indeed stage physical contact, including occasional uses of force, along with the occasional non-violent death.[3] On the other hand, however, violence per se – fisticuffs, swordfights, executions, torture – was almost always avoided onstage. The impaling of Prometheus in *Prometheus Bound* is one certain exception which proves the rule; *Rhesus* includes another possible exception; Ajax may or may not have killed himself onstage.[4] Accordingly, Sommerstein proposes two conventions for the dramatisation of violence in Greek drama: dramatists never – or *almost* never – staged the proximate cause of violent death; tragedians *almost* never staged blows onstage.[5]

Yet Greek tragedy is no stranger to gore, especially in Euripides' report narratives (i.e. 'messenger speeches'). In *Medea*, flesh drips from the princess's bones (1200–1); Creon tears off his own flesh (1216–17). In *Hecabe*, Polymestor describes having his eyes stabbed out (1169–71). In *Electra*, Orestes chops into Aegisthus' back with an axe and the body convulses (841–3). In *Heracles*, the hero smashes his son's blond head with a club (993–4). And in *Rhesus*, the charioteer recalls being splashed by 'a warm stream of fresh blood from my master who had just been slaughtered' (790–1). These and other frequent instances of reported violence reveal both a reticence towards gore and a fascination with it. (Not to mention the bloody tableaux staged on the *ekkuklēma*.) So Sommerstein, reversing the viewing angle: 'It is a cliché that violence, especially violent death, was not presented visually on the Greek tragic stage. Yet violence could be presented *verbally*'; 'nor were the dramatists in the least squeamish about presenting on stage the *results* of violence in the most appalling form'.[6] That is, almost no dramatic representation, but plenty of visual display and verbal description.

This push–pull dynamic between telling and showing culminates in *Bacchae*, a play which is paradigmatic in its treatment of violence, pity, and fear.[7] In the event that I am ever asked to write a pub quiz on Greek tragedy, I already have my first question picked out: *Who kills Pentheus,*

[3] See Kaimio (1988), esp. pp. 69–78 on instances of physical force. Euripides' *Alcestis* and *Hippolytus* contain the only two *certain* onstage deaths in extant tragedy. *Prometheus* contains the only *certain* example of onstage blows.

[4] See Liapis (2013b), 244 on the 'threat of impending stage violence' when the chorus pursues Odysseus in *Rhesus*. On the question of whether Ajax committed suicide onstage in *Ajax*, see Finglass (2011), 376–9 and the essays in Most and Ozbek (2015).

[5] Sommerstein (2010), 44–5.

[6] Sommerstein (2010), 30. See also, e.g., Pathmanathan (1965); Bremer (1976); Petre (1985).

[7] Perris (2011a).

and how?[8] The obvious answer: *His mother Agaue, by decapitating him bare-handed.* But Pentheus dies offstage. Nowhere in *Bacchae* does a reliable eyewitness describe the moment of his death or name the killer(s). Even assuming that Pentheus died when his head parted from his shoulders, we never actually hear whodunnit or how.

Audiences are not entirely in the dark. Dionysus predicts that Pentheus will be 'slaughtered at his mother's hands' (*Ba.* 858).[9] Agaue, holding Pentheus' head in her hands, tells the chorus that she 'caught the little cub without a noose' (1173). Shortly thereafter, she announces that she was the first one to attack (1179–83). The *geras* (war-prize) which she won was the honour of striking the *first* blow – not necessarily the killing blow.[10] All in all, then, Agaue precisely details the preparations for and the start of the process of *sparagmos* (Pentheus' tearing-apart) but not the end. More to the point, she is delusional. She thinks the human head in her hands is a lion cub's. As far as the death of this 'little cub' is concerned, Agaue in her reverie can only assert, 'Mount Cithaeron ... slaughtered it [or *him*]' (1177–8). And right at the important juncture between strophe and antistrophe in the sung exchange, she skips from 'This was a lucky hunt indeed' (1183) to 'Join the feast!' (1184).[11]

Later still, Cadmus tells the attendants who carry Pentheus' jumbled remains – but not the head – that he was killed 'by maenads' (*Ba.* 1226), that is, by the Theban women under Dionysus' control. He later gives Agaue herself, now compos mentis, the sad truth: 'You killed him – you and your sisters' (1289). This is hearsay. Cadmus has heard about his daughters' crimes from 'someone' (1222: του, 1230: τις) in the city (κατ' ἄστυ, 1223), not from an eyewitness.[12] True, the reporting figure (i.e. 'messenger') leaves the stage in order to get himself 'well away from this disaster' (*Ba.* 1148) before Agaue arrives at the palace through one of the side entrances. Audiences might well imagine that he returns to the city via the other side entrance, and that he is the one who spreads the news of

[8] My opening section draws on Perris (2011a). See also Weaver (2009), 35–6, 40–2.

[9] See Roux (1972) on *Ba.* 857–61: 'Il savoure d'avance sa vengeance et en prédit la circonstance la plus atroce' ('He savours his vengeance in advance and foretells its most horrendous aspect'). Gods' predictions usually eventuate, with Euripides' *Ion* (see lines 71–3) furnishing the exception.

[10] Roux (1972) on *Ba.* 1179 prefers the MS reading τίς ἁ βαλοῦσα πρώτα ('who struck first?'). According to Roux, the Lydian Bacchants know well that a *sparagmos* of one victim involves many attackers and ask who struck *first*. Dodds (= Murray, OCT), Diggle (OCT), and Kovacs (Loeb) print Elmsley's correction τίς ἁ βαλοῦσα; Αγ. πρῶτον κτλ ('who struck?' Agaue: 'First ...').

[11] Dodds (1960) on *Ba.* 1181–3 doubts the traditional insertion of a lacuna (i.e. a posited gap, the length of two choral trimeters) at 1183.

[12] Roux (1972) on *Ba.* 1222: Cadmus and Tiresias went to Cithaeron to worship Dionysus but not to take part in the secret, women-only rituals.

Pentheus' death, perhaps as the unnamed 'someone' who then tells Cadmus.[13] But that would be asking, and answering, a question about which *Bacchae* cares not a whit.

Audiences in real time hear the facts of the case from one eyewitness: the reporting figure who accompanied Pentheus. He tells us that Agaue did indeed attack first, followed by her sisters (1125–8). By line 1127, Pentheus has already lost (at least) an arm. At line 1132, he is still alive, shouting with what breath he has left. By line 1137, however, he is reduced from a voice to a dismembered corpse: κεῖται δὲ χωρὶς σῶμα ('his body is lying there in parts'). In his final scene, then, Pentheus morphs from spy to captive to suppliant to victim to mere voice (1131: βοή) to nothing more than hunks of flesh (1136: σάρκα, 1137: σῶμα). At the same time, the verbs abruptly shift from the imperfect tense (to describe the Theban women's ongoing actions) to present-tense or present-force verbs. (The perfect-tense verb κεῖται has the sense 'it is [now] lying [there]'.) This verbal transition to the present moment completes the structural transition from narrative to aftermath – from 'Complication' to 'Coda' in Allan's typology of oral narrative in Greek tragedy.[14] More importantly, the reporting figure elides Pentheus' death, moving from *X was happening* to *Z is where things stand now*, entirely skipping over *Y finally happened*, that is, 'Pentheus died.' In Allan's terms, the speaker omits the 'Resolution' of his narrative. According to Weaver, 'the messenger averts his eyes at certain moments in his description of the *sparagmos*, jumping from one plausible stage in the sequence to a further stage ... The messenger thus evokes what we do not see through explicit narrative.'[15]

In the *Metamorphoses* (3.721–8), by contrast, Ovid expands the Euripidean narrative and includes the actual beheading of Pentheus at line 727: *avulsumque caput* ('ripping off his head'). The same goes for Theocritus' twenty-sixth *Idyll* and Nonnus' *Dionysiaca*.[16] One could also contrast, for example, the report of Neoptolemus' death in Euripides'

[13] As Roux (1972) on *Ba.* 1148–52 reminds us, the actor playing the reporting figure leaves the stage to change mask and costume in order to play Agaue.

[14] R. Allan (2009), 186–9 draws on both Labov's and Fleischman's work to present the following stages: Abstract (summary), Orientation (status quo), Complication, Resolution, Evaluation, Coda (changed circumstances). Euripidean report narratives tend to mark the Coda with present verbs; after κεῖται, all further finite verbs in main clauses in this particular report are present indicative or future indicative.

[15] Weaver (2009), 42. See now De Jong (2014), 203–21 on the second report narrative in *Bacchae*.

[16] See Perris and Mac Góráin (2020), 51–7 on Pentheus' death in *Idyll* 26, the *Metamorphoses*, and the *Dionysiaca*.

Andromache. At lines 1073–5, the reporting figure immediately mentions the details of Neoptolemus' death, including location (Delphi), killers (Delphians and Orestes), and means (swords): this constitutes a complete 'Abstract' in Allan's terms – a summary of the upcoming narrative.[17] *Bacchae* provides a minimal Abstract at best: 'Pentheus, Echion's son, is dead' (1030). In the report narrative from *Andromache*, the reporting figure duly states that Neoptolemus 'fell after being stabbed in the side' (1149–50).[18] Commentators have not hitherto seen fit to note the corresponding omission of Pentheus' death. Just like *Andromache*, *Bacchae* duly produces a corpse onstage. We know, or at least we think we know, that something terrible has happened. Yet the play's reticence about the moment of Pentheus' death remains striking. The final report narrative in *Bacchae* is explicitly supposed to be about Pentheus' death, particularly the precise nature of that death. 'Tell me, tell me how he died, that criminal trying out his crimes!' demand the chorus members (*Ba.* 1040–1).[19] But precisely *how* he dies is one thing we never quite know for sure.

Contrast Ajax son of Oïleus in the *Iliad*, throwing the head of Imbrius 'like a ball' (*Il.* 13.204: σφαιρηδόν) – after he has in fact *chopped off the head* (203: κόψεν). Does Agaue decapitate Pentheus? We cannot say. Does it matter? Not really, at least not after the Theban women, hands bloodied, play 'ball' with chunks of Pentheus' flesh (1136: διεσφαίριζε σάρκα), not unlike Imbrius' head. As Roux, commenting on the second report narrative in *Bacchae* (1043–152), puts it: 'He [Euripides] indulges in an accumulation of gruesomely realistic features, his purpose being no longer to surprise but to horrify.'[20] *Bacchae* shies away from violent death more than other plays, but it also revels in gore as much as any.

Thus we come to our first epigraph: the death of the Trojan Ilioneus at the hands of the Greek Peneleus in *Iliad* 14, a passage which itself recalls the Ajax–Imbrius episode. The poet strings together a grisly sequence of

[17] R. Allan (2009), 189.

[18] This example would be even more apposite were one to retain *Andr.* 1151: Δελφοῦ πρὸς ἀνδρὸς ὅσπερ αὐτὸν ὤλεσεν. But the line, which is superfluous, reads like an interpolation; Hartung was probably right to delete it.

[19] See Perris (2011a), 44–6 on this passage. The chorus members sing in the excited dochmiac rhythm and spice their question with two imperative speech verbs as well as the 'interrogative present' verb θνῄσκει ('he dies'). See also, e.g., Van Emde Boas (2017), 230–1 on Euripidean messengers' concern with not 'what?' but 'how?'.

[20] Roux (1972) on *Ba.* 1125–8: 'Il [viz., Euripides] accumule ici à plaisir les traits d'un réalisme macabre, recherchant non plus un effet de surprise, mais un effet d'horreur.' See Perris (2011a) for the shift in tone from the first to the second report narrative.

graphic details: where weapons strike the body; which body parts are damaged or excised; and in particular, precisely how Peneleus kills Ilioneus (decapitation: 14.498–9). The poppy-head simile adds to the grisliness, visually recalling Ilioneus' head flopping about on the end of the spear and also the redness of his blood. Finally, Peneleus *displays* the head to the Trojans and calls for a response. That is, the scene presents an internal audience's response to physical violence and to the quasi-theatrical display of the aftermath violence in a tableau of sorts; 'its effect is almost as horrendous for us as it is for the Trojans and makes their panic fully apt'.[21] Homeric battle narrative by turns treats bloody warfare as a source of aesthetic pleasure and as a source of horror, for internal *and* external audiences. This is one of many respects in which tragic report narratives may be considered slices from Homer's banquet. Homer and tragedy – the two most elite, serious, public genres of ancient Greek poetic performance – often dwell on blood and guts, violent death, who did what to whom. 'Then the screams and victory shouts of men *killing and dying* mingled, and the earth streamed with blood' (*Il.* 4.450–1). 'Tragedy is a representation not of people but of actions and life' (Arist. *Poet.* 1450a16–17).

Moving to our second epigraph, from *Andromache*, we see tragedy's propensity to hint at violence that never happens. Peleus is all bluster, nothing happens, and his threat is soon forgotten. In this way, Greek tragedy conditions us to expect altercations which it does not stage, substituting words for sticks and stones.

In our third epigraph, we see how verbal violence might appear to focus more on the threat than on the action and, in so doing, replace action with speech. But thanks to the rhetorical figure of aposiopesis, Moe has no need to complete the sentence 'Why, I ought to – *do something bad to you*', because what is unsaid is still perceptible. This is also true of Greek tragedy, in which threats of onstage violence are not carried out as a rule, yet what is kept offstage is also perceptible. Tragedy induces in its audiences a palpable expectation of onstage violence. And what we get, typically, is reported violence. Thus, via a kind of dramaturgical aposiopesis – parasiopesis perhaps – tragedy leaves us with the indistinct impression that we have in fact *witnessed* beatings, murders, and suicides.[22] Hence, the robust cliché that Greek tragedy is violent. Because, in fact, it is.

[21] Janko (1994) on *Il.* 14.489–505. On Imbrius and Peneleus, see now McClellan (2016); Kucewicz (2016).

[22] Aposiopesis: breaking off in the middle of a sentence. Parasiopesis: talking about something by saying that one is not going to talk about it.

II

Now for adaptations. Given the ubiquity of violence in Greek tragedy and the genre's corresponding reputation for bloodshed, adaptors cannot dodge the question of violence. Thence comes the potential for 'dramaturgical parasiopesis' which I have identified, and which relates to what I have elsewhere called 'the aesthetically productive paradox underpinning Greek tragedy's unique brand of formalism'.[23] Tragedy wants what it cannot have: not just 'visible deaths' (οἵ τε ἐν τῷ φανερῷ θάνατοι), physical pain, and wounds (Arist. *Poet.* 1452b12–13), but murder, rape, and suicide. Adaptations can have it all.

In this second section, therefore, we examine the attraction and flexibility of tragic violence in two adaptations of *Bacchae* from the late 1960s: *Rites*, by the British writer Maureen Duffy (premiere 1969), and *Mr O'Dwyer's Dancing Party*, by the New Zealand poet James K. Baxter (written 1967; premiere 1968).[24]

Rites takes place in a women's bathroom, with female dramatis personae and one non-speaking male part 'played' by an anatomically correct, male, pre-school-age doll. Over the course of the play, various women enumerate their problems with men before killing an androgynous woman whom they mistake for a man. The crisis begins when Ada, the ringleader, pointedly asserts, 'We don't need them [i.e. men]. We can do without them!' The other women then start dancing.[25] Still dancing, they surround an Old Woman and taunt her while singing 'Knees Up Mother Brown'. The stage directions continue, '*This is repeated until it reaches a frenzy of menace and the old woman cowers down making little noises of fear. Suddenly a figure appears ... Head bent; it is suited and coated, short-haired and masculine.*'[26] Led by Ada, the women then surround this new figure:

She leads them forward, the OLD WOMAN joining in. They fall upon the figure and it goes under as if drowned. It disappears beneath the flailing crowd. There is frenzied activity and a scream. There is another cry and the crowd breaks apart leaving a tattered and broken figure wrapped in bloody clothing. Only NORMA is left crouching down.[27]

[23] Perris (2011a), 37–8. Gruber (2010), 6 writes of a 'dramaturgically productive tension'; Gruber's section on reportage in modern drama at pp. 35–75 is particularly suggestive.

[24] Duffy (1969); Baxter (1982), 261–91. See Winkler (1993); Davidson (2007).

[25] Duffy (1969), 32. [26] Duffy (1969), 33. [27] Duffy (1969), 34.

After Pentheus' death, *Bacchae* winds down slowly, through lament, laying out the body for burial, Dionysus' appearance 'on high', and the protagonists' farewell and exile. *Rites*, however, winds up towards a final climactic *sparagmos* (prepared for and heightened by a red herring, the 'frenzy of menace' directed at the Old Woman). *Rites* concludes shortly thereafter: after a perfunctory cremation in the basement incinerator, the women go back to their make-up.

This all-female 'orgasm of violence', as Duffy herself describes it, is the play's raison d'être. The characters 'find they have destroyed themselves, and in death there is certainly no difference'.[28] What is more, collective female violence changes nothing; the women remain stuck in broadly conventional gender roles. As spoken by Meg, the play's last line reframes *sparagmos* as a temporary escape and undermines the sense of closure:

(*ADA goes on with her make-up. MEG sits down at the table.*)

MEG: What's he like your Friday feller?[29]

In *Mr O'Dwyer's Dancing Party*, the violence is a little less, well, violent. In the opening scene, the protagonist John Ennis plays chess with his blind neighbour Ephraim Feingold, a rabbi's son. (Like Tiresias in *Bacchae*, Ephraim is a quasi-prophetic voice of reason.) John's wife Mildred joins a women's dancing group led by new arrival Tom O'Dwyer. John confronts Tom, but Tom gets him drunk and takes him to a meeting of the dance group. While dancing, the women strip John, then Mildred rides him like a horse until he collapses with a back injury. In the coda, Tom O'Dwyer and Ephraim Feingold debate religion; O'Dwyer argues for the 'god of the dance', Feingold for Jehovah. No one wins the argument, and O'Dwyer has the last word: 'Remember, Mr Feingold, the spirit of wisdom danced in front of Jehovah before the world was made.'[30]

In both plays, Dionysus triggers a sexual revolution of sorts. For Baxter, the god of the dance, Dionysus (in human form as Tom O'Dwyer), represents sexual liberation after the Summer of Love, with all its mixed blessings for husbands and wives. His *sparagmos* is mildly serio-comic. Duffy, by contrast, allows Dionysiac release only to women through brutal, onstage, in-group violence. In any case, these two examples sharpen their focus on sexuality and gender by concentrating their dramaturgical

[28] Duffy (1969), 7, 'Introduction'. [29] Duffy (1969), 36. [30] Baxter (1982), 291.

energies in an act of violence. The crux of each play is not the aftermath of death, as in *Bacchae*, but the actual moment of violence, enacted onstage.

I draw from translation studies the concept of the *invariant*: that which is invariably translated (literally 'carried over') from source texts to target texts; 'those elements which remain unchanged in the process of translation'.[31] I propose that the invariant of *Bacchae* in adaptation – the transhistorical kernel which is carried over into other genres, other media, and even other stories – is *sparagmos*.[32] Twentieth-century productions of Euripides' *Bacchae*, especially in the 'long sixties' (i.e. 1958–74), enacted cultural revolutions of various kinds; the same holds for adaptations.[33] In particular: adaptations of *Bacchae* (especially from that period) typically stage a revolution which ends in some form of *sparagmos*, to the temporary or permanent benefit of the community. This is observable in other media also, even when *Bacchae* is not an obvious hypotext. Theodoros Angelopoulos' 1980 film *O Megalexandros* (*Alexander the Great*), for example, culminates in a *sparagmos* which leaves behind only a statue head, like the mask which Agaue may well have carried in the original production of *Bacchae*.[34] Duffy's and Baxter's plays certainly illustrate this predilection for enacting cultural revolution.

What is more, violent speech acts cluster around physical violence, doubly contravening tragic decorum. In *Rites*: 'Look a bloody man'; 'Bastard men' (twice); 'Christ!'; 'Oh my gawd!'; 'It was a bloody woman.'[35] In *Dancing Party*, within thirteen lines no less: 'Giddyup, you stupid bugger!'; 'you're breaking my bloody back!'; 'It's your fault – you bastard!'; 'you've bloody well broken it!'; 'it doesn't mean a bugger anyhow'.[36] Indeed, verbal violence is itself an important theatrical phenomenon. Jeanette Malkin, for example, has shown that post-war absurdist theatre directs verbal violence at its characters *and* its audience; Ionesco and Pinter use verbal violence to counteract 'language nausea' caused by a surfeit of language.[37] Adaptations of tragedy, however, tend not to thematise verbal violence in the same way: verbal violence either accompanies moments of physical violence or draws attention to the marked absence of physical violence.

[31] Baker and Saldanha (2009), 269–71 (269).

[32] Perris (2016), *passim* on *sparagmos*, esp. pp. 39–58 on adaptations.

[33] Fischer-Lichte (2014b); Perris (2015); Perris (2016). On 'cultural revolution', see Marcuse (1973), 95. On cultural revolution in the 'long sixties', see Marwick (1998), esp. 3–22.

[34] I thank Prof. Arthur Pomeroy for the Angelopoulos reference. See Perris (2016), 55–6 on *sparagmos* in dramatic adaptations of *Bacchae*.

[35] Duffy (1969), 33–4. [36] Baxter (1982), 287. [37] Malkin (1992), 1–9, 225–6 and *passim*.

Artaud knew the importance of *sparagmos*; *Bacchae* arguably requires its own Theatre of Cruelty.[38] And violent acts committed or simulated by actors on their own or others' bodies, more than any other phenomenon in contemporary theatre, *do* have the power to affect us viscerally. Yet the kind of censorship laws which hobbled Edward Bond's *Saved* (1965) are no longer in force in the developed English-speaking world. What shocks us now is the breaking not of legal or aesthetic restrictions, but of social, ethical, and theatrical mores. To name just a few canonical examples, Howard Brenton's *The Romans in Britain* (1980), Sarah Kane's *Blasted* (1995), and Mark Ravenhill's *Shopping and Fucking* (1996) – which the *New York Times* famously insisted on naming with strategic asterisks – illustrate the persistence of tradition and convention in a post-censorship milieu, especially regarding depictions of rape. Degenring observes:

> While the absence [in post-1968 UK theatre] of pre-censorship and the (so far mostly) unsuccessful attempts at post-censorship through the courts seems to suggest that in a permissive society no taboos are left to be broken, the controversies sparked by the so-called In-Yer-Face Theater of the 1990s and beyond (cf. Sierz) paint a slightly different picture.[39]

Representation – *mimēsis* – is not always the same as enactment. Dahl, for one, offers an aestheticising account of violence in political theatre, in which 'Our realization that actors do not suffer the fate depicted permits us to lower our defenses and enter into the event.'[40] In other words, what really matters is that tragic suffering is not enacted but represented, as *mimēsis*; and that we, the audience, recognise this difference. (Remember: Greek tragedy displays corpses but describes violence.) In Fischer-Lichte's analysis, by contrast, what makes or breaks performance is the 'feedback loop' created by the bodily co-presence of audience and performers.[41] What really matters is what actually happens.[42]

[38] For literal evocations of dismemberment in Artaud's writings, see, e.g., the second 'Post-Scriptum' to *To Have Done with the Judgement of God* and the prologue of *Les Nouvelles revelations de l'etre*. See Lada-Richards (2005), 468–9 for the relevance of the Theatre of Cruelty for Pentheus in *Bacchae*. According to Sampatakakis (2005, 2017), *Bacchae* encodes and elicits modern performance techniques.

[39] Degenring (2010), 239, referring to Sierz (2001). See also Nevitt (2013), 9–10 on *Saved* and *The Romans in Britain*.

[40] Dahl (1987), 132.

[41] Fischer-Lichte (2008).

[42] Nevitt (2013) is an excellent overview of modes and motivations of violence in modern performance; see esp. pp. 49–54 on actuality and simulation. Kubiak (1991), though less relevant, is an important discussion of terror and theatre; cf. also Nevitt (2013), 3–4 on 'terror' versus 'horror'.

So, does violence in adaptation aim at shock – schlock – for its own sake? Is there a point to all this transgression? Ritual, perhaps? It has been argued that ritual structures and ritual actions in post-war Western theatre enacted much-needed social cohesion in the wake of conflict, industrialisation, globalisation, and so on.[43] Radical theatre typically abstracts ritual as *sacrifice.*[44] And sacrifice is a form of violence. Nor can we divorce fifth-century tragedy from ritual, whether that be its putative ritual origins, its cult setting in the Great Dionysia festival, or the *mimēsis* of specific rituals in specific plays.[45] We have seen one manifestation of this in the hypothetical taboo against onstage violent death in Greek drama, which could stem from a taboo on murder, suicide, sex, and childbirth in sanctuaries.[46]

Furthermore, ritual has walked in step with theatres of shock, with non-realist techniques, with stylised actions, and with the avant-garde, and with the breaking of taboos and norms. Postdramatic theatre emphasises not so much 'real-life rituals' as *ritualistic* actions. Performance art, for example, traffics in repetitive, ritualistic violence, including self-harm, exacted on performers' bodies before spectators' eyes.[47] Instances include Marina Abramović's *Rhythm 0* and *Lips of Thomas* and the works of Bob Flanagan. And in addition to its privileged status in theories of drama and performance, ritual violence in a post-censorship era has been reinscribed on drama and performance praxis, no longer hidden away inside the *skēnē* or offstage, as in Greek tragedy, but front and centre. On the one hand, then, we can observe a connection between ancient and contemporary drama: ritual. On the other hand, we can observe a disparity in how those two dramatic traditions approach violence. That difference can also be explained, at least a priori, by way of ritual: tragedy problematises ritual and violence; avant-garde theatre either takes violence out of context or simplistically conflates it with ritual.

Dahl identifies a number of twentieth-century playwrights turning to ritual substructures only to secularise those structures and, more importantly, replace sacrificial violence with post-sacral, secular, *political* violence.[48] This is a suggestive idea; one cannot deny the typological (and possibly also genetic) likenesses between the ancient and modern plays

43 Fischer-Lichte (2005). More generally, see Kershaw (1992) on radical theatre.

44 René Girard's *La Violence et le sacré* (1972; in English as *Violence and the Sacred*, 1977) and Walter Burkert's *Homo Necans* (1972) have been especially influential.

45 On ritual origins, see, e.g., the essays in Csapo and Miller (2007). On the Dionysia, see Goldhill (1987).

46 Sommerstein (2010), 33–7.

47 E.g. Lehmann (1999); Goldberg (2011).

48 Dahl (1987), 1–10; also Dahl (1991).

which she discusses. More to the point, political violence sharpens a paradox facing (secular-) humanist theatre: in a secular milieu, sacrificial violence is not what it was. What if stopping violence requires more violence?[49] Can non-violent tragedy still be meaningful? Adaptation insists on giving meaning to suffering where there was, perhaps, none to be found. War plays become *anti*-war plays; Aristophanic comedy becomes feminist; *Bacchae* ushers in the revolution. Adaptation always interprets, and in recent years, this has typically been through a radical lens. As Revermann argues, though Greek tragedy itself is never utopian, recent receptions of Greek tragedy tend to utopianise the genre along progressive, leftist lines.[50] Viewed in this light, violence is a regrettable but unavoidable consequence.

Generally speaking, performances *of* ancient drama present themselves as facsimiles or reproductions. This is true even when, as is usually the case, the script is a translation. Translations, unlike paraphrases or versions, 'can be said to have the same author as the source text; they can be used as quotations'.[51] At any rate, translations and performances of a play 'by Euripides' or 'by Racine' reach for verisimilitude if not substitution. For example, the Bacchanals theatre company production of '*The Bacchae* by Euripides' (BATS Theatre, Wellington, New Zealand, premiere 6 November 2003) replaced the report narratives with prerecorded film clips, replete with special effects and plenty of fake blood, thereby bringing murder out of the text and onto the stage and screen. In so doing, the Bacchanals, a company explicitly 'dedicated to exploring text-based theatre (none of this devised crap for us!)',[52] both broke ancient convention by depicting murder and respected it by not enacting murder. In so doing, they staged a violent play which was still recognisably 'by Euripides', all thanks to multimedia realism. The Bacchanals' *Bacchae* thus found common ground between ancient and modern convention by way of intermediality.[53]

Published translations and 'versions' likewise enter the reception history of an ancient text as proxies for that text.[54] Out-and-out adaptations with new titles such as *Dionysus in 69, Rites,* and *Mr O'Dwyer's Dancing Party* do not function, nominally or substantively, as substitutes for the original; translations *do*. As such, choosing not to create a 'performance of' or

49 Dahl (1987), 1–2. 50 Revermann (2008), 97–8.

51 Reynolds (2011), 24; see Perris (2016), 12–13.

52 www.thebacchanals.net (accessed 10 June 2014).

53 I owe this observation to Avra Sidiropoulou. See also Peter Campbell, Chapter 8, this volume.

54 Perris (2010), 185–9; Perris (2016).

'translation of' an ancient theatrical work implies a departure from the script – a break with one or more conventions inscribed on a particular text. Choosing to *adapt* an ancient tragedy into a new play with a new name thus implies some willingness to contravene tragic conventions. And of course, together with the chorus, the masks, the limit on speaking actors, and other scenic conventions of Greek tragedy, one major, well-known ancient Greek scenic convention which goes against contemporary practice is that regarding violence. Violence, like sex, is a privileged theatrical phenomenon, doubly so in adaptations of Greek tragedy.[55]

Adaptation, then, is ontologically disposed to break tragic conventions about onstage violence. Martin Revermann, enumerating the appeal of Greek tragedy, identifies among others the appeal of 'bigness' and the appeal of survival; he describes Greek tragedy as 'extreme theater' perfectly suited to a late twentieth- or early twenty-first-century milieu.[56] Indeed, Greek tragedy in our era often overreaches itself, especially in adaptation, and above all when it comes to violence: 'big', 'extreme' words and deeds leave stages littered with corpses – and survivors. Overdetermined in adaptation, tragic violence can encompass actions, words, institutions, and structures; oppression, liberation, and self-destruction. The tragic condition subsumes drama and performance to become a part of (ordinary) life, like sex, ritual, dancing parties, and women's lavatories. Violence, which is part and parcel of tragedy, comes to resemble a necessary and sufficient condition for serious drama per se.

III

Nevertheless: is there anything particularly *Greek*, or *ancient*, or even *tragic* about violence in adaptations of ancient Greek tragedy? With a view to answering the question, we turn now to a selection of canonical adaptations by Steven Berkoff, Sarah Kane, and Marina Carr.[57]

First: how Greek is Steven Berkoff's *Greek* (premiere 1980)? The title projects a prima facie Hellenism, obviously. And *Greek* does in fact dramatise *a* story of Oedipus, right from his youth almost to the end of Sophocles' *Oedipus Tyrannus*. Instead of Oedipus, Eddy; instead of

[55] See in general, e.g., Eagleton (2003); Dahl (1987); more specifically, Ioannidou (2017), 39–71 on the reframing of suffering in postmodern adaptations of Greek tragedy.

[56] Revermann (2008), 110–11, 111–13, 113–14. See E. Hall (2010a), 1–11 on survival in Greek tragedy.

[57] See, respectively, e.g., Berkoff (1992), Cross (2004), Ioannidou (2017), 45–52; Saunders (2009), and Urban (2011); Leeney and McMullan (2003).

Thebes, Thatcher-era Britain. Aside from the large-scale parallels of plot and character, *Greek* also signals its Greekness with an allusively named protagonist ('Eddy' ≈ Oedipus), a riddling Sphinx, and marked references to the 'British plague' and Oedipus.[58]

But *Greek* asserts Greekness most strenuously when characters use the actual word 'Greek'. When Eddy meets his mother and soon-to-be-wife, she says, 'Your face is like all Greek / and carved from ancient marble.'[59] In this case, Greekness means an idealised, static classicism. Upon sighting a bomb victim, however, Eddy exclaims:

> OH, MAGGOT SCRATCHER [*viz.*, Margaret/'Maggie' Thatcher] HANG THE CUNTS / HANG THEM SLOW AND LET ME TAKE A SKEWER AND JAB THEIR EYES OUT / LOVELY / GREEK STYLE ...[60]

'Greek style' here refers not to some classical ideal but to a kind of 'lovely' aestheticised violence. Resonances multiply when Eddy discovers the incest and outright refuses to imitate Oedipus' 'Greek-style' eye-gouging. Once more, 'Greek style' describes a kind of violence:

> Why should I tear my eyes out Greek style, why should you hang yourself / have you seen a child from a mother and son / no. Have I? No. Then how do we know that it's bad / should I be so mortified? Who me. With my nails and fingers plunge in and scoop out those warm and tender balls of jelly quivering dipped in blood. Oedipus how could you have done it, never to see your wife's golden face again, never again to cast your eyes on her and hers on your eyes.[61]

Crucially, amidst all this Greekness, *Greek* keeps its violence offstage. Now, if one were to posit an 'invariant' for adaptations of Sophocles' *Oedipus Tyrannus*, it would surely include not only the parricide and incest, which happen outside the play, but also the suicide and self-blinding of the protagonists, which happen inside it. Yet in the climactic ending of *Greek* (part of which was quoted earlier), Eddy outright refuses to blind himself.

Not that *Greek* is non-violent. In an earlier climax, Eddy unknowingly kills his father in an argument in a café – but with words. Stage directions instruct them to '*mime fight*'. Their threats escalate until Eddy defeats his opponent with a flurry of linguistic jabs:

58 Berkoff (2000a), 114, 139. 59 Berkoff (2000a), 120.

60 Berkoff (2000a), 112. Maggot Scratcher also appears in Berkoff's *Sink the Belgrano!* (premiere 1986).

61 Berkoff (2000a), 139.

EDDY: Haemorrhage, rupture and swell. Split and cracklock jawsprung and neck break
MANAGER: Cave-in rib splinter oh the agony the shrewd icepick
EDDY: Testicles torn out eyes gouged and pulled strings snapped socket nail scrapped
MANAGER: Bite swallow suck pull
EDDY: More smash and more power
MANAGER: Weaker and weaker
EDDY: Stronger and stronger
MANAGER: Weak
EDDY: Power
MANAGER: Dying
EDDY: Victor
MANAGER: That's it
EDDY: Tada
WAITRESS: You killed him / I never realized words can kill.
EDDY: So can looks.
WAITRESS: You killed him / he was my husband.
EDDY: I didn't intend to I swear I didn't / he died of shock.[62]

Eddy literally talks his father to death. 'I never realized words can kill.' In fact, this is doubly Oedipal, for Oedipus kills his *sons* with a curse.[63] Berkoff also uses obscenity to mark Jocasta's recognition, which is itself a prelude to self-harm. In Sophocles' *Oedipus Tyrannus*, Jocasta cries out and leaves the stage immediately when she realises the truth (1071–2). At the corresponding moment in *Greek*, Eddy's wife resorts to inarticulate obscenity:

WIFE: Oh fuck.

. . .

WIFE: Oh shit and piss and fuck. I just pissed my pants. (*She faints.*)[64]

All in all, we can see that Berkoff reifies verbal violence as an alternative to and complement for physical violence.

Along with Berkoff's plays *East* and *West*, *Greek* is part of a loose trilogy of demotic verse dramas, and its representation of action through words is not unique. Here as elsewhere, Berkoff's characters use violent language; they also use archaic diction not unlike, say, that used in Burgess' *A Clockwork Orange* ('But you, O my brothers, remember sometimes thy little Alex that was').[65]

[62] Berkoff (2000a), 116–17.
[63] I owe this observation to Vayos Liapis.
[64] Berkoff (2000a), 136, 138.
[65] Burgess (1962[1972]), 149.

Yet *Greek* is still unique in its relationship to Greek tragedy. Treating language as a proxy for action picks up on a later element in Oedipus' biography (his curse on his sons) while, at the same time, honouring ancient convention. 'Oedipus' talks 'Laius' to death; 'Jocasta' swears and faints instead of committing suicide; 'Oedipus' refuses to stab out his eyes. In this way, the Greek source material of *Greek* elicits a 'Greek-style' approach to violence.

Adaptation heightens the tension between enacted and narrated violence in tragedy. Generally speaking, translations or 'versions' of ancient play scripts (i) narrate offstage violence and (ii) eschew onstage violence in stage directions. Performances of these texts can thus become liminal cases when the director, sometimes the same person as the playwright, introduces stage business not in the script. Adaptations, on the other hand, more often than not, write violence into the script.

Compare Berkoff's two 'versions' – rewritings in the original setting with similar dramatis personae – of Greek tragedy: *Agamemnon* (full premiere 1976) and *Oedipus* (published 2000; premiere 2011).[66] Each text follows its source in keeping violence offstage, namely the murders of Agamemnon and Cassandra, Jocasta's suicide, and Oedipus' self-blinding. Directing *Oedipus*, however, Berkoff changed tack. According to one reviewer of the performance:

> The Greeks knew a thing or two about the terrible power of the imagination – but while Sophocles reported, Berkoff has his own Oedipus blindness moment and insists on illustrating. So we get Jocasta miming putting the noose around her neck, and Oedipus blinding himself like a kids' show-and-tell session.[67]

In the relatively close 'version' of *Oedipus*, violence is represented onstage to accompany the expected report narrative, and it is as though Berkoff the director is adapting Berkoff the playwright. In the adaptation *Greek*, though the mechanism and effect is rather different, the basic setup remains: mimed physical violence accompanied by speech.

Marina Carr's oeuvre is chock-full of rape (*On Raftery's Hill*) and suicide (*The Mai*, *Portia Coughlan*, and *By the Bog of Cats* . . .). But only her adaptations of *Medea* (*Bog of Cats*) and the *Oresteia* (*Ariel*) dramatise murder.[68] Elsewhere, her larger-than-life female protagonists escape their

[66] Berkoff (2012), 9 describes *Agamemnon* as 'Freely adapted from the Aeschylus version'. Berkoff (2000b), 155–6 describes *Oedipus* as a 'version' of *Oedipus Tyrannus*.

[67] Gardner (2011).

[68] See Jordan (2002), 246–7 on violence in Marina Carr's work. An arguable counter-example is Scene Nine from *The Map of Argentina*, in which the Argentinian cuts out the Mother's heart and smashes it with a hammer; see Carr (2015), 177–9.

predicaments through self-harm, but in these classical adaptations, women kill others. In effect, Carr distinguishes between off- and onstage violence along roughly that same fault line between adaptations and other plays. In *By the Bog of Cats . . .* (premiere 1998), Hester kills her daughter Josie, then herself, onstage. In *Ariel* (premiere 2002), the sacrifice of Ariel takes place offstage like that of Iphigenia in Greek tragedy. But the murders of Fermoy and Frances take place onstage, unlike those of Agamemnon and Clytemnestra in the *Oresteia* or the *Electra* plays by Euripides and Sophocles. Carr's non-classical plays, by contrast, do not stage suicide or rape. A last-minute blackout leaves the rape of Sorrel Raftery to the audience's imagination, while the suicides of The Mai and Portia Coughlan are revealed through prolepsis (flash-forward). Carr clearly knows the difference between staged and narrated violence.

Marble (2009) comments, obliquely and self-referentially, on the conventions of stage death and on Carr's own melodramatic plots. Catherine and Ben, husband and wife, are going to see a play:

CATHERINE: I forget the name of it, about the auld one dying.
BEN: Auld ones dying don't interest me. Women who've stopped ovulating should die offstage. Who cares?[69]

Is domestic tragedy ('auld ones dying') of any interest to a male audience? Not enough to make it worth *staging* those deaths which animate domestic tragedy. Classical source material, on the other hand, elevates domestic tragedy so as to encourage staging murder and suicide. That is, classical source material paradoxically encourages the breaking of Greek tragic convention in adaptation. And while rape and suicide elsewhere constitute a climax, but not the conclusion, of the drama, both *By the Bog of Cats . . .* and *Ariel* end, abruptly, in death. All told, classical source material has led Carr towards staging murder and suicide ἐν τῷ φανερῷ (in full view), as Aristotle would put it, and towards making onstage violence, to use again an Aristotelian term, the *telos* (end) of tragedy.

In a sense, Carr's tragedies are less 'Greek' than Berkoff's. Tragedy is a transhistorical, international genre; fifth-century *tragōidia* ('tragedy') was an ancient, Greek one. *Ariel* clearly adapts the *Oresteia*, sprinkling bits of Euripides' *Iphigenia at Aulis* for good measure. Carr acknowledges that it was 'loosely based on the *Oresteia*', and it is hard to see why anyone would call it a 'chilling adaptation of the *Faust* myth'.[70] On the other hand, there is scant justification for claiming, as some do, that *The Mai* is based on

[69] Carr (2009), 296. [70] Carr (2009), 9; Trotter (2008), 189.

Sophocles' *Electra*; Demeter and Persephone or Odysseus and Penelope, though far from obvious, are more plausible models.[71] Above all, I am highly sceptical of the 'Euripidean subtext' which just about everyone else assumes for *By the Bog of Cats* . . .[72] In Euripides' *Medea*, the titular character kills her children offstage and ends the play alive. In Seneca's play of the same title, Medea kills her children onstage (967–1019). In *By the Bog of Cats* . . . Hester Swane kills her daughter, then herself, onstage. (This hyper-Senecan murder–suicide likewise concludes David Vann's 2017 *Medea* novel, *Bright Air Black*.) So: why insist on a 'Euripidean subtext' and not a Senecan one? Presumably because (1) theatre scholars outside classics know their Euripides better than their Seneca and (2) *Greek* tragedy is already such a big deal in Ireland.[73]

I read *By the Bog of Cats* . . . and *Ariel* as Senecan revenge tragedies, along the lines of *Titus Andronicus*. *Titus* is a touchstone for revenge tragedy, and for onstage violence. It also has little or nothing to do with Greek drama.[74] Indeed, *Titus* is Shakespeare's most Latinate, most rhetorical, and most bloody play.[75] That is: his most Senecan. In fact, *any* adaptation of a play which Seneca adapted, or any play in a Senecan manner, could be said to be a 'Roman' rather than 'Greek-style' play – even though modern playwrights, unlike Shakespeare, can access any Greek play in English translation.

Carr does use Greek myths to think and talk about violence.[76] But she also amplifies the violence of Greek myth in a Senecan manner. And given the gravitational attraction, for many modern practitioners, of onstage murder and suicide, can an adaptation of Greek tragedy ever be (purely) Greek anyhow? Berkoff's and Carr's work is violent in general; tragic source material to some extent conditions their treatment of theatrical violence. Not that the trend is universal. Carr's *Phaedra Backwards* (premiere 2011) retreats from the stage violence practised in *By the Bog of Cats* . . . and *Ariel*; it has been criticised for its 'bloodless' presentation of Phaedra's story.[77] Carr's most recent Greek play, *Hecuba* (adapted from

[71] Sophocles' *Electra*: Jordan (2002), 260; McDonald (2002), 81. Demeter and Persephone: Leeney (2002). Odysseus and Penelope: Wallace (2001), 438 (a 'tantalizing structural parallel').

[72] Trotter (2008), 188. Martinovich (2003), 117 assumes a Euripidean intertext; Sihra (2005) insists on one.

[73] E.g. McDonald and Walton (2002); Macintosh (2016).

[74] For Shakespeare's (at most heavily indirect) interaction with Greek drama, see, e.g., Silk (2004); Kenward (2016).

[75] James (1991), 124.

[76] See Jordan (2002), 254–7 on the use of myth in *Bog of Cats*, contrasted with the passage from *Raftery's Hill* in which Isaac presents Zeus and Hera as an aetiology for incest (Carr 2009, 43–4).

[77] Dean (2013).

Euripides), is essentially a rewriting of tragic violence tout court: the entire play explicitly rehabilitates Euripides' Hecuba, and the narrative climax which ultimately rescues her reputation is the murder of Polymestor's sons and blinding of Polymestor himself – but not, as in Euripides, by Hecuba. Yet this is all reported by Polymestor, as in Euripides; the stage directions are silent at this point. In *Hecuba* and *Phaedra Backwards*, therefore, Carr rejects the ancients' negative characterisation of female characters from Euripides while upholding Greek conventions about onstage violence.

Phaedra Backwards may have been bloodless, but the same could never be said of Sarah Kane's *Phaedra's Love* (premiere 1996), which features masturbation, fellatio, rape, castration, disembowelling, cannibalism, and murder – all onstage.[78] *Phaedra's Love* is every bit a contemporary, 'In-Yer-Face' play, as was Kane's explosive debut, *Blasted*. Yet she wrote *Phaedra's Love* specifically as a Gate Theatre commission for a classical play:

> So in the end it was the Gate which suggested something Greek or Roman, and I thought, 'Oh, I've always hated those plays. Everything happens off-stage, and what's the point?' But I decided to read one of them and see what I'd get. I chose Seneca ... I read *Phaedra* and surprisingly enough it interested me.[79]

Phaedra's Love shares much with Seneca's *Phaedra*. Each eschews divine machinery (prologue, *deus ex machina*); in each, Phaedra confesses her passion in person to Hippolytus. On the other hand, she *accuses* him in a note, before committing suicide offstage, just as in Euripides' *Hippolytus*.

Kane claimed that she read Seneca's play once, *Hippolytus* only after finishing *Phaedra's Love*, and Racine's *Phèdre* never.[80] Yet many critics still insist on some Euripidean intertext, hypotext, or subtext. According to one, 'This must be a gap in her memory as she clearly knew Euripides' text when she wrote her play. In fact, she changes some aspects of Seneca's plot construction back to how they are in Euripides' play.' According to another, '*Phaedra's Love* rejects many of the classical conventions of Euripides and Seneca and the even more restrictive rules of the neoclassical Racine.' Yet another calls Kane's oeuvre a 'revision of the Greeks'.[81]

[78] My analysis of *Phaedra's Love* agrees for the most part with that of Campbell (2010), an essay read only after drafting the present chapter.

[79] Sarah Kane, interview with Nils Tabert, 'Gespräch mit Sarah Kane', in *Playspotting: Die Londoner Theaterszene der 90er* (1998), quoted in English in Saunders (2002), 72.

[80] Saunders (2002), 72.

[81] See, respectively, Brusberg-Kiermeier (2001), 168; Campbell (2010), 174; Urban (2011), 318. Bexley (2011) rightly identifies (and analyses) the Senecan intertext.

Should we so casually dismiss what a playwright herself says about her sources and methods? The intertextual relationships *are* fuzzy. In a sense, Kane read Seneca's *Phaedra* as though it were Euripides' *Hippolytus.* As we have seen, she conflated Greek and Roman staging conventions to assume that 'Everything happens offstage.' Paradoxically, she also treated Seneca's Roman play as a vehicle for getting back to the spirit of Greek tragedy: 'I wanted to keep the classical concerns of Greek theatre – love, hate, death, revenge, suicide – but use a completely contemporary urban poetry. I see the writing as poetic. Just not verse.'[82] In any case, *Phaedra's Love* potentially brings about a kind of double (triple? quadruple?) vision in anyone familiar with Euripides, Seneca, or Racine. Brusberg-Kiermeier puts it well: '*Phaedra's Love* can be described as (1) a post-modern re-write (2) in an Elizabethan light (3) of a Roman re-write (4) of a Greek play.'[83]

This 'Elizabethan light' is important. (Remember *Titus.*) As is often remarked, the so-called 'New Brutalists' (alias the 'In-Yer-Face' playwrights) took a Jacobean approach to violence and morality. Indeed, Sarah Kane's work shares deep affinities with Elizabethan–Jacobean tragedy and with Seneca.[84] *Phaedra's Love* subsumes a Greek tragic plot, via its more explicit treatment by Seneca, into a neo-Jacobean play. In particular, the climax of the play, with its smorgasbord of onstage violence, puckishly riffs on the revenge-tragedy tradition.[85] But Kane inverts Seneca's violence, keeping Phaedra's death *offstage* only to put everything else *onstage* – one rape and three murders, all in a single scene.[86]

In this sense, *Phaedra's Love* plays out a conscious intervention in the history of theatrical violence, as reconstructed by Kane herself. Discussing the play, Kane criticised narrated violence: 'The reported deaths in Seneca are incredibly strongly written, conjuring the image really well, but personally I'd rather have an image right in front of me.'[87] (Setting aside the clear examples of onstage murder in Seneca, not to mention Phaedra's suicide.) She also insisted:

82 David Benedict, 'What Sarah Did Next', *Independent*, 15 May 1996, quoted in Saunders (2009), 68.

83 Brusberg-Kiermeier (2001), 165.

84 Saunders (2002), 23, 89–91; Brusberg-Kiermeier (2001), 165–6. See also Bamford (2000).

85 Saunders (2002), 80.

86 Sierz (2001), 109; Campbell (2010), 182–3. Bexley (2011) analyses the show vs. tell dynamic in *Phaedra's Love* vis-à-vis Seneca's *Medea*; see now E. Cole (2019), 61–9 ('Violence and Voyeurism in *Phaedra's Love*').

87 Benedict, in Saunders (2009), 69.

> When I read [Edward Bond's] *Saved*, I was deeply shocked by the baby being stoned. But then I thought there isn't anything you can't represent on stage. If you're saying you can't represent something, you are saying you can't talk about it, you're denying its existence, and that's an extraordinarily ignorant thing to do.[88]

That is: contravening censorship or convention fights for freedom of expression; it also reasserts theatre's necessary function as a *mimēsis* of society – think Aristotle, not Plato. In Kane's view, taboo comes from ignorance; we should be able to *talk* about anything and everything; we should therefore be able to show everything, too.

No surviving ancient play, Greek or Roman, tragedy or comedy, ever stages rape.[89] (A rape takes place offstage during Terence's *Eunuch*.) And one thing which Kane's work consistently talks about, and depicts, is sexual violence. *Blasted*, *Phaedra's Love*, and *Cleansed* all stage rape. Matter-of-fact stage directions in the plainest possible language, without adverbs or other ornament, denote realistic (real?) sexual violence. In *Phaedra's Love*:

> **Theseus** *pulls* **Strophe** *away from* **Woman 2** *who she is attacking.*
> *He rapes her.*
> *The crowd watch and cheer.*
> *When* **Theseus** *has finished he cuts her throat.*[90]

Kane's theatre insists that violence is a fact of life, and therefore of *mimēsis*.

This was already the case in her first play, *Blasted*: 'violence is the most urgent problem we have as a species, and the most urgent thing we need to confront ... When I wrote *Blasted* I tried to discuss what it means to be violent and to suffer violence.'[91] The play includes offstage violence (Cate's rape) and onstage violence both realistic (Ian's rape; the soldier's suicide) and not (Ian eating the baby). *Blasted* thus prompts 'a reconsideration of the function of explicit violence in the theatre'.[92] What is more, *Blasted* shows Kane already working through tensions between text and action, stage directions and stage business: 'Reading *Blasted* is much harder work

[88] Clare Bayley, 'A Very Angry Young Woman', *Independent*, 23 January 1995, quoted in Saunders (2002), 24.

[89] See, however, Rabinowitz (2011) on rape culture in Greek tragedy.

[90] Kane (2001), 101. See Nevitt (2013), 31–5, esp. p. 32, for the way the stage direction 'He rapes her' evokes a long history of sexual violence. Kane is working in the In-Yer-Face tradition here: in *The Romans in Britain*, for example, Roman soldiers anally and orally rape the character Marban, with the actions described in very matter-of-fact stage directions (Brenton 1981, 41, 44).

[91] Rodolfo di Giammarco, interview with Sarah Kane, 16 September 1997, quoted in Saunders (2009), 102.

[92] Carney (2005), 275. See Solga (2007).

than watching it, because when you read it the stage directions say, "*He eats the baby*" (60). When you see the actual play Ian's clearly not eating the baby – it's absolutely fucking obvious!'[93]

Most of the stage directions in *Blasted* can be followed realistically. *Cleansed*, by contrast, takes us right into a world of anti-realistic actions (e.g. cutting off someone's tongue, impaling them). The first production accordingly focused less on *how* violence is performed than *why*.[94] In Kane's view, '[*Cleansed*] can only be done in a theatre. Of course, I knew they were *impossible stage directions*, but I also genuinely believe that you can do anything on stage' (emphasis added).[95] What is more, Kane thought of *Cleansed* as an explicit departure from ancient stagecraft: 'I think with a lot of other plays there are things from Greek drama – a messenger comes in – all of which is much easier to take and gives you time to calm down. But [in *Cleansed*] I didn't want to give anyone time to calm down.'[96]

In turn, *Phaedra's Love* combines the realism of *Blasted* with the stylised anti-realism of *Cleansed*, a fine balance that risks farce. Of Hippolytus' death, for example, one critic wrote: 'It's very difficult to do gonad roasting and penis slicing in a way that inspires horror rather than derisory laughter.'[97] *Phaedra's Love* was a transitional, experimental play in an oeuvre which can itself be described overall as 'unfinished'.[98] It illustrates a transition, in terms of dramaturgy and onstage violence, and a foretaste of *Crave* and *4.48 Psychosis*.

Directed by Kane herself, *Phaedra's Love* thus became an exercise in theatrical violence informed by her own misconceptions about Seneca:

> I thought you *can* subvert the convention of everything happening off-stage and have it on-stage and see how that works ... We made a decision that I would try to do the violence as realistically as possible ... And it turned out to be a lot easier than you would think it is. I mean you write something like *his bowels are torn out*, and that seemed an incredibly difficult thing to do. But actually audiences are really willing to believe something is happening if you give them the slightest suggestion it is.[99]

With *Blasted*, Kane was already exploring the limits of theatrical violence. In *Phaedra's Love*, Greek myth (from a Roman dramatisation) supported a

93 Graham Saunders, interview with Sarah Kane, 12 June 1995, quoted in Saunders (2009), 92.

94 Saunders (2002), 88–9.

95 Dan Rebellato, 'Brief Encounter Platform', interview with Sarah Kane, November 1998, cited in Saunders (2009), 93.

96 Rebellato, in Saunders (2009), 94.

97 Saunders (2009), 130.

98 Sierz (2011), 319.

99 Tabert, in Saunders (2002), 80.

move away from realism and even *mimēsis*. Responding to her own misconceptions about ancient stagecraft, Kane sought an idiom more in tune with the spirit, if not the letter, of *Greek* tragedy. Even for a self-consciously, quintessentially avant-garde, anti-classical dramatist, the tradition of 'Greek' tragedy was an important forerunner in the history of violence.

All of this spirals back to a question posed earlier: are adaptations of tragedies violent in the same way as their source texts? Is the violence in adaptations of Greek tragedy necessarily ancient, Greek, or tragic? The short answer is: no. Violence in adaptation is not always 'tragic'. Carr writes tragedies; Berkoff and Kane wrote violent black comedies.[100] More to the point, the whole notion of onstage violence in *tragōidia* (Greek tragedy) – what we might call 'tragōidic' violence – is an oxymoron, for *tragōidia* keeps murder and (probably) suicide offstage.

Berkoff's *Greek* depicts violence in 'Greek style' yet refuses to stage it (beyond miming a fistfight, that is). In Carr's adaptations, ancient tragedy brings the problem of onstage violence to a head. Finally, in *Phaedra's Love*, tragic myth supports a new approach to onstage violence: a neo-Jacobean dramatist reads a Roman tragedy as though it were Greek, only to reject Greek theatrical convention. Already in a small sample, we see adaptations engaging regularly, directly, and in diverse ways with the problem of violence; and, in many cases, putting it centre stage.[101]

IV

Greek myths are typically violent. More precisely, most Greek myths describe, at some point, human beings intentionally, physically harming other people or themselves, often fatally. Accordingly, the plots of Greek tragedy (which almost exclusively dramatise myth) often include episodes of violence, typically offstage and reported. In narratological terms, it is the mythical *fabulae* of Greek tragedies that include violence. When a *fabula* is rearranged as a *story* and that *story* made into a *text*, Greek tragedy usually renders this violence as narrative.[102] Adaptations, in turn, effectively (and by definition) dramatise these 'tragic *fabulae*' rather than the actual play *scripts*. Now, violence is likewise (for obvious reasons) a staple of

[100] See, e.g, Urban (2007).

[101] One exception worth mentioning is Brian Friel's play *Living Quarters* (written 'after *Hippolytus*'). Friel inverts the myth to have the Theseus character commit suicide, offstage.

[102] See Perris (2011b); Sommerstein (2010).

contemporary theatre, especially in a post-censorship era. Unsurprisingly, adaptations of tragedy frequently translate violence onto the stage – or use words to highlight its absence. Thus, the tension between staged and narrated violence complicates a wider paradox, whereby an 'adaptation of' a specific ancient play stands in for but neither replaces nor translates its source text. Even adaptations which avoid onstage violence cannot escape this tension; turning a tragic *fabula* into a new script always requires a decision about how, and whether, to represent violence. When it comes to Greek tragedy, therefore, violence is part and parcel of adaptation.

It is perhaps unsurprising, then, that the gruesome metaphor of *sparagmos* has assumed special relevance for the reception of tragedy: one critic applies it to postcolonial classical reception in Wole Soyinka's *Bacchae* and Toni Morrison's *Sula*; another describes theatrical performance as *sparagmos*; yet another derives an entire theory of tragedy from it.[103] But one does not need to adopt this metaphor to see that similarity and difference underpin adaptation and reception. 'The spectator or reader must be able to participate in the play of similarity and difference perceived between the original, source, or inspiration to appreciate fully the reshaping or rewriting undertaken by the adaptive text.'[104] The aesthetic pleasure of adaptation 'comes simply from repetition with variation, from the comfort of ritual combined with the piquancy of surprise'.[105]

In this light, violence itself (actual and metaphorical) can be seen as an invariant of sorts, one which opens and at the same time bridges a fissure between ancient and modern drama, and which speaks to the very processes of adaptation. Onstage violence cannot be made to fit (literally 'adapted') in a Greek tragedy without doing 'violence' to the source text. Remember Pentheus, and his mother: Greek tragedy wants to see but refuses to look; adaptation refuses to look away. Ultimately, violence illuminates not only the case studies in the present chapter but also adaptations of Greek tragedy more broadly – and the tragedies themselves. The creative paradox of 'tragōidic' violence animates Greek tragedy as much as adaptations thereof: myth pushes tragedy towards onstage violence even as ancient theatrical convention refuses it. In this way, tragōidic violence activates a dynamic tension between seeing and not-seeing, between *mimēsis* and life.

[103] See, respectively, McConnell (2015); Fischer-Lichte (2014b), 21; Storm (1998).
[104] Sanders (2006), 45. [105] Hutcheon (2006), 4.

Greek tragedy is a radical art form in the best senses of that word,[106] and it retains the capacity to say something radical about violence and those who perpetrate it. By putting problematic Homeric figures on the contemporary stage, tragedy refuses a naively optimistic presentation of heroic ideals, or of human nature.[107] In our era, too, tragedy retains the capacity to reassert the realities of violence in the face of remote warfare, embedded journalism, multimedia saturation, desensitisation, and so on. After all (à la Aristotle), despite its divine machinery and cosmic scope, *tragōidia* focuses on human beings – people like us, say – *doing* awful things to themselves and each other. Like Auden's 'The Shield of Achilles', tragedy reminds us 'That girls are raped, that two boys knife a third'. Adaptations, too, confront us with hard facts: human beings raping, maiming, and killing, out in the open, before our very eyes.

[106] Rehm (2003). On the more general idea that violence in drama can be radical: Kubiak (1991); Nevitt (2013).

[107] See, e.g., W. Allan (2008), 6–8.

CHAPTER 10

Adaptations of Greek Tragedies in Non-Western Performance Cultures

Erika Fischer-Lichte

Although all European, indeed all Western cultures claim that Greek tragedies form part of their own cultural heritage, most of them do not have a continuous, or indeed a long performance history. The performance of *Oedipus the King* that inaugurated the Teatro Olimpico in Vicenza in 1585 remained a unique event for quite some time. Greek tragedy otherwise entered the modern European stages only in surprising transformations: efforts by the Florentine Camerata to revive Greek tragedy resulted in the invention of the opera (1594). However, most libretti were not based on Greek tragedies but drew heavily on books about Greek mythology.

As a result of the 'Querelle des anciens et des modernes' conducted in seventeenth-century France, a number of Greek tragedies – with a preference for those of Euripides – were adapted to prove either that the ancients remained unsurpassable paragons of drama or that the moderns much better suited the new times. Both parties, however, dispensed with the chorus and corrected other 'flaws' of the ancient poets, bringing into being such French classics as Racine's *Iphigénie en Aulide* (1674) and *Phèdre* (1677). For a long time, adaptations were the only form in which Greek tragedies could be staged in Europe.[1] To my knowledge, the first performance of a Greek tragedy to use an unabridged, 'faithful' translation was Tieck/Mendelssohn's *Antigone* in Potsdam in 1841 – besides, of course, the above-mentioned *Oedipus the King* in Vicenza. This *Antigone* was undeniably a brainchild of the latest intellectual wave – historicism.[2] Although this production served as a model for performances of Greek tragedies not only in other German states but also in London, Paris, and

[1] Even in schools, such as in Strasbourg between 1575 and 1609, where Greek tragedies had been performed either in Greek or Latin translation since the late sixteenth century, this did not happen without cuts and changes. Cf. Flashar (1991), 36–7.

[2] Regarding this production and the role historicism played in it, see Fischer-Lichte (2017), 45–68.

even New York, adaptations began to flourish again with the beginning of the twentieth century. They were all realised under very specific conditions and served particular purposes. It therefore makes little sense to assume that such performances took place because of a proclaimed universality of Greek tragedy, i.e. its 'universal truth'.[3] Rather, we must identify the – often very unique – reasons that encouraged the recourse to Greek tragedy.

This not only applies to the overwhelming number of productions of Greek tragedies in Western cultures since the 1960s,[4] but also, if not primarily, to the growing number of productions in other parts of the world. Clearly, there are other reasons and driving forces at work in the former colonised countries than in those that were spared colonisation but acted as colonisers themselves, as in the case of Japan. But even among post-colonial nations, the differences are often stark. A comprehensive analysis of adaptations and performances of Greek tragedies in non-Western cultures would require at least a book-length study, even if one limited the scope of analysis to performances involving local traditions. Dealing with this subject within one chapter therefore entails strict selectivity and focus on very few performance cultures. I have chosen to consider case studies from former colonised countries alongside some that were never colonised. The first group will include West Africa, in particular Nigeria, as well as India; the second comprises Japan and China. As we shall see, the fact and mode of the adaptation can be traced back to very particular conditions unique to each performance culture.

West Africa

In West Africa, these conditions included the educational system established by the British colonisers. Latin and Greek were taught in secondary schools, and Greek tragedy in particular was hailed as the epitome of European culture – one of the coloniser's tools to justify their claims of racial superiority. Performances of Greek tragedies were considered an effective method of letting students embody the 'universal truths' and values seen to be embedded in those texts, even if, as some witnesses suggested, they also allowed the students to reconnect with their indigenous performance cultures. At the beginning of the 1930s, for instance, the Reverend Charles Kingsley Williams, Assistant Principal of the government-funded Achimota School in Accra, completed an English

[3] McDonald (1992), 22. [4] Cf. Hall, Macintosh, and Wrigley (2004).

verse translation of *Antigone,* which he wanted his students to perform. As part of a 1933 report about local performances, he wrote:

> I am anxiously considering whether I could manage to train students to do a version of Sophocles' *Antigone.* My hope is that for the choruses it may be possible to incorporate some of the rhythm movements of genuine Gold Coast community dancing . . . it is very much alive still in the country and can be more impressively beautiful than any description can suggest. (Quoted in Gibbs 2007, 60)

The plan most likely did not materialise. However, the same year a production of *Antigone* took place at Adisadel College on the Gold Coast (Ghana). In an Editorial Note in *Overseas Education* (1934, 116) the event is described as follows:

> We . . . were impressed by the response of actors and audience to the dramatic situations based on the conflict between tribal law and individual conscience. Their bearing on the problems of African tribal life was obviously appreciated. (Quoted in Gibbs 2007, 61)

Gibbs quotes from another review 'that the production adds to the cultural advancement of the country, and sets up a milestone'. There was a repeat performance, and it was later also presented in Sekondi and in Kumasi.[5] Further productions of Greek tragedies in Ghana followed: *Agamemnon* was staged in 1936 and *Alcestis* in 1944/5. While the performances were all in English, the choruses were rendered in Greek – a fact which in itself testifies to the centrality of teaching ancient Greek in the country's educational curricula.

Given the prominent position of Greek tragedies in the British educational system established in West Africa, it does not come as a surprise that after their countries gained independence many African playwrights turned to Greek tragedy in order to transfer it explicitly into an African context. John Pepper Clark's *Song of a Goat,* which by its very title alludes to the etymology of Greek *tragoidia* ('goat song') and draws on Aeschylus' *Agamemnon,* was first performed at the Mbari Centre in 1962, directed by Wole Soyinka. The same year, Kamau Brathwaite's *Odale's Choice,* a new version of *Antigone,* premiered at the Mfantisman Secondary School in Saltpond, Ghana.[6] Efua Sutherland's *Edufa,* featuring themes adapted from Euripides' *Alcestis,* was performed at the Drama Studio, University of Ghana, in 1967. Ola Rotimi's *The Gods Are Not to Blame,* staged in

[5] Gibbs (2007), 62. [6] See Steinmeyer, Chapter 11, this volume.

1968 by Rotimi's own company, the Olakuin Acting Company, draws on Sophocles' *Oedipus the King* and includes lines sung in Yoruba.[7] In all these cases, the Empire was 'writing back', as the now-famous phrase coined by Salman Rushdie goes. By adapting Greek tragedy, that epitome of European culture, and transplanting it into African soil, equality was claimed and manifested.

However, these textual adaptations and their performances were not merely a response to the British educational system and its claim to superiority. They also emphasised and revealed the striking kinship between the Greek pantheon and mythology, and their West African equivalents.[8] Particularly in Nigeria this was often noted, even if it was interpreted differently by different poets, critics, and scholars. In his early essay 'The Fourth Stage' (1969), Wole Soyinka highlights the similarities and also the differences between the Greek and Yoruba gods, focusing on Dionysus and Ogun (the god of war and iron). The striking parallels include Dionysus' thyrsus being mirrored in the *opa*, a willowy pole bedecked with palm fronds and carried by Ogun's male devotees. Also, the rites of Dionysus culminate in the *sparagmos*, the tearing apart of a sacrificial animal, and at the climax of Ogun's rites a sacrificial dog is slaughtered and dismembered in a mock-struggle between the head priest and his acolytes for the carcass. One example of an obvious difference is that Ogun 'is best understood in Hellenic values as a totality of the Dionysian, Apollonian and Promethean virtues'.[9] Soyinka describes him as god of iron, whose powers include war, revolution, liberation, and creativity. He appears as the first actor in the battle fought in 'the fourth area of experience, the immeasurable gulf of transition'.[10] And since 'Yoruba drama is the re-enactment of the cosmic conflict'[11] he is, so to speak, also the god of Yoruba theatre.

In his rewriting of Euripides' *Bacchae* – *The Bacchae of Euripides: A Communion Rite* (1973) – Soyinka linked it to living oral traditions such as masked performances of the *egungun* festival and the worship of the god Ogun, proceeding from one of the affinities between Dionysus and Ogun as explained in 'The Fourth Stage'.[12] Such affinities not only allow for the substitution of one god by the other, they also make this substitution meaningful. It is for this reason that a Dionysian drama can be rewritten and staged as an Ogun drama, and Greek tragedy can merge

[7] See Hardwick (2004); Gilbert and Tompkins (1996), esp. 38–42.
[8] Cf. Disejenu (2007), 72–8. [9] Soyinka (1988), 22. [10] Soyinka in Jeyifo (2001), 134.
[11] Soyinka (1988), 27. [12] Soyinka (1988), 29–30.

with Yoruba ritual. It is therefore small wonder that Soyinka even rejected the idea that tragedy had its origin in ancient Greece: 'What are they talking about? I never heard my grandfather talk about Greeks invading Yorubaland.'[13] As regards tragedy, Yoruba culture was always on a par with its Greek counterpart.

Unfortunately, the first production of Soyinka's *Bacchae* (1973) failed to make any such claim. The play was commissioned by the National Theatre of London and its newly appointed director, Peter Hall.[14] Instead of having the author – who by that time was also an experienced director – direct the play himself, French film director Roland Joffé was entrusted with the production. It was a complete disaster: the African aspects were almost completely eliminated. Instead, Joffé raided Indian and Japanese performance cultures for material.

> Where I had called for some kind of recognizably Aegean music, specifying some composition by Theodorakis as an example, the composer had given a mélange of Indian and Japanese music. Hare Krishna silver bells ... Bamboo percussions and cymbals seemed to promise the eruption of the fierce ghost of a samurai from beneath the causeway, which ran the whole length of the theatre – another oriental pseudism. But the bias came down decidedly on the side of India. Our Dionysus introduced himself onto the stage with the sign of the namaste and the lotus posture; the gestures which accompanied the recitation of his rout of Pentheus was a mixture of the dance of Shiva and Lord Krishna narrating the battle of Arjuna. Plus a touch of Kung Fu. (Soyinka 1988, 73)

The only dramatic characters that were visually associated with Africa were the leading slave and the bacchants – i.e. those characters that were regarded as 'barbarians'. The ending was a fiasco. The transformative, liberating, and communal feast celebrated in the play was here denounced as a barbaric ritual of some 'primitive tribes' to be laughed at with a mixture of amusement and disdain. Instead of triggering a reflection on colonial dynamics, the production re-established it.[15]

After the London debacle, Soyinka became protective of the play, allowing very few productions. It was first performed in Nigeria only many years later, when the National Troupe in Lagos staged it in 2008. Its director, Ahmed Yerima, a former student of Soyinka's, commented as follows on his choice of the play: 'We are concerned with realizing the aesthetic comprehensiveness of the play as well as dislocating it from the

[13] Soyinka in Jeyifo (2001), 134. [14] See Lecznar, Chapter 6, this volume.
[15] See further Fischer-Lichte (2014b), 48–71, and Lecznar, Chapter 6, this volume.

tight grip of Western mythology and planting it in a soil that would give it a colour of its Africanness'.[16] Accordingly, Yerima's production was set in Yorubaland and was 'steeped deeply in the cultural aesthetics of the Yoruba'.[17] As far as can be judged from the reviews, the production was received as that of an African play. The realisation of a deeply Yoruba aesthetics emphasised its Africanness in performance, as did its mythology, for instance, the 'twinning' of Dionysus and Ogun. It also allowed the performance to be related to the contemporary situation in Africa. According to several critics, the performance dealt with 'the misuse and peril of power, especially in developing countries'. This critic went on to state that since the time of the play's inception, 'the crass opportunism of the military elite of that era' had been evident, and, 'nearly 40 years after, little or nothing has changed. Nigeria, like most African countries, is still in the grip of dictatorship and maladministration, while crime, insecurity, nepotism and looting of treasury remain a dominant feature.'[18] Pentheus was no longer likened to the British colonisers but to 'the visionless and purposeless political leaders, many of whom occupy the political space not only in Nigeria but also in Africa and many other third world countries'.[19] The communal rite that concluded the performance could therefore be taken as a celebration of the hope for liberation from dictatorship and a utopian vision of new political communities in Africa.

This is to say that the performance was received in a similar, if not the same, vein as the plays of the second generation of playwrights in Nigeria, particularly regarding their adaptations of Greek tragedies. To understand them within the framework of the Empire writing back, that is, in terms of post-colonial thought, would be deeply misleading. As Femi Òsòfisan puts it: 'It is not so much that the wound of the old colonial empire is not uppermost in our mind; it is, rather, that the notion of that kind of "empire" at all is no longer a current concern.'[20] Therefore, he sharply criticises post-colonialism for talking about the 'Centre', meaning the West: 'our own "Centre" is on the contrary Africa itself'.[21] Further, he argues:

> Post-colonialism will merely take us back to Négritude,[22] whereas our identity crisis in Africa is of a different order entirely, relating to two urgent problems – first, the dilemma of creating a national identity out of our

[16] quoted by Nwachuku (2008) [17] Nwachuku (2008). [18] Asoya (2008).
[19] Nwachuku (2008). [20] Òsòfisan (2016 [1999]), 157. [21] Òsòfisan (2016 [1999]), 159.
[22] Cf. Steinmeyer, Chapter 11, this volume.

> disparate ethnic communities, and secondly, that of creating committed, responsible, patriotic and compassionate individuals out of our civil populations. (Òsòfisan 2016 [1999], 161)

Òsòfisan devotes his theatre work to this mission. In this respect, there is no difference between his two adaptations of Greek tragedies, *Tègònni: An African Antigone* (first performed in 1994) and *The Women of Owu* (premiered in 2004), and his other plays.

As already stated, even the adaptations of the first generation were not merely a response to the British educational system and its claim to superiority. They also emphasised and revealed the striking kinship between the Greek pantheon and mythology and their West African equivalents. Yoruba gods appear in many of Òsòfisan's plays: Yemoya, the goddess of the River in *Tègònni*; Anlugbua, the ancestral founder of Owu Ipole, deified as *òrìṣà*, and his grandmother Lawumi in *The Women of Owu*; Shango, the god of lighting and thunder in *Many Colours Make the Thunder-King* (1997); or Eshu, the trickster god of confusion, chance, and contingency in *Eshu and the Vagabond Minstrels* (1991). As these examples show, the inclusion of Yoruba gods is not a characteristic only of Òsòfisan's adaptations of Greek tragedies. However, while most of Òsòfisan's plays are set in the present day, the two adaptations are located in nineteenth-century Yorubaland. *Tègònni* unfolds during colonial times, while *The Women of Owu* is situated in the pre-colonial era. Both pose questions about the past of the Yorubas. The former does so in order 'to re-invent ourselves, as individuals and as peoples ... for we are after all a people in urgent need of re-inventing – rather than "re-discovering" – ourselves'.[23] The latter, adapted from *The Trojan Women*, not only deals with contemporary war atrocities, clearly alluding to the invasion of Iraq by the US in 2003, but also prominently addresses the problem of slavery as one of Africans selling other Africans. The journey into the past here serves to better understand and deal with contemporary problems.

The 'Africanness' of the plays is further underlined by inserting *oríkìs*, a special genre of Yoruba praise songs devoted to particular individuals, as well as laments and other songs in Yoruba. The productions added to that by having these passages sung and danced in the traditional manner. This way, the Greek chorus was transformed into a Yoruba communal celebration. As far as I know, this happened in all the productions of the two plays. While *Tègònni* was directed by the playwright himself when it

[23] Òsòfisan in Jeyifo (1995), 122.

premiered at Emory College in Atlanta, *The Women of Owu*, commissioned by Chipping Norton Theatre in Oxfordshire, England, was directed by Chuck Mike.[24] Its published version was given its first production by the Okinba Players in a dramatised reading at the Arts Theatre in Ibadan, Nigeria, in January 2005, this time directed by Òsòfisan. The productions were received not so much as adaptations of Greek tragedies (except by classicists), but rather as performances of African plays addressing Yoruban history in order to enable a better and sharper understanding of the contemporary sociopolitical situation. The oft-noted kinship between Greek and Yoruba pantheons and mythologies here allowed for a morphing of Greek tragedy into a Yoruba play without necessarily calling to mind the 'original'. This way, the appropriation of Greek tragedy served a very particular purpose: it allowed, on the one hand, for the process of reinvention, and, on the other, for the adoption of a new perspective on the past without escaping into idealisations. It opened up the possibility for a new access to and understanding of one's history.

India

The social and political conditions in India have been very different. It was the only country colonised by the British where the Greek and Roman classics were not taught from the beginning of colonisation, either in school or in college. As Trivedi argues,

> the most likely reason for such different treatment of India in this respect was that, unlike any of the other colonies, whether White or Black, India had classics of its own, which had been 'discovered' and acknowledged by Britain well before it had, effectively, conquered India and was in a position to promulgate its own educational and cultural policy. (Trivedi 2007, 288)

The study and translation of older Indian texts began as early as the 1770s, introducing Europe to the idea that India had a tradition of ancient literature that ought to be recognised as 'classical' in the European sense. They were written in Sanskrit, i.e. a language that not only surpassed Latin but even Greek, according to Sir William Jones, a former classics scholar at Oxford, who was the first to translate the drama *Abhijñānaśākuntalam* by Kalidasa (fourth century CE). He praised the Sanskrit language for its 'wonderful structure, more perfect than the Greek, more copious than

[24] Cf. Budelmann (2007).

the Latin and more exquisitely refined than either' (1786).[25] In this context, it is not surprising that an annual subsidy of 100,000 rupees was granted by the British administration to native institutions for encouraging the study of Sanskrit. However, Thomas Macaulay, as member of the Governor General's Council, managed to have this policy reversed, and the subsidy withdrawn. Instead, in his 'Minute on Indian Education' (1835) he urged the Governor General of India to have English language and literature taught at schools and colleges in India:

> What the Greek and Latin were to the contemporaries of More and Ascham, our tongue is to the people of India. The literature of England is now more valuable than that of classical antiquity. (p. 243; quotation in Trivedi 2007, 294)

As a result, no Greek tragedies were taught. Hence, after gaining independence in 1947, Indian theatre-makers and playwrights did not feel the need to turn to Greek tragedy. To my knowledge, the first productions of Greek tragedies were realised in the 1960s. The first to do so was Ebrahim Alkazi (born 1925), who would become one of India's leading stage directors. He served as director of the National School of Drama in New Delhi from 1962 to 1977. Already in 1961, he put Euripides' *Medea* on stage for Theatre Unit, then still located in Bombay (now Mumbai), followed by *Oedipus the King* at the National School of Drama in 1964. He is well known for supporting the growth and dissemination of contemporary Indian drama in the 1960s. The reason why he turned to Greek tragedies might well be that they were not loaded with colonial baggage in the Indian context and that he wanted to explore their potential for the contemporary theatre. Since tragedy uses narratives from Greek mythology, this might have seemed an added advantage in terms of the aims of political theatre. The same applies to the two productions of Greek tragedies by another well-known director, Shambu Mitra (1915–97). He staged *The Trojan Women*, with the great actress Tripti Mitra in the leading role, and *Oedipus the King* with his Calcutta-based company Bohurupee in the late 1960s.

In 1980, the Max Müller Bhavan (Goethe Institute) in Calcutta (now Kolkata) invited the German director Hansgünther Heyme, famous in Germany for his provocative, political productions of Greek tragedies,[26] to

[25] Cited in W. Jones (1999 [1807]); here quoted from Trivedi (2007), 289.

[26] Cf. Fischer-Lichte (2017), 228–67, esp. 241–7.

stage *Antigone*.[27] Perhaps inspired by Heyme's production, Kavalam Narayana Panikkar directed another production of *Antigone* at the Avadh Theatre, which was invited to Delphi in 1986 to general acclaim. Also in the 1980s, Amitava Dasgupta (born 1947), a self-proclaimed Brecht disciple, began to stage Greek tragedies with his Delhi-based company Brechtian Mirror. In 1982 he put Euripides' *Electra* on stage, followed three years later by Euripides' *Iphigenia in Aulis*. In 1993 he staged the *Bacchae*, which toured Himachal Pradesh, Lucknow, and Calcutta.

This latter production was quite successful. It was a response to a bloody clash between Hindus and Muslims, highly publicised in India and abroad. In December 1992 the Babri Masjid, a sixteenth-century mosque located in the town of Ayodhya, also known as the location of important Ramlila performances – plays on the life of the god Rama as narrated in the epic *Ramayana* (approximately second century CE) – was destroyed by a mob of Hindu fundamentalists. They believed that the mosque had been erected after the destruction of a Hindu temple on the same site, which had marked the birthplace of Lord Rama. Hundreds of people were killed as tensions between Hindus and Muslims escalated in the aftermath of the demolition, leading to more riots, deaths, and horrendous destruction.

Dasgupta chose to stage the *Bacchae* because he felt that the tragedy told a story of communal, religious riots instigated and stoked by politicians. In his production he emphasised the similarities and references to contemporary Indian politics. He regarded Pentheus as 'a right honest person. He was killed. Take Dhirendra Brahmachari. He used to give all sermons to Indira Gandhi. So, these godfathers, they have tremendous strength over politicians. And in India, the influence of godfathers is very strong.'[28] Accordingly, in his production, Dionysus was not conceived of as a god but as a politician exploiting religion to achieve his cause.

The production was staged shortly after the destruction of the mosque and the riots following it. Since it clearly addressed these events, it exerted a strong influence on its audiences. The performance lasted only one hour and forty-five minutes. The text had been shortened considerably, although the background story was included, with Semele's death being enacted on stage. The central conflict was the triangle between Semele,

[27] At the same time, the German director Fritz Bennewitz from the German Democratic Republic directed Brecht's *Life of Galileo* in New Delhi, claiming that Brecht was for 'the people', while Heyme's production of a Greek tragedy was for the 'elite'. In previous years Bennewitz had already staged Brecht's *The Threepenny Opera* (1970) and *Mr Puntila and His Man Matti* (1979) in New Delhi.

[28] Dasgupta (2009).

Agave, and Dionysus. Throughout the performance, the stage was almost empty. A big oven with fire coming out of it, meant (and probably perceived by the audience) as a sacred object, maybe alluding to Agni, the Vedic god of fire, stood slightly off-centre. A single pillar hinted at the palace. Dasgupta employed two effective staging strategies, the first of which aimed at emphasising the reference to contemporary politics. This was further enhanced by the text. In between, one of the characters remarked: 'Just see what actually happened in the name of religion, 200 persons were killed.' After the final scene, Agave said, 'Please my father, let us go somewhere where the dirty politics is not there.' Mainly, however, this was achieved by some kind of 'Brechtian' device. As Dasgupta relates,

> In one performance we did captions and slides, where we showed headlines from the time, something documentary, for example Babri Masjid, then somebody committed suicide, then Rajiv Gandhi was murdered, then Sheikh Abdullah[29] in Kashmir . . . We stopped the play and this was shown, and then we continued the play . . . (Dasgupta 2009)

According to the director, the audience responded enthusiastically to these slides, with some spectators returning only in order to see them again and complaining when they were removed. Meanwhile, however, the police had interfered, clearly informed of the play's potentially incendiary content by someone in the audience. This strategy demonstrated that it was religion, abused and exploited by politicians, that dismembered communities and perhaps even the whole nation.

The other strategy was the inclusion of different folk and classical dances. When Semele wanted the sun to shine on her love, the sun came out accompanied by Chhau dancers and their music, as was also the case when she died. By contrast, Cadmus and Tiresias were accompanied by Yakshagana dancers, drums, and violin. The chorus consisted of fourteen Kathak dancers.[30] The elements of music and dance allowed for the inclusion of different performance traditions and therefore communities, which were united into one aesthetic whole. This strategy was in some ways reminiscent of India's Republic Day Parade, held annually in New Delhi and featuring, besides a military display, a cultural pageant representing the different folk traditions of the states of the Indian Union and thereby speaking to the Nehruvian ideal of national unity in cultural

[29] Sheikh Abdullah instigated the 1946 uprising in favour of Kashmir's independence.

[30] The Indian tradition of folk dances is very rich. Each has particular characteristics. While the Chhau dance is associated with the military, the other two are used to enact narratives.

diversity.[31] While the representational politics and territorial agenda at work in the parade would have been absent in Dasgupta's production, he did claim to bring together diverse dance traditions ostensibly to form an aesthetic whole, irrespective of ideology. Thus, on the level of what was represented in his production, religious politics was shown as dismembering the community/state/nation, while on the level of representation two different strategies were employed. Firstly, the Brechtian devices, which 'dismembered' the 'unity of action' by interrupting it, underlined, explained, and contextualised what was shown on the level of the things represented. Secondly, the diverse dance traditions juxtaposed on stage formed an aesthetic unity that not only appealed to the particular sensibility of the spectators but, moreover, created a certain sense of harmony. More than fifteen years after that production, Dasgupta reiterated his belief that because of the political situation in India, Greek tragedy was and still is greatly relevant in the country: 'Today's rulers are greedy, just like Agamemnon who sacrificed his own daughter: His ambition was greater than affection. It is here, now also.'[32]

We may therefore conclude that Greek tragedies were put on stage in India in the context of different forms of political theatre. Their performances served this role well for at least three reasons. First, the plays were not connected to the British colonisers and their tendency towards realistic-psychological theatre. Secondly, their mythological framework allowed the inclusion of Indian local aesthetic principles. And, finally, they dealt with subjects easily identified as topical political themes. Even if they were not performed often, their performances served important sociopolitical goals.

There is one notable exception to this rule – a performance of the *Bacchae* by the International Centre for Kathakali in New Delhi, commissioned by the Committee of the Greek Drama International Meetings at Delphi to be presented at the Delphi Festival of 1998. 'Weary of the dangers of having the poetry and tragic wisdom of the ancient texts strangled through the socio-political burden of contemporary Western adaptations', as one Greek critic put it,[33] the performance of a Greek classic text in an Indian classic performance style was envisaged as a remedy against this illness. Guru Sadanam P. V. Balakrishnan responded to the invitation to direct the play by telling the Greek Committee that he would do it only if it would not 'spoil' the tradition. As he emphasised even ten years later, the production did not go against this tradition. Still, because of

[31] Jain (2002). [32] Dasgupta (2009). [33] Matziri (1998).

the encounter between two great theatre cultures, both had to be changed to a certain extent.

One of the necessary changes in his view concerned the chorus. In Kathakali there is no group dancing. Balakrishnan initially suggested leaving out the chorus completely and assigning its songs to the vocalists. Later, he came up with the idea of reducing it to a single character – a device very common among Western directors at that time. However, the representatives of the Greek Committee who sat in on all the rehearsals insisted that a chorus was necessary as it represented the 'essence' of Greek theatre. Consequently, a chorus consisting of eight male and eight female dancers was included for the performance in Delphi, but later, for the performance in New Delhi, it was reduced to four dancers.

The insistence of the Greek host on the inclusion of the chorus as well as the condescending, even arrogant reviews on the performance in Delphi suggest that the purpose of inviting the Kathakali group to stage the *Bacchae* was to reaffirm the superiority of Greek tragedy and its 'eternal truths of mankind'[34] over the classical Indian form of Kathakali that enacted 'local' values. Ultimately, the invitation of the Kathakali group can be understood as an invitation to an *agon* between two 'classical' ancient theatre cultures – an *agon* in which, according to the judgement of Greek critics, their own 'classics' carried the day.[35] Here, finally, the Greek classics, having been excluded from the Indian school and college curricula in colonial times, 'struck back' – at least in the eyes of the Greek critics.

Balakrishnan, on the contrary, remembered only 'that generally the reception in Delphi was fantastic' and quoted a Greek spectator who said 'actually our Greek tragedy fits *only* to Kathakali'.[36] Moreover, the fact that he later staged another Greek tragedy, *Alcestis*, with his own resources invalidates the idea that the production of the *Bacchae* was a failure, let alone that it did any lasting damage to the tradition of Kathakali. *Alcestis* was performed several times in New Delhi and was included in the Kathakali Festival of 2006. It clearly had a great appeal for local audiences. In conclusion, it seems that for Balakrishnan and his company the 'fusion of Kathakali and a Greek play'[37] served as a means to probe into the possibilities and limits of changing their own classical theatre form without spoiling it. It was an attempt to open up to new approaches for

[34] Matziri (1998). [35] Cf. Fischer-Lichte (2014b), 186–205. [36] Balakrishnan (2009).
[37] Krishnan and Pillai (2009).

their own traditional form, albeit carefully – by performing a 'classical' play from another culture.

Japan

Since the 1970s, the most prominent Japanese directors have repeatedly put Greek tragedies on stage. Suzuki Tadashi directed *The Trojan Women* (1974), the *Bacchae* (1978), *Clytemnestra* (1983, based on several tragedies), Sophocles' *Electra* (1995, in cooperation with Miyagi Satoshi and other members of Miyagi's group Ku Na'uka), and *Oedipus the King* (2000). He restaged the *Bacchae* and *Oedipus the King* several times in the following fifteen years. (From 1990 the reworking of the *Bacchae* was renamed *Dionysus*.) Ninagawa Yukio put *Oedipus the King* (1976, 1986, and 2002), *Medea* (1978 and 2005), *Electra* (2003), and *Orestes* (2006) on stage. In addition to *Electra* (1995 together with Suzuki), Miyagi Satoshi did *Medea* (1999), *Oedipus the King* (2000), and *Antigone* (2004). All these productions toured many countries in Asia, Europe, the Americas, and Australia. In Japan they were presented all over the country and performed on very different kinds of stages. Most importantly, it was these productions that turned their directors into celebrities, partly even icons in Japan and beyond.

This might come as a surprise when considering that Japan had almost no performance history of Greek tragedy. After the opening up of the country to the West (1853) and during the Meiji era (1868–1912), one of the reformers of Kabuki, Kawakami Otojirō, belonging to the Shinpa, or 'new Kabuki' school, put *Oedipus the King* on stage in 1894. Between 1899 and 1902 he toured the United States and Europe with his troupe, presenting only Japanese pieces. Since the production of *Oedipus* was staged five years before the tour, it can be safely assumed that it was adapted in the new-Kabuki style of the Shinpa school. In 1916 Kawakami once again staged the tragedy, this time together with the Geijutsuza theatre company founded by Shimamura Hōgetsu (the director of the first production of Ibsen's *A Doll's House* in 1911), and Matsui Sumako, the actress who played Nora in the realistic-psychological style.[38] In this production, Matsui played the part of Jocasta, and it is very likely that this production adhered to a realistic style. In 1913, a production of Sophocles' *Electra* (in Hofmannsthal's version) was staged by the Kōshū Gekidan company led by Matsui Shoyo. Kawai Takeo, a famous *onnagata*

[38] Cf. Fischer-Lichte (2014a), 116–27.

(male actor specialising in female roles) of Shinpa theatre, played Electra.[39] There is no mention of other performances of Greek tragedies before World War II.

We can identify at least three developments that led to the boom of performances of Greek tragedies on Japanese stages from the 1970s onwards. The first resulted from university activities. At the end of the 1950s, a group of professors and students at Tokyo University founded the Girisha-higeki-kenyûkai, or 'Seminar on Greek Tragedy'. It proceeded from an academic, historical interest and aimed at reconstructing the performance style prevalent in Athens in the fifth century BCE. The students were encouraged to translate the texts themselves and then reconstruct the staging, including the costumes, as 'faithfully' as possible. The result of their efforts was shown in a production of *Oedipus the King* at the open-air theatre of the concert hall Hibiya-ongáku-dô in a park in central Tokyo in June 1958, in which the choral songs were sung and accompanied by dancing. Other productions followed on a yearly basis, presented in the same space – *Antigone*, *Prometheus Bound*, *Agamemnon*, *Philoctetes*, *The Trojan Women*, *Heracles*, *The Persians*, the *Bacchae*, *The Suppliant Women*, and *Seven against Thebes.* The performances became very popular. From the performance of *Prometheus Bound* (1960) and until the last performance (that of *Seven against Thebes* in 1968), the 2,500 seats of the theatre were regularly sold out. The performances of the Seminar on Greek Tragedy also seem to have inspired some professional theatres to stage Greek tragedies. The Engekiza Theatre in Tokyo presented *Antigone* in 1959, i.e. in the same year in which the Seminar staged it, and, in the late 1960s, in the context of the protests against the Vietnam War, several theatres performed *The Trojan Women*, albeit in Sartre's version.

The second development was the protests against Westernisation. In the 1960s Westernisation was seen as pure imitation, which brought about a devaluation and negation of traditional Japanese values, customs, habits, and ways of life. The young generation of Japanese rebelled against this situation and demanded decisive cultural changes. New theatre forms sprang up – the so-called *angura*, meaning underground theatre, and, later on, the *shogekijo*, meaning Little Theatre Movement.[40] These new theatre forms were opposed not only to the social and political situation, but also to Shingeki, the spoken theatre, modelled after the European realistic-psychological theatre performed on a box set stage and introduced at the

[39] See Ozasa Yoshio, quoted in Ruperti (2011), 140.

[40] The term refers to the small size of the playhouses used.

beginning of the twentieth century. While it had been founded to enable theatre to deal with the burning social issues linked to processes of modernisation, which the traditional theatre forms did not allow for, Shingeki seemed aesthetically outmoded and sterile by the 1950s.

Among the new groups that emerged in the second half of the 1960s in opposition to Shingeki were the Waseda Shogekijo, which grew out of a students' theatre group under the leadership of Suzuki Tadashi, and the Gendaijin Gekijo (Contemporary Theatre), founded by Ninagawa Yukio and others. These groups disapproved of Shingeki as a mere imitation of text-based, realistic-psychological Western theatre, and instead drew heavily on traditional Japanese theatre forms. Yet they, too, strove to create a new modern theatre, one better attuned than Shingeki to Japanese aesthetics and sensibilities. As we shall see, Greek tragedy seemed to provide a solution.

The third development goes back to the Noh actor Kanze Hisao and his cooperation with Jean-Louis Barrault, made possible by a scholarship from the French government. In 1963 Kanze lived in Paris for six months and studied the local theatre scene. This included Barrault's 1955 'Brazilian' *Oresteia*, into which Pierre Boulez had incorporated Noh music. This performance suggested to Kanze the idea of a certain kinship between Greek tragedy and Noh. This idea was probably further substantiated when Kanze arranged a programme consisting of Noh pieces for the Herod Atticus Theatre in Athens in 1965, where up to that point mostly Greek plays had been performed. In 1971, Kanze, together with his younger brother Kanze Hideo and the celebrated Kyogen actor Nomura Mansaku, founded the theatre company Mei no Kai (Society of Darkness), which staged several Greek tragedies in the style of Noh, Kyogen, and Kabuki: *Oedipus the King* (1971), *Agamemnon* (1972), and *Medea* (1975). In the programme notes to *Oedipus the King*, Kanze Hisao explained that 'the reason we picked a Greek play is possibly because of Jean-Louis Barrault. Noh and Greek drama have common ground between them because their original characteristic is the confrontation between Man and Fate.'[41] This once again confirmed the proclaimed kinship between Noh and ancient Greek tragedy.[42]

41 Cited in Carruthers and Takahashi (2004), 28.

42 This kinship had already been asserted by Ernest Fenollosa, who made comparisons between Noh and Greek tragedy in a manuscript edited by Ezra Pound (Fenollosa and Pound 1916). This kinship is further explored in Smethurst (1989, 2013).

These three developments have to be considered in our discussion of why Greek tragedies have flourished on Japanese stages and become huge national as well as international successes since the 1970s.

It is not certain – although it can be assumed – that Suzuki saw any of the performances staged by the Seminar on Greek Tragedy, in particular their *Trojan Women* and the *Bacchae*, or some of the productions of *The Trojan Women* (in Sartre's version) of the late 1960s. However, his connection to Kanze Hisao, who appeared as Old Man and Menelaus in Suzuki's *The Trojan Women*, and as Dionysus in his *Bacchae*, is well documented.

Those earlier, pre-1970s performances have to be considered, as they form an important part of the context from which Suzuki's and Ninagawa's first productions of Greek tragedies emerged. What did these productions accomplish that neither Shingeki nor the traditional theatre forms were able to achieve? What was/is their particular purpose over the last forty years? This question will be addressed by discussing, even if only briefly, Suzuki's *Trojan Women*, Ninagawa's *Medea*, and Miyagi's *Medea*. These three productions, as also the other productions of Greek tragedies by the three directors, share two characteristic features: first, they deal with a particular sociopolitical problem (and are in this respect comparable to Shingeki) and, secondly, they have ample recourse to, and make use of, devices and elements from traditional Japanese theatre forms. Suzuki's *The Trojan Women* drew on Noh and Kabuki, Ninagawa's *Medea* mainly on Kabuki, and Miyagi's *Medea* in a striking way on Bunraku.

Suzuki embarked on his first production of a Greek tragedy after he had developed a new acting style by performing contemporary Japanese plays and experimental productions, such as *On the Dramatic Passion I* (1969) and *On the Dramatic Passion II* (1970), in which he extensively dealt with Noh and Kabuki as well as with Shintoist rituals. In *The Trojan Women* stomping and squatting – central in Noh as well as in Kabuki – were assigned key importance. In his essay 'Culture is the Body!' Suzuki explains why and how these elements could restore the body's perceptive and expressive qualities, which have been lost in the process of modernisation. Accordingly, his method focused on movements of the feet, e.g. stomping. For

> perhaps it is not the upper but the lower half of our body through which the physical sensibility common to all races is most consciously expressed; to be more specific, the feet. The feet are the last remaining part of the human body, which has kept, literally, in touch with the earth, the very supporting base of all human activities. (Suzuki 2002, 167)

Stomping and squatting were used by the actors in the performance to generate an enormous amount of energy, which was transferred to the spectators. In this respect, the actor came close to the role of a shaman. This new acting style was perfectly embodied by Shiraishi Kayoko as Hecuba – and in later performances, after the death of Kanze Hisao, as Old Woman and Cassandra. The critic Senda Akihiko concludes: 'So it is, then, that we are able to witness this tragedy of ancient Greece and to have the rare experience of a drama set in contemporary Japan.'[43]

Not unlike Shingeki, *The Trojan Women* could address a sociopolitical problem of the greatest relevance, namely, the consequences of an atomic war – not only with refence to the (then) recent Japanese past but also as a constant threat during the Cold War. Unlike Shingeki, however, the production was capable of triggering strong, and even overwhelming emotions in the spectators due to its new rigorous acting style and particular aesthetics as described above.[44]

Like Ibsen's *Doll's House* at the turn from the nineteenth to the twentieth century, *Medea* in the 1970s became the pivotal play of the women's movement in Western cultures as well as in Japan. I do not know whether the *Medea* of the Society of Darkness was already received in this way, but it was certainly the case with Ninagawa's *Medea*. In an interview, Ninagawa even stated that he had produced the play in order to demonstrate to Japanese women that they can be as strong and independent as Medea. For the representation of such a Medea he chose Hira Mikijirô, an *onnagata*, the traditional male impersonator of female roles in Kabuki. In 1987 the *onnagata* Arashi Tokusaburo took over the role of Medea.[45] All other characters were also played by male actors, as is the tradition in Kabuki.

However, this does not mean that Ninagawa staged *Medea* in the style of Kabuki (as in the case of the Society of Darkness production). Rather, the other actors employed a number of different forms and styles. Even Arashi did not strictly adhere to a 'pure' Kabuki style. He deviated from it in certain telling aspects – for instance with his costume, which was reminiscent of (but not identical with) that of a young geisha in Kabuki, as well as with some of his poses and the use of his voice. In fact, all aspects of Arashi's performance brought to mind facets of Kabuki but were actually different from it. After Medea had announced that she would

[43] Senda (1997), 51–2.

[44] Cf. Carruthers and Takahashi (2004), 124–53; McDonald (1992), 21–44.

[45] I saw this production in Tokyo in 1990.

destroy the king, her husband, and his young bride to take revenge, Arashi struck a *mie* pose, which is usually reserved in Kabuki for strong male characters but never for an *onnagata*; what is more, Arashi's *mie* pose was executed faster and lasted a shorter time than in the classical version. Such deviations also occurred in Arashi's use of his voice. When Medea appeared onstage for the first time, Arashi spoke in the 'feminine' voice that is regarded as characteristic of the *onnagata*. Over the course of the performance, however, he let his 'male' voice come through from time to time. When Jason appeared on stage and harshly confronted Medea, Arashi responded in his male voice, this way not only claiming equal status but actually adopting it.

Besides the particular use of elements from Kabuki, the performance's strong emotional impact on the spectators was also due to the music. The performance began with a kind of overture – the song 'Daikanjo' (Deep Emotions), a modern pop song, which Mikami Hiroshi had composed for the production. Then a chorus of sixteen members appeared. They were playing the shamisen, a musical instrument which is typical for Kabuki. After that a flute could be heard playing offstage, accompanied by a string instrument. At prominent moments, a very particular version of 'La Folía' was played, often accompanied by the sound of church bells. It could be heard, for instance, when Medea and the members of the chorus slowly and ceremonially pulled red ribbons from their own mouths – a telling reversal of a Kabuki convention, according to which the actor puts the red ribbon, fastened to his hat, into his mouth in order to indicate that the character, usually a shy young girl, has fallen in love. Here, the reversal suggested the idea that Medea was tearing love from her body or that she was spitting blood. Such scenes, accompanied by music and the sound of the *ki*, wooden rattles, formed the emotional climaxes of the performance.

These processes and moments demonstrated not only Medea's equality with men but also rendered her actions understandable, including the killing of her children. By way of such a very specific transformation of elements, devices, and *kata*[46] from Kabuki, Ninagawa succeeded in portraying Medea as equal to the male characters and, at the same time, to arouse positive feelings in the spectators.[47] The production was thus able to achieve with regard to today's audiences what Shimamura Hogetsu's realistic-psychological Shingeki production of *A Doll's House* in 1911 had

[46] *Kata* means the conventional methods used in the presentation of Kabuki plays. They are fixed forms or patterns of performance. See Leiter (1979), 178.

[47] See also Smethurst (2000).

achieved concerning discussions on the 'new woman' at the beginning of the twentieth century.

More than twenty-five years after Ninagawa's *Medea* premiered, and in the same year in which it was performed for the very last time, Miyagi Satoshi staged his own version of the tragedy (2005). He invented a setting that allowed for linking criticism of the still-patriarchal Japanese society and the subordinate position of women within it to a critique of Japan's colonialism. The setting took the spectators back to the turn from the nineteenth to the twentieth century. A group of men, dressed in long black cloaks and thus characterised as civil servants or judges, visit an elegant restaurant in Tokyo and demand that the women who work there perform *Medea* for them. However, the women were only to carry out the movements, while the dialogue would be spoken by the men, who would each take on a particular role but who would speak the choral parts together.

To Japanese viewers, this separation of language and movement would be an element obviously borrowed from Bunraku, in which there is a clear distinction between the actors who move the puppets and the Gidayū, the black-clad narrator, who kneels on the right side of the stage and reads the lines of the different characters. Miyagi's stage, too, recalled this arrangement, even though the men who read from the book were not sitting on the side but on a separate stage, parallel to the apron and almost extending along the entire breadth of the stage. The men knelt down at its edge, the books in front of them on the floor. Sliding doors featuring traditional scenes from the Edo period (*ca.* 1603–1868) closed off the main stage at the back. Later, they became transparent, so that the drumming women behind them became visible. The space in front of the 'women's' stage was empty except for a tower on the left, on top of which a row of books was arranged as if on a bookshelf.

The recourse to Bunraku, the separation between female 'movers' and male speakers, brought into being a situation in which the women did not have a voice of their own, and the men spoke for them. Moreover, since the woman forced to take on the part of Medea appeared in a traditional Korean garment, Medea was marked as a stranger. But it seemed, particularly in the final scene, that all the women actually were Korean. After Medea (Mikari) had killed her son in a very moving choreography, the women behind the transparent sliding doors took off the Japanese costumes forced on them by the men and suddenly stood there in long, white undershirts. In their hand or mouth they each held a knife as Medea had done before killing her son. To the sound of flutes and drums, they snuck up behind the men and stabbed or strangled them to death. Whoever tried to escape was hunted down. No one was spared. After that there was a moment of complete silence. Then with a loud bang the books fell from the tower's landing onto the floor.

The recourse to Bunraku enabled Miyagi to connect his critique of women's oppression to a critique of colonialism, including the fate of the so-called comfort women. Not only did the men appropriate these women's voices and assign them their roles, but by doing so, the Japanese appropriated the Koreans' voices and assigned them their roles. It was the oppression by the men/Japanese that resulted in the violence of the women/Koreans, through which alone they got access to the books which, presumably, contained their own stories and history.

Staging Greek tragedies in Japan since the 1970s clearly served a double purpose. On the one hand, these performances turned the theatre into a forum for addressing deplorable social and political states of affairs – a purpose fulfilled in the first decades of the twentieth century by Shingeki. On the other hand, because of their aesthetics, which drew heavily on traditional theatre forms, they were able to arouse in the spectators strong, at times even overwhelming emotions. Greek tragedies were particularly suited for this purpose, since they deal with ethical, social, and political problems of great relevance but had not become part of the Shingeki repertoire – maybe because of their special aesthetics, which shies away from psychological or other realisms. This might explain the 'boom' of such productions in Japan since the 1970s. Their international success may require different explanations regarding different cultures. However, the particular fusion of topical ethical, social, and political issues with an aesthetics that arouses strong emotions might work in various parts of the world, albeit perhaps for different reasons.

China

Finally, let us turn to China, where, again, we have very different conditions and intentions to consider. The performance history of ancient Greek tragedies in China is rather short. While the first, roughly ten, translations of tragedies had already been produced in the 1930s, the first performance of a Greek tragedy only took place in the 1980s, i.e. after the Cultural Revolution (May 1966–October 1976). The Cultural Revolution destroyed most of the traditional culture, denouncing it as feudalistic or bourgeois. All *xiqu* companies, i.e. traditional opera companies, were dissolved, and their members were sent to do humiliating forced labour in so-called re-education camps in the countryside. The only operas to be performed were the eight model operas as favoured and introduced by Jiang Qing, Mao's wife, a former actress who had once played the role of Nora in Ibsen's *Doll's House* in the 1930s. Any access to other, particularly Western, cultures was forbidden. In 1980, the so-called Gang of Four, who had taken over after Mao's death in 1976, were arrested and put to trial, and Deng Xiaoping proclaimed the beginning of a new era.

A period of experimentation began for artists. A new style of *huaju*, or spoken drama, introduced to Shanghai at the beginning of the century (shortly after Shingeki had been introduced to Japan), was created by playwrights such as Gao Xingjian, Wang Peigon, Tao Jun, and others. Their forms of spoken drama, quite generally, might be characterised as experimental, each in a different way. The remains of the old traditional theatre forms, *xiqu*, were assembled in the hope of a revival. The first performance of a Greek tragedy happened during this time of experimentation. Luo Jinlin, son of Luo Nian-sheng, one of the three most important translators of Greek tragedy, put *Oedipus the King* on stage using *huaju* in 1986 with students of the Central Academy of Drama in Beijing – a production that might have suggested a parallel between Oedipus and Mao to some spectators. As a matter of fact, *huaju* had to be somewhat adapted to the particular demands of this 'new' genre of drama by sparingly taking recourse to the aesthetics of *xiqu*. This happened in the same year in which Huang Zuolin (1906–94), one of the most admired directors in China (who in 1962 had introduced Brecht in a speech lasting seven hours and who was under extreme pressure during the Cultural Revolution), put *Macbeth* onstage using *kunqu* opera together with the Shanghai *Kunqu* troupe at the First Shakespeare Festival in China. A year later, the Sichuan *xiqu* company in Chengdu performed Brecht's *The Good Person of Szechwan* in their traditional style. Both are to be regarded as experimental productions, transforming – or reinventing – the plays as well as the conventions of their respective style. In 1988, Luo Jinlin continued his experiments by staging *Antigone* in a *huaju* style.

The two performances of Greek tragedies in this style became quite popular in China. Luo's *Oedipus* was even broadcast by the state television company CCTV and reached a large audience. At the same time, an academic symposium was devoted to the production. As such, the production enjoyed a broad resonance throughout different milieus. The response to Luo's *Antigone* was also very positive. The critic Huang Wenjun commented: 'I sense the unique, mysterious, deeply moving and soul-cleansing force of the Greek tragedy. Such tragedy happens without tears and sadness, brings forth a kind of irresistible effect of ethical sublimity'.[48] Huang was enthusiastic about this experiment, which not only introduced a new dramatic genre, radically different from the 'old' realistic plays performed in *huaju* style, but also integrated some aesthetic principles from *xiqu*. He praised Luo's *Antigone* as 'a brilliant and excellent performance that successfully brought together the Chinese character as well as the essence of Greek tragedy'.[49] The experiment in his view resulted in a productive encounter between Greek tragedy and Chinese culture.

Both productions were invited to Delphi. However, they did not garner as much praise there as at home. The Greek director Theodoros Terzopoulos, who was at the time the artistic director of the Greek Drama International Meetings in Delphi, and whose 1986 *Bacchae* had been condemned by most Greek critics for using 'unGreek', 'Asian' movements (such as squatting), suggested to Luo the idea to adapt a Greek tragedy in one of China's many local or regional opera styles. In 1989 Luo adapted *Medea* in the style of the Hebei Bangzi opera (from the province of Hebei), which was presented in Delphi in 1991. This production, by contrast, won international acclaim. The critic Kostas Georgoussopoulos praised it in the highest terms, even while belittling Luo's *Oedipus* and *Antigone*:

> The former 'Oedipus' was a naïve-moving, Western-inspired melodrama. Meanwhile, there was a similar 'Antigone' and now, this year, came the solution, matter-of-factly, natural, simple as a breath. Luo Jin-lin, in the strict but fertile tradition of his country, has breathed and sucked in the language and the traditional customs ... Luo Jin-lin has found his way, and his way is a teaching for us which says: the most successful way to express one's innermost self is to nurture oneself from one's own deepest roots. (Georgoussopoulos 1991; cited in Lin 2010, 267–8)

Ironically, while Luo's *Medea* was seen as a productive encounter of the two cultures by the Greek side, the 'nurturing from one's deepest roots' was not met with the same enthusiasm in China. The Hebei Bangzi *Medea* did not arouse much interest: there were not many performances or reviews. In fact, up until its revival in Beijing in 2002, it was presented only twice. The reasons for the lack of interest in 1989 and even after its great international success in 1991 were manifold, if somewhat contradictory. One of them, no doubt, is the particular woman's image that *Medea*

[48] (Huang 1988, 43; cited in Lin 2010, 252) [49] Huang (1988), 44.

conveys, an image that stands in complete contradiction to the dominant ideas on women in China. Other objections referred to the production's experimental aesthetics. The connoisseurs of Hebei Bangzi opera felt uncomfortable with the changes it had undergone in Luo's *Medea* – changes which had gone unnoticed by the international audiences. Another group of critics were the opponents of traditional opera forms in general. They vehemently fought any attempt to revive them, seeing them as still firmly rooted in feudalism. There was also a third party, which preached 'truthfulness to the text', and took issue with Luo's decision to alter the text considerably in order to meet the demands of the opera form. By 2002, however, these reasons no longer seemed to matter so much. This time, the performance was met with great interest, also from the media, which highlighted and praised the extraordinary performance of the actors.[50]

What exactly had happened in the interim that changed the common opinion on Luo's *Medea* so radically? In 2001, after fourteen years of negotiations with the USA and the European Union, China acquired membership in the World Trade Organization. This opened up China to the global market and vice versa. A year later, Luo's Hebei Bangzi *Medea* was revived, and this occasion was marked by a symposium to discuss the conditions for productive encounters with other cultures – mainly Western ones – through performances of Greek tragedies in the form of *xiqu*. Qin Huashen, director of the Beijing Research Institute of the Arts and chairman of the symposium, stated in his introductory remarks that 'connecting the two theatre traditions in the new century is of utmost importance, especially because there has been a plea to bring Chinese culture into the world ever since China joined the World Trade Organization'.[51]

To internationalise *xiqu* became the official guideline of Chinese cultural politics. The deputy chief editor of the journal *Zhongguo Wenhuabao* (*Chinese Cultural Journal*) Xu Shi-pei strongly supported the idea of such 'meaningful adaptations' of Greek tragedy and defined their goals as follows:

> In view of China's opening up towards the global market and the intensification of multilateral trading processes as well as of cultural exchange, the new task will be to find out how theatre art as a kind of 'global' language can be further developed for the purpose of overcoming the barriers of cultural backgrounds and verbal communication, and to present traditional

[50] See Lin (2010), esp. 251–65. [51] Zhang (2003), 1, cited in Lin (2010), 259.

> Chinese art and culture in foreign countries, so that the market for Chinese art products and Chinese cultural influence can be expanded. (Xu 2003, cited in Lin 2010, 260)

It seemed to be the common belief that these goals could be better achieved when *xiqu* entered the world stage not with performances of traditional Chinese plays but with those from the Western canon, such as Greek tragedies or Shakespeare's plays. After returning from a guest tour to the Sixth International Ibero-American Theatre Festival in Bogotá, Colombia, in 1998, the director of the Hebei Bangzi Company, Li Jiu-yuan, had already formulated this insight as follows:

> In order to carry Chinese theatre art into the world and to take a particular share on the global market, it is mandatory, wherever it is possible, to renounce local content and instead, for an international guest tour, select such plays from the repertoire which are internationally influential and popular. (Li 1998, 57, cited in Lin 2010, 261)

Among these plays Greek tragedies stand out, although they are by no means performed as frequently as plays by Shakespeare, Ibsen, Chekhov, or Brecht. As the critic Xu Shi-pei emphasises, Greek tragedy is regarded as the 'gene bank of Western culture'. Therefore, he advocates a 'crossbreeding' of Chinese and Western culture from which, in his opinion, both sides would profit:

> When *xiqu* adopts and performs ancient Greek classics, which are long since restricted to the text form, it will transform them on today's stages into a living art. This fusion has a much bigger chance of succeeding on the market than it would if we presented to foreign spectators our own works of art unmediated, because with regard to the cultural background, the action, the worldview, etc., they [sc. Greek tragedies] are more accessible to them. In addition, there is the curiosity [of the foreign spectator] and the aesthetic expectation towards a foreign art. (Xu 2003, cited in Lin 2010, 262–5)

On the other hand, Xu not only mentions the argument of the international market, which includes profiting from the West's exoticising gaze; he also believes that such 'meaningful adaptations' will enable a productive encounter between Chinese and Western culture, for they would provide 'new nourishment . . . from the cultural roots of the West',[52] so that a new Chinese culture and art form could evolve. Therefore, he advocates 'bilingual versions':

[52] Xu (2003), cited in Lin (2010), 262–4.

> The version at home should take great care how to explain and interpret the historical Western background and the Western culture with regard to the needs of the Chinese spectator. Concerning the version meant to be presented abroad, the problem that has to be solved is how ancient Greek classics can be represented in the form of *xiqu*, so that this art can unfold its attraction for Western spectators. (Xu 2003, cited in Lin 2010, 263)

To summarise: we can identify two different agenda points to be realised by performances of Greek tragedies in China. The first was characteristic of the beginning of a new era after the Cultural Revolution, and the second gained prominence after China gained membership in the World Trade Organization. The first was meant as an experiment to enrich the possibilities of *huaju*, which, following Stanislavsky, featured a realistic-psychological acting style that posed a challenge for the staging of Greek tragedies. By also referring to the aesthetic principles of *xiqu*, the experiment broke fresh ground, thus opening up new approaches for the future – as did the innovative plays by Gao Xingjian, Wang Peigon, Tao Jun, and their productions. The second agenda that advocated the staging of Greek tragedies in the style of *xiqu* did not, and does not, so much address Chinese audiences but continues to look for a successful way to reach out and sell Chinese culture to the world, particularly to Western audiences.

Conclusion

In the context of this chapter only four different non-Western performance cultures could be considered. However, these four suffice to demonstrate that adapting Greek tragedies to specific performance traditions addresses distinct conditions and thus fulfils very particular tasks in each culture, and that these in turn are determined by various sociohistorical situations and contexts. Within the time span of the last forty to fifty years, the conditions and goals for adapting and performing Greek tragedies changed within each of the cultures addressed here. It might seem easy and convenient to explain the frequency of performances of Greek tragedies in Western as well as non-Western cultures over the last decades via the argument of their inherently universal truths and values. However, this argument does not hold up. It instead links back to bygone times, when the assumption of Greek tragedy's universality was aimed at affirming the colonial ideology of Western culture. To acknowledge that the absorption of Greek tragedy into each of these cultures is based on the specific conditions obtaining in them does not devalue Greek tragedy. Rather, it puts today's frequent and widespread adaptations of Greek tragedies into perspective, allowing a better understanding and evaluation of their effect in each case. Yet even today, the terms 'universality' or 'universal' are often applied to Greek tragedy. In order to avoid their pitfalls, Emily Greenwood has introduced the concept of the 'omni-local for Greek and Roman classical texts that circulate widely in different historical and cultural contexts'.[53] She herself lists as a possible objective of this concept that 'a version of cosmopolitanism or universalism is being reintroduced through the prefix *omni*, from the Latin adjective *omnis* (all, any). After all, isn't labelling something "local to all" (one way of construing omni-local) the same as labelling it universal, or timeless?'[54] Despite her own objective, she continues to favour this concept, because 'to label a classic omni-local is to acknowledge its local, historical origins, some of which are untranslatable, while simultaneously crediting it with a strong degree of cross-cultural adaptability'.[55] I could not agree more with this assessment; however, I would advocate replacing the term 'omni-local' with 'pluri-local', as 'omni-local' will always carry the burden of an implied claim to universality. Moreover, I would not restrict the term 'pluri-local' to Greek tragedies and other classical texts but apply it to Shakespeare's, Ibsen's, Chekhov's, or Brecht's plays as well, to name just the most obvious examples that are used and adapted in various ways in many cultures all over the world to diverse purposes and ends. Quite often, they serve at least two different goals: On the one hand, through this form of localisation they are made productive for one's own local content. On the other, performances of such plays at international theatre festivals appear as both a promising and a popular way to successfully present one's own traditional theatre forms – as well as the latest waves of experimental theatre – to international audiences in different parts of the world.[56]

[53] Greenwood (2016), 43. [54] Greenwood (2016), 43. [55] Greenwood (2016), 44.

[56] Still, a question remains that cannot be discussed in this context, namely, why the quality of being pluri-local is attributed exclusively to plays from the Western tradition, and not to traditional or modern plays from countries such as Nigeria, India, China, Japan, and others. This is all the more surprising as acting methods and devices developed within the performance aesthetics of these cultures, partly over hundreds of years, have been productively received by Western directors since the avant-garde movements at the beginning of the twentieth century, and have thus already proved to be pluri-local in a striking manner.

CHAPTER 11

Cultural Identities

Appropriations of Greek Tragedy in Post-Colonial Discourse

Elke Steinmeyer

Post-Colonialism: Key Concepts

Post-colonialism, post-colonial discourse, and post-colonial studies constitute a lens through which the relationship between (former) colonised cultures and their colonisers can be investigated.[1] Stephen Slemon has identified eight subcategories of the umbrella term 'post-colonialism', of which the last is particularly relevant for this study: 'a category of "literary" activity which sprang from a new and welcome political energy'.[2] Slemon's formulation – 'political energy' – will prove to be one of the key factors in this analysis of appropriations or adaptations of Greek tragedy in a post-colonial context.[3] One could classify this specific field of post-colonial writing as part of what Helen Tiffin calls 'canonical counter-discourse', which she describes as follows: 'This strategy … is one in which a post-colonial writer takes up a character or characters, or the basic assumptions of a British canonical text, and unveils those assumptions, subverting the text for post-colonial purposes'.[4] Her definition is not restricted to British

[1] Some critics use the Latin prefix 'post' (meaning: after, behind; cf. Walde and Hofmann 1954, 347–8) in an expanded sense (meaning: concurrent) with the following explanations: '"Post-colonial" as we define it does not mean "post-independence", or "after colonialism". For this would falsely ascribe an end to the colonial process. Post-colonialism, rather, begins from the very first moment of colonial contact' (Ashcroft, Griffiths, and Tiffin 1995, 117) and 'all post-colonial societies are still subject in one way or another to overt or subtle forms of neo-colonial domination, and independence has not solved this problem' (Ashcroft, Griffiths, and Tiffin 1995, 2). Also Gilbert and Tompkins (1996), 2, feel that the 'term – according to a too-rigid etymology – is frequently misunderstood as a temporal concept meaning the time after colonisation has ceased'. For them 'post-colonialism addresses *reactions to* colonialism in a context that is not necessarily determined by temporal constraints'. See also the definition by Forsdick and Murphy (2003), 5, who differentiate between the hyphenated and non-hyphenated spelling and its implications. I use the hyphenated spelling throughout this chapter.

[2] Slemon (1995), 45.

[3] See also Gilbert and Tompkins (1996), 3: 'post-colonial texts embrace a more specifically political aim: that of the continued destabilisation of the cultural and political authority of imperialism'.

[4] Tiffin (1995), 97.

literature only; it can be applied to any other European canonical text as well.

Tiffin's 'canonical counter-discourse' dovetails with another central concept in post-colonial literature, the phenomenon of 'writing back'. In 1982, Salman Rushdie, punning on the title of the *Star Wars* film *The Empire Strikes Back* (1980), coined the phrase 'the Empire writes back to the centre'.[5] What was originally intended to describe the battle for hegemony in space between the Galactic Empire and the Rebel Alliance was then appropriated to describe the literary combat between the former colonies of the British Empire and their former coloniser. Countries, cultures, and literatures, previously marginalised by the dominant imperial centre, rose up and added their own indigenous voices to the prevailing canon. According to the authors of one of the seminal works on post-colonial literature, entitled *The Empire Writes Back* after Rushdie's phrase:

> a characteristic of dominated literatures is an inevitable tendency towards subversion, and a study of the subversive strategies employed by post-colonial writers would reveal both the configuration of domination and the imaginative and creative responses to this condition . . . Writers have [all] rewritten particular works from the English "canon" with a view to restructuring European "realities" in post-colonial terms, not simply by reversing the hierarchical order, but by interrogating the philosophical assumptions on which that order was based.[6]

Post-colonial studies, however, has also been severely criticised for its almost exclusively Anglophone bias and focus on the former British colonies.[7] It is necessary, therefore, to make reference here to its French counterpart, namely Francophone studies. According to Forsdick and Murphy, 'Francophone Studies is engaged in the same intellectual pursuits as Postcolonial Studies, exploring "postcolonial issues" in relation to France and its former colonies.'[8] The term 'Francophone' itself is controversial – it has been debated whether it includes French language and literature in France itself or if it applies to the use of French in all countries

[5] *The Times*, 3 July 1982, 8.

[6] Ashcroft, Griffiths, and Tiffin (1989), 33. Van Weyenberg (2013), xliv–l, similarly discusses 'canonical counter-discourse' and 'writing back' with reference to the same standard theoretical sources, including Gilbert and Tompkins (1996), but arrives at a completely different conclusion, considering Greek tragedy and Shakespeare not as foreign texts, but as part of African cultures: 'The adaptations I look at do not so much "write back" to the texts they adapt as engage with the dominant Eurocentric discourse that has contained these texts' (xlvii).

[7] Forsdick and Murphy (2003), 7; Britton and Syrotinski (2001), 4; Hargreaves and Moura (2007), 307.

[8] Forsdick and Murphy (2003), 7.

and cultures except for France itself.[9] It is strange that, until recently, there has been almost no exchange between scholars in the two fields and little interest from the two sides, especially given the fact that some of the most eminent thinkers in post-colonial studies such as Frantz Fanon, Albert Memmi, and Aimé Césaire were in fact Francophone writers from former French colonies. Francophone studies also deal, at least partly, with the same questions as post-colonial studies (although sometimes reaching different conclusions),[10] but have their own prominent authors such as Édouard Glissant, Patrick Chamoiseau, and Maryse Condé and address specific issues pertaining to the complex relationship between France and the Francophone world.

Another important question which has been vividly and controversially debated, especially among African writers, in the post-colonial context is the question of which language African literature should be written in.[11] The opposing camps were championed by such prominent figures as the Nigerian writer Chinua Achebe, famous for his novel *Things Fall Apart* (1958), and the Kenyan writer Ngũgĩ wa Thiong'o, who first started to write in English but in the middle of the 1970s switched to his mother tongue, Gĩkũyũ. Achebe is advocating a rather pragmatic position when he favours the use of English, despite it being the language of colonisation, as the *lingua franca* worldwide in order to convey African culture globally. He said in 1964: 'Is it right that a man should abandon his mother tongue for someone else's? It looks like a dreadful betrayal and produces a guilty feeling. But for me there is no other choice. I have been given the language and I intend to use it'.[12] He differentiates between a 'national' literature

[9] Forsdick and Murphy (2003), 3, 7. See also Parker (2003), 91, 97; Hargreaves and Moura (2007), 308.

[10] See, for instance, the conflicting interpretations of the term 'exoticism' and 'orientalism' summarised by Forsdick (2003).

[11] Although this debate has been dominated by African Anglophone writers, it has also been thematised among African Francophone writers. Zabus (1991), 2, has taken West African authors as a case study and used the interesting term 'African Europhone Literature'. She quotes (41) the famous statement by the writer Tchicaya U Tam'si from the French Congo: 'La langue française me colonise: je la colonise à mon tour', or 'the French language colonises me: I colonise it in turn' (my translation).

[12] Achebe (1975), 62. Achebe's position is supported by Zabus (1991), iv: 'Poets and novelists might venture a few vernacular terms in the interest of local colour. But the vast majority of early African Europhone writers in the middle of this century felt bound to write in correct, if possible stylish, standard French, English or Portuguese, the main reason being that their works were targeted at a Western audience and at a tiny readership of highly educated African intellectuals.'

written in English and an 'ethnic' literature written in one of the indigenous languages. Ngũgĩ wa Thiong'o severely criticises this compromising opinion in his book *Decolonising the Mind* (1986). For him, the use of any of the European languages reinscribes the pattern of colonialism. He promotes the use of an African writer's mother tongue in the same way as any other writer worldwide would do, which would also lead to a more normal and less conflict-ridden relationship between an African mother tongue speaker and the English language:

> With that harmony between himself, his language and his environment as his starting point, he can learn other languages and even enjoy the positive humanistic, democratic and revolutionary elements in other people's literatures and cultures without any complexes about his own language, his own self, his environment.[13]

This debate also imposes certain limitations to the scope of this chapter: there is no doubt a multitude of adaptations in indigenous African languages which remain underrepresented as a result of cultural politics and the ensuing inequalities between local and national literatures and world literature, including limited knowledge of African languages and literatures by classics scholars. As these restrictions apply to myself as well, my study will focus only on Anglophone and Francophone adaptations of Greek tragedy.

Appropriations or adaptations of Greek tragedy in post-colonial discourse can be found globally. The use of Greek tragedy by Spanish and Portuguese writers in Latin America, for instance, would warrant more research than I am aware of.[14] In my current study, however, I will focus on post-colonial discourse in Africa and the African diaspora. This chapter will examine selected adaptations of Greek tragedy by mainly African authors and show how the concept of post-colonial discourse expands and changes from the original African context into Caribbean and Afro-American countries in the framework of the so-called First Diaspora and lastly into the suburbs in the countries of the former colonisers as part of the so-called Second Diaspora.

[13] Ngũgĩ wa Thiong'o (1986), 28–9.

[14] A recent attempt to address this shortcoming has been undertaken by Rosa Andújar, the organiser of the international conference 'Greeks and Romans on the Latin American Stage' (London, 24–6 June 2014), with the conference proceedings in Andújar and Nikoloutsos (2020). For an earlier major treatment of the reception of Greek drama in the Americas, see Bosher, Macintosh, McConnell, and Rankine (2015).

Africa

On the African continent, one can observe two geographical hubs where the reception of Greek tragedy has been particularly prominent. One is made up of the countries in West Africa and of some in Central Africa, stretching from Côte d'Ivoire over Ghana, Nigeria, Cameroon, and Gabon to the French Congo. The other hub is South Africa. Each of them features long-established famous authors, whose adaptations of Greek tragedy reached worldwide acclaim during the twentieth century. Perhaps the best-known names among them are the Nigerian Nobel Prize winner (1986) Wole Soyinka, who fuses in his *Bacchae of Euripides* (1973) elements from Greek religion and his native Yoruba culture,[15] and the South African playwright Athol Fugard, who wrote several adaptations of Greek myth during apartheid. His play *The Island*, workshopped together with the actors John Kani and Winston Ntshona ('The Serpent Players') and performed in 1973, is an adaptation of Sophocles' *Antigone* set on Robben Island, South Africa's notorious prison island, where Nelson Mandela spent twenty-seven years of his life. Two fictional inmates rehearse and perform Sophocles' play in their cell as a metatheatrical device, i.e. as 'a play within a play'. During his own imprisonment, Nelson Mandela himself played the role of Creon in a Christmas production of Sophocles' *Antigone* staged by the prisoners on Robben Island at the end of the 1960s.[16] Most scholars classify *The Island* as protest literature, because of its implied criticism of the political situation in South Africa at the time.[17]

Political agendas have been in the foreground also for later generations of African writers, who wrote after independence or – in the case of South Africa – after the end of apartheid. It is interesting to observe that, in these adaptations of Greek tragedy, the focus on political issues dominates other approaches or concerns such as gender or psychology, which are only occasionally dealt with.[18] This might also account for the notable interest in certain ancient plays which prevail in the African adaptations. Although

[15] For a post-colonial interpretation of the play, see Gilbert and Tompkins (1996), 39–41.

[16] Brink (1999).

[17] For a deviating opinion, see Mackay (1989), who argues that the term 'protest literature' oversimplifies the complexity of Fugard's play. She prefers Fugard's own term 'theatre of defiance' (146, 158–9) and elaborates in her article numerous links between Sophocles' and Fugard's plays.

[18] Cf. van Weyenberg (2013), xi: 'Rather than emphasizing Greek tragedy as a metaphysical or existential genre, the playwrights I discuss understand it as fundamentally political.'

African authors cover a fair spectrum of tragedies (including *Oedipus Rex*, *Trojan Women*, *Alcestis*),[19] clear preference is given to three female characters: Antigone, Medea, and Electra. A few representative examples for each of them will be presented in the following sections.

French Congo: Antigone

Within a post-colonial context, Sophocles' *Antigone* must have a special resonance among African people. The conflict between Antigone, who stands up and dies for the rights of the individual and of tradition, and Creon, who represents the official law and the dominating power of the state, mirrors the basic conflict between the indigenous colonised people and the European colonisers, who enforced their imported laws, culture, and self-invented superiority over the already existing traditions, customs, languages of the native population, often in an ignorant, disrespectful, and brutal manner. In this context, Antigone becomes a figure with whom to identify, and a sort of freedom fighter, who does not compromise on her ideals and values. In addition to Fugard, other African writers have engaged with this tragic figure in well-known plays, including Kamau Brathwaite (Ghana/Caribbean) in *Odale's Choice* (1967) and Femi Òsòfisan (Nigeria) in *Tègònni: An African Antigone* (1999). I shall focus on the play *Noces posthumes de Santigone* (1988)[20] by the Francophone writer Sylvain Bemba (French Congo or Congo-Brazzaville), because it seems particularly apt to demonstrate several key concepts of post-colonial discourse's engagement with Greek tragedy.

The action of Bemba's complex and multilayered play takes place in two locations: in Birmingham, England, and in Vangu, the capital of a fictional African republic called 'Amandla', which means 'power' or 'strength' in isiZulu and other Nguni languages.[21] According to Kevin Wetmore, Bemba is 'firmly setting the play in the postcolonial, postindependent

[19] Cf., for instance, the Nigerian Ola Rotimi's 1971 *The Gods Are Not to Blame* (*Oedipus*); the Nigerian Femi Òsòfisan's 2004 *The Women of Owu* (*Trojan Women*); and the Ghanaian Efua Sutherland's 1967 *Edufa* (*Alcestis*). For a comprehensive, introductory overview of the most important adaptations in Africa, see Dominik (2007), 117–23. For detailed discussion of a selection of plays not included or only briefly mentioned in this chapter, see McDonald (1999).

[20] In 1990, the play was translated into English by Ubu Repertory Theatre in New York under the title *Black Wedding Candles for Blessed Antigone*. I have discussed extensively the complex word plays in the French name Santigone (*sainte* + Antigone and / or *sang* + Antigone) and their implications for the overall interpretation of the play, in Steinmeyer (2010a), 137–9, and have incorporated this ambiguity in the title of that article.

[21] For the political background of the word 'amandla', see Steinmeyer (2010a), 124.

troubled political and economic situation in which many African nations have found themselves'.[22] Four expatriates from Amandla, including three young women, Dorothy Mela, Margaret Bintu, and Melissa Yadé, and an elderly man, John Abiola, live in Birmingham. The girls compete for the leading role in an upcoming production of Sophocles' *Antigone*. Sophocles' original confrontation between Antigone and Creon (*Antigone*, 384–525) is performed as a condensed version in a metatheatrical fashion as 'a play within a play' in Act 2, sc. 5 of Bemba's play. Bemba uses the situation of the expatriates in order to explore the post-colonial concepts of hybridity and assimilation. Cultural hybridity is evident in their English names, the multicultural outfits and flat decor of Dorothy and Margaret, and the list of exclusively European characters which Dorothy has performed onstage so far.[23] Assimilation is illustrated in the character of Abiola.[24] He is married to an Englishwoman, but seems to be neither integrated into English society nor accepted by the female expatriates. He is a typical example of what Frantz Fanon (1952) and Albert Memmi (1957) would describe as a colonised black who rejects his own culture in favour of that of the white coloniser, which he tries to adopt and which results in his being rejected by both cultures, since he has betrayed the one and will never be white enough for the other.[25] The fact that he still uses the old colonial name 'Golden Nugget' for his home country is a sign of his neo-colonial outlook, a condition in which the colonised individual, even after independence, still carries his old mind-set into the new nation, as if nothing had changed.[26] The name 'Golden Nugget' is reminiscent of 'Gold Coast', the colonial name for Ghana. Ghana was the first African country to obtain independence in 1957 and the first to fail in an attempt to establish democracy.[27]

Melissa Yadé, who wins the role of Antigone, is drawn more and more into her stage character and eventually completely identifies with it and calls herself 'Antigone', until the very last scene when she breaks with her role and returns to her own name. She is the fiancée of the political leader

[22] Wetmore (2002), 205.

[23] Hybridity is also evident in the use of European music within the African framework of the play: see Steinmeyer (2010a), 127–8.

[24] For a different understanding of the term 'assimilation' in the context of France's colonial policy and in Francophone studies, see Murphy (2003), 221–3.

[25] In colloquial terms, he would be labelled a 'coconut' or 'Oreo', being black on the outside and white on the inside.

[26] According to Murphy (2003), 223, 'France [was] becoming a neo-colonial power that continued to dominate its former possessions economically and militarily.'

[27] For a more detailed historical background, see Steinmeyer (2010a), 124.

of Amandla, Titus Saint-Just Bund,[28] a selfless man[29] who tries to govern the country according to the motto 'essayer de faire une politique juste avec les moyens justes', or 'strive for a politics of justice through just means'.[30] Titus is assassinated during a performance of *Antigone* in Birmingham, and Melissa, who has obtained permission from the church to marry him posthumously, returns as Antigone to Amandla to ensure his burial so that his memory is preserved. On leaving the country again, she dies when her airplane crashes into the ocean. Bemba has introduced into the cast the traditional African figure of a *griot*,[31] thereby placing the European myth into the framework of African storytelling. The *griot*'s primary function is to preserve history, and here he will ensure that the memories of Melissa, Titus, and Amandla will survive.

Bemba has modelled his character Titus on the historical figure of Thomas Sankara, the leader of Burkina Faso (former Upper Volta). Sankara symbolises for Bemba the ideal political leader, who tried in vain to turn his country into a model state but was assassinated in 1987 by the opposition. In the same way as the *griot* in his play, Bemba preserves the memory of Sankara and his failed attempt to create a post-colonial African utopia.

South Africa: Electra

While Sophocles' *Antigone* has inspired modern adaptations throughout Africa, the reception of the Electra myth remains, as far as I know, restricted to South Africa. I have discovered an impressive number of such adaptations by South African playwrights, although not all of them deal with post-colonial issues.[32] Here, I have included three of them which

[28] Titus is a reference to the Roman emperor by the same name (79–81 CE), who was very popular and fought against corruption. Saint-Just evokes Louis Antoine de Saint-Just, a leading member of the French Revolution who was executed together with Maximilien de Robespierre in 1794. For a detailed discussion of the different elements of this name, see Steinmeyer (2010a), 135–6.

[29] Cf. Goff and Simpson (2011), 332: 'His selflessness and dedication have marked him for death.' It would be helpful if Goff and Simpson's work were contextualised more fully from an African perspective, and used the original French text rather than the English translation.

[30] Bemba (1995), 29.

[31] A *griot* is a sort of storyteller and somebody who communicates messages, for instance from the king or chief to the people or from anybody to the audience. He is also somebody who transmits history. He is particularly important in West African culture. For further details and references, see Steinmeyer (2010a), 123.

[32] I leave out Fugard's play *Orestes* (1978) for a number of reasons, mainly because it focuses on Orestes and not on Electra and therefore is only partially relevant to my discussion. The same goes for Tug Yourgrau's play *The Song of Jacob Zulu* (1993), which also deals with an incident during

have a common political background,[33] namely the situation in South Africa after the abolition of the apartheid regime in 1994 and the work of the Truth and Reconciliation Commission (TRC), which was established in 1995 in order to try and come to terms with the past and to find a way forward into the future. In this process, countless traumata from the past needed to be addressed: hatred, pain, the desire for revenge, coping with the murder of loved ones – that is, feelings comparable with those which feature so prominently in the ancient Electra myth. This could explain why this particular character has appealed so strongly to South African audiences. The story of Electra, who can probably be considered as the embodiment of these negative and destructive feelings, offers the possibility to explore alternative scenarios.

The first to undertake this approach was the Cape Town producer Mark Fleishman. In his play *In the City of Paradise* (1998), he questions the foundation on which the TRC was based: can disclosure of the truth lead to forgiveness and reconciliation?[34] By creating his version of the Electra myth, he draws on the four main ancient sources: Aeschylus' *Choephoroi* (*Libation Bearers*), Sophocles' and Euripides' *Electra* plays and Euripides' *Orestes*. Fleishman makes extensive use of so-called workshop theatre, a theatrical genre which emerged in South Africa at the beginning of the 1970s and which can be considered in itself as a post-colonial reaction to the established 'white' theatre world. 'Workshop theatre' is a collaborative enterprise: a play is created by a group, not by a single author; it is an amalgamation of different performance forms (text, music, dance, body language); it incorporates allusions to South African townships and features a multiracial cast.[35] As Lorna Hardwick observes: 'workshop theatre has moved from being a protest and consciousness-raising art-form to one that is actively reconstructing and revising cultural relationships in the new

apartheid and concentrates on the character of Orestes. Mervyn McMurtry's (et al.) play *Family* (2008) does not deal with politics at all, but uses Aeschylus' *Oresteia* and Euripides' *Iphigenia in Aulis* in order to experiment with various performance styles (dance, musical, cabaret) and to explore the concept of a dysfunctional family from various perspectives comparable to modern soap operas. See Steinmeyer (2010b) for a full discussion.

[33] Van Zyl Smit (2010) provides additional insights into these three plays together with some more background information on the Truth and Reconciliation Commission.

[34] For a detailed discussion of the play and more background about the TRC, see Mezzabotta (2000) and Steinmeyer (2007); cf. van Weyenberg (2013), 99: 'perpetrators were asked to reveal what they had done and state the facts, but whether or not they would be given amnesty did not depend on any expression of remorse or guilt; amnesty was linked solely to truth, not remorse'. See also van Weyenberg (2013), 129 with n. 96.

[35] For a detailed discussion of the characteristics of 'Workshop Theatre' and its background, see Steinmeyer (2007), 104, 107, and esp. Fleishman (1990, 1997).

South Africa'.[36] Fleishman's most significant innovation is the end of the play, where he explicitly links the myth with the TRC by having Electra and Orestes stand trial for the murder of Clytemnestra. Fleishman explores the situation from the viewpoint of Clytemnestra's parents, taking his cue from Euripides' portrayal of Clytemnestra's father Tyndareus in his *Orestes*. The parents hope for justice for the murder of their daughter and are devastated when they hear that Orestes and Electra have been given amnesty. While the siblings look forward to a new life, their grandparents feel forsaken by the justice system and leave the stage disillusioned and without forgiveness or reconciliation. Their position is representative of countless South African people who were not able to forgive the deeds of the perpetrators despite the TRC hearings.[37]

In his play *Electra* (2000), the Durban producer Mervyn McMurtry used a postmodern approach in order to explore the question of truth. The fact that truth is not a monolithic concept and that there is no single truth illustrates the dilemma with which the TRC was often faced: there was more than one version of the same story, and it was not always possible to establish the 'real' truth. Each character in his play claims the truth for themselves so that multiple truths exist concurrently. McMurtry uses the same ancient sources as Fleishman with additional material from Euripides' *Hecabe* and *Andromache*, but the plot follows mainly Sophocles' text. Like Fleishman, he workshopped the play together with a multiracial cast. In terms of structure, he has added a prologue which takes place six days after the killings of Clytemnestra and Aegisthus – the play itself is told as a sort of flashback. The prologue is spoken by a forensic pathologist who gives a medical report based on the autopsy of Clytemnestra's corpse. Under the apartheid regime in South Africa, medical reports with questionable findings were common practice. All of the characters, including the chorus, suffer from various forms of post-traumatic stress disorder as a result of the violence they have witnessed or have been exposed to.[38] McMurtry pays special attention to the role of women as victims of male violence. He replaces the choral odes with testimonies from the TRC and media reports about the atrocities in Bosnia-Herzegovina, thus making the experiences both relevant for the situation in South Africa and at the same time universal. His play ends in a multilingual Platonic *aporia* with the words 'I do not know', spoken in

[36] Hardwick (2007a), 50. [37] Cf. van Weyenberg (2008), 38, 41.

[38] For a detailed discussion of the various forms of post-traumatic stress disorder and the use of postmodern concepts in the production, see Steinmeyer (2009).

various languages such as English, Afrikaans, isiXhosa, and Greek. He shows a society whose foundations have been shaken and confused, a traumatised society in need of redefining and consolidating itself.

Yaël Farber also makes explicit references to the TRC hearings in her play *Molora* (2003), the seSotho word for 'ash'.[39] The setting of her play is reminiscent of the town and church halls around the country in which these hearings were conducted. Clytemnestra must account for the murder of Agamemnon before her children and a chorus which consists of traditional Xhosa women wrapped in blankets, depicted as TRC commissioners of sorts. During the interrogation, various kinds of torture are mentioned or even re-enacted, such as the so-called wet bag or black bag method, which was one of the means under apartheid to extract information from a suspect, and which Clytemnestra inflicted on Electra in order to obtain information about Orestes' whereabouts. However, Farber offers an alternative solution to the traditional ending of the myth: Clytemnestra pleads with her children not to kill her, and, as a result, Orestes is unable to go through with the deed. Electra tries to kill her mother, but is overpowered by the women of the chorus. Ultimately the siblings crawl towards their mother and help her to get up. The cycle of vengeance has been broken.

Farber subverts the original myth even further by rooting the play firmly in Xhosa culture. Orestes' return is described as the return of a young Xhosa man after the initiation ceremony into manhood. He also wears the typical traditional clothing. The invocation of Agamemnon's spirit by Orestes and Electra bears many similarities to the ancestor cult in Xhosa culture, including the burning of a special herb and the spitting of sorghum beer on the grave. Clytemnestra's snake dream from Aeschylus' *Libation Bearers* is also linked to the ancestor cult, in which the ancestor is believed to reappear in the form of a snake. The choral odes have been replaced by the traditional Xhosa 'split-tone-singing', whereby one person sings two melodies at the same time through a special vocal technique. This singing is performed by women only and is accompanied by traditional musical instruments. Despite the strong local connotation, Farber tries to create a universal message through the title of the play with its connotation of human mortality.

These African writers all use Greek tragedy as a vehicle to engage with the politics of their time, to subvert European canonical texts by fusing them with elements from their own indigenous African cultures, to

[39] seSotho is one of the eleven official languages in South Africa. For a detailed discussion of the play, see Steinmeyer (2018).

incorporate various concepts of post-colonial discourse as outlined above through the ancient myths, and to 'write back' to their (former) colonisers.[40]

The Caribbean

The slave trade during the sixteenth to the nineteenth centuries from Africa into various places in the world, especially to North and South America and the Caribbean, led to the enforced displacement of millions of African people from their homelands,[41] mainly from Western Africa, into foreign overseas countries. This form of slave trade is referred to by the term 'Middle Passage' which designates a geographical triangle across the Atlantic Ocean between Europe (from where the slave ships embarked), Africa (from where the slaves were transported) and America (where the slaves were sold for goods to be transported back to Europe). The African diaspora is usually classified by scholars as a typical example of the 'classical, victim diaspora – the idea of dispersal following a traumatic event in the homeland to two or more foreign destinations'.[42] It has also been labelled the 'first' African diaspora in contrast to the 'second' one, which will be discussed later.[43] Slaves were used to a great extent for plantation labour – a topic to which Afro-American writers turn time and again – and had to negotiate a new identity, after having lost their freedom and homeland, under new deplorable living conditions.

The Caribbean itself is a complex construct whose constituent islands have different relationships to their former coloniser, France. Martinique is a *département d'outre-mer*, while 'Haiti was post-colonial decades before much of the rest of the world was colonial'.[44] Its colonial past differs from other former colonies: 'For the Caribbean was the site of a particularly brutal and traumatic form of colonialism, beginning with the genocide of the indigenous populations and sustained by the middle passage and the slave trade.'[45] Against this backdrop, the meaning of current post-colonial concepts such as 'identity' needs to be redefined: 'identity, a touchstone of

[40] Hardwick (2007a), 52, suggests additional reasons for the appropriation of Greek tragedy for African counter-discourse: 'the usefulness of Greek drama as a field for experiment by African theatre, similarities between Greek and African . . . theatre, the importance of myth in Greek and African culture, the nature of the themes and debates in tragedy, the difference between the Athenian *arche* and modern imperialism and the mélange of cultures in the ancient Aegean and Eastern Mediterranean from which Athenian culture emerged'.

[41] According to Cohen (2008), 3, some ten million African people became victims of the slave trade.

[42] Cohen (2008), 2. [43] Cohen (2008), 3. [44] Dubois (2003), 34.

[45] McCusker (2003), 112.

postcolonial discourse generally, becomes a particularly obsessive theme in a society which has no continuous link to a pre-colonial era, and in which transportation has shattered any sense of a permanent or essential selfhood'.[46]

Most importantly, the Caribbean, being a melting pot for European, African, Asian, and Middle Eastern influences plus indigenous/native cultures,[47] gave rise to important conceptual developments such as the *négritude* movement initiated by Aimé Césaire (who mentions the term for the first time in 1939 in his *Cahier d'un retour au pays natal*), Léopold Sédar Senghor (the later president of Senegal), and Léon-Gontran Damas,[48] and new concepts such as 'creolisation' and *créolité*, with Édouard Glissant being probably the most important theorist of *créolité* and another related Caribbean concept, *antillanité*.

Although the Caribbean reception of classics in general is widespread and multifaceted,[49] culminating in the towering work *Omeros* (1990) by Nobel Prize winner Derek Walcott (1992), which is loosely based on Homer's *Odyssey*, the reception of Greek tragedy in this region is almost non-existent. Walcott's subsequent play *The Odyssey: A Stage Version* (1993) can hardly be considered as an adaptation of Greek tragedy, since – as the title indicates – it is based on Homer's epic poem.[50] Some scholars may claim that Kamau Brathwaite's play *Odale's Choice* (1962) should be viewed as a Caribbean adaptation of Sophocles' *Antigone*, because Brathwaite, who was born in Barbados and spent the largest part of his life there (and in Jamaica), is Barbadian and Caribbean rather than African. This is problematic, however, because Brathwaite appears to have also spent eight years in Ghana,[51] where the play was created and produced for the first time by Ghanaian schoolchildren. With the exception of some Creole expressions in the text, the play is firmly rooted in an unspecified

[46] McCusker (2003), 112.

[47] E.g. Carib, which is still present in our day in Dominica, and words from Arawak, Taino, etc., which are present in the languages of the modern Caribbean.

[48] According to Britton and Syrotinski (2001), 1, *négritude* is 'the first francophone attempt to "theorise" black culture'. See also Chapter 6 by Adam Lecznar in this volume.

[49] For a thorough introduction into various receptions of classics in the Caribbean, see Greenwood (2005, 2010).

[50] For a detailed discussion of the play, see McConnell (2013), 134–54, who also mentions that Walcott directed an operatic version of the play, *The Burial at Thebes*, an adaptation of Sophocles' *Antigone* by his friend Seamus Heaney in 2008 in London (McConnell 2013, 109, n. 10). See also Friedman (2007).

[51] See Gibbs (2007), 63 with n. 10.

African context.[52] The simple fact that it was restaged nine years later, in 1971, after Brathwaite's return to the Caribbean, in Trinidad by the Trinidad Theatre Workshop (founded by Walcott in 1959) does, in my opinion, not warrant labelling it 'Caribbean'.

A rare example of a 'real' Caribbean adaptation of Greek tragedy can be found in the plays by the Haitian playwright Félix Morisseau-Leroy, *Antigòn an Kreyòl* (*Antigone in Créole*, 1953), *Wa Kreyon* (*King Creon*, 1978), and *Pèp La* (*The People*, 1978).[53] Morisseau-Leroy pursued here a similar goal to that of Ngũgĩ wa Thiong'o in Kenya: he wanted to create a literature written in Haitian Créole and therefore substituted in his plays the official language French by the indigenous Creole language and the official Catholic religion by the pagan animistic-naturalistic Vodou cult.[54] The setting of Morisseau-Leroy's *Antigòn* is a *péristil*, the traditional place for Vodou ceremonies, which is an open space with a roof and central pillar.[55] Antigone and Haemon are saved at the end by, and become the children of, the Vodou serpent spirit Danbala (or Damballa), which means that they have become ancestors. It is very likely that the Creon figure in this play has been modelled on the Haitian dictator François Duvalier (called 'Papa Doc'), who had been a classmate of Morisseau-Leroy.[56] Both were part of a movement which wanted to revive and preserve African roots as an essential part of a national Haitian identity. Fradinger characterises the play *Antigòn* as 'a *Haitian historical drama* in the language of its people'.[57] Through his use of language and by fusing elements from his indigenous culture into the original Greek play, Morisseau-Leroy appropriates and subverts the European canon and 'writes back' to the colonial powers in his unique way.[58]

[52] Cf. Goff and Simpson (2007), 219–44, esp. 236: 'both the time and the place of the first production of Brathwaite's play imply a critique of postcolonial Ghana'. Wetmore (2002), 177, feels that '*Odale's Choice* is arguably just as much a Caribbean play as it is an African one', although in his discussion the African elements clearly outweigh the Caribbean ones. See also Gibbs (2007), 65, 67.

[53] Fradinger (2011) offers an excellent discussion of the play *Antigòn* with background information on the role of Creole and Vodou in Haiti. Morisseau-Leroy also wrote a poem entitled *Antigone* in 1972: Fradinger (2011), 128.

[54] Fradinger (2011), 131, defines Créole as follows: 'Creole's mixture of African, Indian, and European languages was the lingua franca created by slaves to communicate among themselves and, thus, to make revolt possible.'

[55] Fradinger (2011), 132.

[56] According to Fradinger (2011), 129, Duvalier had studied and practised Vodou and considered himself a Vodou priest.

[57] Fradinger (2011), 128.

[58] Gibbs (2007), 67, mentions a production of the play *Antigòn an Kreyòl* in an English translation in Ghana in 1963 during Félix Morisseau-Leroy's stay there.

Afro-American

The curious unpopularity of Greek tragedy among Caribbean writers is evident also among Afro-American writers, who seem in general to favour Latin authors and Homer over the tragic plays. The reception of Greek tragedy is not always a straightforward matter.[59] There are, however, some works which illustrate some of the issues which are important for the descendants of the 'First Diaspora' victims.[60] One of these examples is the play *The Darker Face of the Earth* by Rita Dove. There are several versions of this play, since over the years Dove undertook substantial revisions and changes of her original version of 1979.[61] She transposes the plot of Sophocles' *Oedipus Rex* 'into a plantation setting in South Carolina in the 1820s to 1840s'[62] and into the white master–black slave constellation in the American South. While cotton plantation labour, slavery, racial segregation, and miscegenation are recurring topics in Afro-American writing, Dove undercuts the conventional relationship between master and slave in an unusual manner. Whereas it is traditionally the white master who sexually abuses the female black slaves, here it is the white mistress Amelia who has taken one of the male black slaves, Hector, as her lover. Their relationship results in the birth of the baby boy Augustus. After a failed attempt by Amelia's husband Louis to kill the baby, Augustus is sent away, sold to a sea captain and returns as an adult man, killing his biological father unknowingly on the way, and equally unknowingly engages in a sexual relationship with his biological mother. At the end, Augustus, who has become a leader of a slave revolt, following the model of the famous Haitian (Slave) Revolution in 1797[63] and the revolt on the slave ship *Amistad* in 1839,[64] kills his stepfather, and his mother commits suicide.[65] In the first published edition of the play, Augustus too died at

59 For instance, Cook and Tatum (2010), 135–40, 148–52, refer to a free adaptation of Sophocles' *Oedipus Rex* by Jessie Fauset in the form of a novel entitled *The Chinaberry Tree* (1931) and also to Countee Cullen's *The Medea*, an unfinished and unperformed adaptation of Euripides' *Medea* (1936).

60 Wetmore (2003) discusses a multitude of adaptations, but only a few are relevant in the context of post-colonial discourse.

61 The play was first published in 1994 and was performed for the first time in 1996: see Goff and Simpson (2007), 135. I am grateful to an anonymous CUP reader for pointing out to me that Dove also published a third edition of the play in 2000.

62 Cook and Tatum (2010), 311.

63 According to Dubois (2003), 27, this was 'indeed the only successful slave revolt in the history of the Americas'.

64 For more historical background, see Cook and Tatum (2010), 337.

65 The protagonists meet different endings of their lives in the various versions of the play.

the end, but in the second, 1996 edition Augustus is carried away triumphantly – although there are suggestions that the rest of his life will be overshadowed by sorrow and that his success will be short-lived.[66] As Dove remarked in an interview: 'Augustus does live at the end of the new version; it's just not a life worth living . . . the revolutionaries think that he did what he was supposed to do and he's a hero. But what kind of hero is that, who's just realized that he's lost everything that could make him happy?'[67] Dove also successfully undercuts the literary trope of the 'tragic mulatto' by having a male rather than a female character as the tragic hero of the play. Through the history of other slave characters in the play, common traumata from the historical past, such as the enforced separation of slave families, are explored.[68] Dove elides some of the more recognisably Greek elements from the original play, such as the question of human destiny and the relationship between gods and mankind, to foreground issues which are relevant for black Americans: questions of hybrid identity,[69] race, skin colour, and the consequences of the enforced displacement of their forefathers from their native continent, such as the situation of black slaves in a white society, their desire for freedom, and their ambivalent feelings towards their masters. Thus she transforms Sophocles' original tragic hero into a mulatto Oedipus in the diaspora.

Theatre-for-Development

The international theatre world recently witnessed a trend towards moving theatre culture out of its traditional urban space not only into the 'Off' and 'Fringe' scene (such as in New York's off-Broadway or off-off-Broadway theatres) but much further: into the suburbs, the ghettos, the slums, the shanty towns. This move can be understood in a literal and in a metaphoric sense, both of which have different implications within the framework of post-colonial discourse as will be illustrated below.

It has become fashionable for theatre producers, directors, and theatre companies to literally move theatre productions out of the cities, the traditional centres of high culture, to the – often industrial – outskirts, the margins of the city and the habitats of the underprivileged. Treu has

[66] See Cook and Tatum (2010), 335; Goff and Simpson (2007), 155–6.

[67] Pereira (2003), 148–9. I am grateful to an anonymous CUP reader for pointing out to me the crucial change between the 1994 and the 1996 editions.

[68] See Goff and Simpson (2007), 147–8.

[69] The post-colonial topos of hybridity has been discussed earlier in connection with Sylvain Bemba's play *Noces posthumes de Santigone*.

described the challenges of this postmodern, 'de-centralising' experiment as follows: 'those outskirts are often richly populated, but culturally poor. Their inhabitants seldom go to the theatre, or artistic events, as their difficult economic conditions do not allow them to.'[70] As Treu remarks, such contexts are associated with 'harsh social problems – unemployment, crime, drug dealing, immigration conflicts, violence, riots, and street fighting with policemen'.[71] Most of these problems are universal and can be found to the same extent in the squatter camps of South Africa, in the Projects of New York, in the *banlieues* of Paris, in the *bassifondi* of Naples or Milan. In his book *When People Play People* (1993), the South African author, playwright, and director Zakes Mda describes an earlier similar approach called 'Theatre-for-Development'.[72] In his opinion, theatre can be used to remedy the shortfalls of the current dysfunctional communication media, which focus on the urban population and neglect the needs of people in rural areas. He says: 'Communication technologies need to be decentralised and located among the rural people, who form the majority of the population in African countries. This will give the rural population access not only to the messages produced by others, but to the means to produce and distribute their own messages.'[73] In order to achieve this goal, theatre needs to reach out to its intended audience, in this case the rural population, and involve the spectators in the process of creating 'messages' (to use Mda's terminology) through plays. This can be achieved by going out into the rural areas, by developing awareness of the existing problems, by involving the people in the theatre production, and by 'integrating indigenous and popular systems of communication that already exist in the rural areas'.[74] Theatre production is no longer a top-down enterprise, but it becomes a collaborative exercise between the theatre company, the director, and the audience. Mda refers here to a 'theatre-for-development process' in seven steps, which have been outlined by Ross Kidd:[75]

(a) building a relationship with members of the community and motivating them to participate;
(b) working with them to study their situation and identify issues for in-depth analysis;
(c) learning the indigenous forms of cultural expression of the area, and utilising them for the theatre-for-development activity;

[70] Treu (2009), 83. [71] Treu (2009), 96.
[72] 'Theatre-for-Development' is a theatre practice which evolved after 1950, mainly in developing countries, as an educational tool in order to empower underprivileged communities.
[73] Mda (1993), 1. [74] Mda (1993), 2. [75] Mda (1993), 70; Kidd (1985), 182.

(d) exploring through drama, dance, and song (coupled with discussion) ways of deepening the understanding of the issues and looking for solutions;
(e) organising a performance as a way of bringing the community together and agreeing on solutions and action;
(f) discussing with the villagers ways in which this short-term activity could be continued by villagers on their own (follow-up);
(g) evaluating the whole experience and drawing out the lessons learned.

Mda's 'Theatre-for Development' draws on Augusto Boal's 'Theater-of-the-Oppressed' concept, which also involves underprivileged audiences such as 'peasants, workers, or villagers' in Latin America.[76] Boal's concept comprises four stages, of which the third stage, entitled 'The theatre as language', is particularly interesting. He defines it as follows: 'The spectator is encouraged to intervene in the action, abandoning his condition of object and assuming fully the role of subject.'[77] Boal further subdivides the third stage into three degrees. The last degree, called 'Forum Theater', resembles to some extent Mda's interaction with the audience. According to Boal: 'The spectators intervene directly in the dramatic action and act',[78] which means that he gives the direct participation of the audience in the creative process a greater scope than Mda does. Both concepts can be seen as manifestations of the umbrella term 'Applied Theatre'. According to Prentki and Preston, 'Applied Theatre' describes 'a broad set of theatrical practices and creative processes that take participants and audiences beyond the scope of conventional, mainstream theatre into the realm of a theatre that is responsive to ordinary people and their stories, local settings and priorities'.[79] They further identify some other essential characteristics of Applied Theatre, namely that it takes place in 'informal spaces, in non-theatre venues in a variety of geographical and social settings'[80] and that it involves in most cases the audience and participants in the work.

Although Mda's and Kidd's findings are based on African theatre in a rural African environment, many of their observations are valid for the European urban theatre scene as well. Many of the inhabitants of the suburbs in Europe are immigrants, often from the African former colonies, which adds another range of questions and problems to the existing paradigm. Martina Treu has discussed some Italian theatre productions

[76] Boal (2000), 126. [77] Boal (2000), 132. [78] Boal (2000), 16.
[79] Prentki and Preston (2009), 9. [80] Prentki and Preston (2009), 9.

and also an Italian–Senegalese coproduction of Aristophanes' comedies, especially *Ploutos* (*Wealth*), performed in the *bassifondi*[81] of various Italian cities such as Milan, Rome, and Naples.[82] She thinks that this particular play has been a success in 'industrial countries . . . and the so-called "post-colonial world"' because it 'deals with problems such as wealth, supplies and resources',[83] which are particularly relevant for the people living in these industrial suburbs. The approach used by the Italian directors is very similar to that of the African 'Theatre-for-Development': they work together primarily with young people from the Italian slums, incorporate their respective 'typical forms of expression, slang and music',[84] and allow them to bring in their own experiences and backgrounds, thereby making the production much more relevant for them than a conventional one would have been.

South Africa: Medea

This trend is not restricted to adaptations of Greek comedy only. A good example of an adaptation of Greek tragedy which has been taken to the underprivileged outskirts is Brett Bailey's South African adaptation of Euripides' play *Medea*, which Bailey spells *medEia* (2005). It was performed by the South African theatre company Third World Bunfight, whose director Brett Bailey is. Their mission statement is: 'Our main focus areas are the post-colonial situation in Africa, and historical and contemporary relations between Africa and the West.'[85] Third World Bunfight also reaches out to people from underprivileged areas and countries, as stated on their website: 'We have a strong orientation towards fostering and exposing the talents of both performers and non-performers from disadvantaged and previously disadvantaged communities.'[86]

The director moves the location of this play to a squatter camp (or shanty town) in 'a post-colonial African wasteland'.[87] The actual place of the production outside Cape Town was reminiscent of the one in the movie *uCarmen eKhayelitsha*, an adaptation of Bizet's opera *Carmen* in the

[81] In Italian, the terms *bassifondi* or *quartieri bassi* are more or less the equivalent to the English slums. They also imply a connotation of the low social status of the population and of some ongoing criminal activity. There is another similar Italian term, namely *baraccopoli*, which designates an informal settlement or shanty town. I would like to thank my former postdoctoral student Dr Francesco Lupi (UKZN and University of Verona) for providing me with this information.

[82] She also mentions some productions of Aristophanes' comedies in South Africa: Treu (2009), 85–7.

[83] Treu (2009), 84. [84] Treu (2009), 88. [85] www.thirdworldbunfight.co.za/about-us.html.

[86] www.thirdworldbunfight.co.za/about-us.html. [87] Van Zyl Smit (2007), 3.

township Khayelitsha.[88] Bailey describes the set for his play 'as a site-specific, promenade performance'[89]. According to Van Zyl Smit, who witnessed one of the live performances in the Cape, the audience had been advised to wear walking shoes and had to walk for at least ten minutes from the official meeting point to the first performance site and from there to approximately twenty different sites during the performance.[90] Bailey describes his rationale as follows: 'I have pruned the original text to suit the ritualistic staging that I have given to the piece . . . This production roots the classical Greek tragedy of Medea firmly in the post-colonial present, reanimating the drama with a deep spirituality and with topical themes of immigration, displacement and xenophobia.'[91]

For the duration of the performance, Bailey makes his audience experience life in a squatter camp at first hand. The spectators walk through the dust and bushes of the veldt, they sit on wooden benches, they sample typical township food such as 'soup in tin mugs and "vetkoek", a batter cake fried in oil',[92] they look at the shacks, traditionally made of corrugated iron or of cardboard, in which the inhabitants live, they are surrounded by the sounds of African songs and music. Lighting is provided by fires, torches, and candles, and there is a lot of code-switching between English and isiXhosa. Bailey turns Medea's hometown of Colchis, originally located on the Black Sea, into a fairly primitive African village, which is attacked by 'armed, violent gangs of men [who] move through remote villages looking for booty, sex and adventure',[93] the fate of many villages across Africa, but also part of daily life in the townships and squatter camps, where people often live in fear of marauding bands of so-called *tsotsis* or township gangsters, who break in, steal, and rape. In the case of *medEia*, Jason is the gang leader, and his band are the Argonauts, who have come to seize the Golden Fleece. Despite Jason's violence, Medea falls in love with him, and (in accordance with the Greek myth) hands over the Golden Fleece and follows him to Corinth, which is depicted as the more developed urban settlement in contrast to the rural village of Colchis. Bailey here translates the conflict in Euripides' play, i.e. the assumption by the 'coloniser' Jason that his Greek civilisation is superior to Medea's supposedly barbaric culture of 'colonised' Colchis, to a contrast between the urban world and the supposedly primitive rural village. Like Euripides,

[88] It should be added, however, that the play toured internationally and was performed in several European cities (www.thirdworldbunfight.co.za/productions/medeia.html).

[89] www.thirdworldbunfight.co.za/files/medEia%202012.pdf.

[90] Van Zyl Smit (2007), 3.

[91] www.thirdworldbunfight.co.za/files/medEia%202012.pdf.

[92] Van Zyl Smit (2007), 3.

[93] www.thirdworldbunfight.co.za/files/medEia%202012.pdf.

he undercuts the notion of cultural supremacy by showing that Corinth does not even have running water, displays signs of neo-colonialism through Coca Cola adverts, and that the Corinthians have a xenophobic attitude towards Medea who is an outsider, just as in Euripides' play.

Another interesting post-colonial African allusion is the depiction of King Pelias, who is dressed like a stereotypical African dictator and resides in a shack full of Western goods such as washing machines and TV sets, which are of no use in a place without electricity but which nevertheless represent wealth and power. Pelias embodies the negative image of an African dictator who abuses resources for nobody's good except his own. Other changes by Bailey include the events of the story being told in a non-chronological sequence, Medea being doubled up as a young and an old woman (with both performers being always on stage simultaneously), the use of many elements of the Haitian Vodou cult,[94] and Medea being finally accepted, after the murder of her children, into the community of women, who are represented by the chorus of African women. In almost all previous adaptations of Euripides' original Greek play, Medea was depicted as the *other*, the outsider, the foreigner and the *unheimlich*, because of her magical powers. All of these elements make it easy to appropriate her story in a post-colonial context, where indigenous people were treated as not belonging in their own country and as exotic, second-class human beings displaced by the actual foreigners. The fact that Bailey transposes this myth into an exclusively African framework makes her situation even more tragic.

In his Programme Notes, Bailey explains under the heading 'The Drama' that 'In a foreign city a group of immigrant Africans gathers to dramatise Medea's tale of transcendence over the powers that marginalise and silence them; to enact a harrowing dramatic ritual as a protest against the adversity of their situation.'[95] In another instance of 'metatheatre', *medEia* is staged as a 'play within a play'. Bailey's complex arrangement resembles Chinese boxes or Russian dolls: the original Greek myth is embedded in an exclusively African context, and the African adaptation in turn is embedded in the context of an anonymous metropolis. But by making a 'foreign city' the framework for the fictional setting of his play and a 'group of immigrant Africans' the fictional actors, he moves theatre also in a metaphoric sense to the suburbs, since in most large cities,

94 Van Zyl Smit (2007) analyses in detail the various elements of the Vodou cult and their amalgamation with traditional African rites and customs.

95 www.thirdworldbunfight.co.za/files/medEia%202012.pdf.

immigrants reside rather in the outskirts or peripheries and not in the centre. Bailey's retranslation of his play out of the actual African colonies and the original post-colonial context to new forms of settlement outside Africa, namely Europe, expands it from the original post-colonial discourse into that of present-day African diaspora. In this context, the term designates the migration of formerly colonised people to the countries of their former colonisers after the independence of their countries. Robin Cohen describes this phenomenon as follows: 'Twentieth-century, post-colonial African emigration prompted by civil war, famine, economic failure and political instability can be thought of as generating a "second", incipient, set of "new" African diasporas.'[96] As already mentioned, according to Cohen's definition, the 'first' African diaspora can be classified as a 'prototypical, classical, victim diaspora', and it overlaps to a certain extent also with a different category of diaspora which he calls 'the expanded concept of diaspora'.[97] Another scholar, William Safran, had already defined the latter as 'a metaphoric designation [for] expatriates, expellees, political refugees, alien residents, immigrants and ethnic and racial minorities'.[98] Both definitions are relevant for the position of African immigrants in European countries.

A prominent example of a host land for the 'second' African diaspora is France. The *banlieues* of Paris and other big French cities are largely populated by inhabitants from the former French colonies, particularly from North Africa, and are notorious for unemployment, poverty, crime, drugs, prostitution, and frequent violent clashes with the police. The fact that many immigrants from North Africa are Muslims seems to provide extra potential for conflict.[99] The inhabitants of these ghetto-like settlements are very isolated and exist in a sort of limbo, since they belong neither to their homeland anymore nor are they accepted by (let alone integrated into) the society of their host land.

Côte d'Ivoire and France: Antigone

When Brett Bailey made an anonymous foreign city the platform for his metatheatrical undertaking and some anonymous African immigrants the actors, he made a first step towards a metaphoric move of theatre into the outskirts. The Francophone author Koffi Kwahulé continues this process,

[96] Cohen (2008), 3. [97] Quotations from Cohen (2008), 2 and 4, respectively.
[98] Safran (1991), 83. [99] Cf. Hargreaves (2003), 147.

setting the location and action of his play *Bintou* in an anonymous French *banlieue*[100] among African immigrants from an unspecified country.

Kwahulé was born in Abengourou, Côte d'Ivoire in 1956. He trained as a comedian in Abidjan and later in Paris, where he received his PhD in Theatre Studies at Paris III-Sorbonne Nouvelle and where he lives. He has written approximately twenty plays, which according to Love are 'Generally set in unnamed French suburbs, never in his homeland of Côte d'Ivoire', and 'address territories and themes within the borderlands between the present and the past, Europe and Africa, Parisian and Côte d'Ivoirien French, as well as between contemporary Parisian suburban social problems and ancient tragedy'.[101] The last point is underlined by Virginie Soubrier:

> Koffi Kwahulé's texts seem straight away to bear the mark of Greek Tragedy ... Bintou is a contemporary Antigone, she has her insolence and pride, adamance and clarity. At the end of the play, the young girls – the chorus – who surround the murderous Uncle, embody his guilty conscience and are reminiscent of the Erinyes pursuing Orestes in Aeschylus' play'[102]

Kwahulé wrote an earlier and shorter version of *Bintou* in 1996 during a stay at the thirteenth Festival International des Francophonies in Limoges in Limousin.[103] One year later, in 1997, a revised version was published and staged by Gabriel Garran at the Théâtre International de Langue Française (TILF) Festival in Paris.

Bintou is a very contemporary and rather free adaptation of Sophocles' *Antigone*. In Kwahulé's scenario, Antigone is Bintou, a thirteen-year-old girl, a second-generation descendant from an African immigrant family. She lives in a French *banlieue*, which is described on the blurb of the printed edition as violent (*violente*) and multiracial (*métissée*). She is the leader of a gang called 'les Lycaons' which consists of three youngsters a few years older than Bintou: Bintou's boyfriend Manu, who is white, Kelkhal, who is Maghrébien, and Blackout, who is black. They are

100 Given the biographical background of the author, it is very likely that it is one of the *banlieues* in Paris.

101 Love (2009), 108.

102 Soubrier (2005), 24: 'Les textes de Koffi Kwahulé semblent d'emblée porter l'empreinte de la tragédie grecque... Bintou est une Antigone contemporaine, elle en a l'insolence et la fierté, l'intransigeance et la lucidité. À la fin de la pièce, les jeunes filles – the chœur – qui entourent l'Oncle meurtrier de Bintou, incarnent sa conscience coupable, et rappellent les Érinyes poursuivant Oreste dans la tragédie d'Éschyle' (English translation by Love 2009, 121, n. 3).

103 The title at the time was ... *Et son petit ami l'appelait Samiagamal*, or ... *And her boyfriend called her Samiagamal* (my translation).

mesmerised by Bintou and obey her orders unconditionally; they seem collectively to correspond to the Haemon figure in Sophocles. Bintou loves to dress in a provocative way in very short skirts without underpants and bare-midriff tops showing her navel, since it is her dream to become a belly-dancer like the famous Egyptian belly-dancer Samia Gamal, which is also her nickname (spelt as 'Samiagamal'). She spends her days together with her gang marauding through the *quartier* terrorising people and committing various kinds of crimes including arson and murder. She flatly refuses to accept any form of authority, including that of her own family: her aunt Rokia ('Eurydice'), her unnamed mother ('Jocasta'), and her uncle Drissa, the counterpart to Sophocles' Creon, who has assumed the role of head of the family, since Bintou's father ('Oedipus') spends his life in his room which he never leaves out of shame for having lost his job. Since all of them fail to exercise control over Bintou, they ultimately resort to curbing Bintou's insolence and disobedience by subjecting her to Female Genital Mutilation (FGM), a procedure practised in several African countries in order to control women's sexuality. Since it is unprofessionally executed by a traditional 'knife-lady' (*dame-au-couteau* in French), Bintou bleeds to death. The three girls, who form the chorus, hold Drissa as the mastermind responsible for Bintou's murder and persecute him in resentful silence.

Despite the very different circumstances, the character of Bintou has a lot in common with Antigone. Both are proud, independent teenagers, who stand up for what they believe is right and refuse to accept the authority and the value systems of their respective uncles, both of whom try in vain to keep them in their traditional place. Both are aware that their actions might lead to their untimely death, and neither of them cares. In fact, both playwrights, Sophocles and Kwahulé, emphasise that the actions of their female protagonists are motivated by love and not by hatred.[104]

In Sophocles' play, Antigone stands for tradition and the right of the individual versus Creon, who represents the law and the right of the state. Their positions have been reversed by Kwahulé. Here it is Bintou who turns her back on the traditions of her homeland and advocates a modern lifestyle compatible with that of her host land, while her uncle and the other family members still try to preserve the value systems and customs of their homeland. Their conflict is symptomatic of the problems experienced by people who live in the diaspora. Cohen has identified a list of what he

[104] Cf. Sophocles, *Antigone*, 523; Kwahulé (2003), 18; see also Bemba (1995), 89.

calls 'common features of diaspora'[105] of which the following six or seven[106] criteria can be applied to Bintou's family members, who are first-generation immigrants:

1. dispersed from an original homeland, often traumatically, to two or more foreign regions;
2. alternatively or additionally, the expansion from a homeland in search of work, in pursuit of trade, or to further colonial ambitions;
3. a collective memory and myth about the homeland, including its location, history, suffering, and achievements;
4. an idealisation of the real or imagined ancestral home and a collective commitment to its maintenance, restoration, safety, and prosperity, even to its creation;
5. the frequent development of a return movement to the homeland that gains collective approbation even if many in the group are satisfied with only a vicarious relationship or intermittent visits to the homeland;
6. a strong ethnic group consciousness sustained over a long time and based on a sense of distinctiveness, a common history, the transmission of a common cultural and religious heritage and the belief in a common fate;
7. a troubled relationship with host societies, suggesting a lack of acceptance or the possibility that another calamity might befall the group.

The term 'homeland' (in French: *pays*) occurs frequently in the play;[107] Bintou's family first proposes to send her back to the *pays* under the pretext of a holiday so that she learns the traditional culture and appropriate behaviour for a girl or woman (which might include FGM). This plan fails, because Bintou refuses to go, since she does not feel ready for Africa yet. Despite their infighting, the family holds closely together and has a social network consisting of other equally conservative African immigrants represented by the above-mentioned 'Knife-Lady'. They also display a racist attitude towards Bintou's white boyfriend. Away from their homeland and in the context of the French host society, the highly controversial custom of FGM becomes even more senseless. Kwahulé, who is himself

[105] Cohen (2008), 17.

[106] There is not enough information in the text to determine whether point 1 applies, but it is possible that it does.

[107] In French, the word 'pays' literally means simply 'country', while 'homeland' would be technically 'pays natal'. In the context of the play, however, the term 'pays' is used as a synonym for 'pays natal' – what might be called in English 'old country'.

circumcised, but by his own personal choice, wrote his play at a time when 'France was beleaguered by trials around excision'.[108] The debate then was fuelled further by the personal experiences of two famous models, Waris Dirie from the Somali Desert near Ethiopia and Fatima Siad from Somalia. Dirie's autobiography *Desert Flower*, in which she describes her own ordeal of having been subjected to FGM at the age of five, was published in the same year in which *Bintou* had its premiere (1997).[109] On her website Dirie provides detailed factual information and statistics which provide an important backdrop for a better understanding of Kwahulé's play and the actuality of the topic to date.[110]

Like Dirie, who has become a human rights activist fighting against FGM, Siad, the second runner-up in the American television series *America's Next Top Model* in 2008, condemns the custom. She was circumcised herself at the age of seven,[111] but she takes a more practical approach by suggesting proper medical surgery and counselling for affected girls. Siad was severely criticised in Somalia for her outspoken and critical position. Kwahulé himself makes a clear distinction between male circumcision and female excision, 'because excision touches on the issue of pleasure. With excision, you have the idea of surveillance, of controlling something outside of the ritual'.[112] In his opinion, tradition without context is a 'perverted tradition':

> This is exactly what I call a perverted tradition, meaning that she [the knife-lady] has done a deed outside of context, without any solemnity. In fact, she says so in the play: "I have two more operations waiting for me". This is a sort of assembly line, a mechanical thing. And then, one is not anymore in the tradition.[113]

As Love puts it: 'Drissa calls upon the traditions of his homeland to construct an ideology of the family he undermines by first sexually assaulting and then killing Bintou.'[114] In order to punish his niece because of his inability to control his own sexual desires, Drissa tries to enforce the

[108] Kwahulé (2008), 172. The term 'excision' means 'female circumcision'.

[109] Subsequently, Dirie's book was turned into a movie by the same title in 2008.

[110] www.desertflowerfoundation.org/en/home.html.

[111] For more details and further references on the topic, see Davis (2012), 6.

[112] Kwahulé (2008), 181.

[113] Zabus (2005) (my translation): 'C'est justement ce que j'appelle la tradition pervertie, c'est-à-dire, qu'elle [la dame au couteau] a commis un acte en dehors de son contexte, en dehors de toute fête. D'ailleurs, elle le dit dans la pièce: « J'ai deux autres opérations qui m'attendent ». C'est une chose qu'elle fait à la chaîne, un truc mécanique. Et là, on n'est plus dans la tradition.' This important paragraph in the 2005 original has been unfortunately left out in the English translation (2008).

[114] Love (2009), 114.

traditional patriarchal order outside its original context. As a result, Bintou's death becomes a sort of meaningless collateral damage of an unprofessionally performed routine operation and raises the question of the validity of traditions outside of their original context.[115]

Bintou is a typical representative of second-generation immigrants, comparable to the second (and third) generation of Turkish immigrants in Germany. Sandra Hestermann summarises the latter's dilemma as follows:

> Unlike their parents and grandparents, they do not have any original memories of their home country. For them, Turkish reality gets transformed into a myth in which flourish very vague notions derived from the stories told by their families . . . [They] have grown up in a "vacuum culture" and construct their identity as a consciously "hyphenated" one. For them, Turkey is a foreign country . . . [They] do not share the nostalgia of their fathers' and/or grandparents' generation, but have to create an identity of their own which is no longer exclusive but cross-cultural or even multicultural.[116]

Hestermann adds two serious predicaments:

> In fact, a large majority of second- and third-generation Turks do not maintain any social contacts, or at best, only occasional contacts with Germans in their free time . . . This dilemma of living in two separate worlds is additionally aggravated by the fact that many of the young Turks who experience exclusion, stigmatization and threat from mainstream German society also feel imprisoned by their families.[117]

This parallel to a completely different group of migrants illustrates particularly well how post-colonial concepts and diaspora theory are equally applicable to non-post-colonial contexts, and consequently proves the global relevance of modern adaptations of Greek tragedy: Kwahulé's African Bintou in the French *banlieue* could just as well be substituted by a Turkish Bintou living with her traditional family in an anonymous German city.

[115] For most people, including myself, the practice of FGM is totally unacceptable and a gross violation of human rights. However, one can still find a very traditional patriarchal attitude in various cultures and countries worldwide, also among African black men, who do not recognise gender equity or women's rights. In order to avoid being labelled a 'white racist' and 'Eurocentric', one has to deal with this highly objectionable mind-set, especially in a post-colonial context. Kwahulé's position is ambivalent: although on one hand he has chosen for himself to be circumcised, on the other hand he severely condemns in his play the practice for women, and even more so, if the original cultural context is non-existent.

[116] Hestermann (2003), 340. [117] Hestermann (2003), 341.

Bintou has no emotional ties to her African homeland;[118] she does not want to travel there, because she considers the city, the *quartier*, its concrete and her peers her home. This is where she was born, and she has no desire to experience something else.[119] Her friends are other youngsters from the ghetto, most of them also foreigners, and her family disapproves of them as well as of her activities outside the family home. She speaks a common, often vulgar language in the same way as many young Turks in Germany speak only broken German interspersed with colloquial or vulgar expressions. The *banlieue* is the only world Bintou has: it belongs neither to her home land nor really to her host land, but is a sort of no man's land.

This lack of belonging not only reflects Bintou's conflict as a second-generation immigrant, but it also represents another generation conflict: the conflict between the so-called Generation X or MTV generation, born between 1960 and 1980 and considered to be happy, educated, life-orientated, heterogeneous, and today's generation, the so-called 'Generation Y' or Millennials or YOLO generation, usually born between 1980 and 2000. Madelaine Davis, a former third-year student in Classics at the University of KwaZulu-Natal, has made a fine observation:

> My generation has no Polyneices to bury or tyrannical opposition to oppose. "Generation Y" we are called (The Internet Generation . . .) and we are desperately fighting for something, but we are not quite sure of what it is, the same way Bintou is fighting with the intensity of Sophocles' Antigone for something quite intangible, the greater good perhaps and "Generation Y". That is why she may be paralleled with Antigone. She is the Antigone of "Generation Y".[120]

Davis provides a quotation from the movie *Fight Club* (1999)[121] which in her opinion captures the spirit of 'Generation Y': 'We have no Great war, no Great depression, our Great war is a spiritual war, our Great depression is our lives, we've been raised by television to believe that one day we'd all

[118] Cf. Koser (2003), 9: 'Many African adults in the UK, for example, share with many other migrant adults around the world a concern that their children have become socially, culturally, linguistically and often religiously distanced from their "homeland".'

[119] Cf Kwahulé (2003), 32, where Bintou says: 'Mais mon pays c'est ici, maman. C'est la cité, le quartier, le béton, mes mecs. . . mes "Lycaons", comme dit tante Rokia. C'est ici que je suis née et je n'ai pas envie de connaitre autre chose. Ça me suffit' ('But my home is here, Mum. It's the city, the neighbourhood, the concrete, my pals . . . my "Lycaons", as Aunt Rokia says. I was born here, and I don't feel like experiencing something new. This is enough for me').

[120] Davis (2012), 3.

[121] The movie was directed by David Fincher and is adapted from the novel *Fight Club* by Chuck Palahnuik (1996). See Davis (2012), 3.

be millionaires and movie gods and rock stars, but we won't and we're slowly learning that fact. And we're very pissed off.'[122] Davis' comments are representative of young post-colonial African people today (the so-called 'born-free' generation, which is to say, born after apartheid) and what appeals to them in an African adaptation of a Greek myth. They may relate to Bintou, who does not go to school, wastes her life by hanging out between concrete blocks, gives up her dream of becoming a belly-dancer, has no real purpose in life, and is riddled by conflicting emotions. Her overall frustration and the senselessness of her life seem to mirror the feelings of the young people of 'Generation Y', as Davis suggests.[123] Davis' discussion illustrates how post-colonial issues have shifted over the past decades, at least in the reception of Greek tragedy. Topics such as hybridity, assimilation, political utopias, the Truth and Reconciliation Commission, indigenous cultures, which were crucial for earlier authors, have been replaced by questions of the late twentieth and twenty-first century: the problems which migrants face in foreign countries in a global context not necessarily restricted to a post-colonial background, gender-related issues such as FGM, generation conflicts on various levels. The flexibility with which Greek tragedy can accommodate these developments is probably one of the reasons why a young contemporary audience can still identify with a (female) character from Greek mythology.

In a production of *Bintou* in Brussels in 2003, the director, Rosa Gasquet, used an approach very similar to the ones outlined earlier. Being herself from what Love calls 'the immigrant neighbourhood of Schaerbeck',[124] a suburb of Brussels, she involved some youngsters from this 'quartier populaire'[125] as actors in the performance. She also included some rap and slam poetry, which might also account for the production's success among the audiences from Schaerbeck. In this production, an adaptation of a Greek tragedy was transported both in a literal and in a metaphoric sense from its traditional space and discourse into the diaspora.

Conclusion

There is no single answer to the question why authors, playwrights, and directors from various post-colonial backgrounds have been interested in or even fascinated by fifth-century Greek tragedy. This is a multifaceted and multi-causal phenomenon. Authors who still wrote under colonialism or during apartheid could turn to the ancient Greek texts as a safe vehicle

[122] Davis (2012), 3. [123] Davis (2012), 3, 8. [124] Love (2009), 118. [125] Chalaye (2004).

to express criticism against dictatorial regimes, since Greek mythology was considered to be harmless by state censors. A parallel case can be found in the former German Democratic Republic (GDR), where a vast corpus of East German literature was based on the reception of Greek mythology and Greek tragedy.[126] Furthermore, African writers who grew up in the former colonies (even after they became independent) or in the diaspora were still exposed at school to the European curriculum, including the ancient languages and the reading of Greek tragedy, and also often studied outside Africa. The fact that Greek tragedy deals with problems and questions which are not restricted to a certain time or place but which are fundamentally part of the so-called *condition humaine*, makes the content of the plays universal and relevant for everybody. For a post-colonial writer, Greek tragedy offers the perfect means to engage with the (former) coloniser by appropriating the content and context of the 'European canon' from the perspective of the (formerly) colonised subject. Greek tragedy provides an abundance of topics which are particularly relevant for post-colonial discourse: how to deal with the murder of a loved one, the desire for revenge, hatred, helplessness, betrayal, pain, rejection, the status of being an outsider; how to fight injustice and to stand up for what is right. The works discussed in this chapter offer individual responses to these questions, reflecting the circumstances, concerns, and *Zeitgeist* of each particular writer. They represent the ways in which post-colonial adaptations of Greek tragedy have developed over the past decades and they will hopefully lead the way for the next generations of writers to come.

[126] The Institut für Griechische und Lateinische Philologie at the Freie Universität Berlin, founded by (now Emeritus) Professor Bernd Seidensticker, houses an impressive collection of GDR primary literature and respective scholarship which deals with the reception of classical mythology by GDR writers.

CHAPTER 12

Trapped between Fidelity and Adaptation? On the Reception of Ancient Greek Tragedy in Modern Greece[*]

Anastasia Bakogianni

The reception of ancient Greek tragedy on the world stage underwent seismic changes in the twentieth and twenty-first centuries, gradually moving away from traditional approaches to staging classical plays towards freer, more experimental adaptations. This trend is still going strong in the new millennium, with Greek tragedy now established as a powerful weapon in the service of liberal, feminist, and anti-war agendas.[1] Modern Greece offers us a distinctive example of the reception of ancient drama that testifies to the complications introduced by questions of national identity, vested ideological interests, and deep political divisions. Its study allows us to interrogate our assumptions about the role of theatre today and test the state of our relationship with the classical past. On the modern Greek stage, the performance of ancient Greek drama has been characterised by an ongoing struggle between tradition and innovation. The traditional approach privileges 'authenticity', the attempt to bring the classical past to life on the theatrical stage, as part of a wider intellectual project that seeks to imbue modern Greece with the glamour and cultural capital of ancient Greece. Theatre practitioners in Greece today remain divided, with some seeking to engage in innovative ways with ancient drama, while others continue their search for fidelity.

This chapter investigates the tension between inherently conservative approaches to performing ancient drama and more innovative responses as

* I am very grateful to the editors for their collegiality and assistance in the preparation of this chapter. Many thanks to Professors Helene P. Foley (Columbia University) and Andrew Earle Simpson (Catholic University of America) for commenting on an earlier version of this material. A debt of gratitude is due to Gonda Van Steen (KCL) for her support over many years. Many thanks to the Library of the National Theatre of Greece for access to their archive and in particular to Artistic Director (2015–19) Stathis Livathinos for granting me an interview.

1 Edith Hall identified 1968–9 as a 'watershed' year for this liberal 'turn' in the history of the performance reception of Greek drama: E. Hall (2004a), 1. But in Greece the ancient plays had already become an ideological battleground between the Right and Left in the turbulent post–World War II era. For details, see Van Steen (2011).

exemplified by the work of one of the country's premier theatrical institutions, the National Theatre of Greece. Founded in 1930, the company is a good weathervane of dominant trends in modern Greek theatre.[2] It thus serves as a useful test case for investigating the clash between tradition and innovation. My analysis focuses on four representative examples from two turning points in the new millennium, 2000 and 2015–16. My discussion sets the stage by comparing two very different productions from 2000, funded and performed by two separate branches of the company. On one end of the spectrum, there is a production of Sophocles' *Oedipus Tyrannus*, translated and directed by Vasilis Papavassiliou (b. 1949) and starring the popular theatre and television actor Grigoris Valtinos (b. 1955).[3] Staged in the summer of 2000 and viewed by many theatre critics as the highlight of that year's Athens and Epidaurus Festival, this traditional production performed the 'special relationship' with ancient Greece that modern Greece lays claim to, before a large audience of Greeks and foreign visitors. At the more creative end of the spectrum stands Nikos Perelis' *Traps and Killings: The Machines of Dolos and Terror* (2000),[4] a pastiche that combines narrative strands from five dramas by Euripides. Perelis signalled his connection to the classical past by his use of the word *dolos* ('guile', 'deceit') in his title (as will be discussed further below). It was performed by the Experimental Stage of the National Theatre, which was founded in 1996, with the explicit aim of introducing more innovative approaches to the work of the National Theatre of Greece. Perelis' creative reimagining of the War at Troy and its aftermath sought to intertwine ancient and modern themes and anxieties. This experimental adaptation of Euripides' dramas was performed on a smaller stage and had a mixed reception, with the negative reviews criticising the liberties the production took with its source material.[5]

In the summer of the Greek referendum (5 July 2015), when Greeks were asked to vote on whether their country should accept or reject the

[2] For a brief history of the company, see www.n-t.gr/en/knowus/history (accessed 22 July 2019). The National Theatre was preceded by the Royal Theatre (founded in 1891), which opened its doors to the public on 24 November 1901, but stopped performing in 1908.

[3] www.nt-archive.gr/playDetails.aspx?playID=615 (accessed 24 May 2019).

[4] The Greek title of the play was 'Παγίδες και φονικά (Οι μηχανές του δόλου και του τρόμου)'. Nikos Perelis (b. 1940) is an actor, translator, playwright, and director, who had previously directed Euripides' *Iphigenia at Tauris* (1981), *Hippolytus* (1984), and Aristophanes' *Ploutos* (1989) for the National Theatre.

[5] Fewer reviews of *Traps and Killings* were published in the Greek press than is usual for a National Theatre production. For examples of the negative reviews, see *Radiotileorasi* (12 February 2000) and *Kathimerini* (2000, misfiled in the NT's online archive).

bailout conditions set by the European Commission, the International Monetary Fund, and the European Central Bank, even the fate of the prestigious Athens and Epidaurus Festival hung in the balance. Stathis Livathinos (b. 1960), then newly appointed Artistic Director of the National Theatre (2015–19), went on Greek radio to urge the public to attend the opening performances of the company's production of *The Trojan Women* at Epidaurus (3–4 July 2015),[6] in a translation by K. Ch. Myris, directed by the outgoing Artistic Director Sotiris Hatzakis (b. 1957). This turned out to be something of a missed opportunity, however, as the production offered nothing innovative in terms of how the ancient play was staged, and was totally divorced from contemporary anxieties in the tense lead-up to the referendum.[7] The production avoided drawing any parallels between the ancient tragedy and the contemporary Greek context, a directorial choice that in comparison to other productions of Greek tragedy that summer was a retrenchment. In the turbulent year 2015 Hatzakis chose to retreat backwards into the safety of traditional approaches to staging ancient tragedy.[8] But, in a summer fraught with cancellations and shortened runs for the Athens and Epidaurus Festival, there were some theatre practitioners who were not afraid to create fresh and innovative versions of the ancient plays, which could in fact connect with contemporary audiences.[9] Unfortunately, the National Theatre's showcase production of ancient tragedy that year was not among them.

In the following year, Livathinos' own production of *Antigone* at Epidaurus (15–16 July 2016)[10] adopted a more innovative approach vis-à-vis its source text, testifying to the new Artistic Director's openness to new ideas and his willingness to experiment. This was also the company's first co-production with the National Theatre of Northern Greece and the Cyprus Theatre Organisation. Using a fresh translation by Dimitris

6 http://greekfestival.gr/festival_events/national-theatre-sotiris-hadzakis-2015/?lang=en (accessed 21 May 2019).

7 For a discussion of the impact of austerity on the arts in Greece, see Tziovas (2017).

8 Hatzakis was not alone in adopting a more traditional approach to staging Greek tragedy that summer. Vangelis Theodoropoulos' *Ajax* at Epidaurus (7–18 July 2015), in a translation by D. N. Maronitis, was, in this audience member's view, an uncomfortable mixture of archaising and modern elements that did not fit together. The costuming decisions serve as an indicative example. The production mixed archaic-style costumes and props for the protagonists with Ottoman dress for the chorus – a chronological disjunction which was left unexplained.

9 Katerina Evangelatos' innovative production of *Rhesus* (8 July–9 August 2015), performed in the newly opened archaeological site of Aristotle's Lyceum in central Athens, was a particular standout. YouTube promo: www.youtube.com/watch?v=CGlysZGAksA (accessed 2 June 2019). See also Liapis 2018 (accessed 14 October 2019).

10 www.n-t.gr/en/events/andigoni (accessed 21 May 2019).

Maronitis,[11] this *Antigone* performed the clash of three generations (the elders, Creon, and the youth of the city), thereby reminding its audience that the tragic heroine at the heart of Sophocles' play is little more than a child, as opposed to the fully fledged rebel she is usually portrayed as in modern productions of the ancient drama. This interpretation was further reinforced by the casting of the chorus, which was made up of both older and younger members, the latter closer to Antigone in age. Thus, the chorus itself was portrayed as inherently divided and unsure of its allegiance, a group of people caught up, like the audience, in the conflict between Antigone and Creon. The popular appeal of the production, which sold out its run at Epidaurus, was matched by the political upheaval that the decision to perform the play at the ancient Theatre of Salamis in the self-proclaimed 'Turkish Republic of Northern Cyprus' caused in the Greek and Cypriot media.[12] The performance of Greek tragedy once again became a flashpoint for an ideological and political clash between the Greek Right and Left. Ancient Greek drama matters in modern Greece, and throughout its performance history in the modern nation (including in the lead-up to the successful Independence War of 1821)[13] it has given rise to heated debates, political upheavals, and re-examinations of its role in a modern society. Informed by current debates in adaptation studies, this contextualised study of four productions at different points of the spectrum between fidelity and adaptation acts as a focal point for my examination of the 'creative turn'[14] in the performance reception of Greek tragedy on the modern Greek stage.

Modern productions of ancient Greek drama have to find a theatrical, linguistic, and ideological register that allows them to form an effective bridge between our classical dramatic texts and the preoccupations, problems, and anxieties of today. Otherwise, ancient Greek drama risks becoming an unnecessary relic of the past with nothing of value to say to the present (see Sidiropoulou, Chapter 4, this volume). This is precisely the

[11] Maronitis (1929–2016) was a classical scholar and translator.

[12] The condemnation of this decision in the right-wing and populist media testifies to the resurgence of nationalism in Greece after 2010. For examples of their comments, see Anonymous (2016b), 30, Eleutheroglou (2016), 6 and Anonymous (2016c), 5; Anonymous (2016d), 9; and in the neo-Nazi newspaper *Chrysi Avgi*, Anonymous (2016a), 10. The language in which their criticism is couched also testifies to the strained relationship between Greece and Turkey over what has been euphemistically labelled the Cypriot Question. The right-wing Greek and Cypriot media viewed the National Theatre's decision to perform in the occupied territories as a national betrayal.

[13] For the key role played by theatre in the lead-up to the 1821 revolution, see Van Steen (2010), 67–146, and Puchner and White (2017), 269–300.

[14] For the applications of the 'turns' framework to a discussion of the reception of Greek drama in modern Greece, see Van Steen (2016), 201.

challenge facing theatre practitioners today not only in modern Greece but on a global scale. The popularity of Greek tragedy in the twentieth and twenty-first centuries has given rise to a rich plurality of 'solutions' to the problem of staging these ancient plays in a meaningful way, namely in a way that allows contemporary audiences to connect with them. This chapter focuses on the ideologically, culturally, stylistically, and politically complex modern Greek responses to the problem. In particular, it examines closely the uneasy tension between tradition and innovation that continues to plague Greek theatre in the new millennium as it seeks to move beyond the constructed theatrical 'tradition' that invested the Greek stage with the cultural capital of ancient Greek drama, in order to forge new paths. Even in our post-2008 financial crisis world, plagued as it is by austerity, ancient drama continues to flourish on the modern Greek stage,[15] demonstrating its continuing relevance and appeal in our troubled modern world.

The Modern Greek Context

In the twentieth century, the performance of ancient drama on the modern Greek stage was characterised by an increasing tension between tradition and innovation, but it was not until the end of the century that freer adaptations began to gain traction at the National Theatre of Greece.[16] The traditional approach privileges 'authenticity', the attempt to reproduce as closely as possible the original fifth-century BCE performance, in a quest to revive Greek drama on the modern stage. Any such endeavour, however, is intrinsically futile, given the fragmentary nature of our evidence about how these plays were originally performed. Early productions of ancient drama in the modern Greek state, which date back to the nineteenth century,[17] celebrated their self-proclaimed connection to ancient Greece and ideologically positioned modern Greek theatre as the

[15] Theatre attendance in Greece has actually risen due to reduced ticket prices, a policy introduced by several theatre companies since the eruption of the Greek fiscal crisis to attract larger audiences.

[16] In a personal interview granted to the author (15 August 2015), Livathinos, while acknowledging the work of innovative directors prior to this date, pinpoints 1994 as the year when the company finally changed direction and opened itself up to more creative approaches.

[17] The first performance of Greek tragedy, featuring a mixture of professional actors and students, was organised in 1867 by the University of Athens in the ruins of the Roman Odeum of Herod Atticus. Sophocles' *Antigone* was performed on the occasion of the wedding of King George I. Translated by the diplomat and archaeologist Alexandros Rizos Rangavis, with music by Felix Mendelssohn (first used in the earlier 1841 Potsdam *Antigone*), the performance was a spectacular state occasion, in line with Western models. Less attention, however, was paid to making the drama accessible to the audience as 'living' theatre.

inheritor of ancient Greek theatre. A key element of modern Greek national identity is constructed around this 'special relationship' that it claims to enjoy with the classical past. According to the continuity argument, the modern state is the inheritor of ancient Greece via Byzantium.[18] The early National Theatre directors who staged ancient Greek drama were also heavily influenced by Western models, especially the work of German and Austrian practitioners.[19] Onstage, this attitude translated to archaising productions that did not take full advantage of the performativity of the theatrical medium. Gradually, however, Greek theatre practitioners began to free themselves from the restrictions of 'authenticity' and responded in more innovative ways to the challenge of staging ancient plays in the modern world.

In Greece, there is a widespread and long-standing belief that the modern state, officially founded in 1832, is the rightful inheritor of ancient Greece, a view that dates at least as far back as the eighteenth century and the long lead-up to the Greek War of Independence, which broke out in 1821.[20] Greek intellectuals were instrumental in spreading this message, their outlook conditioned by Western Europe's rediscovery of the ancient world, and the emerging view that ancient Greece was the cradle of Western civilisation. Philhellenes, especially those who belonged to the intellectual and/or upper-class elites of the Great Powers (Britain, France, and Russia), helped to formulate and promote these ideas in an effort to sway public opinion in favour of the Greeks' struggle for independence.

The impact of this historical, ideological, and political baggage on the arts in Greece is still being felt today. Many modern Greek artists creatively processed this 'special relationship' by incorporating classical models and themes into their work. This 'exceptional' relationship, however, is by no means straightforward;[21] some artists felt empowered by this connection,

[18] For a recent analysis of the ideologically charged continuity debate, see Puchner and White (2017), who argue that Greek theatre is a unique 'study in discontinuities' (vii). They believe that a nuanced re-examination of the evidence reveals meaningful commonalities in the history of Greek theatre from ancient to modern times. Moreover, despite the geographical spread of the evidence, the long periods of interruption, the adoption of different styles, and particular themes coming to the fore in different eras, it is still useful to date the history of Greek theatre back to antiquity and forward into the present. For a summary of their arguments, see 1–12 and 315–22.

[19] For example, Dimitris Rondiris, a key figure in Greek theatre, studied at the Max Reinhardt Seminar in Vienna from 1930 until 1933. Rondiris was Artistic Director at the Greek National Theatre in 1946–50 and again in 1953–5. For details, see Arvaniti (2010), 155–272.

[20] In 1822 the First National Assembly of the Provisional Greek Government decided to revive the ancient names of 'Hellas' and 'Hellenes', which Greece still uses today within its own borders and on passports and official documents.

[21] See also Sidiropoulou (2018).

while others rebelled against it, decrying it as the 'burden' of the past. What is significant, however, is that so many felt that they had to engage in this dialogue with the classical past, and nowhere is this more apparent than on the modern Greek stage.[22] The search for authenticity might be doomed from the outset, but analysing both its pursuit and rejection is illuminating and more necessary than ever. As Antonis Petrides has argued: 'Modern Greek national and cultural identities consist, largely, of clusters of cultural memory shaped by an ongoing dialogue with the classical past.'[23] This belief in the continuity between ancient and modern Greeks is a widespread and long-standing attitude, cultivated for centuries by both foreign and Greek intellectuals,[24] which gradually trickled down to the wider public.[25]

The reception of the classical past in the modern state of Greece has received increasing attention in recent decades, but studies tend to focus on specific topics such as modern Greek literature,[26] archaeology and the display of ancient artefacts,[27] the Language Question,[28] modern Greek identity,[29] and the important role that Philhellenes played in fostering the intellectual connection with ancient Greece, their involvement in the struggle for Greek independence, and the ongoing conflict of East and West.[30] The study of the history of modern Greek theatre and its relationship with the past is still being written and is an active area of research.[31] But what are the differences in terms of interpreting and adapting the ancient past between those artists, intellectuals, theatre practitioners, and teachers working within the status quo and those working more independently? Traditionally, successive Greek governments have supported artists who drew on ancient themes or motifs in their work or

[22] The belief in the exceptional access of modern Greeks to the classical past has permeated every facet of the culture and has manifested itself in many different forms in a variety of media.

[23] Petrides (2017), 1–2.

[24] For the role played by intellectuals in shaping modern Greek identity, see Ferris (2000); Güthenke (2008); Beaton and Ricks (2009); Van Steen (2010).

[25] On the reception of ancient Greece in modern Greek folklore and the oral tradition, see Kakridis (1997).

[26] Beaton (1999, 2003); Mackridge (1996); Ricks (1989).

[27] Damaskos and Plantzos (2008); Hamilakis (2007).

[28] Georgakopoulou and Silk (2009); Mackridge (2009).

[29] Tziovas (2014); Beaton and Ricks (2009); Zacharia (2008).

[30] Beaton (2013); Van Steen (2010); Güthenke (2008).

[31] Puchner and White (2017), 320. Key studies in English include, but are not limited to, Ioannidou (2017); Liapis, Pavlou, and Petrides (2017); Van Steen (2000, 2010, 2011, 2014). In Greek: Grammatas (2006); Andreadis (2005); Mavromoustakos (2005); Hatzipandazis (2002); Sideris (1976).

theatre practitioners who revived ancient dramas for the modern stage,[32] but not everyone toed the official line. Left-wing artists employed classical themes to mask politically unsanctioned beliefs and ideas.[33] Philhellenes such as Lord Byron and Percy Bysshe Shelley had already made an important contribution to the way in which the classical past was received in the new state, and their Romantic ideals continue to shape the way modern Greeks view themselves and their country.

In the late nineteenth and early twentieth centuries, modern Greek revivals of ancient tragedy generally used translations in *katharevousa*,[34] an artificially constructed language purged of foreign elements, in order to bring it closer to ancient Greek, as part of an attempt to rediscover the spirit of the 'original' source text (I use the term 'original' with a grain of salt here, given the unstable nature of our ancient texts). *Katharevousa* was the language of officialdom taught at school and university, while *dimotiki*, 'the people's language', was used in everyday interactions. This *diglossia*, the existence of two competing national languages, complicated the practice of both the written and the spoken logos of modern Greece for well over a century (1888–1976).[35] Infamously, the Language Question sparked the so-called *Evangelika* (1901) and *Oresteiaka* (1903) riots, caused by protests against the translation into a more popular idiom of the Gospels and of Aeschylus' *Oresteia*, respectively.[36] Conservative elements saw any such attempt as a corruption of the true logos of these 'sacred' texts and fought fiercely against it.[37] The purists believed that any attempt to dilute *katharevousa* was an attack on the nation itself. Early modern Greek revivals of ancient dramas were thus driven by philological concerns.[38]

In the first half of the twentieth century, a stilted style of performance, spearheaded by the National Theatre, became the gold standard. Actors tended to declaim their lines dressed in archaeologically accurate costumes

32 An indicative example is the state funding given to the National Theatre of Greece.

33 For example, the left-wing prisoners held on the Greek prison islands after the Greek Civil War performed classical drama as a means of resisting their political re-education. For details, see Van Steen (2001).

34 Rangavis' translation for the 1867 production of *Antigone* is one of the earliest examples we know of.

35 On the phenomenon of *diglossia*, see Alexiou (1982) and Fragoudaki (1992).

36 For more information on the *Evangelika*, see Carabott (1993). For the *Oresteiaka* episodes, see Van Steen (2008), 360–72 and, in Greek, Spathis (2005).

37 George Sotiriades' translation of Aeschylus' trilogy for a Royal Theatre production was deemed not 'pure' enough.

38 For a more detailed history of modern Greek dramaturgy in the nineteenth century and the early part of the twentieth, see Hatzipandazis (2002, in Greek).

and were praised by theatre critics for their 'authenticity'. Thomas Oikonomou belongs to this first generation of professionals who directed ancient drama at the National Theatre.[39] The Delphic Festivals of Angelos and Eva Sikelianos in 1927 and 1930 staged Aeschylus' *Prometheus Bound* and *Suppliant Women* outdoors and sought to connect ancient drama to modern Greek folk traditions.[40] However, the dictatorship of Ioannis Metaxas (1936–41), the turbulent World War II years (1941–4), and the Civil War that followed (1946–9) disrupted the development of modern Greek theatre, as did the military dictatorship of 1967–74.[41]

During these turbulent periods and their aftermath, traditional approaches to staging ancient drama were challenged. Directors endeavoured to illustrate the continuing impact of ancient drama not by making a claim to 'authenticity', but by creating an accessible and engaging theatrical spectacle that was meaningful to modern audiences. The decision to adopt the language spoken by 'the people' fostered a climate wherein more innovative approaches to the performance of these ancient plays gradually became more acceptable and in which they were, indeed, encouraged. In the second half of the century, and in particular in its concluding decades, there was a renewed commitment to reviving ancient Greek drama in a way that was engaging to modern Greek audiences. This approach informs the work of Karolos Koun (1908–87),[42] Theodoros Terzopoulos (b. 1949),[43] Spyros Evangelatos (1940–2017),[44] and Yannis Houvardas (b. 1950).[45] A new generation of young directors, including female directors such as Angela Brouskou, Katerina Evangelatou, and Avra Sidiropoulou, deliberately set out to once more challenge the conservative obsession with 'authenticity'.[46] But the clash between the traditional and innovative approaches to the staging of ancient drama in modern Greece is ongoing. Modern Greek productions of the ancient plays both engage with and at times criticise prevailing trends in world theatre. Petrides recognises

[39] For a history of the revival of ancient drama between the years 1817 and 1932, see Sideris (1976, in Greek).

[40] On the Delphic Festivals, see Michelakis (2010b), 155–63.

[41] For the state of Greek theatre under the 1967 dictatorship, see Van Steen (2014). On the ideological challenges after 1976, see Moschonas (2009); Goutsos (2009).

[42] On Koun see Van Steen (2000), 124–89; Varakis (2007, 2013).

[43] On Terzopoulos, see Sidiropoulou (2018), 839–41, and Decreus (2019).

[44] In the 1970s, Evangelatos belonged to the avant-garde of emerging young directors, but later he switched sides and became a traditionalist.

[45] On Houvardas, see Sidiropoulou (2018), 842–4. He served as Artistic Director of the National Theatre of Greece between 2007 and 2013.

[46] On modern Greek directors who challenge traditional approaches to staging Greek drama, see Sidiropoulou (2018).

that the reception of ancient tragic drama in Greece and Cyprus involves 'a process of negotiating both a modern(ist) cultural poetics and a new sense of self'[47] in the shadow of the continuity debate and the valorisation of the classical past.

As the premier theatre company in the country, the National Theatre of Greece lies at the heart of the culture clash between the obsession with fidelity and the search for innovative new approaches. Until fairly recently, the National Theatre's approach to performing these ancient plays aligned it with the traditional approach that seeks to reconstruct Greek drama's substance and spirit through a valorisation of Greek tradition in its entirety by synthesising ancient, Byzantine, and folk elements. Since the National Theatre enjoys significant 'cultural capital'[48] and the financial backing to ensure that its productions can reach large audiences both at home and abroad, its ideological alignment plays a key role in determining popular perceptions of how modern Greece stages Greek drama.[49] Its outreach was further enhanced by the creation of a digital archive (1932–2005).[50] The company's long history of performing ancient drama began rather inauspiciously (as the Royal Theatre) with the controversial 1903 production of Aeschylus' *Oresteia*, briefly referred to above (nn. 36 and 37). Its commitment to performing ancient drama was cemented in 1932 when a revamped National Theatre reopened its doors with Aeschylus' *Agamemnon* as one of its first two productions. The company's first performance of a tragedy in an ancient theatre (Epidaurus) was Dimitris Rondiris' landmark 1938 production of Sophocles' *Electra*. In 1954, Euripides' *Hippolytus* was performed at Epidaurus, again with Rondiris as the director, and a year later the Epidaurus festival was inaugurated, which continues to this day. Since 1955, Epidaurus has become the official venue for the annual premieres of the National Theatre's productions of Greek drama. In 1981, the entire Festival was devoted exclusively to ancient drama, testifying to the National Theatre's belief in the modern Greek stage's classical roots.

[47] Petrides (2017), 1. See also Ioannidou (2017), 1–5.

[48] Van Steen (2010), 22–3. See also Bourdieu (1977, 1986).

[49] The company has a long tradition of taking their productions on tour abroad. For example, Dimitris Rondiris' 1938 production of *Electra* went on tour in the following year with performances in the UK and Germany. Alexis Minotis' production of *Oedipus at Colonus* (1952–3) transferred to Broadway in New York City.

[50] Once funding for the digitisation project ran out, the archive continued its work, but it no longer publishes the results online: www.nt-archive.gr (accessed 22 November 2019).

The history of the National Theatre's reception of Greek drama is littered with violent reactions against new approaches. In 1969, Takis Mouzenidis' production of Euripides' *Electra* caused a scandal because its costumes (designed by Pavlos Mantoudis) were viewed as too 'Slavic', and therefore inauthentic, which was considered a national insult. Yannis Houvardas' 1984 production of *Alcestis* was interrupted by audience members with cries of 'shame', not only because of the director's decision to use modern dress, but mainly because his production featured a wild party and a sex scene.[51] Inviting foreign directors and theatre companies to perform in the Festival and in the 'sacred' ancient theatres of Greece was also met with considerable resistance. Peter Stein's emblematic 1985 *Oresteia* did not meet with favour, while an Eskimo production of *Yup'ik Antigone* in the same year was dismissed as childish.[52] Matthias Langhoff's *Bacchae* (1997) was vilified in the conservative press as an attack on Greece itself.[53] Only in the twenty-first century have the new creative approaches gained more than just a foothold, but even now traditional approaches to staging Greek drama persist.[54]

Reviving Greek Tragedy: A 'canonical' *Oedipus*? (2000)

One example of the traditional approach is Vassilis Papavassiliou's 2000 production of Sophocles' *Oedipus Tyrannus*, the director's first collaboration with the National Theatre.[55] It premiered to great fanfare at the Colosseum in Rome (19–21 June 2000)[56] and was subsequently performed at the Epidaurus Festival (11–12 August). Subsequently it went on tour in the Americas as one of the National Theatre's signature productions and received rave reviews.[57] The National Theatre's conservative

51 The wild party and the sex scene came after Alcestis' funeral. For details see Sampatakakis (2014).

52 On the audience reception of the Eskimo production in modern Greece, see Michael (2015), 205–7.

53 Sampatakakis (2017), 204–7.

54 Foreign directors staging Greek tragedy still meet with resistance from Greek audiences. For example, Anatoly Vassiliev's production of *Medea* caused an uproar in 2008. For details of the negative Greek reaction, see Merkouri (2010), 96–100.

55 Papavassiliou returned in the summer of 2013 with a more creative production of Euripides' satyr drama *Cyclops*, but he also directed and acted in freer adaptations of Greek myth, such as Yannis Ritsos' *Helen* (2001, 2009, and 2018). See www.festivalandros.gr/en/event/helen-giannis-ritsos (accessed 12 June 2019).

56 Papavassiliou was not happy with production conditions at the Colosseum. In an interview with Hatzikiriakos (2000), he expressed his 'bitterness' over not being allowed to use surtitles with an Italian translation, in order for the audience to better follow the performance.

57 See, e.g., www.nytimes.com/2000/10/06/movies/theater-review-private-horror-made-public.html (accessed 26 July 2019).

productions of Greek drama have traditionally received praise abroad and appealed to foreign audiences who tend to 'buy into' the continuity argument and consider modern Greek productions as somehow more 'authentic' than their international counterparts. Still, Papavassiliou's production, with its white statues strategically placed across the stage and a protagonist who adopted the National Theatre's signature acting style (characterised by elevated enunciation and dignified acting), ultimately failed to resuscitate the canonical tragedy.

The tragic hero Oedipus dominates the play named after him, so the eponymous performer is likely to make or break a production. As mentioned above, Papavassiliou cast Grigoris Valtinos as the title character. Valtinos adopted a declamatory style, familiar to audiences from National Theatre productions dating back to the previous century, and some reviewers labelled his performance 'dramatic' (meaning melodramatic) rather than 'tragic'.[58] The star actor's fame and the National Theatre brand ensured the popularity of the production,[59] but it contributed nothing new to the performance history of Sophocles' tragedy. In the climactic scene, when Oedipus appears onstage after his act of self-mutilation, Valtinos failed to do justice to Sophocles' subtle characterisation of the once all-powerful king, who has ended up a social outcast. This is a tragic hero who, while suffering great misfortune, still retains his agency and will, as his decision to blind himself demonstrates.[60] One of the notable theatrical features of the production actually worked against this reading of Oedipus' final appearance on stage. Valtinos, now dressed in white, like a Christian martyr, with copious amounts of blood down his face and garments, was led onstage by a rope tied round his waist. The emphasis in this scene was on his total lack of agency and helplessness, in contrast to his previous arrogance (which included viciously lashing the messenger in full view of the audience until he revealed the name of the older shepherd who was involved in his exposure as an infant). Even when Valtinos got rid of the rope, so that he could enhance his range of movement, it was the pathos of his predicament that was highlighted. In an indicative gesture, the young Ismene patted her father's head in a vain attempt to comfort him. In Valtinos' melodramatic performance, Oedipus' fall is complete and his Oedipus an utterly broken man.

58 Timogiannakis labelled the entire production a drama rather than a tragedy (2000). See also Kaltaki (2000).

59 On the night I attended the performance, the Epidaurus theatre was full, and the audience applauded heartily at the end.

60 Karakantza (2020), 146–7.

The translation, also by Papavassiliou, aimed at elevated poetic diction to lend gravitas to the production. For example, in the final scene Oedipus calls himself 'κακούργος και γέννημα κακούργων' ('evildoer and the seed of evildoers').[61] He uses the rope to lash himself, this time making a violent spectacle of himself in front of the chorus and the theatre audience. The chorus, in their half-masks, were also prone to declaiming their lines, which were even more formal than those of the protagonists. One of the stronger aspects of the production was the sense of ritual atmosphere that the chorus was able to establish. For example, they used their tall rods to accompany their song in the second *stasimon*, dropping them on the floor for emphasis as they concluded their chant. The performance of ritual is, however, a characteristic of many National Theatre revivals of Greek tragedy, so it did not represent an innovation for the company.[62] While the actors were confined to the downward-sloping ramp that dominated the stage, the chorus enjoyed more freedom of movement. When compared to productions by other companies, however, their choreography was rather rigid. In general, rigidity and formality were the dominant characteristics of Papavassiliou's production.

In addition to the white statues that were such a prominent feature of the production, all the actors' faces were covered with white make-up so that they also resembled statues that had come to life, further adding to the impression that this was an overly aestheticised 'theatrical artefact' rather than a living performance.[63] As Worthen argues, 'actors do much more with words than simply utter them',[64] but Valtinos' performance, and the performances of his fellow actors, rarely went beyond a one-note, predictable interpretation. For Greeks and foreigners alike, it is easy to fall under the spell of Epidaurus and the other ancient theatres. Location does after all matter. The Epidaurus Festival acts as a creative space which the modern state utilises to advertise its intellectual credentials and in which it has traditionally performed the aforementioned 'special relationship' with ancient Greece. But that should not blind us to the fact that overly reverent productions do not do justice to the complexity of the surviving tragedies.

[61] All translations from the modern Greek are the author's.

[62] For a discussion of another conservative National Theatre production (Lydia Koniordou's 1996 *Electra*), whose main strength was the performance of ritual, see Bakogianni (2019), 47–52.

[63] I use Raeburn's (2017, 1) term in a negative sense here, but agree with the emphasis he places on the ancient dramatic texts as plays for performance.

[64] Worthen (2010), 9.

A Creative Pastiche of Euripidean Drama (2000)

Creative acts of adaptation may allow a source text to be communicated in a topical way to new audiences,[65] and that was a key aim for the second production under discussion, which serves to exemplify the creative 'turn' in the performance reception of ancient drama at the National Theatre at the turn of the millennium. Nikos Perelis' *Παγίδες και φονικά (Οι μηχανές του δόλου και του τρόμου)*, or *Traps and Killings: The Machines of Dolos and Terror* (henceforth *Traps and Killings*),[66] draws on five Euripidean dramas: *Iphigenia at Aulis*, *The Trojan Women*, *Hecuba*, *Electra*, and *Orestes*. Perelis chose Euripides because of the popular view that he is the 'most modern' of the three ancient tragedians.[67] But in his act of 'dramatic synthesis,' he threw additional passages from Aeschylus, Sophocles, and even Thucydides into the mix. The production was the culmination of a three-year project at the Πειραματική Σκηνή (Experimental Stage) of the National Theatre of Greece, the last year of which was devoted to the exploration of ancient drama, testifying to its importance in shaping modern Greek theatre in general and the National Theatre of Greece in particular. An important aspect of the creative process involved a close collaboration of theatre practitioners and academics. According to the director, the aim of the production was to seek to understand 'the core of the ancient texts'.[68] Perelis' interpretation of his classical source texts, however, testifies to his anti-war and pro-feminist agenda. The take-away message of *Traps and Killings* is that corruption and the abuse of power lead to a cycle of violence that overwhelms both nations and families. This pastiche of the story of the war against Troy and its aftermath offers a three-step synthesis of the myth of the Atreidae: (i) Western Civilisation vs. Eastern Barbarians, (ii) Eastern Civilisation vs. Western Barbarians, and (iii) the destruction of the family. Both Greek and Trojan examples of the impact of war on the family, in particular on noncombatants, are recast in *Traps and Killings* to emphasise the human cost of war.

Traps and Killings emerged out of a long collaborative process, and even the title of the play underwent changes. In 1999 the working title was

[65] Minier (2014), 16.

[66] As discussed in greater detail below, Perelis' choice of the term 'δόλος' for the title of his play is indicative of the production's synthesis of ancient and modern elements, in this particular instance on the linguistic level.

[67] The theatre and film director Michael Cacoyannis helped to popularise this view of Euripides with his Euripidean trilogy: *Electra* (1962), *The Trojan Women* (1971), and *Iphigenia* (1977).

[68] Programme notes, 5.

'*Οι μηχανές του δόλου και του τρόμου: Ο πόλεμος, τα φονικά, το χρήμα*' (*Machines of Dolos and Terror: War, Killings and Money*, 1999). In this earlier incarnation, the title more explicitly revealed the company's interpretation of its ancient source material. During a key moment, Orestes refers to 'η μηχανή του δόλου και του τρόμου' ('the machine of *dolos* and terror'), using the second part of the revised title to refer to the imperative towards matricide. The ancient roots of the term *dolos* (deceit) are a linguistic signal to the story's classical connections, but the reference to machines reminded the audience of the mechanised way modern wars are fought and projected that backwards to the ancient world. The machine is also the trap that Clytemnestra's children prepare for her in order to punish her for her part in the murder of their father. The 'machine',[69] however, also traps Polyxena and the other Trojan women and terrorises them earlier in the play, when the audience witness two Greek soldiers holding a net over Polyxena. Polyxena, on her knees, is surrounded by the other Trojan women, who are also forced to kneel at the feet of their new masters. The spatial arrangement with the Greeks standing menacingly over the women reinforces the life-and-death power they now hold over their captives.

Traps and Killings condemns the suffering that the strong inflict on the weak, but argues that this is balanced by the need for justice. Hecuba laments, 'το ένα κακό πάνω στο άλλο' ('one evil on top of another'), and argues 'πρέπει να τιμωρήσω το φονιά, να λάμψει η δικαιοσύνη έστω για μια στιγμή' ('I must punish the murderer so that justice can shine, if only for a brief moment'). Of course, the particular form that justice takes leads to more violence when Hecuba murders Polymestor's two sons and blinds the king himself, in revenge for his murder of her son Polydorus. Like many other modern productions of Greek tragedy, *Traps and Killings* features onstage violence, as when Orestes kills Aegisthus with a knife. In the fifth century BCE, violence usually took place offstage, but the majority of modern directors, worried about audiences more familiar with graphic depictions of violence in the media, choose to 'show' rather than 'tell' their audiences about these terrible acts of violence and death.[70] The production was also concerned to emphasise the impact of war on

[69] Perelis' emphasis on the 'machine' could be a nod to Cocteau's *La Machine infernale* (1953), but also served as a timely reminder of the human toll of mechanised warfare at the end of the twentieth century. In the large-scale conflicts of the last century, war became increasingly reliant on ever more destructive technological weapons, machines of war that crushed the human beings in their path.

[70] Violence has become 'the lifeblood of contemporary storytelling': Symonds (2008), 2. See also Perris, Chapter 9, this volume.

noncombatants and soldiers alike, and on how it dehumanises both. To modern audiences of Greek tragedy this anti-war emphasis feels very familiar.[71]

In their search for dramatic and emotional impact (the way in which the Aristotelian concept of *katharsis* is usually understood by modern theatrical practitioners), Perelis and his collaborators selected such highlights from their ancient theatrical models as (to name but a few) Clytemnestra's emotional farewell to her daughter Iphigenia, Andromache's reaction to the news that the Greeks have ordered the death of her son Astyanax, and the debate between Electra and her mother Clytemnestra. The production's linguistic register reinforced its accessibility to a wider public, while also signalling its historical connections. The Language Question gave modern Greek theatre practitioners a choice of languages (ancient Greek, *katharevousa*, *dimotiki*, or some combination of the three) in which they could express their engagement with the classical past. Their choice is an indication of their ideological stance towards ancient Greece and the role it plays ideologically in the modern Greek state. Rather than seeking to sidestep this contentious question, *Traps and Killings* paid tribute to the history and evolution of the Greek language itself, moving freely between the ancient and modern registers. To give an indicative example, when Electra witnesses her mother's murder she addresses her brother first in modern Greek and then in ancient Greek.[72] This linguistic synthesis of older and newer forms of Greek is Perelis' acknowledgement of the passing of time, reminding his spectators that they are watching a modern Greek performance of ancient Greek drama. A knowledgeable modern Greek audience (and in winter, in the smaller Experimental Stage, the majority of the audience would have been Greeks) allowed *Traps and Killings* to be bolder. The production's modern mise-en-scène prioritised contemporary connections over 'classical' ones. The costumes were modern, including military uniforms for all members of the Greek army. The Trojan War was portrayed as a story about 'ordinary people', with a chorus that was fully

[71] The British translator, playwright, and director Don Taylor labelled *The Trojan Women* 'the most shattering and complete condemnation of the atrocities of war': Taylor (1990), x. The anti-war interpretation of Euripides' *The Trojan Women*, *Hecuba*, and *Iphigenia at Aulis* has proven particularly popular with theatre practitioners and audiences alike, establishing itself as the proper way to perform these tragedies. The success of this interpretation on stage should not, however, lead us to uncritically adopt it, since it is largely an anachronistic reading. For the complexity of ancient Athenian audience responses to witnessing the suffering of their traditional enemies, the Trojans, in Euripides' *The Trojan Women*, see Mills (2010), 176–83.

[72] For Electra's words, see the following video at 90:33–54: www.nt-archive.gr/playMaterial.aspx?playID=383#videos (accessed 15 January 2020).

integrated into the action of the drama and interacted closely with the protagonists. The production's modern military and civilian dress introduced visual as well as thematic connections (notably the massacre of civilians)[73] to the Balkan wars of the 1990s that had been featured extensively on Greek television. *Traps and Killings* repurposes the story of the Trojan War, reinforced with references to Thucydides' account of the Melian Massacre, to condemn modern conflicts. With its many contemporary historical and political connections and realistic acting style, it also serves as a direct challenge to the traditional approach to staging Greek drama in modern Greece.

Retrenchment in a Crisis: *The Trojan Women* (2015)

Watching the Trojan women curse Greece for their suffering only a few days before the Greek bailout referendum was a deeply unsettling theatrical experience. It led this particular audience member to reflect on the power and relevance of Euripides' ancient drama and more widely on the role of Greek tragedy in today's politically, economically, and culturally fractured world. Even Sotiris Hatzakis' conservative production of the *The Trojan Women* for the National Theatre of Greece in the same year felt like it had the potential to be very timely, precisely because it premiered in that particular moment in a tempestuous summer of political and financial crisis. Watching Hecuba, Cassandra, Andromache, and the chorus of Trojan women lament their cruel fate brought into sharper focus a number of key questions about the future of ancient Greek drama not only in the modern Greek state, but beyond its borders, too. Can Greek tragedy truly offer a measure of consolation during a moment of real crisis? Do its viewers undergo a *katharsis* of emotions that could translate into tangible therapeutic benefits in their life outside the theatre? More generally, is watching theatre a radical act or is it merely an escape from an unbearable reality? And, crucially, from the point of view of this classicist at least, what is the function of ancient drama in a society riven with deep political divisions and facing a deeply uncertain future?

All contemporary productions have to find a theatrical and linguistic register that will help them form an effective bridge between ancient drama and the preoccupations, problems, and anxieties of today. Otherwise, ancient Greek drama risks becoming an unnecessary relic of the past with

[73] For example, the infamous Srebrenica massacre (1995), in which Muslim men and boys were murdered, as the men of Troy were during the Greeks' sacking of their city.

nothing of value to say to the present. This is precisely the challenge facing theatre practitioners not only in modern Greece, but also on the world stage. Hatzakis' *The Trojan Women* was a production that retreated back into the safety of traditional approaches to staging ancient drama. In contrast, that same summer, smaller, more experimental theatre companies sought innovative ways of bringing these ancient plays to the stage. In what follows, I argue that in the politically charged atmosphere of 2015 this represented a missed opportunity for the National Theatre of Greece to make an impactful statement.

The production starred the well-known Greek actress Karyofillia Karabeti in the role of Hecuba. Karabeti, familiar to modern Greek audiences from both stage and small-screen appearances, is usually cast in the role of a passionate woman facing impossible dilemmas.[74] Her portrayal of Hecuba generated sympathy for the former queen of Troy, but at times she ended up encroaching on other performers' space by design. To give an indicative example, during Andromache's famous scene when she is forced to accept that there is nothing she can do to save her son Astyanax, Karabeti's acting distracted the audience from Maria Kitsou's performance as Hector's widow. When Talthybius delivered the terrible news of Astyanax's impending death, this Andromache remained frozen in horror, making room for her mother-in-law to take the lead in lamenting their fate. As a result, Andromache's anticipatory lamentation for her son was overshadowed prematurely by Hecuba, who, according to the text, is not supposed to take centrestage before Astyanax's burial. Karabeti, as the star of the production, proved both one of its highlights and one of the forces that destabilised it. The actress did, however, provide the only moment of political commentary on the then-imminent referendum by making the victory sign while taking her bow and generally trying to raise the spirits of the audience before they left the ancient theatre. Audience members on the first night did applaud enthusiastically, but this was one of the smallest audiences I have ever been part of at Epidaurus. Despite Livathinos' call-to-arms to the public on national radio to attend the performance, the general disruption of the country spilled over into the theatre.

A particularly jarring moment in the production came when Eleni Roussinou arrogantly swanned onto the stage as Helen, in a long blond wig, draped in an evening gown in white and blue (in different shades), reminiscent of the Greek flag (see Figure 12.1). Hatzakis chose to

[74] Bakogianni (2013a), 207.

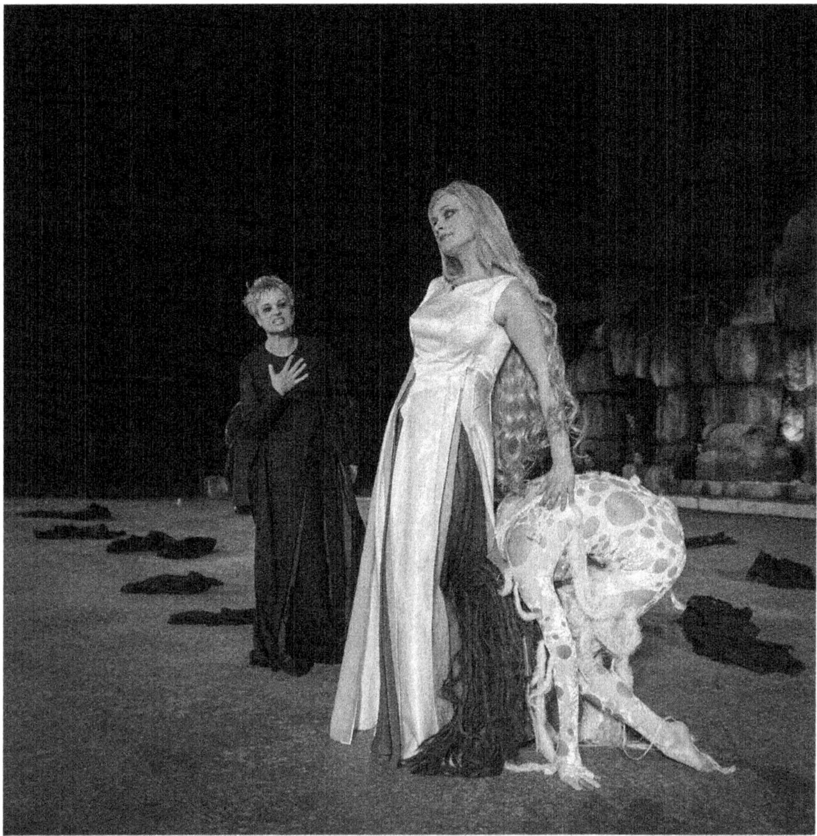

Figure 12.1 Hecuba (Karyofyllia Karabeti), Helen (Eleni Roussinou) and the daemon (Georgina Dalara) in Sotiris Hatzakis' production of *The Trojan Women* (2015). Reproduced with permission of the National Theatre, Greece

underscore his Helen's arrogance and disregard for the suffering of others by this explicit reference to the Greek flag and nationalist ideology. In general, the production was out of sync with all the major political and societal concerns of the day. Even though it was planned months before the referendum was announced on 25 June, the director could have made adjustments during the rehearsals and he certainly could have used the play to comment on the migration crisis that was another burning issue of the day. His production felt completely out of step with the modern world, cocooned in the 'glamour' of the classical past with no connection to the difficult issues that were plaguing the modern state during the crisis.

Hatzakis' Helen was accompanied by a silent female daemon (Georgina Dalara), who played at her feet (Figure 12.1). This was one of Hatzakis' innovations designed to place the blame for the war even more squarely on Helen's shoulders than Euripides' source drama does. In this production women were portrayed as either helpless victims or heartless harlots with little room left for ambiguity. Retreading old ground, without any reference to more recent interpretations of the tragedy as a platform for debating the impact of war on women, it all seemed a bit redundant.[75]

Myris' poetic translation did not aid audiences to connect viscerally with the production,[76] despite the best efforts of the performers and the fact that on a number of occasions the text was cut or simplified in order to make the play more accessible. Judging from Hatzakis' own contribution to the programme, he too is more comfortable in the older registers of the Greek language.[77] For example, his description of the tragedy of the Trojan women reads:

> Διακονούμε το άχραντο. Προσκυνητές ενός Επιταφίου, γινόμαστε στο τέλος οι ίδιοιεμείς επιτάφιοι θρήνοι, που οδηγούν μέσα από τον κάθε Γολγοθά – δρομίσκοι αμέτρητοι – στον Μέγαν θόλο της αρχαίας μήτρας.
>
> We are in the service of the immaculate. Pilgrims in the Funerary Procession, in the end we become ourselves funerary lamentations, which lead us, via countless byways, through each and every Golgotha to the Great domed tomb of the ancient womb.[78]

There are clear religious undertones in these words that suggest that the director understood the Trojan women's lament over Troy as an ancient version of the Greek Orthodox Easter practice of mourning the death of Jesus Christ. Christian interpretations of ancient tragedy have proven very popular in modern Greece in the past, but by 2015 they were yet another sign of the production's obsequious reverence for tradition. If it was Hatzakis' intention to mourn the modern tragedy that had befallen Greece that summer, the message failed to be communicated. His production was too focused on the past for that connection to become activated.

[75] While admittedly anachronistic, such productions have become the norm in world theatre. Katie Mitchell's *Women of Troy* (2007–8) for the National Theatre in London is one example of a more nuanced interpretation that highlights issues of gender. Her Helen, for example, is violently manhandled by a Greek soldier and she, too, suffers in the aftermath of the war.

[76] For an example, see Myris (2001), 30–7 (the Cassandra scene).

[77] Programme notes, 6–7.

[78] Hatzakis' note was not translated into English in the bilingual programme that accompanied his production. My 'Funerary Procession' is an attempt to render Hatzakis' *Epitaphios*, a reference to the religious procession headed by a representation of Jesus' sepulchre performed on Good Friday in the Eastern Orthodox Church.

In the post-2008 financial crash culture of austerity, when funding for the arts is radically reduced and their very survival threatened, the question 'Why Greek Tragedy Now?' is more relevant than ever. Many artists seem to find consolation in ancient tragic narratives of extreme suffering, an overt sign of trust in the 'therapeutic value of the arts'.[79] In the *Poetics*, Aristotle writes that tragedy effects 'through pity and fear the purification of such emotions' (1449b28). Aristotle seems to argue that drama allows us to experience negative emotions such as pity, compassion, and fear/terror without any real-life detrimental effects. Paradoxically, we enjoy weeping over the suffering of characters in tragedy, while the same suffering in the real world would fill us with horror and repugnance. The concept of *katharsis* has proven particularly fertile for practitioners concerned with the ancient dramas' emotional impact and relevance. Watching Hecuba, the former queen of Troy, suffer and be treated as a lowly slave in *The Trojan Women*, for example, can help us put our own problems into perspective. In other words, tragedy can act as a form of 'public therapy'[80] that drains dangerous emotions from the body politic. Hatzakis' refusal to engage in any meaningful way with contemporary societal concerns, however, and his insistence on sterile 'authenticity' made his *Trojan Women* one of the least interesting offerings of that summer. An unintended lesson to be learned from this production is that an overly reverent approach to performing Greek tragedy no longer works, if it ever truly did. Ultimately, archaising approaches to Greek tragedy serve up a theatrically less satisfying experience that is easily forgettable or is memorable for the wrong reasons. For Greek drama to continue to speak to modern audiences, especially to those who are living through a real-life crisis, it has to offer something new and meaningful.

New Directions: The Clash of Generations in *Antigone* (2016)

In artistic endeavours in general, 'adaptation is the norm, not the exception'.[81] As on the stage, so in real life, Stathis Livathinos' *Antigone* of 2016 challenged the National Theatre's way of staging Greek tragedy. It was a clash of generations, older versus newer ways of performing Greek tragedy on the stage of Epidaurus (and on tour across Greece and Cyprus). One of the most prominent, and much discussed,[82] features of the

79 Hartigan (2009), 5. 80 Eagleton (2003), 153. 81 Hutcheon (2006), 177.

82 For examples from the Greek press, see Anonymous (2016e); Mesiskli (2016); Ioannidis (2016). See also Programme notes, 15.

production was its performance by three generations of modern Greek actors and actresses. In an interview, Livathinos stated that each generation needs its own Antigone and that this was the time for a new version that addressed contemporary anxieties.[83] In post-referendum austerity Greece, the production sidestepped the dominant interpretation of the tragic heroine as a fully fledged rebel with a cause, who enters the stage already decided on her course of action. Instead, Anastasia-Rafaella Konidi in the eponymous role played a young girl forced to grow up too quickly when faced with a terrible dilemma. Costuming choices reinforced this impression in her early scenes: she was dressed in a plain blouse with a white collar, shorts, and Dockers boots. We first encounter this Antigone swaying on a swing, a young girl not long out of childhood. Haemon, too, is dressed in short pants, and his youthful idealism and pure, innocent love for Antigone earned actor Vasilis Magouliotis a hearty round of applause by the audience during his confrontation with his father. This Antigone and Haemon represented Generation G, the young modern Greeks who, as a result of the bad decisions of their elders (on stage these are represented by Creon and the older members of the chorus), are faced with Europe's highest unemployment rate and some tough dilemmas. Among young people with 'desirable' skills, many were forced to emigrate in what, ahead of the Greek elections of 2015, was already being referred to as 'the world's biggest brain-drain'.[84]

The mixed chorus mirrored this generational divide by its split into older and youthful male and female members (Figure 12.2). The latter were close in age to Antigone and became her support group over the course of the performance. During Sophocles' famous Ode to Man, the younger members of the chorus gambolled about the stage with great energy and adopted a sing-song communal voice that contrasted with the mature tone of the older half. In Antigone's final lament the younger members of the chorus attempted to comfort her. This was a stark reminder that the youth of Thebes has been very nearly annihilated (many, including Antigone's brothers, have died before the drama's opening in the war with Argos), while over the course of the play, two more youthful members of the royal family perish and are joined in death by the middle-aged Eurydice. This served to explain Antigone's insistence that Ismene's life be spared in Livathinos' production. His heroine wanted her sister to survive, and the pair shared a final embrace. Their relationship was portrayed as more loving than is generally the case in modern productions

[83] Livathinos interviewed by Koukos (2016), 54. [84] H. Smith (2015) (accessed 27 June 2019).

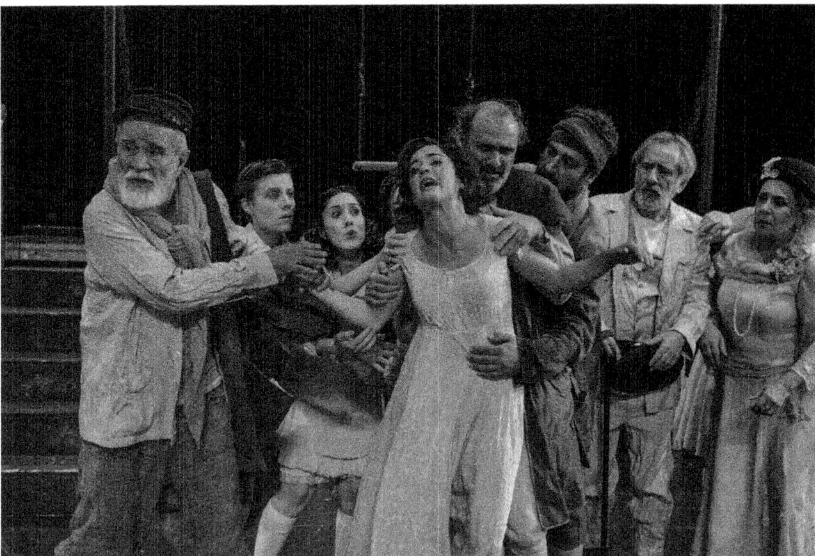

Figure 12.2 Antigone (Anastasia-Rafaella Konidi) and the chorus in Stathis Livathinos' *Antigone* (2016).
Reproduced with permission of the National Theatre, Greece

of the ancient drama, thus resulting in a more humanised Antigone. Livathinos' decision to cast young actors, not only in the eponymous role of Antigone, but also in half the chorus members' roles, strengthened the production's contemporary 'lost generation' resonances, and made the clash of the generations one of the most prominent features of the production.

In her final scene, Antigone changed into a white wedding dress complete with a veil and a crown of flowers: she was ready to become the bride of Hades (Figure 12.2). Significantly, a number of the young members of the chorus who surrounded her, and even physically supported her when she collapsed, clutched dolls in their hands, a visual symbol for the children Antigone will now never be able to have with Haemon, but also of these chorus members' youth. Livathinos wanted to underline Antigone's choice to act alone and to isolate herself from human contact.[85] Ultimately, she rejected the younger chorus' offer of consolation as she also rejected Ismene and Haemon and of course Creon and the

[85] Interviewed by Mastrogiannitis (2016).

elders. Livathinos finds her rejection of Haemon's love 'extreme',[86] but in Sophocles' play Antigone's endogamous devotion to her family is explained by the incestuous nature of her parentage, while on the modern stage her transgressive and unbending nature is part of her appeal as a tragic heroine. These elements were downplayed in the National Theatre's production in favour of emphasising Antigone's youth and her clash with the older generations.

Creon, played by Dimitris Lignadis, was more conventionally portrayed as a tyrant who fails his people – a people symbolically represented on his crown, which was decorated with spikes resembling human figures – and partly redeems himself by his contrition at the end. In Livathinos' production, he memorably used both threats and physical violence against the sisters. It took Teiresias' nightmarish prophetic vision of Antigone's swing turning into a hangman's scaffold, and the two bodies of Antigone and Haemon in nooses, for him to change course. Visually, this was a spectacular and menacing scene, but this raised platform at the back of the stage was the production's most prominent prop. At the beginning of the performance, the swing symbolising Antigone's innocence was prominently displayed on this raised platform, but it was transformed into the noose in this key turning point in the production. Another prominent prop was the benches that dotted the outside ring of the orchestra and provided a touch of metatheatre by placing the play's internal audience in close proximity to the theatre spectators. The production engaged its audience both on an emotional and an intellectual level, with several innovative elements (the contemporary emphasis on the generational divide and metatheatrical touches) that made it more than just another National Theatre of Greece revival of Sophocles' popular tragedy. Some of the signature elements of the company's usual approach to staging Greek tragedy were still present: namely, the occasionally rigid acting and the decision to remain strictly within the confines of the ancient play without any major changes to the dramatic text. However, the openness to new directions and interpretations of the ancient material was a breath of fresh air, especially after the previous year's traditionalist production of *The Trojan Women*. The National Theatre of Greece had finally taken a new creative turn, significantly, with its signature production for the summer of 2016.

[86] Mastrogiannitis (2016).

Conclusion

Modern Greek theatre practitioners return again and again to the tragedies of Aeschylus, Sophocles, and Euripides, some aiming to revive them, while others seek to recontextualise them for the modern stage. Greek drama was gradually radicalised on a global scale in the twentieth and twenty-first centuries, and ancient dramatic texts were and continue to be used to protest against abuses of power, violence, and war. As my four case studies demonstrate, modern Greek theatre practitioners have both reacted and, at other times, failed to respond to the challenge of making these ancient plays relevant for modern audiences in the new millennium. Comparisons between traditionalist and more innovative productions serve to highlight the ongoing clash between the two approaches of staging Greek drama not only in modern Greece, but also globally. I share Avra Sidiropoulou's view that modern Greek theatre practitioners and audiences have become more open to creative adaptations of Greek drama in the twenty-first century.[87] The National Theatre of Greece still has some way to go before it fully embraces this new openness, but it is heading down this creative path.

In 2019, the National Theatre signalled its awareness of current societal concerns by entrusting three female directors, Io Voulgaraki, Lilly Meleme, and Georgia Mavragani, with Aeschylus' seminal trilogy, the *Oresteia* (premiered 27–8 June 2019).[88] Traditionally, few women have directed this trilogy, which has often been among the National Theatre's signature productions of Greek drama at Epidaurus,[89] but it is hoped that this, too, will change in the future in response to the concerns raised by the Time's Up and #MeToo movements. Overall, this production of the trilogy was more traditional than transformative (Georgia Mavragani's *Eumenides* being the most innovative of the three), but it did highlight gender issues.[90] Certainly, the audience's commitment to watching Greek drama was amply manifest in their choice to sit on the less than comfortable stone benches of Epidaurus for four and a half hours without a

[87] Sidiropoulou (2018), 837–9.

[88] http://greekfestival.gr/festival_events/oresteia/?lang=en (accessed 21 July 2019).

[89] For a discussion of the work of female directors staging Greek tragedy, see Sidiropoulou (2018) and Bakogianni (2013a).

[90] For example, Voulgaraki's *Agamemnon* portrayed Clytemnestra as a non-binary figure, a former woman who left her womb back at Aulis and took on masculine features in order to survive in a patriarchal society: www.kathimerini.gr/1028183/article/politismos/8eatro/h-oresteia-se-treis-anagnwseis (accessed 15 January 2020).

break.[91] This is actually one of the most important resources that modern Greek theatre practitioners can draw on, a knowledgeable audience, many of whose members, despite the ongoing economic crisis, return each year to attend not only the summer festival, but also the large and small theatres that make up the modern Greek theatrical scene. Like ancient audiences, these devotees of the modern Greek stage can draw on their memories of earlier performances of tragedy to make comparisons.[92] Coupled with their new openness to new ways of staging Greek tragedy, this is a considerable advantage in the hands of a skilled set of practitioners.

Kamilla Elliott has called the concept of fidelity 'the bane of adaptation studies'.[93] Without a doubt, the search for authenticity remains a powerful lodestone for modern Greek theatre practitioners. The ancient dramatic texts are valorised to the detriment of innovative adaptations, which are framed in terms of what they 'lack' rather than what new layers of meaning they 'add'. But in adopting this position we are deliberately ignoring that the ancients Greeks and Romans did not view the process of reception and adaptation in such negative terms. Ancient Athenian audiences went to the dramatic festivals not to criticise the dramatists for failing to stage a canonical version of the story, but to witness how they adapted, for their own dramatic purposes, a corpus of mythical stories that already existed in multiple versions (see further Meineck, Chapter 2, this volume). If we keep insisting on the primacy of the classical text, we risk isolation and charges of elitism during a time when the arts are in crisis and new ways forward are required. The example of modern Greek audiences' new openness and the National Theatre of Greece's creative turn testify to the rewards of turning our ancient dramatic texts into live, engaging, and accessible theatre.

[91] On the night I attended the performance (27 June), the majority of the audience stayed till the end, although there were a few calls from audience members to get on with it during the latter half of the *Eumenides*, which was the freest adaptation of the three and the most challenging to traditionalists.

[92] Aided by their pedagogical background, especially in the case of *Antigone*, which remains one of the most studied ancient dramas in the modern Greek school curriculum.

[93] Elliott (2013), 22.

CHAPTER 13

Adaptation and the Transtextual Palimpsest
Anne Carson's Antigonick *as a Textual/Visual Hybrid**

Vayos Liapis

To classify Anne Carson's *Antigonick* as an adaptation is to invite scepticism, or even dissent. For *Antigonick* is much more than that; it is also, at places, a little less than that. It is a puzzlingly open-ended artefact, which seems perpetually to resist categorisation; if it invokes traditional categories, such as 'translation', it is only so that it may throw them, almost immediately, into doubt. 'Translated by Anne Carson', we are informed on the book cover, but exactly what has Anne Carson translated? The title 'ANTIGO NICK | (Sophokles)' (see Figure 13.4) seems studiously unspecific: the title of Sophocles' *Antigone* is teasingly alluded to but given an unanticipated ending; and 'Sophokles' (as opposed to '*by* Sophokles') is bracketed, as if to suggest that this is not exactly, or not altogether, a version of Sophocles' play.[1] Carson has produced something that both is and is not a translation of the Sophoclean classic.

As we shall see in detail below, *Antigonick* is a strange beast, a crossbreed between translation, adaptation, and rewriting. For lack of a better term, we might call it a *transtextual palimpsest*: a programmatically composite script, which places itself, to use Gérard Genette's words, in a 'relation (manifest or hidden) with other texts', including 'the transtextual relationship that links a commentary to the text it comments on'.[2] As well as a palimpsest, *Antigonick* is also a kaleidoscope of transtextuality, in which a plethoric variety of discourse types, modes of enunciation, and literary or

* I am grateful to my co-editor and to CUP's anonymous readers for their perceptive reading of this chapter and for comments that improved its content. My thanks go also to my former MA student Ms Angeliki Stylianopoulou for bibliographic information. I am grateful to Mr Christopher Wait, Permissions Editor at New Directions Publishing, for allowing me to use textual quotations and images by Bianca Stone from Anne Carson's *Antigonick* in this chapter. I regret that Alonso 2016 came to my attention only when the present chapter was essentially complete, and I was consequently unable to take her arguments into account. Translations from Greek texts are mine unless otherwise indicated.

[1] Cf. Silverblank (2014), 350–1.

[2] Quotations from Genette (1992), 81–2; cf. also Genette (1997a), 1.

paraliterary genres (including but not limited to citation, parody, commentary, as well as translation) coexist in a sort of symbiotic tension: they superimpose themselves upon each other, complement or antagonise each other, flaunt their transtextual layering, and urge the reader to decorticate it. Finally, *Antigonick* is also, conspicuously, a hybrid object, which amalgamates, on alternating pages, text (or, more precisely, hand-inked blocks of text) and original colour drawings. In so doing, *Antigonick* seems to set itself an unusual challenge: it is a text that wishes to transcend its own textuality; it is a static object that aspires to dynamic movement; it is a typographic artefact that desires to become theatrical (perhaps even to supplant the theatrical) by appropriating the fusion of textual, visual, and even kinetic aspects that is inherent to theatre. We shall have more to say on all of this below.

Before we proceed, we should point out that Carson's *Antigonick* is, to a large extent, indebted to Ezra Pound's much-cited injunction to 'make it new', to breathe new life into old texts, including texts of the Greek and Latin classical canon. For Pound, this rewriting project involves updating the style and language of the source text into a fast-paced, slick, sometimes slangy contemporary idiom,[3] which however is by no means homogeneous but spans several disparate stylistic registers: for it opens itself up just as freely to the language of Elizabethan drama[4] as to jazzy rhymes redolent of Cole Porter.[5] What is more, Pound's translations, like his poetry, are notoriously plurilingual: his and University of Maryland classicist Rudd Fleming's rendering of Sophocles' *Electra*, for instance, introduces Latin quotes from Justinian's *Institutiones* which Pound knew from Dante's *Vita Nuova*,[6] and incorporates entire bits of Sophoclean Greek cited in

[3] Cf., e.g., Pound (2003), 995–6: 'Get goin' quickly. | Sun's risin', birds are a singin' . . . We'll go to dad's tomb, as ordered | with libations an' all my pretty curls' (from Pound and Rudd Fleming's translation of Sophocles' *Electra*). Also, Pound (2003), 1077: "Arf a mo' Ma'am! Better find out | what you're taking in there' (from his translation of Sophocles' *Women of Trachis*).

[4] Cf., e.g., Pound (2003), 1070: 'NORTH WIND or South, so bloweth tireless | wave over wave to flood. | Cretan of Cadmus' blood, Orcus' shafts err not. | What home hast'ou now, | an some God stir not?' (again from his translation of Sophocles' *Women of Trachis*).

[5] Cf. Pound (2003), 1013: 'You can say that I never guess right | a fool born without second sight, | that my head was never screwed tight | But if Justice don't win just this once | I'm a dunce | and before a great time has gone by | My heart's risin now' etc. (from Pound and Rudd Fleming's translation of Sophocles' *Electra*).

[6] Cf. Pound (2003), 1018: 'Now you're talkin', | you did the job, not me, | and things done get names | *nomina sunt consequentia rerum*'. The Latin quote ('names are consequent on things') derives ultimately from Justinian's *Institutiones* 2.7.3 (*sed nos . . . consequentia nomina rebus esse studentes*, 'but we . . . in our wish to have names correspond to things'), but Pound cites it in the form in which he found it in Dante's *Vita Nuova* XIII: 'con ciò sia cosa che li nomi seguitino le nominate cose, sì come

(approximate) transliteration.[7] As we shall have occasion to note later, Carson's *Antigonick* moves along similar lines: her (re)writing idiom is liberally besprinkled with colloquialisms, which may come across as perhaps too conversational and distracting. At the same time, *Antigonick* is also plurilingual, in ways partly comparable to Pound's: it has its own share of faux-Elizabethan idiom in the form of quotations from Sir Richard Jebb's late Victorian translation of *Antigone*; and, like Pound's *Electra*, it sometimes advertises its derivativeness by including Anglicised versions of Greek words culled from the Sophoclean original, or by concocting delightfully discordant words or turns of phrase prompted by bits of Sophocles' Greek.

Antigonick as a Palimpsest

Even as a physical object, the book entitled *Antigonick* makes its palimpsestic nature visible the moment one lays hands upon it. For it looks and feels more like an illuminated manuscript than your average printed book: recto pages imprinted with hand-inked blocks of text (the verso remaining blank) alternate with translucent vellum pages with colour drawings by illustrator Bianca Stone.[8] As well as giving the book a distinctly 'handmade' feel, this alternation between text and image creates ipso facto a quasi-palimpsestic effect: the illustrations are designed to overlay the hand-inked text, so that a reader's first encounter with Carson's text must be mediated by the superimposed semi-diaphanous filter of Stone's designs. This filter may be simply removed by turning the page to get directly to Carson's text; but since the illustrated layering is translucent, a reader can view at least part of the text even before turning the vellum page, so that s/he may approach, if s/he so wishes, Carson's words in tandem with Stone's illustrations as if they were a hybrid, or

è scritto: *Nomina sunt consequentia rerum'* (or, in Dante Gabriel Rossetti's translation, 'seeing that the name must needs be like unto the thing named; as it is written: *Nomina sunt consequentia rerum.'*)

[7] For instance, Pound (2003), 998: 'let everyone hear it | Hell and Persephone | OO DOOM' AIDOU | OO CHTHONI' Hermes, Oh Queen of Avenging | ARA, O Vengeance' (cf. Sophocles, *Electra*, 110–11: ὦ δῶμ' Ἀίδου καὶ Περσεφόνης, | ὦ χθόνι' Ἑρμῆ καὶ πότνι' Ἀρά).

[8] In an interview (Aitken 2004), Carson records her wonder at the historical palimpsests that ancient Greek texts de facto are: 'After all, texts of ancient Greeks come to us in wreckage and I admire that, the combination of layers of time that you have when looking at a papyrus that was produced in the third century BC and then copied and then wrapped around a mummy for a couple hundred years and then discovered and put in a museum and pieced together by nine different gentlemen and put back in the museum and brought out again and photographed and put in a book. All those layers add up to more and more life.'

amalgam, of text and image.[9] Indeed, in certain cases, this sort of amalgamation seems to be invited – or, indeed, imposed – by the physical arrangement of underlying text blocks and overlain illustration. Consider, for instance, the text blocks on page [79][10] and their corresponding illustration (Figure 13.1). Here, the text blocks are arranged on the top and bottom of the page, with the central zone left empty; inversely, on the translucent vellum page the image does not extend beyond the corresponding central register, leaving the top and bottom of the page blank. Thus, the text blocks can be read without hindrance even through the superimposed image; the resulting fusion of text and image is apparently intentional and significant. The image – a horse's lower torso, its two front legs entangled in a red thread that unwinds from a reeling spool – may appear less puzzling once contextualised with help from the underlying text. Indeed, the inauspicious 'Here comes Tiresias', followed by an ominously red-lettered indication 'Episode Five' (the only time that Carson's text offers such a structural marker), leave us in little doubt as to the nature of the ensuing Tiresias scene. In response to the seer's warnings, Creon will rush to liberate Antigone from her underground prison, but his belated diligence will turn out to be inadequate. Rather like Bianca Stone's hobbled horse, Creon will run fast but not nearly fast enough. The red thread – an image which has been running, in several variations, through Stone's illustrations like a red thread indeed[11] – turns out to enshrine notions of encumbrance, failure, and profound distress.

[9] Cf. Stone (2015), 153: 'The drawings and the text could be experienced separately or together. The end result is the reader creates a whole new translation each time she opens the book.' *Antigonick*'s simulation of the material texture of handwritten paper has a fuller and more complex precedent in Anne Carson's *Nox*, a screenfold of a book inside a box, complete with all the traces that suggest the passage of personal time (smudges of ink, tea-stains, stapled photographs, scraps of letters, yellowed pages, etc.); see further Hannaway (2013), 153–7; cf. Stone (2015), 154. On the aesthetics of 'hypermediacy' in *Nox*, see Brillenburg Wurth (2013). A more recent parallel to *Antigonick*, as an anonymous CUP reader points out to me, is Carson's *Norma Jeane Baker of Troy* (The Shed, New York, 6 April – 19 May 2019, dir. Katie Mitchell), a 'melologue' (Carson's term) in which Euripides' Helen is fused with Norma Jeane Baker (aka Marilyn Monroe). Like *Antigonick*, this work is a transtextual and transmedial amalgam involving such disparate components as philological commentary (ruminations on the Greek pronoun τις), a (possibly) traumatised ex-serviceman (Ben Whishaw) transformed onstage into a drag replica of Marilyn Monroe's iconic white-dress figure in *The Seven Year Itch*, a stenotypist (opera diva Renée Fleming) singing experimental musical fragments by Paul Clark, and 'sound effects and background music ... made entirely from a base of recorded clusters of notes sung by Ms. Fleming' (Brantley 2019).

[10] Page numbers in brackets have been assigned by me; there are none in Carson (2012).

[11] See images to Carson (2012), [17], [19], [25]. On 8 February 2008, Carson gave a series of short talks as part of a multimedia performance called 'String Talks', which took place at New York University's Skirball Center and involved, unsurprisingly, a red string which dancers from the Merce Cunningham company wound around the stage, as well as around Carson herself.

NO NOT REALLY

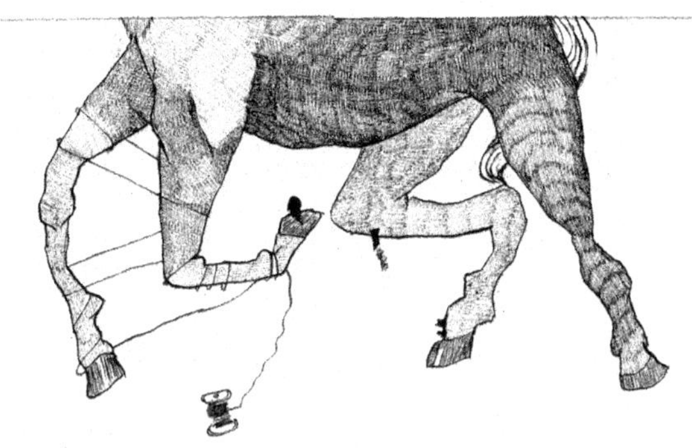

HERE COMES TEIRESIAS

EPISODE FIVE

Figure 13.1 Hand-inked blocks of text on upper and lower page, with superimposed illustration printed on translucent vellum.
From Carson (2012), [79], reproduced with permission of New Directions Publishing Corp

This interaction between image and text, which may originate in graphic-novel aesthetics, transcends conventional typography to achieve a new synthesis of text and image as mutually interdependent components interpreting and illuminating each other. Because the illustrations are not juxtaposed to but superimposed on the text, they appear to animate it, to set it in motion, even when they are of the *nature morte* kind. They force the reader to collate them with the text, thereby intertwining image and text into new and unexpected combinations, forming a fluid nexus that is more than the sum of its parts: it is 'a cross-generic, multimedia manifestation of Sophocles' tragedy', which programmatically defies the logocentrism of traditional translations to arrive at 'an individual choreographic performance through the interplay of text and image for the reader'.[12]

[12] Quotations from Silverblank (2014), 344 and 345 respectively. Silverblank's article offers a sensitive and penetrating discussion of the symbiosis and interaction of text (including typography) and illustrations in *Antigonick*.

The drawings interfere with the text, manipulate the reader's progress through the narrative, and control 'the pacing not unlike the scoring of a live performance, forcing the reader, for example, to ask why a pitcher of kitchen utensils appears in the midst of a choral segment in heightened dramatic language'.[13] Here, too, Carson seems to be operating under the sign of Ezra Pound's translations of Greek tragedy, especially *Women of Trachis* (1957), in which the typographical arrangement of choral verses, their setup and flow upon the page, seems designed to evoke dancing movements, so much so that Pound appears to be 'actually attempting to make printed text embody the motion which its sounds represent'.[14]

The amalgamation of text and image is not the only thing that animates *Antigonick*: the text itself, and its arrangement on the page, appear to take on the attributes of theatrical 'blocking', the physical positioning of actors on the stage. One of the most salient visual features of *Antigonick* as a printed book is the irregular, fluctuating (but far from erratic) disposition of the text on the page: whereas some pages are thickly packed with solid blocks of text, others contain just a handful of words thinly spread out over the entire page. A remarkable case in point is illustrated in Figure 13.2, where a characteristically minor character, Ismene, is given almost a whole page to herself: it looks as if she is restored, if only typographically (and momentarily), to a semblance of dramatic prominence. However, Ismene goes on to squander this unique opportunity by falling back into her traditional character, which is to say by descending 'into miserable, flailing cliché'.[15] Elsewhere, an entire page is occupied by a single line of text – one which is thereby made to stand out in splendid isolation, as it were, its typographic solitariness implying a special semantic status. This is the case with such phrases as the ironically intertextual 'then you notice the soles are on fire' (Figure 13.3), on which see further p. 371 below. In an interview, Carson has stated that 'the spatial aspect' is the primary consideration that motivates and defines her artistic endeavours.[16] Indeed, one of the many things that *Antigonick* can be described as is 'spatial poetry',

[13] Quotation from Souffrant (2014), 121. [14] Quotation from Harrop (2008), 100.

[15] Quotation from Thorp (2013). Cf. also Souffrant (2014), 122: 'The sprawl of emptiness after the density of the lettered pages is visceral. There is an exaggerated relief, perhaps because of the overwrought images and heavy handwritten font, that highlights Carson's use of space itself as a medium for not only dramatic content, but significant conveyance of the central emotional and intellectual drama of the play.'

[16] See Berkobien (2013).

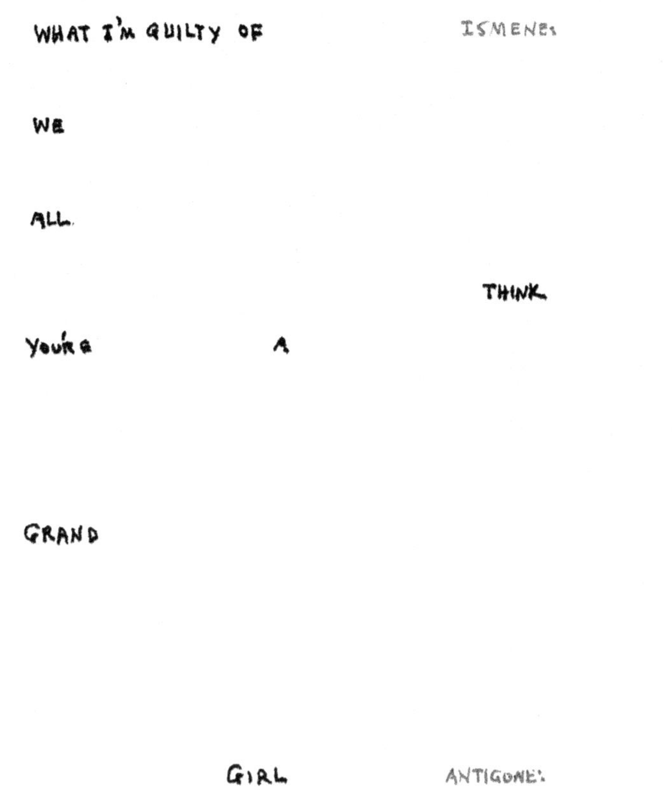

Figure 13.2 Hand-inked blocks of text spread out over the entire page.
From Carson (2012), [39], reproduced with permission of New Directions Publishing Corp

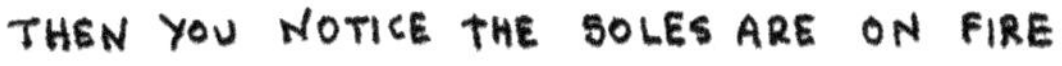

THEN YOU NOTICE THE SOLES ARE ON FIRE

Figure 13.3 A page hand-inked with a single line of text.
From Carson (2012), [47], reproduced with permission of New Directions Publishing Corp

'a staging as well as a rewriting of the text – one can almost see the characters on the stage-space, following her blueprint for abstract, blind, wilful movement'.[17] As a highly spatialised artefact, *Antigonick* is a prime

[17] Quotation from Thorp (2013).

example of the inseparability of (typo)graphic form and literary meaning discussed by Genette.[18]

As an adaptation, then, *Antigonick* goes much farther than the customary rewriting of a source text. Thanks not least to its fusion of text and image, it attempts to recreate, reconstitute, and revivify the essential unity of textuality and visuality that is ancient Greek theatre.

Antigonick: Adaptation, Wordplay, and the Ramifications of Language

Although, for the most part, *Antigonick* has the same dramatis personae as Sophocles' *Antigone*, Carson innovates in one instance, when she introduces a new character whom she calls Nick. As will progressively appear, Nick is a paradox. Textually, he is next to absent, since he is mentioned only twice: once in the list of characters ('cast'), where he is designated as 'a mute part';[19] and once in the final stage direction: 'exeunt omnes except Nick who continues | measuring'.[20] Crucially, measuring is the one activity Nick is given in the list of characters: '*always onstage, he measures things*'.[21] Visually, then, Nick is a perpetual presence: he is onstage even before the first speaking characters make their entrance, and he remains onstage even after all the other characters have departed at the end of the play. In the staged reading of *Antigonick* at the Gallatin School of New York University (22 February 2013), the figure of Nick was omnipresent, constantly measuring 'distances on stage and between the readers with a tape measure'.[22] As we saw above, Nick's overarching presence extends to the book's title itself, where it is enhanced through such peritextual means as design and layout (Figure 13.4). The wide space inserted between the title's two components – 'ANTIGO NICK' – typographically foregrounds Nick's importance and advertises the book as a hybrid construct, roughly three parts Antigo(ne) and one part Nick.[23]

Nick, to repeat, is a paradox. Albeit a non-speaking character, he is a linguistic construct – a composite organism made up of homonymy,

[18] See Genette (1997b), 33–6. In this respect, an early precursor of *Antigonick* is Blaise Cendrar and Sonia Delaunay-Terk's *La Prose du Transsibérien et de la petite Jehanne de France* (1913), a composite modernist work, in screenfold form (like Carson's *Nox*, cf. n. 9), in which text (in various fonts, to suggest the rapid motion of train travel) and images are interlaced, enveloping and interacting with each other. I am grateful to Mr Alexandros Velaoras for the information.

[19] Carson (2012), [5]. [20] Carson (2012), [107]. [21] Carson (2012), [5].

[22] Quotation from Souffrant (2014), 110.

[23] Further on the importance of 'the publisher's peritext', in particular of the book cover, in conveying information (however implicit) about the book, see Genette (1997b), 16–36, esp. 23–32.

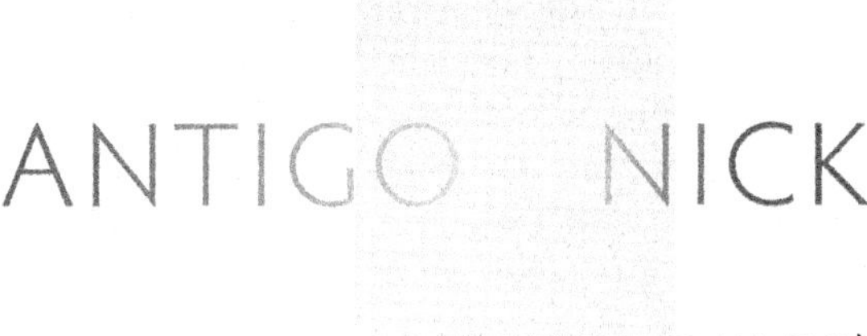

Figure 13.4 Cover of Anne Carson's *Antigonick*.
Reproduced with permission of New Directions Publishing Corp

wordplay, and intertextuality. His name lends itself to a number of linguistic associations, all of which may be prompted by even a cursory reading of the numerous definitions listed under the entry 'nick' in the *Oxford English Dictionary*, a lexicographical work of which Carson is famously enamoured.[24] First of all, Nick's association with the expression 'in the nick of time' is an obvious one and, indeed, is pointed out explicitly

[24] Cf. Silverblank (2014), 358–9.

by Carson's Eurydike ('have you heard | this expression the **nick of time** what is a | nick | I asked my son what | is | a | nick | I asked my son');[25] but even before that, it had already been alluded to by the Chorus on a couple of occasions ('here's Kreon, nick of time', or 'we're standing in | the nick of time').[26] By pointing to the possibilities of homonymy and wordplay inherent in 'Nick', these rather obvious hints fan the flames of linguistic association, thereby alerting us to a central aspect of *Antigonick*'s textuality, which revolves precisely around similar types of intralinguistic or even interlinguistic association.

Let us take as our first example this same expression, 'in the nick of time', and explore how it may lend itself to associative wordplay and thereby give rise to a whole constellation of semantic and interpretive possibilities. 'In the nick of time' implies a last-minute rescue or escape, but both in Sophocles' *Antigone* and in Carson's *Antigonick* timing is almost invariably bad, and time is pervasively an agent of disaster. While Antigone manages to escape 'in the nick of time' after her first 'burial' of Polynices (cf. Sophocles, *Antigone*, 245–77), she is caught in the act during the second 'burial', when a windstorm subsides just in time – in the nick of time indeed – to reveal her to the guards watching over Polynices' body (cf. *Antigone*, 384–440). And when Creon finally heeds Tiresias' warnings and rushes to Antigone's rescue, the fleeting hope that the girl may be saved 'in the nick of time' is belied as soon as it turns out that Antigone has hanged herself in her subterranean prison – or 'nick' in British slang.[27] Creon had hoped that by arresting – or 'nicking' – Antigone he would be able to keep both the city and his own *oikos* in good shape – or 'in good nick' – but has failed miserably: Antigone's suicide precipitates a series of further suicides – Haemon's, Eurydice's – which devastate Creon's house, bringing it down in one fell swoop. Indeed, before stabbing himself to death Haemon, we are told (*Antigone* 1220–43), had attempted to run his father through with his sword: in both cases, Haemon inflicts, or wishes to inflict, much more than a mere 'nick', or small cut. This double sense of 'nick' ('infinitesimal temporal margin' and 'cut') seems to underlie Carson's wordplay just before the announcement of Antigone's and Haemon's deaths in *Antigonick*:

[25] Carson (2012), [93]. Here and elsewhere in this chapter, words in bold typeface (e.g. '**nick of time**') correspond to words hand-inked in red in Carson's text.
[26] See Carson (2012), [27], [87], respectively.
[27] Cf. Steiner (2012): 'Or does the title "Antigo Nick" allude to the heroine's incarceration ("nick" as slang for prison)?'

CHORUS:
. . .
this instant
a second
a split second
a now
a nick
a neck
. . .
the darling you dust
the dust you disperse
the you who does not
does not what
does not
nick here we are we're all fine
[p. 87]
we're standing in
the nick of time

(Carson 2012, [85–7])

Here, the juxtaposition of 'nick' with 'neck' appears designed to evoke the sense 'small cut', which also seems to surface, in its verbal form, a little below, in 'does not | nick' (suggesting, perhaps, that Creon's violence is, eventually, ineffective).

But Carson's Nick is first and foremost a character, a dramatis persona, a proper noun. Spelled with a capital 'N', Nick invites further, and perhaps more sinister associations. Inevitably, he evokes 'Old Nick' himself: he may be the Devil incarnate, or at least a manifestation of that archetypal stage villain, 'old Nick Machiavel', the Elizabethan and Jacobean caricature of Niccolò Machiavelli, who memorably delivers the Prologue in Marlowe's *The Jew of Malta* (1588). Despite what Samuel Butler facetiously suggested in *Hudibras* (III.1313–14), it is not literally true that 'Nick Machiavel' gave 'his Name to our old Nick', the Devil.[28] However, the association between Machiavelli and 'Old Nick' is implicitly made already in Shakerley Marmion's 1641 play *The Antiquary* (Act 3, sc. 1), when a character dismisses another with the words 'Well, go thy ways, old Nick Machiavel, there will never be the peer of thee for wholesome policy and good counsel.'[29] There is, indeed, a distinctly 'Machiavellian' moment both in *Antigonick* and in *Antigone*, when Creon asserts that 'surely a city

[28] S. Butler (1772), 201: 'Nick Machiavel had ne'er a Trick, | (Though he gave his Name to our Old Nick) | But was below the least of these, | That pass i' th' World for Holiness.'

[29] On Machiavelli as the archetypal stage-villain of Elizabethan and later theatre, see Meyer (1897).

belongs | to its ruler'.[30] One cannot help suspecting that Carson's Nick – that constant, ever-occupied silent stage presence – may well be the play's éminence grise, masterminding the action to serve his own dark designs. Indeed, one feels that the designation 'terribly quiet customer', which the Chorus applies to Man in Carson's inventive rendering of the opening lines of *Antigone*'s famous first stasimon,[31] may be equally applicable to the ever-silent Nick. Furthermore, as well as incarnating the Devil, or the devilish element in man, Nick, who 'measures things' all the time, may just as well be an embodiment of 'Man, the measure of all things', in Protagoras' famous formulation (80 B1 Diels/Kranz = D9 Laks/Most πάντων χρημάτων μέτρον ἐστὶν ἄνθρωπος).

Translation as Adaptation in *Antigonick* (I): Greeking[32]

The multiple, often intersecting, and sometimes entangled ramifications of language, as exemplified in the emblematic case of 'Nick' (see previous section), offer a blueprint for the kind of text *Antigonick* wants to be. Albeit deceptively simple, almost trivial, 'Nick', as we have seen, can fan out into a complex nexus of linguistic affiliations. Indeed, wordplay in *Antigonick* is never simple or trivial; it is even less so when it becomes interlinguistic wordplay, that is, when it involves associations between words from different languages, notably English and ancient Greek. In this case, wordplay articulates itself as no less than a statement about the possibilities of translation.

Let us begin with a striking example of interlinguistic wordplay, which has been noted by *The Guardian* critic Charlotte Higgins, and is discussed by Adam Lecznar in Chapter 6 of this volume. In her rendering of the second stasimon of *Antigone* (594–5),

> Carson produces the memorable line 'archives of grief I see falling on this house'. The original Greek refers to 'ancient calamities [sc. of the Labdacids] that are heaped upon the calamities of the dead'. The 'archive' metaphor – original yet absolutely fitting – perhaps suggested itself to

[30] Carson (2012), [57]; cf. S. *Ant.* 738, οὐ τοῦ κρατοῦντος ἡ πόλις νομίζεται; ('isn't it customary to consider a city the possession of its ruler?') On the state as the possession of its ruler in Macchiavelli, see Mansfield (1996), 281–94 (arguing against Quentin Skinner's thesis that *The Prince* offers the first formulation of the idea of the modern state).

[31] See Carson (2012), [21]: 'Many terribly quiet customers exist but none more | terribly quiet than man'; cf. S. *Ant.* 332–3, πολλὰ τὰ δεινὰ κοὐδὲν ἀν-|θρώπου δεινότερον πέλει.

[32] In typography, visual media, and computing, 'greeking' is the display of random bits of Greek or Latin text to facilitate layout preview assessment without the distraction of a meaningful text. Here, I use the term in a substantially different sense, which will be made evident in what follows.

Carson because of its similarity to the word Sophocles uses for ancient, '*archaia*'.[33]

Higgins' conjecture is entirely felicitous: it is, indeed, the phonetic affinity with Sophocles' *archaia* (ἀρχαῖα τὰ Λαβδακιδᾶν οἴκων ὁρῶμαι | πήματα φθιτῶν ἐπὶ πήμασι πίπτοντα)[34] that gave rise to Carson's 'archives of grief'. But there is more to it than mere phonetic free association. Etymologically, English 'archive' comes ultimately (through French and Latin) from Greek *arkheia* (ἀρχεῖα), 'public records', which in turn derives from *arkhē* (ἀρχή), 'government'. The Antigone myth, in its variants from Sophocles to Carson, is a record, or 'archive' (ἀρχεῖα), of the 'ancient evils' (ἀρχαῖα . . . | πήματα) besetting the race of Oedipus, the Labdacids, who have been holding sway, ἀρχή, in Thebes generation after generation.[35]

This is far from being an isolated example. There is a comparable case later on, at the beginning of the Messenger's narrative in which the deaths of Antigone and Haemon are reported:

MESSENGER: o people there is no stanza of
human life that I would praise or blame. luck
sends your powerboat up or down the waves at
any given moment[36]

The startling 'stanza of human life' has in fact been suggested by the near-homonymy with the participle *stant[a]* (στάντ') in the Greek original (Sophocles, *Antigone*, 1156–7):

οὐκ ἔσθ' ὁποῖον στάντ' ἂν ἀνθρώπου βίον
οὔτ' αἰνέσαιμ' ἂν οὔτε μεμψαίμην ποτέ

there is no state of human life that I would praise or blame as though it had come to a stop.[37]

Here, too, Carson's intentional 'misreading' of the Greek original is bolstered by etymological considerations: *stanza* ('group of lines in a

[33] Quotation from Higgins (2015). Higgins is commenting on Carson (2015), 30, a translation of Sophocles' *Antigone* commissioned for a production directed by Ivo van Hove with Juliette Binoche in the title role; but the particular rendering Higgins chooses for comment appears already in identical form in *Antigonick*; see Carson (2012), [43].

[34] S. *Ant.* 594–5: 'From ancient times I see the troubles of the dead of the Labdacid house falling hard upon one another' (trsl. Lloyd-Jones 1994, 59).

[35] Here, too, Carson seems to adopt a technique employed already by Ezra Pound; cf. his rendering of Clytemnestra's prayer in Sophocles' *Electra*, 645–6, with its rather glaring assonance (*Lyk-*, *luck-*): 'O Apollo Lykeios, if it's lucky let the luck come to me' (Pound 2003, 1019). Further on the semantics of the archive, see Lecznar, Chapter 6, this volume.

[36] Carson (2012), [89]. [37] Trsl. Lloyd-Jones (1994), 109.

poem') derives ultimately from Latin *stantem*, accusative present participle of *stare*, 'to stand', just as *stant[a]* in Sophocles' Greek is accusative present participle of *histanai* (ἱστάναι), 'to stand or set down'. A *stanza* is a place where one stands or stops (its everyday meaning in Italian is 'room' in a house), and the meaning 'stanza of verse' comes from the metrical 'stop' at the end of it. In Carson's rewriting of the Sophoclean 'stanza', or group of lines, human life itself is assimilated to a stanza of verse, which may stop momentarily but is always in the end propelled on – by sheer luck. This little word, 'stanza', turns on its head the conventional view of literature as 'a slice of life': now it is life itself that is viewed as a textual construct; it is life that is (re)claimed by literature and turned into a literary mode such as a stanza. Human life 'stands', or remains safely immobile, only for so long as a stanza of verse may be said to 'stand' – that is, for almost no time at all.

A final and much more radical example of Carson's interlinguistic wordplay is to be found towards the end of *Antigonick*, in the context of Tiresias' report of the ill-omened auguries, which will eventually (and belatedly) persuade Creon to change course:

TEIRESIAS: *[to Kreon]*
you're standing on a razor. I hear the birds they
're bebarbarizmenized they're making monster
sounds[38]

In this tour de force of linguistic boldness, Carson 'Greeks up' her English translation by introducing 'bebarbarizmenized', an utterly remarkable coinage, which, in fact, is no more than an Anglicised version of the Greek *bebarbarōmenos*, 'foreign-sounding', which occurs in the corresponding passage of Sophocles' *Antigone* (1001–2):

ἀγνῶτ' ἀκούω φθόγγον, ὄρνιθας κακῷ
κλάζοντας οἴστρῳ καὶ βεβαρβαρωμένῳ

(TIRESIAS:) I hear an indecipherable sound of birds screeching with evil and foreignized frenzy.

Momentarily, Carson seems to deny the translation process itself: for an instant, her English version seems to take a headlong dive back into its Greek source, whence it re-emerges with its language profoundly re-Greeked. Ironically, however, this re-Greeking process is initiated by a coinage – '*bebarbarizmenized*' – which hovers between Greek and English,

[38] Carson (2012), [81].

and which is calqued on a Greek word that actually signifies the very opposite of 'Greek' (in the Sophoclean original, βεβαρβαρωμένῳ describes the screeches of birds as unintelligible to a Greek). If Carson's aim in translating Sophocles is to English him, this must involve un-Greeking him to a considerable extent; but in the process of un-Greeking Sophocles, Carson's translation re-Greeks itself by reintroducing Sophocles' vocabulary – though her specific linguistic choice for this is a word which emblematically performs un-Greekness. Once more, Carson is dealing in subtle and complex paradox: we find ourselves caught in a hermeneutic feedback loop, in a virtuous circle in which translation and original are routed back into each other, influencing and shaping and reformulating each other. All of this goes much deeper than Ezra Pound's chunks of transliterated Greek, which at best create only an ephemeral alienation effect (considerably weakened when supplemented, on occasion, by Pound's own translations of the Greek).

In the examples discussed above, Carson proposes nothing short of a transformed, and transformative, approach to poetic translation. She effectively denies the autonomy of the target text, as she introduces into it lexical elements that hark back to the Greek original by exploiting near-homonymy, assonance, word association, wordplay, or neologism. These insertions act as verbal reminders of *Antigonick*'s derivativeness: it is a translation which seeks neither to supplant the original nor merely to transplant or re-encode it into the target language; it is no mere 'transfer' (the original meaning of *translatio*); rather, it preserves, advertises, and re-energises its dependency on the source language.[39]

Translation as Adaptation in *Antigonick* (II): Updating

We saw in the previous section how Carson un-Greeks Sophocles' Greek, all the while re-Greeking it – by maintaining links with it, by reaffirming its most fundamental semantic parameters, and by pegging her own textual construction on the Sophoclean text's most crucial verbal nodes.

In a number of cases, Carson's text combines faithfulness to the Greek original with the vigorous anachronism of contemporary idiom. In their

[39] Here, Carson would appear to be putting into practice Lawrence Venuti's famous thesis that translation must be a 'foreignizing' endeavour: it must advertise its foreignness, its dependence on an irreducibly foreign source text, thereby 'disrupting the cultural codes that prevail in the target language' (Venuti 1995, 20).

celebration of human achievements, Carson's Chorus introduce a literally electrifying metaphor:

every human exigency crackles as he [viz., Man] plugs it in
every outlet works but
one
: death stays dark
death he cannot doom.[40]

The electrical imagery captures the otherwise untranslatable Sophoclean juxtaposition of etymologically cognate but semantically opposite words in the first stasimon of *Antigone* (360–1):

παντοπόρος· ἄπορος ἔπ' οὐδὲν ἔρχεται
τὸ μέλλον· Ἅιδα μόνον
φεῦξιν οὐκ ἐπάξεται

> ... all resourceful; he meets nothing in the future without resource; only from Hades shall he apply no means of flight[41]

There is no easy way of rendering the antithetical wordplay *pantoporos* / *aporos*. Carson neatly sidesteps the challenge by importing an audaciously anachronistic image, which, as well as injecting ipso facto new life into the text, succeeds in preserving the spirit of technological celebration that pervades the Sophoclean original. This robust translation tactic, a sort of evasive confrontation with the original, manifests itself again, just as intriguingly, in Carson's rendering of an equally challenging Sophoclean passage from the same first stasimon, namely *Antigone* 368–71:

νόμους γεραίρων (Reiske : παρείρων MSS.) χθονὸς
θεῶν τ' ἔνορκον δίκαν
ὑψίπολις· ἄπολις ὅτῳ τὸ μὴ καλὸν
ξύνεστι τόλμας χάριν.

> When he honours the laws of the earth and the sworn justice of the gods he is high in his city; without city is whoever consorts with evil because of his audacity.[42]

Much of the force of Sophocles' Greek here relies on the opposition between *hupsipolis* ('high in his city') and *apolis* ('without city', 'city-less').

[40] Carson (2012), [25]. [41] Translation by Lloyd-Jones (1994), 37.

[42] Cf. also Carson's more recent translation of *Antigone* for Ivo van Hove's production (cf. n. 33 above): 'the man who honours the laws of the land | the man who keeps the justice of the gods | walks high in his high city | cityless | he becomes | if he takes it upon himself | to do wrong' (Carson 2015, 23).

In the corresponding passage of *Antigonick*, Carson resorts to playfully alliterative punning, which turns the high-flown language of the original into (rather heavy-handed) sarcasm:

hilarious in his high city
you see him cantering just as he please [*sic*]
the lava up to **here**.[43]

Here, Sophocles' unreservedly laudatory *hupsipolis* – which Carson herself faithfully renders by 'high in his high city' in her 2015 translation (quoted in n. 42) – gives way to a sneering 'hilarious in his high city', which paves the way, perhaps too overtly, for the culminating irony of 'the lava up to **here**'. However, this image is not chosen at random: the idea that no one suspects what is coming to them until they burn their foot in the fire occurs in Sophocles' *Antigone*, 618–19, and resurfaces twice elsewhere in *Antigonick*.[44] The lava imagery is thus integrated into a broader nexus of related notions, thereby mitigating the somewhat trivialising effect.

This is not to say that *Antigonick* is entirely devoid of moments of triviality, or of seemingly unnecessary chattiness. When in Sophocles' play Creon asks Antigone whether she buried Polynices, she famously replies 'I both confirm this and I do not deny it' (*Antigone*, 443);[45] in Carson's rendering, Antigone's defiant affirmation of guilt is reduced to an incongruously casual 'Bingo'.[46] Shortly before that, the Chorus had greeted Creon's imminent entrance with what might come across as tongue-in-cheek consternation: 'oh perfect | here's Kreon'.[47] And when the Messenger brings news of Haemon's suicide, the Chorus are forced to admit that Teiresias' predictions were right, but they do so with a colloquial 'okay Teiresias, point match game', which leads to the Messenger's 'game's not over'.[48] Such moments may reasonably be put down to the influence of Ezra Pound's slangy translation idiom (see n. 3), which was actually much more jarringly demotic than Carson's. For instance, in the translation of Sophocles' *Electra*, which Pound prepared around 1950 in collaboration with Rudd Fleming, Orestes concludes his opening speech with a robustly enchorial 'Nuff talk. Get in there, old buck, and |

43 Carson (2012), [25].

44 Cf. Carson (2012), [45–7]: 'but of course there is hope look here comes hope | wandering in | to tickle your feet | then you notice the soles are on fire' (cf. Figure 13.3 above); also, Carson (2012), [37]: 'I | think a man knows nothing but his foot when | he burns it in the hot fire.'

45 Cf. Carson (2015), 25: 'I did the deed I do not deny it.'

46 Carson (2012), [29].

47 Carson (2012), [27].

48 Carson (2012), [89], [91] respectively. Cf. Steiner's (2012) strictures against such 'populist witticisms', which sacrifice 'the subtle complexity, the lyric poise of Sophocles' tragic idiom'.

keep steady.' In the same translation, the Chorus comment on Electra's obduracy with a chatty 'Gheez, she's a-goin' it fierce, | right or not she dont care a hang.' And at times, Orestes' Tutor speaks in an approximation of African American Vernacular English, which seems intended (and here, as elsewhere, Pound's fascist-racist bias comes to the fore) to accentuate his low social status: 'and the track wuz narrow, the lot of 'em drivin' togedder | and a-lammin' the horses, each one tryin' to git out of the bunches'.[49]

Thankfully, however, *Antigonick* is devoid of such extravagance, and whatever gratuitous colloquialisms it does possess are few and far between. Much more interesting are those cases in which Carson's use of contemporary idiom, so far from being a concession to untrained tastes, very often succeeds in conveying hidden connotations, nuances, and undertones of Sophocles' Greek. When Antigone tries to convince her sister Ismene to join her in offering burial rites to Polynices, she invokes the delights of lying next to her dead brother in an eternal embrace:

ISMENE: sweet sister
you aim too high ANTIGONE: true sister, yet how
sweet to lie upon my brother's body thigh to thigh[50]

The undisguised eroticism of the phraseology provoked the Olympian thunder of George Steiner, who counted this as one among several 'vulgarities which subvert this most adult, unsparingly formal and radiant of masterpieces'.[51] Steiner was, of course, right to warn that an over-indulgence in ephemeral tastes is, in the end, patronising as well as populist and risks slighting 'the demanding intricacy of the conflicts between public and private, law and justice, between generations, between men and women, between the archaic and the institutional which have fuelled debate and wonder over the millennia' with respect to *Antigone*. However, Carson's sexualised language ('thigh to thigh') does little more than bring out the latent incestuous undercurrent of the Sophoclean original (*Antigone* 73–7):

[49] Pound (2003), 997, 1017, 1021 respectively. The Tutor's idiom in particular has a precedent in an earlier abortive attempt by Pound to translate Aeschylus' *Agamemnon*, in which he tried 'every possible dodge', including 'making the watchman a negro, and giving him a fihn Géoogiah voice' (see Pound's 'Paris Letter', *The Dial*, March 1923, as quoted in Pound 2003, 1330, n. on 993.1). Foley (2012), 20–2 sees in Pound's mixed-style translation a deliberate 'cacophony of linguistic styles and dialects that expressed a painful (by implication national) failure of communication, in which characters talked past each other, along with something close to comic absurdity' (quotation from p. 20).

[50] Carson (2012), [9].

[51] Steiner (2012).

> φίλη μετ' αὐτοῦ κείσομαι, φίλου μέτα,
> ὅσια πανουργήσασ'· ἐπεὶ πλείων χρόνος
> ὃν δεῖ μ' ἀρέσκειν τοῖς κάτω τῶν ἐνθάδε.
> ἐκεῖ γὰρ αἰεὶ κείσομαι

> I shall lie next to him [sc. Polynices], a beloved woman next to a beloved man, having committed a pious crime; because it is to the dead, not to the living, that I must be agreeable for a longer time. For it is down there that I shall lie for ever.

The repeated κείσομαι, 'I shall lie', is sexually charged, as can be seen from, e.g., Aristophanes' *Peace*, 1332–3, μετ' ἐμοῦ καλὴ | καλῶς κατακείσει, 'you, my beautiful lady, shall lie beautifully next to me' (in a nuptial context). The sexual innuendo is a poignant reminder of the incestuous union to which Antigone herself owes her birth and which she seems to perpetuate: as one scholar has perceptively remarked, if Antigone insists so much on burying Polynices, it is because she regards this as the only means of having an eternal post-mortem relationship with him.[52] The incestuous nature of Antigone's attachment to Polynices, notoriously denied in Hegel's influential reading,[53] has been asserted notably by Judith Butler,[54] to whose analysis of *Antigone* Carson is, as we shall see, multiply indebted. Carson's programmatically anachronistic, or updated, translation, unfaithful as it may seem, 'in fact constitutes and performs a challenge to conservative, chronological, teleological temporal frames that constantly threaten to bury the irruptive potential of this text, and this figure, within the deathly chamber of a distant, fixed, "original" past'.[55]

52 Zellner (1997), 316–17. See further Liapis (2013a), 85–6 with bibliography, to which add Griffith (2010), 115–16 and esp. Torrance (2010). The latter investigates intimations of Antigone's incestuous relationship with Polynices beyond Sophocles' *Antigone*, including ancient sources and two French plays (Rotrou's *Antigone* and Gide's *Œdipe*).

53 See esp. Hegel (1986a), 337–8; cf. the translation by J. B. Baillie in Paolucci and Paolucci (1962), 269; see also Honig (2013), 125.

54 See esp. J. Butler (2000), 6, 13, 17–19, 23–4, 60, 66–7, 72, 78; also, Johnson (1997). On Butler's reading of *Antigone*, see also Honig (2013), 41–56, 97–8, 105, 131, 182.

55 Quotation from Hjorth (2014), 136. Not everyone, of course, is happy with such updating strategies. For instance, William Logan, in a review for the ultra-conservative *New Criterion*, found that Carson in *Antigonick* 'has taken one of the most moving plays of the classical world – still charged with pathos despite its remoteness in custom and dramaturgy – and updated it like a new Honda' (Logan 2012).

Translation, Transtextuality, and Pastiche

As well as exploring the limits of translation, and even pushing them to extremes, *Antigonick* also engages in an investigation of its own transtextual nature, which is to say its 'relation (manifest or hidden) with other texts'.[56] *Antigonick*'s transtextuality includes, but is not limited to, its incorporation of a variety of different translation traditions, of philological scholarship, and also of tantalising snippets from the established critical discourse on the play, especially Hegel. *Antigonick*'s 'textual transcendence' (to quote Genette again)[57] is boldly advertised from its very first lines, which, contrary to expectation, do not offer a version of the beginning of Sophocles' *Antigone*, but explicitly present themselves as a *quotation*, whose disputed provenance gives rise to a travesty of philological and critical debate between Antigone and Ismene:

> [enter Antigone and Ismene] ANTIGONE: we
> begin in the dark and birth is the death of
> us ISMENE: who said that ANTIGONE: Hegel
> ISMENE: sounds more like Beckett ANTIGONE: he
> was paraphrasing Hegel ISMENE: I don't think
> so[58]

Hegel's reading of Sophocles' *Antigone* represents a landmark in the history of the interpretation of Greek tragedy, and it is almost de rigueur for much modern criticism on *Antigone* to engage with the Hegelian vision of Antigone and Creon as representing two clashing but equally valid moral forces, the former standing for the rights of the *oikos* and of the nether gods, the latter for the law of the State. Also, it is a commonplace of contemporary philosophical discourse, at least since Foucault's 'Discourse on Language',[59] to think of Hegel as both a point of departure and as an inescapable destination, which is to say as the end-point of a circular course in which 'the death of Hegel is the birth of Hegel, the birth his death – *the birth of his death*. We return back to Hegel in the fashion of this circularity because Hegel's own thought is the thought of that return.'[60]

[56] Cf. Genette's definition on p. 1 with n. 2. [57] Genette (1992), 81. [58] Carson (2012), [7].

[59] See Foucault (1972), 235: 'We have to determine the extent to which our anti-Hegelianism is possibly one of his tricks directed against us, at the end of which he stands, motionless, waiting for us.'

[60] Quotation from Hass (2014), 90 (italics in the original). Carson herself, in an interview to *Asymptote* journal, remarked that Hegel is 'something you can't get around because everyone who writes about *Antigone* has something to say about Hegel's analysis – it's a very polarizing piece' (Berkobien 2013). By beginning her *Antigonick* with an emblematic invocation of Hegel, Carson 'knit[s] the reception of *Antigone* into the play itself, letting us know that our only access to this play is through this present time, and yet showing that this time is still bound to that classical one' (J. Butler 2012).

Antigone's musings, then, on the essential identity of the birth and death 'of us' can also be read as a comment on the eternal rebirth of Hegel. Scarcely has one had time to think about the viability of such a proposition, however, when one realises that this is in fact a comic send-up of critical clichés. The opening quotation, which masquerades as Hegel, turns out to be, as in fact Ismene implies, a paraphrase of the opening lines of Samuel Beckett's *A Piece of Monologue* (1979): 'Birth was the death of him. Again. Words are few. Dying too. Birth was the death of him.'[61] Once established, the Beckettian intertext immediately casts a seriocomic light on the exchange between Antigone and Ismene. As a perceptive reviewer has remarked, Carson 'makes her characters suspiciously like Beckett's Vladimir and Estragon: it works so perfectly, it's a wonder no one has thought of this before'.[62] Indeed, the quotation-burlesque here seems to hark back to *Waiting for Godot*'s extended spoof of philosophical discourse in Lucky's monologue, which comes complete with such grotesque pseudo-citations as 'the labours left unfinished crowned by the Acacacacademy of Anthropopopometry of Essy-in-Possy of Testew and Cunard', or 'the labours of Fartov and Belcher left unfinished for reasons unknown'.[63] In *Antigonick*, the opening Beckett-style travesty of (pseudo-) Hegel sets the tone for much of what follows. The text's palimpsestic transtextuality often takes the form of a Rabelaisian extravaganza, a supremely learned (and unapologetically motley) patchwork of texts or textual allusions, translations and translation styles, critical idioms and philological techniques, sometimes earnest, sometimes tongue-in-cheek, sometimes stirringly despondent, and often all of the above.

References to Hegel are not limited to the opening dialogue. They crop up on two more occasions later in the play – and, interestingly, they do not seem to be always accurate. Here is a prime example:

[61] S. Beckett (1986), 425. The phrasing is reminiscent of Edward Young's *Night-Thoughts*, v.718: 'Our birth is nothing but our death begun'; but the idea goes back to classical antiquity (Manilius, Seneca, Silius Italicus): see Tosi (2018), 524–5, no. 722. The first words of Carson's Antigone – 'We begin in the dark' – may also allude to Beckett's stage directions for *A Piece of Monologue*: '*Faint diffuse light . . . standard lamp, skull-sized white globe, faintly lit . . . Thirty seconds before end of speech lamplight begins to fail. Lamp out.*' In point of fact, there may be *some* genuine Hegel in Carson's pseudo-Hegelian quotation. Hjorth (2014), 136, n. 3, points to a passage in Hegel's *Science of Logic* that seems to prefigure Beckett: 'the being as such of finite things is to have the germ of decease as their being-within-itself: the hour of their birth is the hour of their death' (Hegel 1986b, 140; quoted in the translation by A. V. Miller 1969, 129). However, Hegel himself treats this idea as, originally, a piece of folk, especially Oriental, wisdom; cf. Hegel (1986b), 84.

[62] Quotation from M. H. Miller (2012).

[63] Quotations from S. Beckett (1986), 42.

ANTIGONE: some think the
world
is made of bodies some think forces I
think a man knows nothing but his foot when
he burns it in the hot fire
ISMENE: quoting Hegel again
ANTIGONE: Hegel says I'm wrong
ISMENE: but right to be wrong ANTIGONE: no
ethical consciousness ISMENE: is that how
he puts it[64]

As we saw above (p. 371 with n. 44), the idea that human illusions are short-lived, and last only until shattered by harsh reality (when one 'burns his foot in the hot fire'), is one found already in a choral ode from Sophocles' *Antigone* – but is never, as far as I can see, cited or alluded to by Hegel. Thus, Ismene's 'quoting Hegel again' seems deliberately inaccurate – a continuation, no doubt, of the mood of Beckettian mock-quotation with which the opening of *Antigonick* is infused. Paradoxically, however, this false quote is immediately followed by a more accurate reference to Hegel: 'ANTIGONE: Hegel says I'm wrong ISMENE: but right to be wrong'. This nicely captures the philosopher's analysis of the conflict in Sophocles' *Antigone* as a dialectical clash not between characters but between moral forces. For Hegel, Antigone represents the rights of the *oikos* and of the nether gods, which collide with the law of the State as personified by Creon; each of the two central dramatis personae defends one, and only one, of these contrasting claims, and because of their one-sidedness the two clashing powers are presented as equally just and equally unjust at the same time: 'they both have their own validity, but a validity which is equalized'; and 'it is only the one-sidedness in their claims which justice comes forward to oppose'.[65]

Typically, however, this genuine reference to Hegel is immediately followed, and undermined, by yet another pseudo-quotation: 'ANTIGONE: no ethical consciousness ISMENE: is that how he puts it'. In point of fact, Hegel never says that Antigone possesses 'no ethical consciousness'; on the contrary, in the *Phenomenology of Mind* he states that

[64] Carson (2012), [37].

[65] See Hegel (1986d), 133: 'hier haben sie beide ihr Gelten, aber ihr *ausgeglichenes Gelten*. Es ist nur die Einseitigkeit, gegen die die Gerechtigkeit auftritt'; trsl. E. B. Speirs and J. Burdon Sanderson, as quoted in Paolucci and Paolucci (1962), 325. Cf. further Oudemans and Lardinois (1987), 110–17; Steiner (1984), 19–42; Nussbaum (1986), 51–82.

> the ethical consciousness is more complete, its guilt purer, if it knows beforehand the law and the power which it opposes, if it takes them to be sheer violence and wrong, to be a contingency in the ethical life, and wittingly, like Antigone, commits the crime.[66]

In Hegel, action is an essential continuation of the ethical consciousness, as it actuates the consciousness' perception of what is the true right; and it is precisely on account of this actuality that 'ethical consciousness must acknowledge its opposite as its own actuality; it must acknowledge its guilt' – as indeed Antigone does in Hegel's (mis)translation of line 926 from Sophocles' play: 'Because of our sufferings we acknowledge we have erred.'[67] In point of fact, Sophocles' Greek (παθόντες ἂν ξυγγνοῖμεν ἡμαρτηκότες) makes Antigone much less self-condemnatory: '*if* these things have divine approval', she says, 'then I should acknowledge my error since I will have suffered (my doom)'.[68] To quote Judith Butler's apposite formulation, Hegel appears to assimilate himself to Creon in that, like him, he 'cannot get Antigone to perform a full enough confession for him'.[69] In fact, the Sophoclean Antigone, contrary to Hegel's mistranslation, acknowledges her deed but not necessarily its erroneousness.

In Carson, however, Antigone's apparent misquotation of Hegel ('no ethical consciousness') is, intriguingly, not *entirely* erroneous. For elsewhere in the *Phenomenology of Mind*, Hegel does state that

> the feminine, in the form of the sister, has the highest *intuitive* awareness of what is ethical. She does not attain to *consciousness* of it, or to the objective existence of it, because the law of the Family is an implicit, inner essence

[66] Hegel (1986a), 348: 'Aber das sittliche Bewußtsein ist vollständiger, seine Schuld reiner, wenn es das Gesetz und die Macht *vorher kennt*, der es gegenübertritt, sie für Gewalt und Unrecht, für eine sittliche Zufälligkeit nimmt und wissentlich, wie Antigone, das Verbrechen begeht'; trsl. by J. B. Baillie, as quoted in Paolucci and Paolucci (1962), 279.

[67] Hegel (1986a), 348: '*weil wir leiden, anerkennen wir, daß wir gefehlt*'; trsl. by J. B. Baillie, as quoted in Paolucci and Paolucci (1962), 280.

[68] In the translation by Lloyd-Jones (1994), 89, ἂν ξυγγνοῖμεν is taken to mean 'I should forgive', so that Antigone never positively admits her guilt: 'I should forgive them for what I have suffered, since I have done wrong.' Cf. J. Butler (2000), 34: 'And note the extraordinary suspension of the question of guilt and the implicit rebuke to Hegel that enters with the most reliable translation, that offered by Lloyd-Jones ... Here Antigone seems to know and to speak the wisdom that she cannot quite avow, for Antigone will not admit her guilt.'

[69] J. Butler (2000), 33.

> which is not exposed to the daylight of consciousness, but remains an inner feeling and the divine element that is exempt from an existence in the real world.[70]

Although in this passage Hegel does not explicitly mention Antigone, his remarks are clearly applicable to her insofar as they concern 'the feminine in the form of the sister'. A number of prominent feminist anti-Hegelians, notably Luce Irigaray and Judith Butler, have observed that the two passages from the *Phenomenology of Mind* quoted above are incompatible with each other: Hegel commits the logical fallacy of having the female 'both on the side of the unconscious and on the side of the guilty'.[71] Irigaray puts it most forcefully: '*What an amazing vicious circle in a single syllogistic system.* Whereby the unconscious, while remaining unconscious, is yet supposed to know the laws of a consciousness – which is permitted to remain ignorant of it – and will become even more repressed as a result of failing to respect those laws.'[72] In the same spirit, Judith Butler has remarked that, in the framework of Hegelian ethics, 'Antigone cannot exemplify the ethical consciousness who suffers guilt; she is beyond guilt – she embraces her crime as she embraces her death, her tomb, her bridal chamber.'[73] So, when Carson's Antigone quotes Hegel as saying that she has 'no ethical consciousness', she is in fact echoing such anti-Hegelian criticisms.[74] As Craig Hannaway appositely remarks, the Hegelian debate between Antigone and Ismene in Carson's *Antigonick* is in all likelihood intentionally ironical: 'these words are actually Irigaray's words, who attacked Hegel's reading of Antigone on the basis that he makes her unconscious enough to lack an ethical consciousness, because she is a woman, but, conversely, wants her to be conscious enough to be guilty of committing a crime and to be punished for it'.[75] But in doing so, Carson's Antigone creates a mesmerising vicious circle of the kind Irigaray accuses Hegel of: she misquotes – or at least unilaterally quotes – Hegel,

70 Hegel (1977), 274 (italics in the original). Cf. Hegel (1986a), 336–7: 'Das Weibliche hat daher als Schwester die höchste *Ahnung* des sittlichen Wesens; zum *Bewußtsein* und der Wirklichkeit desselben kommt es nicht, weil das Gesetz der Familie das *ansich*-seiende, *innerliche* Wesen ist, das nicht am Tage des Bewußtseins liegt, sonder innerliches Gefühl und das der Wirklichkeit enthobene Göttliche bleibt.' Further on the Hegelian notion of the family as an unselfconscious, 'natural' substance that 'merely is', see Leonard (2005), 97–9.

71 Quotation from Leonard (2005), 132.

72 Irigaray (1985), 223 (emphasis in the original). Further on Irigaray's effort to salvage Antigone from Hegel's denial of her consciousness, see the lucid analysis by Leonard (2005), 130–3.

73 J. Butler (2000), 34.

74 That Carson is conversant with Butler's work on *Antigone* is evident, e.g., from her quotation of Butler's (2000, 43) memorable formulation 'permanent elsewhere' in Carson (2015), 6, 7, 8 n. 1.

75 Hannaway (2013), 163.

who in turn (as we saw) misquotes Sophocles' Antigone in order to cast her as a sublime expression of ethical consciousness – the same ethical consciousness which he elsewhere denies her, according to Carson's Antigone (and also, of course, according to Irigaray and Butler).[76]

Mesmerising, agonising vicious circles are, of course, the domain of Samuel Beckett, who (as we have already seen) is quoted under the misnomer 'Hegel' at the beginning of *Antigonick*. Indeed, Beckett is a pervasive, if largely unacknowledged, presence in the style and language of *Antigonick*, especially in its astounding neologistic compounds. Whereas the Sophoclean Antigone laments the fact that Polynices' body has been left 'unburied, a rich treasure house for birds as they look out for food' (*Antigone* 29–30),[77] her counterpart in *Antigonick* employs linguistic inventiveness to bring out her own moral and physical execration at the disgraceful treatment of Polynices' body:

ANTIGONE: ... Polyneikes is to lie unwept and
unburied sweet sorrymeat for the little lusts
of birds[78]

The invented compound 'sorrymeat', itself further compounded by oxymoron ('sweet'), at first sight appears to play on the more familiar nouns 'sweetmeat' and 'sweetbread'.[79] On a second level, however, it looks like a nod to Beckettian coinages (such as 'two lashed ovaries with prostisciutto', or 'there were red eggs there | I have a dirty I say henorrhoids'),[80] in which references to food are served in the form of off-puttingly anatomical or sexual wordplay.[81] In the passage cited above, the deflating potential of 'sorrymeat' is implicitly acknowledged and deftly diminished: it is absorbed into, albeit not sanitised by, the pathos of the surrounding rhetoric (by contrast, Beckett unapologetically deploys the comic potential of 'henorroids' and suchlike to its full extent).

[76] There is, in *Antigonick*, one further reference to Hegel (a briefer and, apparently, much less complicated one): 'ANTIGONE: Hegel says people want to see their | lives on stage look at me people I go my last | road I see my last light look'; see Carson (2012), [67]. This may be an allusion to Hegel's view that dramatic art is higher, more complete and more concrete than recitation, because it satisfies our desire for 'a completed vision' (the actors, their demeanour, their surroundings), which recitation leaves unfulfilled; see Hegel (1986c), 510; cf. Paolucci and Paolucci (1962), 36.

[77] Trsl. Lloyd-Jones (1994), 7. The Greek text has οἰωνοῖς γλυκὺν | θησαυρὸν εἰσορῶσι πρὸς χάριν βορᾶς.

[78] Carson (2012), [7–9].

[79] I owe this point to an anonymous reader for Cambridge University Press.

[80] From *Whoroscope* (Seaver 1976, 80) and *Sanies II* (Seaver 1976, 96) respectively.

[81] On Beckett's linguistic inventiveness, see Adams (2011), 173–7.

In another instance, Carson adopts a different strategy: she has the Guard make a show of his plebeian wit by juxtaposing highfalutin' jargon ('putrefaction', 'vermiculation') with yet another Beckettian compound, the viscerally impactful 'noonsunstink', in his report of the conditions in which Polynices' unburied corpse lay rotting:

> left that body bare sat up on the hill was
> it hot yes was there putrefaction and
> vermiculation yes was there noonsunstink yes[82]

But there is more to such coinages than mere Beckett-style wordplay. In the Sophoclean Guard's report, the narrator memorably compares Antigone's bitter cries at finding out that her brother's corpse lay again unburied to 'the piercing note of a bird when she sees her empty nest robbed of her young' (*Antigone*, 423–5).[83] Most translators would not dare to tamper with a description of such harrowing poignancy, but Carson brings this off with a masterstroke:

> there
> she was the child in her birdgrief the bird
> in her childreftgravecry howling and cursing[84]

Once again, it is largely by means of made-up compounds that Carson breathes new life into the familiar text, insofar as her pithy, punchy coinages condense the Greek into more incisive and vivid formulations. Thus, Sophocles' πικρᾶς[85] | ὄρνιθος ('a bitter, sorrowful bird') is encapsulated into a single, powerful 'birdgrief'. And even an entire line-and-a-half – namely, κἀνακωκύει . . . | . . . ὀξὺν φθόγγον, ὡς ὅταν κενῆς | εὐνῆς νεοσσῶν ὀρφανὸν βλέψῃ λέχος ('and she let out . . . a piercing shriek, as when [a bird] sees the bed of its empty nest orphaned of its fledglings') – is compacted into the remarkable quadruple compound 'childreftgravecry'. But Carson's neologistic compounds here are more than the sum of their parts: together, they turn the Sophoclean comparison of Antigone to a bird into an actual *identity* between the keening Antigone ('the child in her birdgrief') and the grieving bird ('the bird in her childreftgravecry') – an identity underlined by the nicely symmetrical repetitions of 'child' and

[82] Carson (2012), [29].

[83] Trsl. by Lloyd-Jones (1994), 41. Cf. Carson's own translation of the passage in Carson (2015), 25, which is less conservative than Lloyd-Jones' but still follows the original closely enough: 'there | she was | the child | making that weird little bird sound you know | how they cry when they see the nest empty | so she cried seeing the body bare'.

[84] Carson (2012), [29].

[85] Thus the paradosis; Bothe emended into πικρῶς.

'bird' in the two juxtaposed parts of the sentence, with each word appearing both independently and as part of a new-fangled compound.

Hegel's comments on *Antigone* and Beckett's verbal pyrotechnics are only a small part of the range of texts (or genres) with which Carson's translation engages as part of its programmatic transtextuality. Another looming presence is Bertolt Brecht, whose own version of *Antigone* (1948) featured Helene Weigel in the eponymous role with, memorably, a door attached to her back. It is precisely this awkward aspect of her Brechtian incarnation that Antigone is reminded of by the Chorus of *Antigonick*:

CHORUS: you're clumsy
it's true clumsy as your
father remember how Brecht
had you do the whole play with a door strapped
to your back[86]

Here, Carson takes her cue from the Chorus of the Sophoclean *Antigone* (853–6), who remark that the heroine went too far in her daring, so much so that she 'stumbled against the lofty altar of Justice'.[87] To turn Antigone's act of self-destructive daring into mere hereditary 'clumsiness', as if her stumbling 'against the lofty altar of Justice' were tantamount to tripping over a piece of furniture, is to risk creating a bathetic effect. The effect, however, is mitigated, if not altogether avoided, by the parallelism with the stage business of Brecht's *Antigone*. The door strapped to Antigone's back might perhaps seem gratuitously comical to the unwary but is in fact a potent visual commentary on important themes of Brecht's play: inside and outside, permanence and itinerancy, home and exile, ownership and dispossession. At the same time, by being attached to the body of the performer, the door signals 'a fundamental aspect of the Brechtian *gestus*', namely an intricate and complex 'relationship between actors and objects on the stage'.[88] Rather than remaining spatially distinct, the actor and the stage object perform a sort of visual fusion and become interchangeable. Indeed, the intimations of interchangeability suggested by Brecht's door-bearing Antigone are exploited by Carson when she has her Eurydice refer to Antigone as 'that girl with the undead strapped to | her back'.[89] So far from allowing her family dead (Polynices but also Oedipus

86 Carson (2012), [69]. 87 Trsl. Lloyd-Jones (1994), 83.
88 All quotations are from Taxidou (2008), 251. My discussion of Brecht's *Antigone* owes much to Taxidou's penetrating analysis.
89 Carson (2012), [93].

and Jocasta) to die, Antigone carries them with her as a vampiric ('undead') extension of her own body.[90]

Another important aspect of *Antigonick*'s engagement with other texts is the way in which it expressly inscribes itself in the history of its own genre, and measures itself against earlier English translations of *Antigone* – specifically, that of Sir Richard C. Jebb. That late-Victorian translation was meant to sound antiquated already at the time of its publication, as it purposely adopted an idiom reminiscent of the prose passages of Elizabethan and Jacobean drama. About halfway through *Antigonick*, Carson makes her Creon suddenly come out with snippets (sometimes adapted) from Jebb's translation, whereas Haemon continues to reply calmly, using a moderate contemporary idiom:

KREON: o shameless thou utter miscreant
to prosecute thine own
father
HAIMON: yes for I see you doing wrong
KREON: wrong to respect mine own
prerogatives
HAIMON: you don't respect you trample on the
prerogatives of the gods
KREON: o polluted
o dastard nature o subject to a woman
HAIMON: but not subject to injustice
KREON: all thy words plead for her
HAIMON: and
for you and me and the gods below
KREON: thou canst not marry her this side the
grave[91]

This last phrase is taken almost word-for-word from Jebb's translation ('Thou canst never marry her, on this side the grave'),[92] whereas other formulations in the same passage are but lightly retouched versions of the same (cf. e.g., 'Do I offend, when I respect mine own prerogatives?', 'Shameless, at open feud with thy father!', 'O dastard nature, yielding place to woman!').[93] It is conceivable that Carson is momentarily casting Creon as an Elizabethan or Jacobean stage tyrant. However, in view of the openly palimpsestic nature of her text, it seems likelier that her near-quotations

[90] *The Un-Dead* is what Bram Stoker, practically the inventor of the archetypal modern vampire, had initially entitled the novel that eventually became *Dracula*, in which the word 'Un-Dead' occurs no less than thirty times.

[91] Carson (2012), [57]. [92] Jebb (1900), 141. [93] Jebb (1900), 139.

from Jebb are meant to bring out the often unacknowledged fact that every translation confronts and assimilates not only the source text but also that text's previous translations. Here, too, Carson takes a leaf out of Ezra Pound's book: in his translation of Sophocles' *Electra*, Pound did not resist the temptation of 'kidding the crib', as he put it – that is, of introducing a waggish reference to Jebb's translation by having his Electra address Orestes with a deliberately anacoluthic 'you "deign" deign to show up here', which contains a clearly signposted jab at Jebb ('O thou who, after many a year, hast deigned thus to gladden mine eyes by thy return').[94]

If the inclusion of Jebb's translation is an acknowledgement of Carson's predecessors ('Translation is once again Carson's core concern, her true theme', says one reviewer),[95] it is not the only act of scholarly self-awareness in *Antigonick*. A reference to the conventions of Greek tragedy, complete with additional intertextual layering, explicitly underlies the one and only appearance of Eurydice, Creon's wife and Haemon's mother, in the play:

[enter Eurydike]

EURYDIKE: this is Eurydike's monologue it's her
only speech in the play. You may not know who
she is that's ok. Like poor Mrs. Ramsay who died
in a bracket of **To The Lighthouse** she's the wife
of the man whose moods tensify the world of
this story[96]

This is a patent reference to Virginia Woolf's novel *To the Lighthouse*, in which the death of Mrs Ramsay is mentioned, as if incidentally, in the final, bracketed paragraph of Chapter 3:

> (Mr. Ramsay stumbling along a passage stretched his arms out one dark morning, but, Mrs. Ramsay having died rather suddenly the night before, he stretched his arms out. They remained empty.)[97]

In Sophocles, Eurydice enters, speaks a mere nine lines (*Antigone*, 1183–91), and then exits without the departing lines customarily uttered by characters of high status in Greek tragedy.[98] We become aware of her

[94] Jebb (1894), 171, translating S. *El.* 1273–4. Pound's 'kidding the crib' comes from a note in the fair copy of his and Rudd Fleming's translation of *Electra*, now at Princeton University Library; see Pound (2003), 1332, n. on 1050.17.

[95] Thorp (2013). [96] Carson (2012), [92–3].

[97] The bracketed text is not in the MS of the novel, and was apparently added at galley-proof stage. The deaths of Mrs Ramsay's children, her daughter Prue and her son Andrew, are also announced in brackets (both of them in chap. 6).

[98] On this convention, see further Taplin (1977), 205, 309–10; Poe (1993), 379–80.

exit only through the Chorus' comment (1244–5): 'What do you make of this? The lady has departed, before uttering a good or a bad word.'[99] The dramaturgic indignity suffered by Sophocles' muted Eurydice is relatively subtle and low-key; by contrast, her counterpart in Carson is implicated in an extended, and conspicuous, play with theatrical convention, whereby she – like Woolf's Mrs Ramsay – encloses herself in brackets from which she appears unable to exit, at least not of her own volition. Thus, while her entrance is announced by a conventionally bracketed stage direction ('[enter Eurydike]'), her exit is not forthcoming, even though Eurydice herself attempts, ineffectually, to bring it about by uttering, in highly untypical fashion, the corresponding stage direction herself:

EURYDIKE: . . . we're all here we're
all fine. why do messengers always exaggerate
exit Eurydike bleeding from all orifices
[Eurydike does not exit][100]

For a stage direction to specify that a character does *not* exit (or enter, for that matter) is against established theatrical convention; the anomaly brings out Eurydice's entrapment, which is at once intratextual and intertextual, since it asks to be collated both to Sophocles' muting of Eurydice and to Woolf's bracketing of Mrs Ramsay. In the end, Carson's Eurydice manages to extricate herself from the brackets of her enforced onstage presence, but only at the instigation of the *male* characters (the Messenger and the Chorus):

MESSENGER: . . . o my queen
I did not see death marry them at last oh so
shyly. but I did I did see it. exit Eurydike
CHORUS: exit Eurydike
EURYDIKE: exit Eurydike
[exit Eurydike] [exit messenger][101]

The stage direction, which had proved ineffective in Eurydice's mouth a short while ago, is now energised back into efficacy, so much so that it becomes essentially a (male-controlled) speech act, whose mere utterance, in and of itself, brings about Eurydice's exit.

Carson's scholarly self-awareness extends even to technical questions that are normally of interest only to the professional philologist. When Haemon is about to break to his father the alarming news of popular

[99] Trsl. Lloyd-Jones (1994), 117. [100] Carson (2012), [95]. [101] Carson (2012), [97].

discontent and possibly imminent insurrection, he is naturally hesitant, but his hesitation is couched in the philological jargon of textual criticism:

> yet I could not would
> not do not know how to say you are wrong
> it may be, some other way, I don't know, might
> turn out, *I delete this line*, I am your defender
> I'm yours . . .
> yet I
> hear there is talk there are shadows this
> girl *here I posit a lacuna* this girl does not
> deserve to die the town is sad[102]

Likewise, an awareness of philological debate regarding the authenticity of lines 904–20 from Sophocles' *Antigone* is required in order fully to appreciate the following passage from Antigone's parting lament in *Antigonick*:

> ANTIGONE: . . . I organized your deaths dear ones all
> of you father mother brother when you died
> you ask would I have done it for a husband or a
> child my answer is no I would not. A husband or
> a child can be replaced but who can grow me
> a new brother is this a weird argument, Kreon
> thought so but I don't know, the words go wrong . . .[103]

This, in a nutshell, is the argument Antigone uses in Sophocles (*Antigone*, 904–20): 'had I lost a child or a husband', she says there, 'I would not have dared to bury them in defiance of the citizens; for whereas I could take another husband or have a child by another man, I could never have another brother, since both my parents are dead'. Unsurprisingly, this passage has long been the subject of disputes among scholars, with not a few of them arguing that these lines are spurious and ought to be excised.[104] By proclaiming the argument of these lines 'weird', Creon seems to join the long line of athetisers, which goes back to the early nineteenth century, although Antigone (perhaps like Carson herself?) remains undecided.

Carson's engagement with the textual problems of the Sophoclean text is not always as manifest; but an awareness of the textual questions that inevitably beset every classical text informs and illuminates some of the

[102] Carson (2012), [53]. Emphasis added. [103] Carson (2012), [71].

[104] For a detailed account of the history of this question, and for a vigorous defence of the authenticity of the disputed lines, see Neuburg (1990). For an account of approaches to these lines by Hegel, Goethe, Lacan, and others, see Leonard (2005), 115–18; Honig (2013), 123–8.

choices in Carson's translation. Thus, in her rendering of the second stasimon, Carson chooses to retain, in translation, a transmitted reading which modern editors usually seek to emend:

> one last root was reaching up for the light in
> the house of Oidipous
> but the bloody dust of death
> hacks her down mows her down
> all the tall mad mountains of her mind[105]

The incongruity of 'the bloody dust of death' hacking down or mowing down is curiously satisfying, but also not Carson's invention: it simply reflects the transmitted reading κόνις, 'dust', in Sophocles' *Antigone* 602, where modern editions generally print Jortin's emendation κοπίς, 'cleaver' or 'scimitar'. Here is the modern *vulgata* of the passage in question:

> νῦν γὰρ ἐσχάτας ὑπὲρ
> ῥίζας ἐτέτατο φάος ἐν Οἰδίπου δόμοις·
> κατ' αὖ νιν φοινία
> θεῶν τῶν νερτέρων ἀμᾷ κοπίς [Jortin: κόνις MSS.],
> λόγου τ' ἄνοια καὶ φρενῶν Ἐρινύς.

For lately the light spread out above the last root in the house of Oedipus; it too is mown down by the bloody chopper of the infernal gods, folly of reasoning and an Erinys afflicting the mind.[106]

From a philologist's point of view, Jortin's emendation is judicious, perhaps even compelling: manuscript copyists tend to replace rare words such as κοπίς with more common ones, such as κόνις, and a 'bloody chopper' can very well 'mow down', whereas 'bloody dust' cannot. But Carson may be right to put sound philological method aside for the sake of what she, as a poet, does best: creating off-key juxtapositions, which tilt our focus of vision and resituate us 'at a slight angle to the universe'.[107] The intermingling of elements, light and earth, may appear incongruous at first sight but it successfully 'confounds boundaries and obscures the senses',[108] just as the

105 Carson (2012), [43]. 106 Transl. Lloyd-Jones (1994), 61 (adapted).

107 I appropriate here E. M. Forster's famous description of C. P. Cavafy: 'a Greek gentleman in a straw hat, standing absolutely motionless at a slight angle to the universe' (Forster 1923, 91).

108 Quotation from Kitzinger (2008), 35, who also argues (36 with n. 49) that καταμᾷ in Sophocles' Greek is ambiguous and carries secondary connotations of 'heaping up' or 'gathering', which would be consonant with the transmitted reading κόνις as an allusion to the ritual sprinkling of dust on mourners' heads. But this would be a linguistic impossibility: κατ' . . . νιν . . . | . . . ἀμᾷ κόνις cannot mean 'dust piles up on Antigone's head'; see further Jebb (1900), 253–4 (Appendix on S. *Ant.* 601f.).

'bloody dust of death' obscures the light which Antigone, the 'last root . . . in | the house of Oidipous', had been reaching for.

Epilogue

This chapter has attempted to show that Anne Carson's *Antigonick* is an exercise in transtextuality, which challenges and expands the limits of both translation and adaptation. It absorbs, transforms, and foregrounds not only its obvious source text, namely Sophocles' *Antigone*, but also earlier translations of the ancient text (notably Jebb's), earlier philological and exegetic work on the play, as well as landmarks of the history of its interpretation from Hegel to Butler. Moreover, it encourages and sustains a continuous engagement with the possibilities (and impossibilities) of language, especially in the form of interlinguistic wordplay, which often redirects the English translation back to its Greek source, thereby unapologetically flaunting its derivativeness but also re-energising it. Finally, *Antigonick* makes its own palimpsestic nature manifest through the physical layering of text and image, which acts as a reminder not only of *Antigonick*'s bold openness to the lowbrow graphic-novel genre, but also of the fact that our access to ancient texts is in itself mediated by the palimpsestic process of successive copying and of critical and interpretive commentary. To quote Souffrant, 'If any text absorbs and transforms another, the translation takes as its overt task this transformation. What Anne Carson more assertively presents in *Antigonick* is the mosaic, the way in which this transformation is a creation from pieces of other texts, these pieced together, absorbed and transformed.'[109]

And what about *Antigonick*'s stage visualisation in performance? As intimated at the beginning of this chapter, *Antigonick* seems first and foremost to want to assert itself as an autonomous, self-standing *typographic artefact* – not as a playscript intended for, and necessarily linked to, performance. It is tempting to see *Antigonick*'s typographical re-enactment of theatrical kinaesthetics – principally through its choreographic arrangement and interlacing of text and image (see p. 359 above) – as an attempt to appropriate for the book format the unique synthesis of textuality and visuality (and even movement) that is the theatre. It is perhaps significant that Carson herself has participated only in staged readings, not fully fledged performances, of *Antigonick*: one at the Louisiana Museum of Modern Art (in Humlebæk, Denmark) on 25 August 2012, and one in

[109] Souffrant (2014), 116.

Stockholm's Moderna Museet on 8 May 2015, both as part of literature festivals.[110] As even a cursory look at the video recordings listed in n. 110 can confirm, these readings are firmly text-centred, with performers simply walking up to a microphone and reading their piece, and without much else in the way of stage business or design.[111] It is as if even these oral performances of *Antigonick* sought to affirm the ascendancy of the printed object, its power to integrate the visual as well as the textual, and its primacy as a virtually all-absorbing medium.

To transform, therefore, a supremely 'bookish' work like *Antigonick* into a stage spectacle would be no small challenge. But it is precisely this challenge that the 2015 Shotgun Players production of *Antigonick* rose to with singular verve and intelligence. The directors, Mark Jackson and Hope Mohr, were fully aware of the uniqueness of *Antigonick* in being 'not your typical script, not just a text',[112] and displayed admirable subtlety and discernment in trying to strike a balance between visuality and textuality and in drawing inspiration from the book's typographic syntax, especially from the white spaces punctuating the text, which they rendered now with stage silences, now with movement. What is more, the directors fully took into account the genre- and category-bending nature of Carson's work: in the words of Hope Mohr, Carson's 'work is not just a play, it's not just poetry, it's not just criticism – it's all of those things'.[113] And in their stage version of *Antigonick*, they likewise involved themselves in 'pushing at the boundaries of what is theatre'. If this chapter has achieved anything, it is precisely to demonstrate how adaptation, with Anne Carson's *Antigonick* as a prime example, can and must 'push the boundaries' of genre, textuality, and visuality towards a new synthesis that may go beyond mere agglutination to capture something of the unity of speech, *opsis*, music, and movement that Greek drama managed, unprecedentedly, to achieve.

[110] For a video recording of the Louisiana Literature Festival staged reading, see www.youtube.com/watch?v=BEfJKjOg3ZU&t=277s; for the Stockholm Literature festival, see www.youtube.com/watch?v=CJsfojZjD9g&t=533s (both accessed 14 March 2017).

[111] The only exception being a banner hanging upstage at the Louisiana Literature Festival reading, with I WAS BORN TO OCCUPY LOVE NOT HATRED printed in black lettering (except for the word LOVE, which was printed in red) against an all-white background.

[112] Quotation from Hope Mohr's interview in the trailer for the Shotgun Players' *Antigonick* (see www.youtube.com/watch?v=RSemjY_n_zc, accessed on 15 March 2017).

[113] See n. 112.

Bibliography

Abrams, J. and Parker-Starbuck, J. (2007) 'Politics and the Classics', *PAJ* 29: 88–100.

Achebe, C. (1975) 'The African Writer and the English Language', in *Morning Yet on Creation Day* (London), 55–62.

Adamitis, J. and Gamel, M. K. (2013) 'Theaters of War', in *Roman Literature, Gender and Reception: Domina Illustris*, ed. D. Lateiner, B. K. Gold, and J. Perkins (Abingdon), 284–302.

Adams, M. (2011) *From Elvish to Klingon: Exploring Invented Languages*. Oxford.

Ahrensdorf, P. J. (2009) *Greek Tragedy and Political Philosophy: Rationalism and Religion in Sophocles' Theban Plays*. Cambridge.

Aitken, W. (2004) 'Interviews: Anne Carson, The Art of Poetry No. 88', *Paris Review* 171 www.theparisreview.org/interviews/5420/the-art-of-poetry-no-88-anne-carson (accessed 18 September 2015).

Albert, W. (1970) 'Structures of Revolt in Giraudoux's *Electre* and Anouilh's *Antigone*', *Texas Studies in Literature and Language* 12.1: 137–50.

Alexiou, M. (1982) 'Diglossia in Greece', in *Standard Languages, Spoken and Written*, ed. W. Haas (Manchester), 156–92.

Allain, P. (2002) *The Art of Stillness: The Theatre Practice of Tadashi Suzuki*. New York.

Allan, R. (2009) 'Towards a Typology of the Narrative Modes in Ancient Greek: Text Types and Narrative Structure in Euripidean Messenger Speeches', in *Discourse Cohesion in Ancient Greek*, ed. S. J. Bakker and G. C. Wakker (Leiden and Boston), 171–203.

Allan, W. (ed.) (2008) *Euripides: Helen*. Cambridge.

Allfree, C. (2016) 'A Somewhat Disjointed, Sometimes Revelatory Evening with Euripides – Review', *Telegraph*, 4 May, www.telegraph.co.uk/theatre/what-to-see/iphigenia-quartet-gate-theatre-review-somewhat-disjointed-someti (accessed 27 February 2020).

Alonso, M. (2016) 'We Are Standing in the Nick of Time: Translative Relevance in Anne Carson's Antigonick', MA thesis, Florida International University.

Andreadis, Y. (ed.) (2005) *Στα ίχνη του Διονύσου: παραστάσεις αρχαίας τραγωδίας στην Ελλάδα, 1867–2000* (*In the Tracks of Dionysus: Ancient Tragedy Performances in Greece 1867–2000*). Athens.

Andrew, D. (1980) 'The Well-Worn Muse: Adaptation in Film History and Theory', in *Narrative Strategies: Original Essays in Film and Prose Fiction*, ed. S. M. Conger and J. R. Welsch (Champaign), 9–17.

Andújar, R. and Nikoloutsos, K. (eds.) (2020) *Greeks and Romans on the Latin American Stage*. London.

Anonymous (2016a) 'Το Εθνικό Θέατρο ανεβάζει «Αντιγόνη» του Σοφοκλέους στα Κατεχόμενα!' ('The National Theatre Presents Sophocles' 'Antigone' in the Occupied Areas!'), *Chrysi Avgi*, 14 September: 10.

(2016b) 'Αντιδράσεις για την Αντιγόνη στα Κατεχόμενα' ('Reactions against *Antigone* in the Occupied Areas'), *Demokratia*, 13 September: 30.

(2016c) 'Οργή των Κυπρίων για το θέατρο στην Αμμόχωστο' ('Cypriots Angry at the Performance in Famagusta'), *Demokratia*, 30 September: 5.

(2016d) 'Θεατρική πρόκληση στα Κατεχόμενα' ('Theatrical Provocation in the Occupied Areas'), *Espresso*, 27 September: 9.

(2016e) 'Η «Αντιγόνη» του Εθνικού Θεάτρου στο αρχαίο θέατρο της Δωδώνης' ('National Theatre's 'Antigone' at the Ancient Theatre of Dodona'), *Proinos Logos Ioanninon*, 30 July: 5.

Anouilh, J. (1946) *Antigone*. Paris.

(1986) *Œdipe ou le Roi boiteux: D'après Sophocle*. Paris.

(2005) *Antigone*, trsl. B. Bray, comm. and notes T. Freeman. London.

Appadurai, A. (1988) *The Social Life of Things: Commodities in Cultural Perspective*. Cambridge.

Appiah, K. A. (1993) 'Thick Translation', *Callaloo* 16.4, 808–19.

Arnds, P. (2001) 'Translating a Greek Myth: Christa Wolf's *Medea* in a Contemporary Context', *Neophilologus* 85: 415–28.

Aronson, A. (2005) *Looking into the Abyss: Essays on Scenography*. Ann Arbor.

Arvaniti, K. (2010) *Η αρχαία ελληνική τραγωδία στο Εθνικό Θέατρο, τ. Α': Θωμάς Οικονόμου – Φώτος Πολίτης – Δημήτρης Ροντήρης* (*Greek Tragedy at the National Theatre, vol. 1, Thomas Oikonomou – Fotos Politis – Dimitris Rondiris*). Athens.

Ashcroft, B., Griffiths, G., and Tiffin, H. (1989) *The Empire Writes Back: Theory and Practice in Post-Colonial Literatures*. London and New York.

(eds.) (1995) *The Post-Colonial Studies Reader*. London and New York.

Asoya, S. (2008) 'Bacchae of Euripides, a Satirical Play by Wole Soyinka Comes Alive at the National Theatre', *A Warning Defied*, 8 April.

Auletta, R. (2006) *The Persians by Aeschylus*. New York.

Auslander, P. (1999) *Liveness: Performance in a Mediatized Culture*. London.

Ayres, S. (2005) 'Helene Cixous's The Perjured City: Nonprosecution Alternatives to Collective Violence', *City University of New York Law Review* 9.1, https://academicworks.cuny.edu/cgi/viewcontent.cgi?referer=https://www.google.com/&httpsredir=1&article=1117&context=clr (accessed 25 October 2018).

Bache, B. (2015) 'Theatre Review: Antigone, Malthouse Theatre', *Herald Sun*, 27 August.

Baker, M. and Saldanha, G. (eds.) (2009) *Routledge Encyclopedia of Translation Studies*, 2nd edn. Abingdon.

Bakogianni, A. (2011) *Electra, Ancient and Modern: Aspects of the Reception of the Tragic Heroine* (*Bulletin of the Institute of Classical Studies*, Supplement 113). London.

(2013a) 'The Triumph of Demotike: The Triumph of Medea', in Hardwick and Harrison (2013), 197–212.

(ed.) (2013b) *Dialogues with the Past 1: Classical Reception Theory and Practice*, Bulletin of the Institute of Classical Studies, Supplement 126-1. London.

(2019) 'Performing Grief: Mourning Does Indeed Become Electra', *Thersites* 9: 45–69.

Balakrishnan, Guru Sadanam P. V. (2009) In conversation with Saskya Jain at the International Kathakali Centre, New Delhi, 28 January.

Balme, C. (2014) *The Theatrical Public Sphere*. Cambridge.

Bamford, K. (2000) *Sexual Violence on the Jacobean Stage*. London.

Banks, D. (2010) 'From Homer to Hip Hop: Orature and Griots, Ancient and Present', *Classical World* 103.2: 238–45.

Bano, T. (2016) 'The Iphigenia Quartet Review at Gate Theatre, London – "Tragedy Through a Prism"', *The Stage*, 4 May.

Barchiesi, A. (2015) *Homeric Effects in Vergil's Narrative*. Princeton.

BareFacedGreek (2017) *The Watchman*, www.youtube.com/watch?v=Vh6gN8nQWSk (accessed 29 January 2017).

Barthes, R. (1972a) *Mythologies*, trsl. A. Lavers. New York. (French original published Paris, 1957).

(1972b) *Critical Essays*, trsl. R. Howard. Evanston.

(1973) *Le Plaisir du texte*. Paris.

(1977) *Fragments d'un discours amoureux*. Paris.

(1978) *Image-Music-Text*, trsl. S. Heath. New York.

(2000 [1988]). 'Death of the Author', in *Modern Criticism and Theory: A Reader*, ed. D. Lodge and N. Wood (Harlow), 146–50.

Bassnett, S. (2002) *Translation Studies*, 3rd edn. London and New York.

(2013) *Translation Studies*, 4th edn. London and New York.

(2014) *Translation*. Abingdon and New York.

Bastian, J. A. B. (2003) *Owning Memory: How a Caribbean Community Lost Its Archives and Found Its History*. Westport and London.

Batstone, W. W. (2006) 'Provocation: The Point of Reception Theory', in Martindale and Thomas (2006), 14–20.

Baxter, J. K. (1982) *Collected Plays*, ed. H. McNaughton. Auckland.

Beard, M. (2014) 'Domestic Violence', *Times Literary Supplement*, 30 July.

Beaton, R. (1999) *An Introduction to Modern Greek Literature*, rev. edn. Oxford. (1st edn 1994.)

(2003) *George Seferis: Waiting for the Angel, A Biography*. New Haven.

(2013) *Byron's War: Romantic Rebellion, Greek Revolution*. Cambridge.

Beaton, R. and Ricks, D. (eds.) (2009) *The Making of Modern Greece: Nationalism, Romanticism, and the Uses of the Past, 1797–1896*. London.

Beckett, F. (2005) *Olivier*. London.

Beckett, S. (1986) *The Complete Dramatic Works*. London.

Bemba, S. (1990) *Black Wedding Candles for Blessed Antigone*, trsl. T. Brewster, in Bemba *et al.*, *Theater and Politics* (New York), 1–62.

(1995) *Noces posthumes de Santigone*. Solignac.

Benedict, D. (1996) 'What Sarah Did Next', *Independent*, 4 May, www.independent.co.uk/arts-entertainment/what-sarah-did-next-1347390.html (accessed 25 February 2020).

Berkobien, M. (2013) 'An Interview with Anne Carson and Robert Currie', *Asymptote*, October 2013, www.asymptotejournal.com/article.php?cat=Interview&id=24&curr_index=36&curPage (accessed 15 July 2015).

Berkoff, S. (1992) *The Theatre of Steven Berkoff*. London.

(2000a) *Plays 1*. London.

(2000b) *Plays 3*. London.

(2012) *Agamemnon; The Fall of the House of Usher*. Charlbury.

Bevan, D. (ed.) (1989) *Literature and Revolution*. Amsterdam.

Bexley, E. (2011) 'Show or Tell? Seneca's and Sarah Kane's *Phaedra* Plays', *Trends in Classics* 3: 365–93.

Billington, M. (1999) 'A Challenge for Our Time: Review of The Oresteia', *Guardian*, 2 December, www.theguardian.com/stage/1999/dec/03/theatre.artsfeatures (accessed 25 February 2020).

(2007) 'The Bacchae', *Guardian*, 13 August, www.theguardian.com/culture/2007/aug/13/edinburghfestival2007.edinburghfestival3 (accessed 10 November 2019).

(2015) 'Oresteia Review: Icke Brings us Aeschylus for the Modern Age', *Guardian*, 7 June, www.theguardian.com/stage/2015/jun/07/oresteia-review-icke-brings-us-aeschylus-for-the-modern-age (accessed 15 January 2020).

Birringer, J. (1998) *Media & Performance: Along the Border*. Baltimore.

(2014) 'The Theater and Its Screen Double', *Theater Journal* 66.2: 207–25.

Blasi, A. (1974) 'On Becoming Responsible: Orestes in Aeschylus and in Sartre', *Review of Existential Psychology and Psychiatry* 13: 70–87.

Blau, H. (1987) *The Eye of the Prey*. Bloomington.

Bloom, H. (1979) 'The Breaking of Form', in *Deconstruction and Criticism*, ed. H. Bloom *et al.* (London), 1–37.

Boal, A. (2000) *Theater of the Oppressed*, trsl. C. A. and M.-O. Leal McBride and E. Fryer. London. (1st edn 1979.)

Boenisch, P. M. (2006) 'Aesthetic Art to Aisthetic Art: Theater, Media, Intermedial Performance', in *Intermediality and Performance*, ed. F. Chapple and C. Kattenbelt (Amsterdam), 103–16.

Bortolotti, G. R. and Hutcheon, L. (2007) 'On the Origin of Adaptations: Rethinking Fidelity Discourse and "Success" – Biologically', *New Literary History* 38.3: 443–58.

Bosher, K., Macintosh, F., McConnell, J., and Rankine, P. (eds.) (2015) *The Oxford Handbook of Greek Drama in the Americas*. Oxford.

Boulogne, J. (2007) 'L'Éclairage de la figure d'Électre par Giraudoux', *Bulletin de l'Association Guillaume Budé* 1: 118–31.

Bourdieu, P. (1977) *Outline of a Theory of Practice*, trsl. R. Nice. Cambridge.

(1986) 'The Forms of Capital', in *Handbook of Theory and Research for the Sociology of Education*, ed. J. G. Richardson (Westport), 241–58.

Boyle, A. J. (1997) *Tragic Seneca: An Essay in the Theatrical Tradition*. London and New York.

Boyum, J. G. (1985) *Double Exposure: Fiction into Film*. New York.

Brantley, B. (2009) 'The Bacchae: God vs. Man in an Open-Air Fight,' *New York Times*, 25 August: C5.

(2019) 'Review: Marilyn Monroe Goes to War in "Norma Jeane Baker of Troy"', *New York Times*, 10 April 2019, www.nytimes.com/2019/04/10/theater/norma-jeane-baker-of-troy-review.html (accessed 2 September 2019).

Bremer, J. M. (1976) 'Why Messenger-Speeches?', in *Miscellanea Tragica in Honorem J. C. Kamerbeek*, ed. J. M. Bremer *et al.* (Amsterdam), 29–48.

Brenton, H. (1981) *The Romans in Britain*, 2nd edn. London.

Brillenburg Wurth, K. (2013) 'Re-vision as Remediation: Hypermediacy and Translation in Anne Carson's *Nox*', *Image [&] Narrative* 14: 20–33.

Brink, A. (1999) 'Mandela, a Tiger for Our Time', *Guardian*, 22 May, www.theguardian.com/world/1999/may/22/southafrica.nelsonmandela (accessed 12 January 2020).

Britton, C. and Syrotinski, M. (2001) 'Introduction', *Paragraph* 24.3: 1–11.

Brodie, G. and Cole, E. (eds.) (2017) *Adapting Translation for the Stage*. London.

(2018) 'Conversations with Iphigenia', *Practitioners' Voices in Classical Reception Studies* 9, www.open.ac.uk/arts/research/pvcrs/2018/iphigenia (accessed 10 March 2020).

Brook, P. (1968) *The Empty Space*. London.

Brown, P. and Ograjenšek, S. (eds.) (2010) *Ancient Drama in Music for the Modern Stage*. Oxford.

Bruckner, D. J. R. (1999) 'Trojan War Victims Lie on Normandy Beaches', *New York Times*, 29 November, www.nytimes.com/1999/11/29/theater/theater-review-trojan-war-victims-lie-on-normandy-beaches.html (accessed 14 January 2020).

Bruhn, J. (2013) 'Dialogizing Adaptation Studies: From One-Way Transport to a Dialogic Two-Way Process', in Bruhn, Gjelsvik, and Hanssen (2013), 69–88.

Bruhn, J., Gjelsvik, A., and Hanssen, E. F. (eds.) (2013) *Adaptation Studies: New Challenges, New Directions*. London and New York.

Brusberg-Kiermeier, S. (2001) 'Re-writing Seneca: Sarah Kane's *Phaedra's Love*', in *Crossing Borders: Intercultural Drama and Theatre at the Turn of the Millennium*, ed. B. Reitz and A. von Rothkirch (Trier), 165–72.

Bryant, J. (2013) 'Textual Identity and Adaptive Revision: Editing Adaptation as Fluid Text', in Bruhn, Gjelsvik, and Hanssen (2013), 47–68.

Budelmann, F. (2007) 'Trojan Women in Yorubaland: Femi Osofisan's Women of Owu', in Hardwick and Gillespie (2007), 15–39.

Burgess, A. (1962) *A Clockwork Orange*. Harmondsworth.

Burian, P. (1997) 'Tragedy Adapted for Stages and Screens: The Renaissance to the Present', in Easterling (1997a), 228–83.

Burke, A. (2003) 'Interviews in Classical Performance Research: Journalistic Interviews', Essay 5 in the series 'Essays on Documenting and Researching Modern Productions of Greek Drama: The Sources', www.open.ac.uk/arts/research/greekplays/publications/essays/burke-journalistic-interviews (accessed 3 March 2020).

(2005) 'Dramatic Techniques in Performing Aeschylus' Agamemnon: The Oresteia at the Royal National Theater', PhD thesis, Queen Margaret University, Edinburgh.

Burke, A. and Innes, P. (2004, rev. 2007) 'Interviews in Classical Performance Research: Academic Interviews', Essay 6 in the series Essays on Documenting and Researching Modern Productions of Greek Drama: The Sources', www.open.ac.uk/arts/research/greekplays/publications/essays/burke-innes-interviews-performance-research (accessed 10 March 2020).

Burton, A. (ed.) (2005) *Archive Stories: Facts, Fictions, and the Writing of History*. Durham and London.

Butler, J. (2000) *Antigone's Claim: Kinship between Life and Death*. New York.

(2012) 'Can't Stop Screaming', *Public Books*, 5 September, www.publicbooks.org/fiction/cant-stop-screaming (accessed 12 September 2015).

Butler, S. (1772) *Hudibras, in Three Parts*, ed. Z. Grey, vol. II. London.

Cairns, D. (2016) *Sophocles: Antigone*. London.

(2017) 'The Destruction of Thebes in Brecht's *Antigone*', in *Aeschylus and War: Comparative Perspectives on Seven against Thebes*, ed. I. Torrance (New York), 186–201.

Calvino, I. (2000) *Why Read the Classics?*, trsl. M. McLaughlin. New York.

Campbell, P. A. (2010) 'Sarah Kane's *Phaedra's Love*: Staging the Implacable', in *Sarah Kane in Context*, ed. L. de Vos and G. Saunders (Manchester), 173–83.

(2011) 'Remaking the Chorus: Charles Mee Jr.'s *Orestes 2.0*', *Comparative Drama* 45: 65–79.

(2012) 'Postdramatic Greek Tragedy', *Journal of Dramatic Theory and Criticism*, 25: 55–74.

Carabott, P. (1993) 'Politics, Orthodoxy and the Language Question in Greece: The Gospel Riots of November 1901', *Journal of Mediterranean Studies* 3.1: 117–38.

Carney, S. (2005) 'The Tragedy of History in Sarah Kane's *Blasted*', *Theatre Survey* 46.2: 275–96.

Carr, C. (2008) *On Edge: Performance at the End of the Twentieth Century*. Hanover, NH.

Carr, M. (1999) *Plays 1*. London.

(2009) *Plays 2*. London.

(2015) *Plays 3*. London.

Carruthers, J. and Takahashi, Y. (2004) *The Theatre of Suzuki Tadashi*. Cambridge.

Carson, A. (2012) *Antigonick: Sophokles*. New York.

(trsl.) (2015) *Sophokles: Antigone*. London.

Cartmell, D. (ed.) (2012) *A Companion to Literature, Film and Adaptation*. Oxford.

Caswell, M. (2014) *Archiving the Unspeakable: Silence, Memory, and the Photographic Record in Cambodia*. Madison and London.

Causey, M. (2001) 'Stealing from God: The Crisis of Creation in Socìetas Raffaello Sanzio's *Genesi* and Eduardo Kac's *Genesis*', *Theatre Research International* 26: 199–208.

Cavendish, D. (2013) 'National Theatre's 50th: The Best Shows from 1973–83', *Telegraph*, 15 October, www.telegraph.co.uk/culture/theatre/10364303/National-Theatres-50th-the-best-shows-from-1973-1983.html (accessed 20 February 2020).

(2015) 'Oresteia, Almeida Theatre, Review: "Bogged down"', *Telegraph*, 6 June, www.telegraph.co.uk/culture/theatre/theatre-reviews/11656622/Oresteia-Almeida-Theatre-review-bogged-down.html (accessed 16 January 2020).

Chalaye, S. (2004) '"Un conte archaïque urbain qui empêche de dormir": Entretien de Sylvie Chalaye avec Rosa Gasquet sur la mise en scène de Bintou (Bruxelles, novembre 2003)', *Africultures*, 29 February, www.africultures.com/php/index.php?nav=article&no=3311 (accessed 24 February 2020).

Cixous, H. (2004) '*The Perjured City: Or, The Awakening of the Furies*', in *Selected Plays of Hélène Cixous*, ed. E. Prenowitz (London and New York), 89–190.

Clapp, S. (2015a) 'A Terrifying Immediacy', *Guardian*, 7 June, www.theguardian.com/stage/2015/jun/07/oresteia-almeida-review-lia-williams-angus-wright (accessed 9 November 2019).

(2015b) 'Robert Icke, Theatre Director: "Oresteia? It's Quite Like The Sopranos"', *Guardian*, 23 August, www.theguardian.com/stage/2015/aug/23/robert-icke-director-oresteia-1984-interview (accessed 10 March 2020).

Clark, A. (2015) *Surfing Uncertainty: Prediction, Action, and the Embodied Mind*. Oxford.

Clark, J. (1991) *The Modern Satiric Grotesque and Its Traditions*. Lexington.

Cobb, S. (2012) 'Film Authorship and Adaptation', in Cartmell (2012), 105–21.

Cohen, R. (2008) *Global Diasporas: An Introduction*. London and New York.

Cole, C. M. (2010) *Performing South Africa's Truth Commission: Stages of Transition*. Bloomington.

Cole, E. (2019) *Postdramatic Tragedies*. Oxford.

Conacher, D. J. (1955) 'Theme and Technique in the *Philoctetes* and *Oedipus* of André Gide', *University of Toronto Quarterly* 24.2: 121–35.

Constantinidis, S. (ed.) (2016) *The Reception of Aeschylus' Plays through Shifting Models and Frontiers*. Leiden.

Conte, G. B. (1994) *Latin Literature: A History*, trsl. J. B. Solodow, rev. D. Fowler and G. W. Most. Baltimore and London.

Cook, W. W. and Tatum, J. (2010) *African American Writers and Classical Tradition*. Chicago and London.

Costa, M. (2013) 'Meet Ben Power – the National Theatre's Secret Weapon', *Guardian*, 24 July, www.theguardian.com/stage/2013/jul/24/ben-power-national-theatre-hush (accessed 5 March 2020).

Craven, L. (ed.) (2008) *What Are Archives? Cultural and Theoretical Perspectives: A Reader*. Aldershot and Burlington.

Croggon, A. (2015) 'Antigone, a Greek Tragedy Plays Out in Paris and Melbourne – Review', *ABC News*, www.abc.net.au/arts/blog/Alison-Croggon/antigone-greek-tragedy-plays-out-melbourne-paris-150901 (accessed 22 September 2016).

Cross, R. (2004) *Steven Berkoff and the Theatre of Self-Performance*. Manchester.

Csapo, E. and Miller, M. C. (eds.) (2007) *The Origins of Theater in Ancient Greece and Beyond: From Ritual to Drama*. Cambridge.

Cutchins, D., Krebs, K., and Voigts, E. (2018) *The Routledge Companion to Adaptation*. Abingdon-on-Thames and New York.

Dahl, M. K. (1987) *Political Violence in Drama: Classical Models, Contemporary Variations*. Ann Arbor.

(1991) 'Stage Violence as Thaumaturgic Technique', in Redmond (1991), 251–9.

Damaskos, D. and Plantzos, D. (eds.) (2008) *A Singular Antiquity: Archaeology and Hellenic Identity in Twentieth-Century Greece*. Athens.

Dasgupta, A. (2009) In conversation with Saskya Jain at Sangeet Natak Akademi, New Delhi, 16 February.

Davidson, J. F. (2007) 'Euripides' *Bacchae* in New Zealand Dress', *Antichthon* 41: 97–108.

Davis, M. (2012) 'The Transcendence of Greek Tragedy and the Suffused Politics into the Modern Theatrical Arena: With Specific Focus on the Adaptation of Sophocles' *Antigone* by Koffi Kwahulé' (unpublished essay).

De Jong, I. J. F. (2014) *Narratology and Classics: A Practical Guide*. Oxford.

Dean, T. (2013) 'Phaedra Backwards', *Irish Theatre Magazine*, 23 October, http://itmarchive.ie/web/Reviews/Current/Phaedra-Backwards.aspx.html (accessed 10 March 2020).

Decreus, F. (2019) *The Ritual Theatre of Theodoros Terzopoulos*. London.

Degenring, F. (2010) 'Taboo, Transgression, and (Self-) Censorship in Twentieth-Century British Theater', in *Taboo and Transgression in British Literature from the Renaissance to the Present*, ed. S. Horlacher, S. Glomb, and L. Heiler (New York), 227–42.

Deleuze, G. and Guattari, F. (1999) *A Thousand Plateaus*, trsl. B. Massumi. London.

Derrida, J. (1996) *Archive Fever: A Freudian Impression*, trsl. E. Prenowitz. Chicago and London.

(2002) 'Archive Fever in South Africa', in Hamilton *et al.* (2002), 38–80.

Disejenu, J. (2007) 'Cross-Cultural Bonds between Ancient Greece and Africa: Implications for Contemporary Staging Practices', in Hardwick and Gillespie (2007), 72–85.
Dodds, E. R. (ed.) (1960) *Euripides: Bacchae*, 2nd edn. Oxford.
Doerries, B. (2015) *The Theater of War: What Ancient Greek Tragedies Can Teach Us Today*. New York.
Dolan, J. (2012) *The Feminist Spectator as Critic*. 2nd edn. Ann Arbor.
Dolce, L. (1560) *Tragedie di M. Lodovico Dolce: cioè, Giocasta, Didone, Thieste, Medea, Ifigenia, Hecuba*. Venice.
Dominik, W. J. (2007) 'Africa', in *A Companion to the Classical Tradition*, ed. C. W. Kallendorf (Oxford), 117–31.
Doolittle, H. (= H. D.) (2003) *Hippolytus Temporizes & Ion: Adaptations of Two Plays by Euripides by H. D.* New York.
Dryden, J. and Lee, N. (1679) *Oedipus: A Tragedy. As It Is Acted at His Royal Highness the Duke's Theatre*. London.
Dubois, L. (2003) 'In Search of the Haitian Revolution', in Forsdick and Murphy (2003), 27–34.
Duffy, M. (1969) '*Rites*', in *New Short Plays 2* (London), 5–36.
Duncan, A. and Liapis, V. (2018) 'Theatre Performance after the Fifth Century', in Liapis and Petrides (2018), 180–203.
Eagleton, T. (2003) *Sweet Violence: The Idea of the Tragic*. Malden and Oxford.
Easterling, P. E. (1997a) *The Cambridge Companion to Greek Tragedy*. Cambridge.
(1997b) 'Form and Performance', in Easterling (1997a), 151–77.
Eastman, H. (2013) 'Greek Tragedy and the Modern Director', in Bakogianni (2013b), 27–37.
Eleutheroglou, N. (2016) 'Ανεβάζουν παράσταση στην κατεχόμενη Αμμόχωστο' ('A Performance to Be Presented in Occupied Famagusta'), *Demokratia*, 29 September: 6.
Eliot, T. S. (1951) *Poetry and Drama: The Theodore Spencer Memorial Lecture, Harvard University, November 21, 1950*. London.
(1964 [1939]) *The Family Reunion*. New York.
Elliott, K. (2013) 'Theorizing Adaptations/Adapting Theories', in Bruhn, Gjelsvik and Hanssen (2013), 19–45.
Ellis, J. (1982) 'The Literary Adaptation', *Screen* 23 (May–June): 3–5.
Elsom, J. (1976) *Post-War British Theatre*. London, Boston, Henley.
Erkelenz, M. (1996). 'The Genre and Politics of Shelley's *Swellfoot the Tyrant*', *Review of English Studies*, n.s. 47.188: 500–20.
Ewans, M. (1984) 'Elektra: Sophokles, Von Hofmannsthal, Strauss', *Ramus* 13.2: 135–54.
Fanon, F. (1952) *Peau noire, masques blancs*. Paris.
Farber, Y. (2008) *Molora*. London.
Fenollosa, E. and Pound, E. (1916) *Noh or Accomplishment: A Study of the Classical Stage of Japan*. London.
Ferrario, S. B. (2016) 'Aeschylus and Western Opera', in Constantinidis (2016), 176–212.

Ferri, R. (2003) *Octavia: A Play Attributed to Seneca*, Cambridge Classical Texts and Commentaries 41. Cambridge.

Ferris, D. S. (2000) *Silent Urns: Romanticism, Hellenism, Modernity*. Stanford.

Findlater, R. (1997) 'The Winding Road to King's Reach', in S. Callow, *The National: The Theatre and Its Work 1963–1997* (London), 79–83.

Finglass, P. J. (ed.) (2011) *Sophocles: Ajax*. Cambridge.

(2015) 'Reperformances and the Transmission of Texts', *Trends in Classics* 7.2: 259–76.

Fischer-Lichte, E. (2004) 'Thinking about the Origins of Theatre in the 1970s', in Hall, Macintosh, and Wrigley (2004), 329–60.

(2005) *Theatre, Sacrifice, Ritual: Exploring Forms of Political Theatre*. Abingdon and New York.

(2008) *The Transformative Power of Performance: A New Aesthetics*. New York.

(2010) 'Performance as Event – Reception as Transformation', in Hall and Harrop (2010), 29–42.

(2014a) *The Routledge Introduction to Theatre and Performance Studies*, ed. M. Arjomand and R. Mosse, trsl. M. Arjomand. London and New York.

(2014b) *Dionysus Resurrected: Performances of Euripides' The Bacchae in a Globalizing World*. Malden and Oxford.

(2017) *Tragedy's Endurance: Performances of Greek Tragedies and Cultural Identity in Germany since 1800*. Oxford and New York.

Fisher, M. (2019) 'Oedipus Review – Robert Icke's Take Exerts Thriller-like Grip', *Guardian*, 16 August, www.theguardian.com/stage/2019/aug/16/oedipus-review-kings-theatre-edinburgh-festival-2019-robert-icke-sophocles (accessed 27 October 2019).

Flashar, H. (1991) *Inszenierung der Antike: Das griechische Drama auf der Bühne der Neuzeit*. Munich.

Fleishman, M. (1990) 'Workshop Theatre as Oppositional Form', *South African Theatre Journal* 4.1: 88–118.

(1997) 'Physical Images in the South African Theatre', *South African Theatre Journal* 11.1–2: 199–214.

Fleming, K. (2013) '"For Everyone Must Answer the Sphinx": Ted Hughes's Translation of Seneca's Oedipus', *Canadian Review of Comparative Literature*, Special Issue, 40.1: 105–22.

Fludernik, M. (ed.) (2003) *Diaspora and Multiculturalism: Common Traditions and New Developments*. Amsterdam and New York.

Foley, H. P. (1999) 'Modern Performance and Adaptation of Greek Tragedy', *Transactions of the American Philological Association* 129: 1–12.

(2012) *Reimagining Greek Tragedy on the American Stage*, Sather Classical Lectures. Berkeley.

Forsdick, C. (2003) 'Revisiting Exoticism: From Colonialism to Postcolonialism', in Forsdick and Murphy (2003), 46–55.

Forsdick, C. and Murphy, D. (2003) *Francophone Postcolonial Studies: A Critical Introduction*. London.

Forster, E. M. (1923) *Pharos and Pharillon*, 2nd edn. London.

Forsyth, A. (2009) 'Pacifist Antigones', in *Performing Adaptations: Essays and Conversations on the Theory and Practice of Adaptation*, ed. M. MacArthur, L. Wilkinson, and K. Zaiontz (Newcastle-upon-Tyne), 25–42.
Foucault, M. (1972) *The Archaeology of Knowledge and The Discourse on Language*, trsl. A. M. Sheridan Smith. New York.
Fradinger, M. (2011) 'Danbala's Daughter: Félix Morisseau-Leroy's Antigòn an Kreyòl', in Mee and Foley (2011), 127–46.
Fragoudaki, A. (1992) 'Diglossia and the Language Situation in Greece', *Language in Society* 21: 365–81.
Freshwater, H. (2003) 'The Allure of the Archive', *Poetics Today* 24.4: 729–58.
Freud, S. (1999) *The Interpretation of Dreams*, trsl. J. Crick. Oxford. (German original published 1899.)
Fried, R. K. (1985) 'The Cinematic Theater of John Jesurun', *Drama Review* 29:1: 57–72.
Friedman, R. (2007) 'Derek Walcott's "Odysseys"', *International Journal of the Classical Tradition* 14.3–4: 455–80.
Fries, A. (2014) *Pseudo-Euripides, Rhesus: Edited with Introduction and Commentary*. Berlin and New York.
Fuchs, E. (1986) 'The *PAJ* Casebook: *Alcestis*', *PAJ* 10: 79–115.
(1996) *The Death of Character: Perspectives on Theater after Modernism*. Bloomington and Indianapolis.
Fuhrmann, A. (2015) 'Antigone (Malthouse, Melbourne)', *Daily Review*, 26 August, https://dailyreview.com.au/antigone-malthouse-melbourne (accessed 22 September 2016).
Gallagher-Ross, J. (2009) 'Postdramatic Stress Syndrome: Dood Paard's *medEia* at P.S. 122', *Drama Review* 53.1: 129–35.
Gamel, M.-K. (2010) 'Revising "Authenticity" in Staging Ancient Mediterranean Drama', in Hall and Harrop (2010), 153–70.
Gardner, L. (2005) '*Phaedra's Love*', *Guardian*, 31 October, www.theguardian.com/culture/2005/oct/31/theatre.art (accessed 9 March 2020).
(2011) 'Oedipus – Review', *Guardian*, 3 March, www.theguardian.com/stage/2011/mar/03/oedipus-review (accessed 10 June 2019).
(2016) 'The Iphigenia Quartet Review: Picking Over a Greek Myth's Bloody Bones', *Guardian*, 4 May, www.theguardian.com/stage/2016/may/04/the-iphigenia-quartet-review-gate-london (accessed 22 February 2020).
Garland, R. (2004) *Surviving Greek Tragedy*. London.
Geertz, C. (1993 [1973]), *The Interpretation of Cultures*. New York and London.
Genette, G. (1992) *The Architext: An Introduction*, trsl. J. E. Lewin. Berkeley.
(1997a) *Palimpsests: Literature in the Second Degree*, trsl. C. Newman and C. Doubinsky. Lincoln, NE.
(1997b) *Paratexts: Thresholds of interpretation*, trsl. J. E. Lewin. Cambridge.
Georgakopoulou, A. and Silk, M. (eds.) (2009) *Standard Languages and Language Standards: Greek, Past and Present*. Farnham.
George, N. (2004) 'Sample This', in *That's the Joint! The Hip-Hop Studies Reader*, ed. M. Forman and M. A. Neal (New York), 437–41.

Georgoussopoulos, K. (1991) 'The Chinese Paradigm: Medea Has Been Liberated and Revitalized by China's Style and Speech', trsl. A. Siouzouli, *Ta Nea*, 7 July.

Gibbs, J. (2007) 'Antigone and Her African Sisters: West African Versions of a Greek Original', in Hardwick and Gillespie (2007), 54–71.

Gide, A. (1925) *Le Prométhée mal enchaîné*. Paris.

(1942) *Théâtre: Saul–Le Roi Candaule–Œdipe–Perséphone–Le Treizième arbre*. Paris.

(1948) *Le Retour de l'enfant prodigue; précédé de cinq autres traités: Le Traité du Narcisse–La Tentative amoureuse–El Hadj–Philoctète–Bethsabé*. Paris.

(2007) *Prometheus Illbound*, trsl. L. Rothermere. New York.

Giesekam, G. (2007) *Staging the Screen: The Use of Film and Video in Theater*. New York.

Gilbert, H. and Tompkins, J. (1996) *Post-colonial Drama: Theory, Practice, Politics*. London and New York.

Gilliatt, P. (1980) 'A Nigerian Original', in *Critical Perspectives on Wole Soyinka*, ed. J. Gibbs (Washington, DC), 106–7.

Glynn, D. (2015) *(Re)telling Old Stories: Peter Brook's Mahabharata and Ariane Mnouchkine's Les Atrides*. New York.

Goetsch, S. (1994) 'Playing against the Text: *Les Atrides* and the History of Reading Aeschylus', *Tulane Drama Review* 38: 75–95.

Goff, B. (2005) 'Dionysiac Triangles: The Politics of Culture in Wole Soyinka's *The Bacchae of Euripides*', in *The Soul of Tragedy: Essays on Athenian Drama*, ed. V. Pedrick and S. M. Oberhelman (Chicago and London), 73–88.

Goff, B. and Simpson, M. (2007) *Crossroads in the Black Aegean: Oedipus, Antigone and Dramas of the African Diaspora*. Oxford.

(2011) 'Voice from the Black Box: Sylvain Bemba's Black Wedding Candles for Blessed Antigone', in Mee and Foley (2011), 324–39.

Goldberg, R. (2011) *Performance Art: From Futurism to the Present*, 3rd edn. London.

Golder, H. (1996) 'Geek Tragedy? Or, Why I'd Rather Go to the Movies', *Arion* 4: 174–209.

Goldhill, S. (1987) 'The Great Dionysia and Civic Ideology', *Journal of Hellenic Studies* 107: 58–76.

(1991) 'Violence in Greek Tragedy', in Redmond (1991), 15–33.

(1997) 'The Language of Tragedy: Rhetoric and Communication', in Easterling (1997a), 127–50.

(2004) *Aeschylus: The Oresteia*. Cambridge.

(2007) *How to Stage Greek Tragedy Today*. Chicago and London.

(2012) *Sophocles and the Language of Tragedy*. Oxford.

(2015) 'Introduction', in Icke (2015), 4–7.

Goodwin, T. (1988) *Britain's Royal National Theatre: The First 25 Years*. London.

Goto, Y. (1989) 'The Theatrical Fusion of Suzuki Tadashi', *Asian Theater Journal* 6: 103–23.

Gould, E. (1981) *Mythical Intentions in Modern Literature*. Princeton.

Goutsos, D. (2009) 'Competing Ideologies and Post-Diglossia Greek: Analysing the Discourse of Contemporary "Myth-Breakers"', in Georgakopoulou and Silk (2009), 321–39.

Grammatas, T. (2006) *Για το δράμα και το θέατρο* (*On Drama and Theatre*). Athens.

Green, A. S. (1994) *The Revisionist Stage: American Directors Reinvent the Classics*. Cambridge.

Greenwood, E. (2005) '"We Speak Latin in Trinidad": Uses of Classics in Caribbean Literature', in *Classics and Colonialism*, ed. B. Goff (London), 65–91.

(2010) *Afro-Greeks: Dialogues between Anglophone Caribbean Literature and Classics in the Twentieth Century*. Oxford.

(2013) 'Omni-local Classical Receptions', *Classical Receptions Journal*, Special Issue, 5.3: 354–61.

(2016) 'Reception Studies: The Cultural Mobility of Classics', *Daedalus: Journal of the American Academy of Arts and Sciences* 145.2: 41–9.

Gregory, J. (ed.) (2005). *A Companion to Greek Tragedy*. Malden.

Grene, D. and Lattimore, R. (trsl.) (2013) *The Complete Greek Tragedies*, 3rd edn, ed. M. Griffith and G. W. Most, 9 vols. Chicago.

Griffith, M. (2010) 'Psychoanalysing *Antigone*', in *Interrogating Antigone in Postmodern Philosophy and Criticism*, ed. S. E. Wilmer and A. Žukauskaitė (Oxford), 110–34.

Gruber, W. (2010) *Offstage Space, Narrative, and the Theatre of the Imagination*. New York.

Gumpert, M. (2001) *Grafting Helen: The Abduction of the Classical Past*. Madison.

Gussow, M. (1985) '*A Seagull* in Washington', *New York Times*, 17 December, www.nytimes.com/1985/12/17/theater/theater-a-seagull-in-washington.html (accessed 5 June 2015).

(1986) 'THEATER: ALCESTIS', *New York Times*, 21 March, www.nytimes.com/1986/03/21/theater/theater-alcestis.html (accessed 19 December 2014).

Güthenke, C. (2008) *Placing Modern Greece: The Dynamics of Romantic Hellenism, 1770–1840*. Oxford.

Hall, E. (1989) *Inventing the Barbarian: Greek Self-Definition through Tragedy*. Oxford.

(2004a) 'Why Greek Tragedy in the Late Twentieth Century?', in Hall, Macintosh, and Wrigley (2004), 1–46.

(2004b) 'Towards a Theory of Performance Reception', *Arion*, 3rd series, 12: 51–89.

(2010a) *Greek Tragedy: Suffering Under the Sun*. Oxford.

(2010b) 'Towards a Theory of Performance Reception', in Hall and Harrop (2010), 10–28.

Hall, E. and Harrop, S. (eds.) (2010) *Theorising Performance: Greek Drama, Cultural History and Critical Practice*. London.

Hall, E. and Macintosh, F. (2005) *Greek Tragedy and the British Theatre, 1660–1914*. Oxford.

Hall, E., Macintosh, F., and Taplin, O. (eds.) (2000) *Medea in Performance 1500–2000*. Oxford.

Hall, E., Macintosh, F., and Wrigley, A. (eds.) (2004) *Dionysus since 69: Greek Tragedy at the Dawn of the Third Millennium*. Oxford.

Hall, P. (1983) *Diaries*. London.

Hamilakis, Y. (2007) *The Nation and Its Ruins: Antiquity, Archaeology and the National Imagination in Greece*. Oxford.

Hamilton, C., Harris, V., Taylor, J., Pickover, M., Reid, G., and Saleh, R. (eds.) (2002) *Refiguring the Archive*. Dordrecht, Boston, London.

Hanink, J. (2014) *Lycurgan Athens and the Making of Classical Tragedy*. Cambridge.

(2018) 'Scholars and Scholarship on Tragedy', in Liapis and Petrides (2018), 324–49.

Hankir, A., Kirkcaldy, B., Carrick, F. R., Sadiq, A., and Zaman, R. (2017) 'The Performing Arts and Psychological Well-Being', *Psychiatria Danubina* 29 (Suppl. 3): 196–202.

Hannaway, C. B. (2013) 'Translations of the Self: A. E. Housman and Anne Carson, between Scholarship and Creativity', PhD thesis, Durham University.

Hardwick, L. (2003) *Reception Studies*, Greece & Rome: New Surveys in the Classics 33. Oxford.

(2004) 'Greek Drama and Anti-Colonialism: Decolonising Classics', in Hall, Macintosh, and Wrigley (2004), 219–42.

(2005) 'Staging *Agamemnon*: The Languages of Translation', in *Agamemnon in Performance 458 BC to AD 2004*, ed. F. Macintosh, P. Michelakis, E. Hall, and O. Taplin (Oxford), 207–21.

(2006) 'Remodelling Receptions: Greek Drama as Diaspora in Performance', in Martindale and Thomas (2006), 204–15.

(2007a) 'Contests and Continuities in Classical Traditions: African Migrations', in Hilton and Gosling (2007), 43–71.

(2007b) 'Translating Greek Tragedy to the Modern Stage', *Theatre Journal* 59.3: 358–61.

(2007c) 'Shades of Multi-Lingualism and Multi-Vocalism in Modern Performances of Greek Tragedy in Post-Colonial Contexts', in Hardwick and Gillespie (2007), 305–28.

(2010) 'Negotiating Translation for the Stage', in Hall and Harrop (2010), 192–207.

(2013a) 'Translating Greek Plays for the Theatre Today: Transmission, Transgression, Transformation', *Target* 25.3, Special Issue, 321–42.

(2013b) 'The Problem of the Spectators: Ancient and Modern', in Bakogianni (2013b), 11–26.

(2015) 'Audiences across the Pond: Oceans Apart or Shared Experiences?', in Bosher, Macintosh, McConnell, and Rankine (2015), 819–40.

(2016) 'Cultural Spaces in the Recent Translation and Performance of Greek Drama', in Monaghan and Montgomery Griffiths (2016), 155–76.

(2018) 'Can Transmission and Transformation be Reconciled?', in Liapis, Pavlou, and Petrides (2018), 9–25.

(2019) 'Thinking with Classical Reception: Critical Distance, Critical Licence, Critical Amnesia?', in *Classics in Extremis: The Edges of Classical Reception*, ed. E. Richardson (London), 13–24.

(2020) 'Aspirations and Mantras in Classical Reception Research: Can there Really be Dialogue between Ancient and Modern?', in *Framing Classical Receptions*, ed. M. de Pourck *et al.* (Nijmegen).

Hardwick, L., Easterling, P. E., Ireland, S., Lowe, N., and Macintosh, F. (eds.) (2000) *Theatre: Ancient and Modern*. Milton Keynes.

Hardwick, L. and Gillespie, C. (eds.) (2007) *Classics in Post-Colonial Worlds*. Oxford and New York.

Hardwick, L. and Harrison, S. J. (eds.) (2013) *Classics in the Modern World: A Democratic Turn?* Oxford.

Hargreaves, A. G. (2003) 'The Contribution of North and Sub-Saharan African Immigrant Minorities to the Redefinition of Contemporary French Culture', in Forsdick and Murphy (2003), 145–54.

Hargreaves, A. G. and Moura, J.-M. (2007) 'Editorial Introduction: Extending the Boundaries of Francophone Postcolonial Studies', *International Journal of Francophone Studies* 10.3: 307–11.

Harrison, T. (1985) *Tony Harrison: Theatre Works 1973–1985*. London.

(1991) 'The Oresteia in the Making: Letters to Peter Hall', in *Tony Harrison*, ed. N. Astley (Newcastle-upon-Tyne), 275–80.

Harrop, S. (2008) 'Ezra Pound's *Women of Trachis*: Modernist Translation as Performance Text', *Platform: Postgraduate eJournal of Theatre & Performing Arts* 3: 90–106.

Hartigan, K. (1995) *Greek Tragedy on the American Stage: Ancient Drama in Commercial Theater, 1882–1994*. Westport and London.

(2009) *Performance and Cure: Drama and Healing in Ancient Greece and Contemporary America*. London.

Hass, A. W. (2014) *Hegel and the Art of Negation: Negativity, Creativity and Contemporary Thought*. London.

Hatzikiriakos, L. (2000) '"Μου αρνήθηκαν τους υπότιτλους": Πικραμένος από την παράσταση στο Κολοσσαίο δηλώνει ο Β. Παπαβασιλείου' ('"I Was Denied Subtitling": V. Papavassiliou Embittered after Colosseum Performance'), *Eleftherotypia*, 24 July.

Hatzipandazis, T. (2002) *Από του Νείλου μέχρι του Δουνάβεως: Το χρονικό της ανάπτυξης του ελληνικού επαγγελματικού θεάτρου στο ευρύτερο πλαίσιο της Ανατολικής Μεσογείου, από την ίδρυση του ανεξάρτητου κράτους ως τη Μικρασιατική Καταστροφή* (*From the Nile to the Danube: A Chronicle of the Development of Greek Professional Theatre in the Context of the Eastern Mediterranean, from the Foundation of the Independent State till the Asia Minor Disaster*), vols. I–II. Heraklion.

Haubold, J. (2013) *Greece and Mesopotamia: Dialogues in Literature*. Cambridge.

Healy, J. F. (1978) *Mining and Metallurgy in the Greek and Roman World.* London.

Hebdige, D. (2003) *Cut'n'mix: Culture, Identity and Caribbean Music*. Abingdon.

Heck, T. F. (ed.) (1999) *Picturing Performance: The Iconography of the Performing Arts in Concept and Practice.* Rochester and Woodbridge.

Hegel, G. W. F. (1977) *Phenomenology of Spirit*, trsl. A. V. Miller. Oxford.

(1986a) *Phänomenologie des Geistes* (*Werke* 3), ed. E. Moldenhauer and K. M. Michel. Frankfurt am Main.

(1986b). *Wissenschaft der Logik I; Erster Teil: Die objektive Logik; Erstes Buch* (*Werke* 5), ed. E. Moldenhauer and K. M. Michel. Frankfurt am Main.

(1986c). *Vorlesungen über die Ästhetik III* (*Werke* 15), ed. E. Moldenhauer and K. M. Michel. Frankfurt am Main.

(1986d). *Vorlesungen über die Philosophie der Religion II: Vorlesungen über die Beweise vom Dasein Gottes* (*Werke* 17), ed. E. Moldenhauer and K. M. Michel. Frankfurt am Main.

(1998) *Aesthetics: Lectures on Fine Art*, trsl. T. M. Knox. Oxford.

Heilman, R. B. (1953) '*Alcestis* and *The Cocktail Party*', *Comparative Literature* 5.2: 105–16.

Helfer, R. and Loney, G. (eds.) (1998) *Peter Brook: Oxford to Orghast.* Amsterdam.

Henerson, E. (2011) 'Trojan Women: Misery under the Stars', *Examiner*, 17 September.

Herbert, J. (1993) *A Theatre Workbook*, ed. C. Courtney. London.

Hermansson, C. (2015) 'Flogging Fidelity: In Defense of the (Un)dead Horse', *Adaptation* 8.2: 147–60.

Hestermann, S. (2003) 'The German-Turkish Diaspora and Multicultural German Identity', in Fludernik (2003), 329–73.

Higgins, C. (2015) 'Death Becomes Her: How Juliette Binoche and Ivo van Hove Remade Antigone', *Guardian*, 18 February, www.theguardian.com/stage/2015/feb/18/juliette-binoche-ivo-van-hove-antigone (accessed 23 July 2015).

Highet, G. (1949) *The Classical Tradition: Greek and Roman Influences on Western Literature*. Oxford.

Hilton, J. and Gosling, A. (eds.) (2007) *Alma Parens Originalis? The Reception of Classical Literature and Thought in Africa, Europe, the United States, and Cuba.* Bern.

Hjorth, B. (2014) 'We're Standing in/the Nick of Time: The Temporality of Translation in Anne Carson's *Antigonick*', *Performance Research* 19.3: 135–9.

Hofmannsthal, H. von (1908) *Electra: A Tragedy in One Act*, trsl. A. Symons. New York.

Holford-Strevens, L. (1999) 'Sophocles at Rome', in *Sophocles Revisited: Essays Presented to Sir Hugh Lloyd-Jones*, ed. J. Griffin (Oxford), 219–59.

Honig, B. (2013) *Antigone, Interrupted.* Cambridge.

Hornblower, S. (2018) 'Hellenistic Tragedy and Satyr-Drama; Lycophron's Alexandra', in Liapis and Petrides (2018), 90–124.
Huang Wenjun (1988) 'Reuxin de lizan-wo kan *Andigani*' ('Praise for Humanity: Seeing a Performance of *Antigone*'), trsl. Kuan-wu Lin, *Chinese Theatre* 7: 43–4.
Hughes, T. (1968) 'The Oedipus of Seneca', *Arion* 7.3: 324–71.
(1969) *Seneca's Oedipus*. London.
Hunt, L. and Wing-Fai, L. (eds.) (2010) *East Asian Cinemas: Exploring Transnational Connections on Film*. London.
Hunwick, A. (1996) 'Tragédie et dramaturgie: Les ambiguïtés dans l'*Antigone* d'Anouilh', *Revue d'histoire littéraire de la France* 96.2: 290–312.
Hutcheon, L. (2006) *A Theory of Adaptation*. Abingdon and New York.
(2012) *A Theory of Adaptation*, 2nd edn. London.
Icke, R. (2015) *Aeschylus: Oresteia*. London.
Ioannidis, G. (2016) 'Ένα αγοροκόριτσο ωριμάζει πριν την ώρα του' ('A Tomboy Matures Before Her Time'), *Efimerida ton Syntakton*, 18 July: 34.
Ioannidou, E. (2017) *Greek Fragments in Postmodern Frames: Re-writing Tragedy 1970–2005*. Oxford.
Irigaray, L. (1985) *Speculum of the Other Woman*, trsl. G. C. Gill. Ithaca, NY.
Isherwood, C. (2002) 'Review: To You, The Birdie!', *Variety*, 25 February, http://variety.com/2002/legit/reviews/to-you-the-birdie-2-1200551138 (accessed 1 February 2017).
Jain, J. (2002) 'India's Republic Day Parade, Restoring Identities, Constructing the Nation', in *India's Popular Culture: Iconic Spaces and Fluid Images*, ed. J. Jain (Mumbai), 62–75.
James, H. (1991) 'Cultural Disintegration in Titus Andronicus: Mutilating Titus, Vergil, and Rome', in Redmond (1991), 123–40.
Jameson, F. (1993) 'Postmodernism, or The Cultural Logic of Late Capitalism', in *Postmodernism: A Reader*, ed. T. Docherty (New York), 62–92.
Janko, R. (1994) *The Iliad: A Commentary. Volume IV: Books 13–16*. Cambridge.
Jebb, R. C. (1894) *Sophocles: The Plays and Fragments. Part VI: The Electra*. Cambridge.
(1900) *Sophocles: The Plays and Fragments. Part III: The Antigone*, 3rd edn. Cambridge.
Jenkins, T. (2013) 'Is There Too Much Rape on Stage and TV?', *Independent*, 28 August, www.independent.co.uk/arts-entertainment/theatre-dance/features/is-there-too-much-rape-on-stage-and-tv-8788256.html (accessed 10 June 2019).
(2015) *Antiquity Now: The Classical World in the Contemporary American Imagination*. Cambridge.
Jeyifo, B. (1995) 'Interview with Femi Osofisan', *Yearbook of Comparative and General Literature* 43: 120–32.
(ed.) (2001) *Conversations with Wole Soyinka*. Jackson.
Johnson, P. J. (1997) 'Woman's Third Face: A Psychosocial Reconsideration of Sophocles' *Antigone*', *Arethusa* 30: 369–98.

Johnston, D. (2011) 'Metaphor and Metonymy: The Translator-Practitioner's Visibility', in *Staging and Performing Translation: Text and Theatre Practice*, ed. R. Baines, C. Marinetti, and M. Perteghella (London), 11–30.

Jones, F. (1957) 'Tragedy with a Purpose: Bertolt Brecht's Antigone', *Tulane Drama Review* 2.1: 39–45.

Jones, R. E. (1965 [1941]) *The Dramatic Imagination*. New York.

Jones, W. (1999 [1807]) 'The Third Anniversary Discourse' (2 February 1786), in *The Works of Sir William Jones: with the Life of the Author, by Lord Teignmouth III*, ed. Guido Abbatista, ELIOHS (Electronic Library of Historiography), www.eliohs.unifi.it/testi/700/jones/Jones_Discourse_3.html (accessed 16 August 2016).

Jordan, E. (2002) 'Unmasking the Myths? Marina Carr's By the Bog of Cats ... and On Raftery's Hill', in McDonald and Walton (2002), 243–62.

Jung, C. G. (1961) *Freud and Psychoanalysis*, trsl. R. F. C. Hull, in *The Collected Works of C. G. Jung*, vol. IV. New York.

Kaimio, M. (1988) *Physical Contact in Greek Tragedy: A Study of Stage Conventions*. Helsinki.

Kakridis, I. T. (1997) *Οι αρχαίοι Έλληνες στη νεοελληνική λαϊκή παράδοση* (*Ancient Greeks in Modern Greek Folklore*). Athens.

Kalb, J. (2001) 'Samuel Beckett, Heiner Müller and Post-dramatic Theater', *Samuel Beckett Today/Aujourd'hui* 11: 74–83.

Kaliss, E. M. (1971) 'Anouilh through Euripides and Seneca', *Classical Folia* 25: 212–17.

Kaltaki, M. (2000) ''Ενας μη τραγικός Οιδίποδας ...' ('A Non-Tragic Oedipus...'), *Ependitis*, 19 August.

Kane, S. (2001) *Complete Plays: Blasted, Phaedra's Love, Cleansed, Crave, 4.48 Psychosis, Skin*. London.

Karakantza, E. D. (2020) *Who Am I? (Mis)Identity and the Polis in Oedipus Tyrannus*. Washington, DC.

Kaye, N. (1994). *Postmodernism and Performance*. London.

Kenward, C. (2016) 'The Reception of Greek Drama in Early Modern England', in Van Zyl Smit (2016), 173–98.

Kershaw, B. (1992) *The Politics of Performance: Radical Theatre as Cultural Intervention*. London.

Kidd, R. (1985) '"Theatre for Development": Diary of a Zimbabwe Workshop', *New Theatre Quarterly* 1.2: 179–204.

Kilvert, I. S. (1968) 'Seneca or Scenario?', *Arion* 7.3: 501–11.

Kirby, J. (2012) 'Aristotle on Sophocles', in *A Companion to Sophocles*, ed. K. Ormand (Oxford), 411–23.

Kitzinger, M. R. (2008) *The Choruses of Sophokles' Antigone and Philoctetes: A Dance of Words*. Leiden.

Kneehigh (2005) *The Kneehigh Anthology: Volume 1*, London.

Komporaly, J. (2017) *Radical Revival as Adaptation: Theatre, Politics, Society*. London.

Koser, K. (ed.) (2003) *New African Diasporas*. London and New York.

Koukos, S. (2016) Interview with Stathis Livathinos: 'Η γενιά της «Αντιγόνης» έχει ανάγκη από ήχο, από φωνή' ('"Antigone's" Generation Needs a Voice'), *Makedonia Kyriakis*, 28 August: 54–5.
Kramer, J. (2007) 'Experimental Journey', *New Yorker*, 8 October: 48–57.
Krebs, K. (2012) 'Translation and Adaptation: Two Sides of an Ideological Coin?', in *Translation, Adaptation and Transformation*, ed. L. Raw (London and New York), 42–53.
(2014) 'Introduction: Collisions, Diversions and Meeting Points', in *Translation and Adaptation in Theatre and Film*, ed. K. Krebs (London and New York), 1–12.
Krishnan, K. P. K. and Pillai, R. (2009) In conversation with Saskya Jain, 16 January.
Krüger, M. (1967) 'Private Existenz und öffentliche Meinung: Zum Antigone-Drama von Jean Anouilh', *Zeitschrift für französische Sprache und Literatur* 77.1–2: 64–89.
Kubiak, A. (1991) *Stages of Terror: Terrorism, Ideology, and Coercion as Theatre History*. Bloomington.
Kucewicz, C. (2016) "Mutilation of the Dead and the Homeric Gods', *Classical Quarterly* 66.2: 425–36.
Kuppers, P. (2005) *Disability and Contemporary Performance: Bodies on the Edge*. Oxford and New York.
Kwahulé, K. (2003) *Bintou*. Carnières-Morlanwelz. (Originally published 1997.)
(2008) 'Men's Business: An Interview with Chantal Zabus', in Zabus (2008), 171–90.
Lada-Richards, I. (2005) 'Greek Tragedy and Western Perceptions of Actors and Acting', in Gregory (2005), 459–71.
Laera, M. (2013) *Reaching Athens: Community, Democracy and Other Mythologies in Adaptations of Greek Tragedy*. Frankfurt am Main.
(2014) *Theatre and Adaptation: Return, Rewrite, Repeat*. London.
(2015) 'On Killing Children: Greek Tragedies on British Stages in 2015', *Critical Stages* 12, www.critical-stages.org/12/on-killing-children-greek-tragedies-on-british-stages-in-2015/ (accessed 1 March 2020).
Laizé, H. (1997) *Premières leçons sur Électre de Jean Giraudoux*. Paris.
Lanfranchi, P. (2006) *L'Exagoge d'Ezéchiel le Tragique: Introduction, texte, traduction et commentaire*. Leiden.
(2018) 'The Exagōgē of Ezekiel the Tragedian', in Liapis and Petrides (2018) 125–46.
Lauriola, R. (2015a) 'Medea', in Lauriola and Demetriou (2015), 377–442.
(2015b) 'Hippolytus', in Lauriola and Demetriou (2015), 443–503.
Lauriola, R., and Demetriou, K. N. (eds.) (2015) *Brill's Companion to the Reception of Euripides*. Leiden.
Lecznar, A. (2014) 'Soyinka's Bacchae: Reading Tragedy in Postcolonial Modernity', PhD thesis, University College London.

(2020) *Dionysus after Nietzsche: The Birth of Tragedy in Twentieth Century Literature and Thought.* Cambridge.

Leeney, C. (2002) 'The Return of Persephone? Missing Demeter in Irish Theatre', in McDonald and Walton (2002), 232–43.

Leeney, C. and McMullan, A. (eds.) (2003) *The Theatre of Marina Carr: 'Before Rules Was Made'.* Dublin.

Lehmann, H.-T. (1999) *Postdramatisches Theater.* Frankfurt am Main.

(2006) *Postdramatic Theatre*, trsl. K. Jürs-Munby. London and New York.

Leitch, T. (2012) 'Adaptation and Intertextuality, or, What Isn't an Adaptation, and What Does It Matter?', in Cartmell (2012), 87–104.

Leiter, S. L. (1979) *Kabuki Encyclopedia: An English-Language Adaptation of "Kabuki Jiten".* Westport and London.

Lensing, L. A. (2006) 'Elektra "antik u. modern": Zu einem Abend der Mittwoch-Gesellschaft im Jahre 1905 (mit einer unbekannten Postkarte Freuds an Paul Federn)', *Luzifer-Amor: Zeitschrift zur Geschichte der Psychoanalyse* 38: 46–75.

Leonard, M. (2005). *Athens in Paris: Ancient Greece and the Political in Post-war French Thought.* Oxford.

(2015) *Tragic Modernities.* Cambridge, MA.

Li, Jin-yuan (1998) 'Shije renmin xihuan Zhongguo xiju yishi' ('Cosmopolitans Love Chinese Theatre Art'), trsl. Kuan-wu Lin, *Da Wutai* (*The Great Stage*) 3: 57.

Lianeri, A. and Zajko, V. (eds.) (2008) *Translation and the Classic: Identity as Change in the History of Culture.* Oxford.

Liapis, V. (2012) *A Commentary on the Rhesus Attributed to Euripides.* Oxford.

(2013a) 'Creon the Labdacid: Political Confrontation and the Doomed Oikos in Sophocles' *Antigone*', in *Tragedy and Archaic Greek Thought*, ed. D. L. Cairns (Swansea), 81–118.

(2013b) 'Staging *Rhesus*', in *Performance in Greek and Roman Theatre*, ed. G. W. M. Harrison and V. Liapis (Leiden), 235–53.

(2014a) 'Orestes and Nothingness: Yiannis Ritsos' "Orestes", Greek Tragedy, and Existentialism', *International Journal of the Classical Tradition* 21: 121–58.

(2014b) '"The Painful Memory of Woe": Greek Tragedy and the Greek Civil War in the Work of George Seferis', *Classical Receptions Journal* 6.1: 74–103.

(2016) 'On the *Hector* of Astydamas', *American Journal of Philology* 137: 61–89.

(2018) 'Blowing Up the Parthenon: Greek Antiquity as a Burden and as a Rival on the Modern Greek Stage', The Niki Marangou Lecture, King's College London, 23 May 2019, www.academia.edu/39978325/Blowing_up_the_Parthenon_Greek_antiquity_as_a_burden_and_as_a_rival_on_the_modern_Greek_stage (accessed 27 February 2020).

Liapis, V., and Petrides, A. K. (eds.) (2018) *Greek Tragedy after the Fifth Century: A Survey from ca. 400 BC to ca. AD 400.* Cambridge.

Liapis, V. and Stephanopoulos, Th. K. (2018) 'Greek Tragedy in the Fourth Century: The Fragments', in Liapis and Petrides (2018), 25–65.

Liapis, V., Pavlou, M., and Petrides, A. K. (eds.) (2017) *Debating with the Eumenides: Aspects of the Reception of Greek Tragedy in Modern Greece*. Newcastle-upon-Tyne.

Lin, Kuan-wu (2010) *Westlicher Geist im östlichen Körper? 'Medea' im interkulturellen Theater Chinas und Taiwans: Zur Universalisierung der griechischen Antike*. Bielefeld.

Llewellyn-Jones, L. (2002) 'Understanding Theater Space', www2.open.ac.uk/ClassicalStudies/GreekPlays/essays/VisualSystems.htm (accessed 1 February 2017).

Lloyd-Jones, H. (1994) *Sophocles: Antigone, The Women of Trachis, Philoctetes, Oedipus at Colonus*, Loeb Classical Library 21. Cambridge, MA (corr. repr. 1998).

Lodewyck, L. and Monoson, S. S. (2015) 'Performing for Soldiers: Twenty-First-Century Experiments in Greek Theater in the US', in Bosher, Macintosh, McConnell, and Rankine (2015), 651–65.

Logan, W. (2012) 'Song & Dance', *New Criterion*, December 2012, www.newcriterion.com/articles.cfm/Song—dance-7511#footnote-34650-1-backlink (accessed 18 September 2015).

Løkse, A. M. C. (1994) 'In Defence of Hellas: An Analysis of Shelley's Hellas and Its Reception', PhD thesis, Universitetet i Tromsø.

Lombardo, S. and Murnaghan, S. (1997) *Homer: Iliad*. Indianapolis.

Love, C. (2009) 'Koffi Kwahulé's Bintou and Sophocles' Antigone: The Silent Form of Adaptation', *New Voices in Classical Reception Studies* 4: 108–22, http://fass.open.ac.uk/sites/fass.open.ac.uk/files/files/new-voices-journal/issue4/6Love.pdf (accessed 20 February 2020).

(2014) 'Ben Power Talks Dramaturgy, Rebranding The Shed and Rethinking Medea', *What'sOnStage*, 13 May, www.whatsonstage.com/london-theatre/news/05-2014/ben-power-talks-dramaturgy-rebranding-the-shed-and_34413.html (accessed 9 March 2020).

Lü, Y. (2004) 'Germany: Myth and Apologia in Christa Wolf's Novel *Medea. Voices*', *Portal: Journal of Multidisciplinary International Studies* 1.1, https://epress.lib.uts.edu.au/journals/index.php/portal/article/view/50 (accessed 12 March 2020).

Maass, E. (1912) *Goethe und die Antike*. Stuttgart.

Macintosh, F. (1997) 'Tragedy in Performance: Nineteenth- and Twentieth-Century Productions', in Easterling (1997a), 284–323.

(2007) 'From the Court to the National: The Theatrical Legacy of Gilbert Murray's *Bacchae*', in *Gilbert Murray Reassessed: Hellenism, Theatre, and International Politics*, ed. C. Stray (Oxford), 145–65.

(2009) *Sophocles: Oedipus Tyrannus*. Cambridge.

(2015) 'Shakespearean Sophocles: (Re)-Discovering and Performing Greek Tragedy in the Nineteenth Century', in *The Oxford History of Classical Reception in English Literature, vol. IV (1790–1880)*, ed. N. Vance and J. Wallace (Oxford), 299–323.

(2016) 'Conquering England: Ireland and Greek Tragedy', in Van Zyl Smit (2016), 173–98.

Mackay, A. (1989) 'Fugard's The Island and Sophocles' Antigone within the Parameters of South African Protest Literature', in Bevan (1989), 145–62.

Mackridge, P. (ed.) (1996) *Ancient Greek Myths in Modern Greek Poetry: Essays in Memory of C. A. Trypanis*. London.

(2009) *Language and National Identity in Greece 1766–76*. Oxford.

Malafouris, L. (2013) *How Things Shape the Mind*. Cambridge, MA.

Malkin, J. (1992) *Verbal Violence in Contemporary Drama*. Cambridge.

Manheim, M. (ed.) (1998) *The Cambridge Companion to Eugene O'Neill*. Cambridge.

Mansfield, H. C. (1996) *Machiavelli's Virtue*. Chicago.

Manuwald, G. (2011) *Roman Republican Theatre*. Cambridge.

Marcuse, H. (1973) *Counter-Revolution and Revolt*. Boston.

Martens, L. (1987) 'The Theme of the Repressed Memory in Hofmannsthal's *Elektra*', *German Quarterly* 60.1: 38–51.

Martindale, C. (2003) *Redeeming the Text*. Cambridge.

(2006) 'Introduction: Thinking through Reception', in Martindale and Thomas (2006), 1–13.

Martindale, C. and Thomas, R. F. (eds.) (2006) *Classics and the Uses of Reception*. Oxford.

Martinovich, M. K. (2003.) 'The Study of Greeks and Ghosts in the Shaping of the American Premiere of By the Bog of Cats . . .', in Leeney and McMullan (2003), 114–27.

Marwick, A. (1998) *The Sixties: Cultural Revolution in Britain, France, Italy, and the United States, c.1958–c.1974*. Oxford.

Mastrogiannitis, D. (2016) 'Στάθης Λιβαθινός "Φτάνει με τα κλισέ στην τραγωδία"' ('Stathis Livathinos: Enough with the Clichés in Tragedy'), *Athens Voice*, 14 July: 30.

Matziri, S. (1998) 'Myth Is a Lie that Tells the Truth', trsl. A. Siouzouli, *Eleftherotypia*, 7 August.

Mavromoustakos, P. (2005) *Το θέατρο στην Ελλάδα 1940–2000: Μια επισκόπηση* (*Theatre in Greece 1940–2000: An Overview*). Athens.

Maxwell, D. (2016) 'Theatre: The Iphigenia Quartet at the Gate Theatre, W11', *Times*, 5 May, www.thetimes.co.uk/article/theatre-the-iphigenia-quartet-at-the-gate-theatre-w11-wzcz9fxc2 (accessed 30 January 2020).

McCall, D. (1969) *The Theatre of Jean-Paul Sartre*. New York and London.

McClain, T. D. (2009) [Review of Torrance 2007], *Classical Review* 59.2: 359–61.

McClellan, A. M. (2016) 'The Death and Mutilation of Imbrius in *Iliad* 13', *Yearbook of Ancient Greek Epic* 1.1: 159–74.

McConnell, J. (2013) *Black Odysseys: The Homeric 'Odyssey' in the African Diaspora since 1939*. Oxford.

(2015) 'Postcolonial Sparagmos: Toni Morrison's *Sula* and Wole Soyinka's *The Bacchae of Euripides: A Communion Rite*', *Classical Receptions Journal* 8.2: 133–54.
McCusker, M. (2003) '"This Creole Culture, Miraculously Forged": The Contradictions of "Créolité"', in Forsdick and Murphy (2003), 112–21.
McDonald, M. (1992) *Ancient Sun, Modern Light: Greek Drama on the Modern Stage*. New York.
(1999) 'Black Dionysus: Greek Tragedy from Africa', in Hardwick, Easterling, Ireland, Lowe, and Macintosh (2000), 95–108.
(2002) 'The Irish and Greek Tragedy', in McDonald and Walton (2002), 37–86.
(2003) *The Living Art of Greek Tragedy*. Bloomington.
McDonald, M. and Walton, J. M. (eds.) (2002) *Amid Our Troubles: Irish Versions of Greek Tragedy*. London.
McGillivray, G. (2011) 'The Performance Archive: Detritus or Historical Record?', in *Scrapbooks, Snapshots and Memorabilia: Hidden Archives of Performance*, ed. G. McGillivray (Bern), 11–28.
McKee, J. (2013) 'Siti Troup Bringing Its Updated Anti-War Trojan Women (After Euripedes*)* to Ann Arbor', *Ann Arbor News*, 23 April, www.annarbor.com/entertainment/siti-company-and-ums-bring-trojan-women-after-euripedes-to-ann-arbor (accessed 10 March 2020).
McMullan, A. (2003) 'Unhomely Bodies and Dislocated Identities in the Drama of Frank McGuiness and Marina Carr', in *Indeterminate Bodies*, ed. N. Segal, L. Taylor, and R. Cook (New York), 181–91.
Mda, Z. (1993) *When People Play People: Development Communication through Theatre*. London.
Mee, C. L. (1998) *History Plays*. Baltimore.
(1999) 'The Theatre of History', in *Conversations on Art and Performance*, ed. B. Marranca and G. Dasgupta (Baltimore), 182–93.
Mee, E. B. and Foley, H. P. (eds.) (2011) *Antigone on the Contemporary World Stage*. Oxford and New York.
Meineck, P. (2006) 'Live from New York: Hip Hop Aeschylus and Operatic Aristophanes', *Arion* 14.1: 145–68.
(2009) '"These Are Men Whose Minds the Dead Have Ravished": Theater of War/The Philoctetes Project', *Arion* 17.1: 173–92.
(2012) 'The Embodied Space: Performance and Visual Cognition at the Fifth Century Athenian Theatre', *New England Classical Journal* 39: 3–46.
(2013) 'Under Athena's Gaze: Aeschylus' Eumenides and the Topography of Opsis', in *Performance in Greek and Roman Theatre*, ed. G. W. M. Harrison and V. Liapis (Leiden), 161–79.
(2016) 'Greek Drama in North America', in Van Zyl Smit (2016), 397–421.
(2017) *Theatrocracy: Greek Drama, Cognition, and the Imperative for Theatre*. Abingdon.

Meineck, P. and Konstan, D. (eds.) (2014) *Combat Trauma and the Ancient Greeks*. New York.

Memmi, A. (1957) *Portrait du colonisé précédé du portrait du colonisateur*. Paris.

Mendelsohn, D. (1997) 'Yo, Achilles', *New York Times*, 20 July, https://archive.nytimes.com/www.nytimes.com/books/97/07/20/reviews/970720.20mendelt.html (accessed 17 January 2020).

(2003) 'The Bad Boy of Athens', *New York Review of Books*, 13 February: 24–9, www.nybooks.com/articles/2003/02/13/the-bad-boy-of-athens/ (accessed 10 March 2020).

Merkouri, A. (2010) 'Medea's Sacrifice and the Unsatisfied Director: Euripides' *Medea* by Anatoli Vassiliev', in *Tragic Heroines on Ancient and Modern Stage*, ed. M. de Fátima Silva and S. Hora Marques (Coimbra), 87–108.

Merola, N. (1981) 'Rileggere Alfieri: La tragedia della politica', *MLN* 96 (Italian Issue): 70–88.

Mesiskli, E. (2016) '«Αντιγόνη» από το Εθνικό Θέατρο' ('Antigone' from the National Theatre'), *Peloponnesos*, 19 August: 14.

Meyer, E. (1897) *Machiavelli and the Elizabethan Drama*. Weimar.

Meyrick, J. (2014) *The Retreat of Our National Drama*. Sydney.

Mezzabotta, M. R. (2000) 'Ancient Greek Drama in the New South Africa', in Hardwick, Easterling, Ireland, Lowe, and Macintosh (2000), 246–68.

Michael, A. (2015) 'Reflections of a Nation: Antigone on the Modern Greek Stage', PhD thesis, Royal Holloway College, University of London.

Michelakis, P. (2010a) 'Archiving Events, Performing Documents: On the Seductions and Challenges of Performance Archives', in Hall and Harrop (2010), 95–107.

(2010b) 'Theater Festivals: Total Works of Art, and the Revival of Greek Tragedy on the Modern Greek Stage', *Cultural Critique* 74.1: 149–63.

Miller, A. V. (ed. and trsl.) (1969 [1835]) *Hegel's Science of Logic*. London.

Miller, J. G. (2007) *Ariane Mnouchkine*. Abingdon and New York.

Miller, M. H. (2012) 'A Matter of Time: Anne Carson Re-Writes "Antigone"', *Observer*, 30 May, http://observer.com/2012/05/a-matter-of-time-anne-carson-re-writes-antigone/#ixzz3fc5FaDr2 (accessed 23 June 2015).

Mills, S. (2010) 'Affirming Athenian Action: Euripides' Portrayal of Military Activity and the Limits of Tragic Instruction', in *War, Democracy and Culture in Classical Athens*, ed. D. M. Pritchard (Cambridge), 163–83.

Milton, J. (1671) *Paradise Regaind: A Poem in IV Books to Which is Added Samson Agonistes*. London.

Minier, M. (2014) 'Definitions, Dyads, Triads and Other Points of Connection in Translation and Adaptation Discourse', in *Translation and Adaptation in Theatre and Film*, ed. K. Krebs (London and New York), 13–35.

Mitchell, K. (2009) *The Director's Craft: A Handbook for the Theater*. London.

Mnouchkine, A. (1992) 'Ariane Mnouchkine's Theater of History', *TheaterWeek*, 5 October.

Moddelmog, D. A. (1993) *Readers and Mythic Signs: The Oedipus Myth in Twentieth-Century Fiction*. Carbondale.

Monaghan, P. (2009) '"I Can Not Act / Cause I'm No Actor" – Dood Paard's Postdramatic medEia', *Didaskalia* 7.2, www.didaskalia.net/issues/vol7no2/monaghan/monaghan.pdf (accessed 15 March 2020).

(2016a) 'Aeschylus as Postdramatic Analogue: "A Thing Both Cool and Fiery"', in Constantinidis (2016), 250–79.

(2016b) 'Tragedy Without Character: Dood Paard's Postdramatic "Cool"', in Monaghan and Montgomery Griffiths (2016), 197–223.

Monaghan, P. and Montgomery Griffiths, J. (eds.) (2016) *Close Relations: Spaces of Greek and Roman Theatre*. Newcastle-upon-Tyne.

Montgomery Griffiths, J. (2015a) *Antigone*. Sydney.

(2015b) 'What Women Critics Know That Men Don't', *Performing Arts Hub*, 1 October, http://performing.artshub.com.au/news-article/opinions-and-analysis/performing-arts/jane-griffiths/what-women-critics-know-that-men-don't-249447 (accessed 22 September 2016).

(2016) 'Inside/Outside: The Problems of Space when Playing Electra', in Monaghan and Montgomery Griffiths (2016), 177–96.

Moroney, M. (2001) 'Katie Mitchell Devastates with Euripides', *Guardian*, 30 March 2001, www.theguardian.com/stage/2001/mar/30/theatre.artsfeatures3 (accessed 10/3/2020).

Morrison, B. (2010) 'Translating Greek Drama for Performance', in Hall and Harrop (2010), 252–66.

Moschonas, S. (2009) '"Language Issues" after the "Language Question": On the Modern Standards of Standard Modern Greek', in Georgakopoulou and Silk (2009), 293–320.

Most, G. and Ozbek, L. (eds.) (2015) *Staging Ajax's Suicide*. Pisa.

Mueller, M. (1980) *Children of Oedipus and Other Essays on the Imitation of Greek Tragedy 1550–1800*. Toronto.

(1986) 'Hofmannsthal's *Electra* and Its Dramatic Models', *Modern Drama* 29.1: 71–91.

Mulhallen, J. (2010). *The Theatre of Shelley*. Cambridge. http://books.openedition.org/obp/744.

Müller, H. (1984) *Verkommenes Ufer; Medeamaterial; Landschaft mit Argonauten*. Frankfurt am Main.

Murphy, D. (2003) 'Beyond Tradition Versus Modernity: Postcolonial Thought and Culture in Francophone Sub-Saharan Africa', in Forsdick and Murphy (2003), 221–30.

Myris, K. Ch. (trsl.) (2001) *Ευριπίδου: Τρωάδες* (*Euripides: Trojan Women*). Athens.

Neely, K. (1987) '*Clytemnestra* by Tadashi Suzuki', *Theatre Journal* 39: 514–16.

Neill, R. (2013) 'Hooked on Classics', *The Australian*, 25 May.

Nestruck, K. (2009) 'At Avignon, the Best Theatre Is All Greek', *Guardian*, 20 July, www.theguardian.com/stage/theatreblog/2009/jul/20/avignon-theatre-greek (accessed 9 June 2016).

Nethercot, A. H. (1960) 'The Psychoanalyzing of Eugene O'Neill', *Modern Drama* 3.3: 242–56.

Neuburg, M. (1990) 'How Like a Woman: Antigone's "Inconsistency"', *The Classical Quarterly* n.s. 40: 54–76.
Nevitt, L. (2013) *Theatre and Violence*. Basingstoke.
Newton, I. (1676) Letter from Sir Isaac Newton to Robert Hooke, Historical Society of Pennsylvania, http://digitallibrary.hsp.org/index.php/Detail/Object/Show/object_id/9285 (accessed 16 December 2016).
Ngũgĩ wa Thiong'o (1986) *Decolonising the Mind: The Politics of Language in African Literature*. Oxford.
(2012) *Globalectics: Theory and the Politics of Knowing*. New York.
Nikoloutsos, K. P. (2012) 'Seneca in Cuba: Gender, Race, and the Revolution in José Triana's *Medea en el espejo*', *Romance Quarterly* 59.1: 19–35.
Nussbaum, M. C. (1986) *The Fragility of Goodness: Luck and Ethics in Greek Tragedy and Philosophy*. Cambridge.
Nwachuku, McPhilips (2008) 'National Troupe Presents Soyinka's The Bacchae *of Euripides* as Parable of Power', *Vanguard*, 29 March.
O'Neill, E. (1988) *Complete Plays 1920–1931*, Library of America 41. New York.
Oosterling, H. and Plonowska Ziarek, E. (eds.) (2011) *Intermedialities: Philosophy, Art, Politics*. Lanham.
O'Reilly, K. (2010) *Program-Notes: The Persians*. Cardiff.
Òsòfisan, F. (2016 [1999]) *Insidious Treasons and Beyond: Forty years of Alternative Theatre in Nigeria*. Ibadan.
O'Toole, E., Pelegri Kristić, A., and Young, S. (eds.) (2017) *Ethical Exchanges in Translation, Adaptation and Dramaturgy*. Leiden.
Oudemans, T. C. W. and Lardinois, A. P. M. H. (1987) *Tragic Ambiguity: Anthropology, Philosophy and Sophocles' Antigone*. Leiden.
Owen, A. S. (ed.) (1939) *Euripides: Ion*. Oxford.
Paolucci, A. and Paolucci, H. (1962) *Hegel on Tragedy*. New York.
Parker, G. (2003) '"Francophonie" and "Universalité": Evolution of Two Notions Conjoined', in Forsdick and Murphy (2003), 91–101.
(ed.) (2018) *South Africa, Greece, Rome: Classical Confrontations*. Cambridge.
Parry, A. M. (1981) *Logos and Ergon in Thucydides*. New York.
Pathmanathan, R. S. (1965) 'Death in Greek Tragedy', *Greece & Rome* 12: 2–14.
Pattie, D. (2012) *Modern British Playwriting: The 1950s. Voices, Documents, New Interpretations*. London.
Pavis, P. (1986) 'The Classical Heritage of Modern Drama: The Case of Postmodern Theatre', *Modern Drama* 29: 1–22.
(2008) 'On Faithfulness: The Difficulties Experienced by the Text/Performance Couple', *Theatre Research International* 33: 117–26.
(2013) *Contemporary Mise en Scene: Staging Theatre Today*, trsl. J. Anderson. London.
Pearce L. (1997) *Feminism and the Politics of Reading*. London.
Peeters, F. (1999) 'Scenography, Iconography and Semiotics: Towards an Analytical Framework', in Heck (1999), 150–62.

Pereira, M. (2003) 'Going Up Is a Place of Great Loneliness: An interview with Rita Dove', in *Conversations with Rita Dove*, ed. E. G. Ingersoll (Jackson), 148–73.

Perris, S. (2010) 'Performance Reception and the "Textual Twist": Towards a Theory of Literary Reception', in Hall and Harrop (2010), 181–91.

(2011a) 'Perspectives on Violence in Euripides' *Bacchae*', *Mnemosyne* 64: 37–57.

(2011b) 'What Maketh the Messenger: Reportage in Greek Tragedy', in *ASCS 32 Proceedings (2011)*, ed. A. Mackay, http://ascs.org.au/news/ascs32/Perris.pdf.

(2015) 'Bacchant Women', in *Brill's Companion to the Reception of Euripides*, ed. K. Demetriou and R. Lauriola (Leiden), 507–48.

(2016) *The Gentle, Jealous God: Reading Euripides' Bacchae in English*. London.

Perris, S. and Mac Góráin, F. (2020) 'The Ancient Reception of Euripides' *Bacchae* from Athens to Byzantium', in *Dionysus and Rome: Religion and Literature*, ed. F. Mac Góráin (Berlin), 39–84.

Petre, Z. (1985) 'La Représentation de la mort dans la tragédie grecque', *Studii Classice* 23: 21–35.

Petrides, A. K. (2017) 'Introduction', in Liapis, Pavlou, and Petrides (2017), 1–8.

Phelan, P. (1993) *Unmarked: The Politics of Performance*. London.

Philipsen, B. (1998) 'Das Zaudern der Macht: Tragödie und Demokratie in Brechts *Antigonemodell 1948*', *Germanistische Mitteilungen* 48: 52–67.

Plastow, C. (2018) 'Conversations with Iphigenia: Two Roundtable Discussions with the Playwrights of the Iphigenia Quartet', *Practitioners' Voices in Classical Reception Studies* 9, http://oro.open.ac.uk/58580 (accessed 27 January 2020).

Poe, J. P. (1993) 'The Determination of Episodes in Greek Tragedy', *American Journal of Philology* 114: 343–96.

Pollmann, K. (2017) *The Baptized Muse: Early Christian Poetry as Cultural Authority*. Oxford.

Pope, A. (1812) *The Works of Alexander Pope Esq. in Verse and Prose*, vol. VI. London.

Poulin, J. (2006) *La Traduction est une histoire d'amour*. Arles.

(2009) *Translation Is a Love Affair*, trsl. S. Fischman. New York.

Pound, E. (2003) *Ezra Pound: Poems and Translations*, Library of America 142. New York.

Powers, M. (2018) *Diversifying Greek Tragedy on the Contemporary US Stage*. Oxford.

Prentki, T. and Preston, S. (eds.) (2009) *The Applied Theatre Reader*. London and New York.

Prins, Y. (2015) 'Translating Tragedy: Robert Browning's Greek Decade', in *The Oxford History of Classical Reception in English Literature*, ed. N. Vance and J. Wallace (Oxford), 509–38.

Pronko, L. C. (1961) *The World of Jean Anouilh*. Berkeley.
Puchner, W. and White, A. W. (2017) *Greek Theatre between Antiquity and Independence: A History of Reinvention from the Third Century BC to 1830*. Cambridge.
Quick, A. (2007) *The Wooster Group Workbook*. New York.
Rabinowitz, N. S. (2011) 'Greek Tragedy: A Rape Culture?' *EuGeStA* 1: 1–20.
Racine, J. (1951) *Théâtre de Racine*, vols. I–V, ed. P. Mélèse, Collection Nationale des Classiques Français. Paris.
Raeburn, D. (2017) *Greek Tragedies as Plays for Performance*. Malden and Oxford.
Ranald, M. L. (1998) 'From Trial to Triumph (1913–1924): The Early Plays', in Manheim (1998), 51–68.
Rebellato, D. (1999) *1956 and All That: The Making of Modern British Drama*. London and New York.
Redmond, J. (ed.) (1991) *Violence in Drama*. Cambridge.
Rees, R. (ed.) (2009) *Ted Hughes and the Classics*. Oxford.
Rehm, R. (2003) *Radical Theatre: Greek Tragedy and the Modern World*. London.
Renger, A.-B. (2013) *Oedipus and the Sphinx: The Threshold Myth from Sophocles through Freud to Cocteau*, trsl. D. A. Smart, D. Rice, and J. T. Hamilton. Chicago.
Revermann, M. (2006) *Comic Business: Theatricality, Dramatic Technique, and Performance Contexts of Aristophanic Comedy*. Oxford.
(2008) 'The Appeal of Dystopia: Latching onto Greek Drama in the Twentieth Century', *Arion* 16.1: 97–117.
Reynolds, M. (2011) *The Poetry of Translation: From Chaucer & Petrarch to Homer & Logue*. Oxford.
Ricks, D. (1989) *The Shadow of Homer: A Study in Modern Greek Poetry*. Cambridge.
Ricoeur, P. (2004) *Memory, History, Forgetting*, trsl. K. Blamey and D. Pellauer. Chicago.
Rodosthenous, G. (ed.) (2017) *Contemporary Adaptations of Greek Tragedy: Auteurship and Directorial Visions*. London and New York.
Roisman, H. M. (2005) *Sophocles: Philoctetes*. London.
Rosenmeyer, T. G. (1989) *Senecan Drama and Its Stoic Cosmology*. Berkeley.
Roux, J. (ed.) (1972) *Euripide: Les Bacchantes*. Paris.
Ruperti, B. (2011) 'Greek Tragedies in/and the Productions of Ninagawa Yukio', in *Japanese Theatre Transcultural: German and Italian Intertwinings*, ed. S. Scholz-Cionca and A. Regelsberger (Munich), 138–56.
Rush, M. (1999) *New Media in Late 20th-Century Art*. New York.
Ryals, C. de L. (1973) '*Balaustion's Adventure*: Browning's Greek Parable', *Proceedings of the Modern Language Association* 88.5: 1040–8.
Sachs, M. (1962) 'Notes on the Theatricality of Jean Anouilh's "Antigone"', *French Review* 36.1: 3–11.
Safran, W. (1991) 'Diasporas in Modern Societies: Myths of Homeland and Return', *Diaspora* 1.1: 83–99.
Sagar, K. (2009) 'Ted Hughes and the Classics', in Rees (2009), 1–24.

Sampatakakis, G. (2005) 'Bakkhai-Model: The Re-Usage of Euripides' *Bakkhai* in Text and Performance', PhD thesis, Royal Holloway at the University of London.

(2014) '«Έξω οι Ούνοι...»: Πολιτισμικές δυσανεξίες και ιδιοκτησιακές ιδεολογίες στα ελληνικά φεστιβάλ (Εθνικό Θέατρο και ΚΘΒΕ)' ('"Out with the Huns...": Cultural Intolerance and Proprietary Ideology in Greek Festivals (National Theatre and State Theatre of Northern Greece)'), in *Πρακτικά Διεθνούς Επιστημονικού Συνεδρίου «Σκηνική Πράξη στο Μεταπολεμικό Θέατρο: Συνέχεις και Ρήξεις»* (*Proceedings of the International Conference on 'Performance Practice in Postwar Theatre: Continuities and Ruptures'*), ed. A. Dimitriadis, I. Pipinia, and A. Stavrakopoulou (Thessaloniki), 435–50.

(2017) 'Dionysus the Destroyer of Traditions: The Bacchae on Stage', in Rodosthenous (2017), 189–211.

Sanders, J. (2006) *Adaptation and Appropriation*. London and New York.

(2016) *Adaptation and Appropriation*, 2nd edn. London and New York.

Saunders, G. (2002) *'Love Me or Kill Me': Sarah Kane and the Theatre of Extremes*. Manchester.

(2009) *About Kane: The Playwright and the Work*. London.

Schechner, R. (ed.) (1970) *Dionysus in 69*. New York.

Scheib, J. (2005) 'Program Note for *The Medea*', www.jayscheib.com/medea/pressmaterials.html (accessed 1 February 2017).

Schober, R. (2013) 'Adaptation as Connection: Transmediality Reconsidered', in Bruhn, Gjelsvik, and Hanssen (2013), 89–112.

Scott, J. (2005) *Electra after Freud: Myth and Culture*. Ithaca, NY.

Seaford, R. (2005) 'Tragedy and Dionysus', in *A Companion to Tragedy*, ed. R. Bushnell (Malden), 25–38.

Seaver, R. W. (ed.) (1976) *I Can't Go on, I'll Go on: A Selection from Samuel Beckett's Work*. New York.

Segal, C. P. (1999) *Tragedy and Civilization: An Interpretation of Sophocles*. Norman.

Semenowicz, D. (2011) 'Man Is a Beautiful Animal', *European Culture Congress*, www.culturecongress.eu/en/theme/theme_lost_in_culture/fabre_interview (accessed 23 January 2017).

Senda, A. (1997) *The Voyage of Contemporary Japanese Theatre*, trsl. T. Rimer. Honolulu.

Shaw, F. and Warner, D. (2001) 'Sympathy for the Devil', *Guardian*, 30 January, www.theguardian.com/culture/2001/jan/30/artsfeatures2 (accessed 11 December 2015).

Shay, J. (2002) *Odysseus in America: Combat Trauma and the Trials of Homecoming*. New York.

Shelley, P. B. (1820) *Prometheus Unbound: A Lyrical Drama in Four Acts with Other Poems*. London.

Shepherd, S. (2009) *The Cambridge Introduction to Modern British Theatre*. Cambridge.

Sheridan, A. (1999) *André Gide: A Life in the Present*. Cambridge, MA.

Shevtsova M. (ed.) (2009) *Directors/Directing: Conversations on Theater.* Cambridge.

Shewey, D. (1984) 'Bogart in Space', www.donshewey.com/theater_articles/anne_bogart_vv.html (accessed 10 August 2016).

Sideris, G. (1976) *Τὸ Ἀρχαῖο Θέατρο στὴ Νεοελληνικὴ Σκηνή, 1817–1932* (*The Ancient Theatre on the Modern Greek Stage, 1817–1932*). Athens.

Sidiropoulou, A. (2011) *Authoring Performance: The Director in Contemporary Theatre.* New York.

(2015a). 'Mise-en-Scène as Adaptation', *Critical Stages* 12, www.critical-stages.org/12/mise-en-scene-as-adaptation (accessed 5 January 2016).

(2015b) 'Adaptation, Recontextualization and Metaphor: Auteur Directors and the Staging of Greek Tragedy', *Adaptation* 8: 31–49.

(2018) 'Negotiating Oblivion: Twenty-First Century Greek Performances of Ancient Greek Plays', in *Συναγωνίζεσθαι: Studies in Honour of Guido Avezzù*, ed. S. Bigliazzi, F. Lupi, and G. Ugolini (Verona), 833–56.

Sierz, A. (2001) *In-Yer-Face Theatre: British Drama Today.* London.

(2011) '*Phaedra's Love*, Arcola Theatre', *the artsdesk.com*, 1 October, www.theartsdesk.com/theatre/phaedra%E2%80%99s-love-arcola-theatre (accessed 28 January 2020).

Sihra, M. (2005) 'Greek Myth, Irish Reality: Marina Carr's *By the Bog of Cats . . .*', in *Rebel Women: Staging Ancient Greek Drama Today*, ed. S. Wilmer and J. Dillon (London), 115–34.

Silk, M. (2004) 'Shakespeare and Greek Tragedy: Strange Relationship', in *Shakespeare and the Classics*, ed. C. Martindale and A. B. Taylor (Cambridge), 239–58.

Silverblank, H. (2014) 'Spectral Presences and Absences in Anne Carson's *Antigonick*', *Logeion* 4: 343–63.

Simons, J. and Lucaites, J. L. (eds.) (2017) *In/visible War: The Culture of War in Twenty-first-century America.* New Brunswick.

Slaney, H. (2015) *The Senecan Aesthetic.* Oxford.

Slemon, S. (1995) 'The Scramble for Post-Colonialism', in Ashcroft, Griffiths, and Tiffin (1995), 45–52.

Smethurst, M. J. (1989) *The Artistry of Aeschylus and Zeami: A Comparative Study of Greek Tragedy and No.* Princeton.

(2000) 'The Japanese Presence in Ninagawa's *Medea*', in Hall, Macintosh, and Taplin (2000), 191–216.

(2002) 'Ninagawa's Production of Euripides' *Medea*', *American Journal of Philology* 123: 1–34.

(2013) *Dramatic Action in Greek Tragedy and Noh: Reading With and Beyond Aristotle.* Lanham.

Smidt, K. (1961) *Poetry and Belief in the Work of T. S. Eliot.* London.

Smith, A. C. H. (1963) *T. S. Eliot's Dramatic Theory and Practice: From 'Sweeney Agonistes' to 'The Elder Statesman'.* Princeton.

(1972) *Orghast at Persepolis: An Account of the Experiment in Theatre Directed by Peter Brook and Written by Ted Hughes.* London.

Smith, H. (2015) 'Young, Gifted and Greek: Generation G – The World's Biggest Brain Drain', *Guardian*, 19 January, www.theguardian.com/world/2015/jan/19/young-talented-greek-generation-g-worlds-biggest-brain-drain (accessed 29 January 2020).

Solga, K. (2007) '*Blasted*'s Hysteria: Rape, Realism, and the Thresholds of the Visible', *Modern Drama* 50.3: 346–74.

Soloski, A. (2014) 'A Double Dose of Chekhov: Jay Scheib Stages Platonov, or The Disinherited', *New York Times*, 5 January, www.nytimes.com/2014/01/06/theater/jay-scheib-stages-platonov-or-the-disinherited.html (accessed 23 January 2017).

Sommerstein, A. H. (2010) 'Violence in Greek Drama', in *The Tangled Ways of Zeus and Other Studies in and around Greek Tragedy* (Oxford), 30–46.

Soubrier, V. (2005) 'La tragédie grecque retrouvée', *Lecture jeune* (Dossier Historique: Qu'est-ce que la tragédie?) 114: 23–7.

Souffrant, L. (2014) '"She Said Plain, Burned Things": A Feminist Poetics of the Unsayable in Twentieth-century Literary & Visual Culture', PhD thesis, City University of New York.

Sourvinou-Inwood, C. (2003) *Tragedy and Athenian Religion.* Lanham.

Soyinka, W. (1973) *Collected Plays Volume 1*. Oxford.

(1976) *Myth, Literature and the African World.* Cambridge.

(1988) *Art, Dialogue and Outrage: Essays on Literature and Culture*. Ibadan.

(1993) 'Between Self and System: The Artist in Search of Liberation', in *Art, Dialogue and Outrage: Essays on Literature and Culture* (New York), 40–61.

Spathis, D. (2005) 'Ο σκηνοθέτης και η παράσταση της Ορέστειας στο Βασιλικό Θέατρο' ('The Director and the Performance of the Oresteia at the Royal Theatre'), in *Ευαγγελικά (1901) – Ορεστειακά (1903): νεωτερικές πιέσεις και κοινωνικές αντιστάσεις* (*Evangelika (1901) – Oresteiaka (1903): Modernizing Pressures and Society's Resistance*) (Athens), 229–66.

Spencer, C. (2015) 'Medea, National Theatre, Review: "Thrilling and Merciless"', *Telegraph*, 4 May, www.telegraph.co.uk/culture/theatre/theatre-reviews/10980862/Medea-National-Theatre-review-thrilling-and-merciless.html (accessed 3 March 2020).

Stam, R. (2000) 'Beyond Fidelity: The Dialogics of Adaptation', in *Film Adaptation*, ed. J. Naremore (New Brunswick), 54–76.

(2005) 'Introduction', in *Literature and Film: A Guide to the Theory and Practice of Film Adaptation*, ed. R. Stam and A. Raengo (Oxford), 1–17.

States, B. O. (1992), 'The Phenomenological Attitude', in *Critical Theory and Performance*, ed. J. G. Reinelt and J. R. Roach (Ann Arbor), 369–79.

Stead, H. (2013) 'Seneca's Oedipus: By Hook or By Crook', *Canadian Review of Comparative Literature* 40.1, Special Issue: 88–104.

Stead, H. and Hall, E. (eds.) (2015) *Greek and Roman Classics in the British Struggle for Social Reform*. London and New York.

Steedman, C. (2001) *Dust*. Manchester.

Steinbeck, J. (1949 [1937] *Of Mice and Men*. Harmondsworth.

Steiner, G. (1961) *The Death of Tragedy*. New York.

(1984) *Antigones*. Oxford.
(2012) 'Anne Carson "Translates" Antigone', *Times Literary Supplement*, 1 August.
Steinmeyer, E. (2007) 'Post-Apartheid Electra: In the City of Paradise', in Hardwick and Gillespie (2007), 102–18.
(2009) 'Post-Traumatic and Post-Modern: A South African "Electra"', *Akroterion* 54: 111–24.
(2010a) 'Blessed of Bloody? Antigone in Sylvain Bemba's "Noces Posthumes de Santigone"', *French Studies in Southern Africa* 40: 121–41.
(2010b) '"The Bold and the Beautiful" in Ancient Athens? The Atreides and "Family"', *Acta Patristica et Byzantina* 21.2: 194–206.
(2018) 'The Reception of the Electra Myth in Yaël Farber's "Molora"', in Parker (2018), 467–484.
Stone, B. (2015) 'Your Soul Is Blowing Apart: *Antigonick* and the Influence of Collaborative Process', in *Anne Carson: Ecstatic Lyre*, ed. J. M. Wilkinson (Ann Arbor), 152–5.
Storm, W. (1998) *After Dionysus: A Theory of the Tragic*. Ithaca, NY.
Sugiera, M. (2004) 'Beyond Drama: Writing for Postdramatic Theatre', *Theatre Research International* 29: 16–28.
Suzuki, T. (2002) 'Culture Is the Body', in *Acting (Re)Considered: Theories and Practices*, ed. P. B. Zarrilli (New York), 163–7.
Symonds, G. (2008) *The Aesthetics of Violence in Contemporary Media*. New York and London.
Tanner, R. G. (1970) 'The Dramas of T. S. Eliot and Their Greek Models', *Greece & Rome* 17.2: 123–34.
Taplin, O. (1977) *The Stagecraft of Aeschylus: The Dramatic Use of Exits and Entrances in Greek Tragedy*. Oxford.
(2006) 'Aeschylus' *Persai* – The Entry of Tragedy into the Celebration Culture of the 470s?', in *Dionysalexandros: Essays on Aeschylus and His Fellow Tragedians in Honour of Alexander F. Garvie*, ed. D. Cairns and V. Liapis (Swansea), 1–10.
Tarvin, W. L. (1990) 'Tragic Closure and "Tragic Calm"', *Modern Language Quarterly* 51.1: 5–24.
Taxidou, O. (2008) 'Machines and Models for Modern Tragedy: Brecht/Berlau, *Antigone-Model 1948*', in *Rethinking Tragedy*, ed. R. Felski (Baltimore) 241–62.
(2017) 'The Dancer and the Übermarionette: Isadora Duncan and Edward Gordon Craig', *Mime Journal* 26.1: 6–16.
Taylor, D. (1990) 'Introduction', in *The War Plays: Iphigenia at Aulis, The Women of Troy, Helen* (London), vii–l.
Terpening, R. H. (1997) *Lodovico Dolce: Renaissance Man of Letters*. Toronto.
Tessman, N. (2010) '"Page and Stage": The Librarian's Perspective', *Classical World* 103.2: 256–60.
Thorp, J. (2013) '*Antigonick* (Bloodaxe) by Anne Carson', *Manchester Review*, April 2013, www.themanchesterreview.co.uk/?p=2393 (accessed 13 October 2015).

Thumiger, C. (2013) 'Hallucination, Drunkenness and Mirrors: Ancient Reception of Modern Drama', in Bakogianni (2013b), 39–60.

Tian, M. (2008) *The Poetics of Difference and Displacement: Twentieth-Century Chinese–Western Intercultural Theatre*. Hong Kong.

Tiffin, H. (1995) 'Post-Colonial Literatures and Counter-Discourse', in Ashcroft, Griffiths, and Tiffin (1995), 95–8.

Timogiannakis, P. (2000) 'Όταν η τραγωδία γίνεται δράμα: "Οιδίπους Τύραννος", Προβληματισμοί για την αμφιλεγόμενη παράσταση του Εθνικού' ('When Tragedy Becomes Drama: "Oedipus Tyrannus", Reflections on the National Theatre's Controversial Performance), *Eleftheros Typos*, 4 September.

Tisdel, F. M. (1917) '*Balaustion's Adventure* as an Interpretation of the *Alcestis* of Euripides', *Proceedings of the Modern Language Association* 32.4: 519–46.

Tobari, T. (1985) 'Une Tragédie provocante: la *Médée* de Corneille', *Cahiers de l'AIEF* 37: 127–36.

Törnqvist, E. (1998) 'O'Neill's Philosophical and Literary Paragons', in Manheim (1998), 18–32.

Torrance, I. (2007) *Aeschylus: Seven Against Thebes*. London.

(2010) 'Antigone and Her Brother: What Sort of Special Relationship?', in *Interrogating Antigone in Postmodern Philosophy and Criticism*, ed. S. E. Wilmer and A. Žukauskaitė (Oxford), 240–53.

Tosi, R. (2018) *Dizionario delle sentenze latine e greche*, 3rd edn., Milan.

Toury, G. (1985) 'A Rationale for Descriptive Translation Studies', in *The Manipulation of Literature: Studies in Literary Translation*, ed. T. Hermans (London), 16–41.

Treu, M. (2009) 'Aristophanes and the Suburbs of the World: The Game of Wealth and Poverty', *New Voices in Classical Reception Studies* 4: 83–101, http://fass.open.ac.uk/sites/fass.open.ac.uk/files/files/new-voices-journal/issue4/5Treu.pdf (accessed 25 February 2020).

Trivedi, H. (2007) 'Western Classics, Indian Classics: Postcolonial Contestations', in Hardwick and Gillespie (2007), 286–304.

Trotter, M. (2008) *Modern Irish Theatre*. Cambridge.

Trouillot, M.-R. (1995) *Silencing the Past: Power and the Production of History*. Boston.

Tynan, K. (2007) *Theatre Writings*, ed. D. Shellard. London.

Tziovas, D. (ed.) (2014) *Re-Imagining the Past: Antiquity and Modern Greek Culture*. Oxford.

(ed.) (2017) *Greece in Crisis: Culture and the Politics of Austerity*. London.

Urban, K. (2007) 'The Body's Cruel Joke: The Comic Theatre of Sarah Kane', in *A Concise Companion to Contemporary British and Irish Drama*, ed. N. Holdsworth and M. Luckhurst (Oxford), 149–70.

(2011) 'Sarah Kane', in *The Methuen Drama Guide to Contemporary British Playwrights*, ed. M. Middeke, P. P. Schnierer, and A. Sierz (London), 304–22.

Vaill, A. (2007) *Somewhere: The Life of Jerome Robbins*. London.

Van Emde Boas, E. (2017) *Language and Character in Euripides' Electra*. Oxford.

Van Steen, G. (2000) *Venom in Verse: Aristophanes in Modern Greece*. Princeton.

(2008) '"You Unleash the Tempest of Tragedy": The 1903 Athenian Production of Aeschylus' *Oresteia*', in *A Companion to Classical Receptions*, ed. L. Hardwick and C. Stray (Oxford), 360–72.
(2010) *Liberating Hellenism from the Ottoman Empire: Comte de Marcellus and the Last of the Classics*. New York.
(2011) *Theatre of the Condemned: Classical Tragedy in Greek Prison Islands*. Oxford.
(2014) *Stage of Emergency: Theater and Public Performance under the Greek Military Dictatorship of 1967–1974*. Oxford.
(2016) 'Greece: A History of Turns, Traditions, and Transformations', in Van Zyl Smit (2016), 201–20.
Van Weyenberg, A. (2008) '"Rewrite this Ancient End!" Staging Transition in Post-Apartheid South Africa', *New Voices in Classical Reception Studies* 3: 31–46, http://fass.open.ac.uk/sites/fass.open.ac.uk/files/files/new-voices-journal/issue3/Weyenberg.pdf (accessed 19 February 2020).
(2013) *The Politics of Adaptation: Contemporary African Drama and Greek Tragedy*. Amsterdam and New York.
Van Zyl Smit, B. (2007) '*medEia* – A South African Medea at the Start of the 21st Century', *Akroterion* 52: 1–10.
(2010) 'Orestes and the Truth and Reconciliation Commission', *Classical Receptions Journal* 2: 114–35.
Van Zyl Smit, B. (ed.) (2016) *A Handbook to the Reception of Greek Drama*. Malden.
Vanden Heuvel, M. (1994a) *Performing Drama/ Dramatising Performance: Alternative Theatre and the Dramatic Text*. Ann Arbor.
(1994b) 'Performing Gender(s)', *Contemporary Literature* 35: 804–13.
Varakis, A. (2007) 'The Use of Masks in Koun's Stage Interpretations of *Birds*, *Frogs*, and *Peace*', in *Aristophanes in Performance 421 BCE–AD 2007: Peace, Birds, and Frogs*, ed. E. Hall and A. Wrigley (London), 179–93.
(2013) 'Aristophanes in Performance as an All-Inclusive Event: Audience Participation and Celebration in the Modern Staging of Aristophanic Comedy', in Hardwick and Harrison (2013), 213–25.
Velle, M. (2011) '"AND FUCK YOU ALL SECOND RATE, THIRD RATE AND FOURTH RATE PSYCHO-FUCKERS": Jan Fabre's *Prometheus-Landscape II*, or The Tragic Hero Dismantled', in *Receptions of Antiquity*, ed. J. Nelis (Gent), 227–31.
Velody, I. (1998) 'The Archive and the Human Sciences: Notes towards a Theory of the Archive', *History of the Human Sciences* 11.4: 1–16.
Venuti, L. (1995) *The Translator's Invisibility: A History of Translation*. London and New York.
(1998) *The Scandals of Translation: Towards an Ethics of Difference*. London and New York.

(2013) *Translation Changes Everything: Theory and Practice*. London and New York.

Wainscott, R. (1998) 'Notable American Stage Productions', in Manheim (1998), 96–115.

Walde, A. and Hofmann, J. B. (1954) *Lateinisches etymologisches Wörterbuch*. Heidelberg.

Walker, M. (2001) 'Rehabilitating Feminist Politics and Political Theatre: Hélène Cixous's *La Ville parjure ou le réveil des Erinyes* at the Théâtre du Soleil', *Modern & Contemporary France* 9.4: 495–506.

Wallace, C. (2001) 'Tragic Destiny and Abjection in Marina Carr's *The Mai, Portia Coughlan* and *By the Bog of Cats . . .*', *Irish University Review* 31.2: 431–49.

Walton, M. (2006) *Found in Translation: Greek Drama in English*. Cambridge.

Ward, A. E. (2013) *Women and Tudor Tragedy: Feminizing Counsel and Representing Gender*. Madison and Teaneck.

Watters, E. (2010) *Crazy Like Us: The Globalization of the American Psyche*. New York.

Weaver, B. (2009) 'Euripides' *Bacchae* and Classical Typologies of Pentheus' *Sparagmos*, 510–406 BC', *Bulletin of the Institute of Classical Studies* 52: 15–43.

Weingartz, G. (2010) '"A Tunnel Full of Mirrors": Some Perspectives on Christa Wolf's *Medea: Stimmen*', *Myth & Symbol* 6.2: 15–43.

Weisstein, U. (1973) 'Imitation, Stylization, and Adaptation: The Language of Brecht's *Antigone* and Its Relation to Hölderlin's Version of Sophocles', *German Quarterly* 46.4: 581–604.

Weltman-Aron, B. (2012) 'Political Betrayal: Hélène Cixous's *The Perjured City*', *CR: The New Centennial Review* 12.3: 67–89.

Wetmore, K. J. (2002) *The Athenian Sun in an African Sky: Modern African Adaptations of Classical Greek Tragedy*. Jefferson.

(2003) *Black Dionysus: Greek Tragedy and African American Theatre*. Jefferson.

(2014) 'Adaptation [review article]', *Theatre Journal* 66.4: 625–34.

(2015) '"Aeschylus Got Flow!": Afrosporic Greek Tragedy and Will Power's The Seven', in Bosher, Macintosh, McConnell, and Rankine (2015), 543–55.

Wiles, D. (2011) *Theatre and Citizenship: The History of a Practice*. Cambridge.

(2016) 'Oedipus: The Chronotope', in Monaghan and Montgomery Griffiths (2016), 95–105.

Williams, J. A. (2014) 'Theoretical Approaches to Quotation in Hip-Hop Recordings', *Contemporary Music Review* 33.2: 188–209.

Wilmer, S. E. (2007) 'Finding a Post-Colonial Voice for Antigone: Seamus Heaney's *Burial at Thebes*', in Hardwick and Gillespie (2007), 228–42.

Wilson, E. (1961) *The Wound and the Bow: Seven Studies in Literature*. London.

Winkler, E. H. (1993) 'Three Recent Versions of the *Bacchae*', *Themes in Drama* 15: 217–28.

Wohl, V. (ed.) (2014) *Probabilities, Hypotheticals, and Counterfactuals in Ancient Greek Thought*. Cambridge.

Wood, D. N. C. (1992) 'Catharsis and "Passion Spent": *Samson Agonistes* and Some Problems with Aristotle', *Milton Quarterly* 26.1: 1–9.

Woodhead, C. (2015) 'Needless Tinkering Disturbs Sophocles' Classic', *The Age*, 26 August.

Woodruff, P. (2005) 'Justice in Translation: Rendering Ancient Greek Tragedy', in Gregory (2005), 490–503.

Worthen, W. B. (1997) *Shakespeare and the Authority of Performance*. Cambridge.

(2010) *Drama: Between Poetry and Performance*. Chichester.

Wright, M. (2016) *The Lost Plays of Greek Tragedy, vol. 1: Neglected Authors*. London.

Wyles, R. (2010) 'Towards Theorising the Place of Costume in Performance Reception', in Hall and Harrop (2010), 171–80.

Xu Shi-pei (2003) 'Cong Hebei Bangzi shuokai qu' ('The Approach of the Hebei Bangzi "Medea"'), trsl. Kuan-wu Lin, *Zhongguo Wenhuabao* (*Chinese Cultural Journal*), 23 January.

Yourcenar, M. (1971) *Théâtre II: Électre ou La Chute des masques; Le Mystère d'Alceste; Qui n'a pas son Minotaure?* Paris.

(1974) *Feux*. Paris.

Zabus, C. (1991) *The African Palimpsest: Indigenization of Language in the West African Europhone Novel*. Amsterdam and Atlanta.

(2005) 'À propos de Bintou: Excision et circoncision. Entretien de Chantal Zabus avec Koffi Kwahulé', *Africultures*, 8 December, www.africultures.com/php/index.php?nav=article&no=4235 (accessed 10 March 2020).

(ed.) (2008) *Fearful Symmetries: Essays and Testimonies around Excision and Circumcision*. Amsterdam and New York.

Zacharia, K. (ed.) (2008) *Hellenisms: Culture, Identity, and Ethnicity from Antiquity to Modernity*. Aldershot and Burlington.

Zanin, E. (2008) 'Early Modern Oedipus: A Literary Approach to Christian Tragedy', in *The Locus of Tragedy*, ed. A. Cools, T. Crombez, R. Slegers, and J. Taels (Leiden), 65–79.

Zeitlin, F. (2004) 'Dionysus in 69', in Hall, Macintosh, and Wrigley (2004), 49–75.

Zellner, H. M. (1997) 'Antigone and the Wife of Intaphrenes', *Classical World* 90: 315–18.

Zenowich, D. (2011) 'Reimagining Euripides: A 21st-Century "Trojan Women" at the Getty Villa', *Iris*, https://blogs.getty.edu/iris/reimagining-euripides-a-21st-century-trojan-women-at-the-getty-villa (accessed 15 September 2019).

Zhang, Y.-Y. (2003) 'Meideya Yanchu chen gong yu yishu-baijing hebei bangzi jutuan "meideyu" yantuo hui congshe' ('The Success and Cultural

Importance of the *Medea* Performance: Summary of the Symposium on *Medea* of the Hebei Bangzi Company from Beijing'), *Journal of College of Chinese Traditional Opera* 24.1: 1–5.

Zinoman, J. (2013) 'Ancient Tragedy, Echoed by a Chorus of Veterans: "Herakles," from Aquila Theater, at BAM Fisher', *New York Times*, 23 March, www.nytimes.com/2013/03/29/theater/reviews/herakles-from-aquila-theater-at-bam-fisher.html (accessed 15 January 2020).

Index

Printed by Printforce, United Kingdom